D0302840

Mixed Metaphors

Mixed Metaphors:
The *Danse Macabre* in Medieval
and Early Modern Europe

Edited by

Sophie Oosterwijk and Stefanie Knöll

CAMBRIDGE
SCHOLARS

P U B L I S H I N G

Mixed Metaphors:
The *Danse Macabre* in Medieval and Early Modern Europe,
Edited by Sophie Oosterwijk and Stefanie Knöll

This book first published 2011

Cambridge Scholars Publishing

12 Back Chapman Street, Newcastle upon Tyne, NE6 2XX, UK

British Library Cataloguing in Publication Data
A catalogue record for this book is available from the British Library

ISBN (10): 1-4438-2900-5, ISBN (13): 978-1-4438-2900-7

CONTENTS

List of Illustrations ix

Preface xxi
Hartmut Freytag

Introduction 1
Sophie Oosterwijk and Stefanie Knöll

Duality and Allegory

Dance, Dialogue and Duality: Fatal Encounters in the Medieval
Danse Macabre 9
Sophie Oosterwijk

Dances of the Living and the Dead: A Study of Danse Macabre Imagery
within the Context of Late-Medieval Dance Culture 43
Frances Eustace with Pamela King

Dance, Music, and Inversion: The Reversal of the Natural Order
in the Medieval Danse Macabre 73
Susanne Warda

From Allegory to Anatomy: Femininity and the Danse Macabre 101
Maike Christadler

Macabre Parallels

Dialogue and Violence in Medieval Illuminations of the Three Living
and the Three Dead 133
Christine Kralik

Mixed Encounters: The Three Living and the Three Dead in Italian Art ... 155
Marco Piccat

Death Personified in Medieval Imagery: The Motif of Death
Riding a Bovine 169
Sylvie Bethmont-Gallerand

Death in Drama and Literature

Romance Macabre: Middle English Narrative and the Dead
in the Codex 191
Kenneth Rooney

Frightened or Fearless: Different Ways of Facing Death in the Sixteenth-
Century Majorcan Play *Representació de la Mort* 207
Lenke Kovács

The Kiss of Death: Death as a Lover in Early Modern English
Literature and Art 237
Jean Wilson

Spatial Contexts

Places for Reflection: Death Imagery in Medieval Choir Stalls 269
Kristiane Lemé-Hébuterne

The Istrian *Danse Macabre*: Beram and Hrastovlje 291
Tomislav Vignjević

The *Danse Macabre* at Bierdzany-Bierdzańska Śmierć (Poland) 311
Jutta Schuchard

The Macabre in Print

A Phenomenon of Parallel Reading in the Office of the Dead 325
Caroline Zöhl

Letters without Words? The *Danse Macabre* Initials by Hans Holbein
and his Followers 361
Winfried Schwab

Mix and Match: Huldrich Fröhlich's *Danse Macabre* Editions 385
Stefanie Knöll

Bibliography 407

Contributors 441

Index 443

LIST OF ILLUSTRATIONS

Text figures (b&w)

Sophie Oosterwijk

1. 'Imago mortis', woodcut by Michael Wolgemut in Hartmann Schedel's *Liber Chronicarum* (*Nuremberg Chronicle*) published by Anton Koberger in 1493. © Graphiksammlung 'Mensch und Tod', Heinrich-Heine-University Düsseldorf.
2. Death and the Nun, woodcut by Hans Holbein the Younger in *Les simulachres & historiees faces de la mort* published in 1538.
3. Incised tomb slab of an unmarried girl named Ingeborch (d. 1429) from the Franciscan friary in Nyköping, now in the Nyköpingshus Museum (Sweden). Photo: F.A. Greenhill Collection.
4. Death playing the shawm at the start of Bernt Notke's 1463 *Danse Macabre* formerly in the Marienkirche, Lübeck. Lithograph after Robert Geissler (1872). © Graphiksammlung 'Mensch und Tod', Heinrich-Heine-University Düsseldorf.
5. Four musical corpses, additional woodcut in the expanded *Danse Macabre* edition published by Guy Marchant in 1486.
6. Woodcut at the start of the *Débat du corps et de l'âme* in the expanded *Danse Macabre* edition published by Guy Marchant in 1486.
7a-b. Brass of John Rudyng, Archdeacon of Lincoln (d. 1481), with a detail of Death, at Biggleswade (Bedfordshire). Rubbing and photo: Martin Stuchfield.
8. Brass of the park-keeper James Gray (d. 1591), Hunsdon (Hertfordshire). Rubbing: Martin Stuchfield.
9. Death and the Knight, woodcut by Hans Holbein the Younger in *Les simulachres & historiees faces de la mort* published in 1538.
10. Wheel of Life, or *Rota vitae alias fortunae*, with seven Ages, woodcut, Middle-Rhine area, *c.*1480 (London, British Library, IC.35). © The British Library.
11. The faces of the two effigies on the double-decker tomb of Alice de la Pole, duchess of Suffolk (d. 1475), Ewelme (Oxfordshire). Photos: C.B. Newham.

12. Death and the Emperor, woodcut by Hans Holbein the Younger in *Les simulachres & historiees faces de la mort* published in 1538.

13. Emperor Maximilian I (d. 1519), woodcut portrait by Albrecht Dürer, 1518.

14. 'Vng roy mort' (*a dead King*) and the Author, final woodcut in Guy Marchant's *Danse Macabre* edition first published in 1485.

15. Portrait of John Isham (1567), by an anonymous artist, oil on panel, Lamport Hall (Northamptonshire). © The Lamport Hall Trust.

Frances Eustace with Pamela M. King

16. The Cardinal and the King, woodcut in Guy Marchant's *Danse Macabre* edition first published in 1485.

17. The Friar and the Child, woodcut in Guy Marchant's *Danse Macabre* edition first published in 1485.

18. The Parson and the Labourer, woodcut in Guy Marchant's *Danse Macabre* edition first published in 1485.

19. The Archbishop and the Knight, woodcut in Guy Marchant's *Danse Macabre* edition first published in 1485.

20. The Clerk and the Hermit, woodcut in Guy Marchant's *Danse Macabre* edition first published in 1485.

21. The Bishop and the Squire, woodcut in Guy Marchant's *Danse Macabre* edition first published in 1485.

22. The Monk, the Usurer and the Poor Man, woodcut in Guy Marchant's *Danse Macabre* edition first published in 1485.

23. The Lawyer and the Minstrel, woodcut in Guy Marchant's *Danse Macabre* edition first published in 1485.

24. The Astronomer and the Burgher, woodcut in Guy Marchant's *Danse Macabre* edition first published in 1485.

Susanne Warda

25. '*Dantz hus*' scene with musical and dancing corpses, opening woodcut in *Der doten dantz mit figuren clage und antwort schon von allen staten der werlt* attributed to the printer Heinrich Knoblochtzer, after 1485.

26. The Abbot and the Canon in the Bern *Danse Macabre* mural by Niklaus Manuel, 1516-19/20, lithograph from Joseph Bergmann, *Niklaus Manuels Todtentanz...* (Bern, c.1823). © Graphiksammlung 'Mensch und Tod', Heinrich-Heine-University Düsseldorf.

27. Death and the *hantwercksman* (Craftsman), woodcut in *Der doten dantz ...* attributed to Heinrich Knoblochtzer, after 1485.

28.   Death and the Pope, engraving by Matthäus Merian the Elder based on the Großbasel *Danse Macabre* mural of *c.*1440, published in 1649.

29.   Death and the *Waldbruder* (Hermit), engraving by Matthäus Merian the Elder based on the Großbasel *Danse Macabre* mural of *c.*1440, published in 1649.

30.   Death and the Queen, engraving by Matthäus Merian the Elder based on the Großbasel *Danse Macabre* mural of *c.*1440, published in 1649.

31.   Death and the Cripple, engraving by Matthäus Merian the Elder based on the Großbasel *Danse Macabre* mural of *c.*1440, published in 1649.

32.   The Widow and the Maiden in the Bern *Danse Macabre* mural by Niklaus Manuel, 1516-19/20. Lithograph from Joseph Bergmann, *Niklaus Manuels Todtentanz...* (Bern, *c.*1823). © Graphiksammlung 'Mensch und Tod', Heinrich-Heine-University Düsseldorf.

Maike Christadler

33.   The Monk and the Abbess in the Bern *Danse Macabre* mural by Niklaus Manuel, 1516-19/20, lithograph from Joseph Bergmann, *Niklaus Manuels Todtentanz...* (Bern, *c.*1823). © Graphiksammlung 'Mensch und Tod', Heinrich-Heine-University Düsseldorf.

34.   Monogrammist M, *Death and the Maiden*, engraving, first half of the sixteenth century. © Graphiksammlung 'Mensch und Tod', Heinrich-Heine-University Düsseldorf.

35.   George Grosz, *The Artist in his Studio*, photograph, *c.*1918. © Grosz-Archiv, Akademie der Künste, Berlin.

36.   Hans Sebald Beham, *Death with Three Women*, engraving, *c.*1540. © Graphiksammlung 'Mensch und Tod', Heinrich-Heine-University Düsseldorf.

37.   Hans Sebald Beham, *Death and the Sleeping Woman*, engraving, 1548. © Graphiksammlung 'Mensch und Tod', Heinrich-Heine-University Düsseldorf.

38.   Niklaus Manuel, *Death a as Mercenary with a Maiden*, drawing on panel, 1517. © Kunstmuseum Basel, Inv. Nr. 419. Photo: Martin P. Bühler.

39.   Niklaus Manuel, *Bathseba at her Toilette*, drawing on panel (reverse of Fig. 38), 1517. © Kunstmuseum Basel, Inv. Nr. 419. Photo: Martin P. Bühler.

40.   Albrecht Dürer, *Blazon of Death*, engraving, 1503. © Kunstmuseum Basel, Inv. Aus K.10.147. Photo: Martin P. Bühler.

41.   'Von buolschafft' *(On Courtship)*, woodcut from Sebastian Brant's *Ship of Fools* published in Basel, 1499. © Universitätsbibliothek Basel, DA III 4a:2.

42a-b. Matthäus Greuter, *Omnis Caro Foenum et Gloria Sicut Flos Agri*, with and without lifted skirt, engraving, 1596. © Staatsbibliothek zu Berlin – Preußischer Kulturbesitz - Handschriftenabteilung: YA 2840 kl.

43.   Title page of Andreas Vesalius' *De humani corporis fabrica* published in Basel, 1543, engraving. © Universitätsbibliothek Basel, Lb I 1.

44.   Flowering foetus, engraving from Adrianus Spigelius' *De humani corporis fabrica libri decem* published in Frankfurt, 1632. © Universitätsbibliothek Basel, Lb III 6:1.

Christine Kralik

45.   The Three Living and the Three Dead, miniature in the De Lisle Hours (New York, Pierpont Morgan Library, MS G.50, fol 6v), *c.*1320-25. © The Pierpont Morgan Library, New York.

46.   Master of the Munich Boccaccio, The Three Living and the Three Dead, miniature in the Hours of Anne de Beaujeu (Paris, Bibliothèque nationale de France, NAL 3187, fol. 139v), *c.*1470. © Bibliothèque nationale de France.

47a.   The Ghent Associates, The Three Living and the Three Dead, miniature in the Berlin Hours of Mary of Burgundy and Maximilian I (Berlin, Kupferstichkabinett-SMPK, 78 B 12, fol. 220v), *c.*1480. Photo: Joerg P. Anders. © Bildarchiv Preußischer Kulturbesitz / Art Resource, NY.

47b.   The Ghent Associates, Corpse with a spear and a coffin, miniature in the Berlin Hours of Mary of Burgundy and Maximilian I (Berlin, Kupferstichkabinett-SMPK, 78 B 12, fol. 221r), *c.*1480. Photo: Joerg P. Anders. © Bildarchiv Preußischer Kulturbesitz / Art Resource, NY.

48.   The Master of the Dresden Prayerbook, The Three Living and the Three Dead, miniature in a Flemish book of hours (Berlin, KK-SMPK, 78 B 14, fol. 277v), *c.*1480. © Bildarchiv Preußischer Kulturbesitz / Art Resource, NY.

Marco Piccat

49.   The Legend of the Three Living and the Three Dead, woodcut in Guy Marchant's expanded *Danse Macabre* edition of 1486.

50a-b. Encounter between death and a group of pilgrims from all walks of life, sometimes described as a 'predica della morte' (*Sermon of Death*) or 'predica dei morti' (*Sermon of the Dead*), fifteenth-century fresco in the abbey of San Michele della Chiusa, Turin. Photo: author.

Sylvie Bethmont-Gallerand

51. Albrecht Dürer, *The Four Horsemen of the Apocalypse*, woodcut, 1498. © The British Library.
52. A blindfolded figure of Death on a cow pursuing a young horseman, marginal decoration in the Amiens Missal (The Hague, Royal Library, KB MS 78 D 40, fol. 154v), 1323. © The Hague, Royal Library.
53. Death riding a bovine, misericord in the church of Saint-Adrien, Pocé-sur-Cisse (Indre-et-Loire), late fifteenth century. Photo: author.
54. Death riding a crocodile, emblem from *Proteus* by the Dutch poet Jacob Cats published in 1618. © Graphiksammlung 'Mensch und Tod', Heinrich-Heine-University Düsseldorf.

Kenneth Rooney

55. Simon Bening and workshop (Southern Netherlands), Raising of Lazarus, miniature at the start of the Office of the Dead in the book of hours of Joanna of Ghistelles (Use of Messines), early sixteenth century (London, British Library, Egerton MS 2125, fol. 64v). © The British Library.

Lenke Kovács

56. *Danse Macabre* mural in the former Franciscan convent of Morella in the province of Castellón (Spain), c.1470. Photo: author.
57. Costumed dancers in a Maundy Thursday procession in Verges (Spain). Photo: author.

Jean Wilson

58. Monument to John Latch and his wife Sarah (both d. 1644), Churchill (Somerset). Photo: Norman Hammond.
59a-b. Details of the monument to John Latch and his wife Sarah (both d. 1644), Churchill (Somerset). Photo: Norman Hammond.

60. Brass to Joan Strode (d. 1649) at Shepton Mallet (Somerset). Rubbing: Martin Stuchfield.
61. Boetius Bolswert, engraving after David Vinckboons, *Unequal Lovers and Death*, early seventeenth century. © Graphiksammlung 'Mensch und Tod', Heinrich-Heine-University Düsseldorf.
62. Eighteenth-century tombstone showing a young girl holding a maiden-garland and being accompanied by Death as a skeleton, Falstone (Northumberland). Photo: Norman Hammond.
63. Detail of the eighteenth-century tombstone to a young girl at Falstone (Northumberland). Photo: Norman Hammond.
64. Tombstone of Deborah Devanport (d. 1774), Little Compton (Rhode Island, USA). Photo: Norman Hammond.
65. Tombstone of Lovis Devanport (d. 1774), Little Compton (Rhode Island, USA). Photo: Norman Hammond.

Kristiane Lemé-Hébuterne

66. Arm-rest with Death in the abbey church of La Trinité, Vendôme (Loir-et-Cher, France), late fifteenth century. Photo: author.
67. Misericord with Death and foliage, Remy church (Oise, France), sixteenth century. Photo: author.
68. Arm-rest with Death and scythe, Saint-Martin-aux-Bois (Oise, France), very end of the fifteenth century. Photo: author.
69. Misericord with Death and young lady, Chaumont-en-Vexin (Oise, France), 1507-15. Photo: author.
70. Arm-rest showing a lady with hourglass and skull, collegiate church of Sainte-Catherine, Hoogstraten (Belgium), *c*.1525. Photo: author.
71. Misericord showing a putto leaning on a skull on top of a coffin, church of Saint-Gervais-Saint-Protais, Paris, *c*.1540. Photo: author.
72. Misericord showing a reclining putto with hourglass and skull, Grote Kerk, Dordrecht (Netherlands), 1538-41. Photo: author.
73a. Pendentive showing a young lady with a mirror, Amiens Cathedral (Somme, France), 1508-19. Photo: author.
73b. Pendentive showing a young man with a skull, Amiens Cathedral (Somme, France), 1508-19. Photo: author.
74. Misericord with Death looking at himself in a mirror, Orbais (Marne, France), *c*.1520-25. Photo: author.
75. Parclose with a jester and bauble, collegiate church of Sainte-Catherine, Hoogstraten (Belgium), *c*.1525. Photo: author.

Tomislav Vignjević

76.   Vincent of Kastav, *Danse Macabre* fresco on the west wall in the church of St Mary, Beram (Istria), 1474. Photo: Science and Research Centre, Koper.

77.   The Merchant and Knight in the *Danse Macabre* fresco at Beram (Istria), 1474. Photo: Science and Research Centre, Koper.

78.   The Knight, woodcut in the Heidelberg Blockbook, *c.*1458 (Heidelberg, Universitätsbibliothek, Cod. Pal. germ. 438). © Universitätsbibliothek Heidelberg.

79.   The Beggar in the *Danse Macabre* fresco at Beram (Istria), 1474. Photo: Science and Research Centre, Koper.

80.   The Beggar, woodcut in the Heidelberg Blockbook, *c.*1458 (Heidelberg, Universitätsbibliothek, Cod. Pal. germ. 438). © Universitätsbibliothek Heidelberg.

81.   Master with the Banderoles, *The Wheel of Fortune and the Tree of Estates*, engraving, 1464. © Vienna, Graphische Sammlung Albertina.

82.   *Danse Macabre*, Venetian woodcut, *c.*1500. © Bremen, Kunsthalle.

83.   The Physician in the *Danse Macabre* fresco at Hrastovlje (Istria), 1490. Photo: Science and Research Centre, Koper.

84.   The King, Queen and Cardinal in the *Danse Macabre* fresco at Hrastovlje (Istria), 1490. Photo: Science and Research Centre, Koper.

85.   The Child in the *Danse Macabre* fresco at Hrastovlje (Istria), 1490. Photo: Science and Research Centre, Koper.

86.   The Child, woodcut in the Heidelberg Blockbook, *c.*1458 (Heidelberg, Universitätsbibliothek, Cod. Pal. germ. 438). © Universitätsbibliothek Heidelberg.

Jutta Schuchard

87.   The *Danse Macabre* scene in the Catholic parish church of St Hedwig in Bierdzan (Bierdzany) near Opole (Oppeln) in Silesia (Poland). Photo: author.

88.   Ground plan of the church of St Hedwig in Bierdzan (Poland). Sammlung Nietsch, 1936/38. © Herder-Institut Marburg, Bildarchiv. Image No. 249576.

89.   Title page of Matthäus Merian the Elder's *Todten-Tantz wie derselbe in der löblichen und weitberühmten Stadt Basel ... zu*

*sehen ist, c.*1725. © Graphiksammlung 'Mensch und Tod', Heinrich-Heine-University Düsseldorf.

Caroline Zöhl

90.   The Three Living and the Three Dead, metalcut by Jean Pichore in a book of hours (Use of Rome) published by Jean Barbier and Guillaume Le Rouge, Paris, 22 August 1509. © Ramsen, Antiquariat Bibermühle, Heribert Tenschert.

91.   The Three Living and the Three Dead. anonymous metalcut in a book of hours (Dominican Use) published by Yolande Bonhomme, Paris, 1542. © Staatsbibliothek zu Berlin.

92.   Expulsion from Paradise: (left) metalcut by Jean Pichore in a book of hours (Use of Rome) published by Jean Barbier and Guillaume Le Rouge, Paris, 22 August 1509, and (right) anonymous metalcut in a book of hours (Dominican Use) published by Yolande Bonhomme, Paris, 1542. © Ramsen, Antiquariat Bibermühle, Heribert Tenschert / Staatsbibliothek zu Berlin.

93.   Adam and Eve in the world and Cain slaying Abel: (left) metalcut by Jean Pichore in a book of hours (Use of Rome) published by Jean Barbier and Guillaume Le Rouge, Paris, 22 August 1509, and (right) anonymous metalcut in a book of hours (Use of Rome) published by Thielman Kerver, Paris, 5 December 1519. © Ramsen, Antiquariat Bibermühle, Heribert Tenschert.

94.   Adam praying to God: (left) metalcut by Jean Pichore in a book of hours (Use of Rome) published by Jean Barbier and Guillaume Le Rouge, Paris, 22 August 1509, and (right) anonymous metalcut in a book of hours (Use of Rome) published by Thielman Kerver, Paris, 24 November 1520. © Ramsen, Antiquariat Bibermühle, Heribert Tenschert / Staatsbibliothek zu Berlin.

95.   The funeral mass of Raymond Diocrès: (left) metalcut by Jean Pichore in a book of hours (Use of Rome) published by Jean Barbier and Guillaume Le Rouge, Paris, 22 August 1509, and (right) anonymous metalcut in a book of hours (Use of Rome) published by Yolande Bonhomme, Paris, 5 December 1519. © Ramsen, Antiquariat Bibermühle, Heribert Tenschert.

96.   Birth, Death and Old Age: (left) metalcut by Jean Pichore in a book of hours (Use of Rome) published by Jean Barbier and Guillaume Le Rouge, Paris, 22 August 1509, and (right) anonymous metalcut in a book of hours (Dominican Use) published by Thielman Kerver, Paris, 24 November 1520. © Ramsen, Antiquariat Bibermühle, Heribert Tenschert / Staatsbibliothek zu Berlin.

97. Souls in Purgatory: (left) metalcut by Jean Pichore in a book of hours (Use of Rome) published by Jean Barbier and Guillaume Le Rouge, Paris, 22 August 1509, and (right) anonymous metalcut in a book of hours (Dominican Use) published by Yolande Bonhomme, Paris, 1542. © Ramsen, Antiquariat Bibermühle, Heribert Tenschert / Staatsbibliothek zu Berlin.

98. Deathbed – *Ars moriendi*: (left) metalcut by Jean Pichore in a book of hours (Use of Rome) published by Jean Barbier and Guillaume Le Rouge, Paris, 22 August 1509, and (right) anonymous metalcut in a book of hours (Dominican use) published by Yolande Bonhomme, Paris, 1542. © Ramsen, Antiquariat Bibermühle, Heribert Tenschert / Staatsbibliothek zu Berlin.

99. Job on the Dung heap: (left) metalcut by Jean Pichore in a book of hours (Use of Rome) published by Jean Barbier and Guillaume Le Rouge, Paris, 22 August 1509, and (right) anonymous metalcut in a book of hours (Dominican use) published by Yolande Bonhomme, Paris, 1542. © Ramsen, Antiquariat Bibermühle, Heribert Tenschert / Staatsbibliothek zu Berlin.

100. The Three Enemies of Man: World, Flesh and the Devil: (left) metalcut by Jean Pichore in a book of hours (Use of Rome) published by Jean Barbier and Guillaume Le Rouge, Paris, 22 August 1509, and (right) anonymous metalcut in a book of hours (Use of Rome) published by Thielman Kerver, Paris, 10 September 1522. © Ramsen, Antiquariat Bibermühle, Heribert Tenschert.

Winfried Schwab

101. Hans Holbein the Younger, *Alphabet of Death*, woodcuts, *c.*1523.
102. Johann Quentel, The Pope (H), woodcut, Cologne, *c.*1550.
103. Johann Quentel, The Knight (N), woodcut, Cologne, *c.*1550.
104. Johann Quentel, Hunting Scene (O), woodcut, Cologne, *c.*1550.
105. Johann Quentel, The Pope and the King Playing Cards (L), woodcut, Cologne, *c.*1550.
106. Johann Quentel, Robbery (M), woodcut, Cologne, *c.*1550.
107. Johann Quentel, Three Elegantly Dressed People (F), woodcut, *c.*1550.
108. Johann Quentel, Nobleman and Noblewoman (I), woodcut, *c.*1550.
109. Johann Quentel, The Cardinal (T), woodcut, Cologne, *c.*1550.

Stefanie Knöll

110. Death and the Senator, woodcut and text from Huldrich Frölich's 1608 edition. © Herzog August Bibliothek Wolfenbüttel (67 Poet.).

111. Death and the Abbot, woodcut from Huldrich Frölich's 1608 edition, with the monogram of the master 'HW' below the Abbot's right elbow. © Herzog August Bibliothek Wolfenbüttel (67 Poet.).

112. Death and the Pope, woodcut from Huldrich Frölich's 1608 edition. © Herzog August Bibliothek Wolfenbüttel (67 Poet.).

113. Death and the Blind Man, woodcut from Huldrich Frölich's 1608 edition. © Herzog August Bibliothek Wolfenbüttel (67 Poet.).

114. Death and the Young Man, woodcut from Huldrich Frölich's 1608 edition. © Herzog August Bibliothek Wolfenbüttel (67 Poet.).

115. Death and the Nun, woodcut after Hans Holbein's *Images of Death* (1554, first ed. 1538). © Graphiksammlung 'Mensch und Tod', Heinrich-Heine-University Düsseldorf.

116. The new illustration of Death and the Abbess, woodcut from the 1870 edition published by Danz in Leipzig. © Graphiksammlung 'Mensch und Tod', Heinrich-Heine-University Düsseldorf.

Colour plates

Pl. 1. Burial scene with a charnel house in the background, miniature at the start of the Office of the Dead with Death on a black horse charging at a Pope and an Emperor in the lower margin, book of hours produced in Paris, *c*.1440 (London, British Library Add. MS 18751, fol. 163r). © The British Library.

Pl. 2a. Death and the Chess-player, wall painting by Albertus Pictor (1440-1507) in the church of Täby, Stockholm County (Sweden), 1480s. Photo: Håkan Svensson (Xauxa)

Pl. 2b. Death and Bishop, sole extant stained-glass panel from a larger *Danse Macabre* window scheme, *c*.1500, in St Andrew's church Norwich. Photo: Mike Dixon.

Pl. 3. The Three Living and the Three Dead, Psalter of Robert de Lisle (London, British Library, MS Arundel 83 II, fol. 127r), *c*.1310. © The British Library.

Pl. 4. The Three Living and the Three Dead, in a compilation manuscript probably produced for Marie de Brabant (Paris, BnF, Bibliothèque de l'Arsenal, MS 3142, fol. 311v), *c*.1285. © Bibliothèque nationale de France.

Pl. 5.   *Danse Macabre* mural in the former Franciscan convent of Morella in the province of Castellón (Spain), *c.*1470. Photo: author.

Pl. 6.   The exemplum of the wicked young Emperor beholding his father's corpse, illustration in the so-called Carthusian Miscellany (London, British Library, Add. MS 37049, fol. 87r), *c.*1435-40. © The British Library.

Pl. 7.   Hans Baldung Grien, *Death and the Maiden*, drawing, 1515. © Kupferstichkabinett, Staatliche Museen zu Berlin, KdZ 4578.

Pl. 8.   Simon Bening and workshop (Southern Netherlands), Raising of Lazarus, miniature at the start of the Office of the Dead in the book of hours of Joanna of Ghistelles (Use of Messines) (London, British Library, Egerton MS 2125, fol. 64v), early sixteenth century. © The British Library.

Pl. 9a. Encounter between death and a group of pilgrims from all walks of life, sometimes described as a 'predica della morte' (*Sermon of Death*) or 'predica dei morti' (*Sermon of the Dead*), fresco in the abbey of San Michele della Chiusa, Turin, fifteenth century. Photo: Renzo Dionigi.

Pl. 9b. Death on a cow assaulting a woman on a lion, marginal decoration in the Amiens Missal (The Hague, Royal Library, KB MS 78 D 40, fol. 91r), 1323. © The Hague, Royal Library.

Pl. 10. Death riding a bovine, miniature with the rubric of the Office of the Dead on a single sheet from a book of hours, French(?), early sixteenth century(?). © Graphiksammlung 'Mensch und Tod', Heinrich-Heine-University Düsseldorf.

Pl. 11. Death on an ox attacking a young nobleman in a cemetery, opening miniature of the Office of the Dead in the De Croÿs book of Hours (Paris, Bibliothèque de l'Assemblée nationale, ms. 11, fol. 93r), late fifteenth century. © Paris, Bibliothèque de l'Assemblée nationale.

Pl. 12. Triumph of Death, in a French translation of Petrarch's *Trionfi* by Simon Bourgouin (Paris, Bibliothèque nationale de France, ms. fr. 12423, fol. 37v), first quarter of the sixteenth century. © Bibliothèque nationale de France.

Pl. 13. Death riding a bovine, in a cortege comprising *Eaige* (Age) as a man playing tambourine, *Maladie* (Disease) holding the banner of 'Atropos', and *Accident* as a man blowing a horn, illustration of Pierre Michault's *La Danse aux Aveugles* (Paris, Bibliothèque nationale de France, ms. fr. 1989, fol. 34r), late fifteenth century. © Bibliothèque nationale de France.

Pl. 14. Vincent of Kastav, *Danse Macabre* fresco on the west wall of the church of St Mary, Beram (Istria), 1474. Photo: Science and Research Centre, Koper.

Pl. 15. John of Kastav, *Danse Macabre* fresco in Holy Trinity church, Hrastovlje (Istria), 1490. Photo: Science and Research Centre, Koper.

Pl. 16. Death and the King, illumination in a French luxury *Danse Macabre* manuscript (Paris, Bibliothèque nationale de France, ms fr. 995, fol. 3r), early sixteenth century. © Bibliothèque nationale de France.

PREFACE

HARTMUT FREYTAG

A book like the present volume is long overdue, for it fills a serious lacuna in this field of study. *Mixed Metaphors* will not only benefit researchers but also the many aficionados of the *Danse Macabre*. This French term that has long since become familiar in all European languages reminds us of the famous cycle that was painted in 1424-25 on the walls of one of the charnel houses in the parish cemetery of Les Saints Innocents in Paris. It is this French mural that appears to have been the origin of all later artistic examples of a medieval motif that has proved to be as inspirational as no other from this period. If I may be permitted a pun, I would say that the *Danse Macabre* still has not died nearly six centuries after its first appearance on the scene.

If the *Danse Macabre* – also known as the Dance of Death, *danza de la muerte, dodendans, Totentanz, Dødedansen* or *Surmatants* – has had such a profound impact all over Europe from its emergence in the later fourteenth century until the present day, it is because text and image meet the criteria of a mass medium and have thus had a widespread impact. The reasons for this success are manifold. The *Danse Macabre* is easily understood by many different audiences because it encompasses both text and image, and even when one component is lacking the other still manages to fill the gap. Furthermore, the language of the *Danse Macabre* is not that of literary and academic texts – *viz.* Latin – but that of the vernacular, which means that nobody is excluded from the lesson transmitted through its words. The *Danse* is of its time, yet also timeless; it is valid for today and for eternity. In the face of plague, poverty, war and suffering in the world, it picks up on the individual and collective anxieties of mankind and by representing both physical and spiritual death it raises fear – but also hope. After all, the *Danse Macabre* never fails to remind us of salvation through Christ and the mercy of God as our final judge. The *Danse* thus appeals to the desire of each individual to fulfil his duty in *ordo christianus* for the benefit of the Christian community during his life on earth. This duty is based on a system of values that applies to all mankind and thus transcends the social hierarchy – a system that nobody could ignore as it was in accordance with the religious beliefs of the time.

As a mass medium that was as familiar in the cities of late-medieval Europe from Paris and London to Basel and Lübeck as well as in remote areas, the *Danse Macabre* exhibits its migratory character. Meanwhile the *Danse* remains constant – but never identical – in its core message of *memento mori* (Remember that you must die). It changes according to location and language, it continues earlier forms of imagery and text, and soon sheds first the one and then the other medium, only to resume it later in another form. The *Danse* reduces and expands its repertoire of characters and contents, and in line with its adaptable character it always finds new and fascinating ways to bring across its key message. And it achieves all this *omnibus locis* (in all places), *omnibus linguis* (in all languages), and at the same time *omnibus mediis* (*i.e.* in text and image), in public as well as in private sacred and profane spaces, on a monumental scale as well as in manuscripts and in print. In its continuation of existing, and appropriation of new and newly combined forms and contents, the *Danse Macabre* is characterised by the principle of an *adaptatio continua*, the ability to change and adapt itself continuously.

It is the great merit of *Mixed Metaphors* that this volume addresses all the above characteristics of the *Danse Macabre*. As its editors, the art historians Sophie Oosterwijk and Stefanie Knöll have chosen English as today's scholarly *lingua franca* in order to reach the widest possible readership – rather in the spirit of the *Danse* itself – and moreover to inspire Anglo-American researchers who until recently showed a comparative lack of interest in the subject. An additional merit of this volume is that the contributors do not devote themselves to just one visual or textual source, or fix their attention solely on the dependence of one version on another, or confine themselves to general overviews of particular motifs. Neither do they address the tedious and unanswerable question of the etymology of the word *macabre* nor the problem of what came first – image or text. The present volume corresponds instead with the principle of an interdisciplinarity that transcends national boundaries. This principle is particularly appropriate not only for the subject but also for the many countries and academic disciplines brought together here. The complex title of 'Mixed Metaphors' likewise suits the *Danse Macabre* very well: it sums up facets of the paradoxical elements that are presented to the viewer in the chain of living and dead dancers.

In addition the title of the book outlines incongruities that are genre-specific: ambivalences, ambiguities, contrasts and contradictions that are all found in the incompatibility of transience and eternity, life and death.

The title 'Mixed Metaphors' also takes into account the principle of adaptability of the *Danse*, while the subtitle indicates not only the central theme but also the time frame and the geographical spread of the examples discussed in this book, *viz.* Europe in the Middle Ages and early modern era.

The contributions by the mostly younger and mid-career scholars in this volume who represent a multitude of languages and countries reflect how the *Danse Macabre* is a pan-European phenomenon that transcends linguistic and national boundaries. The multiple questions they address and their methodological starting points match the many disciplines they cover. They address specifically the *Danse Macabre* as well as wider issues, such as the components of dance, music and dialogue, the inversion of the natural order, violence, gender distinctions, iconographic and related aspects. Moreover, the book introduces sources that have often been neglected, such as the Istrian examples of the *Danse* in Slovenia, the 'Representació de la Mort' from Majorca, and a virtually unknown wall painting in a wooden church in Poland.

By addressing so many different aspects in their contributions the seventeen authors in this volume paint a diverse but also representative cycle that is symbolically reminiscent of its very subject in the number of dancers. In view of the cycle of man and death the *Danse Macabre* reminds both reader and viewer of the Last Judgement when God will determine eternal death and eternal life for all as He weighs justice against mercy, as symbolised by the figures 10 (justice) and 7 (mercy).

Editorial note

The editors would like to thank Sally Badham, Jon Bayliss, Mary Woodcock-Kroble, and the student-assistants at the University of Düsseldorf for their help with preparing images for this volume, and especially Tony Carr for meticulously compiling such a comprehensive index.

INTRODUCTION

SOPHIE OOSTERWIJK AND STEFANIE KNÖLL

In the beginning there was the author. All the evidence suggests that the now lost mural that was created in the cemetery of Les Saints Innocents in Paris in 1424-25 started with an image of the anonymous author who explained to the reader/viewer the nature of the work to follow: 'La dance macabre sappelle' (*the* Danse Macabre *it is called*). The Middle English poet John Lydgate went one step further in his *Dance of Death* by adding his own Preface to his adaptation of the French poem, referring to it as 'Macabrees daunce'.[1] Here it is the editors' task to introduce the theme.

The term 'macabre' is nowadays so familiar that it might seem to need no explanation; it is often used very loosely by the public and scholars alike without full understanding of its origins or meaning. The same applies to the *Danse Macabre*, a theme that most people *think* they know although they are likely to associate the *Danse* with much later interpretations of this medieval motif. There is the 1874 symphonic poem *La Danse Macabre* by the French composer Camille Saint-Saëns, which conjures up a vision of dancing skeletons fleeing back to their graves at the break of day, or Walt Disney's first Silly Symphony animation *The Skeleton Dance* of 1929, which presents a similar scene, albeit with different music. More recently still, there are the films of Tim Burton, while 'Gothic' culture has further increased interest in all things 'macabre'. Among medievalists the most familiar image may be the 'Imago Mortis' woodcut with its frolicking cadavers in Hartmann Schedel's *Nuremberg Chronicle* of 1493 (Fig. 1) – an image that is commonly used as an illustration in the literature on the subject. This woodcut has been deliberately chosen for the cover of this book, although it may not even be a 'true' *Danse Macabre* in that it does not include the living.[2] The fact that Saint-Saëns composed his

---

[1] Florence Warren (ed.), with introduction and notes by Beatrice White, *The Dance of Death, edited from MSS. Ellesmere 26/A.13 and B.M. Lansdowne 699, collated with the other extant MSS.*, EETS, o.s. 181 (London, 1931, repr. Woodbridge, 2000), l. 24. The French quotations are from Guy Marchant's 1485 edition.

[2] See the essay by Sophie Oosterwijk in this volume.

musical interpretation nearly five hundred years after the first mention of the term underlines the enduring yet adaptable quality of the *Danse*.

From relative neglect – at least by anglophone scholars – the *Danse Macabre* is rapidly becoming a fashionable topic of research among scholars from different disciplines. However, it is precisely because of the many transformations over time that the original meaning and reception of the theme in its different manifestations are often misunderstood. Too narrow an approach – be it historical, art-historical or literary – is likely to result in an incomplete or biassed view, quite apart from the fact that one also ought to consider examples of the *Danse* not just in isolation but in both a wider and an international context. Yet the literature has grown so vast that such an approach would now be not just ambitious but almost foolhardy, especially as the bulk of studies on the subject is written in languages other than English.[3]

It was especially the problem of language and inaccessibility that called for a new study in English with essays by international experts in this field. This book not only offers examples of the latest research, but also brings together a variety of approaches to different aspects of the *Danse Macabre* itself and its many parallels. For there were other forms of the 'macabre' in medieval culture that influenced the genesis and character of the *Danse* or were inspired by it in turn. As the authors in this volume demonstrate, there are many comparisons and cross-references between the *Danse* and the Legend of the Three Living and the Three Dead, tomb iconography, the imagery in the Office of the Dead in books of hours, and the presentation of death or Death personified in other contexts.

Part of the problem when studying the *Danse Macabre* is the fact that it is hard to define because it is so many things: a literary text as well as a visual motif – sometimes in combination, but not always – with moreover performative potential, even if it has never been proved conclusively that the theme originated in some type of performance. There is also the possibility of folklore influence about revenants haunting the living, although this likewise remains supposition.[4] A broad contextual approach is needed for a proper understanding of the *Danse*. All too often, the focus among historians is on its *memento mori* message, to the exclusion of its satirical character that literary scholars have long been aware of. Inter-

---

[3] James Clark's 1950 monograph *The Dance of Death in the Middle Ages and the Renaissance* may be flawed and outdated in many respects, but few would dare attempt a similarly succinct new study of the *Danse* across Europe.

[4] Nancy Caciola, 'Wraiths, Revenants and Ritual in Medieval Culture', *Past and Present*, 152 (1996), 3-45, esp. 40-44.

preting the *Danse* as a religious theme – or as 'church art'[5] – can result in a supposed 'discovery' of its profane character and create a false paradox.

Any attempt to distinguish between religious and secular is fraught with danger as medieval morality happily combined both aspects. Even the underlying Christian way of thinking or the occurrence of church representatives in the *Danse* do not make it a religious theme. After all, Chaucer's *Canterbury Tales* can hardly be termed a religious poem despite its pilgrimage motif and the inclusion of a monk, a priest, a pardoner, a friar, a nun and prioress – in fact, far from it! Likewise, the church setting in which the *Danse* frequently occurred needs to be understood properly: there is a vast difference between the more public religious spaces, such as the nave or the cemetery, and the liturgical enclosure of the choir, even though profane imagery can often be found in the choir stalls. Cemeteries likewise had a more public character. The Dutch historian Johan Huizinga painted a vivid – if not wholly accurate – picture of the cemetery of Les Innocents in Paris where the painted *Danse* acted as a backdrop to scenes of trade and prostitution as well as to sermons, processions and festivities.[6] Miniatures of burial scenes in late-medieval books of hours frequently depict similar charnel houses with visible piles of skulls and bones in their roof spaces (Pl. 1), thereby illustrating how contemporaries were confronted almost daily with the prospect of their own mortality and the inevitable decomposition of their remains: *sic transit gloria*. In real life these stark reminders must have been even more poignant – and pungent – than any painting or poem, but they only encouraged artists and authors to conjure up ever more horrifying spectres of death and decay.

It is in some ways futile to debate whether the *Danse* began as a text or as an image, a superstition, a rite or enactment, when in the course of its long recorded history from the fourteenth century to the present day it diversified yet further. It is this diversity that the present volume aims to highlight – the mixing of motifs and metaphors that characterise the *Danse* itself and 'the macabre' at large, both in the medieval period and beyond.

The volume has been divided into five sections but the essays contain many cross-references that are intended to draw attention to parallels and comparisons elsewhere. The first section on Duality and Allegory addresses questions about the nature of the dead protagonists in the *Danse*

---

[5] Cf. Rolf Paul Dreier, *Der Totentanz – ein Motiv der kirchlichen Kunst als Projektionsfläche für profane Botschaften (1425-1650)*, PhD thesis (Rotterdam: Erasmus University/Leiden: Brill, 2010).

[6] Johan Huizinga, 'The Vision of Death': chapter 11 in *The Autumn of the Middle Ages*, transl. Rodney J. Payton and Ulrich Mammitzsch (Chicago: University of Chicago Press, 1996), 170.

Macabre – whether Death personified or the dead as mirror images of the living. In some cases, as Sophie Oosterwijk suggests, the question of identity must be taken even further when real-life portraits are integrated into the *Danse* and supposedly stereotypical protagonists are presented instead as historical figures, thereby strengthening the *vanitas* warning. Mirroring is also evident in the postures and movements of the dead dancers, especially in the woodcuts in the earliest French printed edition of 1485 by Guy Marchant, as discussed by Frances Eustace in her essay written in collaboration with Pamela King. Dance and the musical aspects of the *Danse* are addressed by Susanne Warda. Referring mainly to the German tradition, she stresses the aggressive and chaotic tones, as well as the reversal of the natural order displayed in the *Danse*. Maike Christadler explores the erotic potential of the *Danse* in the early modern period, especially in relation to the allegorical meaning of the female body.

The focus of the second section is on Macabre Parallels with first of all the Three Living and the Three Dead, which was a widespread motif across medieval Europe from the later thirteenth century onwards. The juxtaposition of the two groups of living and dead figures has obvious parallels with the *Danse*, although this does not mean that the older theme directly inspired the latter. Christine Kralik's essay takes the depiction of this moralising tale in medieval manuscript illumination as its starting point to discuss the elements of dialogue and violence that are also important elements in the *Danse*, while Marco Piccat discusses the iconographic variations of the same motif and related imagery (Pl. 9a) in mural paintings in medieval Italy. A very different motif is analysed by Sylvie Bethmont-Gallerand, *viz.* Death riding a bovine mount instead of the more traditional horse. The author traces this enigmatic iconography from its earliest known occurrence in the margins of a French missal of 1325 to much later interpretations and variations in literature and art.

Death in all its forms was furthermore an inspiration to authors and playwrights in the Middle Ages and the Renaissance. Kenneth Rooney examines the role of the dead in two Middle English romances, their nature, and their impact on the living protagonists. Lenke Kovács deals with the performative aspects of the motif in Spanish examples. While the Spanish *Dança general de la Muerte* may be the oldest extant text of the *Danse* – older by perhaps thirty years than the French poem we know from the mural in Paris – the focus of her essay is on a sixteenth-century dramatic adaptation from Majorca. In this play Death summons a range of social representatives, each displaying a different reaction to Death. A special relationship to Death is discussed by Jean Wilson. She deals with the explicit eroticism that can be found in early modern English literature, drama, and in tomb iconography, where sex and violence are closely associated. Death is often presented as a lover, and metaphors of flowers, marriage and death are mixed as in the words of Paris in Shakespeare's *Romeo and Juliet* as he scatters flowers on the tomb of his seemingly dead bride Juliet: 'Sweet flower, with flowers the bridal bed I strew'.

The fourth section focusses on spatial contexts, first of all on choir stalls where profane imagery can be found alongside carvings of a more serious, death-related nature, as discussed by Kristiane Lemé-Hébuterne. The mixing of metaphors is also evident in the two medieval Istrian frescoes examined by Tomislav Vignjević. Here the *Danse Macabre* is juxtaposed with the Wheel of Fortune and the Tree of Knowledge with Adam and Eve – the Fall of Man that brought sin and death to mankind. The latter subject was found in combination with the theme of the old man and Death in a virtually unknown mural that Jutta Schuchard encountered in the wooden church at Bierdzany-Bierdzańska Śmierć in Silesia (Poland), dating to the early eighteenth century.

The art of printing played a crucial role in the later dissemination of the *Danse*, culminating in the famous *Images of Death* woodcut series by Hans Holbein the Younger, first published in 1538. Caroline Zöhl examines the unusual picture cycle of eleven engravings that accompanies the Office of the Dead in a book of hours printed in Paris in 1509 and includes the Tale of the Three Living and the Three Dead alongside images of the Expulsion, Souls in Purgatory, a deathbed scene, Job on the dung heap, and the Three Enemies of Man. The last two contributions deal with the reception of Hans Holbein's macabre series of prints. The focus of Winfried Schwab's essay is Holbein's *Danse Macabre* alphabet and variations on these fascinating initials by followers of the artist. Stefanie Knöll re-examines the importance of Huldrich Fröhlich's *Danse Macabre* editions, which mix motifs from Holbein's *Images of Death* with elements from the Basel *Danse*.

The use of metaphors was very fashionable in the late medieval and early modern period. Lydgate often combined several in one sentence, as in his description of how 'cruel dethe that ben so wyse and sage' slays his victims 'by stroke of pestilence' (ll. 6-7). Throughout this volume a yet wider variety of images and metaphors appear: dance, music, violence, inversion, sin, sex, the Fall, the Wheel of Fortune, the Three Living and the Three Dead. All these fascinating variations allowed authors and artists to remind their contemporaries of the ultimate truth: everything must pass and all men must die. For this is how the author in Marchant's final *Danse Macabre* woodcut (Fig. 14) sums it up with yet another metaphor, 'Cest tout vent: chose transitoire' (*All is but wind, something transient*).

DUALITY AND ALLEGORY

DANCE, DIALOGUE AND DUALITY: FATAL ENCOUNTERS IN THE MEDIEVAL *DANSE MACABRE*

SOPHIE OOSTERWIJK

It is a curious irony that the image probably most often used by modern scholars to illustrate the medieval *Danse Macabre* is the 'Imago mortis' woodcut from Hartmann Schedel's *Liber Chronicarum* or *Nuremberg Chronicle* of 1493 (Fig. 1).[1] At first sight this woodcut seems to have it all: one corpse figure playing a shawm on the far left, three cadavers dancing to his tune in a barren setting (presumably a cemetery), and a fifth corpse emerging from the grave, eager to join the fun. With dance, music and cadavers, how can this be anything other than a *Danse Macabre*? Moreover, the dancers all appear to be equal in death without any signs of their former status in life: only their varying stages of decomposition distinguish them.

Yet there is one important element missing in this woodcut, for the *Danse* is supposed to be a fatal encounter of the living with Death whereas here we have only the dead frolicking among themselves. In fact, many examples of the *Danse Macabre* show anything but a dance, in spite of what the term suggests: the elements of music and dancing are often absent or at best underplayed. Most textual examples consist instead of a dialogue between the living and Death, with little or no reference to dancing. In art we may find an encounter that involves armed violence or at least the threat of aggression: no polite invitation to a courtly dance for the higher-ranking social representatives, but more like an arrest with the victims being marched away, irrespective of their status.

---

[1] See also Johann Tomaschek, 'Der Tod, die Welt(zeit)alter und die letzten Dinge. Bemerkungen zum "Tanz der Skelette" in Hartmann Schedels *Weltchronik* von 1493', in Renate Hausner and Winfried Schwab (eds), *Den Tod tanzen?*, Tagungsband des Totentanzkongresses Stift Admont 2001, Im Kontext: Beiträge zu Religion, Philosophie und Kultur, 19 (Anif/Salzburg: Verlag Mueller-Speiser, 2002), 229-49.

Fig. 1. 'Imago mortis', woodcut by Michael Wolgemut in Hartmann Schedel's *Liber Chronicarum* (*Nuremberg Chronicle*) published by Anton Koberger in 1493. © Graphiksammlung 'Mensch und Tod', Heinrich-Heine-University Düsseldorf.

Modern viewers may find it hard to grasp the character of the *Danse* as it is almost impossible to define what the *Danse Macabre* is really supposed to be. Its meaning is clear, however: Death comes to us all, irrespective of age or rank. In order to convey this message the *Danse* combined different metaphors and formats almost from the start, and continued to develop in a variety of ways. This very adaptability was its strength, as this essay will show.

Death or the dead?

When the 'Imago mortis' woodcut was designed the *Danse* had been in existence in one form or another for over a century. In 1376 Jehan le Fèvre already presumed a familiarity with the motif among his readers when he included the enigmatic line 'Je fis de Macabré la dance [...]' (*I made the dance of Macabré*) in his poem *Le Respit de la Mort*, written after his recovery from a serious illness.[2] Another early example is the Spanish *Dança general de la Muerte*, which is believed to date from *c.*1395-1400, thus predating by more than two decades the mural of 1424-25 in the cemetery of Les Saints Innocents in Paris that appears to have given the real impetus to the spread of the theme across Europe. By 1493 the *Danse* had been widely disseminated in texts, drama, murals, sculpture, manuscripts, memorial art, and print, so readers of the *Chronicle* would have been quite accustomed to images of the dead dancing.

It is therefore no surprise that the 'Imago mortis' woodcut combines elements from different traditions. The dancing component is reminiscent of the *Beinhauskapelle* iconography that we find in other *Danse Macabre* examples, such as the two opening woodcuts in Heinrich Knoblochtzer's edition *Der doten dantz* that was published after 1486 in the wake of Guy Marchant's *Danse Macabre* editions of 1485 and 1486 (see Fig. 25). The occurrence of multiple corpses, their varying states of putrefaction, and the fact that the cadaver on the far right has distinct female characteristics – long hair and the sad remnants of female breasts – indicate that they are meant to be generic representatives of the dead. Yet are all these corpses truly equal or does the shawm-player on the left play a different role: is he perhaps not just another deceased mortal but the orchestrator, *viz.* Death personified?

There appears to have been confusion about the nature of the dead protagonists in the *Danse* from the very start. Much has been written about the terms by which the *Danse* is known, from *Totentanz* in German and *dodendans* in Dutch, *i.e.* dance of the dead, to *Dance of Death* in English and the Spanish equivalent *Dança de la Muerte*. The latter uses the single voice of Death personified, whereas the French poem has *le mort* (the dead person) instead of *la mort* (Death). The text still reads *le mort* in Marchant's 1485 edition and *la morte* (the dead woman) in his 1486 *Danse Macabre des Femmes*, although various manuscript copies of both poems as well as later editions substitute *la mort* throughout. The problem may be partly linguistic. John Lydgate (*c.*1371-1449) could simply have misread *le mort* as Death when he translated the French poem into English during his stay in Paris in 1426: *le* is the feminine article in some French dialects of the period, including Picardian and also the Anglo-Norman dialect with which Lydgate himself would have been familiar.[3] Yet even he is not wholly consistent as we find when Death invites the Squire,

---

[2] Geneviève Hasenohr-Esnos (ed.), *Le Respit de la Mort par Jean le Fevre*, Société des anciens textes français (Paris: A. & J. Picard, 1969), 113, l. 3078.
[3] I am grateful to Jelle Koopmans and Clive Sneddon for this information.

'Daunceth with vs' (*E*:222).[4] Does 'us' imply a host of dead dancers of whom the speaker is but one, or does Death once again act as the choreographer for dead and living dancers combined – like the shawm-player in the Nuremberg woodcut? Perhaps even Lydgate was unsure.

Gender is another vexed question. If each dead dancer is not Death personified but the counterpart or *alter ego* of the living – as is often proposed and also suggested by the use of *la morte* in early text versions of the female *Danse* – one would expect to find female as well as male cadavers. Wolgemut's woodcut does include at least one unmistakably female corpse whose body has lost all its former allure: *sic transit gloria*. Hans Holbein likewise assigned a female corpse with withered breasts to the nun in his woodcut for *Les simulachres & historiees faces de la mort* published in 1538 (Fig. 2). Her ghoulish appearance is in stark contrast to that of the frivolous nun who is still ogling the handsome youth serenading her. The nun is too preoccupied to notice her candle being snuffed by her dead counterpart – a subtle but apt metaphor for both spiritual blindness and life extinguished. Yet the dead are not necessarily mirror images of the living, for some artists (and patrons) were morbidly fascinated by the potential for sexual tension between a male corpse and the luscious body of a young female, or the horror that the decaying female corpse must inspire in a living man.[5]

The gender of personified Death was not always fixed, either. The early association of sin with death meant that Death often assumed a female appearance.[6] A late example is the presentation of Death as a long-haired female demon in the fourteenth-century fresco in the Camposanto in Pisa, nowadays attributed to the painter Buonamico (Buffalmacco).[7] A female Death is also what we find in the Middle English poem *Learn to Die* by Thomas Hoccleve (*c*.1370-1440). Here the dying man explains Death thus:

---

[4] Citations in the text are from Florence Warren (ed.), with introduction and notes by Beatrice White, *The Dance of Death, edited from MSS. Ellesmere 26/A.13 and B.M. Lansdowne 699, collated with the other extant MSS.*, EETS, o.s. 181 (London, 1931, repr. Woodbridge, 2000), with *E* referring to the Ellesmere Manuscript or A version and *L* to the later Lansdowne or B version.

[5] See especially the essay by Maike Christadler in this volume.

[6] Jill Bradley, *'You Shall surely not Die'. The Concepts of Sin and Death as Expressed in the Manuscript Art of Northwestern Europe, c. 800-1200* (Leiden/Boston: Brill, 2008), 2 volumes.

[7] Karl S. Guthke, *The Gender of Death: A Cultural History in Art and Literature* (1997, transl. Cambridge: Cambridge University Press, 1997), 71-75 and fig. 8; also Alberto Tenenti, *La vie et la mort à travers l'art du XVe siècle* (Paris: Serge Fleury, 1952), 20-23.

Fig. 2. Death and the Nun, woodcut by Hans Holbein the Younger in *Les simulachres & historiees faces de la mort* published in 1538.

Deeth fauorable is to no maner wight;
To all hir self shee delith equally;
Shee dredith hem nat þat been of greet might,
Ne of the olde and yonge hath no mercy;
The ryche & poore folk eek certainly
She sesith shee sparith right noon estaat;
Al þat lyf berith with hir chek is maat.[8]

(*Death is not favourable to any creature; she deals with everyone equally; she does not fear those who are of great might, nor does she take pity on the old and the young; indeed, she also seizes rich and poor people and she spares absolutely no estate; she checkmates all who live.*)

---

[8] F.J. Furnivall (ed.), *Hoccleve's Works, I. The Minor Poems, in the Phillipps MS. 8151 (Cheltenham) and the Durham MS. III.9.*, EETS, e.s. 61 (London: Kegan Paul, Trench, Trübner, 1892, repr. 1937), 23, *How to Learn to Die*, ll. 155-61.

Not only does Hoccleve present Death as female, but he also uses a chess metaphor that people nowadays are likely to associate with the iconic image of the knight playing a chess match with Death for his life in Ingmar Bergman's 1957 film *The Seventh Seal*. Bergman is said to have found his inspiration in a 1480s medieval wall painting by Albertus Pictor in the church of Täby in Stockholm County (Sweden), which shows a man playing chess with a cadaver (Pl. 2a).[9] Although their chessboard is rendered inaccurately, the postures of the two players and Death's gleeful grin indicate who is winning. In medieval art chess is usually presented as a courtly game played by a knight and a lady, a symbolic battle with love as the stake. The comparison with the *Danse* is apt as chess is in many ways a metaphor for society with a king, queen, bishops, knights, rooks, and pawns (the lower order) battling for survival, while the colours black and white are again highly symbolic. Lydgate used a similar chess metaphor in his *Dance of Death* where the Amorous Gentlewoman complains, 'To my beaute thou haste I-seide checke-mate' (*E*:459).[10] The chess metaphor may arguably have been used in the sole surviving stained-glass panel from a once larger *Danse Macabre* series of *c*.1500 in St Andrew's church, Norwich: it shows Death and – quite fittingly – a Bishop standing on a tiled floor that resembles a chessboard (Pl. 2b).[11]

Another characteristic that distinguishes the dead dancers and thereby suggests they are separate entities is their varying states of decay. Whereas some are relatively fresh if deadly pale corpses with their skin and shroud intact, others are already being devoured by vermin or have progressed to a (near-)skeletal state, as we can see in the Nuremberg woodcut. Worms are commonly mentioned in *contemptus mundi* texts, just as they are often clearly visible – and in size resembling serpents rather than maggots – in the more grotesque depictions of the corpse, sometimes in combination with toads and other vermin. A good example is the incised tomb slab of an unmarried girl named Ingeborch (d. 1429) in Nyköping (Sweden), which shows the corpse crowned, but with two toads squatting on the torso (Fig. 3). Based on the authority of ancient texts such as Pliny the Younger's *Naturalis Historia*, there was the medieval physiological belief in a natural if paradoxical phenomenon of corpses spontaneously generating

---

[9] I am grateful to Anthony Seaton for drawing my attention to this example.

[10] In the B version it is the Empress who observes that of her riches, nobility and beauty that 'Deth seith chek-mat to al sich veyn noblesse' (*L*:77).

[11] George A. King, 'The Pre-Reformation Painted Glass in St. Andrew's Church, Norwich', *Norfolk Archaeology*, 18 (1913), 283-94. However, chequerboard-tiled floors are a characteristic of East Anglian art at this time, so an actual chessboard may not be implied here. I am grateful to Sally Badham for pointing this out to me.

reptiles and worms that would then proceed to devour the host body –
death thus feeding new life.[12] The ultimate humiliation is voiced in the
Psalter of Robert de Lisle of *c*.1310 by the third of the Three Living whose
body is in the most advanced state of decomposition (Pl. 3), 'Ore su si
hidous et si nuz. / Ke moy uer ne deigne nuls' (*Yet now I am so hideous
and naked that even the worms scorn me*).[13]

Fig. 3. Incised tomb slab of an unmarried girl named Ingeborch (d. 1429) from the
Franciscan friary in Nyköping, now in the Nyköpingshus Museum (Sweden).
Photo: F.A. Greenhill Collection.

---

[12] Sophie Oosterwijk, 'Food for Worms – Food for Thought: The Appearance and
Interpretation of the "Verminous" Cadaver in Britain and Europe', *Church
Monuments*, 20 (2005), 40-80, 133-40, esp. 53.
[13] Lucy Freeman Sandler, *The Psalter of Robert de Lisle in the British Library*
(London and Oxford: Harvey Miller, 1983), 42-43.

Artists also used colour to indicate different stages of putrefaction: brown suggests a greater degree of decomposition than deathly grey, while black is the ultimate hue of the rotting corpse before it is reduced to a skeleton. In the Middle English poem *A Lullaby to Christ in the Cradle* the Virgin conjures up a grim picture of her son's future Passion in the line 'For than thi bodi is bleyk & blak, sone after sal ben driye' (*For then your body is pale and black, and soon after it will be dry*).[14] Yet this suggests another paradox as black is also the colour of evil. When Hoccleve's hypothetical dying man in the poem *Learn to Die* exclaims in his final agony that 'The blake-faced ethiopiens / me enuyrone' (*The black-faced Ethiopians surround me*, ll. 673-74), he refers to the devils waiting to seize his soul, as his subsequent lines make clear.[15] However, the Child in the Latin-German *Totentanz* who cries to his mother that 'me vir trahit ater'/'ein swarzer man ziuht mich dahin' (*A black man drags me away*) is describing not a devil but Death whose colour is that of the putrefying corpse.[16]

Death personified has no fixed appearance or colour, which makes it hard to distinguish Death from the more generic dead dancers whose appearance likewise varies – from naked to shrouded, near-skeletal to still fleshy or putrid. Yet although black is the colour of evil, it would be incorrect to equate Death with the devil for Death is the messenger and executioner, but not the judge. He may criticise his victims, yet he is firmly earth-bound – like the dancing corpses in the 'Imago mortis' woodcut – and he does not determine the ultimate destiny of the dying. The role of Death is thus different from that of the devil, who always lies in wait to carry off souls to Hell. Yet while their shared black hue can be confusing, Death and the devil do have a similar taste in music, which is another key metaphor in the *Danse*.

---

[14] Carleton Brown, *Religious Lyrics of the Fourteenth Century* (Oxford: Oxford University Press, 1924), nr. 65, l. 12. The glossary incorrectly lists 'bleyk' and 'blak' as synonyms for 'pale'.

[15] According to early Christian tradition, Noah's curse meant that his son Ham's descendents inherited Africa and a dark skin, which thus became suspect because of its association with sin. See David Goldenberg, *The Curse of Ham. Race and Slavery in Early Judaism, Christianity and Islam* (Princeton: Princeton University Press, 2003).

[16] For the Latin-German *Totentanz*, of which the earliest extant text survives in a compilation manuscript copied in Augsburg between 1443 and 1447 (Heidelberg University Library, Cpg 314, fols 79r-80v), see Reinhold Hammerstein, *Tanz und Musik des Todes: die mittelalterlichen Totentänze und ihr Nachleben* (Berne/Munich: Francke, 1980), 31-39.

Dance and music

As Susanne Warda and Frances Eustace explain elsewhere in this volume, dance and music are normally expressions of *joie de vivre* that Death manages to pervert into something morbid, threatening and uncouth in the *Danse Macabre*. Dance is also a perfect visual vehicle for human interaction: people can dance in a circle, in a line, or in pairs. The mural of *c.*1470 in Morella (Spain) shows a circle of living dancers who move around a centrally positioned sarcophagus containing a representation of Death, but this is a fairly unusual format (Pl. 5).[17] A long wall is obviously ideal for showing a line of dancers such as we find in many extant and lost murals, including the famous example in Paris. Yet when Marchant adapted this scheme to a book format, he was obliged to split up the long line into two pairs per page, which inevitably altered the erstwhile interaction and contact between the living and dead dancers. Other printers went further still and divided the *Danse* into single pairs per page.

The sense of movement and direction of the *Danse* is obviously dependent on the way it is presented. Some mural schemes show a clear direction of the dancers towards the viewer's left (as in Bernt Notke's painted Reval *Danse* in Tallinn) or right (as in the murals at Beram and Hrastovlje in Istria).[18] However, the living often indicate their reluctance by attempting to turn away, and the sense of direction tends to disappear completely when the *Danse* is reduced to a series of single pairs. There is thus little left of the dance element or of consistent movement and direction in Holbein's woodcuts (Figs 2, 9).

Dancing was frowned upon by the Church, and music was likewise suspect if it induced frivolity and thereby led people astray. In the French *Danse* the Minstrel is reminded by his dead counterpart that he has merely entertained foolish people ('sos et sotes') with his music. The Minstrel himself uses an apt musical metaphor to illustrate his impending death: 'Jay mis soubz le banc ma vielle' (*I have put away my hurdy-gurdy under the seat*) was a colloquial way to describe dying that was also used by the

---

[17] See the essay by Lenke Kovács in this volume. There are later examples of circular *Danses Macabres*, e.g. John Audelay's 1569 broadsheet 'The Daunce and Song of Death' (London, BL, Huth 50 (32)) and on an embroidered pall of 1637 in Kassel: see Imke Lüders, *Der Tod auf Samt und Seide. Todesdarstellungen auf liturgischen Textilien des 16. bis 19. Jahrhunderts im deutschsprachigen Raum*, Kasseler Studien zur Sepulkralkultur, 14 (Kassel: Arbeitsgemeinschaft Friedhof und Denkmal e. V., 2009), I.2, esp. 50-51, 138-39.

[18] See Hammerstein (1980), 154-56, 193-94, and pls 31-33, 132, 130, and Tomislav Vignjević's essay in this volume.

fifteenth-century poet François Villon.[19] Of course, music can be heavenly – musical angels abound in medieval art – as well as seductive in a more sinister and potentially lethal way, if one considers the sirens in classical mythology, mermaids or the Lorelei. The Pied Piper who lured away first the rats and then the children of Hamelin with his music may well have been inspired by the iconic figure of Death playing his shawm, like the corpse with his plumed hat in the Lübeck *Danse* (Fig. 4).

Fig. 4. Death playing the shawm at the start of Bernt Notke's 1463 *Danse Macabre* formerly in the Marienkirche, Lübeck. Lithograph after Robert Geissler (1872). © Graphiksammlung 'Mensch und Tod', Heinrich-Heine-University Düsseldorf.

Whereas music in heaven was believed to be harmonious, devils must naturally prefer disharmony and cacophany: according to theological tradition, hell contains no music – only noise.[20] Music as hellish torture is a common motif in the work of Hieronymus Bosch, with bagpipes being a particular favourite. It is surely no coincidence that Death is also often shown playing the bagpipe in *Danse Macabre* schemes, as suggested by the very words of Death in the Reval/Tallinn *Danse*, 'Went gy moten na myner pypen springen' (*For you must dance to my pipes*).[21] Death likewise favours raucous instruments, to judge by the woodcuts in the

---

[19] I am grateful to Clive Sneddon for this information. Quotations from the French *Danse Macabre* poem are from Guy Marchant's 1485 edition.
[20] Kathi Meyer-Baer, *Music of the Spheres and the Dance of Death: Studies in Musical Iconology* (1970, repr. New York: Da Capo Press, 1984), 271; also Hammerstein (1980), esp. 24-26 and 39-42.
[21] Hartmut Freytag (ed.), *Der Totentanz der Marienkirche in Lübeck und der Nikolaikirche in Reval (Tallinn). Edition, Kommentar, Interpretation, Rezeption*, Niederdeutsche Studien, 39 (Cologne/Weimar/Vienna: Böhlau Verlag, 1993), 144.

Knoblochtzer edition, which could explain why the King in the French *Danse* objects, 'Je nay point apris a danser / A danse et note si sauuage' (*I have never learnt to dance to so savage a danse and tune*).[22]

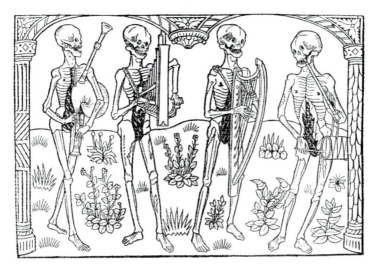

Fig. 5. Four musical corpses, additional woodcut in the expanded *Danse Macabre* edition published by Guy Marchant in 1486.

There are frequent references to dancing in *Danse Macabre* texts, even if music – or dance – is not always evident in the visual tradition: Marchant's woodcut of four musical corpses with an ill-assorted choice of instruments was a later addition and presumably not part of the Paris mural (Fig. 5). There is still a debate about whether the origins of the *Danse* lie in some type of performance or procession. Whereas a procession might be led by Death personified, an alternating chain or circle of living and dead dancers requires more than one representative of death, and it is worth pointing out that in some early depictions of single *Danse* pairs the victim is flanked by two dead companions.[23] Despite what the term *Totentanz* seems to imply, the earliest German *Danse* has *der Tod* (Death) yet the Bishop in the Latin text moans about being constrained by multiple

---

[22] Jane H.M. Taylor. 'Que signifiait *danse* au quinzième siècle? Danser la Danse macabré', *Fifteenth Century Studies*, 18 (1991), 259-77, at 265-66.

[23] An example is the extensive *Danse Macabre* cycle that starts on fol. 123r of a Parisian book of hours of *c.*1430-35 (New York, Pierpont Morgan Library, MS M.359).

dancers: 'nunc distorti praesumunt, me dare morti (*Now the twisting dancers take control of me to give me to Death.*).[24] The Sergeant in the French poem likewise exclaims, 'Je suis pris: deca et dela' (*I am caught from this side and the other*), but the page format allows only a corpse figure on his right. Even if there is just one dead partner per living victim, artists often differentiated them through colour, as discussed above, thereby lending them individuality.

On the other hand, the texts are really dialogues that make more sense as a series of encounters of living victims with one single dead opponent, *viz.* Death personified. In enactments of the *Danse* texts each victim may pass before Death to enter into a dialogue and then make way for the next victim. The format – dance or dialogue – may thus also affect the way that one perceives the core protagonist(s): as a series of dead counterparts to the living, or as successive appearances of Death himself.[25]

Dialogue

Whether the *Danse Macabre* was a dialogue from the beginning is debatable. Some scholars have drawn comparisons with the *Vado Mori* monologue poem, in which a series of living representatives of medieval society lament their imminent death without Death being specifically present.[26] A number of different *Vado Mori* text versions survive, the earliest dating to the thirteenth century. All consist solely of male characters speaking in distich verse, each repeating like a refrain the phrase 'vado mori'. A typical example is the king sighing, 'Vado mori: rex sum. Quid honor, quid gloria mundi? / Est via mors hominis regia: vado mori' (*I am going to die: I am the king. What use is honour, what use worldly glory? Death is the royal road of man: I am going to die*).[27]

---

[24] 'Distorti' is translated in the matching German verses as 'ungeschaffen', *i.e.* misshapen creatures. See also the essay by Susanne Warda in this volume.

[25] For the idea of performativity in the *Danse Macabre*, see also Elina Gertsman, *The Dance of Death in the Middle Ages. Image, Text, Performance*, Studies in the Visual Cultures of the Middle Ages (SVCMA 3) (Turnhout: Brepols, 2010).

[26] For example, see Willy F. Storck, 'Das "Vado mori"', *Zeitschrift für deutsche Philologie*, 42 (1910), 422-28; Eleanor Prescott Hammond, 'Latin Texts of the Dance of Death', *Modern Philology*, 8 (1911), 399-410; Hellmut Rosenfeld, *Der mittelalterliche Totentanz: Entstehung – Enwicklung – Bedeutung* (1954, revised edn Cologne/Graz: Böhlau Verlag, 1968), esp. 38-43, 323-26, and by the same author 'Vadomori', *Zeitschrift für deutsches Altertum und deutsche Literatur*, 124 (1995), 257-64.

[27] Quoted from the so-called Paris version in Rosenfeld (1968), 324, ll. 17-18.

It is impossible to establish a direct link between the *Vado Mori* poem and the *Danse*: both may simply have been separate compositions within the *contemptus mundi* tradition. However, it is interesting that the Latin-German *Danse Macabre* is also a monologue of the dying, with a Preacher providing a prologue and epilogue.[28] The stanzas of Death that we subsequently find in the Basel *Danse* and the Heidelberg Blockbook were added only at a later stage, thereby making it a dialogue and thus a proper encounter.

However, even the *Danse* proper is not always merely a dialogue between dead and living dancers: the reader or spectator is often addressed directly, and not just by the Author or Preacher at the start and conclusion. The first cadaver of the French poem directs his first four lines to 'Vous qui viuez' (*You who are alive*), and the Abbot likewise addresses the reader with 'Vous qui viuez au demorant' (*You who are alive just now*). The audience thus becomes directly involved and reminded even more vividly of their own mortality: they could be summoned next to join Death's dance. In a mural the impact would be yet greater if the painted figures look back at the viewer – something we do not find in Marchant's woodcuts, but which other artists used to great effect.[29] Like a voice from the grave, the words of the dead King at the end of the French mural – 'Vous: qui en ceste pourtraiture / Veez danser estas diuers' (*You who in these likenesses can see the various estates dancing*) – were likewise aimed at those who had just witnessed the *Danse* taking place before their very eyes (Fig. 14). Lydgate not only followed the French poem closely in many respects, but added yet another voice – his own – in the 'Verba Translatoris' at the start and his final Envoy in which he reveals his identity: 'Haue me excused, my name is Jon Lidgate' (*E*:670). The *Danse* is thus not just a dialogue but an interplay between the dead, the living, the author (and translator), and the reader/viewer.

The dialogue format was frequently used for other texts with a *contemptus mundi* message. One example is *A Disputacion betwyx þe Body and Wormes*, of which an illustrated copy can be found in the so-

---

[28] For the text, see Rosenfeld (1968), 308-18 (German) and 320-23 (Latin); Hammerstein (1980), 31-39. For objections to Rosenfeld's spurious 'Würzburg' hypothesis and Hammerstein's misleading amalgamation of the two texts, see Gert Kaiser, *Der tanzende Tod. Mittelalterliche Totentänze* (Frankfurt am Main: Insel Verlag, 1982), 276-77.

[29] For example, the central figure in a Last Judgement altarpiece of *c.*1550-55 by the Münster painter Hermann tom Ring (Utrecht, Catharijneconvent Museum) shows Death aiming an arrow directly at the viewer.

called Carthusian Miscellany manuscript of *c.*1435-40.[30] Another favourite was the *Débat du corps et de l'âme.*[31] This dream poem in which the (dead!) body debates with the soul was included in many *Danse Macabre* editions, *e.g.* in Marchant's expanded 1486 version (Fig. 6). The accompanying woodcut shows the dreamer in bed in the foreground, while behind him a naked child-like soul debates with a shrouded corpse reclining in his tomb – an interesting juxtaposition of sleep and death with the soul at the pinnacle literally having the upper hand in the dispute.

Senfuit le debat dun corps et dune ame.

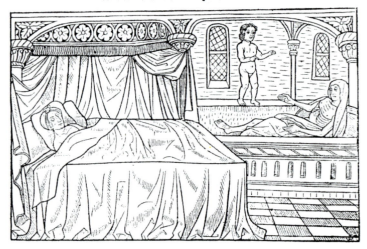

Fig. 6. Woodcut at the start of the *Débat du corps et de l'âme* in the expanded *Danse Macabre* edition published by Guy Marchant in 1486.

Marchant also incorporated the *Dict des trois morts et des trois vifs* into his 1486 edition. The Legend of the Three Living and the Three Dead is an obvious parallel to the *Danse* in presenting a dialogue between the dead and the living, who are often shown as each others' mirror images.[32] This moralising tale became so well known that the encounter was often

---

[30] Klaus Jankofsky, 'A View into the Grave: "A Disputacion Betwyx þe Body and Wormes" in British Museum MS Add. 37049', *Taius*, 1 (1974), 137-59; Jenny Rebecca Rytting, 'A Disputacion Betwyx þe Body and Wormes: a Translation', *Comitatus: A Journal of Medieval and Renaissance Studies*, 31:1 (2000), 217-32.
[31] Rosemary Woolf, *The English Religious Lyric in the Middle Ages* (Oxford: Clarendon Press, 1968), 326 and also chapters III, IX, and Appendices H and I.
[32] See especially Christine Kralik's essay in this volume.

depicted in murals without the accompanying poem: a separation of text and image that we also find quite early on in the development of the *Danse*. However, there is the important difference that the Legend presents a non-fatal encounter: the dead serve as a warning to the living, who are given a chance to mend their ways, unlike the living in the *Danse*.

Variations of the famous saying of the Three Dead, 'As you are, so we once were; as we are now, so shall you be', can also be found on many cadaver monuments of the period. This type of memorial emerged in the later fourteenth century and no doubt drew its inspiration in part from other macabre imagery (Fig. 3), including depictions of the Three Dead. Yet the phrase 'Sum quod eris' was much older: it was used most notably in the popular twelfth-century *Meditationes* commonly attributed to St Bernard of Clairvaux.[33] Every medieval tomb monument was intended to provoke a reaction from the beholder, most importantly prayers for the deceased, and medieval readers were accustomed to reading texts out aloud – it was an acceptable mode of reading. Thus the combination of effigy and epitaph creates a dialogue with the beholder that is curiously similar to the encounter of the Three Living and the Three Dead. For Archbishop Chichele (d. 1441), whose double-decker tomb in Canterbury was completed by 1427, the phrase must have carried even more meaning: every time he passed through his cathedral he would have seen the stone cadaver effigy (or *transi*) lying like a personal premonition of death beneath his own painted effigy *au vif* in full archiepiscopal pomp.[34]

Sometimes the dialogue on such 'macabre' monuments is not between the living beholder and the deceased, however, but with Death himself. A good example is the brass of John Rudyng, archdeacon of Lincoln (d. 1481), at Biggleswade (Bedfordshire), which still features the figure of Death although Rudyng's own effigy has been lost (Fig. 7a-b).[35] The

---

[33] Originally a series of meditations, the *Meditationes* were loosely adapted as a verse sermon called the 'Sayings of St Bernard' at the end of the thirteenth century and inspired such poems as the 'Signs of Death' macaronic. I am grateful to David Harry for this information. See also Kathleen Cohen, *Metamorphosis of a Death Symbol: the Transi Tomb in the Late Middle Ages and the Renaissance*, California Studies in the History of Art, 15 (Berkeley/Los Angeles/London: University of California Press, 1973), esp. 22-32.

[34] Oosterwijk (2005), esp. 44, 48, 55, 69, 71 and col.pl. 11; Cohen (1973), esp. 15-16 and fig. 13. Chichele's epitaph contains the variation 'Tu quod eris mihi consimilis' (*You will be like me*) and a reference to his body being food for worms.

[35] Sophie Oosterwijk, '"For no man mai fro dethes stroke fle". Death and *Danse Macabre* Iconography in Memorial Art', *Church Monuments*, 23 (2008), 62-87, 166-68, at 69-71; also Nigel Saul, 'At the Deathbed of Archdeacon Rudyng', *Monumental Brass Society Bulletin*, 108 (May 2008), 155–57.

lengthy Latin verse epitaph beneath the image of Death is a dialogue between the passer-by and 'Mors' (*Death*); Rudyng himself remains silent. In the first six lines the reader accuses Death of being merciless, to which Death responds with what is in essence the message of the *Danse Macabre*: death is inevitable and all mankind must die eventually, regardless of rank or status. The text reads:

Tu fera mors quid agis . humane prodiga stragis
Cedo . quot offendis . qd' in huic discrimina tendis
Dic . cur tela strius . nature depopulatrix
Dic . cur non metuis . huic trudere vasta voratrix
Cur te non puduit . fatali sorte ferire
Vivere quem decuit . & plebs lacrimatur obire

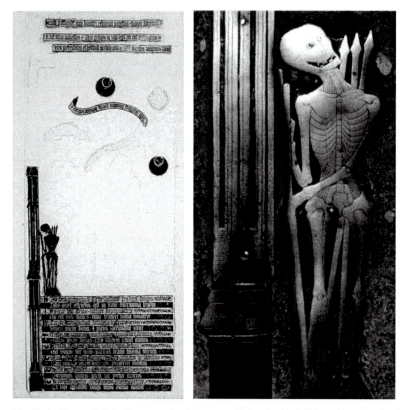

Fig. 7a-b. Brass of John Rudyng, Archdeacon of Lincoln (d. 1481), with a detail of Death, at Biggleswade (Bedfordshire). Rubbing and photo: Martin Stuchfield.

Mors: Crede nec iniurias mortalibus huic dare somnis
Namq' meas furias . caro tandem senciet omnis
Horrida tela fero . morsu necis vrgeo seclum
Nec vulgo nec hero . parcens traho singula mecum
Quid valet altus honos . rex . dux . princeps . q' sacerdos
Hanc subeunt sortem . nequeunt precurrere mortem
Mors ego sum fi nis . lustrantibus hic peregrinis
Terminus itineris . quem nec pretire mereris
In scriptis legitur . caro queuis morte potitur
Et vox applaudit . vulgi mors omnia claudit

(*You savage Death, brimful of human wreckage, what are you doing? Out
with it: how often do you offend! What do you bend your decisions against
this man? Speak! Why do you arrange your spears in ranks, you decimator
of nature? Speak! Why do you feel no qualms about thrusting this man
down, you crude desolate devourer? Why have you not felt ashamed to
strike with fatal lot him who ought to have lived, and whose demise the
people weep tears over?*

*Death: Do not in your dreams believe that this man did mortals any
injustice. Indeed, in the end all flesh shall feel my furies. I carry terrible
spears, I come down upon humans with the bite of death. Sparing neither
the common folk nor the master, I drag behind me every single thing. What
does high honour avail? King, duke, prince, and priest, this lot they shall
all undergo, and they cannot outrun Death. I am Death, the end for all
those strangers wandering about here, the journey's terminus, which you
do not deserve to overstep. In books one reads: all flesh is held in
subjugation by Death and the people's voice applauds: Death finishes off
everything.*)[36]

The sentiments are unmistakably similar to those found in the *Danse*,
including the hierarchical reference to 'King, duke, prince and priest'.
Whereas Rudyng himself does not take part in the debate – he is already
dead – the living reader may still benefit from Death's warning in this
dialogue.

Violence

Apart from the dialogue aspect of Rudyng's brass, there is another
important element that we also find in the *Danse*: violence. 'Mors' not
only mentions his 'horrida tela' (*terrible spears*) but is also shown with
five of these weapons in readiness. We find the same suggestions of

---

[36] I am grateful to Reinhard Lamp for his translation of the Latin text and detailed
comments, and to Jerome Bertram for additional information and suggestions.

violence in depictions of the Three Living and the Three Dead in the
fifteenth and sixteenth centuries, which demonstrate a shift in presenting
death in an ever more terrifying manner. While earlier encounters show
the dead politely debating with the living, later examples show the Three
Living in mortal fear as they are actively pursued by the Three Dead, who
carry a variety of spears or darts and burial-related implements such as
coffins and spades. The same attributes can also be found in the *Danse*.
Whereas Knoblochtzer chose musical instruments for his dead dancers –
perhaps reverting to an earlier idea that remained stronger in the German
tradition – in Marchant's woodcuts we frequently see the dead armed with
coffins or coffin lids, spades and pickaxes, as well as with spears or darts.

Death's choice of lethal weapon is intriguing. Sometimes he is shown
with bow and arrow, as in the small surviving stained-glass quarry in the
church of Stanford on Avon (Northamptonshire). Here local vicar Henry
Williams (d. 1501) stipulated in his will that he wanted several such
representations of himself kneeling 'and the ymage of deth shotyng at
me'.[37] More often, however, Death's preferred weapon is not exactly a
spear or javelin, but rather a large dart ending in a fletch. All these
varieties suggest a similar type of weapon: one that pierces the living flesh
and kills swiftly if the aim is right.

The pickaxe is more problematic. At first sight it may just be a tool
used for digging a grave and thus related to burial, like those that one may
still observe on the wooden frieze surrounding the late-medieval cemetery
of Saint-Maclou in the centre of Rouen.[38] Yet Marchant's dead dancers
carry these tools in different ways. The cadaver addressing the Emperor
holds a pickaxe (here combined with a spade) across his shoulder, as does
the corpse who marches away with the Bishop, and also the one
approaching the Monk, but the dead counterpart of the *Curé* instead
casually leans on his pickaxe. The tool looks the same in all four woodcuts
and the word 'pic' is used several times in the text: for example, the
Emperor recognises that 'Arme me fault de pic. de pelle' (*I must arm
myself with pick and spade*).

Yet there is the possibility of iconographical confusion as Death is
frequently depicted with a scythe – an instrument implied in the
description in Jeremiah 9:21-22 (in the Douai-Rheims translation of the
Vulgate):

---

[37] Oosterwijk (2008), 76-77 and col. pls 2a-b; compare also the two trefoil glass
panels in Nuremberg depicting Death aiming his arrow at Dr Sixtus Tucher (d.
1507), 77 and col. pls 3a-b.

[38] The frieze also illustrates a variety of liturgical instruments, bones and skulls,
while the carved stone pillars below feature worn *Danse Macabre* pairs.

For death is come up through our windows, it is entered into our houses to destroy the children from without, the young men from the streets.

Speak: Thus saith the Lord: Even the carcass of man shall fall as dung upon the face of the country, and as grass behind the back of the mower, and there is none to gather it.

The scythe is also the traditional attribute of Chronos or Father Time, in combination with an hourglass – an emblem found throughout Holbein's woodcut series. Chronos often became conflated with the Greek god Cronus, patron of the harvest, who carries the sickle with which he castrated his father, the sky god Uranus. The female personification of Death in the mural at Pisa also wields a scythe as a weapon as she rushes forward to mow down her victims like a human harvest.

Normally an impediment to dancing, these instruments are apparently there to be used against the living in the *Danse*. Despite the ostensible musical/dancing theme, references to violence abound in *Danse Macabre* texts. While the Emperor merely contrasts his own imperial emblems – the raised sword and orb – with Death's pickaxe and spade, other characters make explicit reference to aggression. Thus the *Curé* (Parson) observes, 'Il nest homme que mort nassaille' (*There is no man whom Death does not attack*), while the bold Sergeant asks indignantly, 'Comme mose la mort frapper' (*So how dare Death strike me?*). The language of aggression is particularly strong in the address to the Constable, as befits his rank: 'Dun cop iabatz le plus estable / Rien nest darmes quant mort assault' (*With one blow I strike down the most solid. Weapons are of no use when Death attacks*). Lydgate uses similar language in Death's words to the Constable, in the Cardinal's lament ('dethe is come me sodeynli to assaile', *E*:99), in the Knight's words ('But dethes stroke hath made me so lame', *E*:183), and especially in his own 'Verba Translatoris' where he describes 'the sodeyne vyolence / Of cruel dethe [...] / Which sleeth allas by stroke of pestilence / Both 3onge and olde of low and hie parage' (*E*:5-8). The reference to pestilence is interesting, but common is the suggestion of a sudden stroke or attack – a motif repeated in Death's closing words to the Squire: 'For no man mai fro dethes stroke fle' (*E*:224).

The allegorical figure of Death as the aggressor can be found from the fifteenth century onwards on tomb monuments across Europe, and in some cases the artists may well have been inspired by the *Danse*. A prime example is the brass of the park-keeper James Gray (d. 1591) at Hunsdon (Hertfordshire), which shows Death despatching both Gray and the stag

that he thought to shoot with his crossbow (Fig. 8).[39] The irony is
unmistakable and, as is often the case in the *Danse*, the manner of death
befits the victim. The latter is particularly true in Holbein's woodcuts
where aggression is much more in evidence than dance, most notably in
the woodcut of the Knight who is here being presented as an emblem of
masculinity and futile pugnacity. Raising his sword in vain, he is being
transfixed not with Death's usual dart or spear, but with a jousting lance
wielded by a gleeful cadaver who wears a cuirass over a mail shirt or
haubergeon (Fig. 9).[40] While the armour on both figures is accurately
depicted, that worn by Death looks late-fifteenth-century in style and
dilapidated, as contemporaries would have recognised. This may imply
that Death is wearing the spoils of a knight killed at an earlier date.[41]

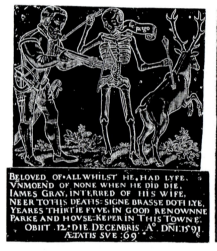

Fig. 8. Brass of the park-keeper James
Gray (d. 1591), Hunsdon (Hertfordshire).
Rubbing: Martin Stuchfield.

Fig. 9. Death and the Knight, woodcut by Hans Holbein the Younger
published in 1538.

Part of this extreme aggression appears to be role-playing by Death to
suit each victim. Holbein's woodcuts also show Death – or his
representative(s) – don a cardinal's hat while approaching the Pope,
assume the role of cup-bearer while pouring the King his final drink, and

[39] See also Oosterwijk (2008), 72-74 and fig. 12.
[40] A woodcut subsequently added to the series shows Death attacking the Soldier
with a femur, which some of Holbein's later followers changed into a dart.
[41] I am grateful to Philip Lankester and the late Claude Blair for this information.

drag away the Queen in the guise of a court jester. Death likewise leads away the Abbot while sporting the latter's mitre and staff. Yet does this make Death the Abbot's *alter ego*, or is he playing the part in mockery? It is worth raising the question of identity once more.

Identity

The idea of the *Danse* as a mirror to the reader/beholder, and the dead dancers as a mirror image of each living victim, is discussed elsewhere in this volume. The mirroring effect in the juxtaposition and postures of the Three Living and the Three Dead is likewise strong, especially in early examples (Pls 3-4).[42] Also related is the motif of the living who behold an image of Death in the mirror instead of their own reflection.[43] Yet what does this macabre mirror image actually mean: is it a foreshadowing of death, *i.e.* Death personified, or does it reveal the viewer's true essence, *viz.* the skull beneath the still fair exterior? Both may ultimately be the same: an image of what the future holds for any human.

Mirroring and symmetry were favourite devices among medieval artists. Whereas the *Danse Macabre* traditionally took the form of a chain of dancers, human life was often presented as a circle or semi-circle in depictions of the Ages of Man to show the cycle of birth, growth, maturity, decline and death. Being born inevitably means dying, as a German woodcut of *c.*1480 of the Wheel of Life demonstrates (Fig. 10).[44] The baby in the cradle mirrors the corpse in his grave, while the toddler with his whirligig mirrors the old man leaning on his staff, as emphasised by the pointing finger. Even the leisurely pursuit of the young man with his hunting bird is compared to the older man's focus on money – both ultimately the kind of vain preoccupations that the living find themselves censured for in the *Danse*. Some sins were considered typical of a particular age group, as is evident in the Three Living who are presented as young nobles out hunting. The Lover (*amoureux*) in the *Danse* is naturally a young man because lust naturally goes with youth, whereas avarice is a typical sin of the old: an old lecher is simply a figure of ridicule, but an image of a young miser is much harder to find.

---

[42] See especially the essays by Christine Kralik and Frances Eustace in this volume, and also Susanna G. Fein, 'Life and Death, Reader and Page: Mirrors of Mortality in English Manuscripts', *Mosaic*, 35:1 (2002), 69-94.

[43] See in particular the essay by Kristiane Lemé-Hébuterne in this volume.

[44] John Winter Jones, 'Observations on the Origin of the Division of Man's Life into Stages', *Archaeologia*, 35 (1853), 167-89.

Fig. 10. Wheel of Life, or *Rota vitae alias fortunae*, with seven Ages, woodcut, Middle-Rhine area, *c.*1480 (London, British Library, IC.35). © The British Library.

What is important in the presentation of the cadaver in medieval art is the idea of loss of identity: beauty, clothes, status, riches – all are lost instantly when Death strikes, as we are incessantly reminded in the *Danse*. Alongside the strongly erotic subtext to Death's exhortation 'Allons nous deshabiller' (*Let us go and take our clothes off*) to the Bride (*espousee*) in the *Danse Macabre des Femmes*, there is a further meaning:[45] many characters in this all-female version of the *Danse*, including the Little Girl (*ieune fille*), express regret for the clothes they must now exchange for a shroud. While this might represent a misogynist's view of female frivolity, clothes are also an indication of status and therefore an obvious way for contemporaries to identify specific social representatives in the *Danse*.

The adage 'you cannot take it with you' was especially true in the Middle Ages when it was custom to bury corpses naked but for a shroud. The Bride therefore has to undress to enter her grave instead of her marriage bed. The Emperor similarly recognises that he must relinquish his sword, orb and heraldic mantle for a shroud: without these trappings his body is just another corpse, no matter how splendid his monument. No funeral pomp or imposing tomb monument may hide this basic fact, however much they impress the beholder. Lydgate reiterated this in his didactic poem *The Debate of the Horse, Goose, and Sheep* of c.1440:

> Tweene riche & poore what is the difference,
> What deth approchith in any creature,
> Sauff a gay tumbe ffresh of apparence?[46]

> (*What is the difference between rich and poor when death comes to any living being, except for a showy tomb fair in appearance?*)

However, the clergy were buried in their vestments, which is ironic if one considers the monuments commissioned by such dignitaries as Archbishop Chichele in Canterbury, Bishop Fleming in Lincoln, Bishop Beckington in Wells, or Cardinal Jean de la Grange in Avignon: all show the corpse naked except for a shroud.

Yet the loss of clothes and status symbols is less hard to bear than the thought of what happens to the body itself after death. This message was conveyed in a number of medieval exempla, such as the story of the

---

[45] Ann Tukey Harrison (ed.), with a chapter by Sandra L. Hindman, *The Danse Macabre of Women: Ms.fr. 995 of the Bibliothèque Nationale* (Kent/London: Kent State University Press, 1994), 113.

[46] *The Debate of the Horse, Goose, and Sheep*, ll. 612-14, in Henry Noble MacCracken and Merriam Sherwood (eds), *The Minor Poems of John Lydgate, II*, EETS, o.s. 192 (London: Oxford University Press, 1934).

wicked young Emperor who repents after being shown the corpse of his dead father. The illustration of their encounter in the Carthusian Miscellany is accompanied by a dialogue between the young Emperor and his father, in which the latter uses the repulsive state of his own stinking corpse as a warning of what awaits his son (Pl. 6).[47] The dead father thus serves his living son as a mirror, just as the Three Dead are the fathers of the Three Living in some versions of the Legend. The son knows that it is his father's corpse because the tomb is recognisable through its heraldry and the imperial effigy, but these only disguise the ultimate brutal truth below, *viz.* the real corpse (not a cadaver effigy!) in its putrid state.

Putrefaction has other implications apart from an unpleasant smell and sight: it erases the possibility of recognising the deceased once the face has been reduced to nothing but a skull, perhaps with just some tufts of hair clinging to it. Skulls are normally anonymous: only modern forensic artists can try to restore a face – and perhaps an identity – to a person long after death. This grim recognition of mortality and transience dawns on Hamlet in the iconic moment in Shakespeare's *Hamlet*, V, i, when he gazes upon Yorick's skull and utters the famous words, 'Alas, poor Yorick. I knew him, Horatio [...]'. The grave-digger is able to identify Yorick only because of location of the grave in which he had buried the fool twenty-three years earlier. Of course, the dead lose not only their identity but even their integrity when their remains are dug up and mixed with those of others in a charnel house or pit. The dancers in the *Danse* and in the 'Imago mortis' woodcut are at least still intact as corpses.

Portraits

Physical appearance is thus always transient. It changes throughout our lives as we grow up and then old, until the final stage of death when one's physiognomy is reduced to just the bare skull – the grim image that medieval artists sometimes used as a reflection in the mirror. It is worth considering that true portraiture in the modern sense of the word – warts and all – really reappeared only in the fourteenth century.[48] In the medieval period portraiture was not usually an important aspect of tomb monuments: heraldry, epitaphs, status symbols and location were the prime means of identifying the deceased, whereas the tomb effigy was just

---

[47] BL Add. MS 37049, fol. 86v; part of the text is quoted in Woolf (1968), 313.

[48] For a recent discussion, see Stephen Perkinson, *The Likeness of the King. A Prehistory of Portraiture in Late Medieval France* (Chicago/London: University of Chicago Press, 2009).

an idealised representation. The same may be said of the figures in the *Danse*: although the dead king in the French poem speaks of 'pourtraiture' the term carries a more general meaning of 'likenesses' or 'types'.

Cadaver monuments were a demonstration of pious humility and a declaration of faith in the Resurrection, as expressed in Job 19:25-26. As such they look ahead to the life hereafter, just as the *Danse* generally looks back at a life lived well or badly, and the Legend looks forward to a new life of repentance. However, cadaver effigies are also a visualisation of the physical self erased: whereas the soul is immortal, the sinful flesh must be annihilated – an essential task that the worms will gladly undertake. This type of monument did not have wide appeal and it may be no coincidence that female examples are especially rare. One such is the incised cadaver slab in Nyköping in which the crown signals Ingeborch's maidenly status (Fig. 3). Another is the late-fifteenth-century double-decker tomb of Alice de la Pole, duchess of Suffolk, at Ewelme (Oxfordshire) with its unmistakably female *transi* that appears to have been intended to resemble the deceased in death (Fig. 11).

Fig. 11. The faces of the two effigies on the double-decker tomb of Alice de la Pole, duchess of Suffolk (d. 1475), Ewelme (Oxfordshire). Photos: C.B. Newham.

Yet are these cadaver effigies always prospective 'portraits' of the deceased? Ingeborch's cadaver image (Fig. 3) is obviously stylised, but it has a crown and long hair as individualistic elements. Therefore, while it is not a 'portrait', it is evidently meant to represent her. Very different is the curious phenomenon of double tomb monuments with two effigies of the

deceased and only a single cadaver effigy below.[49] An example is the
double-decker monument of *c*.1542 at Vianen (Netherlands), which shows
Reynout van Brederode (d. 1556) and his wife Philippote van der Marck
(d. 1537) as shrouded but 'fresh' corpses resting above a particularly
gruesome cadaver. This and other such examples – usually of a cadaver
juxtaposed with effigies of the deceased *au vif* – have raised questions
about the status and identity of the corpse below. Could it be a generic
emblem of mortality or an allegorical image of Death personified – the
same question that is asked about the dead protagonists in the *Danse*?
Evidence against this can be found in the will of Isabel Despenser,
countess of Warwick (d. 1439), which stipulated 'my Image to be made all
naked, and no thyng on my hede but myn here cast bakwardys'.[50]
Unfortunately her monument is lost, unlike Alice de la Pole's, but the text
in her will suggests a self-representation.

   In Renaissance France the naked but not yet decomposing *transi*
figures on five high-status monuments were certainly meant to be
representations of the deceased, as an inspection of the cadaver monuments
at Saint-Denis and Brou will reveal.[51] It should be noted, however, that
Catherine de Médicis rejected the first, more brutally realistic version by
Girolamo della Robbia in favour of Germain Pilon's more flattering *transi*
in a Venus *pudica*-inspired pose that now lies beside the cadaver effigy of
her husband Henri II at Saint-Denis; the first – unfinished – version is in
the Louvre. Yet earlier artists, patrons and viewers may have held different
views on the identity of the cadaver, and views also changed over time:
whereas some monuments may be ambiguous, most later skeletons are
allegorical and represent not the deceased, but Death personified.[52]

   If some cadaver effigies were indeed meant to represent the deceased
after death, rather than a personification of Death himself, the dead in the
Danse Macabre are instead anonymous. Yet what about the living

---

[49] Oosterwijk (2005), 41-42.

[50] Pamela M. King, '"My Image to be made all naked": Cadaver Tombs and the
Commemoration of Women in Fifteenth-Century England', *The Ricardian*, 13
(2003), 294-314, esp. 308-14.

[51] Conrad Meit's two separate double-decker tombs at Brou (Bourg-en-Bresse)
commemorate Margaret of Austria (d. 1530) and her husband Philibert 'le Beau' II
of Savoy (d. 1504), while Saint-Denis houses the double-decker monuments of
Anne of Brittany (d. 1514) and her husband Louis XII (d. 1515); François I (d.
1547) and his first wife Claude (d. 1524); and Henri II (d. 1559) and his wife
Catherine de Médicis (d. 1589). See Cohen (1973), esp. chapter 6 and figs 80-96.

[52] For example, see the ambiguous recumbent skeleton on the incised slab of
Andreas Dix (d. 1711) at Wijk near Maastricht (Netherlands) in Oosterwijk (2008),
62 and fig. 1.

participants in the *Danse*? It is usually assumed that these simply represent social stereotypes, but a number of later examples contain unmistakable portraits of real people whom contemporaries were evidently meant to recognise. One example is the stone relief of 1534-37 in Dresden, which contains portraits of Charles V (as Emperor), his brother Ferdinand I (as King of the Romans), the patron George the Bearded (as Duke of Saxony) and the latter's son Johann (as Count), all wearing the chain of the Order of the Golden Fleece.[53] George the Bearded commissioned the frieze himself for the Georgentor, so he must have intended it to incorporate portraits and thus in a way to have a commemorative function.

Fig. 12. Death and the Emperor, woodcut by Hans Holbein the Younger published in 1538.

Fig. 13. Emperor Maximilian I (d. 1519), woodcut portrait by Albrecht Dürer, 1518.

Other examples can be found in Holbein's woodcut series, most notably the King who bears a striking resemblance to Francis I (d. 1547), one of the three kings commemorated with a cadaver effigy at Saint-Denis: even the cloth behind the figure is decorated with fleurs-de-lys. It is also conceivable that Holbein's Emperor was modelled on Albrecht Dürer's 1518 famous woodcut portrait of Maximilian I (Figs 12-13). Apart

---

[53] Marius Winzeler (ed.), *Dresdner Totentanz: das Relief in der Dreikönigskirche Dresden* (Halle an der Saale: Verlag Janos Stekovics, 2001), 4-5, 13, and figs 4-5.

from the facial resemblance, the Emperor wears the chain of the Order of the Golden Fleece – a sign not just of individuality but of status, especially with the hat in Dürer's woodcut replaced by a crown, and the inclusion of the imperial emblems, *viz.* the raised sword, the orb and sceptre. Holbein thus appears to have cast real people in the roles of two of Death's archetypal victims in the *Danse*, albeit one living and one already dead.

Such incorporation of portraits in the *Danse* may be much older: the Basel-born engraver Matthäus Merian the Elder recorded a tradition that the *Danse Macabre* mural of c.1440 in the Dominican cemetery in Basel featured 'cryptoportraits' of antipope Felix V (elected 1439), Emperor Sigismund (1368-1437), and his Habsburg son-in-law and successor Albrecht II (1379-1439).[54] Heraldry and imperial/royal insignia may well have played a role here, too, to indicate the double nature of these victims of Death. It should be noted that Sigismund and Albrecht were probably dead when the Basel *Danse* was painted, but not so Felix V who lived until 1451: perhaps it was possible to portray both dead and living persons in the *Danse*, just as some patrons (*e.g.* Chichele) commissioned their own cadaver effigy during their lifetime. While it is debatable whether Niklaus Manuel intended the Pope in his *Danse Macabre* mural of 1515-17 in Bern to resemble Leo X (1513-21), he did include himself as the Painter at the very end, complete with his own coat of arms as further proof of his identity.[55] The painter Hans Hug Kluber, who renovated the Basel mural in 1568, also added a portrait of himself at the very end; the Mother and Child in the preceding scene are thought to be Kluber's wife and son.[56] Jakob Hiebeler likewise incorporated his own portrait in his *Danse Macabre* mural of 1602 at Füssen[57] as did Jakob von Wyl in his painted *Danse* on canvas of c.1615 in the Jesuit college in Luzern.[58]

Even though the existence of cryptoportraits in Basel can no longer be ascertained, these later examples are suggestive. Lydgate revealed his

---

[54] Kaiser (1982), 194-95.

[55] Johannes Tripps, *'Den Würmer wirst Du Wildbret sein.' Der Berner Totentanz des Niklaus Manuel Deutsch in den Aquarellkopien von Albrecht Kauw (1649)*, Schriften des Bernischen Historischen Museums, 6 (Berne: Verlag Bernisches Historisches Museum, 2005) 32-33, 98-99.

[56] See Kaiser (1982), 272 and 274 for Merian's engravings.

[57] Reinhold Böhm, *Sagt Ja Sagt Nein. Der Füssener Totentanz und das Fortwirken der Totentanzidee im Ostallgäuer und Außerferner Raum: Oberstdorf, Füssen (St. Sebastian), Breitenwang, Elbigenalp, Elmen, Schattwald, Pfronten (Lithographien)* (Füssen: Historischer Verein Alt Füssen, 1990), 13-14, 38; Hammerstein (1980), 220 and pl. 226.

[58] Hammerstein (1980), 220-22, pl. 223.

identity at the end of his poem, although this need not imply that his portrait was included in the *Danse Macabre* cycle painted around 1430 at Old St Paul's Cathedral, London. However, Lydgate did introduce the enigmatic figure of a hitherto unidentified court magician, 'Maister Jon Rikelle some tyme tregetowre / Of nobille harry kynge of Ingelonde / And of Fraunce the myghti Conquerowre' (*E*:513-15) – a rare occurrence of a named character in the *Danse*, or actually *two* named characters. It is usually assumed that the inclusion of the 'some tyme tregetowre' Rikelle in Lydgate's poem means that he was already dead, but nobody of that name has so far been identified in the accounts of Henry V. However, more important than Rikelle himself was the opportunity for Lydgate to name the late king whose demise was considered a national tragedy: Henry V, who had died in the prime of life in 1422.

Fig. 14. 'Vng roy mort' (*a dead King*) and the Author, final woodcut in Guy Marchant's *Danse Macabre* edition first published in 1485.

Just as the King is the pivot in chess, he may also have been the key player in the *Danse Macabre* mural in Paris and in Lydgate's adaptation. The French *Danse Macabre* proper ends with the closing words of the final cadaver who praises the hermit's acceptance of his fate and offers a grim reminder to the reader/beholder, 'Il nest qui ait point de demain' (*There is nobody who has any tomorrow*). Yet the final twist of the *Danse* is the added figure and stanza of a recumbent cadaver who represents 'Vng

roy mort' (*A dead King*): his single stanza is not part of the preceding
dialogue and appears to be an interpolation between the *Danse* and the
author's epilogue. Like the dead dancers before him, this corpse is
nameless yet he is unmistakably a King: not only does Marchant's
woodcut show his fallen crown (Fig. 14) but the figure also refers
explicitly to his former status, 'Si ay ie este roy coronnez' (*As once I was a
crowned king*).

At first sight, these words and the figure itself may seem just another
morbid commonplace with echoes of the medieval Wheel of Fortune,
which also traditionally showed the rise and fall of kings with the words
''Regnabo' (*I shall reign*), 'Regno' (*I am reigning*), 'Regnavi' (*I have
reigned*) and 'Sum sine regno' (*I am without a kingdom*). One mural of
*c.*1350-1400 in the church of Birkerød (Denmark), not only shows the four
kings in their rise and fall, but also a worm-riddled figure of Death next to
a fifth king in the centre of the Wheel.[59] It is worth noting that the first full
printed version of Lydgate's *Dance of Death* was as an appendix to his
Fall of Princes in the edition published by Richard Tottel in 1554, and the
association of the *Danse* with the fall of kings was widespread: in the
fresco of 1474 in Beram (Istria) the *Danse Macabre* is juxtaposed with a
Wheel of Fortune.[60] Yet the recumbent figure of the 'roy mort' in the
Danse is also reminiscent of a cadaver effigy, which is all the more
interesting when one realises that the church of Les Saints Innocents was
situated on the rue Saint-Denis, the main thoroughfare that ran from
central Paris to the royal abbey of Saint-Denis in the north. It was there
that the kings and queens of France were buried and their funeral
processions would have led past the church.

The *Danse Macabre* mural in Paris was begun in August 1424 and
finished in Lent 1425, according to the anonymous author known only as
the 'Burgher of Paris'.[61] This means that the mural was created when
France had no crowned king and the city was ruled by an English regent,
John duke of Bedford, for Charles VI had died in Paris on 21 October
1422 while his son-in-law and heir – the victorious English king Henry V
– had predeceased him on 31 August. Since then the country had been torn

---

[59] See the Mills-Kronborg Collection of Danish Church Wall Paintings on
http://ica.princeton.edu/images/mills/04-039.jpg (accessed 29 October 2010).

[60] See the essay by Tomislav Vignjević in this volume.

[61] Janet Shirley (transl.), *A Parisian Journal 1405-1449* (Oxford: Clarendon Press,
1968), 204. For a discussion of the mural in Paris and its historical context, see
Sophie Oosterwijk, 'Of Dead Kings, Dukes and Constables: the Historical Context
of the *Danse Macabre* in Late Medieval Paris', *Journal of the British
Archaeological Association*, 161 (2008), 131-62.

once again between the Armagnacs led by the disinherited dauphin (the later Charles VII) and the English on behalf of the infant Henry VI, son of Henry V and heir to the dual kingdom of England and France.

If heraldry, status symbols, epitaphs and location enabled contemporaries to identify memorials, then the figures of the dying King towards the start of the mural in Paris and the 'roy mort' at the end must have seemed obvious allusions to the late lamented king Charles VI at a time when France was without a crowned and anointed king. Although Marchant's woodcuts are in many ways an updated version of the mural, the King does wear the French royal mantle decorated with fleurs-de-lys (*cf.* Fig. 16 and Pl. 16), which is what we find in the illuminated *Danse Macabre* border decoration in a book of hours produced in Paris not long after the creation of the mural (Paris, BnF ms. Rothschild 2535, fol. 107v). Moreover, the words of the King appear to contain allusions to a notorious incident that occurred on 28 January 1393 when Charles VI barely escaped being burnt to death while dressed in the highly inflammable costume of an 'homme sauvage' (*wild man*). Although the King ostensibly complains about the raucous quality of Death's music ('Je nay point apris a danser / A danse et note si sauuage') and his last line 'En la fin fault deuenir cendre' (*In the end we must all turn to ashes*) reads like a commonplace about the inevitability of death, the words in the mouth of the King cannot but have reminded contemporaries of this notorious episode.

Although the destruction of the mural in 1669 means we can no longer inspect the figure of the King for signs of likeness, the combination of heraldry, poem and context suggests that it was intended to be a cryptoportrait of Charles VI. The political circumstances in Paris and London at this time cannot be discussed at length here. However, there is reason to believe that Lydgate likewise included allusions to the late Henry V in his poem, which may have been matched by a similar cryptoportrait in the painted scheme in London.[62] If these hypotheses are correct, then the *Danse* scheme at Les Saints Innocents in Paris and the slightly later one at Old St Paul's Cathedral in London were not just moralities but also metaphors for two royal deaths and the trauma suffered by two nations bereft of their kings. The inclusion of cryptoportraits in the *Danse* schemes in Paris, London and possibly Basel may have given the impetus to the wide dissemination of a motif that had been in existence in some form since at least the later fourteenth century, but without having

---

[62] Sophie Oosterwijk, 'Death, Memory and Commemoration: John Lydgate and "Macabrees Daunce" at Old St Paul's Cathedral, London', in Caroline M. Barron and Clive Burgess (eds), *Memory and Commemoration in Medieval England*, 2008 Harlaxton Symposium Proceedings (Donington: Shaun Tyas, 2010), 185-201.

the impact it was to have from 1425 on. In addition, these cryptoportraits may well have inspired the proven inclusion of real-life portraits in other schemes, such as in Dresden.

More tentatively, one could even wonder whether recognisable portraits in the *Danse* played a role in the development of the Renaissance *vanitas* portrait that shows the sitter at his best, but with a skull as a *memento mori* for the beholder – or perhaps playing the role of the sitter's future *alter ego*? This type of portrait emerged in the sixteenth century and was still in vogue in the seventeenth.[63] It shows the living sitter with a skull and perhaps other emblems of time and mortality, such as a clock or watch, wilting flowers, an empty glass, a lute with a broken string, or a newly extinguished candle. In exceptional cases there may even be the personification of Death himself looming up behind the sitter, an example being the painted portrait of Sir Brian Tuke in Munich (Bayerische Staatsgemäldesammlung) which, in a variation on Hans Holbein's original *c.*1527 portrait of Tuke in Washington (National Gallery of Art), shows Death with his scythe looking at Tuke while pointing at the hourglass on the desk before him.[64]

Skulls are more than just symbolic objects. They represent both a once living – and recognisable – human being and a portent of our own future condition. Although the inclusion of skulls and other death emblems may signal a posthumous portrait, the majority of *vanitas* portraits are contemplative in nature, *i.e.* a demonstration of the sitters' awareness of their own mortality and a recognition that their portraits will outlive them. This is evident in the 1567 portrait of John Isham (1525-96) at Lamport Hall (Northamptonshire), which shows the founder of the dynasty resting his right hand on a skull (Fig. 15). A clock on the wall behind him serves as a warning about the passage of time, while Isham is moreover wearing a skull-ring on the left index finger with which he points at the skull. This

---

[63] See the brief discussion of *vanitas* portraits by Pierroberto Scaramella and Maria Giulia Aurigemma in Alberto Tenenti (ed.), *Humana Fragilitas. The Themes of Death in Europe from the 13th to the 18th Century* (2000, trans. Clusone: Ferrari, 2002), esp. 61-62, 78-79, 179-81, and figs 38-40, 54-55, 136-37. Also Tarnya Cooper, 'Memento Mori Portraiture. Painting, Protestant Culture and the Patronage of Middle Elites in England and Wales 1540-1630, unpublished PhD thesis (University of Sussex, 2001), and Niklas Gliessmann, 'Memento mori in der Tafelmalerei der Südniederlande zwischen 1450 und 1520', in Andrea von Hülsen-Esch and Hiltrud Westermann-Angerhausen with Stefanie Knöll (eds), *Zum Sterben schön: Alter, Totentanz und Sterbekunst von 1500 bis heute* (Regensburg: Schnell & Steiner, 2006), vol. 1, 321-28.

[64] Tuke had been ill not long before Holbein painted him, and his sense of his own mortality is indicated by the folded sheet before him with a text from Job 10:20.

painting thus serves both as a portrait and as a *vanitas* reminder about Death coming to us all, thereby echoing the message of the *Danse*. After all, every portrait eventually becomes a memorial to the sitter whose features will ultimately be reduced to just that – a skull – once he has had his own fatal encounter with Death, as Isham makes clear in a mute but telling dialogue with the beholder.

Fig. 15. Portrait of John Isham (1567), by an anonymous artist, oil on panel, Lamport Hall (Northamptonshire). © Lamport Hall Trust.

Conclusion

The woodcut in the *Nuremberg Chronicle* is what the caption 'Imago mortis' declares it to be: an image solely of death, and a reminder of the physical fate that awaits us all once death and the decomposition process have turned our bodies into anonymous cadavers. The corpse that rises from its grave does not represent the resurrection on Judgement Day but a temporary state of macabre 'revitalisation' with the didactic purpose of confronting the viewer with a stark *memento mori* warning. Whether or not readers of the *Chronicle* truly believed in revenants, they were familiar enough with the idea of dancing corpses to grasp the message. The question of whether this woodcut represents a true *Danse Macabre*, or whether it is deliberately ambiguous, is thus largely an academic one.

Whatever the origins of the *Danse* may have been or wherever it originated, it outlived other medieval forms of 'the macabre', such as the Legend of the Three Living and the Three Dead that had largely run its course by the mid sixteenth century. A more individual contemplation of death came to be favoured, and the *vanitas* portrait is part of that development. The strength of the *Danse* – and probably the reason for its endurance – is no doubt its adaptability: it was capable of incorporating or emphasising different metaphors from dance and music to violence, pious thought and social satire, stereotypes and individual portraits. Like the Legend it lent itself well to dissemination both as a text and as a visual image, but unlike the Legend with its rigid structure – its juxtaposition of two groups of three protagonists, all male and of equal rank and age – the *Danse* could be expanded or reduced, altered and updated. It may well have been the historical circumstances in Paris and London – the deaths of Henry V and Charles VI – that gave the *Danse* a topical new relevance to contemporaries. Yet even when the memory of incorporated historical portraits faded, the *Danse* still sent out a strong message about mortality that had the power to shock each new generation.

Acknowledgements

I should like to thank Martin Stuchfield, Cameron Newham, the Lamport Hall Trust, and my co-editor Stefanie Knöll for their help in providing me with illustrations. I am also grateful to Sally Badham for reading and commenting on an earlier draft of this paper, and to Julian Luxford for discussions on the subject.

DANCES OF THE LIVING AND THE DEAD: A STUDY OF *DANSE MACABRE* IMAGERY WITHIN THE CONTEXT OF LATE-MEDIEVAL DANCE CULTURE

FRANCES EUSTACE WITH PAMELA M. KING

> The origins of *The Dance of Death* have been traced in poetry, painting and sermon, but none of these 'sources' helps explain why it should have been a dance.[1]

Beginning with a brief study of the execution and reception of dance and dance-song in the Late Middle Ages, this essay provides a context for an understanding of why Death danced in the allegory of the *Danse Macabre* and consequently also the reason for the powerful resonance of the allegory. For the modern reader the text in an edition such as Guyot Marchant's *Danse Macabre* is accompanied by images. However, it could be argued that for most fifteenth-century readers the opposite would have been the case: the body-language of the dance, expressing the interactions between Death and his reluctant partners, would have been more easily readable than the written word.

My understanding and experience of dancing and dance history allow me to explore in this essay how the shared common language of dance may account for the universal appeal of the *Danse Macabre* across a range of different cultures and media in the late Middle Ages, and suggest possible readings of the imagery of the allegory. As illustrative examples I shall use the Paris *Danse Macabre* as reproduced in the 1485 and later woodcut editions by Guyot Marchant (excluding the *Danse Macabre des Femmes*, which was a separate later composition), and John Lydgate's Middle English *Dance of Death* of *c.*1426 that once accompanied the

---

[1] Richard Axton, *European Drama of the Early Middle Ages* (London: Hutchinson, 1974), 58.

painted scheme at Old St Paul's Cathedral, London.[2]

Dancing was arguably the most popular and widespread communal activity during the Middle Ages, comparable with religious ceremony in the numbers of participants involved. At all ages and levels of society, from courts to commons, from childhood to old age, people had a shared experience of this language through participation or observation. One dimension of the development of the doctrine of purgatory in the twelfth century was that ritual life developed the symbiotic relationship between the living and the dead. Moreover, under the influence of Franciscan piety, there was a gradual shift from a collective response to that relationship towards a focus on the journey of the individual spirit and the need to prepare for that journey. Everyday objects, images, and shared experiences were pressed into didactic service, particularly by mendicant preachers.[3] Reflection on those shared experiences and memories was rendered in both Latin and English sermons and devotional texts through the pervasive image of the *speculum* or mirror;[4] an idea taken up by John Lydgate in his *Dance of Death*:

> In this myrrow[r]e / eueri wight mai fynde
> That hym behoueth / to go vpon this daunce (ll. 49-50)

Amongst the array of imaginatively realised mirrors, the *Danse Macabre* sought to provide one that used the universal language of the bodily experience of the dance to help the reader reflect. One could argue that a focus on an animated personified Death freed the minds of observers from a preoccupation with the manner of their dying and helped them concentrate on their spiritual readiness for the moment of their death.

The role of dance in late-medieval culture

Dancing in its various forms at entertainments and festivals was integral to the cultural and social life of the European Middle Ages. In Italy in 1490, at the wedding of Giangaleazzo Sforza and Isabella of Aragon, one

---

[2] All Lydgate quotations in this essay are taken from version A (Ellesmere MS) in Florence Warren (ed.), *The Dance of Death*, Early English Text Society, o.s. 181 (Oxford: Oxford University Press, 1931).

[3] G.R. Owst, *Literature and Pulpit in Medieval England* (Oxford: Blackwell, 1961), 305.

[4] See the essay by Kristiane Lemé-Hébuterne in this volume, and also H. Leith Spencer, *English Preaching in the Late Middle Ages* (Oxford: Clarendon Press, 1993), 153, 372.

hundred of the richest and most beautiful ladies of the court danced and, in a truly international cultural exchange, performances were given by dancers from Spain, Poland, Hungary, Germany and France.[5] Away from the court, pilgrims of all ranks danced to the songs of the *Llibre Vermell de Monserrat*, a codex of mainly liturgical material compiled in the late fourteenth century and containing ten musical pieces notated between 1396 and 1399.[6] The vocabulary needed to describe an evening of carolling and dancing at an inn in France was considered important enough to be included in a fourteenth-century conversation manual for Englishmen:

> Doncques viennent avant ou presence du signeur les corneors et clariouers, ou leur fretielles et clarions, et se commencent a croulent, balent, dancent, houvent et chantent de biaux karoles sanz cesser jusques a mynuyt.[7]

> *(Therefore horn-players and trumpeters came into the presence of the gentleman with their flutes and trumpets and began to jig, dance, shout and sing beautiful caroles without ceasing until midnight.)*

The frustration for the dance historian lies in the lack of detail relating to what was danced, what steps were executed, or how the dancers were organised. For example, did those one hundred Italian ladies at the Sforza wedding in 1490 dance *en masse* or did they take turns in pairs or in groups? Just as the vast majority of the melodies of the troubadours have been lost, contained as they were only in the minds of the performers and audiences, so the movements of actual medieval dancers have left scant trace.

There are surviving treatises that give specific choreographic instructions, although the earliest were written by Italian dancing teachers in the fifteenth century.[8] The most accessible of these, which also includes

---

[5] Guglielmo Ebreo of Pesaro, *On the Practice or Art of Dancing / De Practica seu Arte Tripudii*, ed. and trans. Barbara Sparti (Oxford: Oxford University Press, 1993), 52.

[6] E.K. Chambers, *The Medieval Stage* (Oxford: Clarendon Press, 1954), 2 vols, I, 163. The songs from the *Llibre Vermell* are widely available and can be downloaded at http://www.emusic.com/album/Egidius-Kwartet-El-llibre-Vermell-de-Montserrat-MP3-Download/11034214.html (accessed 22 July 2009).

[7] Richard Leighton Greene, *The Early English Carols* (Oxford: Clarendon Press, 1935), xliv (London, BL MS Harley 3088).

[8] Domenico da Piacenza wrote *De Arte Saltandi et Choreas Ducendi* around 1425; see Paris, BnF, ms. ital. 972, downloadable version available at

complete dances, is *De Practica Seu Arte Tripudii* by Guglielmo Ebreo of Pesaro (born *c.*1420), who was also known as Giovanni Ambrosio.[9] For the fourteenth century and earlier we have only literary sources, which are by their nature technically less reliable, although they do illustrate the vital social functions of the dance.

Dancing as an integral part of courtship occurs in numerous texts, for example in the thirteenth-century *Jeu de Robin et Marion* by Adam de la Halle.[10] Here, after Robin has asked Marion for love tokens, she in return requests that he prove himself adequate to dance at the evening festivities. This is a thinly disguised opportunity for her to admire his best features, from head to toe.

> Robin, par l'ame ten pere, / sés tu bien baler du piet? [...]
> Robin, par l'ame ten pere, / car nous fai le tour dou chief. [...]
> Robin, par l'ame ten pere, / car me fai le tour du bras. [...]
> Robin, par l'ame ton pere, / sés tu fere le touret? [...]

> *(Robin, on your father's soul, do you know well how to dance with your foot? [...] Robin, on your father's soul, make for us the turn of the head. [...] Robin, on your father's soul, make for me the turn of the arms. [...] Robin, on your father's soul, do you know how to do the turn (pirouette)? [...])*

Illustrations of this passage highlight the difficulties facing the dance historian when interpreting a static two-dimensional representation of the three-dimensional kinetic nature of dance. For example, in Aix-en-Provence, Bib. Méjanes MS 166 (Rés. MS 14), the first miniature (fol. 4r) shows Robin turning a nicely shaped calf and left foot while Marion raises her hands in modest admiration; *le tour dou chief* and the *touret* are equally subdued, whereas the illustration of the *tour de bras* shows Robin's right arm raised high in a flamboyant gesture, while his left hand is drawing back his tunic to expose his crossed legs as he stands on his toes. It is difficult to distinguish between expressions of surprise or admiration on the faces of Marion and her sheep, and equally impossible to surmise what movements preceded the position depicted. Marion is

---

http://www.pbm.com/~lindahl/pnd/all.pdf (accessed 6 August 2009). Antonio Cornazano's treatise *Libro dell'Arte del Danzare* (Vatican, Bibliotheca Apostolica Vaticana, capponiano 203) dates from *c.*1455.

[9] See n. 5 above.

[10] Adam de la Halle, *Jeu de Robin et Marion*, Aix-en-Provence, Bib. Méjanes Ms. 166 (Rés MS 14), fols 3v and 4r. See http://toisondor.byu.edu/dscriptorium/aix166/ (accessed 20 October 2008).

certainly impressed as she encourages Robin to lead the *treske* at the evening festivities.

Literary allusions also show that dancing was not only an opportunity for courtship but also a means of entertainment for people of all ages and all estates: for the commoner a way of passing a pleasant evening at an inn or, at the other end of the social scale, a courtly pastime as described by the fifteenth-century Scottish poet William Dunbar (*c.*1460-1520) in *A Dance in the Queen's Chamber*.[11] Again, there is no clue in Dunbar's poem as to what dance was being performed, but clearly the manner of performance was expected to show breeding and refinement, such as Geoffrey Chaucer commends for ladies in his *Book of the Duchess* (l. 849);[12] characteristics sadly lacking in Dunbar's burlesque account. Just as Chaucer's clerk Absalon in *The Miller's Tale* shows his Oxford credentials by being able to 'trippe and daunce' in twenty ways 'after the scole of Oxenforde' (ll. 3328-30), so Dunbar's Sir John Sinclair is expected to exhibit French *chic* as he 'begowthe to dance, for he was new cum owt of France' (ll. 1-2). Unfortunately 'the an futt yeid ay onrycht and to the tother wald nocht gree' *(one foot always went awry and would not agree with the other)* and he is shouted off the floor. Dame Dounteboir, with her swaying hips and uncontrollable farting, is disastrously even less impressive (ll. 38-41). The contrast is stark between these dancers' antics and the 'trimlye dance' of Maesteres Musgraeffe who displays the desired attributes of 'guid convoy and contenance' (l. 33).

Behind its grotesque effects, Dunbar's poem demonstrates the elements of both participation and observation that were an essential part of the experience of dance in the medieval period, and also the crossing of national boundaries in the vocabulary of dance styles. The abilities, or lack of abilities, thus caricatured by Dunbar, correspond with the instructions given by Ebreo:

> The movement of her body should be humble and meek, and her carriage dignified and stately; her step should be light and her gestures shapely [....] and when she moves she should be nimble, light and restrained.[13]

Ebreo also has a comment on the relationship between dancer and audience that Dunbar's dancers would have done well to observe:

[11] William Dunbar, *The Complete Works*, ed. John Conlee (Kalamazoo, Michigan: Medieval Institute Publications, 2004).
[12] All references to the works of Chaucer are from Larry D. Benson (ed.), *The Riverside Chaucer* (Oxford: Oxford University Press, 1987).
[13] Ebreo (1993), 109.

> Further, it should be so composed and well-measured with fine airiness
> that it bestow delight and pleasure on the onlookers and on those who take
> delight in this art. And above all it should please the ladies. For dancing is
> considered more beautiful the more it pleases the multitude of spectators,
> who pass judgement according to their pleasure and instinct rather than
> according to the art [...][14]

An example from the visual arts shows in turn that dance was
considered to display not only good governance of self, demonstrating
aspects of balance, self-control and ordering of the body, on an individual
level, but was also used as an allegory to show the good and orderly
governance of state. The fresco known as *The Effects of Good Government
in the City and the Country* was commissioned for the Palazzo Publico in
Siena (1338-39) from Ambrogio Lorenzetti.[15] It shows a group of nine
women dancing a *farandol* to the accompaniment of a tenth woman with a
tambourine, whose open mouth indicates that she is singing or carolling.
The dancing is taking place in the commercial centre of the city,
conveying an atmosphere of peaceful tranquillity amidst industrious order.
The dancers are not 'performing'; indeed they are not being watched by
the other inhabitants of the picture, who are attending to their own
business, but the impression conveyed is that there is room for gentler
pastimes amidst the bustling commercial life of the well ordered city.
Furthermore, the picture's message that dancing was considered a good
expression of order and social harmony is borne out by real examples.[16] In
1308 when Edward II returned to London with his queen, Isabella of
France, the mayor himself and his dignitaries went 'coram rege et regina
karolantes' (*carolling in the presence of the king and queen*), and in 1312
they ordered 'carolling in the church and street' to celebrate the birth of
their son and heir to the throne, Edward.[17]

If these secular witnesses testify to the social function of the dance in
wholly positive terms, the attitude of the contemporary Church was more

---

[14] Ebreo (1993), 105.

[15] Randolph Starn, *Ambrogio Lorenzetti: the Palazzo Pubblico, Siena* (New York:
George Braziller, 1994); also available online at http://www.wga.hu/frames-
e.html?/html/l/lorenzet/ambrogio/ governme/ (accessed 4 May 2010).

[16] For more information about the links between the development of *Danse* and the
process of civilisation, see Irmgard Jungmann, 'Warum ausgerechnet "Tanzen"?
Musiksoziologische Aspekte der Totentanzikonographie', in Andrea von Hülschen-
Esch and Hiltrud Westermann-Angerhausen with Stefanie Knöll (eds), *'Zum
Sterben schön!' Alter, Totentanz und Sterbekunst von 1500 bis heute* (Regensburg:
Schnell & Steiner, 2006), vol. 1, 119-32, at 119.

[17] Chambers (1954), 164.

ambivalent. The clergy of Sens Cathedral were allowed to dance at festivals 'non tamen saliendo' (*however, without leaping*), and in fifteenth-century Besançon the clergy were recorded dancing a *bergerett*e at Easter to the tune of *Fidelium Sonet Vox Sobria*.[18] However, many preachers fulminated against dancing, including the fourteenth-century Dominican John Bromyard who said, 'In place of the clerk who rings the bell to call people to worship, they have a flute player'.[19] Another fourteenth-century writer accused slothful priests of rushing through their devotions 'more entendynge to haukynge and to huntynge and wrastliynge and to daunsynge and to waste so here tyme amys'.[20] A recurring theme is that of comparing and contrasting dance with religious ceremony, and a fear that the former may act as a rival attraction to the latter.[21]

The Church appears to have cautiously sanctioned some dancing within the specific context of pilgrimage, however. The anonymous scribe of the *Llibre Vermell de Montserrat*, mentioned above, explains how his songs are specifically written to serve the needs of those who desire to sing and dance on pilgrimage in an appropriate manner.[22] The scribe's recognition of the 'need' to dance is echoed rather differently in Chaucer's portrait of Perkin Revelour in *The Cook's Tale*, who is unable to resist dancing (ll. 4370-80). Yet Perkin and his apprentice friends may well have sung and danced at processions of a more sinister kind, 'sometyme lad with revel to Newgate' (l. 4402), accompanying criminals to the gallows, or dancing them to their deaths.[23]

Both Chaucer's *Cook's Tale* and the *Llibre Vermell* point to dance as not only a social grace, but also a compelling need in emotionally heightened circumstances. The most telling evidence of this function of dance can be found in the celebrated outbreaks of *choreomania* that occurred throughout northern Europe in the late-medieval and early modern periods.[24] It has been suggested that *choreomania* is a form of

---

[18] John Stevens, *Words and Music in the Middle Ages* (Cambridge: Cambridge University Press, 1986), 180.

[19] Owst (1961), 394.

[20] BL MS Harley 2398, fol. 7r, quoted in Owst (1961), 278.

[21] Owst (1961), 395.

[22] *Llibre Vermell de Montserrat*, http://www.amaranthpublishing.com/Llibre Vermell.htm (accessed 22 July 2009).

[23] Claire C. Olson, 'Chaucer and the Music of the Fourteenth Century', *Speculum*, 16 (1941), 64-91.

[24] See for example Robert E. Bartholomew, 'Rethinking the Dancing Mania', *Skeptical Inquirer*, 24:4 (July/August 2000), available on http://www.csicop.org/ si/show/rethinking_the_dancing_mania/ (accessed 11 June 2010). Also Klaus Bergdolt, 'Der spätmittelalterliche Veitstanz', in Andrea von Hülschen-Esch and

psychosomatic conversion disorder whereby mentally susceptible subjects, following trauma or an extremely stressful episode, fall into a trance-like state and act out movements and behaviours with a disinhibition that is beyond the constraints and norms of acceptable behaviour.[25] Fifty years after the most celebrated occurrence of *choreomania* in the Rhine and Moselle valleys in 1374, the *Danse Macabre* sought to express a more decorous choreography for the journey to the grave.

Dance-song or dance accompanied by text

Whether associated with courtship, social harmony, religious jubilation, or release from stress, in many examples from the period dancing is intimately connected with singing. The fundamental complementarity and inseparability of dance and text in contemporary dance-song supply another clue to the evocative imagery of the *Danse Macabre* and its reception, where the interaction of the figures through dance is accompanied by the verbal interaction conveyed in the text: a static, and silent, two-dimensional representation of dance-song. The umbrella term used during the fourteenth century to denote dance-song was *carol* or *carole*, 'the secular music of the North'.[26] The term was used to describe any dancing of an informal nature, both at court and at popular festivities, and also the singing that accompanied it. As John Stevens explains, the *carole* was not a single form but a 'dance-idea waiting to be realised in various forms'.[27]

The common ingredient of dance-song is a strong rhythmic underlay and the repetition of some lines in the form of a *burden* at the beginning and possibly a *refrain* throughout. A *burden*, sometimes called a *fote*, is usually two lines long, written at the head of the song, and is not always essential to the rhyme scheme of the following stanzas; indeed, some *burdens* are found attached to several different lyrics. Examples of this

---

Hiltrud Westermann-Angerhausen with Stefanie Knöll (eds), *'Zum Sterben schön!' Alter, Totentanz und Sterbekunst von 1500 bis heute* (Regensburg: Schnell & Steiner, 2006), vol. 1, 85-93.

[25] John Waller, *A Time to Dance, A Time to Die* (Cambridge: Icon Books, 2008), 187. Waller also covers the related topics of St Vitus' Dance and the Tarantella, which will not be discussed here.

[26] Christopher Page, *The Owl and the Nightingale: Musical Life and Ideas in France 1100-1300* (London: Dent, 1989), 77. The Chaucerian spelling of *carole* will be used throughout to distinguish from the later usage of carol to refer to predominantly Christmas songs.

[27] Stevens (1986), 175.

form can be found in French, Italian, English and German lyrics.[28] The scene in the garden at the beginning of the *Roman de la Rose* provides a well-known description of courtly carolling from which some elements of the form can be deduced, both as regards the text and the many extant illuminated copies. Following Chaucer's translation we note that the lead singer is a lady, Gladnesse, and her qualifications for this role are her strong, clear sweet voice and her ability at *refreininge* (l. 749). She sang 'first folk to solace' (l. 756), which in this context could mean either to amuse the dancers or to facilitate the dance. It is clear that she knew some popular songs 'of Loreyne' (l. 766), but her skill at *refreininge* may also imply an element of improvisation or extemporisation.

Dance-songs were not singled out for either approval or disapproval any more than other forms of dance by the Church. Indeed, in certain circumstances they were danced in churches as an expression of devotion and worship, as indicated by the clergy performing an Easter dance in Besançon.[29] The accompaniment of words offered opportunities for the marrying of devotional or moralising material with occasions of dancing, and there is also evidence that dance-song texts were written in Latin as *contrafacta* to vernacular songs. Further examples will show that the topos of death was voiced in *caroles* by both preacher and victim.

Montserrat in northern Spain was a major European pilgrim destination during the late Middle Ages and, because of its geographical position, a crossing point for influences from Spain, France and Italy. One of the ten dance-songs in the *Llibre Vermell de Montserrat*, *Ad Mortem Festinamus Peccare Desistamus*, offers commonplace warnings against the dangers of sin and conveys a message similar to that of the allegory of *The Three Living and the Three Dead*, a precursor of the *Danse Macabre*.[30] The title line is repeated between each stanza and the words *peccare desistamus* are said twice, perhaps providing an opportunity for the pilgrims to echo the lead singer. There are ten stanzas, the last of which reads:

> Vile cadauer eris. Cur non peccare uereris.
> Vile cadauer eris. Cur intumescere queris.
> Vile cadauer eris. Vt quid pecuniam queris.
> Vile cadauer eris. Quid uestes pomposas geris.
> Vile cadauer eris. Vt quid honores queris.

---

[28] Richard Leighton Greene, 'The Carol as Dance-Song', in Greene (1935), xix-lix.
[29] See n. 18 above.
[30] See also the essays by Marco Piccat and Christine Kralik in this volume.

Vile cadauer eris. Cur non penite*ns* confit*eris.*
Vile cadau*er* eris. Cont*ra prox*imum non leteris.

*(You will be a worthless cadaver, so why do you not guard yourself against
sinning? Why do you want to be angry? Why do you search for money?
Why do you wear splendid clothes? For what reason do you seek honours?
Why do you not confess in repentance? Why do you not give joy to your
neighbour?)*

There are comparable surviving English *caroles*, such as the following
fourteenth-century example, which begins with the *burden* 'God, that alle
mytes may, Helpe us at our ending day' and includes the following:

Now I hope, and now I synge;
Now I daunce, now I sprynge;
Now I weyle, and now I wrynge;
    Now is wel, and now is way.

Now I hoppe, and now I daunce;
Now I prike, and now I praunce;
This day heyl, te morwe, perchaunce,
    We mown be ded and leyd in clay.[31]

(Now I hope and now I sing;
Now I dance, now I spring;
Now I wail and now I wring [my hands];
    Now is well and now is woe.
Now I hop and now I dance;
Now I strut and now I prance;
This day healthy, tomorrow perhaps
    we will be dead and buried in the earth.)

In these verses dancing is used as a metaphor to epitomise the essence of
life and to emphasise the contrast between vitality and mortality; a
juxtaposition that recurs in the *Danse Macabre.*

Dance forms: circles, lines and processions

The association of dance-songs with circle or ring dances in many contexts
is recognised by scholarship, frequently with reference to the legendary
carollers of Kölbigk.[32] Some accounts of carolling are illustrated in

---

[31] BL MS Sloane 2593, ll. 6 and 7, as quoted in Greene (1935), 246.
[32] This story, set in the time of Emperor Henry II (r. 1002-24), is retold as a
Middle-English exemplum about the 'hoppyng' dancers of 'Colbek' in Robert

contemporary sources, and show a closed circle of four or more dancers holding hands and facing inwards.[33] The depiction of closed circle-dances in allegorical paintings such as Andrea da Firenza's fresco of 1350 in Santa Maria Novella, Florence, may be designed to emphasize the harmony of circular movement, however, rather than to reflect the popularity of that particular dance form.[34]

Christopher Page cites the *Summa de Vitiis et de Virtutibus* of *c.*1249/50 by the Dominican preacher Guillaume de Peyraut (*c.*1190-1271) as 'by far the richest source of information available, the dancers often moved "in a circular motion" (*motu circulari*) which led to the left'.[35] The movement of a circle towards the left, with dancers facing inwards, creates a clockwise motion and is preserved in the *bransles* (country dances) of the sixteenth century, which begin with a step to the left. The allegorical association of the left hand (*sinestra*) with Hell, as found in visual art of the period, was picked up by Bishop Repingdon of Lincoln (1405-20) who condemned carollers thus:

> For as the clergy go in procession on feast days, singing around the church in honour of God, so these women go in procession upon the left foot towards hell.[36]

The link between a dance going round the church and the religious procession has a resonance with the 'procession' of the *Danse Macabre* moving along the walls of the bays beneath the *charnier des Lingères* in the churchyard of Les Innocents. It is important to note that in Marchant's edition the dancers are moving on the right foot towards their right (*i.e.* the viewer's left), so that each figure of *le mort* appears to be encouraging his partners to dance towards God in Heaven and not towards the devil in

---

Mannyng's *Handlyng of Sinne*. See Frederick J. Furnivall (ed.), *Robert of Brunne's 'Handlyng Synne'*, EETS, o.s. 119, 123 (1901, 1903, repr. Montana: Kessinger Publishing, 2007), ll. 9015-260. The story is also discussed in James M. Clark, *The Dance of Death in the Middle Ages and the Renaissance* (Glasgow: Jackson, Son & Company, 1950), 106-07.

[33] Froissart's *Chronicles of England*, Paris, BnF ms. fr. 2807, fol. 13r, shows a circle of fifteen dancers facing inwards, accompanied by a pipe and tabor player, at the feast at Windsor Castle in 1344.

[34] Fresco by Andrea di Bonaiuto in Santa Maria Novella church, Cappellone degli Spagnoli, Florence: see Kathi Meyer-Baer, *Music of the Spheres and the Dance of Death* (Princeton: University Press, 1970), 131 and fig. 54.

[35] Christopher Page, 'The Carole, the Pulpit and the Schools', in Page (1989), 115.

[36] Owst (1961), 395.

Hell.[37]

Close examination of several versions of the garden scene in the *Roman de la Rose* reveals a wider variety of formations and relationships between dancers during the carolling in the garden, which casts some light on our interpretation of the imagery of *Danse Macabre* and the relationship between *le mort* and his partners. In the text, the dance involves a 'chain' or *treche*, more commonly associated with line-dancing, and which Chaucer translates ambiguously as 'turning' in his version of the scene in *The Romaunt of the Rose*:

Lors veïssiès carole aler
Et gens mignotement baler
Et fere mainte bele treche
Et maint biau torsor l'erbe frèche. (ll. 743-46)

Tho mightest thou caroles seen,
And folk [ther] daunce and mery been,
And make many fair tourning
Upon the grene gras springing. (ll. 759-62)

Several references to *caroling* begin with an indication simply to 'take hands' as in Jean Froissart's *Poésies*:

Cils et celes qui s'esbatoient
Au danser sans gueres atendre
Comencierent leurs mains a tendre
Pour caroler.[38]

(This one and that who enjoy dancing, without waiting long, began to hold hands for carolling.)

---

[37] Hammerstein's argumentation is different. See Reinhold Hammerstein, *Tanz und Musik des Todes: die mittelalterlichen Totentänze und ihr Nachleben* (Bern/Munich: Francke, 1980), 59: 'die linke Seite beim Weltgericht [ist] von Christus und beim Totentanz vom Beschauer her zu verstehen'. For a discussion of the symbolism of dancing in graveyards and churches with reference to the *Danse Macabre*, see Valeska Koal, 'Zur Praxis von Totentänzen in Mittelalter und Früher Neuzeit', in Andrea von Hülsen-Esch and Hiltrud Westermann-Angerhausen with Stefanie Knöll (eds), *'Zum Sterben schön!' Alter, Totentanz und Sterbekunst von 1500 bis heute* (Regensburg: Schnell & Steiner, 2006), vol. 1, 110-18, at 110.
[38] Curt Sachs, *World History of Dance*, trans. Bessie Schonberg (1937; repr. New York: W.W. Norton and Company, Inc., 1963), 270.

Peyraut refers to *tactu manuum* and Christopher Page mentions the phrase '*a la touché de karoles*'.[39]

It is, of course, difficult to illustrate a three-dimensional ring of dancers on a two dimensional page, and the illuminator always has to choose one movement or figure from the dance to illustrate. An illustration in an early fourteenth century manuscript of the *Roman de la Rose* in the Royal Library, The Hague, shows a chain of alternating male and female dancers holding hands only with one person and connected to the other by holding a handkerchief.[40] Another version of the same scene in a French *Roman de la Rose* manuscript of *c*.1380, shows one woman holding another by her long sleeve.[41] We shall return to this important detail by looking at how, in Marchant's illustrations of the Paris *Danse Macabre*, Death frequently holds his partners by their sleeves or other parts of their garments, rather than their hands. Another very clear example of a 'line dance' in a *Roman de la Rose* manuscript of *c*.1320 (London, BL MS Stowe 947, fol. 7r) shows six dancers holding hands in a line, while the ones at either end have their free hands raised in the air.[42]

In his study of twentieth-century French folk dance from the Vendée region of Poitou, an area renowned for its dancing in the Middle Ages, Conrad Laforte found what he believed to be surviving examples of medieval dance-songs without instrumental accompaniment in the repertoire.[43] The dance is initiated by a *chante-avant* singing a two-line *vers signal* (similar to the *burden* of the *carole*). This is repeated by the dancers as they stand holding hands in a circle beating the time with their arms and *balancing* from foot to foot.[44] As the *chante-avant* begins the main stanza of the song, sometimes with a call such as 'Hé! la la!', the dancers break the ring, take hands with their partners, and dance in pairs around in a circle in a couple-dance. This may suggest that in *carolling* and dance-songs, an initial closed circle formation would enable the

---

[39] Page (1989), 115.

[40] *Roman de la Rose* (The Hague, Royal Library, KB MS 120 D 13, fol. 6v): see http://racer.kb.nl/pregvn/MIMI/MIMI_120D13/MIMI_120D13_006V_MIN.JPG (accessed 3 May 2010).

[41] BL Yates Thompson MS 21, fol. 8v: see http://www.bl.uk/catalogues/ illuminatedmanuscripts/ILLUMIN.ASP?Size=mid&IllID=7822 (accessed 24 April 2010).

[42] BL Stowe MS 947, fol. 7r: see http://www.bl.uk/catalogues/ illuminatedmanuscripts/ILLUMIN.ASP?Size=mid&IllID=8957 (accessed 17 February 2010).

[43] Conrad Laforte, *Survivances Medievales dans la Chansons Folklorique* (Quebec: Presse de Université Laval, 1981), 75.

[44] Laforte (1981), 75: 'se tiennent par la main et font balancer leur bras et leurs jambes'.

dancers to 'tune in' to the tempo and character of the dance before separating and moving further away from the singer, something that would ameliorate problems inherent in dancing in the open air without the help of loud instruments or the emphasis of a drum beat.

Therefore, a closed circle may have been a 'signature image' associated with dance-songs, without implying that the entire dance was restricted to this form. Indeed, the circle may have reformed at each repetition of the burden or the refrain or at the change-over between lead singers, with episodes in between of couple-dances.[45] In Marchant's *Danse Macabre*, *le mort* is perhaps leading his partner out of the circle-dance of the living *carollers*?

Dance steps

Moving from the formation of dance-song to its steps, we find that dance steps may be difficult to recognise for the modern-day viewer. Kathi Meyer-Baer thus commented that

> in all versions [of the *Danse Macabre*] the skeletons usually stand or walk and are only rarely shown in livelier action [...] I would say that in the typical forms of the fifteenth and sixteenth centuries, no one is dancing.[46]

Meyer-Baer was apparently unaware of scenes where dead dancers – not actual skeletons – are visibly jumping and hopping. Yet in her scepticism, she also failed to take account of the courtly dance style known as *basse-dance*, which was popular in the period and appropriate to the dignified figures at the start of the *Danse Macabre*. Some extant fifteenth-century choreographies of *basse-dance* show that the steps are executed close to the ground, without hopping or jumping, to create a gentle rising and falling, gliding motion.[47] The dancer's steps remained low even in the more rapid sections, on the ball or the flat sole of the foot. When depicted frozen in time, in a painting or an illumination, the impression can only be of standing or walking, so the observer must seek other indications of the kinetic intent.

---

[45] A couple dance illustrates the carolling scene from the *Roman de la Rose* in the later BL MS Harley 4425, fol. 14v, of *c*.1490-1500.

[46] Meyer-Baer (1970), 306.

[47] Arnold Dolmetsch, *Dances of England and France from 1450 to 1600* (London: Routledge, 1949), 1. The *Livre de Basses Danses de la Bibliotheque de Bourgogne (c. 1450)* is thought to have belonged to Mary of Burgundy, daughter of Charles the Bold.

In short, dancing and dance-songs accompanied every aspect of medieval life from the cradle to the grave and appear, unsurprisingly, to have included a variety of formations and steps. Courtship and marriage, birth and death, journeys and pilgrimages, were all celebrated with dancing, and references to these subjects are to be found in the texts of the *caroles* themselves. Music and dance underpinned not just the grand occasions but also more modest entertainments at the local hostelry or in peoples' homes, and they were to be enjoyed at every level by spectators and dancers alike.

The expression of relationship through dance

Having established that the context, subject, and physical realisation of the *Danse Macabre* can all be accommodated within what is known of contemporary dance practice, I shall now focus on three specific dimensions of dancing as they relate thematically to Marchant's woodcuts and to Lydgate's poem: the selection of partners, processing, and mirroring.[48]

So how does Death choose his partners? According to Caesarius of Heisterbach's story of how a band of devils appeared to some students in Toledo, it was conventional among *carollers* for the women to choose their partners.

> [...] in puellas speciosissimus se transformantes, choreas circa illos ducebant, variis anfractibus iuvenes invitantes. Ex quibus una forma ceteris praestantior unum ex scholaribus elegit.

> *([they] transform themselves into surpassingly beautiful girls and dance caroles around them, inviting the young men with their many lithe movements. One of them, more beautiful than the rest, chooses one of the scholars.)*[49]

In the *Danse*, Death chooses his partner in each case, inviting him or her to join the dance, and in Marchant's illustrations the subtlety of the level of persuasion employed for each person within the metaphor of the dance is evident. To say, as Kathi Meyer-Baer does, that 'the figure is usually leading his partner quietly – very seldom is he in lively action, almost

---

[48] All references to the French text are from BL Add. MS 38858, as edited in Warren (1931). References to Lydgate's text are likewise from Warren's edition.

[49] As quoted in Page (1989), 124.

never is he dancing or fighting with his partner', is a considerable over-simplification of the particularity of what is shown.[50]

In fifteenth-century dance, the man's place was on the left of the lady, with her left hand in his right. This meant that the man's sword was on the outside of the pair, on his left hip, and not between them. It also required him to relinquish control of his sword hand to his partner's grasp. In the case of two men dancing or processing together, it was courteous to honour the superior partner by placing him in the woman's position, thus deferring to him by giving him a potential advantage to use a weapon.[51] Therefore, there are two possible interpretations of the positioning of *le mort* on the female side of the couples in Marchant's *Danse Macabre* woodcuts. He may indeed be 'leading' in the position of a superior, but he may also be 'choosing' or inviting a partner as we have seen was the custom of female *carollers*. The *Clerc* laments in his stanza in the French *Danse*, 'La mort ma pris a son loisir' (l. 487) *(Death has taken me at his leisure)*, thus expressing feelings of helplessness and impotence, despite being in the man's or 'leading' position but deprived of the use of his sword hand.

Describing the scenes in Marchant's edition, Meyer-Baer stated, 'The skeleton hardly touches the figures. They are standing or walking, but never dancing'.[52] The following analysis of the postures and holds of *le mort* again contests this interpretation. The dancing partner of *le Roy* (Fig. 16) is depicted with his left knee bent, thigh parallel to the ground and the foot raised up, as he courteously invites his victim:

Venes, noble roy couronnes,
Renommes de force & de proesse (ll. 65-66)
O noble Kynge / moste worthi of renown
Come forth a-noon / for al ʒowre worthinesse (ll. 105-06)

Death's courteous form of address is at odds with his posture, however, and indeed the King responds:

---

[50] Meyer-Baer (1970), 301.
[51] Johan Huizinga, *The Waning of the Middle Ages: a Study of the Forms of Life, Thought, and Art in France and the Netherlands in the Fourteenth and Fifteenth Centuries* (transl. 1924, repr. New York: Dover Publications, 1998), 37.
[52] Meyer-Baer (1970), 299.

Fig. 16. The Cardinal and the King, woodcut in Guy Marchant's *Danse Macabre* edition first published in 1485.

Je nay point apris a danser
A danses & nottes si sauuage;
Helas, on peut veor & penser
Que vault orgeuil, forche, lignage.
Mort destruit tout, chest son vsage (ll. 73-77)

I have not lerned / here-a-forne to daunce
No daunce in sothe / of fotynge so sauage
Where-fore I see / be clere demonstraunce
What pride is worth / force or hye lynage
Dethe al fordoth / this is his usage (ll. 113-17)

The King's death-dance is not going to be a genteel, undulating *basse-danse* but an undignified, lively high-stepping 'savage' affair, reminiscent of the wild, leaping victims of the dancing manias, and he is powerless even to choose the steps.

The *Cordelier* (Sire Cordelere), a Franciscan friar, is shown holding his hands protectively away from Death, who is tugging at his sleeve and saying, in Lydgate's poem:

Sire Cordelere / to ȝow my hande is rawght
To this daunce / ȝow to conueie ande lede
Whiche yn ȝowre prechynge / hau ful ofte tawght (ll. 561-63)

Fig. 17. The Friar and the Child, woodcut in Guy Marchant's *Danse Macabre* edition first published in 1485.

The Friar may have often preached that 'dethe eche owre is present & redy' (l. 568), but now it has come for him he is not ready to go (Fig. 17). The Friar's right leg is crossed over the left, away from his dead partner, and in synchrony with the movement of his arms. He is turning towards his left, showing clearly his reluctance to be led in the direction of the dance, to his right (*i.e.* the viewer's left). His whole body is expressing his desire to dance in the opposite direction.

A close look at the handholds employed by *le mort* further illuminates his role and also the victim's response to the invitation. It is only the infant whom he actually holds firmly by the hand; the other illustrations show a range of familiarity, firmness or coercion. Surely *le mort* is being over-familiar with the king by resting his hand on the ermine-clad royal shoulder, thereby reinforcing the impression of vulgarity implied by what Lydgate calls his 'savage footing'? Death has his bony hand on several other shoulders, including the *Marchant*'s, but most firmly of all on the shoulder of the *Curé* (Fig. 18) where his elbow is bent high above his head in order to exert maximum pressure through his forearm, perhaps in order to remind the priest of the heavy burden his 'tithing' has placed on the shoulders of his flock (ll. 541-44).

Fig. 18. The Parson and the Labourer, woodcut in Guy Marchant's *Danse Macabre* edition first published in 1485.

In the pairing with the King (Fig. 16), *le mort* has taken hold of the cape of the Cardinal in his other hand, while the Cardinal's own *mort* has caught hold of a fistful of fabric from the front of the Cardinal's cassock as if to feel the quality of the cloth described in the text as his 'cappe de pris' (l. 61) or 'vesture of grete coste' (l. 94). Indeed, several of the images show *le mort* holding his partner by items of clothing. As discussed above and illustrated in the *Roman de la Rose*, this was an acceptable hold for dancing. *Le mort* is grasping the *Chevalier*'s hanging sleeve exactly in the manner shown in contemporary romances, though the Knight's arms (which are folded firmly across his chest) signal his unwillingness to respond to the invitation (Fig. 19). If he were being invited, in Death's words, 'with ladies to daunce yn the shade' (l. 174), the Knight would no doubt gladly offer his hand, as in miniature of Courtesye inviting the Dreamer in a French *Roman de la Rose* manuscript produced in Paris *c.*1405 (Getty MS Ludwig XV 7, fol. 9v).[53] The *Amoureux* also refuses to give his hand to *le mort*, who holds him rather more coercively by the belt. The *Medecin* has his hands full, raising a urine bottle as he searches vainly for a cure; *le mort* holds the front of his robe.

---

[53] See http://www.getty.edu/art/gettyguide/artObjectDetails?artobj=5668 (accessed 24 April 2010).

Fig. 19. The Archbishop and the Knight, woodcut in Guy Marchant's *Danse Macabre* edition first published in 1485.

Fig. 20. The Clerk and the Hermit, woodcut in Guy Marchant's *Danse Macabre* edition first published in 1485.

When *le mort* holds a cloak or a robe, the folds of the fabric are carefully observed in the woodcuts and show the degree of force and resistance being exerted. His grip on the reluctant Friar is firm and involves both hands, while the cloak of the Patriarch is held on both sides but still sits comfortably on his shoulders, unlike that of the *Clerc* (Fig. 20). The latter's dead counterpart is clutching a large bunch of the material of his cloak in his hand, behind his back, and without a glance at his victim who is holding on to his cloak to stop it being pulled from his shoulders: the tension can be clearly seen in the fabric stretched over his right shoulder.

In contrast, the *Ermite*, who is depicted in the same woodcut, needs only a gentle guiding hand on his back as he moves forward, rosary and prayer book in hand, thanking God 'with humble chere & face / Of al his ʒiftes and grete habundaunce' (ll. 621-22). Death holds the *Laboureur* by his elbow, but the arm hangs down passively, with only a crick in his wrist indicating slight resistance. Death's attitude to the poor Labourer, who has often wished for death, is gentle as he points out that only a fool would want to live forever in such a false world.

Fig. 21. The Bishop and the Squire, woodcut in Guy Marchant's *Danse Macabre* edition first published in 1485.

The *Esquier* (Fig. 21) is trying to decline the invitation to the dance with a politely raised palm and his feet pointing firmly in the opposite direction. However, *le mort* has his hand linked around the Squire's upper arm, though its fingers are open and not in a closed grip. Both their arms are relaxed and *le mort* seems to have adopted a cajoling manner appropriate to a young peer. The grip of *le mort* on the upper arm of the *Usurier* is quite different, with his fingers right up near the armpit and leaning his body weight outwards, as the Usurer tries to pull away to clinch a final deal with a Poor Man (Fig. 22). The grip shifts from the upper arm to the forearm of the Bailiff, whose raised fist seems to threaten a punch, or perhaps he is just showing his ring to signify his authority. However, judging by the way *le mort* is moving his head and chest as far away as possible, leaning backwards in a defensive stance, he is perhaps anticipating a forceful rebuttal. For an audience accustomed to reading nuances of relationship from the manner of holds, these images would have eloquently told them of the subjects' readiness to meet their maker.

Fig. 22. The Monk, the Usurer and the Poor Man, woodcut in Guy Marchant's *Danse Macabre* edition first published in 1485.

Reading the signs and symbols of the processional dance

The processional dance form – either as a complete dance as in the *basse-danse*, or occurring as a section within a *carole* – provided an opportunity through its formations to display status and to demonstrate order. It was a choreographed version of the processions and parades that punctuated medieval life. The procession was not purely an ecclesiastical form of communal expression or an aristocratic one, but was used at every level of society. Pilgrims and penitents processed to exhibit their spirituality and piety. These un-choreographed processional 'dances' were taken to extremes by the flagellant sects of the fourteenth century who, far from running around in a frenzy, processed solemnly according to a set of behavioural codes described in detail by Froissart.[54] The singing of songs by pilgrims, as they walked through towns and villages, also transformed their movements from an unsynchronised group of individuals into a harmonious, processional, un-choreographed dance-song.

In a society where codes of dress and hierarchy of status were so universally accepted and understood, the dividing line between processions, parades and performances was very thin indeed.[55] People's clothes proclaimed their status, profession, religion and allegiances by means of colours, badges, rings, chains, trimmings and styles. Banners, swords, staffs and batons were carried to assist immediate identification in peacetime and in war. In Marchant's edition, the illustrations of the *Cardinal*, the *Patriarche*, the *Advocat* and the *Clerc* all show *le mort* holding an arrow. A sense of the suddenness and unpredictability of death is conveyed by these pictures and the accompanying texts; however, the image of the arrow held firmly in *le mort*'s grasp eliminates any possibility of a chance or random victim. The choice of target and the moment for the unleashing of the arrow are entirely in the hands of the Death figure just as, in the *carole* the choice, and time of choosing, of partners was in the hands of the maidens. The essential specificity of the experience of death is therefore expressed in Marchant's images.

The visual vocabulary of symbols, emblems and attire was an essential element in the reading of processions, used not only to identify living individuals but also to interpret allegorical personifications in art and literature.[56] In the *Roman de la Rose* the people dancing inside the garden represent the ideals of love, beauty, youth, truth, nobility and courtesy. However, before he enters the walled garden, the Dreamer also sees 'portraitures' showing all the evils of the real world: Hate, Felonye, Vilanye,

---

[54] Jean Froissart, *Chronicles*, selected and translated by Geoffrey Brereton (Harmondsworth: Penguin, 1968), 111-12

[55] Sumptuary laws existed throughout Europe during the fourteenth century, being introduced into England in 1336-37 by Edward III. Specific styles of hats distinguished Muslims and Jews, and the choice of fabrics, furs and trimmings was prescribed. This had the dual purpose of controlling imports of foreign textiles and attempting to curb the efforts of the rising mercantile classes to emulate the aristocracy.

[56] Sarah Kay (ed.), *The Romance of the Rose*, Critical Guides to French Texts, 110 (London: Grant & Cutler, 1995), 24.

Coveityse, Avarice, Envye, Sorowe, Time, Pope-holy (*i.e.* hypocritical piety), and Poverty.[57] These female personifications of the worldly vices are each described, and recognised, by their manner, bearing and apparel. The procession of figures in the mural at Les Innocents in Paris would have struck a chord with all those steeped in the *Roman* tradition, and the connection is surely alluded to in *le mort*'s words to the *Chevalier*:

> Vous qui entre les grans barons
> Auez eu renon, cheualer,
> Oublies tromppettes, clarons,
> Et me suyes sans sommeiller;
> Les dammes solies resueiller
> En faisant danser longue piece,
> A aultre danses faoult veiller;
> Ce que lun fait lautre despiece. (ll. 129-36)

> ʒe that amonge / lordes and barouns
> Hau had so longe/ worship & renoun
> Forʒete ʒowre trumpettes / & yowre clariowns
> This is no dreme / ne symulacioun
> Somme-tyme yowre custome & entencioun
> Was with ladies / to daunce yn the shade
> But ofte hit happeth / In conclusioun
> That oo man breketh / that another made. (ll. 169-76)

It lies outside the scope of this study to consider the specific contemporary political resonances of the *Danse Macabre* in Paris or in England.[58] However, it will have become evident that within a culture of shared visual vocabulary for interpreting processions and processional dances emblematically, the *Danse* also offered reminders to all, of the ideal of order of the Estates, and of the human condition understood according to a culturally specific and hierarchically nuanced way. The Paris order of the Estates, as illustrated by Marchant, is replicated, with remarkably slight variations of local or contemporary significance, in all the derivative fifteenth-century versions of the *Danse Macabre*.[59]

---

[57] Chaucer, *Romaunt of the Rose*, ll. 147-474.

[58] For this, see Sophie Oosterwijk, 'Of Dead Kings, Dukes and Constables: The Historical Context of the *Danse Macabre* in Late Medieval Paris', *Journal of the British Archaeological Association*, 161 (2008), 131-62.

[59] Processional aspects of later versions of the *Danse Macabre* are discussed in Jungmann (2006), 124-29.

Mirroring in movement to demonstrate empathy

Having briefly touched upon the general symbolic clues in the imagery of the *Danse*, I shall now look more closely at the detail of the individual pairs of dancing couples and the interpretation of relationships, using the visual language of dance and the shape of the space between their bodies. As soon as the human infant achieves a stable upright posture it expresses the desire to dance.[60] It is initially a solitary activity, but just as the first smile is mirrored back by the primary carer so do the infant's first efforts at dancing elicit a response from those around it, and immediately dance is established as a form of communication. It seems to be an inherent capability of *homo erectus* to communicate through body movement and to 'entrain' to each other's rhythms.[61]

This form of communication occurs in its simplest form when two people endeavour to maintain a conversation whilst walking. In order to sustain contact they will 'fall into step' with each other and thus begins the dance. A feeling of harmony and empathy, which is created by being 'in step', is not only felt by the participants but is also observable to onlookers. It is thus possible to 'read' the relationship between two people by seeing the level of empathy between them. In dance the term 'mirroring' can be used to mean the exact reflection of posture or movement face to face, using opposite body parts, or it can refer to side-by-side imitation. However, it can also refer to part of a movement, a rhythm or the quality of a movement, *e.g.* a tapping foot might be reflected back by a partner as a tapping hand. The relationship between a pair of dancers, or *dyad*, can be expressed in movement through an entire range in this way, from total empathy in exact imitation of movement, rhythm, quality of movement and energy level, through slight variations or exaggerations to highlight individuation, to complete disharmony and disintegration of rhythm and synchrony.

There are examples of empathy in the *dyads* of the *Danse Macabre*, as illustrated most clearly in the final pairing of *le mort* and the *Ermite* (Fig. 20). The figures are side by side with feet equally spaced and the weight slightly over the left foot. The left arm of *le mort* is bent across his body in

---

[60] Jeanette Macdonald, 'Dance? Of Course I Can', in Helen Payne (ed.), *Dance Movement Therapy: Theory and Practice* (London: Routledge, 1992), 202-17, at 204.
[61] *Why do we sing?* BBC Radio Four programme (19 August 2008). Entrainment was discovered by Christian Huygens in 1665 when he observed that the movements of two unsynchronised pendulum clocks placed close together side by side always became synchronous after a short time.

exact imitation of that of the hermit holding his prayer book. The *dyad* is unique in that Death is behind his partner, on his left side, not leading him but accommodating and reflecting his serene demeanour and calmness. Death and the *Laboureur* are also 'in step', both leading with the right foot in the direction of the dance, thus expressing a unity of intention, in contrast to the opposition expressed in the adjoining *dyad* of the *Curé*. Death and the *Menestrel* mirror each other face to face with their feet equally spaced but their bodies forming opposing convex shapes (Fig. 38). This shows a degree of empathy but with some reservation, as the Minstrel explains in his opening lines, 'De danser ainsy neusse cure, / Certes tres enuis je men melle' (ll. 401-02), or in Lydgate's version:

This newe daunce / is to me so straunge
Wonder dyuerse / and passyngli contrarie
The dredful fotyng / doth so ofte chaunge
And the mesures / so ofte sithes varie (ll. 505-08)

Fig. 23. The Lawyer and the Minstrel, woodcut in Guy Marchant's *Danse Macabre* edition first published in 1485.

A similar mirror image links Death and the *Chevalier* (Fig. 19). They face each other with opposing feet and inside legs bent; however, Death shows a higher level of engagement as he bends towards his partner with his left leg lifted. The *Chevalier* is not responding; his foot is flat on the ground and his arms are folded, his hands in his sleeves. He would no doubt lean closer and unlock his arms if his partner were a beautiful woman. Comparing these *dyads* to Death and the *Escuier*, we see the bodies taking a similar mirroring form but not facing each other. Instead they are turned away and the closest body parts are their buttocks; not a very empathetic contact. Their bodies make convex shapes in opposition and their feet are moving in opposite directions so that, although they form a mirror image, the intention expressed is one of disagreement.

Fig. 24. The Astrologer and the Burgher, woodcut in Guy Marchant's *Danse Macabre* edition first published in 1485.

The mismatch of Death's *fotyng* has already been referred to with reference to the King's dead counterpart, but it is even more exaggerated in the *dyad* of the *Bourgois* who stands demurely on two feet, hip width apart, with his hands crossed on his chest, showing gravitas and self-importance (Fig. 24). He is partnered by the highest stepping dead dancer of them all, who breaks every code of seemly conduct by leaning his upper body towards his partner, jutting his head out and looking in the opposite direction as he hurries the stately Merchant along, saying 'Bourgois, hastes vous sans tarder' (*Burgher, hurry without delay*). Thus *le mort* shows his disregard for the Burgher's worldly position by failing to mirror him in any way and disregarding the conventions of graceful dancing, described by

Guglielmo Ebreo as *aiere* (air) which 'should be employed and put into practice at the right place and time with unfailing discretion'.[62]

In some of the images a link is made in the folds of the shroud of *le mort* rather than by his posture; for example, the Archbishop has gathered his richly decorated vestments protectively in his left hand and Death's plain shroud mirrors this by being gathered in the opposite direction under his right arm, serving both to create a sense of pairing but also to highlight the vanity of the richly embroidered cloth by the contrast with the blank white shroud. In the illustration of the Infant, the swaddling bands in the cradle are mirrored in the crossing of Death's shroud from right shoulder to left hip and then back down to his right foot, while the free end flies off in the air above their heads, creating a sense of movement in the otherwise static picture.

In the partnership of the *Maistre* or Astrologer, the exact mirroring of the figures is also reflected in the text (Fig. 24). The two figures reflect each other, arm in arm, as peers, apart from the spade in *le mort*'s left hand emphasising the reference to the Fall 'And al shal dye / for an appil rounde' (l. 288). The French and English texts differ in detail, but both are couched in academic language referring to the 'ologies' of *astrologie*, *genealogie*, and *theologie* in Paris, and *astrologie*, *genelegye* and *theologie* in Lydgate. The verse concludes with the final *logie* or logic, 'Qui vo[ul]dra bien morir bien viue' (l. 224), 'Who lyueth a-right / mote nedes dye wele' (l. 296). This is the essential message of the teaching of a contemporary *Maistre*, the Chancellor of the University of Paris, Jean Gerson (1363-1429), in his treatise *De Arte Moriendi*, presented to the Council of Constance in 1415 – a message that the images of the *Danse Macabre* were to convey so vividly to the people of Paris a decade later.[63]

Conclusion

When the spectre of Death stepped out of its separate frame in the allegory of *The Three Living and the Three Dead* and into the *Danse Macabre*, it entered into a very specific and stylised relationship. The *Danse Macabre* imagery takes the commonplace activity of dancing and, drawing on universal experience, is able to express thereby a critical dimension of the relationship between man and God. As in a country-dance that changes partners at every repeat, each encounter is unique, but the dance and the

---

[62] Ebreo (1993), 97.
[63] Eamon Duffy, *The Stripping of the Altars: Traditional Religion in England 1400-1580* (New Haven/London: Yale University Press, 1992), 316.

music remain the same. One partner may glide across the floor while another whirls his partner round fast and furiously. Some may hold their partners too closely for comfort while others ignite a spark of attraction between them.

Likewise, in Marchant's *Danse Macabre* illustrations, *le mort* responds to each of his partners according to his or her state, but the outcome is always the same. The experience of art, music and dance is beyond language and can convey a depth of meaning that is beyond words. The prospect of a *pas de deux* with Death opens up the possibility of a relationship of subtle dimensions. Through the common experience of dance, the observer could interpret the solicitous hand on the *Ermite*'s back or the force through the hand on the *Curé*'s shoulder and, by somatic association, feel personally the tenderness of God's love or the burden of his judgement.

Acknowledgements

This essay is based on the author's MA dissertation of the same title (supervised by Professor Pamela M. King and Dr Emma Hornby), with which she successfully completed her MA in Medieval Studies at the University of Bristol in 2009. The author is very grateful to the editors, Sophie Oosterwijk and Stefanie Knöll, for their help and advice in the preparation of this work for publication.

DANCE, MUSIC, AND INVERSION: THE REVERSAL OF THE NATURAL ORDER IN THE MEDIEVAL *DANSE MACABRE*

SUSANNE WARDA

'Nun ziehen mich die Ungeschaffnen / An ihren Tantz / alß einen Affen' (*Now the miscreants are drawing me into their dance like an ape*).[1] These verses are the Bishop's answer to the summons of Death in the Basel *Danse Macabre* mural of *c.*1440.[2] The words 'miscreant' and 'ape' highlight one of the most significant characteristics of the *Danse Macabre*: the element of inversion. 'Ape' may recall the medieval tradition of calling the devil *simia dei* (God's ape),[3] *i.e.* a mock imitation of God, or even a mirror image – a 'perversion' in the original Latin meaning of the word (the state of being the wrong way round, or inverted).

Since Death and the devil are closely related, not least iconographically, this choice of words is possibly an instance of the two spheres of death and devil merging. The Bishop expresses his abhorrence of the cadaver figures approaching him and calls them 'miscreants', thereby

---

[1] The Basel text is quoted from the Merian edition as reproduced in Gert Kaiser, *Der tanzende Tod. Mittelalterliche Totentänze* (Frankfurt am Main: Insel Verlag, 1982), 194-275, at 210.

[2] In this article I do not always distinguish linguistically between personified *Death* (spelled with a capital D) and *the dead*. The distinction can be highly relevant for the discussion and analysis of certain aspects of *Danses Macabres* which require a way of separating the terms and their underlying concepts, but in my own research I avoid dwelling on this distinction.

[3] Cf. Hartmut Böhme, 'Imagologie von Himmel und Hölle. Zum Verhältnis von textueller und bildlicher Konstruktion imaginärer Räume', in Barbara Naumann and Edgard Pankow (eds), *Bilder-Denken. Bildlichkeit und Argumentation* (Munich: Fink, 2004), 19-45, at 31: '[...] der Teufel ist *simia dei*, ein Affe Gottes, der in seinem Raum, der Hölle, die himmlischen Formen in genauer Umkehrung, als Perversion also, choreographiert' (*the devil is God's ape, who in hell – his realm – choreographs the heavenly forms, distorting them into a perversion*). We could transfer this to the *Danse Macabre* where Death is the choreographer.

emphasising their repellent appearance. By referring to himself as an ape, he not only indicates that he is being forced to join in and mimic the other dancers, but also implies that sooner or later he will look as repulsive as the corpses surrounding him.

In these few words, we thus encounter some of the most salient and vital components of the medieval *Danse Macabre*. In the following discussion, I will look at these issues in greater detail by considering examples mainly from the German *Danse Macabre* tradition.

Music and musical instruments

Undoubtedly, music is one of the fundamental elements in the *Danse Macabre*. The theme has even been described as 'perhaps the most famous connection of music with death'.[4] The dance movement itself depends to a certain extent on music. Consequently, musical instruments play an important role in the iconography of the *Danse Macabre* and music is used in a variety of ways to establish the inverted order.[5]

First of all, it is mainly the dead who play musical instruments in depictions of the *Danse*.[6] Death thus not only usurps the dance itself – normally a genuine expression of the joy of living – but also claims the right to lead the dance by taking charge of the accompanying music. This

---

[4] Kathi Meyer-Baer, *Music of the Spheres and the Dance of Death: Studies in Musical Iconology* (Princeton: University Press, 1970), 298.

[5] On the topic of musical instruments in the *Danse Macabre* in general, see Reinhold Hammerstein, *Tanz und Musik des Todes: die mittelalterlichen Totentänze und ihr Nachleben* (Bern/Munich: Francke, 1980), 41-42, 51-55 and 112-46. Also Meyer-Baer (1970); Heiko Maus, 'Musikinstrumente in den Totentänzen des 15. Jahrhunderts', *L'art macabre (Jahrbuch der Europäischen Totentanz-Vereinigung)*, 1 (2000), 135-51; Bertha Antonia Wallner, 'Die Bilder zum achtzeiligen oberdeutschen Totentanz. Ein Beitrag zur Musikikonographie des 15. Jahrhunderts', *Zeitschrift für Musikwissenschaft*, 6 (1923), 65-74; Stefanie Knöll, '"Der Pfeifen Schall verkündet euch des Todes Fall". Zur Darstellung des musizierenden Todes in Einzelszenen', *L'art macabre (Jahrbuch der Europäischen Totentanz-Vereinigung)*, 9 (2008), 95-107.

[6] The only case I know of instruments being played by the living occurs in the fifteenth-century *Danse Macabre* manuscript that belonged to the humanist Sigismund Gossembrot in Augsburg. See Michael Stolz, *Artes-liberales-Zyklen. Formationen des Wissens im Mittelalter*, Bibliotheca Germanica, 47, 2 vols (Tübingen: Francke, 2004), 578-622, and appendix 10, 838-51 (illustrations); Susanne Warda, *Memento mori: Text und Bild in Totentänzen des Spätmittelalters und der Frühen Neuzeit*, Pictura et Poesis, 29 (Cologne: Böhlau, 2011), esp. chap. 3.3.1.4.

inversion is often paralleled by a contrast between the static posture of the living and the convulsive and contorted dancing movements of the dead.

Fig. 25. '*Dantz hus*' scene with musical and dancing corpses, opening woodcut in *Der doten dantz mit figuren clage und antwort schon von allen staten der werlt* attributed to the printer Heinrich Knoblochtzer, after 1485.

Fig. 26. The Abbot and the Canon in the Bern *Danse Macabre* mural by Niklaus Manuel, 1516-19/20, lithograph from Joseph Bergmann, *Niklaus Manuels Todtentanz...* (Bern, *c.*1823). © Graphiksammlung 'Mensch und Tod', Heinrich-Heine-University Düsseldorf.

Furthermore, in some cases Death plays the instruments in an incorrect manner, *e.g.* by holding them upside down or the wrong way round. The printed *Danse Macabre* edition commonly known as the 'Knoblochtzerdruck' or *Doten dantz mit figuren* (Heidelberg, after 1485) contains good examples of this, such as the scene at the '*dantz hus*' (dancing house) (Fig. 25).[7] Here three of the four corpse figures are playing medieval wind instruments known as shawms; the one on the left is possibly a bombard. The musician plays his instrument without using the grip holes which, according to Hammerstein, is a common negative

---

[7] The '*dantz hus*' in the Knoblochtzer edition is sometimes referred to as 'Beinhaus' (*charnel house*), but I doubt that in this case the two terms are interchangeable. Proper charnel houses are shown in Knoblochtzer's second and final woodcuts, whereas the '*dantz hus*' does not exhibit the characteristics of a charnel house. Meyer-Baer (1970), 310, proposes that this '*dantz hus*' might be interpreted as 'the dance hall of the gravediggers' guild'. Although instruments are not mentioned in the text, nearly every single scene of the Knoblochtzer edition contains one: see Warda (2011), 152-55.

symbol.[8] Similarly, in one of the scenes of the Bern *Danse Macabre* by Niklaus Manuel (1516-1519/20), a female corpse figure plays a bladder pipe (Fig. 26), but the way the instrument is constructed makes it impossible for her to produce a sound: the inflated bladder is situated below the finger holes, whereas in a properly built instrument it should be directly below the insufflation tube.[9] Moreover, the way the old hag holds the bladder pipe – between her legs – probably has sexual implications.

Fig. 27. Death and the *hantwercksman* (Craftsman) in *Der doten dantz ...* attributed to Heinrich Knoblochtzer, after 1485.

In some cases, the dead do not use their instruments for the sake of making music, but instead handle them almost like weapons. The cadaver accompanying the '*hantwercksman*' (Craftsman) in the Knoblochtzer *Danse* carries a *Trumscheit* (nun's fiddle), yet he does not actually play it; he does not even have a bow (Fig. 27). Instead he seems to wield the

---

[8] Hammerstein points out that improper use of musical instruments is common in Last Judgement depictions, which he sees as precursors of the *Danse Macabre*. See Reinhold Hammerstein, *Diabolus in Musica: Studien zur Ikonographie der Musik im Mittelalter*, Neue Heidelberger Studien zur Musikwissenschaft, 6 (Bern: Francke, 1974), 35-37; Hammerstein (1980), 85.

[9] Cf. Hammerstein (1980), 134.

instrument as if ready to deliver a blow with it. Moreover, the instruments are sometimes not proper instruments at all: for example, in the Basel *Danse,* the cadaver leading away the Pope has a skull attached to his waist that he uses as a kind of drum, substituting the drumstick with a bone (Fig. 28). Similarly, the corpse accompanying the Hermit wears a lantern round his waist, which he works with two bones (Fig. 29). In a lavishly illustrated *Danse Macabre* manuscript of *c.*1470 in Kassel (Landesbibliothek, 4° Ms. poet. et roman. 5), Death blows on a spade as if it were a trumpet.[10]

Furthermore, it is worth pointing out that many of the instruments employed in the *Danse* can be used to produce very loud or strident sounds. Typical are the percussion instruments, which come in a variety of forms, and the various wind instruments such as trombones, trumpets, flutes, and bagpipes. The trumpets would have reminded contemporaries of the Last Judgement, which in German culture are usually trombones. There are string instruments as well, but they are a minority.

As we have seen, the instruments not only appear in their own right but are also used to suggest deeper layers of meaning. They can have a covert relation to the person whom Death accompanies, such as the harp which he carries in the scenes with the '*bose monich*' (Evil Monk) and the '*dumherr*' (Canon) in the Knoblochtzer edition. The instrument was probably chosen because of its connotations with heavenly music or with King David, the biblical prototype of the harp-player. Yet the image of Death playing string instruments such as harps and psalteries can also be intended as a travesty of the heavenly music played by angels.[11] Similarly, as an instrument belonging to the church sphere the portative organ occurs in connection with clerics.[12] However, these assignations are often inconsistent and therefore remain in the realm of speculation, since in different *Danse Macabre* examples the same instrument can appear in a variety of – sometimes contradictory – contexts.[13] Kathi Meyer-Baer has observed that occasionally the instruments are simply an expression of the social customs of a certain estate. In other cases, there may be an acoustic reason; for instance, a xylophone can be reminiscent of the sound of rattling bones.[14]

---

[10] Hammerstein (1980), 119-28, speaks of 'as-if instruments' in this context.

[11] On this topic in general, see Meyer-Baer (1970).

[12] The portative was also used in secular music, but in the present context it is most likely an allusion to the clerical sphere.

[13] Compare Knöll (2008), 104-05. As Knöll points out, there does not seem to be any definite system underlying the assignment of instruments to specific persons, neither for a given period of time nor for any single *Danse Macabre* cycle.

[14] Meyer-Baer (1970), 304-05.

❄] 65 [❄

Der Tod zum Pabſt.
Komm, heiliger Vatter, werther Mann!
Ein Vortanz müßt ihr mit mir han:
Der Ablaß euch nicht hilfft davon,
Das zweyfach Creutz und dreyfach Cron.

Antwort des Pabſts.
Heilig war ich auf Erd genannt,
Ohn Gott der Höchſt führt' ich mein Stand:
Der Ablaß that mir gar wohl lohnen,
Nun will der Tod mein nicht verſchonen.

Fig. 28. Death and the Pope, engraving by Matthäus Merian the Elder based on the Großbasel *Danse Macabre* mural of *c.*1440, published in 1649.

✻] 107 [✻

Der Tod zum Waldbruder.

Bruder! komm du aus deiner Claus;
Halt still, das Licht lösch ich dir aus;
Drum mach dich mit mir auf die Fahrt,
Mit deinem weissen langen Bart.

Antwort des Waldbruders.

Ich hab getragen lange Zeit
Ein härin Kleid, hilfft mich jetzt nit:
Bin nicht sicher in meiner Claus;
Die Stund ist hie, mein G'bett ist aus.

Fig. 29. Death and the *Waldbruder* (Hermit), engraving by Matthäus Merian the Elder based on the Großbasel *Danse Macabre* mural of *c.*1440, published in 1649.

Alternatively, the choice of instruments may be grounded in contemporary music theory. Thus, instruments such as the bagpipe, which is very common in the *Danse Macabre*, were seen as 'perverse' because they were made of animal skin and bladders.[15] Moreover, most of the instruments used in the *Danse* belong to the domain of the minstrel – a profession that was not highly esteemed.[16]

The great variety of the instruments used together in the *Danse* certainly does not make a proper ensemble. We can therefore imagine some sort of cacophony, noise rather than music, which may be a travesty of the harmonious music played in heaven.[17] Death therefore parodies Jesus Christ, the heavenly minstrel who leads the righteous in a dance to eternal life; a motif which can be linked to the *Danse Macabre* and has recently been explored in depth.[18]

As Meyer-Baer has previously observed, instruments in *Danse Macabre* schemes are used 'for a variety of reasons'.[19] It falls to the reader or beholder, respectively, to decide which interpretation fits the given context best.

Hierarchy

The structures at work in the *Danse Macabre* bear a strong relation to the aspect of hierarchy. Hierarchical configurations are very important in the

---

[15] Hammerstein (1974), 22-37. Compare Maus (2000), 137: '[...] eine Todessymbolik ist nachvollziehbar – schließlich wird die Sackpfeife aus toten Tieren hergestellt. Wie der Spieler seinen Atem in den leblosen Tierkörper bläst und somit den Ton angibt, so gebietet der Tod über den Sterbenden' (*the death symbolism is understandable, since the bagpipe is made from dead animals. When the musician blows his breath into the lifeless animal body, thereby setting the tone, Death presides over the dying person*).

[16] Cf. Hammerstein (1974), 50-53.

[17] According to Meyer-Baer (1970), 309, 'In none of the examples of the *Danse Macabre*, either in the pictures or in the poems, is there any suggestion of a reference or link to the dance of the blessed or resurrection through music'. Although the connection cannot be proven, I think the allusion is sufficiently clear, as different studies have shown (see also n. 18).

[18] See Walter Salmen, 'Jesus Christus, der himmlische Spielmann', *Music in Art*, 22:1-2 (2008), 5-10; Holger Eckhardt, 'Von Leichen, vom Leichaerer oder: Wie der Tanz zum Tod kam,' *Wirkendes Wort*, 44 (1994), 177-88, esp. 178. Eckhardt lists several theories about the much discussed origins of the *Danse Macabre* and calls the minstrel theory the 'religious-mystical explanation'; see also Hammerstein (1974), 60-61, and Meyer-Baer (1970).

[19] Meyer-Baer (1970), 304.

Danse as the impact of its message can only work in the face of *inverted* hierarchies. The persons shown in the *Danse* are arranged according to the medieval *ordo*, the social order that was universally acknowledged because, according to a contemporary argument commonly given as justification, it was ordained of God. Therefore, the people who must die range from the Pope to the Beggar, comprising the clergy, the secular dignitaries, and also the populace, as well as some figures who are exempt from the *ordo*: criminals or heathens (such as the Turks in the Basel *Danse* or the Thief in the Knoblochtzer edition).

In the German *Danse Macabre* tradition women usually appear only as female counterparts to certain male personages such as the King (Queen), Count (Countess), and Duke (Duchess).[20] Furthermore, women can be included as an Abbess or Nun, matching the male ranks of Abbot and Monk. Alternatively, they may make an occasional appearance as a Mother with her little children. The only other cases in which women are not presented as mere counterparts for male figures occur when they appear as girls and young women in the motif of Death and the Maiden, or when they are used as personifications of vices that were seen as typically female, such as vanity or a predilection for wordly pleasures like dancing. An example of the latter is the *Edelfrauw* (Noblewoman) in the Basel *Danse Macabre*, who is pictured looking in a mirror. In the printed editions of the Basel *Danse Macabre* by Huldrich Frölich, the Noblewoman is not called *Edelfraw*, as in the later editions by Merian, but instead bears the inscription '*Hoffart*'.[21] This archaic term is commonly translated as

---

[20] Relatively early in the course of the development of the genre, a *Danse Macabre des Femmes* was composed probably by the French poet Martial d'Auvergne (*c.*1420-1508). See Patrick Layet, 'La *Danse Macabre* des Femmes', in Winfried Frey and Hartmut Freytag (eds), *'Ihr müßt alle nach meiner Pfeife tanzen.' Totentänze vom 15. bis 20. Jahrhundert aus den Beständen der Herzog August Bibliothek Wolfenbüttel und der Bibliothek Otto Schäfer Schweinfurt*, Ausstellungskataloge der Herzog August Bibliothek, 77, (Wolfenbüttel: Harassowitz, 2000), 35-41; J.A. Wisman, 'Un miroir déformant: hommes et femmes des Danses macabres de Guyot Marchant', *Journal of Medieval and Renaissance Studies*, 23 (1993), 275-99; Ann Tukey Harrison (ed.), with a chapter by Sandra L. Hindman, *The Danse Macabre of Women. Ms. fr. 995 of the Bibliothèque Nationale* (Kent/London: Kent State University Press, 1994). However, discussion in this essay will focus on the German tradition.

[21] Huldrich Frölich's compilation was printed three times, in 1581, 1588 and 1608, with several variations, *e.g.* in the assortment of images. My observations are based on the third edition: Huldrich Frölich, *Der Hochloblichen und weitberümpten Statt Basel kurtze aber nützliche Beschreibung* [...] (Basel: Sebastian Henricpetri, 1608). See also the essay by Stefanie Knöll in this volume.

'pride', though it also means something like 'arrogance' or 'vanity'; it has particular overtones in evoking the mortal sin of *superbia* and is sometimes used as its German equivalent.

The person leading the dance is almost always the Pope, the highest church dignitary. This is often a prime theme in the dialogue between Death and the Pope when the latter is reminded that his high position is no longer of any use. Thus, in the Knoblochtzer *Danse* Death says to the Pope:

HErr baibst dyssen dantz must yr begynnen
Vor alle die da ere gewynnen.
Aller werlt yr gebot
Nu synt kommen yr in den dot
Vwer herschafft hat nu eyn ende[22]

(Sir Pope, you must begin this dance
before all others who are of high standing.
You had dominion over the whole world,
Now you have come to your death,
Your command is at an end.)

The invitation to the Pope to lead the dance has a certain ambivalence. By being in front, he is still granted prime status, but not in a positive sense: he is also the first one to die – a questionable privilege, quite apart from the fact that dancing ill befits a Pope.

It is interesting to see how this hierarchical order is intertwined with the direction that most *Danse Macabre* examples take: they lead their characters to the left. This direction is not a coincidence, but of the utmost importance,[23] and another instance of the inversion so ubiquitous in the *Danse Macabre*. In the Bible, right and left are associated with good and evil.[24] At the Last Judgment, the sinners are banished towards Christ's left, whereas the righteous are assigned a place to his right. The *Danse Macabre*, so close to the sphere of the devil, Evil and all things chthonic, moves to the left because it potentially leads to damnation. This is also the reason why *Danse Macabre* paintings were often placed on northern walls

---

[22] Quoted from Manfred Lemmer (ed.), *Der Heidelberger Totentanz von 1485. 42 Holzschnitte* (Frankfurt am Main/Leipzig: Insel Verlag, 1991), 49-50.

[23] Hammerstein (1980), 59-65, links the origins of the *Danse Macabre* to the iconography of the Last Judgement; see n. 8 above, and also the essay by Frances Eustace with Pamela King in this volume.

[24] For example, see Proverbs 4:27: 'vias enim quae a dextris sunt, novit Dominus, perversae sunt quae a sinistris sunt'.

in the church buildings – the north is the direction where Evil has its
realm; an idea that goes back to the Bible.[25] By moving to the left, the
dancers on a north wall are thus facing west instead of east – the location
of the altar and ultimately the Resurrection.

Yet we have to take into account another twist concerning direction.
The left side may be linked to a number of negative associations and
connotations, but it is still a technical necessity that the *Danse* leads to the
left. Since the Pope is the one dancing in front, and since the reader or
viewer has to proceed from the left to the right when looking at the
painting (in keeping with the normal reading direction), there is simply no
other logical way to construct a *Danse Macabre*.

There are very few *Danse Macabre* examples that move towards the
right, and the ones known to me do not feature a text, *e.g.* the *Danse
Macabre* mural in Hrastovlje (Slovenia).[26] The *Danse Macabre* mural in
the Marienkirche in Berlin, which is structured in a unique way, consequently
poses some problems. Here the *Danse* 'revolves' around a depiction of
Christ crucified; the secular estates are arranged to the right of the cross
(from the viewer's perspective), while the clergy are positioned on the left,
beginning with their lowest-ranking representative, the Sexton. The Pope
does still lead the dance, but he is the last clerical representative that the
viewer encounters, being situated close to the cross and opposite the
clerical estates starting with the Emperor. Nonetheless, Death addresses
him in the following way:

> gy hebben in der stede gades ghestan
> dar vmme schole gy vor an den dantz gan (lines 171-72)[27]

> *(You have held the place of God;*
> *therefore you shall go in front of the dance.)*

Of course, this ironic statement makes sense only in a conventionally
structured *Danse Macabre*. The author probably employed it quite
unthinkingly because it was just a common phrase in the *Danse*, a more or
less stereotypical comment by Death when facing the Pope.

---

[25] Cf. Jer. 1:14: 'Et dixit Dominus ad me: 'Ab aquilone pandetur malum super
omnes habitatores terrae'. On the topic of the left side as the place of Evil in the
Bible in general, see Hartmut Freytag, *Kommentar zur frühmittelhochdeutschen
Summa Theologiae*, Medium Aevum, 19 (Munich: Fink, 1970), 58-59, with
examples.

[26] See the essay by Tomislav Vignjević in this volume.

[27] Quotations from the Berlin *Danse Macabre* are from Peter Walther, *Der
Berliner Totentanz zu St. Marien* (Berlin: Lukas-Verlag, 1997), 69-84.

It is worth pointing out that neither the office of pope itself nor the social order as a whole are called into question in the *Danse Macabre*.[28] On the contrary, the *Danse* has an affirmative function because everyone is exhorted to fill his place in this order in an adequate and God-fearing way. The *ordo* as such is not considered faulty, but rather the way the humans violate it by exploiting their position and status.

The problem of the *ordo* is also related to the postulated conjunction of the *Danse Macabre* with the plague, or Black Death. It has been proposed that the cycles first evolved after one of the major outbreaks of this epidemic, when the social order was in danger of total disintegration because everybody strove to protect himself without paying any regard to his social duties any more. There is no proof for a firm link between the plague and the *Danse*, although Meyer-Baer pointed out that one of the most common attributes of Death – the scythe – 'makes sense only in periods of great catastrophes like the plagues in the fourteenth and fifteenth centuries, when death reaps crowds'.[29] However, only in the Lübeck *Danse Macabre* of 1463 may we see a possible connection, for parts of its text were re-used in the Redentin Easter Play, which was probably intended for performance at Easter 1464. This may not actually have taken place, however, as the Black Death was ravaging northern Germany at the time and the mass of spectators would have contravened the policy against gatherings of people during times of plague.[30]

Whatever the connection between the *Danse* and the plague, Death acts out the role of the great leveller. He shows mankind that their social standing is of no importance to him, thereby turning the man-made world order upside down. This idea is iconographically imparted in a variety of ways. One of the most meaningful assets are the status symbols: in the case of the Emperor and King these are the regalia or sovereign insignia, while for the clergy it is often the staff or typical headgear of their office.

---

[28] Anti-papal criticism already occurs in the medieval *Danse*, but it grew much harsher after the Reformation. For example, in a *Danse Macabre* manuscript from the early seventeenth century in Wismar (north-east Germany), the Pope is called 'Anti-Christ', a term also employed by Luther. See also the essay by Winfried Schwab in this volume.

[29] Meyer-Baer (1970), 296.

[30] Maike Claußnitzer, Hartmut Freytag and Susanne Warda, 'Das Redentiner – ein Lübecker Osterspiel. Über das Redentiner Osterspiel von 1464 und den Totentanz in der Marienkirche in Lübeck von 1463', *Zeitschrift für deutsches Altertum*, 132 (2003), 189-238; also Maike Claußnitzer, *Sub specie aeternitatis. Studien zum Verhältnis von historischer Situation und Heilsgeschichte im Redentiner Osterspiel*, Mikrokosmos, 75 (Frankfurt am Main: Peter Lang, 2007), 147-60.

In some *Danse Macabre* scenes, these attributes of status are depicted as having fallen to the ground, thereby demonstrating that they are no longer of any significance. The Basel *Danse* shows how the Emperor has lost his *globus cruciger* (cross-bearing orb), which has rolled between Death's feet, while the sceptre seems to be falling to the ground as well. Likewise, at the feet of the Pope there is a useless letter of indulgence, and Death remarks fittingly:

> Ein Vortantz müßt ihr mit hir han:
> Der Ablaß euch nicht hilfft darvon[31]
>
> (*You must lead the dance with me,*
> *the letter of indulgence does not help you.*)

Sometimes, the insignia are not trampled on the ground but simply taken away. Death often snatches the headgear of his clerical victims and dons it himself. In the Basel *Danse*, he steals the Abbot's mitre, puts it on and says, 'Herr Apt ich zieh euch die Yfflen ab' (*Sir Abbot, I pull off your mitre*). [32]

The Munich blockbook of *c.*1465/70 (Munich, Cod. xyl. mon. 39) similarly employs the headgear motif to illustrate the vanity of wordly ambitions. Its last scene (fol. 14v) shows a preacher meditating on death. Assembled in front of him are twenty-two skulls, four of them wearing different types of headgear that can be assigned to dignitaries shown earlier in the *Danse*, viz. a papal tiara, a mitre, a royal and an imperial crown. [33] This is quite an original way of showing the reversal of high status to nothingness. Ironically, the dead dignitaries are allowed to keep their headgear and thus their status symbols, but they are obviously no longer of any use: they only have value in the human world, and not in the

---

[31] Kaiser (1982), 198.

[32] The mitre is also known as an *infula*. The expression *Yffel* in the *Danse Macabre* text is a 'Germanised' version of this word; it is still in use in Switzerland, albeit with a slightly different meaning.

[33] The Munich blockbook is now available online at http://daten.digitale-samm lungen.de/~db/0003/bsb00038191/images/. See also the minute description in Wilhelm Ludwig Schreiber, *Handbuch der Holz- und Metallschnitte der XV. Jahrhunderts*, IV (Leipzig: Hiersemann, 1927), 442, and Patrick Layet, 'Die bimediale Münchner Totentanzhandschrift Xyl. 39', *L'art macabre (Jahrbuch der Europäischen Totentanz-Vereinigung)*, 1 (2000), 80-96 (with a few illustrations).

reversed world of Death. In this way, the social position of the victims is affirmed and denied at the same time.[34]

In many ways, the *Danse Macabre* illustrates the futility of men's endeavours to establish distinctions in this life – distinctions which eventually are of no avail because Death overthrows them, along with all plans engineered by men. Everyone is made aware of the relativity of his position, be it the Usurer who has to realize that his riches will not impress his ghastly dance partner, or the Lawyer who must abide by the laws of Death while human laws are thwarted. The issue of social standing is explored further in Urs Martin Zahnd's study of the Bern *Danse Macabre*. He points out that the *Danse* depicts a model of a society that at first sight appears to be arranged according to the estates, but by reiterating the identical existential situation (*viz.* everyone must die) the basic equality of all human beings is highlighted.[35]

In many ways, the figure of Death resembles the figure of the Fool because he can 'mock [the humans] with impunity' and is 'no respecter of rank, either; he treats everyone alike, irrespective of their social status'.[36] The Fool appears in several German *Danse Macabre* schemes, *e.g.* in Basel and in Bern. Yet the concept of the Fool is important for the *Danse* in a much more profound sense. As Sophie Oosterwijk has observed, 'in the *Danse Macabre* the dead dancers themselves assume the role of the fool as they mix freely with all ranks of the living while by their mockery and appearance they show every man what he really is and what he will become.'[37] All humans are fools if they do not grasp the ultimate truth. The *sot* in Guy Marchant's expanded *Danse Macabre* edition puts it succinctly, 'sages et sotz [...] Tous mors sont dun estat commun' (*the wise and fools alike, all the dead share the same condition*).[38]

---

[34] Christian Kiening, 'Totentänze – Ambivalenzen des Typus', *Jahrbuch für Internationale Germanistik*, 27 (1995), 38-56, at 56, also speaks of the 'Balance zwischen der Bestätigung und der Aufhebung von ordo' (*the balance between the affirmation and the abolition of the ordo*).

[35] Urs Martin Zahnd, 'Niklaus Manuels Totentanz als Spiegel der Berner Gesellschaft um 1500', *L'art macabre (Jahrbuch der Europäischen Totentanz-Vereinigung)*, 4 (2003), 265-80, at 278.

[36] Sophie Oosterwijk, '"Alas, poor Yorick": Death, the Fool, the Mirror and the *Danse Macabre*', in Stefanie Knöll (ed.), *Narren – Masken – Karneval: Meisterwerke von Dürer bis Kubin aus der Düsseldorfer Graphiksammlung 'Mensch und Tod'* (Regensburg: Schnell & Steiner, 2009), 20-32, at 20.

[37] Oosterwijk (2009), 22-23.

[38] Oosterwijk (2009), 26, and also 134-35. The Fool did not appear in the original mural in Paris.

Moreover, Death seems to topple the natural order when he does not only limit his victims to the old and infirm, but also calls away young people or mothers with their babies. The toddler who is forced to dance, although he has not even learned to walk yet, is a universal topos in the *Danse Macabre*. The final line 'Nw mus ich tantzen vnd kan noch nicht gan' (*Now I must dance, and I am not able to walk yet*) of the small Child in the Heidelberg blockbook is a formula that occurs throughout the southern German group of the 'Oberdeutscher vierzeiliger Totentanztext'. With slightly different emphasis, the Child in Marchant's 1485 edition of the Paris *Danse Macabre* complains:

A. a. a. ie ne scay parler
Enfant suis: iay la lange mue.
Hier nasquis huy men fault aler
Je ne faiz quentree et yssue
[...]
Lordonnance dieu ne se mue.
Aussi tost meurt ieusne que vieux.

(A, a, a, I cannot speak,
I am a child, I am dumb.
Born yesterday, I have to go today.
I exit as soon as I have entered.
[...]
God's verdict is irrevocable.
The young one dies as quickly as the old one.)

It is certainly possible to see the death of children as a perversion of the normal course of nature where old people are supposed to die before the young.[39] However, there is an added twist. In the Middle Ages infant mortality was so high that the death of children might almost be said to have been a 'normal' occurrence. Viewed in this way, the depiction of Death fetching babies and toddlers would not be something particularly cruel, but just an apt description of a given fact of life. Nonetheless, the scenes of Death preying on small children are designed in such a way as to make the reader/viewer experience some kind of disparity, which is also

---

[39] See Sophie Oosterwijk, '"Muoz ich tanzen und kan nit gân?": Death and the Infant in the Medieval *Danse Macabre*', *Word & Image*, 22:2 (2006), 146-64, esp. 161; Thorsten Halling, Silke Fehlemann and Jörg Vögele (eds), 'Vorzeitiger Tod: Identitäts- und Sinnstiftung in historischer Perspektive', special issue of *Historical Social Research – Historische Sozialforschung*, 34:4 (2009); Stefanie Knöll, 'Schwangerschaft, Geburt und Tod', in Daniel Schäfer (ed.), *Hebammen im Rheinland 1750–1950* (Kassel: Kassel University Press, 2010), 285-300.

expressed by the contradiction in the line 'Nw mus ich tantzen und kan noch nicht gan'.

In some pictures Death is leading these small children by the hand, thereby parodying the stereotypical image of a caring parent. Thus, Death distorts the gesture of protection into a 'cruel joke',[40] fitting it into the overall scheme of inversion that is discussed here as one of the salient features of the *Danse Macabre*. Furthermore, the innocent nudity of the infant may be reminiscent of Baby Jesus.[41] This would add yet another layer of meaning to the motif, making the mockery of Death all the more poignant.[42]

Nonetheless, the power of Death is far from all-encompassing. In the *Danse Macabre*, he is obviously the one who sets the tone (in the literal sense), but one has to bear in mind that he is only the executioner of God's will. Death cannot pass judgement: that is the prerogative of God and God alone, as the Child in the Paris *Danse Macabre* points out correctly when it speaks of '*lordonnance dieu*'. Death has been conquered by Christ and relegated to a secondary role. Some *Danse Macabre* schemes even include representations of Christ on the cross, *e.g.* the murals in Berlin (as discussed above), Bern, Klingental,[43] and Pinzolo (Italy). The latter is an interesting case because here Death is shown shooting his victims with a bow, and one of his arrows has pierced the body of Christ. In this painting Death and his conqueror are present simultaneously and in spatial contiguity, which is not necessarily a contradiction but again rather a question of hierarchy. By dying on the cross, Christ has won his victory over Death – this is what the image shows. In this sense, Death has made his own defeat possible. That is also more or less what Death himself says in the Bern *Danse*, where he stands next to the cross (the position usually reserved for St John the Evangelist), pointing at Jesus:

---

[40] Oosterwijk (2006), 154.

[41] As Oosterwijk (2006), 156-59, shows, the motif of the naked toddler led by Death may ultimately derive from the iconography of the *Infantia Christi*.

[42] Compare the post-war adaptation of the Lübeck *Danse Macabre* by Alfred Mahlau, where the Child plays a prominent role and is stylised as Baby Jesus. See Dorothy von Hülsen, 'Alfred Mahlau, Die Totentanz-Fenster der Marienkirche in Lübeck', in Hartmut Freytag (ed.), *Der Totentanz in der Marienkirche in Lübeck und der Nikolaikirche in Reval (Tallinn)*, Niederdeutsche Studien, 39 (Cologne/Weimar/Vienna: Böhlau, 1990), 385-403.

[43] The *Danse Macabre* of Klingental was located in a former nunnery in Basel. To distinguish it from the Basel *Danse* (also known as 'Großbasel') in the Dominican cemetery, it was sometimes called 'Kleinbasel'. The Klingental *Danse* was a replica of the Basel *Danse* and was probably painted in the second half of the fifteenth century, some decades after its model. See Hammerstein (1980), 188-89.

Allein der Herr über all Herren
Mocht sich selbs wol mins Gwallts erweren,
Sin Tod ist gsin min Tod und Stärben,
Dadurch er üch wollt Gnad erwärben.[44]

(Only the Lord of Lords
was able to withstand my power.
His death was my death and dying,
with this, he has obtained mercy for you.)

The technique of mirroring

Another motif which appears in many places in the *Danse Macabre* and is
quite significant in the context of inversion is the mirror, or mirroring as a
technique.[45] When it comes to medieval book titles, the metaphor of the
speculum or mirror is ubiquitous (*e.g. Speculum Humanae Salvationis,*
Speculum Ecclesiae, etc.) and can be found in various languages.[46] The
unknown author of the *Danse Macabre* of Paris uses it in his opening
lines:

En ce miroer chacun peut lire
Qui le conuient ainsi Danser,
Saige est celuy qui bien si mire.

(In this mirror everyone can read
that he must dance in this way,
He who looks at himself well is wise.)

---

[44] Quoted from Wilfried Kettler, *Der Berner Totentanz des Niklaus Manuel.*
Philologische, epigraphische sowie historische Überlegungen zu einem Sprach-
und Kunstdenkmal der frühen Neuzeit (Bern: Peter Lang, 2009), 73-81, at 73,
stanza 6.
[45] Bettina Spoerri, 'Die Spiegelmetapher und das Spiegelbild in den Totentänzen
von 1400 bis zur Mitte des 15. Jahrhunderts. Ein historischer Abriß', in Markus J.
Wenninger (ed.), *Du guoter tôt: Sterben im Mittelalter – Ideal und Realität*
(Klagenfurt: Wieser, 1998), 157-80. See also the essays by Kristiane Lemé-
Hébuterne and Frances Eustace with Pamela King in this volume.
[46] See also Horst Wenzel, *Spiegelungen: zur Kultur der Visualität im Mittelalter,*
Philologische Studien und Quellen, 219 (Berlin: Schmidt, 2009), 64-96; Fein
(2002), 73; Jane H.M. Taylor, 'Un Miroer Salutaire', in Jane H.M. Taylor (ed.),
Dies Illa: Death in the Middle Ages, Proceedings of the 1983 Manchester
Colloquium, Vinaver Studies in French, 1 (Liverpool: Cairns, 1984), 29-43, at 29.

The Lübeck *Danse Macabre*, which is partly based on the Paris *Danse*, consequently employs this metaphor, too, when it exhorts the beholder, 'Seet hyr dat spegel junck vñ olden' (*Look in the mirror, young and old*).[47]

A *Danse Macabre* incunabulum with the title *Des dodes dantz*, also from Lübeck (printed in 1489 by the famous *Mohnkopfdruckerei* publisher), which in turn adapts certain passages of the above-mentioned monumental painting, even calls itself a 'mirror of death'. The text urges the reader:

> So merke he ut sines herten grunde
> Den speigel des dodes, de hir navolgende is (ll. 88-89)[48]
>
> (*Thus he shall understand from the bottom of his heart
> the mirror of death, which follows here.*)

The *Danse Macabre* is a mirror insofar as it serves as a reflection of virtually everyone. It addresses everybody, no matter whether they are young or old, beautiful or ugly, rich or poor. The people in the *Danse* are typified; they usually do not have any individual traits, which makes identification easy for the viewer: in this way, he can look at himself.

Since the human figures of the *Danse* are often sinners or at least people who have been remiss in honouring God, the viewer or reader is presented with an image of what he is *not* supposed to do – a distorted picture. The *Danse Macabre* is *exemplary* in a negative sense. Thus, the viewer may realize that for him – in contrast to the living participants of the *Danse* – it is not too late to convert to a devout and virtuous lifestyle.[49] Some *Danse* schemes contain figures who serve as examples in a positive way, but the majority are presented as guilty of some sin or other, albeit sins that are ever-present in society: vanity, greed, self-conceit and lust are not only common in real life, but also in its mirror-image, the *Danse Macabre*.

---

[47] Quoted from Hartmut Freytag (ed.), *Der Totentanz in der Marienkirche in Lübeck und der Nikolaikirche in Reval (Tallin). Edition, Kommentar, Interpretation, Rezeption*, Niederdeutsche Studien, 39 (Cologne/Weimar/Vienna: Böhlau, 1990), 137-39.

[48] Quoted from Hermann Baethcke (ed.), *Des dodes danz. Nach den Lübecker Drucken von 1489 und 1496* (Tübingen: Laupp, 1876), 13-93. The verb *merken* is difficult to translate because it can have a variety of meanings; here it means something like 'realise', but also 'pay attention (to something)'.

[49] Taylor (1984), 33, speaks of the 'notion of duality' which combines an admonitory (negative example) and an exemplary (positive model) function.

❊] 73 [❊

Der Tod zur Königin.

Frau Königin! euer Freud ist aus,
Springet mit mir ins Todten-Haus,
Euch hilfft kein Schöne, Gold noch Geld,
Ich spring mit euch in jene Welt.

Antwort der Königin.

O Weh und Ach, o weh und immer!
Wo bleibt jetzund mein Frauenzimmer?
Mit denen ich hatt' Freuden viel:
O Tod, thu g'mach, mit mir nicht eil.

Fig. 30. Death and the Queen, engraving by Matthäus Merian the Elder based on the Großbasel *Danse Macabre* mural of *c.*1440, published in 1649.

Yet these are not the only possible ways of linking the metaphor of the mirror to the *Danse Macabre*. The image of the mirror has further layers of meaning to offer, which may throw light on some of the aspects relevant for the *Danse*. Sometimes, the dance partners are mirror images themselves. In some cases, the pictures seem to imply that the dead figures are not only counterparts of the living in a general sense, but rather the same person, albeit looking as if already dead, 'likenesses of themselves as they shall be, a *Doppelgänger* of stark, macabre immediacy'.[50] The scene of Death and the Queen in the Basel *Danse* can serve as an example (Fig. 30). Beautiful and wearing the magnificent attire that her position demands, the Queen is accompanied by a female corpse in an advanced state of putrefaction with hanging breasts and straggly long hair, a snake curling around her neck. It seems reasonable to suppose that the corpse is meant to mirror the Queen, depicting her in her future state as if to visualise the well-known phrase 'Sum quod eris' (*I am what you will be*).[51]

This brings us back to the figure of the Fool discussed earlier. Sophie Oosterwijk described Death as the *alter ego* of the living and drew a comparison with the role of the Fool: 'Visually each dead dancer serves his living counterpart as a distorted mirror, just like the fool who holds up an allegorical mirror to his betters through a semblance of folly or [...] through a portrayal of himself as a victim of Death.'[52] Susanna Fein likewise observed how the Three Living are confronted 'with a startlingly strange [...] "other" who forces one to self-recognition and maturation.'[53]

Jane Taylor distinguishes the notions *La Mort de Toi* versus *La Mort de Soi*, relating the latter to the *Danse Macabre*:

> [...] the living of the *Danse Macabré* are not characters but types, individualised only by externals such as clothes or symbols of office and with their faces carefully anonymous. The mechanism is therefore the following: the spectator looks into the mirror of the *Danse Macabré* and recognises self [...]; he next identifies the partners also as self, but as self tranformed so that the illusion of youth and immortality is stripped away, leaving the reality of the mortal man.[54]

Taylor calls this function of the mirror the 'mirror as transformer': 'the understanding that within the mirror itself there takes place a metamorphosis

---

[50] Fein (2002), 69.

[51] *Cf.* Spoerri (1998), 165.

[52] Oosterwijk (2009), 23.

[53] Fein (2002), 71.

[54] Taylor (1984), 35.

of the onlooker, so that he sees not himself, but himself altered'.[55] In other cases, the dead are outright mirror-images of the living in the true sense of the word, as in the image of Death and the Cripple (Fig. 31). Death mimics his victim, who is missing his left foot, and the way the two figures face each other is very close to true mirror reflection.

Fig. 31. Death and the Cripple, engraving by Matthäus Merian the Elder based on the Großbasel *Danse Macabre* mural of *c.*1440, published in 1649.

---

[55] Taylor (1984), 35.

Since the motif of the mirror is very popular in didactic literature in general, it can be found in various forms of art and literature, not least those that have death as their primary subject. In her study on the theme of the Three Living and Three Dead, Fein makes a number of interesting observations which can also be applied to the *Danse Macabre*. She identifies the pictorial design of the motif as 'essentially binary, with the space between the [... persons ...] established as a mirror-point, the site of inversion between the realm of the Living and that of the Dead.'[56] She also speaks of the crossover point between these two spheres, the 'divide between the here and the hereafter, between time and atemporality. The symmetry of the binary image sets this divide before the viewer, at the centre.'[57] This is true for many *Danse Macabre* images, especially the ones showing separate pairs of corpse figures with living humans. They basically consist of two parts, namely the dead (mostly on the left) and the living (on the right side), in this way forming a symmetrical configuration, underpinned with the oppositions that Fein names.

Stefanie Knöll has pointed out additional meanings that the mirror often has. Not only can it be used as a means towards self-knowledge – exhorting the beholder to see the *Danse* as a reflection of his true nature, *viz.* a mortal and fallible creature – but it may also be a symbol of vanity. This is the reason why it mostly occurs in connection with female figures, who are often employed as personifications of vanity. Knöll furthermore shows that this way of implementing the symbol of the mirror necessarily links it to death: 'Dieser Narzissmus, der keine christliche Nächstenliebe zuläßt, verbindet den Spiegel unausweichlich mit dem Tod' (*This narcissism, which does not permit any Christian charity, inevitably links the mirror to death*).[58] The *Edelfraw* (Noblewoman) in the Basel *Danse Macabre* looks into her mirror and exclaims, 'Den Todt hab ich im Spiegel g'sehen' (*I have seen Death in the mirror*):[59] instead of her own face, the

---

[56] Fein (2002), 70.

[57] Fein (2002), 70.

[58] Stefanie Knöll, 'Zur Entstehung des Motivs *Der Tod und das Mädchen*', in Andrea von Hülsen-Esch and Hiltrud Westermann-Angerhausen with Stefanie Knöll (eds), *Zum Sterben schön: Alter, Totentanz und Sterbekunst von 1500 bis heute*, (Regensburg: Schnell & Steiner, 2006), vol. 1, 65-72, at 68. On the association of mirrors with death, also see Taylor (1984), 37-38, and Oosterwijk (2009), 30, who observes that a mirror can 'reveal truth, and a man who recognises his folly – or, in some cases, mortality – in his own reflection is well on the road towards attaining wisdom'.

[59] Kaiser (1982), 232.

mirror reflects the cadaver standing behind her. Taylor points out that in contexts like these, the mirror is a

> gateway to a truth not discernible on a surface level, to a reality deeper than that provided by superficial observation. It is the instrument which enables the spectator to move from the plane of everyday reality, to a plane of profounder reality concealed deep in his heart and soul.[60]

As has been shown above, the reflecting function of macabre images directly relates to the spectator in a number of ways. Fein describes the way these pictures 'function' in an insightful passage that deserves to be quoted in full, because it illuminates the underlying structure of the iconography of the dead and the living. A mirror effect comes about

> because the motif exploits symmetry. Typically according equal space and/ or text to each half, Living and Dead, it *looks* like a mirrored reflection. At the same time, it operates as a reflection for the viewer [...] by a process that depends on an even more crucial binary divide, that is, the line between the viewer and the work. In this relationship, the page (or painted wall) operates as the demarcated point of encounter. The spectator embodies, in *actual* living flesh, the living half of the icon, while the artistic work remains a monitory sign frozen in timelessness. The image thus takes primal hold upon anyone who would contemplate it.[61]

One could thus state that there are four different ways in which the mirror appears in the *Danse Macabre*. First, it works in a linguistic way, *viz.* as a metaphor in the texts themselves. Secondly, the whole *Danse* serves as a mirror for the viewer in a parenetic, didactic way. And finally, the dead are mirror images of the living on two different levels: in a figurative way, and in the geometrical sense.[62]

---

[60] Taylor (1984), 32.

[61] Fein (2002), 71-72.

[62] Spoerri (1998) identifies three distinct ways of employing the motif of the mirror, albeit slightly different from my classification: 1) the *Danse* as a whole is a mirror of society; 2) the estates mirror the separate social groups of this society; 3) the individual dance partners are mirror images. Compare the functions named in Taylor (1984), esp. 30-32 and 38-39, as 'the mirror as exemplar' (supplying an *exemplum*, a model or pattern for the spectator), 'the mirror as reflector' (providing an exact reflection of reality) and 'the mirror as *repoussoir*' (showing a distorted image, a reflection with negative connotations).

Ambiguities

The impact that the *Danse Macabre* has on its viewers – medieval and modern alike – is partly based on the ambivalences it rests on. It relies on the grotesque and often repellent way in which the corpse figures are depicted: they are not skeletons but either putrefying corpses or 'mummies'. Skeletons would be comparatively 'clean', or even 'clinical', as it were. The corpses in the *Danse* often have some hair left, however; they are covered with remainders of wrinkled skin, and there are even examples of figures with noses or still intact faces. Since they are in the process of putrefaction, the dead are often infested with various forms of worms, snakes, reptiles such as toads – the type of vermin that corpses were thought to engender spontaneously – and sometimes phantastical creatures, *e.g.* the 'serpents' twisting around the bodies of the cadavers in the Munich blockbook, which look like snakes or worms but have small pricked-up ears or horns protruding from their heads. Cadaver imagery is not exclusive to the *Danse Macabre*, but these works of art exhibit some of the most vivid examples of this iconographic tradition.[63]

The *Danse Macabre* undoubtedly exerts some sort of aesthetic fascination, not in spite of these grotesque features, but rather because of them. The synthesis of morbid and alluring elements is probably the reason why the motif of Death and the Maiden became so omnipresent in art and literature. [64] One of the most compelling scenes in the *Danse Macabre* is surely the picture of Death and the Maiden in Niklaus Manuel's mural in Bern, because here eroticism and grisly death are intertwined – literally – in such a way as to repulse and beguile at the same time (Fig. 32).

However, this is not the only form of ambivalence to be found in the *Danse Macabre*. The genre as a whole is based on contradictions, polarity and ambiguities. A central question of scholarship is the relation between

---

[63] See Sophie Oosterwijk, 'Food for Worms – Food for Thought: the Appearance and Interpretation of the 'Verminous' Cadaver in Britain and Europe', *Church Monuments*, 20 (2005), 40-80, 133-40, especially 48-49, 57, 64-66, 68 and 70; also see p. 50 with observations about the negative associations linked with reptiles.

[64] See Knöll (2006). Knöll shows that the motif of Death and the Maiden did not derive from the *Danse Macabre* (as has often been postulated), but did indeed spring from earlier sources and was later introduced into the *Danse*, probably by Niklaus Manuel in the Bern *Danse*.

Death as a personification and *the dead*.[65] Stephan Cosacchi went so far as to divide the *Danse Macabre* into three different groups according to whether they show Death, the dead or a mixture of both; he consequently called them *Totentänze* (dances of the dead), *Todestänze* (dances of death), and *Todes-Toten-Tänze* or *Todtentänze* (essentially untranslatable, but a mixture of the first two).[66] His suggestion has not been widely accepted and the common German term is still *Totentanz*. It is interesting to note that the English term 'Dance of Death' is actually the equivalent of the other German form, *viz. Todestanz*, which has become obsolete. French usage avoids this dilemma by employing the term *Danse Macabre*.

Fig. 32. The Widow and the Maiden in the Bern *Danse Macabre* mural by Niklaus Manuel, 1516-19/20. Lithograph from Joseph Bergmann, *Niklaus Manuels Todtentanz...* (Bern, *c.*1823). © Graphiksammlung 'Mensch und Tod', Heinrich-Heine-University Düsseldorf.

---

[65] Wilhelm Fehse, *Der Ursprung der Totentänze. Mit einem Anhang: Der vierzeilige oberdeutsche Totentanztext. Codex Palatinus Nr. 314 B. 79a-80b* (Halle: Niemeyer, 1907). See also n. 2 above.
[66] Stephan Cosacchi, *Makabertanz. Der Totentanz in Kunst, Poesie und Brauchtum des Mittelalters* (Meisenheim am Glan: Hain, 1965), 7.

Christian Kiening observes fundamental ambivalences rooted in the origins of the genre. He supplies several examples of the *Danse Macabre* where the figures seem to vacillate between a personification of *Death* and *the dead*, *i.e.* cadavers, but he also cites some instances where certain strategies of disambiguation are employed.[67] Erwin Koller, in contrast, speaks of a 'pseudo-problem'.[68] Indeed, the difference between *Death* and *the dead* loses its discriminative value somewhat when we take into account that the easiest and most natural way to depict Death is by painting a dead person, although there have been other approaches both in Antiquity and after the Middle Ages (*e.g.* as Cupid with an inverted torch or Death as the brother of Sleep), especially in the wake of Lessing.[69] Considering this, one has to realize that the concepts of *Death* vs. *the dead* are bound to mix and blend into each other.

Conclusion

In the world of the *Danse Macabre*, everything is 'wrong', upside down, reversed: a realm of chaos and disorder. The *Danse* employs various techniques to establish this 'topsy-turvy' world.[70] Death violates hierarchy and levels distinctions; the music accompanying his gruesome dance is not only noisy and inharmonious, but the musicians themselves are utterly

---

[67] Kiening (1995), 49, states that in several *Danse Macabre* schemes it is possible to distinguish between personifications of Death and depictions of dead persons, but he also admits that the latter may be identical to executioners or messengers of Death himself, to the effect that both the personification and the actual corpse figure (as dance partner) may overlap with Death's henchmen.

[68] See Erwin Koller, *Totentanz. Versuch einer Textembeschreibung*, Innsbrucker Beiträge zur Kulturwissenschaft, Germanistische Reihe, 10 (Innsbruck: Institut für Germanistik der Universität, 1980), 10-11 and 21-24.

[69] Gotthold Ephraim Lessing's essay 'Wie die Alten den Tod gebildet' (*How the ancients represented death*) was published in 1769.

[70] See Gert Kaiser, 'Totentanz und verkehrte Welt', in Franz Link (ed.), *Tanz und Tod in Kunst und Literatur*, Schriften zur Literaturwissenschaft, Germanistische Reihe, 10 (Berlin: Duncker & Humblot, 1993), 93-118. Kaiser explores the motif of the 'topsy-turvy' world, relating it to carnival, Shrovetide and the figure of the fool. See also Knöll (ed.) (2009); Dietz-Rüdiger Moser, *Fastnacht, Fasching, Karneval: das Fest der verkehrten Welt* (Graz: Ed. Kaleidoskop im Verl. Styria, 1986); Werner Mezger and Irene Götz (eds), *Narren, Schellen und Marotten: elf Beiträge zur Narrenidee. Begleitband zu einer Ausstellung in der Universitätsbibliothek Freiburg im Breisgau vom 9. Februar bis zum 14. März 1984* (2nd edn, Remscheid: Kierdorf, 1984).

terrifying. The living are forced to join in and, even worse, endure mockery and scorn.

These instances of inversion are not an end in themselves or just a means to enliven the art form stylistically. On the contrary, they all serve the same objective: to expose beauty, riches, social status and any form of man-made distinctions in all their worthlessness and to show man what he will become in the face of death. The multi-layered meanings underlying the *Danse Macabre* can only be gauged to their full extent if basic motifs and themes (such as the mirror or the ambiguities which run through the texts and images) are explored through all their ramifications.

The ambivalences cannot always be resolved, and perhaps this explains some of the fascination that the *Danse Macabre* still exerts. Another reason for this ongoing allure may be that it is almost impossible for the viewer to evade the message of the *Danse Macabre*, since it is valid for each and every one of us. The *Danse* forces the reader into a dialogue, refusing to grant him any form of respite, like Death himself. As Fein so aptly puts it, 'the viewer is participant, willing or not'.[71]

Acknowledgements

I am very much indebted to the editors for their valuable help with sources and illustrations, and for their knowledgeable and patient feedback during the editing process of this essay. I also want to thank Professor Hartmut Freytag (Hamburg) for his helpful comments and suggestions.

---

[71] Fein (2002), 72.

FROM ALLEGORY TO ANATOMY: FEMININITY AND THE *DANSE MACABRE*

MAIKE CHRISTADLER

Equality in the face of death is often described as one of the characteristics of the *Danse Macabre*. It refers to the social standing of the figures whom Death comes to fetch from their place in society in order to take them to his world. Moreover, it refers to gender as the Queen, the Duchess and the Abbess are torn from life just as their male counterparts are.[1]

There appears to be even further equality: the figure of Death in the *Danse Macabre* is not without gender: he is sometimes a she, or should we say that she is sometimes a he? Visual evidence is very clear in this respect: many of the most famous *Danses Macabres* of the fifteenth and sixteenth centuries include female corpses accompanying men and women to the other world. Corpse figures with long wavy hair and hanging breasts indicate 'femaleness', their behaviour being exactly the same as that of their male counterparts. While the cadavers dancing in Hartmann Schedel's *Weltchronik* or Nuremberg Chronicle of 1493 depict various stages of decay, the one on the right with its bowels flowing out of the abdominal cavity is recognisable as female by her hanging breast and long hair (Fig. 1). In the Basel *Danse Macabre* of *c.*1440 it is the Queen who has to face a female Death, and the Empress is also faced by a long-haired cadaver, although we cannot see whether it has breasts. In the *Danse Macabre* mural of 1516-19 by Niklaus Manuel Deutsch (*c.*1485-1530) in

---

[1] I do not want to go into detail here but the so-called equality is very much one of degrees. Thus the whole procession is neatly ordered along social hierarchies that are profoundly anchored in early modern society: first come the Pope, clergy and wordly rulers, men before women, followed by the hierarchically differentiated nobility and public officials, and finally the humbler artisans and soldiers – who are included or not according to local interests. See Dagmar Eichberger, 'Close Encounters with Death. Changing Representations of Women in Renaissance Art and Literature', in Bernard J. Muir (ed.), *Reading Texts and Images. Essays on Medieval Art and Patronage in Honor of Margaret M. Manion* (Exeter: University of Exeter Press, 2002), 273-96, at 276-78.

Bern, the *Domherr* (Priest) follows the flute and dance of a decrepit, mummy-like old hag who easily compares to contemporary representations of witches and whose musical instrument is placed between her legs in a very suggestive way.[2] Still in the Bern *Danse*, the Merchant is confronted by a corpse with one breast who playfully releases his girdle. This kind of erotic interplay between the figures of Death and the people confronted by them is not limited to the female corpses and their followers.

Fig. 33. The Monk and the Abbess in the Bern *Danse Macabre* mural by Niklaus Manuel, 1516-19/20, lithograph from Joseph Bergmann, *Niklaus Manuels Todtentanz...* (Bern, *c*.1823). © Graphiksammlung 'Mensch und Tod', Heinrich-Heine-University Düsseldorf.

Referring to the Bern *Danse Macabre*, Christian Kiening has recently drawn attention again to the role inversion of the figures of Death and those still living who have to face their end.[3] Here the corpses are dancing in a lively manner and playing music, they are lascivious and sexually interested, and actually prompting their – often reluctant – living counterparts

---

[2] See the essay by Susanne Warda in this volume.
[3] Christian Kiening, *Das andere Selbst. Figuren des Todes an der Schwelle zur Neuzeit* (Munich: Wilhelm Fink Verlag, 2003), 58-63.

into very ambivalent actions. Thus in the double arcade of Monk and Abbess the corpse guiding the latter seems to be a bride's attendant delivering her to a future husband – who can only be the Monk to the left, himself desperately trying to escape from Death and in doing so turning to the Abbess and her bony companion who is entering the scene from the right (Fig. 33). The figures of Monk and Abbess not only match in their respective movements towards one another, but they are also unified by the corresponding colours of their clothes. Unrighteous desire and immorality in the eyes of contemporary society are here suggestively and ironically brought to the surface.

Liminality and ambiguity are evident throughout Niklaus Manuel's *Danse* and they are particularly elaborate in erotic moments. Dancing itself sends out erotic messages and this is especially true of the Morris Dance which is explicitly mentioned in one of the verses added to the Bern *Danse Macabre*, 'Tod und Burger' (*Death and Burgher*):

Der tod spricht zum Burger.
Burger nun mach din Testament
Din läben ist zum tod gewendt
Din Huß und Hoff must du verlan
vnnd Ein Marischgentänzli han.[4]

(Death addresses the Burgher.
Burgher, make your testament:
Your life has turned to death.
You must leave your house and court
And take part in a morris dance.)

The Morris Dance ('Marischgentänzli') is executed with excited and ecstatic movements. It probably derives from a sword dance, and at the end of the fifteenth century and throughout the sixteenth it was strongly connoted with sexuality and connected to male-female courtship.[5]

Some of the couples in the Bern *Danse* are more explicitly eroticised and these are more frequently women led to the dance by a 'male' cadaver. The Abbess has already been mentioned. The Empress, too, offers her hand to her bony companion so that he may lead her. However, her eyes

---

[4] Quoted from Johannes Tripps, *'Den Würmern wirst Du Wildbret sein'. Der Berner Totentanz des Niklaus Manuel Deutsch in den Aquarellkopien von Albrecht Kauw (1649)* (Bern: Bernisches Historisches Museum, 2005), 75.

[5] Johanna Müller-Meiningen, *Die Moriskentänzer und andere Arbeiten des Erasmus Gasser für das Alte Rathaus in München* (Regensburg: Schnell & Steiner, 1998), 35.

are coquettishly directed towards the viewer of the painting to whom she also seems to expose her brilliantly red underskirt – visible only because she has to lift her robe for dancing. Even though her foot is not actually exposed, her gaze reminds the viewer of things other than death. Even the Widow glances out of the painting into the viewer's space as she dances with a dead companion characterised by a long moustache and typical war instruments, who is thus easily recognisable as a *Landsknecht* (Lansquenet). Here the painting refers to a contemporary discourse of the particular virility of soldiers and the lasciviousness of widows – both morally reprehensible.[6]

Most openly eroticised, however, is the *Tochter* (Daughter) whose breasts Death is fondling, almost exposing them to the viewer who is also the target of the girl's glance (Fig. 32). Her long braids and her girdle end in decorative and swirling ribbons often found in drawings by Manuel and Urs Graf (1485-after 1529) where they are attributes of Venus who threatens to tie up lovelorn men.[7] The young girl is a promised bride, and both Death and the viewer are ready to share the bridegroom's privileges and to 'have' the girl, as she herself makes clear: 'Ich was verpflicht Einem Jungen knaben, / So wyl mich der tod mit Im haben' (*I was promised to a young lad, but now Death will take me with him*).[8] Whether the *Tochter* is horrified by her fate or rather pleased with the attention she is provoking is impossible to tell, and this adds to the ambivalences and blurring of too neat and too easily drawn separation lines and confinements present in the *Danse*.[9]

It is exactly this ambivalence that opens up the spaces of signification that interest me: the *Danse Macabre* is a forceful sign of moral control, and one that cannot be nailed down to just one meaning. The metaphor of dancing which pairs a suitor and his/her beloved creates an erotic suspense that necessarily compromises the *Danse*'s moral intents. In the Bern *Danse* some of the female dancers establish a relation with the viewer by glancing at him, thereby inviting him to become involved in the scenes he

---

[6] Matthias Rogg, *Landsknechte und Reisläufer: Bilder vom Soldaten. Ein Stand in der Kunst des 16. Jahrhunderts* (Paderborn: Ferdinand Schöningh, 2002), 36-39.

[7] Christiane Andersson elaborated this argument in a conference at the Annual Meeting of the Renaissance Society of America in Venice 2010.

[8] Quoted from Tripps (2005), 79. In my opinion, the words 'mit Im' are deliberately ambiguous and may suggest that Death and the young lad will both 'have' the girl.

[9] Tripps (2005), 78, on the contrary does not see any lascivious ambiguity in the attitude of the Daughter.

is looking at; they thus not only address his fear of death but also his sexual desire.[10]

In this double signification of moral reprehension and active arousal of lust 'femininity' becomes invested with multiple meanings: women are seduced by male corpses and in turn seduce (male) viewers. Images of women, and particularly images of woman's gazes, establish the viewer as part of the intricate functioning of art. He becomes involved in the playful blurring of the realms of 'reality', death and art that creates the polyvalence of meaning intrinsic in any 'reading' of art. Femininity is a semiotic link between the world of the viewer and the 'other' worlds – of death and of art. It is the ambiguity intrinsic in the representations of erotic encounters between femininity, the spectator and death of which the *Danse Macabre* is a prototypical formulation that will be at the centre of my following analysis.

Death and the Maiden

The extent to which the motif of the triangulation of female figure, cadaver and viewer appealed to a late medieval/early modern public becomes obvious when one considers further evidence of such pairing.[11] Besides the *Danse Macabre* the iconography of the 'Death and the Maiden' motif functions in a similar code. Stefanie Knöll has convincingly refuted the common claim that the motif of 'Death and the Maiden' has been singled out from the *Danse Macabre*.[12] She has instead shown that

---

[10] Gert Kaiser, *Der Tod und die schönen Frauen, Ein elementares Motiv der europäischen Kultur* (Frankfurt/New York: Campus, 1995), 121, 123, has drawn attention to the fact that in the *Danse Macabre* Death comes to fetch men who are characterised through their professional attributes whereas the female representatives are usually characterised by their physical (sexualised) presence.

[11] Jean Wirth, *La fanciulla e la morte. Ricerche sui temi macabri nell'arte germanica del Rinacimento* (trans., Roma: Istituto della enciclopedia italiana, 1985), 37-38, has already observed that the development of the *Danse Macabre* tends to isolate the couples who in the first place all belong to a long procession of dancers. However, architectural framing or the separation of the confrontation of Death and his victim on single sheets in book illustrations use this formal way to create a more dramatic and individual story between the individual person and his or her death. The representation of young girl and cadaver is one of the very effective pairings that develop a life of their own.

[12] Stefanie Knöll, 'Zur Entstehung des Motivs *Der Tod und das Mädchen*', in Andrea von Hülsen-Esch and Hiltrud Westermann-Angerhausen with Stefanie Knöll (eds), *Zum Sterben schön. Alter, Totentanz und Sterbekunst von 1500 bis heute*, exhibition catalogue, 2 vols (Regensburg: Schnell & Steiner, 2006), vol. 1,

around the year 1500 the motif of a young girl together with a bony personification of Death has a different genealogy, *viz.* it may stand for either a *vanitas* or a *voluptas* allegory, sometimes coupled with an admonition against *superbia* or pride.[13] However, the two traditions seem to conflate and inspire one another. Thus the young girls being taken by Death are brilliantly gruesome visualisations of the *memento mori* idea – as naked shining and youthful flesh is contrasted with the abject cadaver. The iconography serves the moralising exhortations not to succumb to sin, and the *Danse Macabre* adds a social dimension in representation and in reception. The *Danse* in turn takes up the erotic connotation of the allegories of the vices. Both sets of images are integrated and share common strategies of representation. Here, too, Knöll has already made the point that they both play with the viewer's involvement by creating and guiding the glances to be exchanged between him and them. The Bern *Danse* takes up and releases the motif of the young girl and the cadaver, while owing its representation of 'intercourse' between girl and viewer to the earlier scenes of 'Death and the Maiden' and linking the young spouse with the seductive naked bodies of the personifications of *voluptas* and *vanitas*.

The formulation of the motif by Hans Baldung Grien (*c.*1484/85-1545) in a drawing of 1515 (Pl. 7), actually shows Death as a 'demonstrator' for the beautiful nakedness of the young woman, who is completely unaware of anybody looking at her as she is entirely absorbed in looking at herself in a mirror.[14] The corpse 'looks' (as far as eye-sockets in a skull are capable of looking) out of the drawing at the viewer, thus involving him in the scene. Standing behind the girl, he has one hand on her hip whereas the other touches her breast and somehow proffers it to the viewer. Her whole body is turned almost frontally towards the viewer, leaving him free in his enjoyment of looking at her. Although it is to her that the sins of *superbia* and *vanitas* are attributed – thus mitigating the spectator's own lustful involvement in watching her – he cannot escape the dreadful gaze of Death who reminds him of the perils of seduction and desire, of his (respective) sins, and with that of his own end.

65-72, esp. 66-68. Authors like Kaiser (1995) and Eichberger (2002) have referred to the motif as a derivative of the *Danse Macabre*.

[13] Knöll (2006), 67-69.

[14] Kiening (2003), 118, gives further examples of young women watching themselves in the mirror as representations of superbia and caducity. Yet he also describes the glance into the mirror as a refined play with perceptions and cognition – inside and outside the image.

However, the triangle of gazes privileges the (male) viewer. While she is looking at herself as a mirrored – naturalistic – reflection and the cadaver is looking out of the drawing at the 'real' world, the viewer is the only one who is authorised to interpret what he is seeing. His 'reading' of the image may focus on its moral message, or he may let himself be seduced and aroused. In any case he is the only one able to sublimate what he is seeing into the cognition of art. His gaze empowers him to enter the playground of shiftings between the 'real', the 'imaginary', the 'moral' or the 'artistic' keys of interpretation. The painting offers the metaphor of death in a 'realistic' portrayal of naked female beauty – and in an equally 'realistic' portrayal of horrifying decay. The image visualises the 'realistically' impossible in the mode of 'realism', thus consciously making the painting's artistic qualities its central theme. The mirror that the girl is studying herself in also reflects a self-referential play of signifiers: in her hand it is a moralising symbol of *vanitas*, whereas in the artistic discourse it epitomises the act of looking, analogising mirror and image.

Art(ist) and Death

The Monogrammist M (active in the first half of the sixteenth century) has made visual self-reflexivity a central theme of his version of the 'Death and Maiden' motif, giving yet more complex meaning to the *Danse Macabre*. A young naked woman, almost frontally exposed to the viewer, looks over her shoulder at her reflection in a mirror, which is placed in such a way as to allow the viewer also to see the young girl's back (Fig. 34).[15] Her body is presented in a serpentine movement, almost as if she were dancing. A wing at her feet leads the viewer's gaze into the drawing where a wheel takes up the iconography of fortune and destiny. Right behind the wheel in the dark background, peeping out from behind the wall in front of which the mirror is placed, is a still slightly fleshy cadaver holding an hourglass and looking at the girl, who is absorbed in her reflection. The allegorical dimension of the work is made explicit in the attributes present. As in the Baldung Grien drawing, the self-love of the young woman stands for the vices of *vanitas* and *superbia*, giving the composition a moral message as a *memento mori*.

---

[15] The identity of the Monogrammist M is far from certain, mostly because he elaborates the 'Death and Maiden' motif iconographically on the basis of northern art, but stylistically in an Italian manner. The engraving is usually dated to the beginning of the sixteenth century. For an exhaustive discussion of these problems, see Von Hülsen-Esch *et al.* (eds) (2006), vol. 2, cat. no. 121, 217-19.

Fig. 34. Monogrammist M, *Death and the Maiden*, engraving, first half of the sixteenth century. © Graphiksammlung 'Mensch und Tod', Heinrich-Heine-University Düsseldorf.

Yet what strikes the viewer foremost is the very muscular body of the young woman. Her scarf and the way she turns her head are quite obviously based on a Michelangelesque model.[16] With this reference to style in general and specifically to one of the most cited works of art in particular, *viz.* the figure of Aurora in the Medici Chapel, the engraving becomes a reflection about art as well.[17] The Michelangelesque ideal

---

[16] Von Hülsen-Esch *et al.* (eds) (2006), vol. 2, cat. no. 121, 218.
[17] See Raphael Rosenberg, *Beschreibungen und Nachzeichnungen der Skulpturen*

evokes a *paragone* situation that is present in the mirror, too, where her body is reflected from behind, thus making it possible to see it from all sides at once.[18] It is the frame of the mirror that the artist uses to introduce a further moment of artistic theory: the right hand of the young woman should be reflected in the mirror, but it is not. The frame becomes a threshold between different image spaces, between different artistic realities. The woman's hand blurs the perfect illusion and makes the artistic creation visible. The viewer of this engraving is not only a voyeur or a penitent; he is first and foremost a connoisseur. Even the presence of Death becomes a warning on two levels: as a *memento mori* it refers to the transience of human life, but together with the inscription even the usual projection of survival in art is contested. The phrase 'Mortalia facta peribunt' (*What humans make will perish*) actually seems to refer to the art work itself rather than to human lives.

The rendering of the female nude while citing Michelangelo also evokes studies in anatomy. Together with the cadaver, the two bodies refer to the artistic and scientific mode of creating representations of the human body: the artist does not only copy nature for his images but his creative process is analogous to the working of nature. This analogy is part of the sixteenth-century discourse of the artist's geniality and its topical dimension is a further context for the reading of the engraving.[19] In a self-reflexive loop the artist makes a statement about creation and transience – in life and in art – and he empowers himself as author. The tablet with his monogram M is placed at the right hand bottom of the engraving with an inclination that indicates three-dimensionality and helps to define space. Yet it is also close to the inscription, thus participating in the dimension of the written word, evoking the plane of the sheet of paper. The Monogrammist M partakes in a discourse of authorship that is intimately linked to questions of art and death. The author is supposed to render immortal what he represents, but in the process of transferring life into art he also kills off what he represents.[20]

Michelangelos. Eine Geschichte der Kunstbetrachtung (Munich/Berlin: Deutscher Kunstverlag, 2000), 14-15.

[18] Lars Olaf Larsson, *Von allen Seiten gleich schön. Studien zum Begriff der Vielansichtigkeit in der europäischen Plastik von der Renaissance bis zum Klassizismus,* Acta Universitatis Stockholmiensis, 26 (Stockholm: Almqvist & Wiksell International, 1974).

[19] Maike Christadler, 'Kreativität und Genie: Legenden der Kunstgeschichte', in Anja Zimmermann (ed.), *Kunstgeschichte und Gender. Eine Einführung* (Berlin: Reimer, 2006), 253-72, at 257.

[20] Georges Didi-Huberman, *La Peinture incarnée, suivi de 'le chef-d'oeuvre*

Fig. 35. George Grosz, *The Artist in his Studio*, photograph, *c.*1918. © Grosz-Archiv, Akademie der Künste, Berlin.

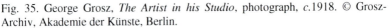

The artistic discourse at the beginning of modernity in the first years of the twentieth century committed itself to revealing the intrinsic relation between death and artistic production, *i.e.* the idea of the author as murderer.[21] The moment of transience between the worlds of life, death and art and the active role of the artist is made explicit in a photo by George Grosz (1893-1959) of a young woman looking at herself in a mirror (Fig. 35). The composition of the image is quite similar to the

inconnu' par Honoré de Balzac (Paris: Les Éditions de Minuit, 1985); Elisabeth Bronfen, *Nur über ihre Leiche. Tod, Weiblichkeit und Ästhetik* (Munich: Antje Kunstmann Verlag, 1994), here esp. chapter 4, 'Das "poetischste" aller Themen: Edgar Allan Poe, die Schönheit und der Tod', 89-113.
[21] See also Kathrin Hoffmann-Curtius, *Im Blickfeld: John, der Frauenmörder von George Grosz*, exhibition catalogue (Stuttgart: Gerd Hatje Verlag, 1990).

engraving of the Monogrammist M: a young woman (dressed in a bathing suit) is placed in a slightly mannerist movement in front of a mirror, looking at herself in a second mirror that she is holding in her hand. From behind the large mirror the artist is peeping out himself, a knife in his hand, directed towards the young woman. Grosz conflates in his position that of Death, of the Author and of the voyeur. In the artful positioning of the knife and the hand-mirror – both intersecting the frame of the large mirror – Grosz reveals the process of how life is made art. The mirror becomes the projection plane of art, author-ised by the photographic self-portrait of Grosz stuck on the mirror. The knife becomes the instrument of the artist to cut out representation from 'reality', to kill the (female) body by transposing it into art. The doll sitting at the bottom of the easel is a metaphor for the result of this transferral. The explicit presentation of the whole scene to the viewer reveals its constructedness – and his complicity. The revelation of the presuppositions of the creative process functions through author and model performing their respective roles, staging them as a theatrical event the spectator is invited to perceive as such.

In the sixteenth-century engraving the author presents death on two levels, *viz.* as a moral and an artistic problem, subject to annihilation. In contrast the modern photograph makes the author perform a kind of *Danse Macabre* where he himself personifies the figure of Death, thus revealing representation as a fatal engagement and the female body as its signifier.

The spectator and Death

In the engraving of the Monogrammist M the closeness of femininity and death in the process of image production is shown in the self-reflexive mode of looking into a mirror. However, the cadaver with a young girl is a motif generally linked to the reflection of art, sometimes in more mediated ways. About the same time Hans Sebald Beham (1500-50) and Barthel Beham (*c.*1502-40) treated the juxtaposition of a female body with a corpse in a variety of prints that have long been interpreted in a mostly moralising key.[22] Yet besides the moral connotation – which is always an opportune explanation for the existence of these pieces – the body of the nude woman is used as a projection screen for the (male) viewer's desire,

---

[22] Bob Scribner, 'Ways of Seeing in the Age of Dürer', in Dagmar Eichberger and Charles Zika (eds), *Dürer and his Culture* (Cambridge: Cambridge University Press, 1998), 93-117, at 109, interprets erotically arousing images as a kind of trap: the spectator is caught with his sexually interested reaction which he immediately has to transform into a recognition of his sinfulness.

thus on the one hand insisting on the moralising contents but on the other hand transforming the sinful voyeur into a connoisseur of art.[23]

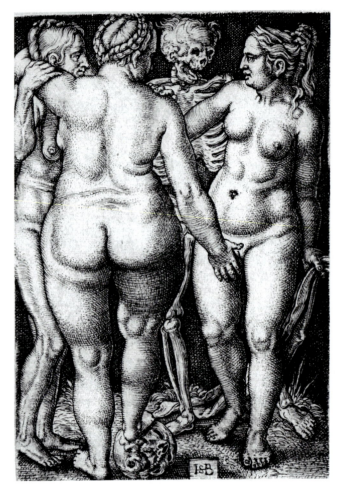

Fig. 36. Hans Sebald Beham, *Death with Three Women*, engraving, *c*.1540. © Graphiksammlung 'Mensch und Tod', Heinrich-Heine-University Düsseldorf.

---

[23] Janey L. Levy, 'The Erotic Engravings of Sebald and Barthel Beham: a German Interpretation of a Renaissance Subject', in Stephen H. Goddard (ed.), *The World in Miniature. Engravings by the German Little Masters, 1500-1550*, exhibition catalogue (Lawrence/Kansas: Spencer Museum of Art, 1988), 40-53, *passim*.

One way of appealing to the spectator's conoisseurship is to refer to other images and to develop a playful contest with one's predecessors. Albrecht Dürer (1471-1528), above all, served as a model for many of the artists in the first half of the sixteenth century, particularly in Nuremberg. An example is Sebald Beham's transformation of Dürer's famous four witches into three voluptuous Graces joined by a skeleton (Fig. 36).[24] In the Dürer engraving a hell fire is burning at the left side, showing the direct connection between the women's supernatural forces and the devil. In Sebald's interpretation Death has directly joined the women and his main interest is in the most beautiful of them, the one also singled out for the viewer to whom she is turned frontally. Whereas Dürer had covered her pubis with a veil, Sebald 'covers' her pubis with the right hand of her plump companion, thereby almost suggesting sexual contact. It is she more than the other women who is sexualised and who is most explicitly linked to Death. Her companion, who presents her impressive posterior to the viewer, has placed her right foot on a skull. This skull alludes to its tiny counterpart in Dürer's print where it had actually established contact with the viewer, reminding him of the dangers of femininity. Sebald copies the skull into his own image but presents it as totally vanquished. The voyeur-connoisseur may recognise his own defeat when confronted with voluptuous femininity. Bound together with their ghastly opposite – Death – female corporeality and sexuality become figurations of nature itself. The reference to Dürer naturalises the connotation of women with witchcraft, and it establishes the female nude as a field of *paragone* where allusion, transformation and artistic execution turn the viewer into a connoisseur.

For Baldung Grien's eroticised witches Bodo Brinkmann has reconstructed a spectator's context that locates the images in an early kind of collection that allowed male viewers to wallow in their voyeuristic desire while transforming this desire into a refined appreciation of artistic quality.[25] Baldung Grien's images are ever so far removed from a *Danse Macabre* setting: they are consciously not popular but elitist, and they make the discourse of morality and sinful desire a problem of art as they turn the female nude into a metaphor for painting in general.[26]

---

[24] Anne Röver-Kann, *Albrecht Dürer. Das Frauenbad von 1496,* exhibition catalogue (Bremen: H.M. Hauschild, 2001), 83.

[25] See Bodo Brinkmann, *Hexenlust und Sündenfall. Die seltsamen Phantasien des Hans Baldung Grien / Witches' Lust and the Fall of Man. The Strange Phantasies of Hans Baldung Grien*, exhibition catalogue (Frankfurt/Petersberg: Michael Imhof Verlag, 2007), 36-49.

[26] For this discussion, see Lynda Nead, *The Female Nude: Art, Obscenity, and Sexuality* (London: Routledge, 1992), and Silvia Eiblmayr, *Die Frau als Bild. Der*

Fig. 37. Hans Sebald Beham, *Death and the Sleeping Woman*, engraving, 1548. ©
Graphiksammlung 'Mensch und Tod', Heinrich-Heine-University Düsseldorf.

However, the engravings of the Beham brothers do not offer gorgeous
layers of brilliant colouring and their minuscule dimensions are certainly
not conceived for the same discussions in front of the work of art. They
rather seem to demand a very close scrutiny, thus provoking a *tête-à-tête*
of subject and viewer.[27] In the case of Beham's engraving *Death with
Sleeping Woman* of 1548 (Fig. 37) the approaching viewer/voyeur is
confronted with an exposure of female genitals as well as a second
spectator inside the image: a winged skeleton lurking behind the sleeping
beauty. Kiening has suggested that the viewer may identify with his inner
visual counterpart, transferring his own phantasies of power onto him.[28]
Yet to my mind the connoisseur seems to be rather absent from the scene:
the image functions as an Albertian window through which the observer

---

weibliche Körper in der Kunst (Berlin: Reimer, 1994).

[27] See Stephen H. Goddard, 'The Origin, Use, and Heritage of the Small Engraving
in Renaissance Germany', in Goddard (1988), 13-29, at 17, and Levy (1988) 47.
Both correctly insist that the audience of the Behams must have been rather
educated and literate, recognising and appreciating even visual 'quotations' from
earlier Italian prints.

[28] Kiening (2003), 116.

watches without being seen. To him Beham offers his sleeping beauty and exposes her sex. The skeleton behind the bed, trying to creep in and holding the hourglass over the beauty's head, is obviously a reminder of the viewer's moral integrity. However, in its bony presence it also stands for the artist's capability to render the 'natural' essence: the structure of the human body.

Furthermore, it recalls the famous composition of the satyr watching the sleeping nymph from the romance *Hypnerotomachia Polifili* (*Poliphilo's Strife of Love in a Dream*, published by Aldus Manutius in Venice in 1499), thus quoting and transforming an artistic invention again.[29] This woodcut has come to embody an entire artistic theory about the gaze, reflecting on the relationship between the spectator and the figure of the lecherous satyr.[30] In Beham's engraving this satyr inside the image has been moralised into a skeleton, but the observer is empowered to look on both, nude and death, with the distanced look of art. It is quite striking that the skeleton in Beham's engraving does not touch the girl he is looking at. This careful omission seems to be aimed at active concentration on the sense of vision, encouraging the viewer to use his eyes to enjoy – girl and art. Yet the images are not always so abstinent: sometimes the bony suitor has the privilege of not only touching the beautiful maiden, but even kissing her.

In his painted version of *Death and Maiden* of 1520 (Kunstmuseum Basel) Baldung Grien shows the woman in an entirely frontal position, thereby presenting her perfect white body to the viewer without obstacles.[31] She is weeping at her gruesome destiny as Death approaches her from behind, having perhaps emerged from the grave below. He holds her tight and, turning her head towards him, places the kiss of death on her face. Her weeping heightens the violence of the scene and appeals to the viewer's compassion, while at the same time satisfying his voyeuristic inclinations.

The interdependence of desire, tactility, the male gaze and death is further developed in Niklaus Manuel's drawing *Death as Mercenary with a Maiden* of 1517 (Fig. 38). Here, the kiss that the decaying corpse of a lansquenet places on the mouth of a pretty young girl is not just the evocation of a tactile dimension of desire; in its reciprocity and the shamelessness of the girl guiding the cadaver's hand to her pubis, the image is also overtly sexualised. As the male lover is here recognisably

---

[29] See Goddard (1988), cat. 47.
[30] See Maria Ruvoldt, *The Renaissance Imagery of Inspiration, Metaphors of Sex, Sleep, and Dreams* (Cambridge: Cambridge University Press, 2004), 110-15.
[31] Illustrated in Brinkmann (2007), 231.

dressed as a Swiss mercenary, it is easy to imagine the girl to be a prostitute, which would socially legitimise the representation of a sexual act. The lasciviousness of soldiers was notorious and women getting involved with them were easily associated with prostitution.[32]

Fig. 38. Niklaus Manuel, *Death as a Mercenary with a Maiden*, drawing on panel, 1517. © Kunstmuseum Basel, Inv. Nr. 419. Photo: Martin P. Bühler.

---

[32] Barton C. Hacker, 'Women and Military Institutions in Early Modern Europe: a Reconnaissance', *Signs*, 6 (1981), 643-71, at 650-52.

Yet what on the one hand is an almost 'realistic' image of a young prostitute represents on the other hand the mercenary's unsuccessful attempt to corrupt the goddess Fortune. The allegorical key of the interpretation lies in the tiny statue of Fortune in the background that evokes such associations for the viewer, who would have been trained in the contemporary iconography of the goddess Fortune as a whore herself. For example, in one of Urs Graf's drawings Fortune is shown on her sphere or wheel, her skirt blown in the air to allow a glance at her sex.[33] She stands for the soldier's destiny which is as fleeting as a woman – and which the soldiers would like to be as corruptible.[34] Manuel's picture thus also visualises the allegorical embrace of Fortune and Death.

Fig. 39. Niklaus Manuel, *Bathseba at her Toilette*, drawing on panel (reverse of Fig. 38), 1517. © Kunstmuseum Basel, Inv. Nr. 419. Photo: Martin P. Bühler.

---

[33] For an illustration see Christian Müller (ed.), *Urs Graf. Die Zeichnungen im Kupferstichkabinett Basel* (Basel: Schwabe Verlag, 2002), 268.
[34] Christiane Andersson, *Urs Graf. Dirnen, Krieger, Narren. Ausgewählte Zeichnungen* (Basel: GS-Verlag, 1978), 44-49.

However, Manuel's panel in Fig. 38 has a drawing on the reverse as well, which shows the story of David who falls in love with Bathsheba, struck by her beauty as he watches her as a voyeur (Fig. 39). This biblical narrative has proved prototypical for the danger of the gaze.[35] In Manuel's version the beautiful female nude, taking a bath in a fountain, is exposed to the viewer who takes the king's place – as the figure of David gets lost in the perspectival vastness of the pictorial space. Thus it is the spectator whose desire is aroused; he is the addressee of the erotic programme of the fountain where cheeky little putti are spilling water from all their (sexual) openings. The viewer is encouraged to imagine the yielding to his desires – unless he turns the panel around to find himself confronted instead with the Kiss of Death that is the gruesome fulfilment of his desire. Looking at the panel and following its invitation to relate the messages on both sides, the viewer himself becomes a protagonist in a *Danse Macabre*.

Perilous femininity

Whereas Manuel makes the viewer turn his panel around to incite him to ponder about the relationship between death and desire, Urs Graf visualises the whole in his woodcut *Lansquenet, Swiss Mercenary and Prostitute with Death* of 1524.[36] The latter is sitting in the tree right above the two soldiers, holding an hourglass as further reminder of the hour to come. The two soldiers are taking no notice of one another's or even Death's presence; they are just looking into space without communicating. Sitting on the ground beside the tree is a woman, richly adorned and wearing a hat decorated with feathers, while holding a little lap dog in her arms. She turns around to look over her shoulder out of the image into the viewer's space. She is placed in the same picture plane as the bony representation of Death, separated from the soldiers and yet related to them. The aloofness of everybody involved gives the composition the dignity and weight of a timeless truth: just as in the *Danse Macabre*, Death comes for everyone.

Yet here the composition suggests that the haughty soldiers do not fear anything – other than death and women. Just like the skeleton sitting in the tree, the woman – allegory of lust and lechery – does herself stand for death, perhaps even in the very concrete form of syphilis. Like Manuel, Graf succeeds in blending an allegorical dimension with an almost anecdotal one; he leaves an interpretative space between a 'realistic' representation

---

[35] Kiening (2003), 103-05, discusses the two sides of the panel as a visual conception of the relation between desire and the glance.
[36] See Müller (2002), 291.

and its 'allegorical' signification, thereby creating productive ambiguities.

Fig. 40. Albrecht Dürer, *Blazon of Death*, engraving, 1503, © Kunstmuseum Basel, Inv. Aus K.10.147. Photo: Martin P. Bühler.

Graf's woodcut recalls an earlier engraving by Dürer, *The Promenade* of 1498.[37] A young couple walking and conversing are observed by a grinning cadaver behind a tree, holding the traditional hourglass. In his figure the spectator is reminded of the lascivious dangers that the young couple is engaging in. As in Graf's woodcut, the cadaver as a representation of death seems to be doubled by the presence of the woman, herself representing death; an idea that Dürer's takes up again in his engraving *The Blazon of Death* of 1503 (Fig. 40). Femininity, uncontrolled libido and death are once more tied together: a young, carefully dressed woman is teased and caressed from behind by a furry wild man. The wild man seems tender and the young girl rather pleased by his advances. In front of both of them, turned to the beholder, is a large blazon with an enormous skull on it. Girl, blazon and wild man are linked by a leash fixed to the crest of the blazon, thus making the young woman, who is holding it in her hand, 'pull the strings'. Like the Fates she controls the 'thread of life': her light touch of the cord foreshadows the male spectator's impending loss of self-control – as he admires her beautifully inviting body that lures him, the skull is a reminder of the deadly dangers of lust.

As a model for his engraving Dürer playfully adapted an earlier invention of his own that had been designed, though, to give a slightly different interpretation.[38] The thirteenth chapter of Sebastian Brant's *Ship of Fools*, 'Von buolschafft' (*On courtship*), presents a beautifully adorned winged woman – Venus – together with a skeleton (Fig. 41). She, too, is holding reins in her hand, binding men who are chained to their desire. Brant's version highlights their foolishness in succumbing to their bestial urges, as indicated by the ape and donkey in the image.[39] For the author of the *Ship of Fools* 'buolschafft' is linked directly to death, as shown in the unity of Dame Venus and the skeleton. In Brant the moral message is

---

[37] Staatliche Kunsthalle Karlsruhe, illustrated at http://commons.wikimedia.org/wiki/File:D%C3%BCrer-Spaziergang.jpg (accessed 27 September 2010).

[38] For a discussion of Dürer as author of the woodcut illustrations in Brant's *Ship of Fools*, see Konrad Hoffmann, 'Wort und Bild im Narrenschiff', in Ludger Grenzmann and Karl Stackmann (eds), *Literatur und Laienbildung im Spätmittelalter und in der Reformationszeit* (Stuttgart: Metzler, 1984), 392-422. Hoffmann, 396-97, was also the first to notice that Dürer took up some of his inventions for Brant in his later works, *e.g.* the figure of Venus in 'Von buolschafft' inspired *The Blazon of Death*.

[39] Cf. Michael Overdick, 'Zur Darstellung von Tod und Verdammnis in den Illustrationen zu Sebastian Brants *Narrenschiff*', in Stefanie Knöll (ed.), *Narren – Masken – Karneval. Meisterwerke von Dürer bis Kubin aus der Düsseldorfer Graphiksammlung 'Mensch und Tod'* (Regensburg: Schnell & Steiner 2009), 33-42, at 39.

clearly dominant although the radiant beauty of the female figure leaves space for the viewer's lascivious imagination.[40] However, Dürer's *The Blazon of Death* explores exactly the seductive impact of the erotic confrontation between the woman and the wild man, thus intimately linking the moral message with a visualisation of desire. The 1503 engraving is a formulation of the ambiguities that proliferate in the context of liminality between life and death, between desire and morals. It visually suggests the intimate relation of normative morals and their immediate subversion in the image.

Fig. 41. 'Von buolschafft' *(On courtship)*, woodcut from Sebastian Brant, *Ship of Fools* (Basel, 1499). Universitätsbibliothek Basel, DA III 4a:2.

---

[40] In Jacob Locher's Latin version of Brant's *Ship of Fools* a further woodcut has been added to the discussion between Voluptas and Virtus that shows Hercules dreaming the famous Y-crossroads, one leading to Dame Venus, a beautiful young woman, the other towards virtue, an old hag. In this image, too, just as in 'Von buolschafft', the young woman is accompanied by a cadaver that leaves no doubts about the dangers of sexual desires and women incarnating them. See Kiening (2003), 107.

The illustration to 'Von buolschafft' has yet another context that refers back to the *Danse Macabre*. In an engraving of 1475 by Israhel van Meckenem (*c*.1440-1503) a group of men dance ecstatically around a woman who herself is moving only slightly with her eyes chastely cast to the floor.[41] Here no leash and no reins are necessary to tie the men to the female figure: the woman in the centre of the circle seems to possess gravitational forces. The engraving shows a Morris Dance, which we have come across already in the Bern *Danse Macabre* where it is explicitly cited in the verses underneath the representation of the *Burger*. In the Morris Dance the male dancers enact a highly ritualised and very eroticised form of courtship that is performed by acrobatic leaps and wrenches and is honoured with a ring given to the most successful of the dancers. The Morris Dance has an allegorical interpretation as well, however: the female figure becomes identified with *Frau Welt* (Lady World) – allegory of *vanitas*, decay, and fugacity – around which the seven deadly sins perform their dance of seduction.[42] The circle dance even evokes a dance with the devil.[43] The analogy between Brant's Venus and the women personifying *Frau Welt* as the centre of a circle dance is quite striking. In both cases the female figure attracts her male suitors who lose their wits due to their sexual arousal. Just as in Meckenem's Morris Dance, a fool in Brant's woodcut characterises the exposed behaviour as ridiculous and morally reprehensible. Together with the skeleton that Dürer integrates in his 'Von buolschafft', the female figure of Venus connects the scene to the *Danse Macabre*: Death and Woman make you lose your life and your wits, respectively, which for Brant is equally bad.[44]

The iconography of *Frau Welt* continues to be used as a moral admonition and reminder of the futility of things, and it remains charged with sexual connotations. The 1596 engraving *Omnis Caro Foenum et Gloria Eius Sicut Flos Agri* by Matthäus Greuter (*c*.1564-1638) shows a lavishly adorned and richly clad woman underneath the title line taken

---

[41] Munich, Staatliche Graphische Sammlungen. For an illustration see www.artknowledgenews.com/Israhel_van_Meckenem.html (accessed 27 September 2010).

[42] Compare Dominicus Custos's engraving *Frau Welt* of *c*.1600 in Werner Mezger, *Narrenidee und Fastnachtsbrauch. Studien zum Fortleben des Mittelalters in der europäischen Festkultur* (Konstanz: Universitätsverlag, 1991), 123.

[43] Irmgard Jungmann, *Tanz, Tod und Teufel. Tanzkultur in der gesellschaftlichen Auseinandersetzung im 15. und 16. Jahrhundert* (Kassel: Bärenreiter, 2002), 71.

[44] See Barbara Könneker, *Wesen und Wandlung der Narrenidee im Zeitalter des Humanismus. Brant – Murner – Erasmus* (Wiesbaden: Franz Steiner Verlag, 1966), 2-3.

from Isaia 40:6-8 (Fig. 42a). The female figure is framed by an ornamented porch whose figural programme gives further interpretations of the scene.[45] To her left and right Adam and Eve expose their (near-) nakedness with easily comprehensible reference to their sexual experience and the Fall. Four putti are placed in the four corners of the frame, all with such *vanitas* attributes as an hourglass or soap bubbles that refer to transience and death. In the arch of the architectural frame vine leaves and grapes allude to Dionysian (sexual) excess but also to the Christian doctrine of salvation. The image of the woman is thus surrounded by suggestive symbolism, while the spectator is erotically titillated and morally admonished at the same time. Just when curiosity wins from the moral warning, the observer will notice that the print incites him to become active: the skirt of the woman may be lifted to allow a glimpse underneath (Fig. 42b).

Fig. 42a-b. Matthäus Greuter, *Omnis Caro Foenum et Gloria Sicut Flos Agri*, with and without lifted skirt, engraving, 1596. © Staatsbibliothek zu Berlin – Preußischer Kulturbesitz - Handschriftenabteilung: YA 2840 kl.

---

[45] Jörn Münkner, 'Tote Li/ebende – li/ebende Tote. Blick unter Röcke und in Schädel', *L'art macabre (Jahrbuch der Europäischen Totentanzvereinigung)*, 8 (2007), 161-76, has given an exhaustive analysis of the print on which my observations are based.

Yet what the image reveals below the skirt is certainly not what the curious spectator had hoped to see: instead of intimate female secrets he sees the lady stripped of all her flesh onto the bare bones. This skeletal vision is matched by the coffin with a skull that have equally found their place under the skirt, thereby forming a kind of underskirt *cum* burial-chamber. The image of the woman here refers to the representations of *Frau Welt* who is beautiful when viewed from the front but rotten behind and, as we have seen, she is at the centre of a circle of dancers. Thus her engraved image functions like the cadaver that comes to invite the living to the *Danse Macabre*: by looking under the skirt the spectator is confronted with Death waiting to take him. All these imaginary moves of the spectator at least return to the print and uncover its medial functioning. The print's involvement of the observer, who is even challenged to touch and not just to look, playfully demonstrates its own qualities.

As in the prints by Urs Graf or Dürer, death and femininity are intimately linked, the latter becoming almost synonymous for the first. Together with death, femininity is qualified as dangerous and morally condemnable. Yet the moral conviction never goes without the pleasure of desire – and it never goes without the appreciation of artistic qualities.

The *Danse Macabre* of anatomy

The glimpse underneath the skirt of *Frau Welt* opens up a further and completely different pictorial theme. The lower part of her body is shown as mere bones, but this skeletal lower half is very slightly brought into a contrapposto position, thereby lending it – as in a *Danse Macabre* – a life of its own. There is another pictorial tradition that makes cadavers move: the representation of anatomy.

The famous illustrations in *De Humani Corporis Fabrica* of 1543 by Andreas Vesalius (1514-64) have been called a *Danse Macabre* before.[46] The partially dissected corpses are in movement with the landscape setting, which is only visible in its entirety once the single sheets are put one beside the other, and thus reminiscent of the *Danse*. Here Death and the person he was going to take for the last dance have been conflated, and only the corpse 'dance' has remained – its movement being induced and controlled by the anatomist (and the artist!). These dancing cadavers are without a specific gender. In anatomical practice it was rare to dissect

---

[46] Reinhard Hildebrand, 'Anatomische Darstellungen zwischen Kunst und Wissenschaft', in Von Hülsen-Esch *et al.* (2006), vol. 1, 181-96.

female bodies, so that knowledge about the structure of the human body in general was based on male bodies.[47]

Yet there was a keen interest in the reproductive female body, so representations of the opened female womb are not as rare. Even on the title page of *De Humani Corporis Fabrica*, Vesalius chose to place a female corpse (Fig. 43).[48] The anatomist himself is shown standing beside the dissecting table amidst an enormous crowd attending this public event. On the table, which is placed in rather daring foreshortening in the centre of the page, is a female corpse and the onlookers are permitted to glance into her already opened abdomen. Vesalius is making a gesture of demonstration and most of the gathered crowd are eagerly looking into the partially dissected body. The first impression is one of a cramped place with an exciting and rather chaotic event. Only two lines strike the observer's eye immediately: the first is the long transversal line guiding the eye into the perspectival opening of the third dimension of the space represented that is formed by the corpse of the woman. This line is taken up by a second one with a slightly changed angle at the head of the woman by a rod that leads the viewer's attention to the skeleton exposed directly above the female corpse.

In the context of an anatomical treatise this skeleton above the corpse is easily understood as the essence of the anatomist's art of dissection. However, in the context of images and cultural traditions, and together with the female body below, it also refers to the cycle of reproduction that initiates with birth from the woman's womb and ends with death and decay – here all present in the same image to illustrate the *memento mori* message of 'nascentes morimur' (*From the moment we are born, we begin to die*).[49] As a 'personification' of Death, however, it is as easily seen as the skeleton of the *Danse Macabre* who has come for the last dance with the woman on the dissecting table. Yet the anatomist changes the traditional constellation. His intervention has somehow immobilised both figures: neither the skeleton nor the woman are representations of vitality anymore. The act of giving and taking life has been transferred onto the scientist who by disclosing the interior of the body is able to copy the functioning of life itself. Moreover, it is the artist who is able to visualise this claim of the anatomist. The co-production of anatomist and artist invests both of

---

[47] Jonathan Sawday, *The Body Emblazoned. Dissection and the Human Body in Renaissance Culture* (London: Routledge, 1995), 221.

[48] Sawday (1995), 68-73, gives a beautiful analysis of the title page on which my own observations are partially based.

[49] Sawday (1995), 71.

them with the authority of the discourse of generation: one by opening the body, the other by (re)creating its surface.

Fig. 43. Title page of Andreas Vesalius' *De humani corporis fabrica* published in Basel, 1543, engraving. © Universitätsbibliothek Basel, Lb I 1.

Fig. 44. Flowering foetus, engraving from Adrianus Spigelius' *De humani corporis fabrica libri decem* published in Frankfurt, 1632. © Universitätsbibliothek Basel, Lb III 6:1.

As much as in Greuter's moralising broadsheet where the viewer is confronted with the lower part of a skeleton beneath the skirt of *Frau Welt*, the *Danse Macabre* remains visually present in anatomical illustrations well into the seventeenth century. Using a rich iconography, anatomical treatises participate in the creation of the principle of generation and particularly the part played by women in this notion: their contribution is organic and vegetative matter that is brought to growth and formed by male sperm. Congruent to these ideas, the anatomy of a pregnant woman is visually conceived in a flower-metaphor, as Jonathan Sawday has observed (Fig. 44):

> In Spigelius's work on the formation of the foetus (*De formato foeto* of 1627), for example, we can see the metaphor of vegetative growth in pictorial form. The foetus lies, couched like Spenser's Adonis, a flowering bud encircled by petals.[50]

In fact, the woman's abdomen is covered by the openings of her own flesh and skin that form the flower whose centre is the foetus. Yet the image adds further layers of symbolic meaning. The woman holds an apple in her hand that evokes the Fall and Eve's sexual appetite. Furthermore, the tree-stump on which she rests her knee also refers to the Christian metaphor of the Old and New Testament as it has a shoot of new growth that alludes to the birth of Christ from a woman; biologically it is a symbol for the cycle of life as well. Another branch is growing from the stump right where it might be placed to cover the woman's pubis, but visually it rather seems to gently tickle and stimulate her, thus eroticising the female body.

To the viewer the woman is exposed as a signifier of sexuality, of its moral ambiguity and of reproduction/generation. A closer look at the image brings forth further information. The shipwreck in the background takes up the mythological narrative of Fortune who, as we have seen, was the agent of the Wheel of Fortune, *i.e.* of ever changing destiny. Yet she has also been conceived as a whore, and thus as highly sexualised and corruptible.

Conclusion

In Spigelius the shipwreck seems to indicate that Fortune has lost her fatal powers and that she has been converted from the dangerous agent of the Wheel of Fortune into a symbol of the natural cycle of life. Under the knife of the anatomist and the line of the artist, Fortune has died while giving life to the child on her belly. She has turned out to be an object of dissection and of representation. The body displayed in the print can finally be recognised as dead; it depends on science and art to be rendered (seemingly) alive. This conflation of life and death, of imaginary and represented, is intrinsic to the imagery of the *Danse Macabre*.

---

[50] Sawday (1995), 216.

In Vesalius's title page the opened womb of the woman was surmounted by the skeleton to remind the viewer of the *Danse Macabre*. In Spigelius's plate the viewer has become the dancing partner of the woman: her inviting hand and fluttering pony tail as well as her pose indicate that her body is in movement. In John Brown's *A Complete Treatise of the Muscles* of 1681, the dancing of the represented female figure is combined with the coquettish glance that the woman – whose partially dissected back is on display – casts at the viewer. Like the Vesalian anatomical studies where the corpses are displayed in movement, both these later models allude to the *Danse Macabre* tradition and its ambiguity between life and death, between morals and erotics: the spectator becomes involved in these spaces of the 'in-between' where meaning and signification are generated.

What is today generally considered the beginning of scientific illustration, *i.e.* the visual rendering of the functioning of the human body, is still informed by visual models that are based on the *Danse Macabre* formula. The *Danse* in its iconographic tradition was coined to conflate moral reprehension and erotic arousel in its representation of female figures. By merging allegorical figures with 'portrayals' of women, the perception of what one really saw was blurred and the separation lines between imaginary and 'real' femininity were just as confounded as the neat separation between living and dead. It is exactly this conflation of different iconographic formulas and their polyvalent resemantisation, the simultaneous presence of the dimensions of death, sexuality and art that have made the *Danse Macabre* such a persistent motif in the production of meaning.

MACABRE PARALLELS

DIALOGUE AND VIOLENCE IN MEDIEVAL ILLUMINATIONS OF THE THREE LIVING AND THE THREE DEAD

CHRISTINE KRALIK

The Legend of the Three Living and the Three Dead, a medieval moralising story, tells of three young men on their return from a hunting trip who come across three dead. In some versions of the tale, the animated dead tell the living: 'As you are, so we once were; as we are now, so shall you be'. The story is likely to have first emerged in the secular context of the court in late-thirteenth-century France, from which it spread across Europe and was told and recorded in various forms over the course of the late Middle Ages.[1] The Legend of the Three Living and the Three Dead is linked to the *Danse Macabre* with respect to the interaction that occurs between living and dead, and the themes were not infrequently depicted together. However, the notion that the Three Living and the Three Dead served as the source for the later tradition of the *Danse Macabre* has long

---

[1] Key studies for the story of the Three Living and the Three Dead include Karl Künstle, *Die Legende der drei Lebenden und der drei Toten und der Totentanz* (Freiburg im Breisgau: Herdersche Verlagshandlung, 1908); Willy Storck, *Die Legende von den drei Lebenden und von den drei Toten* (Tübingen: Druck von H. Laupp Jr., 1910); Stefan Glixelli, *Les cinques Poèmes des Trois Morts et des Trois Vifs* (Paris: Librairie Ancienne Honoré Champion, 1914); E.C. Williams, 'Mural Paintings of the Three Living and the Three Dead in England', *Journal of the British Archaeological Association*, 7 (1942), 31-40; Willy Rotzler, *Die Begegnung der drei Lebenden und der drei Toten: Ein Beitrag zur Forschung über die mittelalterlichen Vergänglichkeitsdarstellungen* (Winterthur: Verlag P.G. Keller, 1961); Pavel Chihaia, *Immortalité et décomposition dans l'art du Moyen Age* (Madrid: Fondation culturelle Roumaine, 1988), 43-70; Paul Binski, *Medieval Death: Ritual and Representation* (Ithaca, NY: Cornell University Press, 1996), 134-40. For a recent in-depth study of the French wall paintings of the story, see Groupe de Recherches sur les Peintures Murales (eds), *Vifs nous sommes... morts nous serons: La Rencontre des trois morts et des trois vifs dans la peinture murale en France* (Vendôme: Éditions du Cherche-Lune, 2001).

been rejected, although it is recognised that both participated in the tradition of the so-called 'Macabre'.[2]

Numerous poetic versions of the story of the Three Living and the Three Dead survive in the vernacular, including Old French, Anglo-Norman, Early New High German and Italian, as well as in two versions in Latin, each of which reflects a rich and diverse tradition of storytelling. Most of the poems that have come down to us are accompanied by illustrations that also represent an interesting variety. Early investigations of the pictorial record of the story by scholars such as Willy Rotzler were primarily concerned with establishing a chronology and identifying iconographic types. Art-historical investigations have generally moved beyond such iconographical and typological studies in recent decades and have focussed more on function, reception, contextualisation, and the relationship between text and image – issues that inform my own work. Yet what the initial investigations clearly demonstrate is that, early on in the tradition of illustrating the story of the Three Living and the Three Dead, emphasis was placed upon the dialogue and communication that occurs either directly between the living and the dead in many French and English texts and images, or through a mediator in the person of a hermit in the case of many Italian examples.[3]

The emphasis on verbal interaction is ubiquitous in illuminations of the tale in the late thirteenth and fourteenth centuries, not only in images that accompany poetic texts of the story but also in images that appear independent of the poetic text. This suggests that the tale was becoming so well known by the mid fourteenth century that an image of the story could function on its own without an extended textual exposition or explanation.[4]

---

[2] The texts and images of the Three Living and the Three Dead generally restrict the action to young male aristocrats and offer the living a chance to improve their lives before it is too late, while the *Danse Macabre* displays individuals of different social strata and sometimes both genders being dragged away by death without hope of reprieve.

[3] The tradition of illustration in which three young men converse with three dead has come to be described as the French type, while images in which three young men on horseback observe the corpses lying in three open coffins, while a hermit serves as mediator between the living and the dead, has come to be known as the Italian type. See Storck (1910), 27-43; Rotzler (1961), 10, 73-167. Rotzler used these labels of the French type and the Italian type in order to organise his discussion, even grouping some images together according to how they combined aspects of the French and Italian types. See Rotzler (1961), 167-83.

[4] For example, the early-fourteenth-century English legal manuscript known as the Smithfield Decretals (London, British Library, MS Royal 10 E. IV) includes an extended narrative pictorial cycle that runs along the bas-de-page between fols

By the early fifteenth century, the imagery of the Three Living and the Three Dead had become a mainstay as the miniature accompanying the liturgical prayers of the Office of the Dead in books of hours, the prayerbook of choice for the laity in this period.[5] Interestingly, when serving as the main miniature introducing the prayers for the hour of Vespers in the Office of the Dead, representations of the dead in images of the story started to exhibit aggressive qualities. In some examples, the dead – animated and existing in the same physical space as the living – seem to stalk the living, while in others the encounter has become downright frightening (see Figs 46 and 47a-b below). The dead close in on the living, laughing and mocking them, while the horses of the living rear and the young men have looks of terror on their faces. In such examples, conversation has given way to violence.

251r-268r accompanying the decretals in Book Five having to do with crime. For more on this manuscript, see Lucy Freeman Sandler, *Gothic Manuscripts 1285-1385, vol. 1, Text and Illustrations* (New York: Harvey Miller Publishers, 1986), 111-12; Andrew Taylor, *Textual Situations: Three Medieval Manuscripts and their Readers* (Philadelphia: University of Pennsylvania Press, 2002), 137-96; Alixe Bovey, *The Smithfield Decretals: Tales from the Margins of a Fourteenth-Century Law Book* (Toronto: University of Toronto Press, forthcoming). The image of the confrontation between the Three Living and the Three Dead itself occurs across the opening of fols 258v-259r. In another example, the image of the Three Living and the Three Dead accompanies a lauda in a Florentine laudario, likely produced for the Compagnia delle laude di Santo Spirito, a small laudesi company that met at the Florentine church of Santo Spirito. This manuscript is now in the Biblioteca nationale centrale in Florence (Banco Rari 18, formerly Magliabecchiana II.I.122, fol. 134r). For a catalogue entry on the manuscript, see G. Mazzatinti, *Inventari dei Manoscritti delle Biblioteche d'Italia, 8: Firenze, Biblioteca nazionale centrale* (Florence, 1898), 46-49. For a reproduction of fol. 134r, see Fernando Liuzzi, *La Lauda e I Primordi della Melodia Italiana, 1* (Rome: Libreria dello Stato, 1935), colour plate following p. 73. For a transcription and translation of the lauda, see Blake Wilson (music) and Nello Barbieri (text) (eds), *The Florence Laudario. An Edition of Florence, Biblioteca nazionale centrale, Banco Rari, 18* (Madison: A-R Editions, 1995), c.

[5] For the illustration of the Office of the Dead, see Millard Meiss, 'La mort et l'office des morts a l'epoque du Maitre Boucicaut et des Limbourgs', *Revue de l'Art*, 1 (1968), 17-25; Gabrielle Bartz and Eberhard König, 'Die Illustration des Toten-offiziums in Stundenbüchern', in Hansjakob Becker *et al.* (eds), *Im Angesicht des Todes: ein interdisziplinäres Kompendium, I* (St. Ottilien: EOS Verlag, 1987), 487-528; Roger Wieck, 'The Office of the Dead', in *Time Sanctified: the Book of Hours in Medieval Art and Life* (New York: George Braziller, 1988, repr. 2001), 124-48. See also the essay by Caroline Zöhl in this volume.

How can we account for the shift from dialogue to fear-inspiring aggression in these images? Much has been written about the emergence of the imagery of death – often termed 'the Macabre' – in the medieval period and the place of the Three Living and the Three Dead in that tradition of description and illustration.[6] However, very little attention has been paid to the shift in the appearance of the iconography of the story itself over the course of the late Middle Ages. This paper will argue that the function served by the image within the context of the manuscript and in the devotional life of the viewer offers keys to understanding why the dead are very frequently depicted as aggressive and violent in fifteenth-century representations.

Before turning to a close examination of several images that exemplify the aggressive encounter between living and dead, and then assessing how such images would have functioned, it will be necessary to examine earlier texts and images of the story to set the stage for tracking the shifts that occurred between the late thirteenth and late fifteenth centuries in the pictorial rendering of the story. Several French and English examples will first be examined, for these are representative of the tradition known north of the Alps in the early history of the dissemination of the tale.

Conversing with the dead

The earliest representations of the Three Living and the Three Dead tend to be relatively benign in appearance. The late-thirteenth-century MS 3142 now in the Bibliothèque de l'Arsenal in Paris, which was probably produced for Marie de Brabant around 1285, is a compilation of courtly tales and stories, and contains the 162-line-long version of the poem attributed to Baudouin de Condé. The poem is accompanied by a representation of two groups of three figures that are seemingly engaged in conversation (Pl. 4).[7] This Baudouin version, which is one of the earliest

---

[6] See Johan Huizinga, *The Autumn of the Middle Ages*, trans. Rodney J. Payton and Ulrich Mammitzsch (Chicago: University of Chicago Press, 1996), 156-72; Emile Mâle, *Religious Art in France: the Late Middle Ages. A Study of Medieval Iconography and its Sources*, ed. Harry Bober, trans. M. Mathews (Princeton: Princeton University Press, 1949, repr. 1986), esp. 324-28; T.S.R. Boase, *Death in the Middle Ages: Mortality, Judgment and Remembrance* (New York: McGraw Hill, 1972), 104-09; Binski (1996), 123-63, esp. 134-38.

[7] For a discussion of the Baudouin version of the Three Living and the Three Dead that appears in Bibliothèque de l'Arsenal MS 3142, see Glixelli (1914), 6-8, 14-15 53-63 and 113-15, and Rotzler (1961), 22-26. For the miniature, see Rotzler

known renditions of the story, was popular in aristocratic circles and survives in at least five other manuscripts from the period.[8] The appearance of the story alongside other texts by Baudouin and additional courtly tales that were brought together in the Arsenal compendium suggests that the story of the Three Living and the Three Dead was rather well known in aristocratic circles by the final quarter of the thirteenth century.[9]

The Baudouin poem begins with an introduction that tells how the Three Living, when they were out one day as a group hunting, came to encounter the Three Dead. Each of the young men then speaks in turn, the first living youth describing what he sees to his companions, while the second claims that what they see is a mirror sent to them by God to cause them to reflect on their mortal state and to free them of their pride. The third young man describes in great detail the gruesome appearance of the dead figures before them. This is followed by the responses of the Three Dead. The first addresses the living, saying 'As you are, so we once were; as we are now, so shall you be!' He claims that he and his companions once looked just as the young men now do, and that Death took everything away from them. He confirms the suspicion of the second young man that the dead were sent to the living as a mirror from God to encourage them to improve their ways, and states that death levels all in the end. The third reminds the young men that they must be ready for death at all times, and asks the living to pray to God for them.[10]

The text appears in several columns across fols 311v and 312r, and the representation of the Three Living and the Three Dead occupies the top of fol. 311v, taking up the width of two columns. This is unusual, as images elsewhere in the manuscript take up the width of only a single column on their respective pages, and it suggests that the encounter of the Three Living and the Three Dead was given special significance visually,

---

(1961), 73-77. Both scholars treated the text and the image as separate entities, even though they appear together in the manuscript.

[8] For the surviving manuscripts that contain the Baudouin version of the poem, see Glixelli (1914), 4-8.

[9] See *Catalogue des Manuscrits de la Bibliothèque de l'Arsenal, III* (Paris, 1887), 256-64, for a discussion of the contents of the manuscript; also Susan Ward, 'Fables for the Court: Illustrations of Marie de France's Fables in Paris, BN, MS Arsenal 3142', in Jane Taylor and Lesley Smith (eds), *Women and the Book: Assessing the Visual Evidence* (London: British Library and Toronto: University of Toronto Press, 1996), 190-203.

[10] For a full transcription of the Baudouin version of the poem, see Glixelli (1914), 53-63.

perhaps because of the popularity of the story in its day.[11] The image presents three elegant young men on the left, dressed almost identically and apparently of a comparable age. The living youth furthest to the right, who clasps the hand of the figure behind him, stands holding a hawk which evokes the hunting trip from which the young men were understood to be returning when they encountered the dead, but also symbolises the pleasures of life against which the dead warn the young men. The dead appear in similar stages of advanced decay, while it is their shrouds – either intact, ragged or entirely absent – which seem to communicate gradations of difference between the three corpses.

The illumination accompanying Baudouin's poem suggests that two groups of three figures appear before each other, and we understand that the figures communicate verbally with each other, although the figures are not depicted performing gestures associated with speaking. No direct conversation takes place, however, since the text of the poem indicates that, while the dead speak directly to the living, the living speak only amongst themselves. No physical barrier has been depicted on the page, suggesting a momentary rupture between two separate worlds that has allowed living and deceased to interact with each other while the separation between the living and the dead is maintained through the distance at which the groups are kept from each other and through the lack of a two-way conversation. This image, and Baudouin's telling of the story as it was recorded in Marie's manuscript, seem to reflect the popular belief that it was possible for the dead to visit the world of the living as revenants and to seek prayers from the living for the benefit of those souls languishing in Purgatory.[12] We might also understand that the dead are depicted as caught between worlds since, according to another popular belief, the body could not truly die until it had fully decayed.[13]

---

[11] The imagery of the Three Living and the Three Dead appears to have been given special emphasis in other manuscripts in which it is found as well. For example, the lauda 'Chi vuol lo mondo disprezare' contained in a mid-fourteenth-century Florentine laudario (Florence, BNC Banco Rari, 18) is accompanied at the top of fol. 134r by a framed miniature of the Three Living and the Three Dead. The miniature takes up the width of the text block and is the only image in the manuscript to do so. All other images in the manuscript are inhabited initials. See Rotzler (1961), 136-39. See also note 4 above.

[12] Nancy Caciola, 'Wraiths, Revenants, and Ritual in Medieval Culture', *Past and Present*, 152 (1996), 3-45, esp. 28. See also the essay by Kenneth Rooney in this volume.

[13] Caciola (1996), 31-37.

While no physical separation divides the two groups in the illumination in Arsenal MS 3142, similar compositions elsewhere make a point of dividing the space into two halves and distinguishing between the separate realms, as is the case with the illumination found in the Psalter of Robert de Lisle.[14] The version of the story found in the De Lisle Psalter is an abbreviated version of the so-called Anonymous IV text.[15] It appears on fol. 127r in two columns in Anglo-Norman French, with headings in Latin and a line in Middle English expressing the thoughts of the living and the dead running along the top of the framed illumination at the top of the folio (Pl. 5).[16] The verses of the poem uttered by the Three Living are arranged in the left-hand column below the figures of the Three Living while the words of the Dead are set in the right-hand column, inscribed directly below the depictions of the Dead. While in most textual renditions of the Anonymous IV poem the Three Living speak first, followed by the Three Dead, here the verses have been arrayed on the page in such a way as to provoke a performative engagement with the text. The arrangement of verses allows the reader to alternate between the words of the living and those of the dead, as if to participate in the conversation.[17]

---

[14] London, BL, MS Arundel 83 II, *c.*1310. This English manuscript contains a number of devotional and moralising texts and images in addition to the story of the Three Living and the Three Dead that might have been studied and consulted with the guidance of a Franciscan confessor. For the manuscript, see Lucy Freeman Sandler, *The Psalter of Robert de Lisle in the British Library* (London: Harvey Miller, 1983, repr. 1999), esp. 44-45; Susanna Greer Fein, 'Life and Death, Reader and Page: Mirrors of Mortality in English Manuscripts', *Mosaic*, 35:1 (2002), 69-94.

[15] The Anonymous IV text, with the incipit 'Conpains, vois tu ce que je voi?', is one version of the story that was fairly popular in England in the late thirteenth century. The verses found in the Psalter of Robert de Lisle are excerpts, translated into Anglo-Norman, of parts of the French Anonymous IV poem. For the Anonymous IV version, see Glixelli (1914), 9-10; Rotzler (1961), 37-38. For a translation, see Binski (1996), 136.

[16] The unusual intermingling of three different languages on the page suggests a hierarchy of languages that associated them with different functions. The poem itself has been recorded in Anglo-Norman French, the language of the aristocracy and of courtly literature, with Latin labels introducing each verse. Middle English, associated with the spoken word and performance, records the initial unfettered sentiments of the living and dead, even as they ironically lose that status as they are inscribed on the page. See Richard Emmerson, 'Visualizing the Vernacular: Middle English in Early Fourteenth Century Bilingual and Trilingual Manuscript Illustrations', in Kathryn A. Smith (ed.), *Tributes to Lucy Freeman Sandler: Studies in Illuminated Manuscripts* (London: Harvey Miller, 2007), 187-204.

[17] Glixelli (1914), 83-91; Fein (2002), 69-94.

Fig. 45. The Three Living and the Three Dead, miniature in the De Lisle Hours
(New York, Pierpont Morgan Library, MS G.50, fol 6v), *c.*1320-25. © The
Pierpont Morgan Library, New York.

The abridged Anonymous IV text of the poem is similar to the Baudouin version in terms of how the interaction between living and dead is described, but it omits the prologue and jumps straight into the words uttered by the protagonists.[18] The versions also differ in the nature of the message that the dead bear to the living. While the Baudouin text found in the Arsenal manuscript describes the dead seeking prayers from the living, in the abridged Anonymous IV text the dead emphasise the importance of preparing the soul for death that is necessary to avoid suffering the torments of hell, suggesting that the dead already reside there and attempt to prevent the same fate from befalling the living.

The image at the top of fol. 127r of the De Lisle Psalter shows an arrangement of the Three Living and Three Dead in postures very similar to those found on fol. 311v of the Arsenal manuscript, with the exception of the living figure shown furthest to the left who seems to have turned his body to face the viewer and yet has his head cocked to one side as he eyes the dead warily. The living, who might be interpreted as kings or aristocrats, are distinguished by their robes of different colours and trims. Two of the three hold attributes: the first a hawk, which symbolises the hunt, and the last a sceptre. All wear crowns.[19]

The living and the dead both speak and the dead address their comments directly to the living, but the living do not answer them; they speak only amongst themselves. A metaphorical wall exists between the two groups that prevents them from interacting directly with each other, and this is visualised in the illumination by a frame that not only surrounds the composition as a whole but also divides the groups from each other. This has the added effect of giving the illumination the appearance of a devotional diptych, linking it to other representations of the story that existed in other English devotional manuscripts, such as in the book of hours that was made for Margaret de Beauchamp, the wife of Robert de Lisle, which will be discussed below (Fig. 45), as well as painted diptychs, such as that which we know was purchased in London by Count Amadeus

---

[18] As is also the case with Anonymous III and V, the poems are so called due to a paucity of information about the original authors, audiences or contexts of production. For an analysis of the French poems, see Glixelli (1914).

[19] The Latin rubrics that introduce each of the verses of the text describe the figures as kings, and yet the living seem to be dressed as fashionable young noblemen, with each wearing a crown and one holding a sceptre. While it is possible that the figures were intended to be understood as kings, the labels may also refer to an earlier tradition of describing the kings that no longer corresponds to the figures as they were intended to be viewed in this manuscript commissioned by a nobleman.

of Savoy around 1303.[20] The monochrome foil set behind the living is in marked contrast to the green background studded with thistles – symbolising remembrance – against which the dead are depicted. This pictorial device further enhances the notion that the living and the dead are to be understood as existing in different spheres. Despite the division between the two groups emphasised by the framing elements in the image, the viewer senses that a rupture has occurred. Indeed, the tail of the hawk held by the first living breaks through the frame into the space of the dead. This seems to offer the dead the symbolic point of entry into the world of the living, for the living could not enter the world of the dead.

Robert de Lisle commissioned a book of hours for his wife Margaret de Beauchamp only a few short years after he commissioned his own psalter.[21] The De Lisle Hours contains a prefatory cycle of images that includes a fragmentary representation of the Three Living and the Three Dead, which is preceded by a depiction of St Christopher and followed by a representation of St Nicholas. That each of the De Lisle manuscripts contains representations of the Three Living and the Three Dead reflects a strong interest in the story on the part of the couple, although the illuminations were produced by different artists, as a stylistic analysis of the images reveals. The incomplete representation of the Three Living and the Three Dead appearing on fol. 6v of the De Lisle Hours (Fig. 45) is set against a diapered foil and is punctuated in the four corners of the frame by heraldic shields of several ruling houses.[22] The lost facing folio would presumably have shown the Three Dead enframed in a similar way.[23] That the scene of the Three Living and the Three Dead appears independent of poetic text shows that the image was likely intended to stand alone; it is

---

[20] Binski (1996), 135.

[21] New York, Pierpont Morgan Library, MS G.50, *c*.1320-25. See John Plummer, *The Glazier Collection of Illuminated Manuscripts* (New York: Morgan Library, 1968), 29-30, no. 37; Lucy Freeman Sandler, *Gothic Manuscripts 1285-1385. A Survey of Manuscripts Illuminated in the British Isles*, vol. 2, Catalogue (New York: Harvey Miller, 1986), 83-84; Kathryn A. Smith, *Art, Identity and Devotion in Fourteenth Century England: Three Women and their Books of Hours* (Toronto: University of Toronto Press, 2003), esp. 152-58 and 297-301.

[22] The heraldic shields likely served a commemorative function in this context, encouraging the viewer to be mindful of praying for members of the families represented on the page by means of their heraldry. See Michael Michael, 'The Privilege of "Proximity": Towards a Re-definition of the Function of Armorials,' *Journal of Medieval History*, 23:1 (1997), 55-74.

[23] A stub for a missing leaf appears next to fol. 6v on which the Three Living are depicted, showing that there was once a facing page which most likely presented a representation of the Three Dead. See Sandler (1986), 83.

also an early indication of how the Three Living and the Three Dead would come to serve a devotional function rather than a strictly moralising one in books of hours in later years. In the context of this prayerbook, the image would have encouraged Margaret to contemplate her own mortality and to pray for loved ones, both living and deceased. The now-missing image of the dead might have been intended to stand for deceased loved ones for whom Margaret should pray.[24] The firm division existing between living and dead, enforced by the organisation of the image across the gutter of the manuscript, suggests a perpetuation of the approach to illustration found in Robert's manuscript, in which the dead are understood to reside in Hell, according to the Anonymous IV version of the text. And yet, as a devotional image in a book of hours, it might have been used by Margaret as she prayed for the souls of the deceased residing in Purgatory. It may be that the representation of the story in this manuscript could reflect aspects of more than one textual tradition, a result of the absence of a particular accompanying text that would otherwise have restricted the artist's choices with respect to how to illustrate the story.

The violent dead

Thus far, this paper has explored several illustrations of a well-known tale that appeared in different textual contexts. The courtly compendium produced for Marie de Brabant included an illustrated text of the Three Living and the Three Dead, while the psalter made for Robert de Lisle included a shortened version of a different text of the same story, also accompanied by an illustration. Finally, an illustration of the story, independent of the poetic text, was included in a prefatory cycle of images in a book of hours intended for daily prayer and the remembrance of the dead. Illustrated poems of the tale did continue to appear in England and on the Continent as accessory texts in prayerbooks such as the mid-fourteenth-century Psalter of Bonne de Luxembourg[25] and the late-fourteenth-century Petites Heures of Jean de Berry.[26] However, by the

---

[24] Ashby Kinch, 'Image, Ideology and Form: the Middle English Three Dead Kings in its iconographic context', *Chaucer Review*, 43:1 (2008), 48-81, esp. 70.

[25] New York, Metropolitan Museum of Art-The Cloisters, MS 69.86. The illustration is found on fols 321v-322r, while the text begins on fol. 321v and continues over the succeeding folios. This manuscript is dated to before 1349. See Florens Deuchler, 'Looking at Bonne of Luxembourg's Prayerbook', *The Metropolitan Museum of Art Bulletin* (February 1971), 267-78.

[26] Paris, BnF, ms. lat. 18014, fol. 282r. François Avril has argued that the Petites Heures was commissioned by Jean de Berry in the early 1370s and was completed

early fifteenth century the imagery of the story was consistently appearing independently of the text of the story and was instead accompanying prayers for the dead in books of hours. Along with the changing context came a change in the character of the pictorial tradition, as the nature of the interaction between living and dead had undergone a decided transformation. By the mid fifteenth century, the appearance of Death as a personification appeared more ominous and insidious, and the interaction between living and dead began to appear more sinister.

The encounter depicted in the Hours of Anne de Beaujeu, attributed to the Master of the Munich Boccaccio and dated to *c*.1470 (Paris, BnF, nouv. acq. ms. lat. 3187, fol. 139v), represents a departure in the tradition of illustrating the story (Fig. 46).[27] Not only are the living and the dead depicted as inhabiting the same physical space, but the interaction has also become more ominous. The scene is set in a clearing just outside a city wall and on the edge of a wood. Three walking and sneering corpses enter the picture plane from beyond the left border of the framed image. They move forward toward the young riders who are returning to the city after their hunting trip, which had presumably taken place in the woods depicted to the right. In response to the appearance of the dead, the first horseman raises his right hand as if in acknowledgement, while the other two riders seem to respond more dramatically. The second rider has completely turned his horse around, while the third rider has thrown both his hands up in surprise and his horse has reared.

---

in the late 1380s, contesting earlier views that the manuscript was commissioned by Charles V and only later completed for Jean de Berry. Avril's analysis of the illuminations has identified Jean le Noir, Jacquemart de Hesdin and the Pseudo-Jacquemart as the artists responsible for the illuminations in the manuscript. See François Avril, 'Beschreibung der Miniaturen', in François Avril *et al.* (eds), *Les Petites Heures du Duc de Berry. Kommentar zu MS lat. 18014 der Bibliothèque nationale, Paris* (Luzern: Faksimile Verlag, 1989), 225-387, esp. 381-83. The Baudouin version of story of the Three Living and the Three Dead was illuminated in the Petites Heures by the Pseudo-Jacquemart in the late 1380s, while the same text in his mother Bonne's Psalter was illuminated by Jean de Noir. The similarities in textual and pictorial inclusions that exist between the two manuscripts must have, at least in part, to do with familial tradition, allowing devotional practices to be passed from one generation to the next. See Margaret Manion, 'Art and Devotion: The Prayerbooks of Jean de Berry', in Margaret M. Manion and Bernard J. Muir (eds), *Medieval Texts and Images: Studies of Manuscripts from the Middle Ages* (Chur: Harwood Academic Publishers, 1991), 177-200.

[27] François Avril (ed.), *Jean Fouquet. Peintre et enlumineur du XVe siècle* (Paris: Bibliothèque nationale de France, 2003), 328-33.

Fig. 46. Master of the Munich Boccaccio, The Three Living and the Three Dead, miniature in the Hours of Anne de Beaujeu (Paris, Bibliothèque nationale de France, NAL 3187, fol. 139v), *c*.1470. © Bibliothèque nationale de France.

Fig. 47a. The Ghent Associates, The Three Living and the Three Dead, miniature in the Berlin Hours of Mary of Burgundy and Maximilian I (Berlin, Kupferstichkabinett-SMPK, 78 B 12, fol. 220v), c.1480. Photo: Joerg P. Anders. © Bildarchiv Preußischer Kulturbesitz / Art Resource, NY.

Fig. 47b. The Ghent Associates, Corpse with a spear and a coffin, miniature in the Berlin Hours of Mary of Burgundy and Maximilian I (Berlin, Kupferstichkabinett-SMPK, 78 B 12, fol. 221r), *c*.1480. Photo: Joerg P. Anders. © Bildarchiv Preußischer Kulturbesitz / Art Resource, NY.

The young men on horseback appear to be of similar age and social standing, and each of the three is beautifully dressed. There are slight differences in their attire, including the distinctive hats that they wear, but the different colours of the horses are probably the most striking feature distinguishing the young men from each other. The dead also seem to be depicted rather uniformly and all appear to be in the same state of decay, but the employment of the shroud in different ways distinguishes the dead.

Just behind the curving footpath on which each of the dead and the first of the living have stepped is a monumental cross that serves several functions in this image. It creates a visual boundary between the living and the dead who encroach upon them, and yet it does not physically separate the two groups, as the hand of the first dead and the hind legs of the horse that has been turned around by its master pass in front of the cross. The shadows cast by the bodies of the dead express in pictorial terms their physicality and suggest their real presence in the world of the living. This seems to give visual form to popular beliefs in ghosts and the idea that the dead could be caught between worlds.

Why might such a dramatic transformation have occurred in the nature of the relationship depicted between living and dead? In order to answer this question, the function that such an image served in its new context must be addressed, necessitating an examination of the text that the images accompanied. The Office of the Dead first emerged in the ninth century in a Benedictine context as a central text of the Divine Office.[28] The Office was made up of prayers to be said at the three canonical hours of Vespers, Matins and Lauds in the evening and morning before the performance of the Requiem mass over the body of the deceased, after which would follow the funeral service. In later centuries, the prayers of the Office of the Dead were introduced into lay devotional manuals, most notably the book of hours. As the Office found its way into a book intended for lay devotional use, its function changed slightly. While it was still prayed the night and morning preceding a funeral, it was also recommended that the Office of the Dead be said regularly, on a daily basis if possible, not only for the preparation of the reader's soul for death but also for the sake of deceased loved ones. The establishment of the Doctrine of Purgatory at the Second Council of Lyons in 1274 asserted that the prayers of the living could assist the dead, and this doctrine was reasserted at the Council of

---

[28] See Edmund Bishop, 'On the Origins of the Prymer', in Edmund Bishop, *Liturgica Historica: Papers on the Liturgy and Religious Life of the Western Church* (Oxford: Clarendon Press, 1918, repr. 1962), 211-37.

Florence in 1439-45.[29] This doctrine granted the laity agency in assisting their deceased loved ones and encouraged them to say their prayers, especially those of the Office of the Dead, more frequently.

From the late thirteenth century, the first hour of the Office was usually accompanied by depictions of real-life moments that preceded and followed the death of an individual.[30] Quite typical selections were images of the recitation of the Office of the Dead, the performance of the Requiem Mass, and the burial in the graveyard. There were other categories of images as well, such as depictions of certain biblical figures, including Job, an appropriate inclusion since the Book of Job provided many of the passages of text that formed the prayers of the Office of the Dead. Job was also a model of faith, hope and patience, important virtues in the preparation for death and qualities that were promoted in the *Ars Moriendi*.[31] The figure of Lazarus, whose resurrection by Christ prefigured the resurrection of all at the end of time, was also a common inclusion (Pl. 8). Arguably most striking were the allegorical images of death, including Death personified and the Three Living and the Three Dead. An embodiment of the idea of death, which paradoxically gives tangibility to the ephemeral, emphasised the ever-present threat of death's advent. Such images were visually persuasive and would have encouraged a more ardent contemplation of the prayers accompanying them. This was especially true when the images were personalised with heraldry, insignia or portraiture. While we have seen an example of the use of coats of arms in the four corners of the frame surrounding the representation of the Three Living and the Three Dead in the De Lisle Hours, in later representations the personalisation of the image became much more emphatic and, arguably, even more effective.

With the function of the Office of the Dead in mind, let us turn to look at another illustration of the Three Living and the Three Dead that accompanied that text in a book of hours made for a young duchess. The representation of the tale found in the Berlin Hours of Mary of Burgundy and Maximilian I is one of the most dynamic and striking of all (Fig. 47a).[32] The scene is set in a naturalistically rendered landscape, situated in

---

[29] Jacques LeGoff, *The Birth of Purgatory*, trans. Arthur Goldhammer (Chicago: University of Chicago Press, 1984), 237.

[30] Wieck (2001), 124-36.

[31] Wieck (2001), 132. For the *Ars Moriendi* tradition, see Hiram Kümper, *Tod und Sterben: lateinische und deutsche Sterbeliteratur des Spätmittelalters* (Duisburg: Wiku Verlag, 2007).

[32] The identification of the illuminator of this image has been the subject of much debate. In the early scholarship on this manuscript, the illuminator of the image of

the Low Countries. The presence of ravens and the dark clouds overhead creates a foreboding atmosphere. The only woman in the group, riding her horse at the centre of the image, has been identified as the original owner of the manuscript, Mary of Burgundy, duchess of Burgundy and wife of the future Habsburg emperor Maximilian I.

A young woman dressed in a very similar fashion appears on fol. 355r of the same manuscript, accompanying a suffrage incipit reading 'Angele qui meus es custos' (*Oh angel, who is my guardian*).[33] This woman, who kneels at a *prie-dieu* with a visualisation of an angel before her, must be the same as the female rider depicted earlier in the same manuscript. The repeated appearance of the initial M on the harness of the horse on fol. 220v suggests that the female rider should indeed be identified as Mary of Burgundy. Of the three living protagonists, the two male riders have turned away from the road and seem intent on riding into the woods to escape the menacing corpses. One of the men, who might be identified as Mary's husband Maximilian, beckons her to follow him.[34] She takes no notice, however. She has turned her head and seems to direct her gaze in the direction of the spear-wielding corpse chasing after her.[35]

In his discussion of the image from the Berlin Hours, Otto Pächt suggested that the picture of Mary of Burgundy being chased down by a corpse was probably painted after her untimely death following a riding

---

the Three Living and the Three Dead was believed to be the same as that of the famous window pages of the Vienna Hours of Mary of Burgundy. See Friedrich Winkler, *Die flämische Buchmalerei des XV. und XVI. Jahrhunderts. Künstler und Werke von den Brüdern van Eyck bis zu Simon Bening* (Leipzig: E.A. Seemann, 1925, repr. Amsterdam: B.M. Israël, 1978), 103-05. More recently, Bodo Brinkmann assigned the artist with the title the Master of the Berlin Hours of Mary of Burgundy, to distinguish the painter from the better-known Master of Mary of Burgundy. See Eberhard König, Fedja Anzelewsky, Bodo Brinkmann, and Frauke Steenbock, *Das Berliner Stundenbuch der Maria von Burgund und Kaiser Maximilians*, exhibition catalogue (Berlin: Kupferstichkabinett, Staatliche Museen zu Berlin Preussischer Kulturbesitz, 1998), esp. 147-53. Anne van Buren has attributed the image of the Three Living and Three Dead to the Ghent Associates, an attribution that I maintain here. See Anne Van Buren, 'The Master of Mary of Burgundy and his Colleagues: the State of Research and Questions of Method', *Zeitschrift für Kunstgeschichte*, 38 (1975), 286-308.

[33] For this image, see König *et al.* (1998), 108-09.

[34] König *et al.* (1998), 36.

[35] It is interesting that, by the late fifteenth century, representations of the Three Living and the Three Dead often showed the dead sporting spears and arrows, which had apparently become their attributes, reinforcing their dangerous and horrifying nature.

accident in 1482. Pächt argued that the image was most likely commemorative since the subject was rare in Flemish illumination; that representations of the story did not include female participants; and, of course, that she had died while horse-riding.[36] However, an examination of an image from another Flemish manuscript of comparable date undermines Pächt's assertion that the image of the encounter of the Three Living and the Three Dead in Mary's manuscript must be interpreted as a commemorative image. Attributed to the Master of the Dresden Prayerbook, the representation of the story found in this other book of hours in Berlin (MS 78 B 14) presents a group of riders, including three men and one woman, who are stalked by three dead (Fig. 48).[37] The young people respond in different ways; while one turns away and tries to flee, another has stopped and has placed his hands over his face in a gesture of terror. This image successfully conveys the notion that death is inescapable and inevitable, and the only recourse is to be ever ready for death through prayer, symbolised by the cross that stands in the lower right corner of the picture field and to which the young man and woman on horseback have turned.

Anne van Buren followed Pächt in suggesting that the image of the Three Living and the Three Dead in the Berlin Hours of Mary of Burgundy and Maximilian I was most likely executed after Mary's death, a contention based on a greater degree of personalisation observed on the folio displaying the Three Living and the Three Dead than elsewhere in the manuscript.[38] Insignia, mottos and heraldic imagery were often employed in devotional images, including portraits of donors, however, even if this was more common in France than in the Netherlands.[39] The decision to include the duchess's initials within the composition of the image could also alternately be read as a reflection of the desire to personalise the image and to heighten its power as a devotional tool.

Eberhard König interpreted the representation of Mary of Burgundy as fearless in the face of death and that her participation in the action strengthened the image's status as both a *memento mori* and a devotional image.[40] The duchess was an avid rider, in fact, and was depicted on

---

[36] Otto Pächt, *The Master of Mary of Burgundy* (London: Faber and Faber, 1966), 50.

[37] The Master of the Dresden Prayerbook, 'The Three Living and the Three Dead', from a Flemish Book of Hours, Berlin, Kupferstichkabinett-SMPK, 78 B 14, fol. 277v, *c.*1480. See Bodo Brinkmann, *Die Flämische Buchmalerei am Ende des Burgunderreichs. Der Meister des Dresdener Gebetbuchs und die Miniaturisten seiner Zeit* (Turnhout: Brepols, 1997), 301-05, 383.

[38] Van Buren (1975), 308.

[39] König *et al.* (1998), 31.

[40] König *et al.* (1998), 36.

horseback for hunting or hawking on a number of occasions during her lifetime.[41] I contend that the representation of Mary was integrated into the composition as one of the aristocratic riders in order to personalise her devotion and make the image a stronger *memento mori* for her own use.

Fig. 48. The Master of the Dresden Prayerbook, The Three Living and the Three Dead, miniature in a Flemish book of hours (Berlin, KK-SMPK, 78 B 14, fol. 277v), *c.*1480. © Bildarchiv Preußischer Kulturbesitz / Art Resource, NY.

---

[41] An example of an image of the duchess as a hawker may be found in a manuscript copy of the *Chronijke van Vlaenderen*. 'Mary of Burgundy as a Hawker', Bruges, Openbare Bibliotheek, MS 437, fol. 372v, *c.*1481. See Eberhard Freiherr Schenk zu Schweinsberg, *Die Illustrationen der Chronik von Flanderen – Handschrift Nr. 437 – der Stadtbibliothek zu Brügge und ihr Verhältnis zu Hans Memling* (Strasbourg: Verlag von J.H.Ed. Heitz, 1922), 19.

The power of the image would have been enhanced by its juxtaposition with the miniature on the opposite recto, however (Fig. 47b). The full-length corpse depicted on fol. 221r of the Berlin Hours of Mary of Burgundy and Maximilian I is shown draped with a shroud, holding a coffin in its left hand and a dart in its right, apparently preparing to strike. The figure seems to be moving forward, in the direction of the scene of the Three Living and the Three Dead represented on the verso, and yet it has turned its gaze out to the viewer that was originally Mary of Burgundy herself. Unlike the naturalistic Netherlandish landscape depicted as the backdrop for the image on the verso, the corpse rendered on the recto is set against a monochrome foil. The orange background is evocative of the purgatorial fires in which the souls of the deceased languished while the living laboured through their prayers to gain respite for them. The corpse shown here is unlikely to represent a soul, which is normally given the form of a small naked figure, but seems rather to reflect the idea of death coming for the individual who is unprepared, thus necessitating a stay in Purgatory. This image encapsulates the need to prepare for death as well as the importance of remembering and praying for those who have passed on.

What sets the representation of the Three Living and the Three Dead in this manuscript apart is how it works together with the image of the animated corpse on the facing recto.[42] The representation of Mary of Burgundy in the image of the Three Living and the Three Dead depicts the duchess about to encounter her own death. Unlike the corpse that the painted Mary encountered on the page, the corpse on the recto looked out from the confines of the picture plane to confront the viewer, Mary of Burgundy, in the flesh. The interchange between the depiction of Mary of Burgundy and the corpse chasing after her on the verso paralleled the encounter that the flesh-and-blood duchess was intended to experience with the corpse depicted on the recto. As she prayed the Office of the

---

[42] A codicological analysis of the Berlin Hours has shown that fol. 220v is on a single leaf that has been tipped into the manuscript. See König *et al.* (1998), 167-72, esp. 170. It is therefore possible that the bifolio on which the image of the Three Living and the Three Dead was painted was altered in some way before the page was sewn into the manuscript, or that it was a later addition to the book. There is no reason to believe that the image was not conceived of as part of the original program, however. An examination of the manuscript's programme of illustrations shows that major textual divisions of the manuscript were all introduced with two facing illuminations, and thus the pairing of the images on fols 220v and 221r fits in nicely with the layout of the manuscript in its entirety. König *et al.* (1998), 31.

Dead and contemplated that very complex pictorial composition, she would be encouraged to experience a spiritual vision of death in her mind, intensifying her devotional experience and encouraging her to prepare herself as fully as possible for death and the life after death.

Conclusion

Between the late thirteenth and late fifteenth centuries, the imagery of the story of the Three Living and the Three Dead underwent a striking transformation. From initially accompanying the text of the story and depicting a dialogue between two parties, one living and one dead, the tradition of illustration took a turn. The imagery, now divorced from its original textual context, regularly began to accompany the prayers for the Office of the Dead in books of hours, and in this new context the imagery displayed a more sinister, aggressive temper. The dead began to be shown as creeping up up on, or even openly attacking, the living.

While popular beliefs in revenants and the heightened fear of death brought about by the experience of famine and plague might all have played some part in this development, it seems probable that a systematic shift was at play. It would appear that in the context of prayers that were said for the good of the soul of the reader as well as for those of the deceased, the more striking and persuasive the accompanying image, the more successful it was. A representation of an attack on the living by the dead was likely to move the reader-viewer to recognise the urgency of fervent prayer and preparation for death more effectively than a representation of simple dialogue.

Acknowledgements

I would like to thank Guita Lamsechi for her careful reading of this text and for her helpful suggestions. I am also grateful to Sophie Oosterwijk for her invitation to contribute to this volume and to both editors for their editorial input.

MIXED ENCOUNTERS:
THE THREE LIVING AND THE THREE DEAD
IN ITALIAN ART

MARCO PICCAT

The motif of the encounter between the Three Living and the Three Dead starts to appear in medieval literature and art in the thirteenth century.[1] This Legend became widespread throughout Europe, and particularly in France, at a time when a new awareness of 'the macabre' was making itself felt. Apart from the texts, examples of the encounter can be found in illuminated books of hours, murals and other works of art. The Legend was particularly widespread throughout the whole of the fifteenth century, which means that it was still current while the *Danse Macabre* was emerging rapidly as another macabre motif. In fact, in France the two themes are often found in juxtaposition, which is fitting as both illustrate a confrontation of the living with death. In Italy the two themes share another element, however, *viz.* the figure of the Hermit who is the last living representative in the French *Danse Macabre* poem and also the commentator after the encounter of the Three Living with the Three Dead. The hermit is shown in the woodcut illustration of the Legend in Guy Marchant's expanded 1486 edition of the *Danse*, in which he chose to add the Legend (Fig. 49). However, this essay will focus on the Italian tradition.

The Legend in Italian art

The oldest records of the written tradition of the Legend can be found in Latin commentaries to the Bible (passages from the Book of Job, Isaiah, Genesis and Ecclesiastes) and, within the context of the Italian vernacular,

---

[1] Introduction in Groupe de Recherches sur les Peintures Murales, *Vifs nous sommes ... morts nous serons. La rencontre des trois morts et des trois vifs dans la peinture murale en France* (Vendôme: Éditions du Cherche-Lune, 2001), 7-10. See also the essay by Christine Kralik in this volume.

in *Laudi* modelled on the texts of Hélinant or Innocent III.[2] In art, this iconographical motif enjoyed wide appeal; there are more than ninety murals in France, fifty in England and twenty in Italy, and new examples continue to be discovered. The iconographic tradition of the Legend soon made use of a polite form of the *maxim*, a short narrative poem of the exemplary type, sometimes written in the vernacular, in which the words of the Dead and the reactions of the Living are contrasted; different versions exist of these dialogues.[3]

Fig. 49. The Legend of the Three Living and the Three Dead, woodcut in Guy Marchant's expanded *Danse Macabre* edition of 1486.

The iconographic canon used to illustrate the encounter is usually organised within two different scenes that are confronted in a rhythmic alternation and situated on two opposing or contiguous walls. From one side a cortege of three men advances: kings, princes or nobles mounted on handsome steeds and carrying a falcon, with hounds following. This is the

---

[2] Mariantonia Liborio, 'Il sentimento della morte nella spiritualità dei secoli XII e XIII', in *Il dolore e la morte nella spiritualità dei secoli XII e XIII*, Todi, 7-10 October 1962 (Todi: Accademia Tudertina, 1967), 45-65.

[3] The Italian text is preserved in two compilations: the codex of the Biblioteca Communale, Ferrara, ms. cl. II, 211 (first half of the fifteenth century), and the Laurentian codex, plut. 90 inf. 13 (fifteenth century).

incipit of an adventure that has yet to become apparent. The characters are men of the world and, whether on foot or on horseback, they are determined to enjoy the good things in life. Even though they all belong to different age groups, they resemble each other in some way: they are either kings or nobles or gentlemen. In any case, they all belong – and this is the first notable difference with the participants of the later representations of the *Danse Macabre* – to a similar social category.

The fleeting moment represented in the initial scene in Italian depictions of the Legend is one of enjoyment which then gives way to confusion and terror: generally speaking, the animals are even more perturbed than the men themselves. One moment the hounds follow the cortege in festive mood and the falcons sit calmly on their masters' wrists; the next moment the scene changes. The men make stereotyped gestures as though preparing to flee from the sight of something unpleasant or an encounter with a deadly foe. They may express their horror or fear by stretching out their arms or raising one to heaven, holding their nose at the stench, or wringing their hands. It is futile for them to turn around or speak to their companions since the horrible vision will not vanish without having first spoken. One of the men sometimes tries to turn away, another follows suit, while the third starts praying. In rare cases, the person most affected by the scene appears to be the figure in front; sometimes the second man shows signs of preoccupation since he has not yet seen the apparition clearly; more often than not, it is the third man who shows signs of horror. They remain silent, although sometimes one of them seems about to break into a lament or to make a gesture of distress. They do not possess the words to defend themselves and thus resemble mute mannequins. It is this behaviour that further differentiates them from the protagonists of the *Danse Macabre* who have individual voices with which they try, albeit in vain, to convince Death to act out of character by showing mercy.

The cortege of three kings or noblemen bears a striking resemblance to what, in Christian art, is the royal cortege *par excellence*: that of the Magi on their journey to the manger of the Christ Child in Bethlehem. However, the visual journey of the approach of the Three Living leads to a completely different reaction: disgust and fear instead of adoration. Many of the physical gestures made by the three men can also be found in frescoes of the Magi: the act of turning back; speaking to a companion; looking into the distance (in the case of the Magi looking for the star); the same method of proceeding, on horseback and then on foot. Both corteges discover the truth; what distinguishes them is the method of the encounter. Whereas the Magi have set out to search the truth, for the Three Living the encounter is essentially fortuitous. On the other side of the fresco we have the Three Dead, not Death personified. As at least two of them have arisen and wish to speak, they might even be called living dead. The Dead are horrible to behold, and their depiction clearly aims to evoke disgust in the spectator. They do not belong to this world and their bodies indicate the more or less recent decay of their flesh with evident signs of putrefaction; they are not masquerading figures but real corpses, their decaying bodies being almost reduced to mere skeletal structures. The one advantage they have over the living is that they can speak: their banderoles which, unfortunately for us, are for the most part illegible, clarify the meaning of their appearance on the scene.

The juxtaposition of the two episodes illustrates the encounter between the three living figures and the three living-dead. Its aim is of a didactic, catechetic sort: the vision occurs in such a way that the people directly involved – the kings, nobles or gentlemen – turn over a new leaf through repentance. The intervention of the Three Dead is designed to provoke a reaction and to stimulate a new and different mode of behaviour. The cadaver figures do not wish to punish or to summon the living, but to warn. They are dead, or living-dead, and not Death: they speak and gesticulate, but they do not threaten or pose a mortal danger to the living. In comparison, the situation depicted in the *Danse Macabre* is quite different in that it is Death who instigates the dance, who determines the rhythm, and who registers the altogether useless responses of the living. For the characters who follow Death's lethal rhythm there is no way out: the game is over and the settling of accounts is inevitable.

The figure of the hermit and the depiction of the dead

Scholars who examined the typology of the scenes in question have shown how, in France, the location of the two groups on opposite sides visualises the confrontation between the Three Living and the Three Dead with the aim of arousing horror in the viewer and encouraging an examination of one's conscience, repentance, and new resolutions.[4] In Italy, however, it became customary from the beginning of the fifteenth century to insert a

---

[4] Stefan Glixelli, *Les cinq poèmes des trois morts et des trois vifs* (Paris: Librairie Ancienne Honoré Champion, 1914), 92-95; Liliane Guerry, *Le thème du 'Triomphe de la Mort' dans la peinture italienne* (Paris: Librairie orientale et Americaine, 1950), 'Le thème de la rencontre des vifs et des morts', 38-57, at 50-55.

new figure as a pivot between the two parties, *viz.* the hermit.[5] Liliane Guerry has suggested that the hermit was introduced to play 'le rôle de l'historien des mystères ou du récitant des oratorios' *(the role of the historian of sacred plays or of the singer of oratorios).*[6] In the opinion of Chiara Frugoni, it was the hermit's role to comment – as if from the wings of a stage – on the story represented in the fresco.[7] Furthermore, by assigning to the figure of the hermit the difficult task of presenting the story, the living-dead are reduced to silence: in the presence of the hermit, any intervention on their part would seem pleonastic.

In Italy this introduction of the hermit as the active agent meant that it was no longer necessary to represent the Dead as standing figures. Instead they became inactive recumbent figures, lying in their tombs and assuming a new character of the dead-dead. Thus developed the motif of the varying stages of bodily corruption that, in the Italian context, focused in particular on the visualisation of actual putrefaction.[8] Hence, the encounter gradually came to be interpreted in Italy as a meditation on death, its effects, and its victory over time, thereby giving rise to the theme of the Triumph of Death.[9] The iconography continued to develop. In the course of the fifteenth century, starting from central Italy, the often brutal image of the decay of the flesh was gradually replaced by the return of sepulchres and the more conventional image of skeletons. Indeed, in the early decades of the fifteenth century the skeleton had become the new and definitive form of Death personified in other 'macabre' contexts. In outlying areas and along the roads that led across the Alps, however, the inclusion of images of decaying corpses persisted for some time.

The situation in Italy is thus a curious one. Across the Angevin territories the depictions are mostly in accordance with the French typology that shows the Three Dead actively engaging the Three Living, whereas the purely Italian version with the hermit as the active agent

---

[5] Anna Maria Finoli, 'La figura dell'eremita nella letteratura antici-francese', in *L'eremitismo in Occidente nei secoli XI e XII,* Pubblicazioni dell'Università Cattolica del Sacro Cuore (Milan: Vita e Pensiero, 1965), 581-89, at 582-83.

[6] Guerry (1950), 38-57.

[7] Chiara Settis Frugoni, 'Il tema dell'incontro dei tre vivi e dei tre morti nella tradizione medievale italiana', *Memorie dell'Accademia dei Lincei, Classe di Scienze Morali,* series VIII, XIII, fasc. III (1967), 145-251, at 168.

[8] Compare also the depiction of cadaver effigies in Sophie Oosterwijk, 'Food for worms – food for thought: the appearance and interpretation of the "verminous" cadaver in Britain and Europe', *Church Monuments,* 20 (2005), 40-80, 133-40.

[9] Pierroberto Scaramella, 'The Italy of Triumphs and of Contrasts', in Alberto Tenenti (ed.), *Humana Fragilitas. The Themes of Death in Europe from the 13th to the 18th Century* (2000, trans. Clusone: Ferrari, 2002), 25-98.

almost disappears. In the south of Italy, the French influence favoured the diffusion of the Legend. The oldest example within the Italian tradition is probably the fresco in the church of St Margarita in Melfi, which cannot be dated exactly but must be c.1290.[10] The scene in the fresco appears to be of the 'French' type: opposite the three upright Living, the second of whom is wearing a small regal crown, we find the figures of the three living-dead standing outside their tombs and preparing to engage the Living in dialogue. The first of the Living, bearded and older than the others, is holding his falcon. All three Living are carrying a short sword and some type of money-bag hanging from their arm – perhaps a reference to their worldly preoccupations that is also often found in the *Danse*.[11]

Similar to the Melfi fresco, although of a later date, is the fresco in the abbey church of Fossanova (Latina), which can be dated to the beginning of the fifteenth century. Of the original fresco there remain the standing figures of the three noblemen who are facing two corpses emerging from their tombs. The movement of the hands of both groups suggest a willingness to enter into dialogue. In the same tradition, albeit with variations, is the fresco of c.1396 in the church of St Fermo in Verona. Here the three kings are standing up and scrutinising the tombs and their awful inmates. The words on the remaining banderole '[...] in omnibus rebus tuis ricordare [...]' (*remember in all your things*) echo the words of the central Living character who, with his right hand resting on the shoulder of his younger companion, seeks to comfort him. The motif of directing the gaze onto the contents of tombs was made popular at this time by the recitation of liturgical-type passages such as:

> Cum apertam sepolturam
> viri tres aspicerent
> ac horribilem figuram
> intus esse cernerent
> quendam scilicet jacentem
> hic recenter positum
> Immo totum putrescentem
> squalidum et fetidum

---

[10] For Melfi, see Roberto Ciasca, *La rappresentazione della vita e della morte nella 'laura' di Santa Margherita sul Vulture* (Todi: Accademia Tudertina, 1963), 335-64. The examples mentioned follow those cited in Frugoni (1967), with the additional insertion of new evidence that has recently come to light. My analysis in this case concentrates only on the mural representations, leaving a discussion of the iconographic examples on panels and triptychs for another occasion.
[11] See especially the essays by Tomislav Vignjević and Jutta Schuchard in this volume.

ossa inter et aliorum
jam nudata totaliter[12]

(When the tomb was opened
the three men saw
this horrible figure and immediately
understood that the corpse had not been
recently buried but was already
putrescent, squalid and stinking
with bones that had already been laid bare [...])

In these texts, attention was drawn to the impact of the scene on the senses of the living: visual, but also olfactory, and even almost tactile.

The figure of the hermit – popular in the Middle Ages because of the devotion to St Anthony Abbot – was himself a telling emblem of the vanity of earthly things. After all, hermits have renounced all worldly pleasures to seek a life of abstinence and solitude, as the Hermit in the French *Danse* also underlines with his mention of a 'vie dure ou solitaire' (*hard or solitary life*). Within depictions of the Three Living and the Three Dead it is the hermit's role to explain the meaning of an encounter that would otherwise be incomprehensible. His appearance within the Italian tradition renders the dead mute insofar as it is his exclusive task to explain the event. He has become the preacher *par excellence* and hence comes to occupy a vital role in the Christian tradition, halfway between the figure of the Old Testament prophet and he who will bear witness of what is to come. He is surrounded by the banderoles with texts that present the true meaning of the apparition. The hermit, probably in the guise of a member of the mendicant and preaching orders of monks, is the Church's response to the ever-growing taste for the horrible. Once the hermit makes his official appearance in the early fifteenth century, he plays an increasingly important role, as is shown by the examples of the Legend in Vezzolano, Subiaco and, most important of all, Pisa. The hermit becomes the only actor to speak on the scene: all the others listen to his words.

The progenitor, so to speak, of the group of frescoes of the Three Living and the Three Dead that show a mixture of the French and the Italian traditions, is the fresco in the cathedral of Atri (Teramo), dated between 1260 and 1270. In this case the juxtaposition of the upright noblemen and standing dead appears to be maintained but, in the background,

---

[12] The poem is preserved in two versions, one dating to the first half of the fifteenth century (Ferrara Central Library, MS class. II, 211) and the other also fifteenth-century in date (Florence Central Library, Laurenziano, Plut. 90 Inf. 13). See Frugoni (1967), 176-77.

the added figure of the hermit can also clearly be seen. The inscription running above the heads of the nobles partially refers to the discourse: '[...] quod sumus hoc eretis [...]' (*what we are you shall be ...*). Dating from almost a hundred years later, around 1362, is a fresco in the monastery of St Benedict in Subiaco. It is similar to that in Atri in that the nobles are in an upright position, the first with the traditional falcon, and also because it shows the variation of the hermit who gestures to the tomb in order to induce the Living to a contemplation of the Dead. At the same time, the Subiaco fresco is different to that in Atri in that the Dead are lying down, each in his own tomb, and with evident signs of the varying stages of the decomposition of their bodies.

At least one of the frescoes preserved in the church of Santa Maria at Vezzolano (Albugnano) clearly follows the Italian tradition. In fact, on the walls of the ancient cloister, there are two frescoes on the theme of the encounter between the Three Living and the Three Dead, of which the older one is only partially preserved.[13] The words that can still be made out – 'O res orida, res orida et stupenda' (*O horrid things, horrid and wondrous things*) – would seem to represent words spoken by the Living. In the church of Santa Maria at Vezzolano, the position of the knights, elegantly dressed and mounted on spirited steeds with their falcons ready to take flight, recalls that of the only living figure, a king, who can still be observed in the mural in the church of St Paolo in Poggio Mirteto (Rieti). This fresco, which can be dated between the end of the thirteenth and the beginning of the fourteenth centuries, also displays an inscription, just as at Vezzolano. This time in the Italian vernacular, the text relates to man's state of mind; '[...] perduto aio risu / e gioia, iocu et ale/gretia non m'è voglia [...]' (*I have lost laughter and joy, and do not want merriment*). Before him is the frightful spectacle of crowned corpses lying in their tombs. The inherent lesson of one of the *Laudi* of Jacopo da Todi 'Quando t'aliegre omo d'altura' (*When you rejoice, proud man*) finds, in this case, a solid and consistent application:

> Or me contempla oi omo mondano,
> mentr'èi nel mondo non esser pur vano;
> pènsate, folle, che a mano a mano
> tu serai messo en grande struttura [...][14]

---

[13] Lina Bolzoni, *Gli affreschi della Morte del Camposanto di Pisa e la predicazione domenicana*, in *La rete delle immagini. Predicazione in volgare dalle origini a Bernardino da Siena*, (Turin: Einaudi, 2002), 3-38. The remaining part that is still visible shows two knights on horseback, carrying falcons.
[14] Jacopone da Todi, *Laude*, ed. Franco Mancini (Bari: Laterza, 1974).

(Just think, worldly man
and do not pursue vain things,
think, fool, that bit by bit
you will be laid in your tomb.)

Even more important within the Italian context is the testimony provided by the second of the frescoes at Vezzolano, dated to the end of the thirteenth century. Here, in a single scene, we find juxtaposed to the left the three noble horsemen distraught at the sight of three bodies in varying states of decomposition, two of which are rising from the communal grave. At the centre of the scene, holding an explanatory banderole in one hand and pointing with the other to the grave, is a bearded monk in front of his chapel.[15] All the elements mentioned here can be found in the painting of the encounter of the Three Living and the Three Dead in the church of St Flaviano at Montefiascone (Viterbo), which can be dated to the early thirteenth century. On the left we see the three mounted knights enter, while on the opposite side there are two corpses with evident signs of putrefaction. The hermit is seen emerging from a grotto, holding in his hand a banderole of which the words have been lost but which may have begun with the word 'Pregate' (*Pray*).

We can include within the same narrative structure the remaining fresco in the chapel called Conte a San Giorio, in Val di Susa.[16] The cycle, dateable to the fourteenth century and currently undergoing restoration, shows the cortege of the three kings blocked by the frightful spectacle of two corpses who rise from their tombs and whose bodies show different degrees of putrefaction. As customary by now, the hermit is assigned the task of explaining, by means of banderoles, the meaning of the vision. We can also find quite nearby in the church of St Francesco in Val di Susa another fresco dateable to the fifteenth century, which follows the same composition as the one already discussed. It is highly significant in that it represents the iconographic development of the Legend of the Three Living and Three Dead along the routes that led pilgrims to Rome and to Santiago de Compostela.[17] Furthermore, also in Susa, on one side of the church of the Madonna del Ponte there can be seen another fresco dealing with the same subject.

---

[15] The combination with the scene of the three Magi in the Adoration of the Child above serves to justify the positioning of the characters in the Legend.

[16] Luisella Ceretta, *Vita del Medioevo nei dipinti della Val Susa tra X e XV secolo* (Sant'Ambrogio, Turin: Susalibri, 2004), 97-104.

[17] Ceretta (2004), 124.

At the beginning of the fifteenth century, with the advent of Humanism, skeletons – once a common motif in Antiquity but not in earlier medieval art – came back into fashion as opposed to decomposing bodies. The signs of decomposition disappear and the focus shifts instead to the more attractive imagery of the elegant art of hunting and the nobles enjoying this pursuit. The Church itself, which was keen to teach respect for the body as the temple of the Holy Spirit, could not countenance its being treated so brutally in art. In the same way the figures in the *Danse Macabre* were to become skeletons over time – as fleshless as their message.

The large fresco of the Triumph of Death in the Camposanto of Pisa, painted by Buonamico Buffalmacco in the early decades of the fourteenth century, also deals with the encounter of the Three Living and the Three Dead against a background of grandiose scenery.[18] On the left, separated by a ridge of rocks, a merry band of knights and ladies are brought up short by the sight of three open coffins. Three of the most elegant knights in the foreground, riding horses that are fully decked out, are wearing a crown: one of them is holding his nose because of the stench, just as in the fresco of Poggio Mirteto.[19] The Dead, of whom at least one is a prelate and one a king, clearly show signs of varying degrees of putrefaction as they lie in their coffins, suffering the progressive decay of the flesh. Near the coffins stands the hermit, bearded and stooping, and holding a banderole to the content of which he is pointing with the other hand.[20] In the woods behind him another four of his companions are intent on carrying out separate activities; they recall the time of the great hermits such as St Anthony of the Desert and St Paul the Anchorite, emphasising as they do by the simple fact of their presence the lesson of the vanity of earthly things.

We find a variation of the above elements in a fresco in the church of Santa Maria dos Regnos Altos at Bosa (Sardinia), datable to between 1340 and 1345.[21] Here the kings are standing and the first of them is holding a

[18] Luciano Bellosi, *Buffalmacco e il Trionfo della Morte* (Turin: Einaudi, 1974); Lina Bolzoni, *La Rete delle Immagini*, translated as *The web of images: vernacular preaching from its origins to St. Bernardino da Siena* (Farnham: Ashgate, 2004), chapter 1.

[19] This was quite a widespread motif that can also be found in scenes of the Raising of Lazarus.

[20] The hermit in the Camposanto fresco is sometimes interpreted as St Macarius. For other suggestions, see Frugoni (1967), 171.

[21] Fernanda Poli, *La chiesa del Castello di Bosa: gli affreschi di Nostra Signora de Los Regnos Altos* (Sassari: EDES, 1999); see Corrado Zedda, 'Gli Arborea e gli

falcon, while the hermit is holding a long banderole and the three Dead are in their tombs, as in the Camposanto fresco. The cycle in the church of St Luca in Cremona is much more simplified in its narrative rhythm but it repeats the same scene. Dateable to 1425, it shows the cortege of three knights on horseback at a crossroads where they find an uncovered communal grave. At least one of the knights is a king who is also carrying a cheetah on his horse; he is turned towards the knight beside him, while the third is holding out his arms in amazement. The corpses are recumbent and each show different stages of decomposition. The hermit displays the banderoles that explain the vision and there is a small church behind him. The fresco in the church of Santa Maria in Sylvis at Sesto al Reghena, dateable to the middle of the fifteenth century, also belongs to the same typology. The king on horseback is looking back at his companions, one of whom is carrying a falcon while the other is wringing his hands. The corpses are once again recumbent, as in the previous examples. The hermit, standing in front of his hut, is presenting his banderole. The halo round his head is a sign of the growing importance of this character.

Apart from the typologies of the Three Living and the Three Dead that we have mentioned, there is yet another variation of representing an encounter between the living and the living-dead. This new variant bears similarities both with the encounter of the Three Living and with the *Danse Macabre*. This time the encounter is between the living-dead and a group of pilgrims, sometimes incorrectly called a 'predica della morte' (*Sermon of Death*). The fifteenth-century fresco that depicts this is preserved in the old choir of the abbey of San Michele della Chiusa in Turin (Fig. 50a-b and Pl. 9a). In this fresco two living-dead – one standing and the other lying in his tomb – are displaying the messages on their banderoles to a compact, dumbstruck crowd that consists of a pope, a king and queen, a cardinal, a bishop, noblemen and poor people, ecclesiastics and laymen: an ensemble of stereotypes from different layers of society that we also find in the *Danse Macabre*. One of the banderoles, written in French, reads 'O vous qui pour ici passe prie Dieu pour les trapasse, car leur donne comme vos avoint ete et leur comme nous sare' (*Oh you who pass this way, pray God to pardon the dead as you have been pardoned and as we shall be pardoned*).

affreschi della chiesa di Nostra Signora de Los Regnos Altos a Bosa', *Archivio storico e giuridico sardo di Sassari*, 3 (1996), 135-65.

Fig. 50a-b. Encounter between death and a group of pilgrims from all walks of life, sometimes described as a 'predica della morte' (*Sermon of Death*) or 'predica dei morti' (*Sermon of the Dead*), fifteenth-century fresco in the abbey of San Michele della Chiusa, Turin. Photo: author.

Conclusion

The examples discussed here illustrate the popularity between the thirteenth and fifteenth centuries of the Legend of the Three Living and the Three Dead within a geographic area that appears to stretch from Piedmont to Sardinia and along the pilgrimage routes to France, Rome and Bari. The theme evidently enjoyed a greater popularity than the *Danse Macabre* ever did in these same territories from the fifteenth century on.

The encounter between the living and the living-dead is less critical of religion and the Church, and contributed – alongside other manifestations of popular piety and spirituality – to a Christian reflection on the inevitable necessity for preparing for death. The interpretation of the motif of the encounter in Italy shows a particular sensitivity towards the figure of the hermit and the idea of the passage of time represented by the putrefaction of the body, thus adhering to a heightened sensitivity to which the *Laude* of Jacopo Da Todi contributed in no small measure. Over time, the image lost its ability to shock and became more domesticated and oriented towards a more sober and 'politically correct' catechesis.

Of course, medieval Italy could also boast an encounter between a living man and a dead woman. In this case, however, the dead woman was beautiful and splendidly luminous, and still open to a smiling dialogue with a man: in short, she was Dante's Beatrice in Paradise. There is nothing in her of the mortal, the horrid or the macabre; not a sense of an end, but of a beginning. Naturally in Beatrice we are dealing with a celestial personage, light years away from the problems and fears of the world, and one who lived exclusively in the memory of her beloved, and to him alone showed herself as a pilgrim of heaven: 'res stupenda'.

Acknowledgements

I am grateful to the editors for their invitation to contribute an essay and for their editorial input. Unfortunately it was not possible to provide more illustrations of the murals discussed in this paper.

DEATH PERSONIFIED IN MEDIEVAL IMAGERY: THE MOTIF OF DEATH RIDING A BOVINE*

SYLVIE BETHMONT-GALLERAND

In his *Dialogus Miraculorum* Caesarius of Heisterbach (*c.*1180-*c.*1240) has a novice make an interesting observation: 'Quidam putant mortem esse personam, quibus concordat quod mors in specie hominis cum falce in picturis repraesentatur' (*Some people think that Death is a person, in accordance with the pictorial representation of Death as a man holding a scythe*).[1] Although Caesarius does not accept this representation, which he considers to be an error originating in the Old Testament, the excerpt proves that this now familiar personification of Death was already anchored in the minds of medieval people and in the fine arts.

Different personifications of Death have been in use since the early Middle Ages. Unlike German where *der Tod* is masculine, French uses the feminine *la mort*, although the gender of Death varies in medieval art and literature throughout Europe. Early representations of Death in monstrous guises made way for the image of Death as a woman, based on the early association of death with sin.[2] Depictions of Death personified occur in murals dating back to the thirteenth century in churches in Atri near Rome and in Santa Margherita in Melfi. At that time, on the portals of French cathedrals such as in Paris, Amiens and Reims, Death is portrayed as a blindfolded cadaverous woman falling from an emaciated horse.

---

* There is no English equivalent for the French noun *bœuf*, which covers all varieties of bovine animals. As this paper will show, Death's mount is sometimes an unmistakable cow with udders, but in other depictions an ox may be implied.

[1] Caesarius Heisterbacensis, *Dialogus Miraculorum*, XI, 61, ed. Joseph Strange (Cologne, Bonn, Brussels: J.M. Heberle, 1851), vol. 2, 312 ; Jean Wirth, *La jeune fille et la Mort, recherche sur les thèmes macabres dans l'art germanique de la Renaissance* (Geneva: Droz, 1979), 31, n. 65.

[2] See the discussion in Jill Bradley, *'You Shall surely not Die'. The Concepts of Sin and Death as Expressed in the Manuscript Art of Northwestern Europe, c. 800-1200* (Leiden/Boston: Brill, 2008), 2 volumes.

In the later Middle Ages one single image – the cadaver – condensed different meanings. A lifelike responsive cadaver could represent the deathlike counterpart or *alter ego* of a living person, as in illustrations of the Legend of the Three Living and the Three Dead (*Dict des trois morts et des trois vifs*) and arguably in the *Danse Macabre*, but also a ghost, a revenant, or Death personified.[3] Even if we ignore the debate about the nature of the protagonists – whether Death or the dead – in the *Danse*, it is evident that Death could adopt many different guises in medieval art. This essay will focus on one specific and rather unusual iconographic motif within the wider spectrum of macabre imagery, *viz.* that of Death riding a bovine mount – either a cow or an ox. There are other variations of Death riding an animal in medieval iconography, however, which need to be addressed first.

Death as a rider

The various medieval personifications of Death share one important characteristic: they evoke the idea of 'unbridled, invisible and harsh Death armed with a sharp scythe' who bursts in unexpectedly to strike 'him who thought he was safe from his impending blows', to use the words attributed to Archbishop Ubaldino Buonamici by Coluccio Salutati in the late fourteenth century.[4]

However, a slow, natural demise seems to have been commonly preferred to a sudden death as it offered the dying a chance of a good *translatio* from this life into the next. This is why the most graphic expression for the terror of sudden death seems to have been that of Death riding a galloping horse. Thus sudden death – the worst of all calamities – comes as if flying, riding the pale horse (*equus pallidus*) of St John's Book of Revelation in the Vulgate Bible: 'And behold a pale horse, and he that sat upon him, his name was Death, and Hell followed him. And power was given to him over the four parts of the earth, to kill with sword, with famine, and with death, and with the beasts of the earth' (Revelation 6:8).

---

[3] The earliest images of the Legend of the Three Living and the Three Dead may have appeared in France in mural paintings at Mont Saint-Michel Abbey and Notre-Dame-des-Doms in Avignon. For the Legend, see Groupe International de Recherches sur les peintures murales (eds), *Vifs nous sommes, morts nous serons. La rencontre des trois morts et des trois vifs dans la peinture murale en France* (Vendôme: Editions du Cherche-lune, 2001), and also the essays by Christine Kralik, Marco Piccat and Kenneth Rooney in this volume.

[4] Coluccio Salutati, *Epistolario*, II, ed. Fr. Novati (Rome: Forzani, 1891-1911), 125, letter of 30 October 1383.

Representations of Death personified riding a pale horse occur in Flemish illuminations around 1400 and early printed Bibles such as the Quentell-Koberger incunable of *c.*1479, as well as in woodcuts published in Strasburg in 1485 and Albrecht Dürer's engravings dating from 1497-98. The horse may be swift or walking with confidence, as in the series of Apocalypse Tapestries at Angers from the end of the fourteenth century.[5] It may also be near-skeletal itself to match its rider (Fig. 51).

Fig. 51. Albrecht Dürer, *The Four Horsemen of the Apocalypse*, woodcut, 1498. © The British Library.

---

[5] In the first of these Tapestries, Death features as a rider in the twelfth panel that shows the opening of the fourth seal (I.12).

Either way, the apocalyptic horse that carries Death in triumph is an image conceived by artists in the mid fourteenth century, most notably in Italy where the *Trionfi* had developed as a separate motif. With a scythe, bow and arrows as her attributes, Death is painted as an old but strong woman riding a galloping black horse in a fresco by Bartholomeo de Fredi at Lucigiano near Arezzo, dating to the second half of the fourteenth century. At the same time, artists begin to portray Death in her triumph as a skeleton, as we can see in the fresco of the Scala Santa of the Sacro Speco at Subiaco (Rome). Triumphal Death is also galloping on the *equus pallidus* in the centre of the mid-fifteenth-century mural from the Palazzo Sclafani, Palermo (now in the Galleria regionale della Sicilia).[6] An interesting variation because of its relevance to the *Danse Macabre* is the marginal scene on fol. 163r at the start of the Office of the Dead in a Parisian book of hours of *c.*1440 (Pl. 1).[7] It shows Death on a horse galloping towards the Emperor and the Pope – traditionally the first two characters in the *Danse* – while raising a red dart for the attack. His mount is both strong and swift here, and its coat not pale but black: the colour of evil and decay.

We may also find Death progressing slowly while riding a worn-out – but not necessarily skeletal or pale – horse in other contexts. It is in this manner that Death approaches Provost Sixtus Tucher (1459-1507) in two stained-glass windows originally made for Tucher's study in the country house to which he retired in 1504.[8] Pieter Bruegel the Elder chose to give his representations of Death both an emaciated but speeding mount and an exhausted cart-horse in his *Triumph of Death* (1562-63, Prado, Madrid). However, to express his slow but inexorable way of coming, artists sometimes prefer to give Death a less noble mount.

---

[6] See also the rich iconographic variety presented in Alberto Tenenti (ed.), *Humana Fragilitas. The Themes of Death in Europe from the 13th to the 18th Century* (Clusone: Ferrari, 2002), esp. in the essay by Pierroberto Scaramella, 'The Italy of Triumphs and of Contrasts', 25-98, esp. figs 21-23 for the frescoes at Lucignano, Subiaco and Palermo, respectively.

[7] I am grateful to Sophie Oosterwijk for drawing my attention to this example.

[8] Two trefoil stained-glass panels, attributed to an artist in the circle of Albrecht Dürer, probably the Benedict Master, Germanisches Nationalmuseum, Nuremberg. See Sophie Oosterwijk, '"For no man mai fro dethes stroke fle". Death and *Danse Macabre* Iconography in Memorial Art', *Church Monuments*, 23 (2008), 62-87, 166-68, at 77 and col.pls 3a-b; Corine Schleif, 'The Proper Attitude Toward Death: Windowpanes Designed for the House of Canon Sixtus Tucher', *Art Bulletin*, 69 (1987), 587-603.

Fig. 52. A blindfolded figure of Death on a cow pursuing a young horseman, marginal decoration in the Amiens Missal (The Hague, Royal Library, KB MS 78 D 40, fol. 154v), 1323. © The Hague, Royal Library.

Death riding a bovine

If he is riding neither the swift and terrifying pale horse of the Apocalypse, nor an exhausted thin horse matching its skeleton-like rider, Death can ride an animal very common in the countryside and the loyal bovine companion of the ploughman: a cow, an ox or an heifer. It was the Dutch historian Johan Huizinga[9] who first cited, as evidence for earlier occurrences of the motif, *Der Ackermann von Böhmen* (*The Ploughman of Bohemia*) of *c.*1400 by the Bohemian author Johannes von Tepl (or Johannes von Saaz, *c.*1350-*c.*1415).[10] This important early humanist poem, which was first printed in 1460 and also survives in a number of manuscript copies, is a dialogue between Death and the Ploughman who has recently lost his wife Margaretha. The grieving widower accuses Death of having bereft him of his wife, while Death replies with cynicism. Their debate centres on key

---

[9] Johan Huizinga, *L'Automne du Moyen Age* (transl. 1932, new edn Paris: Payot, 2002), n. 1, 220, with a reference to Konrad Burdach, *Der Ackermann aus Böhmen*, Vom Mittelalter zur Reformation, III, 1 (1917), 243-49. This brief paragraph does not occur in either the early or the more recent English translations of Huizinga's book.

[10] James C. Thomas, *Johannes von Tepl. Der Ackermann aus Böhmen* (Berne: Peter Lang, 1990); R.M. Kully, 'Le laboureur de Bohème et son process contre la Mort', in Claude Sutto (ed.), *Le sentiment de la Mort au Moyen Age*, Fifth Colloquium of the Institute for Medieval Studies, University of Montreal (Montreal: l'Aurore, 1979), 140-67. For a modern English translation online, see the website http://www.michaelhaldane.com/Husbandman%20and%20Death.pdf; a manuscript version of *c.*1470 with illuminations is available online at http://diglit.ub.uni-heidelberg.de/diglit/cpg76/ (both accessed 23 September 2010).

questions about life, humanity and morality, so there are obvious parallels with the *Danse.*

Huizinga also mentioned that the motif of Death riding an ox or a cow can be found much earlier still in the Amiens Missal of 1323 (The Hague, Royal Library, KB MS 78 D 40). This festal missal was copied by Garnerus de Morolio with Petrus de Raimbaucourt as the illuminator and made for Johannes de Marchello, abbot of the Premonstratensian abbey of Saint-Jean-sur-la-Celle in Amiens.[11] It contains not one but two examples of the motif. In the margin of fol. 154v, a skeleton-like blindfolded figure of Death armed with a spear and a coffin is pursuing a young horseman (Fig. 52). Death's bovine mount is unmistakably a cow, for its udders are clearly visible.

Another marginal image on fol. 91r of the Amiens Missal shows a galloping cow as a mount for Death, again with udders clearly in evidence (Pl. 9b). However, its skeleton-like rider is aiming its spear at a rather peculiar opponent, *viz.* a woman mounted on a lion and carrying a hunting bird. This woman seems like an inversion of the traditional opponent of Death: the allegorical figure of Fortitude. The chicken foot in the woman's right hand was used in the medieval training of birds of prey, here perhaps a goshawk: it is called a *tiroir* as it was used to train the bird to pull the rein (jess), but it also served to distract its attention as a tasty light snack while keeping it hungry and ready for hunting. The fact that we observe the hawk face-on suggests a satirical purpose.[12] The date of the Amiens Missal proves that the motif predates *Der Ackermann.*

The Amiens Missal is not just unusual in featuring two examples of the motif of Death riding a bovine, but also because of the exceptionally early date of their occurrence. Tracing the motif thereafter is difficult until around 1460 when the motif spread to the Office of the Dead in books of hours, which did not have a fixed iconography.[13] It appeared in the

---

[11] These examples are also discussed in Hellmut Rosenfeld, *Der mittelalterliche Totentanz, Entstehung, Entwicklung, Bedeutung*, Beihefte zum Archiv für Kulturgeschichte, no. 3 (Münster/Cologne: Böhlau Verlag, 1954) 8, 15, 18, 24-27, and figs 2-3, 9.

[12] Hubert Beaufrère, *Lexique de la chasse au vol. Terminologie française du XVIe au XXe siècles,* Bibliotheca cynegetica, 4 (Nogent-le-Roi: Laget, 2004), vol. 23, 357-58. Images of the *tiroir* can be found in Frederick II of Hohenstaufen's *L'art de chasser avec les oiseaux* of c.1305-10, illuminated for Guillaume de Dampierre by Simon of Orléans (BnF, ms. fr. 12400, fols 151-157), as reproduced in Marie-Hélène Tesnière, *Bestiaire médiéval, enluminures* (Paris: BnF, 2005), 175-92, figs 93-95.

[13] See especially the essay by Caroline Zöhl in this volume.

margins alongside images of Death seizing the living, the Legend of the Three Living and the Three Dead, the *Danse Macabre*, the resurrection of Lazarus, the repentance of King David, the story of Job, and scenes of funeral masses and burials. A single illuminated page with the rubric of the Office of the Dead, probably from an early-sixteenth-century book of hours (now in the graphic collection 'Mensch und Tod', University of Düsseldorf), is a late, somewhat naive example of this motif (Pl. 10).

The brutal obviousness of inexorable Death – visualised as a sudden gallop – is also the message of the opening miniature of the Office of the Dead in the fifteenth century De Croÿs book of Hours (Paris, Bibliothèque de l'Assemblée nationale, Ms. 11, fol. 93r, Pl. 11). Two characteristic motifs of the Amiens Missal, *viz.* the nobleman and the galloping cow, are brought together in this miniature. A hawk is flying away as its owner (a young nobleman) is transfixed by Death, who looks rather like a Moorish knight with his spurs, scimitar and buckler. Death is riding a galloping ox, which has a shroud tied around its neck. Perhaps to emphasise speed, the ox is saddled and Death even wears spurs. This scene of aggression is set in a cemetery, as indicated by the tomb on the right below Death's elbow, the ossuary on the left, and the chapel of the dead in the background. Some flowers in full bloom – traditionally an emblem of transience – may reinforce the idea of the suddenness of death.

The De Croÿs image of a young nobleman surprised by Death can be linked with depictions of the Legend of the Three Living and the Three Dead. Like the Three Living, he is young, noble and out hunting, *i.e.* in the midst of life when confronted by Death. However, there are also similarities with the *Danse Macabre* in which dancers become isolated in single pairings with Death when the *Danse* is developed as a decorative motif in marginalia and sculpture – a development that has made scholars question the application of the term *Danse Macabre*.[14]

Variations of the motif of Death on a cow or an ox occur elsewhere. One example is the miniature illustrating the Office of the Dead in another French book of hours (use of Poitiers) of *c*.1455-60 (Paris, BnF, nouv. acq. lat. 3191, fol. 100v). It is reminiscent of King René's famous *memento mori* miniature in the Hours of René d'Anjou of *c*.1442-43 (London, British Library, Egerton MS 1070, fol. 53r) in showing an improbably gigantic corpse emerging from a coffin and holding a shinbone in its

---

[14] See also the essay by Jutta Schuchard in this volume.

hand.[15] Below this miniature in the lower margin of fol. 100v, Death has once again chosen an ox as his mount for a joust at walking speed with a man who is already defeated: he is shown with his spear broken and arrows deeply embedded in his body.

Fig. 53. Death riding a bovine, misericord in the church of Saint-Adrien, Pocé-sur-Cisse (Indre-et-Loire), late fifteenth century. Photo: author.

The motif of Death riding a cow or ox was first recognised and published by Alexandre de Laborde, who claimed that it originated in *La danse des aveugles* (Dance of the Blind) by the fifteenth-century rhetorician Pierre Michault.[16] As we have seen, he was corrected by Huizinga regarding the source. Amongst other examples of this motif, de Laborde described a misericord in the choir stalls at Pocé-sur-Cisse as follows: 'Il y a au-dessous de la Dame de Miséricorde [*sic*] un motif de la Mort tenant de la main gauche une faux [*sic*] portant sur l'épaule droite un cercueil, elle chevauche un boeuf très caractérisé' (*There is beneath the*

---

[15] See http://molcat1.bl.uk/illcat/TourPopup.asp?TourID=159 (accessed 30 September 2010), also illustrated in T.S.R. Boase, *Death in the Middle Ages: Mortality, Judgment and Remembrance* (London: Thames and Hudson, 1972), fig. 108.

[16] Laborde was unaware of examples prior to 1460. See Comte Alexandre de Laborde, *La Mort chevauchant un bœuf, origine de cette illustration de l'Office des Morts dans certains livres d'heures du XVe siècle* (Paris: Francisque Lefrançois, 1923), 21.

Lady of Mercy [read: the misericord] *a motif of Death holding by his left hand a scythe* [*sic*: it is a dart] *and carrying on the right shoulder a coffin, while riding a cow full of character*). This motif in the church of Saint-Adrien in Pocé-sur-Cisse (Indre-et-Loire) is unique in the art of misericord carving (Fig. 53). The misericord originally came from the ancient Cistercian abbey of Fontaine-les-Blanches and dates to the late fifteenth century. The carving shows a sniggering eviscerated cadaver holding the traditional attributes of Death, a coffin, and a spear, javelin or dart. This allegorical representation of Death is riding a seemingly good-natured ox whose legs are bent under its body as if it is about to kneel down. Unfortunately the nature of this unusual motif has often been misunderstood, which has resulted in either the rider or the mount being misinterpreted. The misericord has been described as a woman with her cow by some, while others misidentified Death as a witch.[17] Moreover, while the animal is unmistakably bovine, one recent author considered the possibility of its being a horse instead.[18]

One might assume that this new iconographical variation was intended to emphasise the obstinacy of Death who always ends up as the winner. Although arrows and coffins had been attributes of Death in pictures and texts since the fourteenth century, they took on a new moral value in the fifteenth century, as we can see in the misericord at Pocé-sur Cisse. The coffin that Death carries on his shoulder reflects burial practice at that time: the use of coffins was abandoned from the fifth century until the late fourteenth century, when it became common once again.[19] More than a mere indication of changes in social custom, this coffin not only symbolises

---

[17] For the claim that the misericord shows a woman and her cow, see Dorothy and Henry Kraus, *Le monde caché des miséricordes* (Paris: Les Éditions de l'amateur, 1986), 206 (translated from The *Hidden World of Misericords* (New York: Braziller, 1975). The alternative explanation of a witches' Sabbath was proposed by the editors of *Stalles, miséricordes, spiritualité et truculence*, *Arts Sacrés*, Cahiers de l'association 'Rencontres avec le Patrimoine Religieux', 12 (2000), 183.
[18] Elaine C. Block, *Corpus of Medieval Misericords: France* (Turnhout: Brepols, 2003), 77, fig. 302: 'Death rides horned animal [...] The horse, or bull, is lying, with its feet tucked under'. The misericord at Pocé-sur-Cisse is not realistic: the animal has a small head on a long neck, and short legs, similar to another such unrealistic mammal on a misericord of the mid fifteenth century in the chapel of All Souls' College in Oxford, which suggests the use of patterns.
[19] According to Victor Gay and Henri Stein, *Dictionnaire archéologique du Moyen Age et de la Renaissance* (Paris: Picard, 1928), 299, the earliest known occurrence of the use of a coffin for burial was in 1317.

death but also suggests a new moral sense.[20] There is an analogy with the allegory of Prudence, who is represented as a shrouded corpse in an illuminated manuscript of the *Nicomachean Ethics* that was translated into French by Nicolas Oresme (1376).[21] Since the fifteenth century, the virtue of Prudence has been represented with a sieve and a coffin because she sifts things of this world without ever forgetting the Four Last Things (Death, the Last Judgement, Heaven and Hell).[22]

Likewise, a spear, a long arrow or a bundle of arrows visualise the sting of Death in the majority of images of Death personified from the late fifteenth century on. For St Paul this sting, this stimulus that excites and pushes us, is sin since 'the sting of death is sin' (1 Cor. 15:56). The arrow is also the emblem of punishment, an instrument of God as much as of Satan (Eph. 6:16). God sends cursed arrows and Job experiences their bitterness, 'For the arrows of the almighty are in me, my spirit drinks their poison; the terrors of God are arrayed against me' (Job 6:4). Such arrows that cause painful wounds can actually be salutary for a person wounded by sin, for they warn him of the peril of death, thereby making him full of remorse so that he mends his ways.

Riding an ox, holding a dart and a coffin, the image of Death on the misericord at Pocé-sur-Cisse can likewise be understood as a combination of related messages to the viewer: a pious reminder about the Four Last Things, a call to the virtue of prudence, and an invitation to meditate on salvation.

Sources and parallels

Improbable as the motif of Death riding such an unusual mount might seem, it must be remembered that oxen and cows have long been associated with Death. In the Bible a red heifer is the animal chosen for the sacrifice in the Temple (Num. 19:1-10). The ox is one of the four animals, the Tetramorph, described by Ezekiel and the Book of Revelation (Ez.:1, 5; Rev.: 4, 7-8). The Fathers of the Church saw the four animals as symbols of the Evangelists; the ox stands for St Luke and as such it refers to the

---

[20] Compare the figure of Death as a woman with a coffin in *Miroër de vie et de mort* (1266), Paris, Sainte-Geneviève Library, ms. 2200, fol. 166r.

[21] The Hague, Museum Meermanno Westreenianum, ms. 10 D. 1, fol. 110r.

[22] Illustrating the *Pélerinage de la vie humaine*, the fourteenth-century Paris illuminator Pierre Remiet gave Death a coffin as his attribute (Paris, BnF ms. fr. 823, fol. 94): see Michael Camille, *Master of Death. The Lifeless Art of Pierre Remiet, Illuminator* (New Haven and London, Yale University Press, 1996).

Passion of Christ.[23] Furthermore, an ox may be slaughtered for the funeral meal. In order to save fodder, butchers kill many oxen in November – the month of the dead, as celebrated on All Souls' Day – which is illustrated by scenes of slaughter in calendar images in books of hours. Moreover, since Carolingian times a cart pulled by oxen has been used for funerals irrespective of the rank of the deceased – whether a peasant or the relics of an illustrious saint [24]. During the Middle Ages a cow could also take its place in the funeral cortege of peasants in northern European countries.[25]

Yet for the visual origins of the motif we should perhaps look not at Northern European death imagery, but at the development of the theme of the Triumph of Death in Italy.[26] Whereas Death originally rode a horse, as envisaged in the Book of Revelation, a new type of imagery was introduced that saw him riding on a cart instead. In fifteenth-century Italian mural paintings, illuminated manuscripts and easel paintings of the Triumph, the triumphal carriage of Death is commonly pulled by black oxen which are progressing slowly while trampling a crowd of people from all walks of life, rather like the victims in the *Danse Macabre*.

This particular variation of Death riding on a triumphal carriage pulled by oxen had its origins in the *Trionfi* by the poet Francesco Petrarca or Petrarch (1304-74). In the *Trionfi* the poet has a vision of a series of allegorical pageants reminiscent of ancient Roman triumphal processions. The work consists of separate parts, the earliest of which are *The Triumph of Love* and *The Triumph of Chastity*, both probably written in the 1340s. It was after the outbreak in 1348 of the Black Death (which killed Petrarch's muse Laura) that the poet wrote *The Triumph of Death*, which was followed first by *The Triumph of Fame* and finally by *The Triumph of Time* and *The Triumph of Eternity*. Petrarch continued working on the different parts so that the *Trionfi* were still unfinished at his death.

---

[23] F. Cabrol, *Dictionnaire d'Archéologie Chrétienne et de Liturgie (DACL),* vol. 5, (Paris, Letouzey et Ane, 1922-23), col. 845-52.

[24] For example, the power over death of St Vincent and his companions, whose corpses are too heavy for oxen to pull, as illustrated by Pierre Remiet in the *Miroir historial* (Paris, BnF, ms. fr. 312, fol. 219v): see Camille (1996), 205, fig. 152.

[25] Danièle Alexandre-Bidon, ' Le bœuf de saint Luc', in *Aurochs, le retour: aurochs, vaches et autres bovins de la Préhistoire à nos jours*, museum catalogue (Lons-le-Saulnier: Centre jurassien du Patrimoine, 1994), 131-37.

[26] While Death rides swiftly in the Pisa and Clusone paintings, it rides a slow and brutish ox in the illuminations of his triumphs. Compare Paris, BnF, ms. lat. 1377, 87v, ms. fr. 223, fol. 123v, and ms. fr. 594, fol. 135; Avignon, BM, ms. Rés. 203, fol. 3v G3v.

Written in *terza rima*, the *Trionfi* were probably Petrarch's most popular and highly regarded work at the time: over 300 manuscript copies are known, many of them lavishly illuminated with individual miniatures of each of the triumphs, while a printed edition appeared as early as 1470. Moreover, the *Trionfi* were highly influential in inspiring artists working in all media: related imagery can be found not just in woodcuts and engravings, but also in tapestries, stained glass, frescoes,[27] and even on decorated armour.[28] There are thus many illustrations of the *Triumph of Death* that involve Death riding on a cart, such as a miniature in a French manuscript that shows Death wearing a black shroud and holding his scythe like a standard (Pl. 12).[29] In another manuscript dated 1503 (BnF, ms. fr. 594), the French translation of Petrarch's text is accompanied by the commentaries of Bernardo da Pietro Lapini da Montalcino (called Illicino) that were first published in 1475 and then frequently re-edited. The luxurious BnF manuscript was produced at Rouen for King Louis XII (1462-1515). The anonymous artist, now known as the Master of Petrarch's *Triumphs*, introduced here an innovation by dividing each triumph into a type of diptych. Death is shown thrice, each time with a black bovine. The first miniature on fol. 134v shows the victory of Death over Reason, in which Death on a black bovine mount is being preceded by Laura holding a banner, the Roman commander Scipio Africanus, Penelope, and the allegorical figure of 'Bon vouloir' (*Goodwill*). This is followed by the second image of the 'diptych', which shows the actual triumph of Death as he is trampling Laura's body while riding his cart pulled by four black bovines (fol. 135r). In these two images, Death is holding a black scythe and wearing a black shroud, while a snake is wound round his body – a detail derived from Illicino's commentaries on Petrarch's text. The first image of the next diptych shows the victory of Fame over Death (fol. 178v), with Fame blowing a trumpet and bringing down Death who is riding Laura's hearse pulled by four black bovines.[30]

---

[27] In Lorenzo Costa's 1490 painting of the *Triumph of Death* (San Giacomo Maggiore, Bologna), Triumphal Death holding a scythe has climbed onto a carriage pulled by two black oxen, both of which are ridden by a skeleton-like riders. See Scaramella (2002), 47-49 and fig. 28.

[28] For an illustration of this scene in an illuminated *Trionfi* manuscript, see Paris, BnF, ms. fr. 12423, fol. 37v.

[29] Examples include Florence, National Library, cod. Pal., fol. 22r, copied in Naples (1456); Paris, BnF ms. ital. 545, fol. 30v; and Francesco of Antonio del Chierico's illumination in Milan, Bibliotheca Trivulziana, cod. 905, fol. 171v.

[30] François Avril and Nicole Reynaud, *Les manuscrits à peintures en France, 1440-1520* (Paris: Flammarion/Bibliothèque nationale de France, 1994), 415-17.

Transfixed by a man behind the hearse, the greyish body of Death defeated is no longer wrapped in his triumphal shroud.

According to Liliane Guerry, however, the carriage of Death in the illustrations of the *Trionfi* of Petrarch is most probably based not on examples from Antiquity but on the type of theatrical cart processions that took place in Italy during carnival in *charivaris* from the fourteenth to the sixteenth centuries.[31] These processions featured a cart containing a crowd of corpses who carry the attributes of death, such as coffins, arrows, the scythe and the hourglass, whereas in Italian illustrations of the *Trionfi*, Death is perched alone on his cart, wielding a scythe.

Yet there are other parallels or potential sources for the motif of riding a cow or an ox, most notably the above-mentioned *La Danse aux aveugles*, written by Pierre Michault who was attached to the Burgundian court in the later fifteenth century. This rhetorical play of 1464 is a variation on the *Danse Macabre* and features *Amour*, *Fortune* and *Mort* as the three dancing blind.[32] They are the protagonists of chance and the ever-changing world, and although 'l'homme chaste' (*the chaste man*) does not let them have any grip on him, eventually it is Death who triumphs. Only the Fate *Atropos*, followed by *Accident* as the unpredictable and blind murderous misfortune, retains some power over human beings, who are not clear-sighted either because they behave like blind creatures without a guide.

'Mort' herself describes the animal she is riding when introduced in the play:

Sur ce beuf cy qui s'en va pas à pas,
Assise suis et ne le haste point;
Mais sans courir je mets a grief trespas
Les plus bruians quant mon dur dart les point.[33]

See also Helène Verougstraete and Roger van Schoute, 'Bruegel et Pétrarque: une évocation de Laure dans le *Triomphe de la mort* de Pierre Bruegel l'ancien?', in Alessandro Rovetta and Marco Rossi, *Studi di Storia dell'arte in onore di Maria Luisa Gatti Perer* (Milan: Vita e Pensiero/Universita Cattolica del Sacro Cuore, 1999), 247-52, at 248.

[31] Liliane Guerry, *Le thème du 'Triomphe de la Mort' dans la peinture italienne* (Paris: Maisonneuve, 1950), 31-56.

[32] Christine Martineau-Genieys, *Le thème de la mort dans la poésie française 1450-1550* (Paris: Honoré Champion, 1978); Balmedie Folkart, 'Structures lexicales et idéologie au quinzième siècle la *Danse aux aveugles* de Pierre Michault', *Sagi e memorie, Neolatina*, 1:2 (1977), 41-74.

[33] *La danse aux aveugles*, lines 41-44, as quoted by Martineau-Génieys (2009), 242, and by Emile Mâle, *Religious Art in France: the Late Middle Ages. A Study of Medieval Iconography and its Sources*, ed. Harry Bober, trans. M. Mathews

(*On this ox which is going step by step*
I sit and do not hurry him along;
But without running I give a painful death
To the most noisy men when my dart pierces them.)

This description by Michault of the entrance of Death is illustrated in a number of manuscripts and printed books of *La danse aux aveugles* at the end of the fifteenth century (Pl. 13). One of these woodcuts, depicting Pierre Michault's entrance of Death, was re-used as an illustration in the *Livre des bonnes moeurs* (Lyon, Bibliothèque municipale, incunable 342, fol. 6r): its author Jacobus Magni (Jacques Legrand) was an Augustine monk in Paris and confessor to Charles VII, king of France. Legrand wrote the *Sophologium* (*c*.1475), which was translated into French as the *Livre des bonnes moeurs* and printed at Chablitz (or Chablies) by Pierre le Rouge in 1478. [34] A woman, carrying a banner with the name 'Atropos', precedes Death who is riding a black ox similar to those in Petrarch's *Trionfi*. As Michault's play was later than the earliest known images of this motif, it seems likely that the author was inspired by the iconography discussed here, *viz*. the isolated figure of Death riding an ox, the *chorea* of the *Danse Macabre*, and illustrations of Petrarch's *Trionfi*.[35]

However, Michault's play was not the last phase of the motif of Death riding a bovine. Between the end of the fifteenth century and the beginning of the sixteenth, the ineluctable figure of Death driving an ox features in a collection of proverbial sayings called by modern authors *Dits moraux et proverbes* (Moral sayings and proverbs*)* or *Dicts moraux pour faire tapisserie* (Moral sayings to make tapestries). Henri Baude was a rhetorician like Michault and his *Dictz* are illustrated in a number of manuscripts, of which the earliest (*c*.1500-05) was produced as a presentation manuscript for François Robertet, secretary to Duke Pierre II of Bourbon

---

(Princeton: Princeton University Press, 1949, repr. 1986), 345-46, from BnF Ms. fr. 22922, fol 173v. Like de Laborde, Mâle considered Michaut's poem as the origin of the iconography: 'I have no doubt that his poem gave artists the idea of representing Death mounted on an ox and threatening men with a long arrow'.

[34] In England, this French version was translated under the title *Book of good manners* (*By the venerable Frere Jacques le Graunt, in Latin, Jacobus Magnus*) and printed by Caxton (1487).

[35] Catherine Ingrassia, Christophe Deslignes and Xavier Terrasa, *La danse médiévale*, vol. 1 (Beauchamp: Le Local, 2009); Catherine Ingrassia and Sylvie Bethmont, 'L'art de bien danser et de bien vivre', *Histoire et Images médiévales*, 29 (2010), 66-69.

(BnF, ms. fr. 24461, fol. 59).[36] It is now considered as a pattern book 'pour faire tapisserie' (*for making tapestries*), despite the fact that very few tapestries seems to have survived.[37] On fol. 59, a full half-page picture shows Death as a cadaverous archer or crossbow-man shooting a hare. He has climbed onto a cart pulled by oxen, reminiscent of the triumphal carriages discussed above. This beautiful pen drawing is accompanied by short poems consists of eight lines of French verse enclosed in a scroll and accompanied by a *motto*, 'Mors Nemini Parcet' (*Death spares nobody*):

> Le lievre va courant qui tres vistement fuit,
> Et dessus la charrette a pas de beuf le suyt
> Larbalestrier tout beau, sans faire nul effroy,
> Lequel te lassera, comme seurement croy,
> Tout fin voir a la longue par espasse de temps
> Et mort il te rendra dont sur ce mot entens
> Tout homme et toute femme que ty vault fouyr
> Devant la mort, helas, car tous nous fault mourir.

> (*The hare who quickly flees goes running*
> *And following him, on the cart that is pulled at ox pace,*
> *Is the handsome crossbow-man, without causing fright,*
> *Who will exhaust you, as I surely believe,*
> *All will end at the end, as time is longing*
> *And he will give you death, as hearing this word*
> *Every man and every woman says they want to flee*
> *Before Death, alas, because we must all die.*)

Alison Saunders considered this manuscript as an 'emblem book in all but name' as she mentioned the visual resemblance 'between these

---

[36] This manuscript (BnF, ms. fr. 24461) contains illustrated *Dictz* and proverbs, Petrarch's *Trionfi*, figures of gods, goddesses, the muses, sybils, various famous women, and colour symbolism. For a description of this manuscript, see Avril et Reynaud (1994), 354-55; and Florence Buttay-Jutier, *Fortuna, usages politiques d'une allégorie morale*, (Paris: Presses de l'Université Paris-Sorbonne, 2008), 324-30. It is called 'D' for '2246' (*sic*) in the edition of Henri Baude's *Dictz moraux pour faire tapisserie*, ed. *Annette Scoumane* (Geneva/Paris: Droz-Minard, 1959), 24.

[37] 'New Material on some Old Topics', in Jean-Michel Massing, *Studies in Imagery* (London: The Pindar Press, 2004), vol. 1, 175-87. See also 'La pirouette', a tapestry bought in 2003 by the Musée National du Moyen Age at the Hôtel de Cluny, Paris. It seems to be identical with the 'Dict moral XLIII' of Baude (BnF, ms. fr. 24461, fol. 48r), according to Maxence Hermant, 'Recueil de poèmes et dessins variés', in *France 1500: entre Moyen Age et Renaissance*, exhibition catalogue (Paris: RMN, 2010), 290.

illustrated manuscripts and the rather later printed Emblem Books'.[38] The first French emblem books dating to *c.*1550 (Guillaume de la Perrière's *Théâtre des bons engins* and *Morosophie*) are visually similar to the *Dicts* manuscripts.

Conclusion

The origins of the motif of Death riding a bovine remain unclear and research remains in progress. To widen the search, it would be necessary to trace the sources of the first occurrences of the motif. A late-twelfth-century panel painting of the Last Judgment in the Vatican collection shows the Earth personified releasing its Dead as the pagan figure of a semi-naked woman seated on a bovine.[39] She is flanked by another semi-naked female who personifies the Sea releasing the dead it has swallowed up, who straddles a sea monster. This bovine mount of Earth personified appears here in the context of the end of time and illustrates the continuity of macabre motifs from antiquity, but one would need to understand the origins and possible developments in this motif.

The examples discussed in this essay are not the *terminus ad quem* of the motif of Death riding or leading a bovine. The iconography of Petrarca's *Trionfi* stretched beyond the sixteenth century and beyond Europe. Petrarch poems crossed the Atlantic alongside their iconography, as is illustrated by the frescoes of 1580 in the dining room in the house of the dean of Puebla Cathedral in Mexico City. The Triumph of Death is presented as a cart pulled by two white oxen, crushing people of all estates and all ages of life. Seated on the triumphal cart are the three Fates, who spin and cut the thread of life.[40]

---

[38] Alison Saunders, 'Is it a Proverb or is it an Emblem? French Manuscript Predecessors of the Emblem Book', *Bibliothèque d'humanisme et de Renaissance,* 55:1 (1993), 83-111.

[39] Vatican, Pinacoteca, originally from the monastery of Santa-Maria-di-Campo-Marzio, Rome. A date of 1061-71 for this picture is proposed in Robert Suckale, 'Die Weltgerichtstafel aus dem römischen Frauenkonvent S. Maria in Campo Marzio als programmatisches Bild der einsetzenden Gregorianischen Kirchenreform', in Robert Suckale, *Das mittelalterliche Bild als Zeitzeuge: Sechs Studien* (Berlin: Lukas Verlag, 2002), 12-122. See also Stefano Riccioni, 'La décoration monumentale à Rome, XIe-XIIe siècles', *Perspectives, Actualités de la recherche en Histoire de l'art* (2010-2011/2), 332-34, 359.

[40] Bernard Utzinger, 'Art macabre au Mexique post-colombien', *Danses Macabres d'Europe Bulletin*, 42 (February 2011), 8; Serge Gruzinski, 'Les Sibylles de Puebla, le triomphe de la Renaissance', in Serge Gruzinski, *L'aigle et la Sibylle,*

Fig. 54. Death riding a crocodile, emblem from *Proteus* by the Dutch poet Jacob Cats published in 1618. © Graphiksammlung 'Mensch und Tod', Heinrich-Heine-University Düsseldorf.

Although the motif of Death riding a bovine seems not to have survived beyond the sixteenth century, some memory of it can be found in emblem books. Interesting for our purpose is the emblem 'Nescit Habere Modum' (*Without having the measure of it*) from the emblematic work *Proteus* of 1618 by the Dutch poet Jacob Cats (1577-1660). A crocodile replaces the ox as Death's mount, and Death is shown holding an arrow while perched on the scaly back of a crocodile which 'knows the place and the time' (Fig. 54).[41] The moral lesson is kept but the symbolic animal, the mount of Death, had changed.

---

fresques indiennes du Mexique (Paris: Éditions de l'Imprimerie nationale, 1994), 143-46.
[41] See http://emblems.let.uu.nl/c162746.html (accessed 8 October 2010).

The texts underlying the motif of Death riding a cow or an ox may also shed a new light on a painting of Pieter Bruegel the Elder that art historians see as his spiritual testament. His 1567 painting known as *The Blind Leading the Blind* (Naples, Museum of Capo di Monte) shows a *chorea* of six blind men heading towards a ditch that symbolises their downfall. The scene illustrates a proverb derived from the Gospel of Matthew, 'If a blind man leads a blind man, both will fall into a pit' (Mt. 15:14). The moving bodies of the blind men follow an oblique line that comes down from the left of the picture, suggesting that the fall will not be a single one but a multiple one, a choreography going crescendo from the verticality in the left towards a fatal horizontality. Viewing the scene, we know that the last blind beggar still blithely moving forward on the far left will share the fate of the first beggar who has already landed in the ditch. With his empty eye sockets the third beggar from the left, whose movement appears halted, resembles a cadaver; his silent cry suspends the inevitable fall for a while. This man calls upon our understanding and our imagination. Bruegel gives here his own version of Michault's dance of the blind that leads to the still waters of death.

There is one final detail in Bruegel's painting. Almost invisible beneath the tree by the water's edge, just above the point where the diagonals of the water and the row of beggars meet, is a compact and obscure mass that can still be recognised as a cow or an ox. More than a mere rustic touch in a country scene, this witness of the fall of the blind men – an opaque point of silence within a desperate movement – might be a late reminder of the subject of Death riding a cow or an ox.[42]

Acknowledgements

This paper is an updated and translated version of my earlier article 'De l'illustration à la leçon' that was published in *Reinardus*, 16 (2003), 47-62, and of my contribution to the fourteenth International Congress of *Danses Macabres d'Europe* (Ghent, 2005). I am grateful to Sophie Oosterwijk for her invitation to extend this research and for being a constant and helpful editorial guide, and also to Stefanie Knöll for her input. The late Christa Grössinger, Bertrand and Hélène Utzinger, and Rémy Cordonnier, Danièle

---

[42] In the work of Pieter Bruegel the Elder, the most hidden detail is often the most meaningful: for example, in *Icarus* (Brussels, Musée Royal des Beaux-Arts, 1558) the only indication of Icarus' fall are some feathers and two small legs sinking into the water – a tiny detail in the immense landscape.

Alexandre-Bidon, Michel and Sandrine Bethmont, Elisabeth Blanchon and Nicolas Charpentier were also of great assistance to me.

Appendix:
Illustrations of Death riding a bovine[43]

The following list – though inevitably incomplete as research is still in progress – offers an idea of the frequency of occurrence of the motif of Death riding a bovine.

FRANCE
● **Avignon**
– Bibliothèque municipale, ms. Rés. 203, f3v G3v, Petrarch's *Triumph of Death.*
● **Paris**
BnF:
– ms. lat. 1377, fol. 87v, Petrarch's *Triumph of Death*: the ox tramples the corpses of a young man and a young woman in front of a spectator.
– ms. fr. 594, fol. 134v, Petrarch's *Triumphs*, with a commentary by Bernardo Illicino, illuminated for King Louis XII by the Master of Petrarch's *Triumphs* (Rouen, 1503). Victorious Death is preceded by diverse figures such as Laura holding a banner, the Roman commander Scipio Africanus, Penelope, and the allegorical figure of 'Bon vouloir' (*Goodwill*).
– ms. nouv. acq. lat. 3191, fol. 100v, book of hours, use of Poitiers, (*c.*1455-60): the triumph of Death, with in the lower margin the tournament of the knight and Death riding an ox.
- ms. fr. 1989, fol. 34, Pierre Michault, *La Danse aux aveugles*, allegory of Death.
– ms. fr. 12594, fol. 179v, *Voie d'enfer et de Paradis* by Jehan de la Mote (1340), 'pour l'amour de Symon de Lile, Bourgeois de Paris, seu maistre orfeure du Roy de France': Death riding an ox 'moult lent' (*very slowly*).
Bibliothèque du Sénat:
– ms. 11, fol. 93, Heures de Croÿ: Death riding a galloping bovine.
Bibliothèque Mazarine:
– Rés. 34959: Death riding an ox.
Bibliothèque de la Chambre des Députés:
– AC, III, 38: Death riding an ox.

---

[43] Extended notices can be found in comte de Laborde (1923).

● **Lyon**
– Bibliothèque municipale, incunable 342, fol. 06, Jacobus Magni, *Le livre des bonnes mœurs* (Geneva, *c.*1480), woodcut illustrating the entrance of Death from Pierre Michault's *La danse aux aveugles.*

ENGLAND

● **London**
– British Library, Add. MS 28962, fol. 378, prayer book of Alphonso of Aragon, king of Naples and Sicily: Death wears a tiara and rides an ox while aiming his arrow at a man.

NETHERLANDS

● **The Hague**
– Royal Library (Koninklijke Bibliotheek), MS 78 D 40, fols 91r and 154v, festal missal of Amiens (1325): a man jousting with Death riding an ox. Garnerus de Morolio is the writer and Petrus de Raimbaucourt the illuminator, made for Johannes de Marchello, abbot of the Premonstratensians abbey of Saint-Jean-sur-la-Celle, Amiens.

GERMANY

● **Düsseldorf**
– Graphiksammlung 'Mensch und Tod, University of Düsseldorf, unprovenanced single sheet from a French(?) book of hours, early sixteenth century(?): miniature showing Death riding an ox.

DEATH IN DRAMA AND LITERATURE

ROMANCE MACABRE:
MIDDLE ENGLISH NARRATIVE
AND THE DEAD IN THE CODEX

KENNETH ROONEY

The *Danse Macabre* arguably constitutes for modern audiences the most recognisable encounter of living and dead from the Middle Ages. However, dialogues with the dead were nothing new by the time the *Danse Macabre* crystalised (to use Huizinga's term) the *contemptus mundi* language of the senescent and corrupt human body in a visual idiom. Medieval audiences would have had many models – rhetorical and imaginative – for encounters with the dead; encounters which would not always have been directed solely towards didactic ends.

One such encounter – an encounter altogether at poles from the *Danse* in language, decorum and intention – appears in one of the so-called 'Cambridge Songs' (*Carmina Cantabrigiensia*), a collection of Latin poems of the twelfth century (Cambridge University Library, MS Gg.5.35). In the poem 'Foebus Abierat' the ghost of a young man appears to his beloved at dawn:

> Aprillis tempore quod nuper transit
> Fidelis imago coram me adstiit,
> Me vocans dulciter pauxillum tetigit;
> Oppressa lacrimis vox eius deficit,
> Suspirans etenim loqui non valuit.
> Illius a tactu nimis intremui
> Velud exterrita sursum insilui,
> Extensis brachii corpus applicui,
> Exanguis penitus tota derigui –
> Evanuit enim! Nichil retinue!

> (*This very April just past, the image of my true love stood before me, calling me softly, touching me gently, his voice failed; his sighs forbade speech. At his touch I trembled, rose in fear, extending my arms to embrace him; then I froze, and paled. He had vanished. I held nothing –* my translation).

First edited by Peter Dronke in the 1960s, this ghostly *alba* (a parting of the dead lover from the living partner at dawn) can match *Danse Macabre* in its prominence and memorability for modern audiences.[1] The poem can afford us a casual sense of everything which the *Danse Macabre* is not: a narrative based on an emotional interest in the dead themselves, and the human responses available to them, whether those of bereavement or supernatural fear of the unknown. Of course, this lyric is an example (perhaps the earliest extant) of the perennial ballad and folklore motif known as 'The Unquiet Grave' where the only *affect* for the audience is sentimental, not moral.

Such affective responses, divorced from the didactic, constititute a different mode of experiencing the dead from that encountered in the *Danse*, however much the art of the *Danse Macabre* can astonish audiences now (as it presumably first did) by its sheer sensuality. In the *Danse* we usually encounter the dead as metaphor, rather than as agent; as signs of mortality rather than as representative human figures who have encountered death. The *Danse Macabre* is evidently conceived as a meeting of the living and the dead. Yet the iconography of the theme, and the impersonal abstractedness of the dialogue of each 'dead being' (who speaks of the moral implications of death for the living, and not as a being who has himself encountered it) purposely suggests allegory – an encounter with man and an abstraction (death) – rather than a supernatural encounter of the living and the dead. Thus, even if every living being in the *Danse* encounters *le mort* (the corpse) and not *la mort* (Death), we as spectators can still be primed to receive the spectacle of the *Danse* as an encounter not with dead people, but with allegorical death multiplied. In the *Danse Macabre* we see the stylised dead confronting the living as little more than particularly decrepit sermonisers, and the *Danse* in essence is very concerned to underplay its supernatural resonances beyond the obvious fact of the articulation of a naturally decomposed corpse. These 'dead' of the *Danse Macabre* have little need to *be* dead to utter their well-worn commonplaces of personal and corporate mortality, yet the effect and affect of the *Danse* are strengthened by their appearance as cadavers: entities with the appearance of dead people.

Nonetheless, medieval audiences could easily expect, from a variety of literary and narrative precedents, the 'supernatural' confrontation and the interaction of the living and the dead, and not just from (rare) sentimental lyrics such as 'Foebus Abierat'. These narratives allow us to gauge the

---

[1] 'Foebus Abierat', in Peter Dronke (ed.), *Medieval Latin and the Rise of the European Love-Lyric* (2nd edn, Oxford: Clarendon, 1968), 334.

imaginative and recreational contexts medieval audiences had for encounters between the living and the dead, and their object is less the mortification of the living (the theme of the *contemptus mundi* tradition) than the narrative *enjoyment* of the dead as supernatural other.

This essay will briefly explore these contexts in a single late-medieval vernacular, Middle English, by focusing on two texts from a single manuscript no earlier than the mid fifteenth century: *Sir Amadace* and *The Awntyrs off Arthure* (the Adventures of Arthur), which are both contained in the so-called Ireland-Blackburne Manuscript (now Princeton, MS Taylor 41). This manuscript consists of two contemporary manuscripts bound together. It is the first of these which contains the three romances; the second contains the records of the manorial court of Hale (Lancashire), the seat of the family of Thomas Yrlonde, who has left his signature on fol. 48r of the first manuscript and fol. 68r of the second manuscript. The manuscript, like the manor, remained in the Ireland family – Ireland-Blackburne from the eighteenth century – until its auction at Sotheby's in 1945. It is now preserved in the Taylor Collection in Princeton (USA), after a spell in Switzerland.[2]

Based on a reading of these two romances in their textual environment, this essay will gauge the importance for these texts of portraying the dead in narratives designed to entertain more than admonish. It will assess how the represented appearances of those dead figures accord with the presentation of the dead formalised in the *Danse*: the 'macabre' or decayed dead. The aim is to judge how audiences might have been disposed to receive such an 'offensive' idiom for imagining the dead in unexpected narrative contexts. Narratives such as these allow medieval audiences the sensational experience of the living dead, now lent agency by the narrative necessity of their having died.

Adventures with the dead

'Foebus Abierat' lends us one scenario in which the dead are sentimentalised, but this goes hand in hand with a strategy of making the dead intangible, evanescent, and, if not physically horrifying, then at least surprising. In this lyric, no somatic properties are evident apart from the defining absence of them. Here we have one way of imagining the dead, with a spiritual body imitative of the deceased as he was in life, decorously

---

[2] Ralph Hanna III (ed.), *The Awntyrs off Arthure at the Terne Wathlyn* (Manchester: Manchester University Press, 1974), 7.

adumbrated with notions of spectrality.[3] Nonetheless, medieval audiences were at times richly served by representations of the anomalous and monstrous corporeal dead in writing.[4] By the same token, whereas in most medieval writing the dead have no need to appear as cadavers (as they must do in the *Danse Macabre* to demonstrate human transience), on occasion they appear as such in unexpected contexts, *e.g.* in the two English romances which are explored in this essay. Here the dead are fully-fledged revenants, deliberately macabre in their configuration, who are seen to be active agents in their narratives; narratives whose dramatic and didactic structures are predicated on their nature as dead people.

As stated earlier, the dead have ordinarily no need to appear 'macabre' in order to function as elements of a narrative. In most medieval narrative scenarios (generally the exemplary tale), the dead must indeed appear in other forms – such a burning soul from Hell or Purgatory – where somatic representation is based on their appearance not as decaying but as they appeared in life, implicitly recognisable to their living interlocutors. Nevertheless, it is to eschew the altogether vast corpus of such representations in favour of a more restricted 'body', as it were, of macabre dead in ostensibly 'secular' literary contexts that we address ourselves here; to explore, in the context of what has earlier been described rather blithely as 'the macabre spirit', the contexts and implications of the homiletic language and art of death of the late Middle Ages for two Middle English romances. These two romances raise significant questions in their apparent responsiveness to 'macabre' iconography and language in their idiosyncratic deployment of a range of exemplary themes. These themes are common to both iconography and narrative, and include the figure of Lazarus and his mourners (inferred in *Sir Amadace*), and the Legend of the Three Living and the Three Dead (an iconographic forerunner of the *Danse Macabre*) in *The Awntyrs off Arthure*. Both texts also deploy the 'Grateful Dead' and 'Pope Trental'

---

[3] On ways of seeing the dead, and their categories, from the spectral to grotesquely physical, see Jean-Claude Schmitt, 'Describing Ghosts' in his *Ghosts in the Middle Ages: the Living and the Dead in Medieval Society*, trans. by Teresa Lavender Fagan (Chicago: Chicago University Press, 1998), 195-219. See Kenneth Rooney, *Mortality and Imagination. The Life of the Dead in Medieval English Literature* (Turnhout: Brepols, 2010) for the vernacular implications of imagining and describing the dead in Middle English.

[4] See Nancy Caciola, 'Wraiths, Revenants, and Ritual in Medieval Culture', *Past and Present*, 152 (1996), 3-45, on the wealth of narratives concerning the often anomalous and unpredictable dead in medieval Latin writing.

motifs, which are folkloric and exemplary tropes, respectively.[5] In the former a dead individual returns from death to reward a benefactor, while the second (a distinctly medieval variant) has an individual return to the living to beg for suffrages such as a Trental (thirty masses), an idea derived from the founding (and apocryphal) legend of Pope Gregory the Great's intercession for his dead mother.

As well as being patently responsive to wider cultural influences, the two romances in their shared manuscript context raise programmatic questions in their mutual thematic alignment of the dead and the poor. *Sir Amadace*'s narrative concerns with financial destitution are emblematised in the physical dereliction of the corpse of a financially ruined knight consigned to the dogs in a manner symbolic of his 'being torn apart' by creditors. In *Awntyrs* we find in the representation of Guinevere's revenant mother, a virtuosic verbalisation of a macabre corpse. This macabre figure employs rhetoric equally consonant with the *Danse*, levying criticism against a corrupt social order which neglects charity to the poor as much as suffrages to the dead (the lack of which constitutes the immediate cause of the ghost's appearance). The same text inscribes an Arthurian and romance world gone to ethical rot in the physical presentation of the putrescent body of Guinevere's revenant mother.

Both romances combine the energetic and ambiguous language of sermon-tales concerning the living (and grateful) dead with language redolent of the medieval lyrics of mortality, resulting in a darkening of the providential patterns expected of romance – a genre predicated on good endings. In *Sir Amadace* death, and the threat of death, jarringly dominate the text as the recurring symbols and consequences of bourgeois destitution. The titular hero here must realise that, with marriage, the ruinous consequences of a bachelor's unbridled generosity will fall no longer merely on him but in future especially upon his wife and child. *Sir Amadace* yields a disturbing bourgeois mirror of financial prudence in marriage, realised through an unexpectedly bloodthirsty deployment of the Grateful Dead trope (discussed below) that is complemented in the same manuscript by a wider social eschatology in *Awntyrs*. This latter text too is concerned with the poor in the world and frames their vulnerability in an Arthurian world certain (one day) to fall.

---

[5] See Hanna (1974), 24-25, on the Trental Legend and other analogues for *Awntyrs*, and on the grateful dead motif (and the best analysis of its operation in this text) Elizabeth Williams, '*Sir Amadace* and the Undisenchanted Bride: the Relation of the Middle English Romance to the Folktale Tradition of The Grateful Dead', in Rosalind Field (ed.), *Tradition and Transformation in Medieval Romance* (Cambridge: D.S. Brewer, 1999), 57-70.

A reading of both romances in their shared manuscript suggests a themed anthology where each romance informs and alters the reading of the other, offering audiences a sense of the generic capacities of romance and of the narrative pliability of the dead. The unifying theme is the life of the dead – how they affect the living in both the most doctrinally, eschatologically sound manner, and also in the most entertaining ways. The Ireland-Blackburne Manuscript is in fact a unique combination of these anonymous texts, both of which have more than one manuscript witness.[6] The scribe is unknown, though we might well like to know who put together such a potentially provocative programme of romance reading that would serve not just Thomas Irlande but any medieval reader as a mirror of magisterial conduct and social obligation. A third romance, *The Avowying of Arthur*, is attested only in this manuscript and is something of a joker in the pack of this deal of three romances. Like *Awntyrs* it is an Arthurian romance of two distinct halves and also a Tarn Wadling romance – another adventure of Arthur and his knights at the same Cumbrian lake that was drained in the eighteenth century. Yet unlike *Sir Amadace* and *Awntyrs*, its relationship to the dead (if any) is strictly one of burlesque. Furthermore, it shows that the language of describing ghosts, which is put to such serious and challenging uses in *Sir Amadace* and *Awntyrs*, can also be wielded with the utmost inconsequentiality, thereby illustrating the ability of romance both to suggest serious thematic concerns and to eschew them altogether. In other words, the dead are the index of intellectual engagement in these three romances, not merely sensational devices, and I want to turn now to describing how this might be the case.

The Awntyrs of Arthure's first half is, simply put, a ghost story that deals with the apparition of Guinevere's dead mother to her daughter (and Sir Gawain, who is warding her) to plead her relief in Purgatory. The second half is a far more conventional Arthurian episode, *viz.* the challenge of a Northern knight to Arthur's court. Yet both episodes achieve a single romance that is provocative in its adoption of the language of social complaint, from the ghost who speaks both for the plight of the souls in Purgatory and for the poor, to the Northern knight Galeron who must petition Arthur for justice. This bipartite structure in the context of the Ireland-Blackburne Manuscript can stimulate an audience

---

[6] *Sir Amadace* is contained in one other fifteenth-century manuscript (Edinburgh, National Library of Scotland Advocates MS 19.3.1), an anthology of romance and religious works. *Awntyrs* is found in three others: the Lincoln Thornton MS (Lincoln Cathedral Chapter Library MS 91), which is another large and important anthology of romance and devotional narratives; London, Lambeth Palace Library MS 491; and Oxford, Bodleian Library MS Douce 324.

awareness of the potential of discrete texts to provocatively complement one another, and guide the audience to a subsequent reading of all three texts in the manuscript as a whole as episodic instalments of a thematised romance world. This is a world marked by the presence of the dead, and particularly in *Awntyrs* their presence registers something rotten in the state of its own romance world. In their foregrounding of the presence of the bodies of the dead, *Awntyrs* and *Sir Amadace* are both, as I have suggested, stimulated by contemporary iconographic conventions to represent the dead. In *Awntyrs*, the macabre description of the ghost of Guinevere's mother aligns her unmistakably with the stylised iconographic representation of the cadaver that became popular in Europe in the fourteenth and fifteenth centuries, a popularity confirmed by the *Danse Macabre*.

For the closest visual analogue to *Awntyrs*, however, we should look to The Legend of the Three Living and the Three Dead, the exemplum of transience that first became associated with macabre iconography in the late thirteenth century. Here in many vernacular iterations (including the sole English one in the manuscript of John Audelay) the narrative resolves itself as the story of how the dead parents of their living interlocutors present themselves as the embodied warning of death.[7] This was a highly popular theme in medieval England (far more than the *Danse Macabre*) promulgated more, it seems, by church murals rather than by vernacular texts (of which only one is extant in English). Very distinguished examples of such parochial murals survive in Wickhampton (Norfolk) and Raunds (Northamptonshire). The theme enjoyed higher status also in those lavish products for personal devotion – books of hours – in which it was

---

[7] The sole (anonymous) English version of the Legend, *De tribus regibus mortuis* is extant in Oxford, Bodleian Library MS Douce 302, a compilation by the early-fifteenth-century poet John Audelay (who is not generally believed to be the composer of the English Three Dead text). The text shares the same date, language and metre (a thirteen-line stanza combining rhyme and alliteration) of *Awnytrs*, and closely echoes its formulaic and ekphrastic 'macabre' imagery in its presentation of the dead. See E.K. Whiting (ed.), *The Poems of John Audelay*, Early English Text Society, o.s. 184 (Oxford: Oxford University Press, 1931), 217-23. More recent scholarly editions of the English Three Dead poem are found in Thorlac Turville-Petre (ed.), *Alliterative Poetry of the Later Middle Ages* (Washington DC: Catholic University of America Press, 1989), 148-57; and Susanna Fein (ed.), *John the Blind Audelay: Poems and Carols* (Kalamazoo: TEAMS, 2009), no pagination. On the place of the text of the English Three Dead at the 'end' of Audelay's book (aptly suggesting last things), see Susanna Fein, 'Good Ends in the Audelay Manuscript', *Yearbook of English Studies*, 33 (2003), 97-119.

habitually used as one of several decorative motifs (including the *Danse Macabre*) in the Office of the Dead.[8]

Written no later than the early fifteenth century, *The Awntyrs off Arthure* guides our imagination, in its description of the dead, to recall these contemporary iconographic models for the unburied, corrupt, talkative corpse. The English poem delivers the appearance of the body in the conventional blazon, describing beauty from top to toe, but now jarringly in its macabre mirror negative. Its naked body reveals bones protruding through the skin: we are told how 'Bare was the body and blak to the bone' (l. 105) – a ready index of the discoloration of the body in macabre iconography. The corpse is similarly encrusted with the filth of the tomb: 'Al biclagged in clay uncomly cladde' (*all clogged in earth, unpleasingly clothed*, l. 106). Its voice is female and the body, with due 'realism', unrecognisable: 'Hit waried, hit wayment as a woman,/ But on hide ne on huwe no heling hit hadde' (*It wailed, it screeched like a women, but in skin and complexion there was nothing covering it*, ll. 106-07). It is also infested by 'serpents' or worms (ll. 115, 120), again verbalising the visual idiom of the macabre. What ultimately emerges from this figure is a suggestion of the corruption of the world in which it appears, as much as its own physical decay. According to the ghost, the flowers of chivalry are over-proud and neglecting their duties to the poor. Even the knight Gawain by his own words acknowledges that they are abusing their temporal power under a king insatiable for conquest and (for now) invincible. He asks how he and his brothers in chivalry will get to Heaven:

'How shal we fare,' quod the freke, 'that fonden to fight,
And thus defoulen the folke on fele kinges londes
And riches over reymes withouten eny right,
Wynnen worshipp in werre thorgh wightnesse of hondes?'
'Your King is to covetous, I warne the sir knight,
May no man stry him with strenght while his whele stondes.' (ll. 261-66)

'How shall we fare', said the fellow, 'that live to fight, and thus despoil the people of many a king's lands, and appropriate wealth with no right thereto, and thereby win renown in war through strength of hands?' 'Your king is too covetous, I warn thee, sir knight; no man may oppose him with strength while his wheel stands.'

---

[8] See the essay by Christine Kralik in this volume. On the presence of the Legend of the Three Living and Three Dead in English medieval parochial murals, see E.W. Tristram, *English Wall Paintings of the Fourteenth Century* (London: Routledge and Kegan Paul, 1955), 112-14, and Anne Marshall's very helpful online catalogue of English medieval murals at www.paintedchurch.org.

Making appropriate response to the souls in Purgatory as prescribed in other popular medieval legends of Purgatory, Guinevere promises 'a myllion of masses to make mynning!' (*a million masses to make remembrance!*, l. 236). This satisfies the ghost, who departs, and life goes on – but only for the time being, and not without its discontents, for later in the poem the knight Galeron accuses Arthur of wrongful suzerainty over his lands; an accusation anticipated by Gawain's acknowledgment of Arthurian 'imperialism', as we have just seen. Middle English alliterative poetry has a habit of broaching social criticism, but seldom does alliterative romance stray as here beyond a tendency to quasi-cinematic descriptions of the horrors of war (*e.g.* the *Alliterative Morte Arthure*) and offer instead searching criticism of misrule.

The narrative potential of using the dead as both admonishment and as entertainment and, furthermore, as stimulus to wider ethical criticism is therefore clear in *Awntyrs*. Also evident is its concomitant strategy of suggesting iconographic formulae in its narrative art, one which the second romance of the manuscript, *Sir Amadace*, can be seen to accord with. The latter's story can be quickly summarised. Amadace is an impoverished knight (but, crucially, penniless because of his habit of spending on good causes, *viz.* the poor) who chances upon a foul-smelling cadaver on his self-imposed exile to escape his creditors. It is the body of a man who, like Amadace, was in debt and inordinately generous to the poor, but *so* in debt on his death that his widow has been prevented by a creditor from committing him to burial for the past sixteen weeks. Amadace pays for the dead man's burial and suffrages with the very last of his own wealth. Alone and in despair, Amadace then meets a mysterious knight in white who shows him the path to recovery. The lavish spoils of a shipwreck equip him for entry into the lists for a tournament to win the hand of a kingdom's heiress. Once Amadace is married to her and has a child, the White Knight returns to claim his reward in accordance with the bargain made earlier with Amadace: for the White Knight's aid (essentially a treasure map predicated on the normal expectations of romance) Amadace must now yield half of what he has gained in wealth. It is only now that we realise what the White Knight has in mind: half, not of Amadace's property or money, but his other 'winnings', *viz.* half his wife and child each. At the last minute, as Amadace raises his sword over his wife, the seemingly implacable White Knight bids him stop and explains both who he is (the dead merchant whom Amadace had helped in death, by giving him Christian burial) and, more obliquely, his ambiguous 'reward' for Amadace (see below).

Fig. 55. Simon Bening and workshop (Southern Netherlands), Raising of Lazarus, miniature at the start of the Office of the Dead in the book of hours of Joanna of Ghistelles (Use of Messines), early sixteenth century (London, British Library, Egerton MS 2125, fol. 64v). © The British Library.

The most 'macabre' episode of *Sir Amadace* is where we begin: the titular hero's stumbling across the corpse of the figure who becomes, later, the transformed White Knight. The results of his prodigious term of unburial (sixteen weeks) are lent no uncertain evidence as Amadace's squire relates emphatically upon investigating the scene:

'Suche a stinke as I had thare,
Sertis thenne had I nevyr are
Noquere in so stid.
For this palfray that I on ryde,
Ther myghte I no lengur abide;
I traue I have keghte my dede.' (ll. 91-96)

(*Such a stink I had there, certainly I never had before, nowhere, in no place. By the horse I ride on, there I could not stay; I would have caught my death.*)

The narration of the physical consequences of death in *Sir Amadace* can be associated, like that in *Awntyrs*, with the postures of iconography, but here of a different trope – the medieval iconography of the raising of Lazarus, from the gospel of John. We are told in the text how the squire must cover 'his nase with his hude' (*his nose with his hood*, l. 73), thereby adopting the manner of the mourners of the dead Lazarus who cover their faces as they look upon the corpse – a formula repeated frequently in later medieval representations of the story of Lazarus of Bethany. This gesture is, of course, the most instinctive and automatic human response to the dead. Inevitably, in the discourse of *contemptus mundi* of human corruption, the human response – physical horror – must make way for meditative responses. In this context the sketching of such an inconsequential reflex becomes for audiences a reminder and cue, as it were, for productive, contemplative reflection on transience. Just as the crucified Christ was always presented as a stimulus to reflection, so too was Lazarus (his forerunner in resurrection) a prompt to react usefully to mortality.

Nonetheless, there are many precedents for associating the image of the mourners of Lazarus with the idea of the macabre. Lazarus is one of the recurring motifs that illustrate the Office of the Dead in books of hours (Fig. 55 and Pl. 8). The image and its association with themes of mortality is popularised (if for a geographically discrete audience) in its appearance in the vast mid-fourteenth-century mural sequence of The Triumph of Death in the Camposanto in Pisa (embedded in a plenitude of mortal themes), where the three living cover their noses before the three recumbent, putrid corpses (in three carefully adumbrated phases of decay). Lazarus' gagging mourners seem not to have had any appreciable currency in insular parochial murals (to judge from surviving evidence), but imaginative associations could still have been readily made in wider audiences (not just those with lavish books of hours) who would have heard 'stinking Lazarus' being invoked in the liturgy of the Office of the Dead in the responsory to the second Lesson of first Nocturnes in highly recognisable Latin: 'Qui Lazarum resuscitasti a monumento foetidum' (*You who raised Lazarus from the stinking tomb*).

Furthermore, Lazarus is a byword for the moribund corpse in medieval English writing. The Towneley play of Lazarus gives us a corpse who describes his own irreversible decay from first-person experience. The central figure of *The Gast of Guy* (the Middle English redaction of the French ghost story *Spiritus Guidonis*) traduces his own dead body as a Lazarus, and this invective is taken to the furthest extremes in two Middle Scots texts, *viz.* William Dunbar's poetic contest *The Flyting of Dunbar and Kennedie* and Robert Henryson's narrative poem *The Testament of Crisseyde*. Though still alive, Crisseyde becomes in her leprosy every bit as ghastly as a corpse, thereby serving as a vindictively misogynistic *memento mori* for her counterpart in Chaucer's *Troilus and Crisseyde*. This conflation – leper and corpse – is derived from two biblical authorities: the story of Dives Malus and Lazarus the Leper, as well as the story of the resurrected Lazarus of Bethany. The text of *Sir Amadace* itself pays great attention to this latter kind of 'Lazarine' corruption but also to its counterpart – resurrection. It furthermore shows an interest in using such familiar stimuli to morbid reflection and in making its audiences think about, and be surprised by, the consequences of death. In its portrayal of its central figure of death (the corpse of the destitute knight) the text suggests a knowing invocation of the narrative of Lazarus, who was brought back from far beyond the brink; resurrected by Christ even after he had begun to stink. This is the narrative crux of *Sir Amadace*. The dead man – unacceptably, offensively putrid – is raised to life as a transfigured knight in white (though it must be admitted that the text decorously suggests incorporeality in this transfigured figure).

The text implicitly promotes the body's transformation in death and resurrection as suitably emblematic of its genre's concerns: the familiar romance pattern of loss and recovery. In this new context, financial and material loss become altogether too unacceptable in this mirror for bourgeois readership, leaving audiences with the language of morbid realism to remind them of the consequences (and plausibility) of sudden, irreversible economic catastrophe and, moreover, of the rather implausible prospects for recuperation from such a fall. Indeed, the text traces an exemplary pattern for audiences of the pitfalls of unregulated and undiscriminating charity after it has been the very absence of charity in the rich that has been condemned in *Awntyrs* in the same manuscript. Now, in this new text and new romance world, charitable acts are simply poor financial decisions in a romance marked by encounters not with chivalrous knights but rather with merchants and number-crunching stewards. Coming back from financial failure as Amadace does, *Sir Amadace* offers the stuff of fairytales, or romance – narratives predicted on a recovery for every loss. Here such recovery requires nothing less than a fairy godmother in the form of the Grateful Dead – the resurrected dead merchant in the transcendent form of an incognito White Knight.

As in *Awntyrs*, the corpse in *Sir Amadace* becomes a surrogate for the poor of this world, but now the *nouveau* poor as it were – a mirror and *memento mori* for those in debt, as Amadace is. Upon seeing the corpse, Amadace draws appropriate pieties from the spectacle:

> Unnethe he myghte forgoe to wepe,
> For his dedus him sore forthoghte;
> Sayd, 'Yondur mon that lise yondur chapell withinne,
> He myghte full wele be of my kynne,
> For ryghte so have I wroghte.' (ll. 206-09)

> (*Scarcely might he forbear to weep, for his deeds troubled his thoughts. He said, 'That man that lies in that chapel might well be my kin for right so have I done.'*)

Heedless of this mirror's ostensive warning about the ruinous consequences of generosity, however, Amadace expends the last of his wealth to ensure the dead man's burial. It seems the hero will follow his brother in generosity to the same conclusion – possible ruination – in the spirit of chivalric brotherhood, unless habitual romance providence intervenes. And it does: the dead man returns from death as the White Knight to aid his brother in charitable profligacy. Yet just as the dead man's generosity was punished with non-burial in the ultimate configuration of the social ostracism of poverty, so too will Amadace be punished temporarily for his career of giving and not counting the cost. This occurs in the romance's cumulative episode – the abortive execution of Amadace's wife and child – where we understand a second implied mirror for Amadace of the conse- quences of unbridled generosity. Now we have the prospect of a dead wife and son, cruelly symbolising a very bourgeois fear of ever sinking so low as to leave your family destitute. Implicitly Amadace's romance career has been one of induction to the responsibilities of matrimony and social achievement. His days of not counting the cost are over; from now on, the material consequences of improvidence fall first on his family.[9]

The White Knight reveals himself as the revenant of the man Amadace buried, and his speech of identification to Amadace recalls the horrors of the body's experience of death witnessed in *Awntyrs*. Averting with Amadace's charitable burial a post-mortem destiny as 'howundus mete' (*food for hounds*), he has avoided an ordeal which morbidly rewrites the sense of being torn to pieces by one's creditors. His dual reward for Amadace is material in his 'itinerary' to recovery, and moral in his brutal way of making Amadace realise where his wealth truly lies, *viz.* a loyal wife and a child who will live or die by his financial prudence. In a secular idiom it offers admonishment that is unpleasant but useful to the internal characters, and entertaining if ambiguous for the audience. The dead man here can speak as a character both monstrous and unpredictable – as supernatural agents can be in the best medieval romances – and familiar in its capacity as a homiletic organ. Yet, more than this, he is a figure unique in the Middle English corpus of romance for advantageously exploiting the sense of being dead. He absorbs both pious and unauthorised responses to the dead – familiar pieties in his instructive, unburied rotting; supernatural dread as an unpredictable, implacable, anomalous agent from beyond the grave; and finally, it seems, a romance hero and engineer of the romance process, who departs from the living forever in a mode both sentimental and dramatically satisfying. To use a modern cliché, there would not have been a dry eye in the house as the Grateful Dead departs, renewing the bonds of chivalric fraternal identity, generosity and debt that bound him and Amadace:

> 'Fare wele now,' he sayd, 'mynne awne true fere!
> For my lenging is no lengur her,
> With tunge sum I the telle.
> Butte loke thu lufe this lady as thi lyve,
> That thus mekely, withouten stryve,
> Thi forwardus wold fulfille.'
> Thenne he wente oute of that toune,
> He glode away as dew in [d]owne,
> And thay abode ther stille. (ll. 817-25)

> (*'Farewell now', he said, 'my own true companion, for my abode is no longer here, I tell you true, with my tongue. But see to it that you love this lady as your life who would thus meekly, without strife, fulfil your commands.'* Then he went out of that town, he melted away as dew on the down, and they remained there still.)

---

[9] For a more detailed discussion, see Rooney (2010), 82-90.

He vanishes as decorously and evanescently as the dead beloved in 'Foebus Abierat', as dew on the down (1. 824).[10]

Conclusion

In reading *The Awntyrs off Arthure* and *Sir Amadace*, two romances from a nondescript mid-fifteenth-century anthology (the Ireland-Blackburne Manuscript), we have seen romances which exploit to a virtuosic and idiosyncratic degree the appearance and placating of the dead, and which raise implicit questions as to the appropriate interpretation of episodes that both entertain and admonish. Both texts exhibit an adaptive artistry to register the dislocating presence of the dead in their differently regulated romance worlds. *Awntyrs* proceeds by an ekphrastic verbal preciseness imitative of macabre iconography in its eschatological and doctrinal certainties. *Sir Amadace* – always a more ambiguous narrative – proceeds by obliqueness of visual reference and moral interpretation. However, both *Awntyrs* and *Sir Amadace* highlight a concern for the social and spiritual implications of wealth and its use in society, a use that is regulated in both cases not by the poor, but by those who should be more voiceless than the poor and yet paradoxically are not – the dead.

I want to conclude briefly by suggesting how the opening episode of the third text in the manuscript, *The Avowying of Arthur*, might permit us to register possible implied commentaries on the romances of death with which it is compiled. Like *Awntyrs*, *Avowing* opens with the narration of the subjection of the Arthurian world to another terror – this time not the dead but, rather more bathetically (and conventionally), a wild boar. Intriguingly this boar is lent the epithets 'corse' (*corpse*) and 'black': a jolting approximation of the language of dead bodies with blackened bones that is found in *Awntyrs*, but now mandated by the unhappy requirements of rhyme (emphases are mine). Arthur's knights are warned by a hunter that:

> 'He is hegher thenne a horse,
>   That uncumly *corse*;
>   In fayth, him faylis no force
> Quen that he schalle feghte!
> And therto, *blake* as a bere'. (ll. 49-53)

---

[10] A possible crux in the Ireland-Blackburne text is whether *toune* (town) should be read as *doune* (down). I have favoured the latter in my interpretation.

(He is taller than a horse, that ugly corpse; in faith, he does not lack
strength when he fights, and he is moreover as black as a bear.)

'Corse' could just be 'body' and not distinctly 'corpse', while 'black' here
simply governs the inelegant simile 'black as a bear'. Based on our
reading of the other romances, however, we are primed to respond with a
sense of recoil at these words – a response perhaps justified here: 'Butte
sette my hed upon a store / Butte giffe he flaey yo all fawre, / That
griselich *geste!*' (*But chop off my head if he does not flay you all four, that*
grisly ghost, ll. 110-12). Is this 'guest' or 'ghost'? It could be both, and as
we read on we seem to be more and more confronted with a narrator who
is conducting his own Harrowing of Hell in deriving a lexicon for the wild
boar, who becomes 'Sathenas' (*Satan*) at line 120.

We might conclude, in a temptingly quasi-Chaucerian mode of textual
and generic juxtaposition, that we have here tacit, burlesque commentary
on the hyperbole of macabre description elsewhere in the manuscript, and
on the possibilities of the romance genre to register criticism not only of
its reflected worlds but also of its own narrative excesses, as well as wider
currents – the commonplaces of the macabre imagination and spirit.

Acknowledgements

I would like to thank Elizabeth Williams for generously sharing her
insights on *Sir Amadace* with me, and also express my thanks to the
editors of this volume for their helpful criticism and advice. I would also
like to thank the staff of the British Library for their patient and efficient
handling of queries and requests for images.

FRIGHTENED OR FEARLESS:
DIFFERENT WAYS OF FACING DEATH
IN THE SIXTEENTH-CENTURY MAJORCAN
PLAY *REPRESENTACIÓ DE LA MORT* *

LENKE KOVÁCS

Death has been a common subject in various forms of art in European culture from late-medieval times to the present day. The *Danse Macabre* is a literary, choreographic, pictorial and dramatic genre, that probably first emerged in the later fourteenth century although it became a truly widespread theme only in the fifteenth. One of the earliest examples in literature is the Spanish *Dança general de la Muerte* of *c.*1390-1400, which used to be considered an adaptation or translation from a fourteenth-century French poem, but is probably related to an Aragonese or Catalan model.[1]

The earliest pictorial example of a *Danse Macabre* on the Iberian Peninsula is the mural in the former Franciscan convent of Morella (Fig. 56 and Pl. 5). Dated *c.*1470, it is the only extant monumental *Danse Macabre* where male and female dancers are dancing in a circle around a skin-covered skeleton lying in a sarcophagus, who represents Death. The dancers, who follow the usual hierarchically descending order, can be divided into two groups: representatives of the clergy to the right and secular representatives to the left. In the centre is the Pope crowned with the tiara.

---

* Throughout this essay, Catalan place-names will be used; English equivalents (where available) are given in brackets. The English translations of cited Spanish passages in this essay are mine – LK.
[1] See Joan Solá-Solé, 'El rabí y el alfaquí en la *Dança general de la Muerte*', *Romance Philology*, 18 (1965), 272-83; Joan Solá-Solé, 'En torno a la *Dança General de la Muerte*', *Hispanic Review*, 36:4 (1968), 303-27; Francisco Rico, 'Pedro de Veragüe y fra Anselm Turmeda', *Bulletin of Hispanic Studies*, 50 (1973), 224-36; Víctor Infantes, *Las danzas de la muerte. Génesis y desarrollo de un género medieval (siglos XIII-XVII)*, (Salamanca: Ediciones Universidad de Salamanca, 1997), 238.

Fig. 56. *Danse Macabre* mural in the former Franciscan convent of Morella (Els Ports, Valencian Community, Spain), *c.*1470. Photo: author.

To his right are a King, a Queen, a Duke and a Duchess, a Nobleman and a Noblewoman. To his left are a Cardinal, a Bishop, and several tonsured figures, *viz.* a Dominican Friar, a Benedictine Monk, and perhaps two Franciscans. In the foreground, facing the Pope, we see a Monk in a black cowl, a Woman and a Child to the left, and to the right a Scholar, a Burgher and a Nun. Apart from the *Danse Macabre* scene and the accompanying musical notation (another unique feature), the mural includes another scene of Death personified, who is shown as an archer pointing his arrow at the Tree of Life and the fragmentarily surviving scene of the Wheel of Fortune.[2]

A reference to another *Danse Macabre* mural in the area of Léon is found in the satirical novel *Corbacho o Reprobación del amor mundano* (1438) by the Castilian writer Alfonso Martínez de Toledo, also known as the archpriest of Talavera (*c.*1398-*c.*1470).[3] Martínez hints in his novel at a *Danse* comprising male and female dancers in the usual hierarchical order from pope to cobbler, and at Death occurring in two different ways: on the one hand in a dialogue with the social representatives, and on the other hand armed with either bow and arrow, a knife or a lance. The description occurs in a speech where Martínez tries to fight against deeply rooted pre-Christian ideas about death and the world of the dead:

> And people believe death to be an invisible person, walking around and killing men and women. They shall not believe this, because death is nothing else but the separation of body and soul. And it is called death or the parting from present life, when the body, hence embellished by the soul, becomes a corpse. This is death. So nobody shall say: 'I saw death in the shape of a woman, in the shape of a man, talking to kings, etc. as it is painted in León', because this is natural fiction against nature. Natural because it is natural to die, but it is unnatural that death should be anything that kills, as it is shown in fiction, which would be against nature, *e.g.* stabbing the living with a knife or a lance or shooting arrows at them. Yet I know for sure that the king, the pope and the shoemaker all have to pass through that gate. [...] So nobody shall think of death as being a man or a

---

[2] Francesc Massip and Lenke Kovács, 'Ein Spiegel inmitten eines Kreises: der Totentanz von Morella (Katalonien)', *L'art macabre (Jahrbuch der Europäischen Totentanz-Vereinigung)*, 1 (2000), 114-33, and 'La Danse macabre dans le royaume d'Aragon: iconographie et spectacle au Moyen Âge et ses survivances traditionnelles', *Revue des Langues Romanes*, 105:2 (2001), 202-28. See also Enrica Zaira Merlo, 'Death and Disillusion. An Iconographic and Literary Itinerary in Christian Spain', in Alberto Tenenti (ed.), *Humana Fragilitas: The Themes of Death in Europe from the 13th to the 18th Century* (Clusone: Ferrari Editrice, 2002), 219-68, at 228-32 and figs 182-83.

[3] This work was inspired by Boccaccio's late work *Corbaccio*.

woman, neither a body nor a fantastic spirit, but the parting and separation of body and soul: this is what death is.[4]

For Martínez de Toledo the personification of Death was not in accordance with Christian belief. Death personified is also unknown in ancient Greece and Rome: Persephone and Hades may rule over the Underworld but they are not Death. In the *Dança general de la Muerte*, which is a possible source of inspiration for the murals in Léon, Death is shown as an abstract personified entity. This is in contrast to the French *Danse Macabre* from 1424-25 as known from the mural in the *Cimetière des Innocents* in Paris, where it is the dead who are addressing the living.

An extremely spectacular personification of Death is known from a detailed description that is one of the earliest records from the territory of the Catalan-Aragonese confederation to refer to this type of performance. It took place at the coronation of Ferdinand d'Antequera and his wife, which was celebrated in the Aljafería Palace in Saragossa in 1414. The chronicler Álvar García de Santa María describes the event as follows:

> And when the Angel had finished speaking, the heavens revolved, and in the very middle of the room there appeared a cloud in which came Death, who was very hideous, with plenty of skulls, serpents and tortoises, and he came in this shape.[5] A man was dressed in yellow cloth clinging to his

---

[4] 'E piensan las gentes que la muerte es persona invisible, que anda matando ombres e mugeres; pues non lo piensen, que non es otra cosa sinón separaçión del ánima al cuerpo. E esto es llamado muerte o privaçión desta presente vida, quedando cadáver el cuerpo que primero era ornado de ánima. Esta es dicha muerte. Así que non diga ninguno: 'Yo vi la muerte en figura de muger, en figura de cuerpo de ome, e que fablava con los reyes, etc. como pintada está en León' que aquello es ficçión natural contra natura. Es natural porque natural es el morir; peron non que la muerte sea cosa que mate, segund que la pintan en fecçión, que sería contra natura, como dar cuchillas, lançadas o saetadas a los bivos la muerte. Emperó sé cierto que el Rey, e el Papa, e el çapatero, todos pasan por aquel vado [...] Así que non piense alguno que la muerte es muger ni ombre, nin cuerpo, nin espíritu alguno fantástigo, salvo privaçión de vida e apartamiento de cuerpo e de ánima. Esta es dicha muerte.' Alfonso Martínez de Toledo, *Corbacho o Reprobación del amor mundano*, Selecciones bibliográficas, 5 (Barcelona, 1949), 271-73.
[5] In Romance languages the word for 'death' is feminine, yet in texts such as the *Dança general de la Muerte* or the Majorcan *Representació* Death switches gender according to the victim who is being summoned. In the *Dança*, for instance, Death refers to the two maidens with 'son mis esposes' (*they are my wives*, l. 72), while the abbot is addressed as 'seredes mi esposo' (*you will be my husband*, l. 259). In the latter, the lady is encouraged to see Death as 'un marit prompta, / més valent

body so as to look like his own skin, and his head was a skull with a skin of hides, completely fleshless, lacking nose and eyes, which was hideous and ghastly, and he was indicating by gestures in all directions that he would carry off everyone in the room.[6]

Thus, according to the chronicle, Death appears in this performance in the form of an eviscerated corpse, and not as a skeleton. This typology is also to be found in the above-mentioned wall painting in the former Franciscan monastery of Morella (Fig. 56 and Pl. 5).

The second part of the performance took place three days after the crowning of the king, at the banquet celebrated on the occasion of the queen's coronation:

And at that time the King of Aragon had a jester called Monseigneur Borra, and this man was extremely comical: he would not speak ill of anyone except when they made fun of him, which everyone did [...] And this jester was in the feasting chamber where the Queen was having dinner when Death arrived in a cloud as had been arranged by the King, in the manner we have described. Borra showed his great shock at this sight and screamed that Death should stay away. And therefore the Duke of Gandia sent word to the King who was at a window watching the Queen dine, to say that when Death descended and he [Borra] screamed, the he [the duke] would seize him [Borra] from below and he [the duke] would give orders to Death to rope him [Borra] and to take him up, and so it was carried out. Thus when Death came in its cloud before the table, Monseigneur Borra began to scream, the duke seized him from below, and Death threw the rope, and they tied it to the body of the said Borra, and Death hoisted him up. Here you saw marvels in the things that Monseigneur Borra did and the

---

que duch ni compta' (*a prompt husband, / more courageous than a duke or a count*, l. 488-98). In the same play, when Death says he has come to put a 'sabata justa' (*tight shoe*, l. 699) on the bandit's foot, the victim claims never to have seen such a shoemaker ('may tal sabater jo viu', l. 701). Throughout this essay, the masculine pronoun will be used to refer to Death, except where the character's gender is clearly identified.

[6] 'E acabado de dezir el ángel luego se revolvieron los cielos, e en medio de la sala salió una nube en la qual venía la Muerta la qual era muy fea llena de calaveras e culebras e galápagos e venía en esta guisa: un hombre vestido en baldreses amarillos justos al cuerpo que parecía su cuero, e su cabeça era una calavera e un cuero de baldrés toda descarnada sin narizes e sin ojos que era muy fea e muy espantosa, e con la mano faziendo semejanças a todas partes que llevaba a unos e a otros por la sala. E acabado esto de fazer, la nube tornose a los cielos.' See Álvar García de Santamaría, *Historia de la vida e echos del muy alto e esclarecido Rey don Fernando el I° de Aragón, tutór del rey don Juan el 2° de Castilla*, Paris, Bibliothèque nationale de France, ms. esp. 104, fol. 201r.

tears and the great terror that he felt, for as he was being lifted he wet his trousers so that it rained on the heads of those below, who wished that he were carried off to Hell. And our Lord King watched this, and he and those who saw it were highly amused by it. And Monseigneur Borra went up to the heavens in the clutches of Death.[7]

The terrifying vision of Death appearing in a cloud was very likely to cause unrest among the audience at the Aljafería Palace. However, the potentially negative impact on the onlookers was mitigated by the jester's frantic reaction to the ghastly appearance. Thus, after an initial shock, the spectators were able to calm down once they realised that Death's attention was directed at the court jester, who exteriorised his fear in a most expressive and extremely human way, first by screaming and finally by emptying his bladder. By playing the 'frantic fool', who gets completely out of control when confronted with Death, the court jester Monseigneur Borra turns out to be the 'wise fool', who portrays people's fears so graphically that he seems to hold up a mirror in which the spectators can recognise the foolishness and uselessness of their resistance towards Death.[8]

Whereas in Saragossa the audience was not directly addressed by Death and the initially frightening action was changed into a parody, the *Danse Macabre* served as a harsh reminder of man's mortality and as a

---

[7] 'E en esta sazón tenía el rey de Aragón un albardán que dezían mossén Borra, e este era muy gracioso que non dezía mal de ninguno, salvo que tenía gracias que le daban todos [...]. E este alvardán estava en la sala do comía la señora Reyna, e quando vino la Muerte en la nube, segund que fizo el Rey, según que diximos, mostraba gran espanto en la ver e dava grandes bozes a la Muerte que no veniese; e por ende el Duque de Gandía enbió dezir al Rey, que estaba en una ventana mirando el comer de la reina, que quando la Muerte descendiese e él diese bozes, qu·él lo llevaría de yuso e que mandase a la Muerte que le echase una soga e que lo subiría consygo. E fue echo asy. E quando la Muerte sallió en la nube ante la mesa, començó Mosén Borra a dar bozes, e el Duque lo llevó allá de yuso, e la Muerte hechó la cuerda e atáronla al cuerpo al dicho Borra, e la Muerte lo guindó arriba. Aquí veríades maravillas de las cosas que Mosén Borra fazía, e del llorar e del gran miedo que le tornava; e subiendo fizo sus agues en sus paños que corrió en las cabeças a los que de yuso heran, que bien tenía que lo llevavan al ynfierno, e el señor Rey miraba e obo grand plazer és e los que lo vieron. E Mosén Borra fue en poder de la Muerte a los çielos', fol. 204v.

[8] For the close relation between the figures of Death and the Fool, see Sophie Oosterwijk, '"Alas, poor Yorick". Death, the Fool, the Mirror and the *Danse Macabre*', in Stefanie Knöll (ed.), *Narren-Masken-Karneval: Meisterwerke von Dürer bis Kubin aus der Düsseldorfer Graphiksammlung "Mensch und Tod"* (Regensburg: Schnell & Steiner, 2009), 20-32.

warning to bear in mind the risks of a sudden, unprepared death. Gert Kaiser speaks in this context of the 'big chimera' ('das große Angstgespenst') of the fourteenth and the fifteenth century, which is decisive for the understanding of the late-medieval *Danse Macabre*.[9] The idea of transitoriness and the motif of equality in the face of death, which are present in the *Vado Mori* tradition and in the Legend of the Three Living and the Three Dead, are also central ideas in the *Danse Macabre* whose core message is the necessity to be conscious of the unpredictability of one's own death and to change one's life accordingly.

After this brief introduction to the earlier *Danse Macabre* tradition in Spain, we shall now turn to a Majorcan play that exemplifies the perpetuation of the *Danse* in sixteenth-century drama.

The Majorcan *Representació de la Mort* and the Llabrés manuscript

The most important collection of Catalan late-medieval drama, copied at the end of the sixteenth century, is held in the Biblioteca de Catalunya (Ms. 1139) in Barcelona. The so-called Llabrés manuscript contains as its thirty-sixth text (fols 149r-157v) an anonymous play that is a particularly original reworking of the medieval *Danse Macabre* motif.[10] Entitled *Representació de la Mort*, the dramatic piece survives in a fragmentary state of 1,575 lines. According to its first editor, Josep Romeu i Figueras, the missing conclusion may not have comprised more than approx. fifty lines, to judge from the blank space left on the *verso* of the last folio used by the scribe to copy this play.[11]

---

[9] Gert Kaiser (ed.), *Der tanzende Tod. Mittelalterliche Totentänze* (Frankfurt am Main: Insel Verlag, 1982), 48.

[10] The codex, copied in the Majorcan village of Búger between 1598 and 1599 by Miquel Pasqual, is named after the scholar who discovered the manuscript in 1887 and subsequently edited several of its forty-nine plays. See Gabriel Llabrés, 'Repertorio de 'Consuetas', representadas en las iglesias de Mallorca. Siglos XV y XVI)', *Revista de Archivos, Bibliotecas y Museos*, 5 (1909), 920-27. With regard to the four Spanish plays contained in this collection, see William H. Shoemaker, 'The Llabrés Manuscript and Its Castilian Plays', *Hispanic Review*, 4 (1936), 239-55.

[11] Josep Romeu i Figueras, 'La 'Representació de la Mort', obra dramática del siglo XVI, y la Danza de la Muerte', *Boletín de la Real Academia de Buenas Letras de Barcelona*, 27 (1957-58), 181-225. For a Catalan version of this study with a bibliographic addendum, see Josep Romeu i Figueras, *Teatre català antic*, vol. 3 (Barcelona: Curial, 1995), 17-95, at 32. The edition cited here is on pp. 45-

Most of the dramatic pieces in the codex are called 'consueta', a term which describes both Latin and vernacular plays that used to be staged in the Middle Ages in churches in a customary way. Apart from the *Representació de la Mort*, eight more plays in the manuscript include the word 'representació' in their title. These plays deal with a variety of topics, such as Christ's Temptations in the Desert (No. 10), the Life of St Francis (No. 29), the Nativity (No. 37), the Last Supper (No. 42), the Life of St Peter (No. 46), the Old Testamentary motif of Judith and Holofernes (No. 47), the Conversion of St Paul (No. 48) and the Descent from the Cross (No. 49). As the manuscript contains a number of similar plays on the same subject which are indistinctively designated by either of these two terms, 'consueta' and 'representació' seem to be used as synonyms, whereas none of the plays in the manuscript is entitled 'misteri', which is an equally common designation for medieval Catalan drama.[12]

The authorship of the *Representació de la Mort*

One of the aspects of the play which has centred scholarly attention during the last few decades is its authorship. Josep Romeu i Figueras maintains that the play might be the work of the Majorcan writer Francesc d'Olesa

---

94. The play has also been included in the volume on Catalan medieval and Renaissance drama in the popular collection 'Les Millors Obres de la Literatura Catalana' (*Masterpieces of Catalan Literature*), 'La Representació de la Mort', *Teatre medieval i del Renaixement* (Barcelona: Edicions 62 and 'la Caixa', 1983), 98-137, edited by Josep Massot i Muntaner, who follows Romeu i Figueras in attributing the authorship of the play to the Majorcan writer Francesc d'Olesa (1485-1550).

[12] There are five more Nativity Plays in the Llabrés Manuscript (Nos 1, 2, 5 and 6), all of which are entitled 'consueta'. With regard to the hagiographic plays, there are six plays designated as 'consuetes' that stage the lives of St George (Nos 30 and 31), St Christopher (Nos 32 and 33), St Matthew (No. 44) and St Crispin and St Crispinian (No. 45). As for the term 'representació', this designation is documented in 1360, for instance, in relation to two consuetudinary plays staged in the cathedral of Girona: a play on the Martyrdom of St Stephen ('repraesentatio martyrii beati Stephani') and a Nativity Play ('representatio partus beatae Virginis'). The term is also used to refer to the earliest Catalan play on the Assumption of the Virgin Mary, dating from the late fourteenth century, the 'Representació de l'Assumpció de Madona Sancta Maria'. Among the plays, called 'misteris', there are, for example, the assumption plays from València and Elx or the Valencian Corpus Christi plays on the Fall of Man ('Misteri d'Adam i Eva'), King Herod ('Misteri del Rei Herodes') and the Life of St Christopher ('Misteri de sant Cristòfor').

(1485-1550), who is also considered to be the author of the *Nova art de trobar* (The New Art of Writing in Verse), a treaty of poetry still strongly influenced by troubadour lyrics.[13] Another work which is attributed to Francesc d'Olesa is the poem known as *Menyspreu del món* (Scorn of the World), which was written and published on the death of his wife in 1540. According to Jordi Roca, the frontispiece of this edition is illustrated with a very expressive macabre engraving that shows Death holding a bow in one hand and a long arrow in the other, while a serpent is coiled around one of his legs and four skulls are lying scattered on the ground, one of them crowned with a papal tiara. The inscription in the upper part of the engraving reads: 'Nemini parco qui vivit in orbe' (*I spare nobody who lives in the world*).[14]

Among the reasons given by Romeu to prove d'Olesa's authorship of the *Representació* is the fact that some of its verses are also to be found in the *Nova art de trobar* and that the Franciscan spirit impregnating the play is a characteristic feature of the author's other writings. Moreover, if d'Olesa was indeed the author of the *Representació*, this would provide a possible answer to the question why the Emperor – one of the most frequently represented characters in the *Danse* – is not included in the Majorcan play. D'Olesa, who had been knighted by Emperor Charles V, might have wanted to express his gratitude by saving his protector from having to answer Death's call.[15]

Yet Albert Rossich, who embraced Romeu's thesis that the *Representació* and the *Nova art de trobar* are works by the same author, proved that the *Nova art de trobar* must have been written after the death of d'Olesa. Therefore, he concluded that the *Representació de la mort* ought to be considered an anonymous play.[16] Yet even if Romeu, faced with the

---

[13] Josep Romeu i Figueras, 'Francesc d'Olesa, autor dramàtic: una hipòtesi versemblant', *Randa*, 9 (Homenatge a Francesc de B. Moll, 1) (1979-80), 127-37. The study has been re-edited with some additional notes in Romeu (1995), 96-112.

[14] The first two words of this Latin inscription constitute the message written on the scythe which is being carried by the main dancer in the famous 'Dansa de la Mort' during the procession that takes place every Maundy Thursday night in the small town of Verges (Fig. 57). For an English description of this 'unique treasure', as Xavier Fàbregas describes it, see Jordi Roca, *The Verges Procession and the Dance of Death*, translated into English from the original Catalan *La processó de Verges* and with commentary by Simon Furey (Melksham: F.E.P., 1997).

[15] The omission of this figure is even more remarkable if we consider that the near-contemporary Dresden Totentanz relief includes a cryptoportrait of Charles V.

[16] Albert Rossich, 'Francesc d'Olesa i la *Nova art de trobar*', in Antoni Ferrando and Albert G. Hauf (eds), *Miscel·lània Joan Fuster*, vol. 3 (Barcelona: Departament

evidence brought forward by Rossich, accepted that the *Nova art de trobar* dates from the second half of the sixteenth century, he nevertheless continued to consider the *Representació de la mort* to be from the first half of the century and did not rule out that it might yet be a work by d'Olesa.[17]

The *Representació* in the context of Catalan drama in the medieval tradition

The whole *Representació* play is written in seven-syllabic stanzas of five lines each, following the rhyme pattern *abaab*, with the exception of lines 656-60 (*aabba*) and lines 1026-30 (*aaaab*). In the introduction to his edition of the play, Josep Romeu i Figueras points out that the errors and deficiencies that mostly affect the number of syllables and an excessive use of the hiatus are common for this type of literature. He adds that even if such inaccuracies are frequent in old Catalan narrative and dramatic texts, a rather high percentage of these has to be attributed to the scribe. One of the play's assets he acknowledges to be the playwright's expressive agility, which manifests itself in the use of a fluent language and a lively tone, created by colloquial expressions and popular sayings.[18]

In the classification of sixteenth-century Catalan religious drama established by Joan Mas, the *Representació* occupies an intermediate stage, which includes plays that are more developed and contain some allegorical elements, characters of a more discursive type, metrics with stanzas of four or five lines, and some original traits that denote the individual style of an author (stage c).[19] According to this classification, the *Representació* is situated halfway between – on the one hand – those dramatic pieces that either maintain the traditional dramatic schemes and, moreover, tend to stick to the metric pattern of rhyming couplets called 'noves rimades' (stage a), or those that considerably expand the traditional way of staging with material from diverse religious or profane sources (stage b). On the other hand, there are those plays that are divided into 'passos', *i.e.* a number of dramatic episodes, and that can be defined as

---

de Filologia Catalana de la Universitat de València, Associació Internacional de Llengua i Literatura Catalanes and Publicacions de l'Abadia de Montserrat, 1991), 267-95, at 290-91.

[17] A brief summary of this discussion is included in the additional notes in Romeu (1995), 111.

[18] Romeu (1995), 41.

[19] Joan Mas, 'El teatre religiós del segle XVI', in Albert Rossich, Antoni Serrà and Pep Valsalobre (eds), *El teatre català dels orígens al segle XVIII*, (Kassel: Edition Reichenberger and Universitat de Girona, 2001), 17-33, at 30-32.

plays of transition towards Renaissance drama (stage d), and, finally, the so-called 'autos sacramentals' by Joan Timoneda (stage e).

The importance and singularity of the play

Different scholars have pointed out the play's singularity in the panorama of Catalan plays from the sixteenth century. In 1964 Josep Romeu directed a staging of the play as part of the Fourth Cycle of Medieval Drama in the emblematic fourteenth-century 'Tinell Hall' ('Saló del Tinell') in Barcelona.[20] Romeu acknowledges the important role of this play in the transition from medieval to humanist drama, but at the same time he criticises what he considers to be the author's inability to detach himself from the dramatic and conceptual force of the medieval genre of the *Danse Macabre*.[21]

Josep Massot i Muntaner, who published this play in a new edition in the popular collection *Les Millors Obres de la Literatura Catalana* (Masterpieces of Catalan Literature), stresses that the play presents a large number of easily detectable references to the Old and the New Testament that still remain to be specified.[22] Albert Rossich comments that although the play follows a repetitive scheme in its scenic development, it contains fragments of great dramatic power, especially the scenes of Death's encounter with the Youth and with the Lady.[23] Enric Cabra sustains that the play might have been staged in the eastern part of Menorca.[24] Joan Mas considers the *Representació* to be the Catalan play with probably the highest dramatic quality of the whole period.[25] He characterises it as a remarkably elaborated *Danse Macabre*, written by an author who creates

---

[20] This is the place where Christopher Columbus was received by King Ferdinand and Queen Isabella after his first voyage to America.

[21] Romeu (1995), 41.

[22] Josep Massot i Muntaner, 'Notes sobre el text i l'autor de la "Representació de la Mort"', in *Serta philologica F. Lázaro Carreter natalem diem sexagesimum celebranti dicata*, vol. 2 (Madrid: Cátedra, 1983), 347-53, at 351.

[23] Albert Rossich, 'Dues notes sobre la Dansa de la Mort als països de llengua catalana', in Josep Lluís Sirera (ed.), *La Mort com a personatge, l'assumpció com a tema, Actes del VI Seminari de Teatre i Música medievals, Elx, 29 al 31 d'octubre de 2000* (Ajuntament d'Elx, 2002), 337-46, at 338.

[24] Enric Cabra, 'Reminiscències de la Representació de la Mort i d'altres peces teatrals en el cançoner de Francesc d'Albranca', *Revista de Menorca*, 2 (1990), 157-76, at 168.

[25] Joan Mas, 'Els mites autòctons en el teatre català antic', *Revista de Menorca*, 1 (1990), 45-60, at 47.

his personal work on the base of pre-existent material.[26] Víctor Infantes describes it as one of the best achieved examples of the perpetuation of the *Danse Macabre* in drama.[27] Finally, Francesc Massip, taking into account that the play is to be seen in the broader context of the Franciscan preaching practice, relates it to other literary and pictorial examples created under the auspices of this religious order.[28]

It is clear that the *Representació de la Mort* is indebted to the medieval *Danse Macabre* tradition, but its adherence to the model is evidently quite flexible. As in the *Danse*, the Majorcan play shows the coming of Death to man as a sudden and inevitable reality that nobody can escape from. What is new is that sixteenth-century drama no longer follows the characteristic pattern of the genre according to which Death or the dead seize their victims in a fixed order, usually starting with the Pope or the Emperor and descending hierarchically until the lowest rank of society, and often alternating clerical with lay figures. Instead, in this play the successive metaphorical encounters between the allegorical figure of Death and the living take place in what seems to be an arbitrary order. Yet on the stage the play reflects quite graphically that in real life it is impossible to predict who will be the next to be summoned to dance with Death.

The range of characters appearing in the *Representació* is another innovative feature in the play. Whereas in the *Danse Macabre* tradition the characterisation of the victims is usually rather stereotyped, the characters in the Majorcan play are not simply portrayed according to the social group or age they represent. Instead they are also shown as human beings with their own fears, hopes and ambitions.

It goes without saying that this greater complexity in characterisation also affects the way in which the victims are treated by Death. When addressing them, Death takes their uniqueness into account. He thus interacts with them on a much more personal basis than we find in the medieval *Danse Macabre* tradition. In the *Representació* the centre of interest is no longer the levelling power of Death in society, although this

---

[26] Joan Mas i Vives, 'El gènere de la "moralitat" en el teatre català antic', *Llengua & Literatura*, 7 (1996), 91-104, at 100.

[27] Infantes (1997), 288.

[28] Francesc Massip, *Història del teatre català*, 1 (Tarragona: Arola Editors, 2007), 257-59. See also Francesc Massip and Lenke Kovács, 'Les Franciscains et le genre macabre: Les Danses de la Mort et la prédication', *European Medieval Drama*, 8 (2004), 91-105, and Francesc Massip and Lenke Kovács, *El baile: conjuro ante la muerte. Presencia de lo macabro en la Danza y la Fiesta Popular* (Ciudad Real: Consejo Internacional de organización de festivales de folklore and Instituto Nacional de las Artes Escénicas y de la Música, 2004), 119-20.

topic is explicitly referred to in the play, as in 'Papa, rey, jove y vell, / tot o port a un llivell' (*Pope, king, young and old, / All of them do I bring to the same level*, ll. 58-59). The play's core message focuses on how mortality affects man's conscience, thoughts and actions, as exemplified in the different characters that appear on stage. There is a shift from a collective to an individual approach to the subject of dying in accordance with the growing conscience of individuality in the Renaissance period.

As its title indicates, the *Representació de la Mort* is not a dance. However, in a metaphorical sense the image of dancing can indeed be applied to the steps and movements performed on stage by the allegorical figure of Death and each of the dancing partners chosen to join what turns out to be a final tête-à-tête. There is no reference to music or dance in the play – neither in the stage directions nor in the texts spoken by the characters – but the very structure of the dramatic development can be seen as a framework for a very special type of dance performance. Like a dancer addressing a prospective dancing partner without knowing if he or she is willing to accept the invitation, Death calls upon the characters destined to die and listens to their response. In some of the dramatic sequences, the victim's reaction differs from what might be expected. For example, the Poor Man prefers to continue living in misery instead of rejoicing that Death has come to end his troubles, and the Friar shows no eagerness at all to leave his mortal coil behind.

If we regard a dance as being a repeated set of figures, this is a characteristic which is also to be found in the *Representació*, as the sequences that make up the distinct parts of the play follow a common pattern, like the steps and movements in a series of dance figures.

Scenic development

Taking up the medieval stage tradition, the play opens with a prologue in which the audience is exhorted to pay attention and the subject of the play is introduced (ll. 1-40). These introductory lines are spoken by someone who professes to feel responsible for the successful reception of the performance: 'Déu vulla que jo aserta / y los sperits desperta / de tot aquest auditori' (*May God help me to make a point / and to stir the spirits / in this whole audience*, ll. 38-40). The following monologue of self-presentation by Death personified (ll. 41-85) contains an enumeration of the wide range of possibilities to bring man's life to an end: 'A uns mat per malaltia / de febra o de cadarn, / de gota o lebrosia, / axí qu·en l'any no reste dia / ni ora sensa fer carn. / De coltell per violènsia / y en la mar ofegats / messes fas, ab pestilènsias. / Altres moren per sentènsias, / per los jutges condemnats.' (*Some do I kill by sickness, by fever or by chill, by gout or by leprosy, so that in the year there is no day nor hour without slaughter. By violence with the knife and drowning in the sea, plenty do I kill with plagues. Others await their sentences, condemned by judges*, ll. 71-80).

The subsequent encounters between Death and the living always follow the same structure. In the first place, an individual enters the stage and pronounces a monologue which serves to present the character to the audience; then, all of a sudden, Death appears and a verbal confrontation takes place between the two figures in which sometimes physical violence is used. At the end, Death gains the victory and hides so that he remains unseen by the next victim who enters the stage. In this way, Death unexpectedly calls upon the Young Man (ll. 86-155), the Rich Man (ll. 156-270), the Poor Man (ll. 271-370), the Gambler (ll. 371-460), the Lady (ll. 461-560), the Young Boy[29] (ll. 561-660), the Brigand (ll. 661-745), the Old Man whose death is commented by the Gravedigger (ll. 746-900), the King (ll. 901-1010), the Friar (ll. 1011-1115), and the Pope (ll. 1116-75).

Stage directions

There are very few explicit stage directions and these are, moreover, far from extensive; in fact, they are rather simple and repetitive. Because of their strictly functional character they can easily be classified in the following groups: a) speech prefixes that specify the name of the speaker, b) rubrics that indicate that a character enters the stage, c) stage directions that indicate that a character leaves the stage and d) rubrics that give some details about symbolic elements that help us recognise the characters (see

---

[29] In the original, this character is called 'fadrinet', which is the diminutive form of 'fadrí'. In old Catalan, this word is used to refer to a 'young boy under fifteen'. Cf. *Diccionari Català-Valencià-Balear*, 10 vols (Palma de Mallorca: Editorial Moll, 1988). Another meaning of the word is 'bachelor', which Simon Furey uses in his translation of one of the dialogues between Death and the Young Boy (ll. 595-602) in the English version of Jordi Roca's book about the Maundy Thursday Procession in Verges (Roca, *The Verges Procession*, 111). However, the play text leaves no doubt about the fact that the portrayed character has not yet reached adulthood: 'Molt tendra y delicat / mon pare y ma mare em crien.' (*My father and my mother bring me up with great tenderness and delicacy*, ll. 560-61); 'Quina onra guanyaràs / de matar a un minyó?' (*What kind of honour can you obtain from killing a youngster?*, ll. 616-17); 'No me'n puch aconortar / que, quan comens are obrir los ulls, / que·ls age tencar' (*I cannot take it that now that I've just begun to open my eyes I shall close them*, ll. 621-22).

Appendix). As a rule, the scribe does not include speech prefixes when the name of the character can be inferred from the context.[30]

There are also only very few implicit stage directions, *i.e.* deductions that can be made from the text about how the play was intended to be performed or how the characters were expected to be shown. Thus, both the Rich Man and the Poor Man allude to the way in which they are dressed. Whereas the Rich Man boasts, '[Tinc] moltes sedas y brocats!' (*[I own] plenty of silk and brocades!*, l. 154), the Poor Man complains, 'Vestit vaig ten pobrament / que vergonya tinch de la gent.' (*I am so poorly dressed that I feel ashamed when people look at me*, ll. 291-92). Likewise, the use of theatrical props is implied in the text, *e.g.* when Death exclaims, 'No·m fàltan tretas ni darts / per fer del home dos parts' (*I have plenty of projectiles and arrows to divide man into two halves*, ll. 68-69). Likewise the Brigand shows off by enumerating the different types of weapons he is wearing: 'Jo aporta pedranyal, / arcabús y escopeta, / coltell, daga i punyal, / jaco de malla i bresal, / llança, fletxa y ballesta.' (*Here I am with my carbine, arquebus and musket, knife, dagger and small sword, doublet and arm shield, lance, arrow and bow*, ll. 686-90).

Another noteworthy aspect is the way in which the killing is to be performed. The stage direction after line 745 specifies that Death kills the Brigand by means of an arrow. However, this is the only explicit reference throughout the play to how the victim is killed, and it is precisely after a scene of extreme violence that Death makes use of this deadly weapon. The manifold ways used by Death to despatch the living that are listed in the initial monologue suggest that on stage the killing need not always have been portrayed in the same way, and that the arrow might only have been used exceptionally in response to the Brigand's attack with a knife. In this regard, it is interesting to note that the speech of the Poor Man contains an implicit stage direction when he pleads: 'Mort, no·m cobres en ton manto' (*Death, do not cover me in your coat!*, l. 318). The act of killing might in this case have been performed in a metaphorical way by covering the victim with a large piece of cloth, perhaps a shroud, simulating an embrace, like the one that is indicated in the stage direction of the Valencian *Misteri d'Adam i Eva* when the two main characters are being expelled from Paradise: 'Ara la Mort los abraça' (*Now Death embraces them*, rubric after l. 258).[31]

---

[30] In his edition, Josep Romeu i Figueres lists all the cases in which the speech prefixes are omitted. Cf. Romeu (1995), 47, note 40.

[31] 'Misteri d'Adam i Eva', in Ferran Huerta (ed.), *Teatre bíblic. Antic testament* (Barcelona: Editorial Barcino, 1976), 101-18, at 116.

In the Majorcan *Representació*, Death seems to execute all the victims on the spot without giving them time to offer any resistance, except for the Brigand who is killed in a fierce fight. Once a character has been killed, the rubrics state quite plainly that the victim falls to the ground. The absence of any further reference to them suggests that they may have simply remained lying on the stage floor until the end of the performance. However, there are some exceptions to this scenic development, *e.g.* in the case of the Lady who is supposed to hide after having been killed: 'La dama cau morta, y amague's.' (*The Lady falls down dead, and hides*, rubric after l. 560), or in the case of three especially reproachable characters – the Rich Man, the Gambler and the Brigand – who are carried away by devils, according to the rubrics after lines 270, 460 and 745.[32]

The motif of postponed death

What could have been a rather monotonous play because of its regularity and predictability is livened up by some digressions from the main line of action, whereby the emotional impact and the didactic effectiveness for the audience are increased. In this regard, the most outstanding feature in the *Representació* is the introduction of the motif of postponed death. This favour is granted to the Young Man, who is the first person to be summoned to die but who manages to obtain a postponement of his death practically without any effort. At first sight, it might seem quite surprising that Death is so easily ready to concede, as his words indicate: 'Lo que demanas faré / verament, sense falsia' (*What you ask for will be done by me / truthfully and without treachery*, ll. 125-26). However, a closer look at the Young Man's speech reveals a plausible explanation to this unexpected twist of action.

What is most convincing in the Young Man's attitude is his fearlessness. He starts his speech by reproaching Death that he frightens the world in his gruesome shape: 'O Mort, que lo món spantas / ab te molt cruel figura!' (ll. 86-87). Then he asks Death to 'tame himself' a little bit ('Prech-te un poch te amanses.', l. 88) and to add some sweetness to his

---

[32] However, the reference to the hiding of the Lady might also be attributed to a lapsus of the scribe, if we bear in mind that many of the rubrics follow the pattern 'X cau morta, y amague's la Mort' (*X falls down dead, and Death hides.*). The scribe might have reproduced the pattern, writing: 'La dama cau morta, y amague's.' (*The Lady falls dead, and hides.*), before adding redundantly: 'se amague la Mort' (*Death hides.*) Another reason to explain why the actor who played the Lady was supposed to hide would be that he was cast in more than one role of the *Representació*.

menaces ('En tes amanases tantas, / mescle-y un poch de dulsura.', ll. 89-90). Death's answer to these suggestions is the avowal that he ignores any kind of pleasure and that he can bring people nothing but distress:

> No sé què vol dir dolsor
> May gustí sucra ni mel.
> Causa só de gran dolor,
> de tristura i de plor.
> Més amarga só que·l fel. (ll. 91-95)

> *I do not know what sweetness means.*
> *I have never tasted sugar or honey.*
> *I am the cause of great pain,*
> *sadness and crying.*
> *I am more bitter than gall.*

Unimpressed by these words, the Young Man tells Death that he sees no reason why his youthful strength should be destroyed, why he should join him, and why he should end up resembling him in his disfigurement (ll. 96-100). Death's reply to his objection consists in emphasising the inevitability of the body's decay as a common feature of human nature. To illustrate this, Death cites the motif of the Three Living and the Three Dead and refers the Young Man to the skulls, ribs, spines and shinbones in the graveyard that used to belong to people as handsome as he, but who are now as hideous as he will be: 'Lo que tu ets, aquells foren; / tu seràs lo que ells són.' (*That what you are, they were; you shall be what they are*, ll. 105-06).

Yet, even this most dreadful vision does not seem to frighten the Young Man, who still asks Death as a favour that he will be notified when his last hour has come, a request which denotes the medieval preoccupation with a sudden death that leaves no time for contrition. Most notably, the Young Man neither shows fear nor does he make any promises to achieve his goal. He simply looks Death in the eye and asks him to stop addressing him, quietly assuming that he will be granted the favour to go on living until he has grown old. Indeed, the Young Man proves to be right as Death is willing to accede to his wishes, not without telling him that he considers his desire to stay alive a foolish mistake: 'Molt desencaminat vas / saguint del món la follia.' (*You are quite mistaken to follow the world's foolishness*, ll. 116-17). Finally, he promises to keep on reminding him of his death and tells him to be constantly on his guard: 'molts avisos te daré; / mes tu vel·la nit y dia' (*I shall give you many warnings; but watch out night and day*, ll. 129-30), which is a quite obvious allusion to Matthew 24:42.

Immediately after Death has left him, the Young Man expresses his determination to live a life full of pleasure now that he knows that Death will not kill him without prior warning: 'Viure puch ab libertat, / puis de la Mort avisat / sere antes de morir' (*I can live in freedom as Death will warn me before I die*, ll. 133-35). He thus fails to take advantage of Death's promise to act as a constant reminder of his mortality. Instead of opting to lead a virtuous life as a sign of gratitude for this privilege he lulls himself into a false sense of security and nourishes the idea that a feeling of repentance just before his death will be enough to escape from eternal damnation:

Quan la Mort me avisarà,
a la hora em penadiré.
Sols una hora em bastarà
y encara·m sobrarà:
en aquella em salvaré. (ll. 151-55)

When Death comes to call upon me
At that very hour I shall repent
And I shall still have time enough:
At that very hour I shall be saved.

In the figure of the Young Man, the anonymous playwright takes up the issue of justification, a highly polemic topic in the confrontation between Protestants and Catholics, which was much discussed in the Council of Trent (1545-63).[33] The Young Man is presented as a heretic who expects to obtain salvation on his deathbed 'sola fide', *i.e.* by his faith alone, with disregard of his deeds. However, it is evident that his supposed faith is nothing but a farce, since he expresses himself in similar terms to those who do not believe in the resurrection: 'Puis remey no té la mort / [...] / Menjar, beure y jugar / serà lo meu axercisi' (*For there is no remedy against death / [...] / it will be my pastime / to eat, to drink and to gamble*, ll. 135, 141-42), in allusion to the biblical verse: 'Let us eat drink, for tomorrow we die' (1 Corinthians 34). His self-righteous and calculating attitude shows that he ignores the nature of repentance and the concept of salvation by God's grace, two fundamental elements of the Christian creed.

---

[33] 'Konzil v. Trient: Dekret über die Rechtfertigung', in Heinrich Denzinger, *Enchiridion symbolorum definitionum et declarationum de rebus fidei et morum. Kompendium der Glaubensbekenntnisse und kirchlichen Lehrentscheidungen*, ed. Peter Hünermann (Freiburg/Basilea/Vienna: Herder, 2005), 502-21.

The Young Man is the only figure – apart from Death himself – to have more than one entry on stage, because after having been temporarily spared from dying he meets Death again once he has grown old. In his initial monologue, he boasts that at the age of ninety he is still able to chew dry bread. He shows off the merry life he has led and claims that, if it were not for his white beard, he would think of himself as still young. Moreover, he presents himself as a widower who aspires to marriage for the seventh time, yet not to a woman of his own age but to a young, rich, pleasant maiden (ll. 746-70).[34] At this moment, Death makes his appearance to tell the Old Man that he had better stop making plans, because it is time for him to follow him (ll. 771-75), whereupon the Old Man starts to protest energetically and accuse him of treachery (ll. 776-80); an accusation Death repudiates (ll. 781-85). He then reminds Death of his promise to give him some warning (ll. 786-90) and Death replies that he has been doing so over the years, but that he has always chosen to ignore them (ll. 791-95). When the Old Man retorts that he would have recognised his dreadful, bony, naked figure (ll. 796-800), Death tells him that he neither listened to the church bells calling him to mass, nor to the ones announcing the celebration of the last rites (ll. 801-05). The Old Man then admits to having noticed these and other signs that Death enumerates, but he remembers that these reminders of his own mortality always made him cling even more tightly to worldly pleasures (ll. 806-30).

When Death tells the Old Man that he should have taken his salvation seriously and that once in hell he will be beyond salvation, he starts to tremble and pleads with him to let him prepare properly for his demise (ll. 831-40). However, Death accuses him of making false promises from fear and states that he does not believe in his ability to change: 'Qual ets stat fins así, / tal seràs d'aquí avant.' (*Such as you have been up to the present day / You will continue to be from now on*, ll. 841-42). There is no use in his blaming the world for his failure, because Death makes him responsible for his own actions and laughs at him for having believed that he could live merrily and still hope to die a good death. Before he kills him, his final admonition is that anyone who aspires to die peacefully should start serving God at a young age (ll. 843-70).

---

[34] This type of mismatching is a common motif in Catalan popular literature until the present day. For example, in Tarragona there is a traditional dramatic performance of bawdy dialogues called 'Dames i vells' (*Ladies and Old Men*), in which both the male and the female parts are played by men. A medieval precedent for this play is the dialogue *El procés de les olives*, in which a group of people discusses the advantages and inconveniences of old men marrying young women.

Another character that stands out from the rest is the Gravedigger whose main function consists in commenting on the Old Man's foolish behaviour the moment he has died. However, instead of blaming the dead man for having led a life of sin when he should have known better, the Gravedigger does not express a moral judgement. Instead, he shows himself surprised that somebody can be as unwise as the Old Man who has just died. He begins his speech by exclaiming:

Com estave descuydat
de la mort aquest bon vell,
enmig dels visis posat,
de Déu serè oblidat
y mal amicat per ell!

En mals dias és envellit,
minyó de vuytanta anys! (ll. 871-77)

How careless this old fellow was!
Stuck in the middle of vices,
Having forgotten God
And not being close to Him!

How badly you have grown old,
Young boy of eighty years!

The Gravedigger's words denote a certain sense of pity for the victim, but at the same time it is made quite clear to the audience what a bad example it is to follow the character of the Old Man. Even more than the allegorical figure of Death, the Gravedigger does not pretend to anticipate a judgement which only corresponds to God. Instead, he limits himself to lament the foolishness of somebody who spent night and day causing harm to himself ('de dia I de nit / mai t'ets deixat de fer gran dany', ll. 879-80) and who was incautious enough to claim for his 'share of bad life', even if this meant having to 'abandon the precious stone [of virtue]' ('per un tros de vida dolent / dexe l'ome imprudent / la excel·lent pedra fina', ll. 898-900).

There is no hint in the stage directions to indicate that the Gravedigger performs any gestures, movements or actions that suggest the burial of the corpse, apart from his comments on the Old Man's foolishness. Neither do the rubrics specify any stage props (*e.g.* a digging tool such as a spade or trowel) or the type of clothing to characterise this figure. It is true that, throughout the play, the stage directions mostly consist of mere speech prefixes, but when one of the corpses is carried away (as in the cases of the

Rich Man, the Gambler and the Brigand) the rubrics do say so. For this reason, it seems logical to assume that the Old Man's body remains lying on the ground until the end of the play, instead of being removed by the Gravedigger.

Death personified in the Catalan drama tradition

The personification of Death occurs not only in the *Representació* but also elsewhere in the Llabrés play manuscript. At the start of the first play, which is one of the five Nativity Plays in the codex, Death appears very briefly on stage at Lucifer's command. In addition, the fortieth play in the compilation, which is entitled *Consueta dels Set Sagraments* ('The Play of the Seven Sacraments'), also contains a short stage appearance by Death. However, none of the explicit stage directions of these two plays give any details about the character's portrayal on stage. Related to performances in Valencia, there is a reference from 1643 to '.ii. vestits de morts cruet a modo de botargues' (*two undyed costumes for the dead in the form of overalls*). This may relate to the *Misteri d'Adam i Eva* as it is the only one of the Valencian Corpus Christi plays to include the character of Death personified.[35] Moreover, an inventory of the 'Casa de les Roques', where the costumes where kept, mentions in the entry for 23 December 1716: 'un sayo con su capucha para la Muerte' (*an overall with a hood for Death*).[36]

The scenic portrayal of Death in a skeletal appearance is equally documented in the Catalan tradition of the *Danse Macabre*. This is the form that is adopted in the aforementioned Maundy Thursday Procession in Verges (Fig. 57), where the dancers wear close fitting body-stockings made in one piece and painted to resemble skeletons. On their heads they wear skulls in the manner of helmets, which were originally of papier-mâché and very simply made. In the 1980s the costumes and the skull masks were redesigned and at present their aspect is appallingly realistic. In the neighbouring village Rupià, a much simpler *Danse Macabre* with only one dancer used to be performed until 1935.[37] This character, who

---

[35] Manuel Carboneres, *Relación y explicación histórica de la solemne procession del Corpus que anualmentmente celebra la ciudad de Valencia* (Valencia: J. Doménech, 1878), 88.

[36] Hermenegildo Corbató, 'Los misterios del Corpus de Valencia', *University of California Publications in Modern Philology*, 16:1 (1933), 1-172, at 159.

[37] Both the performance in Rupià and the recently discovered dance in La Bisbal d'Empordà were part of the Holy Friday procession. The latter was performed at least until 1867 and included a 'ball rodó' (*circle dance*), which according to the

danced while swaying a scythe, wore a costume consisting of two pieces painted to look like a skeleton and his head covered by a skull-like helmet. This typology of a costume for Death personified is documented for the first time in Europe in the early sixteenth century, *viz.* in a macabre mummery designed by Piero di Cosimo for the Carnival of Florence in 1510. In this context, reference should also be made to the famous skeleton costumes from the seventeenth century preserved in Bern.[38]

Fig. 57. Costumed dancers in a Maundy Thursday procession in Verges (Spain). Photo: author.

---

records took place in the Carrer Ample (*Broad Street*). See Jordi Frigola and Pep Vila, 'La Bisbal tenia Dansa de la Mort', *Diari de Girona* (3 July 2005), 8-9.
[38] Massip and Kovács (2004), 37 and 151, Fig. 87.

As for the way Death is to be portrayed in the *Representació*, there is very little evidence to be found in the text, where the protagonist is referred to as 'lletja figura' (*ugly figure*, ll. 317, 796), 'cuca fera' (*dreadful beast*, ll. 491, 789), and 'fera monstruositat' (*savage monstrosity*, l. 946), apart from being described as 'seca, magra, tota nua' (*bony, gaunt, completely naked*, l. 799) and 'desencarnade, / seca y desfigurade' (*fleshless, bony and disfigured*, ll. 1053-54). Its first editor, Josep Romeu, assumes that the actor representing Death must have worn a clinging one-piece black costume with a skeleton painted on it in white, and that his head and face must have been covered by a helmet and a mask resembling a skull.[39] However, the character's appearance might as well have been similar to that of the Death figure described by the chronicler of the coronation ceremonies in 1414, *i.e.* the typology of an eviscerated corpse.

The individual's response when facing death

With regard to the interaction of Death and the living, not all the victims are treated in the same way in the Majorcan play. Apart from the Young Man who is granted the privilege of a delayed death, each of the other characters who are summoned to die also receives an individualised call by Death. In this respect, the *Representació* differs from the medieval *Danse Macabre* tradition where the emphasis is put on the levelling power of Death, whereas the individual's response fails to have any effect on the course of action.

The first character to appear on stage after the Young Man has left is the Rich Man, who presents himself by boasting of his extraordinary wealth and fortune, and exposing his plans to amass even greater riches.[40] The reason for his excessive pride is to be found in the humble origins from which he managed to rise through his own cunning and frugality ('Rich me só feta ab mas mañas / Turriburri é menjat', ll. 182-83). He finishes his speech in a high-spirited tone, claiming that even if he lived for two hundred years, he would not be able to spend all that he possesses. Death thwarts these futile plans by telling him that it is time to leave and that everything he owns will be given to strangers. In answer to the Rich

---

[39] Romeu (1995), 42.

[40] This passage recalls Jeremiah 9:23: 'Let not the rich man boast of his riches', and Psalm 49:16-19: 'Do not envy a man when he grows rich, / when the wealth of his family increases; / for he will take nothing when he dies, / and his wealth will not go with him. / Though in his lifetime he counts himself happy / and men praise him in his prosperity, / he will go to join the company of his forefathers / who will never again see the light.'

Man's protests, Death reproaches him for his carelessness which made him lead his life without thinking about God, about himself, and about his death.

This is when the Rich Man remembers the sick and the poor, asking Death to take them instead of him as they are living in pain, whereas he himself has plenty of goods to spend. Death wonders how he dares speak for those who he had always treated with disdain, but the Rich Man goes on arguing the appropriateness of their death instead of his own. When he is told that he should not have indulged his greed, the Rich Man desperately implores his money to deliver him from Death. He then offers all his belongings to Death and asks him to leave him naked, but alive. Death announces that, indeed, the Rich Man will have to follow him naked to a place where he will remain until Doomsday. Once again the Rich Man begs his money for help, admitting that he has adored, served and loved money as his god.[41] Death answers by paraphrasing Job 1:21, 'Nuu ets vingut en lo món / y nuu te n'as de tornar' (*Naked you came into the world and naked you shall return*, ll. 246-47), thereby reminding him that his riches belong to God and that he has made a bad use of his wealth. The Rich Man recognises his mistake and expresses his regret, even if he knows that it is now too late. Finally, Death sentences him to permanent loss of both invaluable riches and enduring paradise, all as a result of his wish to be rich for a single moment.

As a contrast to Death's first victim, the next character to appear on stage is the Poor Man, who starts presenting himself with a bitter lamentation about his situation which is so desperate that he has no choice but to work as the gravedigger's dogsbody. He feels miserable, knowing that he will never earn enough money to feed his family, let alone be able to provide dowries for his daughters. Abandoning hope, he believes that the longer he lives the more he will suffer ('Quan más craxaran mos dias / craxaran las penas mias', ll. 303-04). Interpreting these words as a covert desire to die, Death tells the Poor Man that his wish will be fulfilled ('Vòstron desig és complit', l. 315). In response, however, Death's victim states that he has changed his mind and that instead of dying he prefers to go on living even in misery, an attitude which Death considers to be nothing but foolish.

Once the Poor Man has been struck down and Death has hidden himself, the Gambler enters the stage to present a vivid picture of himself

---

[41] This passage recalls Psalm 62:10: 'though wealth breeds wealth, set no your heart on it', and Matthew 6:21: 'where your treasure is, there will your heart be also', a verse which is also to be found in the *Danse Macabre* mural in Morella as an inscription on the banderole issuing from the corpse's mouth.

as somebody so strongly addicted to gambling that nothing can refrain him from following a passion that he knows to be destructive and antisocial. So ruthless that he would even sell his own children in order to obtain money ('A voltas vinch a pensar / mos infants encativar / sols que·m donassen rayals', ll. 423-35), he is not in the least afraid when Death calls upon him, but invites him to gamble with him if he possesses gold or silver. Outraged by this offer, Death shouts at him, calling him 'blind, foolish and unreasonable' ('sego, foll i insensat', l. 446), but the Gambler is determined to go on gambling even with the devil. Consequently, he is carried away by devils once Death has put an end to his life.

Next comes the Lady, who according to her own words is 'gracious and gentile' ('gentil só y graciosa', l. 461). As the apple of her parents' eye ('los meus pares me adoren', l. 466), she presents herself as full of pride and with a strong sense of superiority due to her status, wealth and style of life. When she boasts of having plenty of admirers who wish to marry her, Death turns up as her prospective husband, telling her that she has no choice but to accept him as her spouse. As has been pointed out by Josep Romeu i Figueres, this part of the play incorporates topics taken from courtly love and suggests also the literal use of fragments from the folk song 'La mort i la donzella' (Death and the Maiden).[42]

Some of the verses of this episode have survived in the oral tradition in the song 'Davant es mirai' (*In front of the mirror*), one of many examples collected by Francesc Camps i Mercadal, a researcher in folklore.[43] In the play, the verses that in the song correspond to the Maiden are distributed among two characters: the Lady and the Young Boy. Born with a silver spoon in his mouth like his predecessor, the latter most ungratefully asks Death to spare him and to take away his parents instead: 'Vés a ma mare, qui·s vella, / mata mon pare ab ella, / sols jo age libertat' (*Go and get my mother, who is old and kill my father with her, if only I may be granted freedom*, ll. 603-05). However, he is told by Death that there is no remedy against God's will ('axí·u à Déu definit', l. 658) and that he should accept his fate as mercy and not as disdain.

The Brigand, who is the next to appear in front of the audience, has been interpreted as a reference to the robberies after the Revolt of the Brotherhoods ('Guerres de les Germanies', 1521-23), as he complains

---

[42] Romeu (1995), 39.
[43] According to Cabra (1990), 167, this song, which is similar to 'Death and the Maiden', presents the same structure as the play and might have originated from the stage practice. With regard to a possible place of representation, he suggests that the play, inscribed in the Franciscan tradition, might have been staged in the Convent of Jesus in Maó, which was already important in the sixteenth century.

about the injustices suffered by his kinsmen.[44] Like the Young Man and the Gambler, he is surprised but not afraid when confronted with Death. Heavily armed, he even has the courage to fight; when he attacks Death with a knife, he is finally struck down by an arrow and carried away by devils.[45]

The play then continues with the episode of the Old Man, whose death is commented on by the Gravedigger and precedes the appearance of the King. The latter presents himself in self-indulgence as a godlike sovereign ('[Jo sóc] com una divinitat', *[I am] like a deity*, l. 925), who has the power to decide over life and death ('Jo mate, jo perdona / de la manera que jo vull.' *I kill and I grant pardons in the way that pleases me*, ll. 931-32). Like the characters before him, the King has to learn the hard way that his plans are about to be thwarted by Death, who comes to take him away without mercy.

The following character to enter the stage is a Friar, who looks back at his life of devotion to God. He makes reference to the sacrifices and the hardship he has experienced over the years, but he seems confident that it was for his own good. In fact, his speech of self-presentation can be seen as an invitation to the audience to follow his example. Summing up what he considers to be the ideal attitude, he addresses the audience saying: 'Com a mort, sens resistència, / simplement, ab pasiència, / eu a fer lo que eus és manat' (*As if you were dead, without offering resistance, simply with patience, you have to do what you are being told*, ll. 1033-35). The anonymous playwright makes the Friar stand out from the rest of the characters in this play by showing him as conscientious. However, what turns the Friar into a credible character is the weakness he shows when actually confronted with Death. At this stage, he recognises that there is a gap between theory and practice that is not easily bridged: 'Molt y·à del dir al fer / y del veure an el tocar' (*There is a long way from saying to doing, and from seeing to touching*, ll. 1061-62). When Death tries to comfort him by reminding him of the afterlife, the Friar expresses his fear of having to answer before God as a 'supreme governor' and a 'righteous judge': 'tinc, empero, més temor / del suprem governador, / jutge just, sense respecta' (*yet I am more afraid of the supreme governor, the righteous judge without any respect*, ll. 1083-85).

Death's last victim in this play is the Pope, who emphasises his status as St Peter's successor and lists his privileges, such as the power to grant

---

[45] The editors have kindly drawn my attention to the fact that robbers and gamblers are also part of Holbein's *Images of Death*, but only after 1547 when the original edition was expanded with new woodcuts based on further designs by Holbein.

indulgences, order crusades and religious jubilees, commutate votes, restore frauds, decide upon matrimonial dispensation, and legitimise offspring. He ends his speech saying that he feels so sublimated by his virtue, honesty and studies that he fears nothing but Death. Prompted by this word, Death steps forward to tell the Pope that it is time for him to die. In the only part of the pontiff's reply that is preserved, the Pope confesses that he has always been afraid of this moment and he expresses his sadness in the face of the inevitability of his situation.

The play ends abruptly after a final stanza in which Death reminds the Pope that where he is bound to go he will be all on his own ('A loch qu·eveu de aribar / a on tot sol au de aribar / del vostro papal lo feix', ll. 1171-75). As the final part of the play is not preserved, the interpretation of these lines is difficult. The allusion to the pope's post-mortem state of loneliness might be seen as a reference to his having to leave behind his counsellors, rather than as anti-clerical satire, and a reference to the splendid isolation for the pope to reflect his former status on earth.

Conclusion

By showing the different ways in which people in the play face death, the Majorcan *Representació de la Mort* is related to the *Ars moriendi* or 'Art of Dying' treaties. At the same time, the play represents an adaptation of the fifteenth-century *Danse Macabre* tradition for a sixteenth-century audience. As in the *Danse*, Death summons a number of representatives of the different states in society and the different Ages of Man. At the same time, however, the importance of the individual's response is stressed, which is especially exemplified in the case of the Young Man who is the only one to be granted the privilege of continuing his life until old age. The anonymous playwright introduces this character to squash people's hope of obtaining salvation through last-minute repentance, thereby taking up the polemic issue of justification by faith alone (Romans 3:22-25) or by good deeds (James 2:15-26). Another character which stands out from the rest is the Friar who is presented as an example to follow, not so much because he practises what is known as the 'scorn of the world' in his life but because he is the only character who lives conscientiously. Yet he does not lack human frailty and feels afraid in the face of death, which adds credibility to his portrayal.

It has been pointed out that some passages of the *Representació* use fragments of the Catalan translation and sequel of the French *Danse Macabre* by Pere Miquel Carbonell and Gaspar Nadal at the end of the fifteenth century. There are also coincidences with the Stanzas of Death

(*Cobles de la mort*) reproduced at the end of the Book of the Venturous Pilgrim (*Llibre del venturós pelegrí*), a narrative poem from the late fourteenth or early fifteenth century, which was very popular until the nineteenth century.[46] Nevertheless, the Majorcan play goes far beyond these sources and is a creation in its own right which stands out from the rest of the plays of this genre. In the present state of investigation, any questions related to the play's popularity, its wider influence and performances still remain unanswered.

Acknowledgements

This essay is dedicated to the late Bob Potter (Santa Barbara, † 2010); it was written within the framework of the Research Group 2009 SGR 258 'Literatura, Art i Representació a la llarga Edat Mitjana', coordinated by Francesc Massip, Universitat Rovira i Virgili, Tarragona. I am grateful to Sophie Oosterwijk and Stefanie Knöll for their helpful suggestions and comments on an earlier draft of this essay.

---

[46] Romeu (1995), 39-40.

Appendix:
Types of rubrics in the *Representació*

a) Speech prefixes that specify the name of the speaker
There are one hundred twenty-two rubrics of this type: 'Pròlech' (*Prologue*, inicial rubric), 'la Mort' (*Death*, rubrics after ll. 90, 100, 115, 125, 205, 215, 225, 235, 245, 255, 265, 320, 330, 340, 350, 365, 445, 495, 505, 515, 525, 535, 545, 555, 595, 600, 605, 610, 617, 625, 635, 645, 655, 705, 720, 740, 780, 790, 800, 810, 820, 830, 840, 850, 860, 865, 950, 960, 967, 975, 985, 995, 1005, 1055, 1065, 1075, 1085, 1095, 1110 and 1170), 'Lo Jove' (*The Youth*, rubrics after ll. 95, 110 and 120), 'Lo Rich' (*The Rich Man*, rubrics after ll. 200, 210, 220, 230, 240, 250 and 260), 'Lo Pobre' (*The Poor Man*, rubrics after ll. 325, 325, 335, 345 and 355), 'Lo Jugador' (*The Gambler*, rubrics after ll. 440, 450 and 455), 'La Dama' (*The Lady*, rubrics after ll. 460, 490, 500, 510, 520, 530, 540 and 530), 'Lo Fadrinet' (*The Young Boy*, rubrics after ll. 560, 590, 597, 602, 607, 615, 620, 630, 640 and 650), 'Lo Bandoler' (*The Brigand*, rubrics after ll. 700 and 710), 'Lo Vell' (*The Old Man*, rubrics after ll. 775, 785, 795, 805, 815, 825, 845, 855 and 862), 'Lo Rey' (*The King*, rubrics after ll. 945, 955, 965, 970, 975, 980, 990, 1000), 'Lo Frare' (*The Friar*, rubrics after ll. 1050, 1060, 1070, 1080, 1090 and 1100) and 'Lo Papa' (*The Pope*, rubric after l. 1165).

b) Rubrics that indicate that a character enters the stage
There are eighteen rubrics of this type: 'Ix la Mort, y diu' (*Death enters and says*, rubrics after ll. 40, 195, 310 and 435), 'Ix la Mort' (*Death enters*, rubrics after ll. 485, 585, 695, 770, 940, 1045 and 1160), 'Y entre un pobra, y diu lo pobra' (*And a Poor Man enters and says*, rubric after l. 270), 'Y entre una donzella' (*And a Maiden enters*, rubric after l. 460), 'Y entre un fadrinet y diu' (*And a Young Boy enters and says*, rubric after l. 560), 'Y entra lo foser, y diu' (*And the Gravedigger enters and says*, rubric after l. 870), 'Entre un rey, y diu' (*A King enters and says*, rubric after l. 900), 'Y entre un frare, y diu' (*And a Friar enters and says*, rubric after l. 1010) and 'Y entre un papa' (*And a Pope enters*, rubric after l. 1115)

c) Stage directions that indicate that a character leaves the stage
The six rubrics of this type are 'Amague's la Mort' (*Death hides*, rubric after l. 130), 'Va-se'n lo jove' (*The Young Man leaves*, rubric after l. 155), 'Lo rich cau mort, y aporten-lo-se'n diables. Y la Mort se amague' (*The Rich Man falls dead, and devils carry him away. And Death hides*, rubric

after l. 270), 'Lo pobra cau mort, y la Mort se amaga' (*The Poor Man falls dead, and Death hides*, rubric after l. 370), 'Cau mort lo jugador, y aporten-lo-sse'n diables' (*The Gambler falls dead, and devils carry him away*, rubric after l. 460) and 'La dama cau morta, y amague's; se amaga la Mort' (*The Lady falls dead and hides; and Death hides [as well]*, rubric after l. 560).

d) Rubrics that specify the characters' attributes
There are four rubrics of this type: 'Entre un jove molt ben vestit' (*A Young Man enters, very well-dressed*, rubric after l. 85), 'Y entra un jugador en cartas en las mans' (*And a Gambler enters, holding playing cards in his hand*, rubric after l. 370), 'Y entra un bandoler tot carregat d'armes' (*And a Brigand enters, heavily armed*, rubric after l. 660), 'Lo bandoler arranca lo coltell anant envés la Mort am grans crits, y la Mort tira la setgeta y cau mort, pòrtant-lo-se'n dimonis. Entra lo jova que la Mort havia asegurat, ab una barba blanca com a vell, y diu' (*The Brigand draws his knife and runs towards Death fiercely yelling, and Death draws his arrow, and [the Brigand] falls dead, and devils carry him away. And the Young Man, who had been reassured by Death, enters with a white beard, like an Old Man, and says*, rubric after l. 745).

THE KISS OF DEATH:
DEATH AS A LOVER IN EARLY MODERN
ENGLISH LITERATURE AND ART

JEAN WILSON

At Corsham Court (Wiltshire) is a posthumous portrait of Queen Elizabeth I by an anonymous artist, dated c.1610.[1] The elderly queen sits at a table, her head resting in her left hand, her left arm supported by a cushion, while her right hand marks her place in the book which she has been studying. She faces the viewer, but her expression is abstracted. In the background Time has fallen asleep, his scythe in his arm, and two cherubs or *amorini* hover over her head, the sinister holding a sceptre while both are supporting a crown. Leaning intimately over the back of her chair, Death – shown as a skeleton, hourglass in hand – seems to murmur into her right ear. Is she listening to him, or facing her (brief) future? She is clothed in a crimson ermine-lined robe over a white bodice and gown, her jewels are pearls and diamonds, and more pearls and diamonds crown her hair: her ensemble proclaims that she is a royal virgin.

This is a picture of Death and the Maiden, Death posed as though he were one of the lovers/courtiers of earlier years, whispering intimacies.[2] Time may have been lulled asleep and forgotten about her, but she must still attend to Death. Elizabeth I may have been exceptional, but this

---

[1] An illustration of this portrait can be found at the following website: http://www.corsham-court.co.uk/Pictures/Elizabeth.html.

[2] For Death's invitation to women of all ranks to dance with him, see Stefanie Knöll, 'Death and the Maiden', in Helen Fronius and Anna Linton (eds), *Women and Death: Representations of Female Victims and Perpetrators in German Culture 1500-2000* (Studies in German Literature Linguistics and Culture) (Rochester, New York: Camden House, 2008), 9-27, esp. 13-14. For Death and eroticism in early modern German culture see *ibid.*, *passim*. For a more general treatment of Death as a lover in the early modern period, see Karl S. Guthke, *The Gender of Death: a Cultural History in Art and Literature* (Cambridge: Cambridge University Press, 1999), 92-110. I am grateful to Dr Stefanie Knöll for these references.

representation of the late queen with Death is firmly rooted in the art of the period. The trope of Death as lover, the intimate association of the Reaper and the beautiful corpse, is one that is relatively common in early modern England, occurring in painting, poetry, drama and funerary monuments.

Love and Death

At the most superficial level the image of Death as lover is encouraged by the interpenetration of the vocabularies of love and death – to die, as in the modern French *petite mort*, is to have an orgasm. In *Troilus and Cressida*, a play in which Shakespeare explores the association between sex and violence, or the sexiness of violence, Pandarus' song sums up this meaning of 'death':

> Love, love, nothing but love, still love, still more!
> For, oh, love's bow
> Shoots buck and doe;
> The shaft confounds
> Not that it wounds,
> But tickles still the sore.
> These lovers cry, O ho, they die!
> Yet that which seems the wound to kill
> Doth turn O ho! to ha! ha! he!
> So dying love lives still ... (III, i, 108-17)[3]

In *Much Ado About Nothing* Benedick announces to Beatrice, with obvious sexual meaning, 'I will live in thy heart, die in thy lap, and be buried in thy eyes' (V, ii, 88-89). Other poets use the same vocabulary. Richard Crashaw's 'The Flaming Heart',[4] which combines mysticism with sexual imagery, uses the idea of death throughout to express both sexual and religious ecstasy. The Seraph in this poem is envisaged as an Eros figure, but is armed with a dart, and so conflates Love and Death:

[3] William Shakespeare, *Troilus and Cressida*, in *Complete Works*, ed. Peter Alexander (London/Glasgow: Collins, 1951), 787-826. All references to the works of Shakespeare are to this edition.
[4] Richard Crashaw, 'The Flaming Heart Upon the Book and Picture of the seraphical saint Teresa, (As she is usually expressed with a Seraphim biside her.)', in M.H. Abrams and Stephen Greenblatt (eds), *The Norton Anthology of English Literature, Seventh Edition, Volume 1* (New York: W.W. Norton & Company, 2000), 1640-43. All citations from this poem are to this edition.

Whate'er this youth of fire wears fair,
Rosy fingers, radiant hair,
Glowing cheek and glistering wings,
All those fair and fragrant things,
But before all, that fiery dart
Had filled the hand of this great heart (31-36)

In Crashaw's loaded vocabulary (the male Seraph is initially described as a 'fair-cheeked fallacy of fire', 4), St Teresa's ecstasies are equated both with death and with orgasm – the death produced by love:

O heart! the equal poise of love's both parts,
Big alike with wounds and darts,
Live in these conquering leaves, live all the same;
And walk through all tongues one triumphant flame.
Live here, great heart; and love and die and kill,
And bleed and wound; and yield and conquer still.
Let this immortal life, where'er it comes,
Walk in a crowd of loves and martyrdoms.
Let mystic deaths wait on't, and wise souls be
The love-slain witnesses of this life of thee. (75-84)

The connection between sex and death is commonly made in early modern plays, and it segues into the idea of Death as a rival lover. In *Romeo and Juliet* it is a constant *motif*, signalled in the Prologue:

From forth the fatal loins of these two foes
A pair of star-cross'd lovers take their life;
Whose misadventur'd piteous overthrows
Doth with their death bury their parents' strife.
The fearful passage of their death-mark'd love,
And the continuance of their parents' rage,
Which, but their children's end, nought could remove,
Is now the two hours' traffic of our stage. (*R&J, Prologue*, 5-12)

Romeo's love for Rosaline, before he sees Juliet, is marked by its association with darkness:

But all so soon as the all-cheering sun
Should in the farthest east begin to draw
The shady curtains from Aurora's bed,
Away from light steals home my heavy son,
And private in his chamber pens himself,
Shuts up his windows, locks fair daylight out,
And makes himself an artificial night.

Black and portentous must this humour prove,
Unless good counsel may the cause remove (*R&J*, I, ii, 132-40)

Romeo and Juliet themselves are able to meet and talk only at night or in
secret: at Capulet's feast, in Capulet's garden, in Juliet's bedroom where
they spend their wedding-night together, in the Capulets' tomb where they
are finally united in death. Their meeting before their marriage ceremony
is their sole daylight encounter. The message of the opening Prologue –
that love is associated with Death – is reinforced in the seldom-performed
Prologue to the second Act:

Now old desire doth in his death-bed lie,
And young affection gapes to be his heir;
The fair for which love groan'd for and would die,
With tender Juliet match'd, is now not fair (*R&J*, II, *Prologue*, 1-4)

The clichés of love-poetry are about to become real as Romeo and Juliet
will die from and of love, which the audience knows, but the characters in
the play do not. They speak unthinkingly, but their thoughtless words will
be enacted on stage. Romeo in love with Rosaline declares that

She hath forsworn to love, and in that vow
Do I live dead that live to tell it now (*R&J*, I, i, 221-22)

and, anticipating his own imminent change of affection, asserts

When the devout religion of mine eye
Maintains such falsehood, then turn tears to fires;
And these, who, often drown'd, could never die,
Transparent heretics, be burnt for liars! (*R&J*, I, ii, 88-91)

When he first sees Juliet, Romeo's reaction is 'Beauty too rich for use, for
earth too dear!' (*R&J*, I, v, 45) – an unthinking anticipation of the premise
that the darlings of the gods die young,[5] which will be played out in his
own fate.

This unthinking invocation of love and death is paralleled with a more
serious sense of foreboding in connection with the love affair between

---

[5] Ben Jonson uses almost identical vocabulary in his 'Epitaph on S.P., a Child of Q
El Chapel': 'being so much too good for earth, / Heaven vows to keep him' (23-
24). See Ben Jonson, *The Complete Poems*, ed. George Parfitt (Harmondsworth:
Penguin Books Ltd, rev. edn 1996), 81. All references to the poems of Jonson are
to this edition.

Romeo and Juliet. Romeo is uneasy at the proposed gatecrashing of Capulet's feast:

> [...] my mind misgives
> Some consequence, yet hanging in the stars,
> Shall bitterly begin his fearful date
> With this night's revels, and expire the term
> Of a despised life clos'd in my breast,
> By some vile forfeit of untimely death. (*R&J*, I, iv, 106-11)

When he learns Juliet's identity his reaction is 'my life is my foe's debt' (*R&J*, I, v, 116). Likewise, Juliet's ironic statement as she seeks to know Romeo's identity, 'If he be married, / My grave is like to be my wedding bed' (*R&J*, I, v, 132-33), anticipates the end of the play where she is laid in her grave in her wedding garments (*R&J*, IV, v, 79-81). All their encounters are marked by presages of death. In the balcony scene Juliet has

> no joy of this compact to-night:
> It is too rash, too unadvis'd, too sudden;
> Too like the lightning, which doth cease to be
> Ere one can say 'It lightens'. (*R&J*, II, ii, 117-20)

As they part after their wedding night, Juliet sees Romeo as he will appear on their next encounter

> O God, I have an ill-divining soul!
> Methinks I see thee, now thou art below,
> As one dead in the bottom of a tomb (*R&J*, III, v, 54-56)

Death is constantly present in the play, the frequent mentions of him in the text make him a player in the drama, and when the intervention of death affects the action he is seen as a rival suitor. Capulet announces Juliet's death to her presumed fiancé Paris in terms of her seduction by a rival:

> O son, the night before thy wedding day
> Hath Death lain with thy wife. There she lies,
> Flower as she was, deflowered by him.
> Death is my son-in-law, Death is my heir;
> My daughter he hath wedded; I will die,
> And leave him all; life, living, all is Death's (*R&J*, IV, v, 35-40)

Romeo's reaction to Juliet's supposed corpse in the Capulets' monument is again that Death has been his rival:

> Ah, dear Juliet,
> Why art thou yet so fair? Shall I believe
> That unsubstantial Death is amorous,
> And that the lean abhorred monster keeps
> Thee here in dark to be his paramour? (*R&J*, V, iii, 101-5)

Juliet's funeral is articulated in terms of her wedding. Capulet realises that his daughter's marriage will celebrate only her marriage to death:

> All things that we ordained festival
> Turn from their office to black funeral:
> Our instruments to melancholy bells,
> Our wedding cheer to a sad burial feast,
> Our solemn hymns to sullen dirges change;
> Our bridal flowers serve for a buried corse (*R&J*, IV, v, 84-90)

This image is paralleled by Paris's obsequies at her tomb, which imitate the strewing of the bridal bed:

> Sweet flower, with flowers the bridal bed I strew –
> O woe, thy canopy is dust and stones! –
> Which with sweet water nightly I will dew;
> Or, wanting that, with tears distill'd by moans.
> The obsequies that I for thee will keep,
> Nightly shall be to strew thy grave and weep. (*R&J*, V, iii, 12-17)

Like the brides stolen by the Fairies in folklore,[6] Juliet has become married to a rival lover – one who will keep her eternally in his dark kingdom. The idea of Death as a lover to be embraced appears in *Measure for Measure* where Claudio declares that he will

> encounter darkness as a bride
> And hug it in mine arms (*MfM*, III, i, 85-86)

---

[6] The connection between the fairies and death appears in both folklore and literature, for instance in the fourteenth-century romance *Sir Orfeo*. The Fairies live underground, wear green, and one of their manifestations is the Wild Hunt – all motifs associated with death.

His resolution turns out to be as false as the cliché in which it is expressed, when he learns that his sister could save his life by having sex with his judge.

The sexualised corpse

The idea of the sexualised corpse is present in much more explicit form in plays by authors other than Shakespeare – notably in three tragedies associated with Thomas Middleton, *The Revenger's Tragedy*, *The Lady's Tragedy* and *The Changeling*.[7] In these plays Death is not so much a rival, as in *Romeo and Juliet*, but embodied in the person of the lover, so that the love affair is in effect with Death himself.

The relationship of *The Revenger's Tragedy* to the *Danse Macabre* has been extensively discussed,[8] particularly with reference to the motif of the confrontation of one's own mortality – skeletal Death presents us with what we are and what we will become. The play, indeed, opens with what seems to be a clichéd picture of the melancholy hero – or perhaps the dead hero[9] – as Vindice enters, holding a skull, and proceeds to anatomise the corrupt court as it passes across the stage. It shortly becomes apparent, however, that the skull Vindice holds is not (for him) an emblem of his own mortality but of love triumphing over death

> Thou sallow picture of my poisoned love,
> My study's ornament, thou shell of death,
> Once the bright face of my betrothéd lady (*RT*, I, i, 14-16)

---

[7] Although they have been ascribed to various dramatists, Middleton's authorship of these plays is accepted by his latest editors: see Thomas Middleton, *The Collected Works*, 2 vols, general editors Gary Taylor and John Lavagnino (Oxford: Clarendon Press, 2007). All references to the works of Middleton are to this edition.

[8] Michael Neill, *Issues of Death: Mortality and Identity in English Renaissance Tragedy* (Oxford: Clarendon Press, 1997), 84-85 and *passim*.

[9] The use of a skull as a death-marker on funerary monuments is too common to need comment, and has been particularly associated with *Hamlet*. For striking examples, see the monument to Sir Giles and Lady Mompesson (d. 1633) at Lydiard Tregoze (Wiltshire), which is ascribed to the workshop of Samuel Baldwin, and that to Katherine Steward (d. 1590) at St Peter and St Paul, Swaffham (Norfolk). Vindice's and Hamlet's appearances with skulls in hand effectively show them as they will (imminently) appear on their tombs, and signal that they are marked for death.

Vindice is still in love with the woman whose skull he holds, and it is her face that he sees when he looks at it

> When life and beauty naturally filled out
> These ragged imperfections;
> When two heaven-pointed diamonds were set
> In those unsightly rings; – then 'twas a face
> So far beyond the artificial shine
> Of any woman's bought complexion
> That the uprightest man, (if such there be
> That sin but seven times a day) broke custom
> And made up eight with looking after her. (*RT*, I, i, 17-25)

Vindice turns Gloriana's skull into an instrument of revenge and re-enacts the cause of her death – the Duke poisoned her because she would not agree to be his mistress (*RT*, I, i, 31-33) – by using it as the head of a puppet-lady which the Duke believes is a woman willing to serve his lusts, and by poisoning it: Gloriana posthumously avenges herself, and Vindice evokes the image from the *Danse Macabre* of Death using a toy to reflect the status of the person he is calling. The image of the Duke kissing the disguised skull equally evokes those moments in the *Danse* when Death assumes a disguise to surprise his victim: in the enaction of this moment the *Danse Macabre* becomes if not flesh at least bone.[10]

The corpse-as-puppet motif reappears in *The Changeling*, at the moment when de Flores kills his mistress and instigator of his murders, Beatrice-Joanna. They are locked into a closet by her wronged husband Alsemero, and it is unclear whether what those on stage hear is the noise of Beatrice-Joanna and de Flores making love, or of him killing her, or both. When they emerge De Flores is supporting the dying Beatrice-Joanna in a manner reminiscent of the manipulation of Gloriana in *The Revenger's Tragedy* and the dead Lady in *The Lady's Tragedy*:

> TOMAZO How is my cause bandied through your delays!
> 'Tis urgent in my blood, and calls for haste.
> Give me a brother alive or dead:
> Alive, a wife with him; if dead, for both
> A recompense – for murder and adultery.
> BEATRICE (*within*)
> O! O! O!

---

[10] See Sophie Oosterwijk. '*For No Man Mai fro Dethes Stroke Fle*': Death and *Danse Macabre* Iconography in Memorial Art', *Church Monuments*, 23 (2008), 62-87, 164-66.

ALSEMERO
          Hark, 'tis coming to you.
DE FLORES (*within*)
Nay, I'll along for company!
BEATRICE (*within*)   O, O!
VERMANDERO What horrid sounds are these?
ALSEMERO Come forth, you twins of mischief.
          Enter De Flores, bringing in Beatrice
(*The Changeling*, V, iii, 135-41)[11].

This is a moment in which the slang usage of 'death' to mean orgasm is encapsulated on stage: Beatrice-Joanna dies in both senses, and her body – which has been the instrument of De Flores' corruption (she has seduced him into murdering her unwanted suitor) – now becomes his accessory in his confession of their crimes.

The use of the poisoned corpse as a means of death and revenge is even more explicit in *The Lady's Tragedy* than it was in *The Revenger's Tragedy*.[12] This disturbing play about necrophilia involves the Tyrant exhuming the corpse of the Lady who has committed suicide to avoid becoming his mistress and, believing that she does not look as healthy as he would wish, getting a Painter – who is in fact the Lady's betrothed, Govianus, in disguise – to paint her face to improve her appearance. Govianus uses poison on the lips, and the Tyrant, in kissing the corpse, meets his well-deserved end. Govianus regains his throne (which the Tyrant has also usurped) and has the Lady crowned as his queen before returning her to her violated sepulchre. The scenes of tomb-robbing and the manipulation of the Lady's corpse articulate the anxieties expressed in the *Danse Macabre*. The Tyrant's first reaction on hearing that the Lady has killed herself rather than submit to him is that she has taken Death as her husband

O, she's destroyed, married to death and silence,
Which nothing can divorce (*TLT*, IV, ii, 27-28).

---

[11] *The Changeling*, text edited and annotated by Douglas Bruster, introduced by Annabel Patterson, in Thomas Middleton, *The Collected Works*, vol. 1, 1632-78, vol. 2 (Commentary), 1094-1104.

[12] *The Lady's Tragedy* is the title given to the play previously known as *The Maiden's Tragedy* and *The Second Maiden's Tragedy* in the new *Collected Works* of Middleton: see Thomas Middleton, *The Lady's Tragedy*, ed. Julia Briggs, in Thomas Middleton, *The Collected Works*, vol. 1, 833-906, vol. 2 (Commentary), 619-26. This is a parallel-text edition of two versions of the play. All quotations are from this edition, using the original-text version. For an explanation of its multiple titles, see Briggs' Introduction, 833 and 835-36.

In deciding to steal her body from the grave he articulates his decision in terms of seizing her back from a rival who has wrongfully imprisoned her

> Death nor the marble prison my love sleeps in
> Shall keep her body locked up from mine arms (*TLT*, IV, ii, 45-46).

The soldiers who accompany the Tyrant on his grave-robbing expedition are horrified by his actions, but his relationship to the Lady's body hovers queasily between a denial that she is dead and necrophilia – there is a suggestion that he finds her even more attractive now that she is dead:

> O blest object!
> I never shall be weary to behold thee.
> I could eternally stand thus and see thee.
> Why, 'tis not possible death should look so fair;
> Life is not more illustrious when health smiles on't.
> She's only pale, the colour of the court,
> And most attractive (*TLT*, IV, iii, 61-67).

The comments of the soldiers who witness the Tyrant's actions make it clear that his actions are perverse and damnable: 'Here's a fine chill venery' (*TLT*, IV, ii, 91).

The Lady's costumes during the play reinforce the thematic distinction between body and soul. It is not clear whether the corpse of the lady was played by a second actor, or by a puppet manipulated by Govianus and the Tyrant, as Gloriana's skull becomes a puppet in *The Revenger's Tragedy*. She appears in a triple form: as a living woman, as a corpse, and as a disembodied spirit, which the action makes clear has been disjoined from her body by the Tyrant's violation, and which is integrated with the body as it is reinterred (V, ii, 206-7). Her costume is either black or white – she wears black when she comes to court to reject the Tyrant (I, i, 112), and her disinterred corpse is also sumptuously clothed in black:

> *They bring the body in a chair, dressed up in black velvet, which sets out the paleness of the hands and face, and a fair chain of pearl across her breast and the crucifix above it* (*TLT*, V, ii, 12).

The jewellery symbolises the Lady's piety and innocence – she is to be seen as a martyr rather than a suicide. She is buried in white, as a bride, as is clear in the stage-direction when her spirit appears to Govianus. This is a white version of the costume she will wear as the Tyrant's consort:

> *On a sudden in a kind of noise like a wind, the doors clattering, the tombstone flies open, and a great light appears in the midst of the tomb;*

> *his lady, as went out, standing just before him all in white, stuck with jewels and a great crucifix on her breast (TLT,* IV, iv, 42).

Her reintegration is signalled when her spirit appears clad in the same garments as her corpse:

> *Enter the Ghost in the same form as the Lady is dressed in the chair. (TLT,* V, ii, 153-54).

The dualism of the lady's appearances reinforces a disgust for the body which is also apparent in *The Revenger's Tragedy*: the Lady's body is abused, but it is ultimately just meat and, moreover, meat that is fast rotting. The Tyrant's comment as he replaces the lid on her sarcophagus,

> 'Tis for all the world
> Like a great city-pie brought to a table
> Where there are many hands that lay about.
> The lid's shut close, when all the meat's picked out *(TLT,* IV, iii, 132-35).

simply serves to reinforce the idea that the Lady's carcass is just that – dead meat.[13] When the Tyrant kisses the made-up corpse and so receives his own death he is indeed kissing Death: he is in love with Death, rather than (as is the case with Govianus) the Lady herself – her spirit, which is eternal, as opposed to her transient and changeable (decaying) body.

The monumental body

The anxiety which is expressed in early modern drama is echoed in contemporary sepulchral commemoration. This may have its roots in a growing uncertainty about the physical resurrection of the body. Although there are assurances in the New Testament that the resurrected body will

---

[13] The editor of the play in the *Complete Works* suggests that the Lady may have been represented on her tomb and illustrates the suggestion with a picture of Nicholas Stone's 1629 tomb for Dame Katherine Paston (d. 1629) at Paston, Norfolk (unidentified and unascribed, although this is one of Stone's best-known works: there is also no mention of the epitaph). The wording of the play makes this suggestion improbable: the image evoked is of an aniconic sarcophagus, like that which supports the urn on the monument of her husband Sir Edmund Paston (d. 1632) in the same church. See Thomas Middleton, *The Collected Works*, vol. 1, 15, 838; Nikolaus Pevsner and Bill Wilson, *The Buildings of England, Norfolk 1: Norwich and North-East* (Harmondsworth: Penguin Books Ltd, 1997), 637-38.

not be the same as the mundane one and that marriage will not exist,[14] the words of the Creed, 'I believe in [...] the Resurrection of the Body', became more difficult to sustain as understanding grew of the workings and nature of that body. The heart, once the seat of love, became a pump.[15] In this context it became even more impossible to look forward with certainty to a full post-mortem reunion: the souls of lovers might be reunited but their bodily relationship would never be revived.[16] This was compounded by the traditional dichotomy – and perhaps antipathy[17] – between body and soul, and by a consequent querying of what precisely was loved in a relationship. The easy (and theologically correct) answer is that given by the supposedly bereaved lover Argalus when presented with

---

[14] *I Corinthians* 15:44: 'It is sown a natural body; it is raised a spiritual body'; *Mark* 12:25: 'when they shall rise from the dead, they neither marry nor are given in marriage; but are as angels in heaven'. Milton attempts to deal with the paradox of bodiless physicality in his description of the congress of angels:

> Whatever pure thou in the body enjoy'st
> (And pure thou wert created) wee enjoy
> In eminence, and obstacle find none
> Of membrane, joint, or limb, exclusive barrs:
> Easier then Air with Air, if Spirits embrace,
> Total they mix, Union of Pure with Pure
> Desiring; nor restrained conveyance need
> As Flesh to mix with Flesh, or Soul with Soul
> (*Paradise Lost*, VIII, 622-29)

See John Milton, *Poetical Works*, ed. Helen Darbishire (London: Oxford University Press, 1958), 180-81. All references to the works of Milton are to this edition.

[15] William Harvey announced his findings about the circulation of the blood at the College of Physicians in 1616 and published *Exercitatio Anatomica de Motu Cordis et Sanguinis in Animalibus* in 1628. The actual (and now metaphorical) associations of the viscera with emotion has a good physiological basis: strong emotion may be felt as a thud or pain in the chest, as in 'heart-stopping' or 'heart-broken'. The phrase 'bowels of compassion' may now seem risible, but 'gut-wrenching' locates fear or pity where they are physically felt – modern science has disconnected the emotional from the corporeal in a way that did not prevail when the organs which responded to emotions were seen as the seats of those emotions.

[16] This is discussed in Jean Wilson, 'I Dote on Death: the Fractured Marriage in English Renaissance Art and Literature', *Church Monuments*, 11 (1996), 42-60.

[17] As in Andrew Marvell's 'A Dialogue between the Soul and Body', in which the Soul complains that it is imprisoned in the body, and the body that the soul – responsible for feelings – afflicts it with pain consequent on the emotions. See Andrew Marvell, *The Complete Poems*, ed. Elizabeth Story Donno (Harmondsworth: Penguin, 1972), 103-04.

a potential bride who is the facsimile of his dead lover Parthenia in Sir Philip Sidney's romance *Arcadia*:

> I hope I shall not long tarry after her, with whose beauty if I had only been in love, I should be so with you who have the same beauty. But it was Parthenia's self I loved and love, which no likeness can make one, no commandment dissolve, no foulness defile, nor no death finish.[18]

Other writers recognise the necessity of the physical expression of emotion. In John Donne's 'The Extasie', a poem supposedly celebrating non-corporeal love,

> This Extasie doth unperplex
>   (We said) and tell us what we love,
> Wee see by this, it was not sexe,
>   Wee see, we saw not what did move, (29-32)[19]

the poet ends by affirming that the body is essential to a fully integrated human love:

> On man heavens influence workes not so,
>   But that it first imprints the ayre,
> Soe soule into the soule may flow,
>   Though it to body first repaire.
> As our blood labours to beget
>   Spirits, as like soules as it can,
> Because such fingers need to knit
>   That subtil knot, which makes us man:
> So must pure lovers soules descend
>   T'affections, and to faculties,
> Which sense may reach and apprehend,
>   Else a great prince in prison lies.
> To'our bodies turne wee then, that so
>   Weake men on love reveal'd may looke;
> Loves mysteries in soules doe grow,
>   But yet the body is his booke (57-72)[20]

---

[18] Sir Philip Sidney, *The Countess of Pembroke's Arcadia*, ed. Maurice Evans (2nd edn, Harmondsworth: Penguin, 1987), 105. All references to *Arcadia* are to this edition.

[19] 'The Extasie', in John Donne, *Poems*, ed. Herbert Grierson (London: Oxford University Press, 1933), 46-48. All references to Donne's poetry are to this edition.

[20] For a full examination of Donne's attitude to the relationship between body and soul, see R. Targoff, *John Donne: Body & Soul* (Chicago: University of Chicago Press, 2008). This contains an excellent survey of contemporary attitudes to the

Fig. 58. Monument to John Latch and his wife Sarah (both d. 1644), Churchill (Somerset). Photo: Norman Hammond.

resurrection of the body, 16-24, 169-71, for which see also Peter Sherlock, *Monuments and Memory in Early Modern England* (Aldershot: Ashgate, 2008), 73-78. Donne's fullest exposition of the body/soul problem in the context of marriage is his sermon preached on 19 November 1627 at the marriage of Lady Mary Egerton, daughter of the earl of Bridgwater, to Richard Herbert, eldest son of Lord Herbert of Cherbury. See *The Sermons of John Donne*, ed. Evelyn M. Simpson and George R. Potter, 10 volumes (Berkeley: University of California Press, 1956), vol. 8, 94-109.

Fig. 59a-b. Details of the
monument to John Latch and his
wife Sarah (both d. 1644),
Churchill (Somerset).
Photo: Norman Hammond.

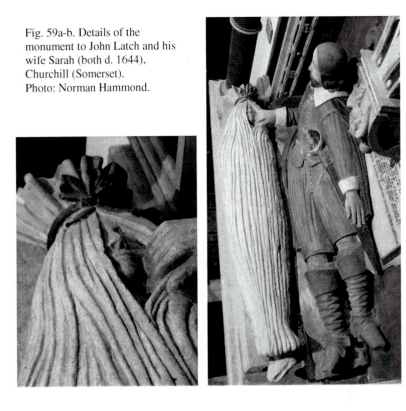

If true love is formed of the union of both souls and bodies, then a
post-resurrection reunion of lovers which no longer involves the body, or
involves only a spiritual body, can never be the same as their earthly
relationship: part of this is irrevocably gone. This consciousness of the
mortality of the body produces an anxiety evident in some monuments
about the nature of love – if it is for the body which is doomed to die, may
it not be a love directed to death as surely as the Tyrant's necrophilia? The
tomb monument to Sara Latch (d. 1644) at Churchill (Somerset) (Figs 58-
59), on which the bereaved husband contemplates the shrouded body of
his wife, parting the cloth over her face so that he may take his last
glimpse (or kiss) from her, raises this question:

> Lyveing and dead thou seest how heere wee lie
> I doate on Death preparing how to die [...]

Since his wife has, as a shrouded corpse, become an embodiment of Death, John Latch is now in love with Death itself.[21] Latch is, of course, expressing an idea common in funerary inscriptions of the period – that the couple were so united that one cannot be said properly to live without the other. At Eyeworth (Bedfordshire) the monument erected by the widow of Edmund Anderson (d. 1638) shows them holding a single heart and proclaims that

> THESE LIVD IN THAT THEY LOVD
> GOD MADE THEM ONE:
> HE DIES AND THUS DISSOLVED
> LOE SHE IS NONE
> DELAY NOT THEN TILL FATE
> SHALL STOPPE HER BREATH
> TO TELL WHAT DAY SHE DIED
> HIS WAS HER DEATH

The inscription adds that his widow

> WITH HIM HATH/ INTOMB'D HER HEART.

The clergyman and poet Henry King in his memorial poem to his dead wife, 'An Exequy to His Matchless, Never-to-be-Forgotten Friend', promises her that he is

> [...] Content to live
> Divided, with but half a heart
> Till we shall meet and never part (119-20)[22]

However, King's poem configures his wife's interment as a wedding-night; she is laid in her grave as in a bridal-bed,

> So close the ground, and about her shade
> Black curtains draw: my bride is laid. (79-80)

Moreover, because she is now married to another (*i.e.* Death), that other is the husband's rival:

---

[21] For a fuller exploration of this motif, see Wilson (1996).

[22] Henry King, 'An Exequy to His Matchless, Never-to-be-Forgotten Friend', in Alastair Fowler (ed.), *The New Oxford Book of Seventeenth Century Verse* (Oxford: Oxford University Press, 1991), 288-90. All citations from this poem are to this edition.

Meantime thou hast her, earth: much good
May my harm do thee. Since it stood
With heaven's will I might not call
Her longer mine, I give thee all
My short-lived right and interest
In her, whom living I loved best:
With a most free and bounteous grief
I give thee what I could not keep.
Be kind to her; and prithee look
Thou write into thy Domesday Book
Each parcel of this rarity
Which in thy casket shrined doth lie:
See that thou make thy reck'ning straight,
And yield her back again by weight;
For thou must audit on thy trust,
Each grain and atom of this dust,
As thou wilt answer him that lent,
Not gave thee, my dear monument. (61-78)

Although King segues into the imagery of the pawn-shop, he begins this passage in the tones of a lover forced to concede his bride to a rival. His perception is that of Romeo as he looks at the 'body' of Juliet, and as with Romeo and John Latch, there is an erotic charge to his vision of his wife's corpse. This eroticising of death may also be found in the art of the period. In Anthony van Dyck's picture of the corpse of Venetia Stanley, she is presented as though asleep, wearing her pearls, in a bed strewn with roses: this might be a bride sleeping after her wedding-night, when the bed was strewn with flowers.[23] Her husband Kenelm Digby kept with him a bust of Venetia by George Larson inscribed 'VXOREM VIVAM AMARE, VOLUPTAS EST: DEFUNCTAM, RELIGIO'.[24]

Another example of the eroticisation of the corpse may be found in the Cotton monument, designed by Inigo Jones, at Norton-in-Hales (Shropshire), in which the body of Lady Cotton (d. 1606) is shown semi-shrouded, after the manner of the royal corpses on the Valois tombs at Saint-Denis, but without their obvious indications of putrefaction, so that the figure

---

[23] Venetia Stanley died in her sleep at the age of 33 on 1 May 1633, and the Van Dyck portrait is supposed to represent her as she was found by her husband. See Ann Sumner (ed.), *Death, Passion and Politics: Van Dyke's Portraits of Venetia Stanley and George Digby* (Dulwich: Dulwich Picture Gallery, 1995), 31, and Clare Gittings' essay 'Venetia's Death and Kenelm's Mourning' in the same volume, 54-68, which provides an invaluable survey of the deathbed portrait convention.

[24] Sumner (1995), 113.

becomes attractive rather than repellent. The juxtaposition of Sir Rowland Cotton's armoured effigy with his wife's semi-naked one telescopes the convention of the monument in which the 'social body' is placed above the 'natural body' with the *Danse Macabre* juxtaposition of the knight with a figure of Death.[25]

In cases such as the Latch monument and the Stanley portrait, love for the deceased comes close to the necrophilia of *The Lady's Tragedy*. The shrouded corpse, a common personification of Death, is the object of the mourner's affection. From here it is easy to move to the characterisation of Death as a rival lover, one who has snatched the beloved from her true companion. The epitaph of Lady Throckmorton in the Lord Mayor's Chapel, Bristol, indeed plays on the idea that the ruler may take his subjects' wives for his own sexual pleasure:

A PRECIOVS JEMME, A MARGARITE WAS LENT
TO CROWNE THROCKMORTON WITH A RICH CONTENT
CONTENTED HE HIS MARGARIT DID SET
INS FAITHFVLL BREAST HIS CHOISEST CABANET,
SHEE WISHT NO BETTER TILL HER LVSTRE DREWE
THE KING OF HEAVEN TO LIKE HER GRACIOVS HEWE,
WHO DEEMING IT VNFIT A SVBIECT SHOVLD,
LONGER ENJOY A JEMME OF THAT RICH MOVLD,
TOOKE BACK HIS LOANE ANND FIXING HER ABOVE
LEFT TO THROKMORTON THIS SOLE PLEDGE OF LOVE,
    HER STATVE TOOMBE AND HOPE IN HEAVNLY LIGHT
        TO MEETE AGAINE HIS BLESSED MARGARITE

MORS RAPAX VRNA CAPAX SED SPES TENAX

The brass at Shepton Mallet (Somerset) to Joan Strode (d. 1649) visually incorporates the same idea (Fig. 60): Death, emerging from an altar/tomb, strikes at Joan with his dart, while her husband tries to restrain him, pleading that 'Parum fuit' (*it was too little*) to which Death replies 'diu vixit' (*she has lived long enough*).[26] As both Oosterwijk and Sherlock

---

[25] The monument as executed differs from the surviving Jones design, which shows the recumbent figure of Lady Cotton fully clothed in classical draperies, supported by a cherub. This does not have the erotic charge and *Danse Macabre* associations of the monument which now exists. See John Harris and Gordon Higgot, *Inigo Jones: Complete Architectural Drawings* (London: Royal Academy of Arts, 1990), 42-44.

[26] Translation from Oosterwijk (2008), 79; the brass is discussed 79-80. See also Sherlock (2008), 71-72. Donne himself may use the image of Death as rapist in his epitaph on his wife, which reads in part, 'Immane Febre correptæ', translated in

note, Death holds out a wreath to Joan Strode – identified in the inscription as a crown of glory ('corona illa gloriæ') – and can tempt the wife with rewards that the husband cannot give. He is richer and can offer a better life than Joan's husband.

Fig. 60. Brass to Joan Strode (d. 1649) at Shepton Mallet (Somerset). Rubbing: Martin Stuchfield.

Death may even be identified with divorce (as well as with decapitation), as on the brass inscription to Sarah Walcot (d. 1651) at Langtoft (Lincolnshire), which reads:

HERE LYETH THE BODY OF SARAH THE WIFE OF
BERNARD WALCOT OF LANGTOFT IN THE COVNTY
OF LINCOLNE ESQ, BY WHOME HE HAD ISSVE FOWER
SONNES AND THREE DAVGHTERS, WHO DYED THE
        24TH OF AVGVST A[O] DÑI 1651
THOV BEDD OF REST RESERVE FOR HIM A ROOME
    WHO LIVES A MAN DIVORC'D FROM HIS DEARE WIFE
THAT AS THEY WERE ONE HART SOE THIS ONE TOMBE
    MAY HOLD THEM NEER IN DEATH AS LINCKT IN LIFE
SHE'S GONE BEFORE AND AFTER COMES HER HEAD
    TO SLEEPE WITH HER AMONGST THE BLESSED DEAD.

Targoff (2008), 76, as 'By a ravishing fever carried off suddenly'.

The larger font size given to the initial letters of the words 'Divorc'd' and 'Tombe' visually associates them for readers of the inscription. Since the only grounds for divorce was infidelity, this inscription implicitly identifies Death with the co-respondent.

An inscription recorded by the antiquarian William Dugdale on a since destroyed monument in St Michael's, Coventry, figures Death as a seducer. Sir William Bulstrode's tribute to Anne Newdigate, Lady Skeffington (d. 1637 aged twenty-nine), read in part (see also Appendix I):

> HER LIFE WAS SUCH AS FEARED NO STING OF DEATH,
> BUT DAR'D HIM BY SO STRONG UNDOUBTING FAITH,
> AS THAT HE DID BUT MILDLY STEAL UNTO HER,
> AND GENTLY WHISPER' AS HE MEANT TO WOE HER.
> AND SHE AS GENTLY YEILDED STRAIT TO GOE [...]

Whether as a tyrant forcing the wives of his subjects, a rich superior offering better prospects, or a practised wooer whispering seductive intimacies, Death steals away the wife from her bereft husband.

Joan Strode died at the age of forty-two at the birth of her sixteenth child. Anne Donne died aged thirty-two after the birth of her twelfth child in fifteen years. Anne King died at twenty-four, having borne seven children in less than eight years of marriage. At their deaths, the husbands of these women were faced with the paradox that their love for their wives – or at least, the physical expression of their love for their wives – was what was responsible for their deaths. The association between Love and Death, so that Death may indeed be seen as a rival lover and Love as a force as irresistible as Death, is enforced by their iconographic parallels. [27] Death is usually armed with a dart, but may be shown with the bow and arrows carried by Love. Love and Death may even use the wrong weapons so that Love kills and Death inflames with desire, as in the engraving by David Vinckboons, *Unequal Lovers and Death* (Fig. 61). The mourning cherubs who are a cliché on early modern funerary monuments may equally be seen as *amorini*. [28] When the deceased is a virgin, the idea that Death became her lover resonates with particular force. Marvell threatens

---

[27] See Oosterwijk (2008), 72-78. For the motif of Death and Love using the wrong arrow see Guthke, *The Gender of Death*, 106-07.

[28] Their similarity may be seen on two Cambridgeshire monuments: to the Bennet brothers (d. 1658 and 1667) at Babraham, and to Sir Thomas Baines (d. 1681) and Sir John Finch (d. 1682) in Christ's College Chapel, Cambridge (by Joseph Catterns).

his coy mistress with the possibility of violation in death: 'Then worms shall try / That long-preserved virginity' ('To his coy mistress', 27-28).

Fig. 61. Boetius Bolswert, engraving after David Vinckboons, *Unequal Lovers and Death*, early seventeenth century. © Graphiksammlung 'Mensch und Tod', Heinrich-Heine-University Düsseldorf.

The seizure of the virgin by Death is central to the epitaph of Lady Katherine Neville (d. 1613) at East Ham (Essex):

AN EPITAPH

VPON THE DEATH OF THE RIGHT VER⁻ VS
FAIRE & NOBLE LADIE KATHERIN NEVILL
FIRST DAVGHTER OF EDMVND EARLE OF
WESTMERLAND, & IANE HIS WIFE, WHO DIED
A VIRGINE THE FIFT OF DECEMBER 1613
BEING OF THE AGE OF XX3 YEARES

SVRVIVING MARBLE CHOYSLY KEEPE,
THIS NOBLE VIRGINE LAYDE TO SLEEPE

A BRANCH VNTYMLEY FALN AWAY
FROM NEVILLS ROYALLIZED TREE
GREAT WESTMERLAND TOO DEERE A PRAY
FOR DEATH IF SHE COVLD RANSOMD BEE
HIR NAME WAS KATHERIN NOT IN VAINE,
HIR NATVRE HELD TRVE REFERENCE
HIR BEVTIE AND HIR PARTS AGAINE
WERE ALL COMPOSD OF EXCELLENCE

BLVD, BEVTY, VERTVE, DID CONTEND
ALL THEIS ADVANCED IN EMINENCE
WHICH OF THEM COVLD HER MOST CO‾ MEND,
WHEN DEATH ENAMORD TOORE HER HENCE,

YET MARBLE TELL THE TYME TO COME
WHAT EARST SHE WAS WHEN I AM DVMBE.[29]

This same theme of a virgin seized by Death may be seen in later monuments both in England and in Colonial America. At Falstone (Northumberland) a tombstone of the early eighteenth century shows a girl holding what is probably a maiden-garland in the company of Death (Figs 62-63).[30] At Little Compton (Rhode Island) the stones of Lovis and Deborah Devanport (who died within two weeks of each other in 1774, aged five and seven) are crowned by representations of their heads framed by Death's scythe and an hourglass (Figs 64-65).[31]

---

[29] From Frederic Chancellor, *The Ancient Sepulchral Monuments of Essex. A Record of Interesting Tombs in Essex Churches and Some Account of the Persons and Families Connected with Them* (London: C.F. Kell, 1890), plate cxxxv.

[30] For maiden-garlands or crants in Britain, see Rosie Morris: 'The "Innocent and Touching Custom" of Maidens' Garlands: A Field Report', *Folklore*, 114:3 (2003), 355-87. For German instances see Zentralinstitut und Museum für Sepulkralkultur Kassel (eds), *Totenhochzeit mit Kranz und Krone. Zur Symbolik im Brauchtum des Ledigenbegräbnisses* (Kassel: Arbeitsgemeinschaft Friedhof und Denkmal, 2007); Anna Linton, 'Der Tod als Brautführer: Bridal Imagery in Funeral Writings.', *Daphnis*, 29:1/2 (2000), 281-306, and Anna Linton, *Poetry and Parental Bereavement in Early Modern Lutheran Germany* (Oxford: Oxford University Press, 2008). I am grateful to Dr Stefanie Knöll for the last three references.

[31] I am grateful to Professor Norman Hammond for drawing these to my attention. Other tombtones in the area use the same pattern. The names on the stones are as recorded above, although the spelling has been regularised to Lois and Deborah Davenport in most U.S. gravestone studies.

Fig. 62. Eighteenth-century tombstone showing a young girl holding a maiden-garland and being accompanied by Death as a skeleton, Falstone (Northumberland). Photo: Norman Hammond.

Fig. 63. Detail of the eighteenth-century tombstone to a young girl at Falstone (Northumberland). Photo: Norman Hammond.

Fig. 64. Tombstone of Deborah Devanport (d. 1774), Little Compton (Rhode Island, USA). Photo: Norman Hammond.

The personification of Death as the rival who has snatched the woman from her earthly lovers is relatively uncontroversial, but in a Christian context the recognition that it is not Death, but God, who has chosen to take her produces a certain queasiness in funerary imagery. In some cases, God is substituted by a pagan deity or deities: the Fates, as in the memorial to Thomas Welshe (d. 1639) in Alverdiscott (Devon) and in Ben Jonson's 'Epitaph on S.P., a Child of Queen Elizabeth's Chapel', or, more controversially, Jupiter, on the brass to Meneleb Rainsford (d. 1627) at

Henfield (Sussex), where the boy is figured as Ganymede.[32] Where the convention of the deceased's being the Bride of Christ is used there is an uneasiness about the sentiment, although this is less marked in the case of unmarried young women. For example, the parents of Cecily Puckering (d. 1636) are urged on her memorial at Warwick to

> Cease sorrowing then sith Saints & Angels sing
> To see her matcht with an eternal King.[33]

Fig. 65. Tombstone of Lovis Devanport (d. 1774), Little Compton (Rhode Island, USA). Photo: Norman Hammond.

---

[32] For the full texts of these memorials, see Jean Wilson, 'The Darlings of the Gods: Monuments to Adolescents in early Modern England', *Church Monuments*, 18 (2003), 65-89, 67-68, 75. For representations of deceased boys as Ganymede in Dutch paintings of this period, see also the examples in Jan Baptist Bedaux and Rudi Ekkart (eds), *Pride and Joy: Children's Portraits in the Netherlands, 1500-1700*, (New York/London: Harry N. Abrams, 2001). I am grateful to Dr Sophie Oosterwijk for supplying me with this reference.

[33] See Wilson (2003), 69-70.

If the woman who has become the bride of Christ was married, like Anna Elford (d. 1639/40, aged twenty) at Newton St Cyres (Devon), there is an awkwardness in the image. As her epitaph explains, Anna Elford has effectively widowed her husband so that she may marry Christ:

> To the pious memorie of ANNA the daughter
> of IOHN NORTHCOT OF Hayne Esqr wife to IOHN
> ELFORD of Shitstor Esqr their issue, WALTER, GRACE
>
> Short was her life that long may heer lye dead,
> Who dyed to live and raigne wth Christ her head.
> Old ANNA crept to Christ, young ANNA flyes
> Into his bosome: for to wedd him dyes:
> If grace or vertue could have life retayn'd,
> She'ad beene immortall: and heer still remayn'd
> Then heaven should want one to sing in her quire,
> The saints sweet Antheame wch let's all desire.
> Where ere shee came true loue of all shee gott,
> Deprauing Enuye could her fame ne'r blott,
> Her mate that left her, found her of that prise,
> As shee gain'd heauen's, hee lost earth's paradise.
> Yet mourne not too much, for she does but sleep,
> To wake and meet thee, where eyes ne'r shall weep.
>
>   Anag^r. ANNA ELFORDE
> All for an Eden, als All for an ende
>
> (EDEN and END, both to one marke applye)
> (Her END below, mounts her to EDEN hye,)
> (EDEN was heauens first type: AL for AN ENDE,)
> (Were both her births: AL FOR AN EDEN tende.)
>
>   Crn. A^o Ætat. Vt obIIt Ita
>   VIVIt.

The epitaph is unclear about who has left whom: has Anna Elford run off from her husband to wed Christ, or has the husband left her, in failing to accompany her to heaven? This uneasiness reflects the potential offensiveness of equating Christ with a stealer of wives. Such imagery is not unknown in literature either, however; in his Holy Sonnet 'Batter my heart three-personed God', Donne segues from images of violence to images of sex and ends with the startling demand that God should rape him:

Yet dearely'I love you, 'and would be loved faine,
But am betroth'd unto your enemie:
Divorce mee, untie, or breake that knot againe,
Take mee to you, imprison mee, for I
Except you'enthrall mee, never shall be free,
Nor ever chast, except you ravish mee. (9-14)[34]

This fusion of religious and sexual intensity continues in the poetry of Crashaw (whose combination of the two, derived in part from the mystical writings which inspired him, has already been mentioned), and to a lesser degree in the marriage imagery of Henry Vaughan in poems such as 'The Dawning' and 'The World', and in his celebration of 'Dear, beauteous death!' in 'They are all gone into the world of light',[35] but it is a fusion which is largely confined to art and literature – in Britain, with few exceptions, eroticism is absent from later tomb sculpture.[36]

The *Danse Macabre*

European tombs of the nineteenth and early twentieth centuries echo the obsession of some contemporary artists (such as the Belgian artist Félicien Rops, 1833-98) with the fusion of sex and death, but this is less true of Great Britain. The cemeteries of Europe provide many examples of a combination of the funerary with the erotic, but where it does occur in a British context it is either the inadvertent product of an unfortunately conceived piece, such as the tomb monument to Bernard Brocas (d. 1777) at Bramley (Hampshire), on which a stout gentleman in classical dress finds heaven in the arms of a soulful female allegory, or located in works which are excluded from public view, such as Alfred Gilbert's monument to the Duke of Clarence (d. 1892) in the Albert Memorial chapel, Windsor.

Where British artists and writers in the nineteenth and twentieth centuries have attempted to confront the fusion of Eros and Thanatos it has

---

[34] For this poem see Targoff (2008), 120-23.
[35] L.C. Martin (ed.), *Poetry and Selected Prose of Henry Vaughan* (Oxford: Oxford University Press, 1963), 283, 299, 318.
[36] This is reflected in works dealing with eroticism in funerary monuments of the nineteenth and twentieth centuries. André Chabot's *Érotique du Cimetière* (Paris: Henri Veyrier, 1989) contains only two examples from Britain (137, 154) both from London cemeteries and among the least startling images. David Robinson and Dean Koontz, *Beautiful Death: Art of the Cemetery* (Harmondsworth: Penguin Books Ltd, 1996) has seven images from England, most of which show gravestones surrounded by flowers; by comparison there are twenty-three images from Italy, most of which show representations of figures.

tended to be in the context of marginalised genres, such as fantasy and science fiction (Bram Stoker's *Dracula* and its descendants, the personifications of Death who appear in the works of Neil Gaiman and Terry Pratchett), or in the works of marginalised artists such as Thomas Lowell Beddoes (1803-49), author of *Death's Jest-Book* (1850), or Aubrey Beardsley (1872-98), principally known for his work for *The Yellow Book* and his illustrations of the works of Oscar Wilde.

For the artists of the sixteenth and early seventeenth centuries, however, the fusion of sex and death in their vocabulary and the eroticisation of Death himself were a fruitful development of the *topos* of the *Danse Macabre*. From infant to queen, all must accept the inevitable invitation to dance with death. Just so, in the Corsham painting, Elizabeth I is invited by her lover to the last dance.

Acknowledgements

I am extremely grateful to the editors for their comments on this paper and for their helpful suggestions for further references.

Appendix I

As recorded by William Dugdale, the tribute by Sir William Bulstrode to Anne Newdigate, Lady Skeffington (d. 1637), on her monument in St Michael, Coventry, reads in full:

AN ELEGIACALL EPITAPH MADE UPON THE DEATH OF THAT MIRROR OF WOMEN, ANN NEWDIGATE LADY SKEFFINGTON, WIFE TO THAT TRUE MOANING TURTLE SIR RICHARD NEWDIGATE KT. & CONSECRATED TO HER ETERNAL MEMORIE BY THE UNFEIGNED LOVER OF HER VERTUES, WILL. BULSTRODE KNIGHT.

VERTUE HUMBLE, BEAUTY CHAST, PIOUS WIT,
HUSBANDS HONOUR, WOMENS GLORY SWEETLYE KNIT,
AND ALL COMPRISED FAIRELYE IN THIS ONE,
SAD FATE HATH HERE INSHRINED WITH THIS STONE.
VIRTUE TRIUMPH, FOR THOU, HAST WON THE PRIZE,
BEAUTIE TEACH WOMEN TO BE CHAST & WIZE;
MAKE HER YOUR PATTERNE OF A VERTUOUS LIFE,
WHO LIV'D & DYED A FAIR VNSPOTTED WIFE.
SHE WAS THE MIRROR OF HER AGE AND DAYS,
AND NOW THE SUBJECT OF TRANSCENDANT PRAISE.
O WHAT A HARMONIE MANS LIFE WOULD BE,
WERE WOMEN ALL BUT NEARE SO GOOD AS SHE!
HER LIFE WAS SUCH AS FEARED NO STING OF DEATH,
BUT DAR'D HIM BY SO STRONG UNDOUBTING FAITH,
AS THAT HE DID BUT MILDLY STEAL UNTO HER,
AND GENTLY WHISPER' AS HE MEANT TO WOE HER.
AND SHE AS GENTLY YEILDED STRAIT TO GOE,
BEFORE 'TWAS KNOWN IF SHE WERE DEAD OR NO.
NOR IS SHE DEAD, HER SOULE TO HEAVEN STEPT,
THE REST STAYES HERE TILL IT A WHILE HATH SLEPT.
AND HER FAME HERE STILL LIVES & STILL SHALL WAKE,
TILL ALL GOOD MEMORIE SHALL EARTH FORSAKE.
THRICE BELSSED SOUL, WEE'LE NOT OUR GRIEF BELYE,
WEE WAYLE NOT THEE, BUT OUR OWN DESTINYE.
YET IN OUR LOSSE OF THEE THIS IS OUR GLORYE,
THAT 'TIS THY HAPPINESS THAT MAKES US SORYE.
                    W.B.

Obiit. Maii 21 Aetatis suae 29
            Anno Dni. 1637

Bulstrode uses the image of the dead wife's being married to Christ in his epitaph on his own wife, which formerly hung in the parish church of St John, Hackney, by the tomb of her first husband, Henry Banister. It read:

An Epitaph,
Made by Sir William Bulstrode, Kt. upon the Death of his most dear Wife
Anne Lady Bulstrode; and consecrated to the Memory of her excellent
Vertues, and his faithful Affection.

Sad Fate! Here lies interred Woman's Glory:
Whose rich and rare Endowments were a Story,
Fit for the shrill and golden Trump of Fame
To make eternal: That her vertuous Name
Might be a sober Pattern, Rule, and Guide,
To all her frailer Sex: In whom, beside
Her modest Beauty, grave, and pious Wit,
Wisdom, and Judgment, so enthron'd did sit,
And so unnatur'd in her female Passion,
As all the Actions of her Life, Discretion
Did always measure: And to crown her Praise,
Religion was the Pilot of her Ways.
Nor did she her great Zeal as fruitless smother,
But by her Practice still incited other.
Her Nature sweet, fix'd with a Mind so even,
As here on Earth her Soul enjoy'd a Heaven.
Which to Perfection her strong Faith hath carried,
And to the Lamb for ever blessed married.
So that her Death's but Jacob's Dream exprest,
A Ladder to convey her Soul to rest.
Rest then, dear Soul, ne'er to return to me,
While I here mourn, and long to come to thee.
She dyed Jan. 4, 1633.[37]

---

[37] Recorded in John Stow, corrected [...] by John Strype, *A Survey of the Cities of
London and Westminster, and the Borough of Southwark* (London: printed for W.
Innys and J. Richardson, J. and P. Knapton [and 10 others], 1754-55), 127.

SPATIAL CONTEXTS

PLACES FOR REFLECTION:
DEATH IMAGERY IN MEDIEVAL CHOIR STALLS

KRISTIANE LEMÉ-HÉBUTERNE

Some years ago, scholars in France organised a conference in Conques entitled 'Le Miroir des Miséricordes (XIIIᵉ-XVIIᵉ siècles)' or 'The mirror of the misericords (13th-17th centuries)'.[1] However, this title did not do justice to the diverse imagery to be found on the different parts of choir stalls that survive in churches and cathedrals to this day. In fact, it is not only misericords that can be seen as mirrors, because the various elements that form the stalls – arm-rests, *jouées*[2] and dorsals, when they are carved with imagery – can all be said to act as mirrors to the beholder, sending back reflected images that are more or less faithful, more or less deceptive.

The conference in Conques aimed to show how modern-day viewers can discover images of medieval society by studying medieval stalls. Yet the title of the conference also conveyed the idea that, for medieval people, stalls could serve as a mirror and show them their own reflection. This fits very well with what we know of late-medieval ways of thinking: by the end of the Middle Ages, artists were keen to depict in stained-glass windows, tapestries, manuscript illuminations, wall painting and sculpture, the society around them in all its different aspects. Although the stalls are seats reserved solely for use – and thus inspection – by the clergy, they likewise follow this trend of illustrating contemporary society. Towards the end of the Middle Ages we see an increasingly large number of images of medieval social life depicted in the stalls: craftsmen at work, scenes of

---

[1] Conference organised by the 'Groupe de recherche Images et Sociétés et la section d'Histoire de l'Art de l'Université de Toulouse – Le Mirail' in Conques, 27-28 May 1994. See 'Le Miroir des Miséricordes (XIIIᵉ-XVIIᵉ siècles)', *Les Cahiers de Conques*, 2 (February 1996).

[2] *Jouées* are the lateral panels that end each row of stalls, high or low. The French term is preferred to the English term 'stall-ends' in Elaine Block and Frédéric Billiet (eds), *Lexicon of Medieval Choir Stalls*, Profane Arts of the Middle Ages (Turnhout: Brepols, 2010).

daily life, games, music, and proverbs, as well as religious life. Yet this imagery does not relate just to life: death found its place on the choir stalls, too.

By the end of the Middle Ages, people regarded any form of mirror as vehicles for moral confrontation, rather than as merely passive instruments for narcissistic purposes. The many medieval texts that have 'mirror' in their title show us this interest in reflection. Already in the thirteenth century, the various instructive *Mirrors for Princes* offered rulers an ideal image of their own function; an image that they were supposed to imitate. On the other hand, the 'miroers salutaires pour toutes gens' (*salutary mirrors for all people*) offered in the *Danse Macabre* texts aimed to teach people of all stations how to behave well during one's life in order to attain a 'good death'.[3] These didactic and moralising texts thus aimed to provide every man and woman with food for thought on living as well as dying.

Yet there is an important difference between sets of choir stalls and texts regarded as mirrors of instruction: the texts were deliberately written to convey a moral and didactic purpose, just as wall paintings in churches could be viewed and explained in ways that bring out a religious purpose. We do not know if choir stalls could have had the same function, however. First of all, choirs were closed spaces, and only clergy had access to the choir stalls. Secondly, although some sets of stalls were certainly executed with the aim of assisting monks or canons in their theological contemplations – for their iconographical programmes seem particularly elaborate[4] – with most choir stalls it is difficult to be quite so certain about any such

---

[3] Compare *La grant danse macabre des hommes et des femmes avec les dis des trois morts et trois vifs, le débat du corps et de l'âme*, printed by Guyot Marchant in 1486 (Paris, Bibliothèque nationale de France, ResYe 189). Presenting the *Danse Macabre*, the *actor* (in French texts, the author is called either *auteur* or *actor*) explains in his prologue (fol. aii), 'En ce miroer chascun peut lire / Qui le convient ainsi danser / Saige est celuy qui bien si mire' (*In this mirror everyone can read that he must dance thus. Wise is he who observes this well*). The same idea can be found in most of the prologues to printed *Danse Macabre* editions where one reads, 'Ce present livre est appelé / Miroer salutaire pour toutes gens' (*This present book is called the salutary mirror for all people*).

[4] This is certainly the case for the Amiens choir stalls (constructed 1508-19). See Kristiane Lemé-Hébuterne, *Les stalles de la cathédrale Notre-Dame d'Amiens* (Paris: Picard, 2007). One can also point to the stalls from the abbey of Saint-Victor (Paris), constructed around 1531 and now dispersed across several churches in Ile-de-France and Normandy, or to the stalls of 1530-40 from Notre-Dame-aux-Dominicains in Louvain (Belgium). All misericords in these stalls depict stories derived from the Old Testament.

intended purpose as a moralising mirror. Nonetheless, even if this were not the prime intention of the clergy who commissioned the stalls and the craftsmen responsible for producing them, the carvings provide us with a reflection of medieval society, its occupations and preoccupations.

Macabre motifs in choir stalls

Thoughts and troubles that occupied medieval minds – and that are evident in contemporary literature as well as in different forms of art – are thus echoed in the imagery that we find on choir stalls. Macabre motifs form only a relatively small part of these carvings, albeit a part that was becoming increasingly important at the end of the fifteenth and the beginning of the sixteenth centuries. Yet carvers, and also the clergy who guided them, seem to have had little interest in representing the *Danse Macabre*, despite this being the very time when *Danse*-related imagery was proliferating on the painted walls of churches and charnel houses, as well as in illuminated manuscripts and early printed books. Only the carvers who sculpted the misericords of the – no longer extant – stalls in the medieval church (now cathedral) of St Michael in Coventry (England) chose to show a series of *Danse Macabre* scenes of living figures paired with Death.[5] Furthermore, the principal subject of each of these misericords was not death: the *Danse Macabre* was merely relegated to the supporters – a typically English arrangement of minor carvings flanking the central scene. Instead, the central carvings of these misericords were devoted to depictions of the Acts of Mercy, while other recorded misericords in Coventry are known to have featured major religious subjects such as the Last Judgement and the Tree of Jesse. In other words, the *Danse Macabre* served as a marginal motif supporting the central carving, in the literal as well as in the figurative sense.

---

[5] See Sophie Oosterwijk, 'Totentanzikonographie auf Chorgestühlen und Miserikordien des Mittelalters', *L'art macabre (Jahrbuch der Europäischen Totentanz-Vereinigung)*, 6 (2005), 199-214, and by the same author 'Money, Morality, Mortality: the Migration of the *Danse Macabre* from Murals to Misericords', in Peregrine Horden (ed.), *Freedom of Movement in the Middle Ages*, Proceedings of the 2003 Harlaxton Symposium, Harlaxton Medieval Studies, 15 (Donington: Shaun Tyas, 2007), 37-56. The ensemble of Coventry misericords was already incomplete when it was destroyed in 1940; they are now only known from photographs. One misericord in the stalls of *c.*1477-84 in St George's Chapel, Windsor, contains three *Danse Macabre* scenes but was never part of a larger series.

One may ask why other carvers and clergy did not choose the same source of inspiration, especially when the theme was evidently popular in other media. Of course, carving a whole *Danse Macabre* on a single misericord was technically difficult because of the limitations of space: misericords are sometimes no more than 30 x 20 cm in size. The use of supporters by the Coventry carvers was one way of resolving this difficulty. Because French misericords have no such supporters, carvers could have filled the centre of the misericord with a single pairing of Death with a living figure, as we find in some printed books of hours where the *Danse* is divided into small marginal vignettes alongside the prayers, unfolding itself on successive folios.[6]

The reason for the near-absence of the *Danse Macabre* on misericords can perhaps be found in the way that medieval choir stalls appear to have been conceived and realised: misericords (as well as arm-rests) must be read as separate entities, without any link from one to the other. Even if we can sometimes find some form of connection between one seat and another, there is no overall continuity between misericords.[7] By the end of the Middle Ages, most choir stalls comprise misericords that, each by themselves, convey a rich and often complex idea very tersely, and even elliptically.[8]

Even if Continental carvers did not represent the *Danse Macabre* proper on choir stalls, death was nonetheless a preoccupation for the artists and for their patrons. It did inspire some sculptures; at times in a straightforward manner, but also in ways more complicated and difficult to understand for the modern viewer. The most recognisable visual reminder of death – and one frequently found – was the skull. The format of the arm-rest is particularly suitable for carving faces and half-length portraits, so skulls naturally take their place amidst the figures on which the clergy

---

[6] For example, *Les grandes Heures de Simon Vostre à l'usage d'Amiens*, printed in Paris around 1508. See Jean Desobry, 'Les Heures de Simon Vostre d'Amiens imprimées à Paris vers 1508', in *Liber Amicorum, Etudes historiques offertes à Pierre Bougard*. co-édition *Commission départementale d'histoire et d'archéologie du Pas-de-Calais*, 25, *Revue du Nord*, hors-série, collection Histoire, 3 (Arras : Université Lille 3, 1987), 123-39, figs 1, 3 and 5.

[7] In contrast, the Amiens choir stalls are innovative in that the misericords here depict different stories of the Old Testament, verse by verse, and are thus meant to be read in sequence.

[8] This makes the understanding of misericords difficult nowadays: there is no context to help the modern viewer when faced with a no longer familiar proverb, for example. Viewers feel often more confident when studying the *jouées*: in the French examples known to us, the iconographical programme of the *jouées* generally illustrate more familiar and more easily understandable religious ideas.

would rest their hands. Among the thirty-two choir stalls in the abbey church of La Trinité de Vendôme, which date from the end of the fifteenth century, are two skulls serving as arm-rests, symmetrically placed (at least in the present arrangement). The two carvings are very close to one another, both showing a skull covered with a veil and with strongly pronounced eye sockets and other facial features (Fig. 66).

Fig. 66. Arm-rest with Death in the abbey church of La Trinité, Vendôme (Loir-et-Cher, France), late fifteenth century. Photo: author.

In the cathedral of Saint-Bertrand-de-Comminges, the macabre motif of the skull inspired three different carvings.[9] The first is an arm-rest comprising the upper part of a naked death's head, which is situated between two seats with misericords that show, on one side, a chubby angel and, on the other, a warrior. A little further along, a misericord features a skull surrounded by three long bones. Here too, only the cranium has been carved; the upper jaw (with some teeth missing) is lying on a horizontal bone as if about to devour it. There is a hole at the top of the head, but it is unclear whether this is later damage to the misericord or a feature intentionally added by a carver as a reminder of Golgotha where the Cross

---

[9] The cathedral of Saint-Bertrand-de-Comminges has sixty-seven stalls, which were completed in 1535, thanks to the liberality of Bishop Jean de Mauléon (1523-51). See Sylvie Augé, Nelly Pousthomis, Michèle Pradalier-Schlumberger and Henri Pradalier, *Saint-Bertrand-de-Comminges, le chœur Renaissance – Saint-Just-de-Valcabrère, L'église romane* (Graulhet: éd. Odyssée, 2000), 86 and 92.

was believed to have been placed precisely on the spot where Adam died. The third example is a misericord of a complete skull with strongly marked features, and with drapery behind – either a veil or a shroud. Clearly feminine, this head no longer represents Death personified, but rather a single individual deceased woman. Another misericord among the eighty-one choir stalls from the late fifteenth century in the cathedral of Saint-Jean-Baptiste in Saint-Jean-de-Maurienne (Savoye) depicts a half-length representation of either Death or a cadaver: the upper part is decaying yet covered by skin, and the left ear is still intact.[10] Isolated skulls also occur on arm-rests or misericords in choir stalls elsewhere.[11]

An accumulation of skulls in a single set of stalls may have been intended to convey a particular message to the beholder. The church of Remy (Oise) now houses a set of twenty-six stalls of the sixteenth century, which are originally from the ancient Benedictine nunnery of Saint-Jean-aux-Bois (Oise). Only the lower structure of the choir stalls survives, complete with misericords and arm-rests; the jouées have disappeared. Among these twenty-six misericords we find three skulls with human bones, which suggests a particular insistence on death; the more so as other misericords in the set are adorned with foliage and Renaissance ornaments, i.e. much lighter motifs. One of these skulls shows only the cranium viewed from the front, surrounded by one flat bone and several long bones. Another skull is shown in profile and fully carved: eye sockets, nasal cavity and ears are especially pronounced. The lower jaw is wide open, which suggests a smile on the skull's face – the typical rictus.

The third misericord at Remy (Fig. 67) illustrates an intimate link between life and death: the upper part of the misericord shows a skull placed on a ledge, with fine branches descending on either side which sprout on the left a plump human torso and head, and on the right a skeletal head and neck – both emerging from the foliage like ripened fruit. Is this just a simple carver's play with Renaissance motifs, or does this represent the juxtaposition of a putto and skeleton, on each side of an invisible mirror: the skeleton offering a reflection to this chubby child of what he will one day become?

---

[10] Nathalie Pineau-Farge, 'Les stalles de la cathédrale Saint-Jean-Baptiste à Saint-Jean-de-Maurienne', special issue of *Société d'Histoire et d'Archéologie de Maurienne*, 34-35 (2000-1).

[11] Examples include a misericord with a skull among the fifteenth-century choir stalls at Distre (Maine-et-Loire), another from the early sixteenth century in the collegiate church of Saint-Jean-Baptiste in Montrésor (Indre-et-Loire), and skulls among the sixteenth-century choir stalls in Goupillères (Eure) and Solesmes (Sarthe), but this list is not exhaustive.

Fig. 67. Misericord with Death and foliage, Remy church (Oise, France), sixteenth century. Photo: author.

Such mingling of carved motifs, and their juxtaposition in choir stalls, underscore their expressive nature in an almost provocative way. Only one example evokes death among the choir stalls of the Augustinian abbey of Saint-Martin-aux-Bois (Oise):[12] an arm-rest, unfortunately mutilated, still allows us to understand its intention to evoke the figure of the Grim Reaper by means of one of its attributes (Fig. 68). Skull and upper body are carefully carved with the bony hand gripping the handle, but the upper part of the scythe – the blade – has broken off. The details are carefully observed and almost realistic, which makes our confrontation with Death here very vivid. This confrontation is especially striking when compared to the other arm-rests, which show amusing monsters in acrobatic positions, animals playing music (an ape with a hurdy-gurdy and a sow suckling her young while playing bagpipes), and human beings shown full- and half-length (such as a monk with an open book, or a woman

---

[12] The choir stalls were created at the end of the fifteenth century on the instruction of Guy de Baudreuil, who in 1492 became *abbé commendataire* (not a 'regular' abbot, *i.e.* not elected by the canons, but chosen by the king in order to restore life in the abbey after the wars of the fifteenth century – a method of nomination that became usual after the Concordat in 1516). Only twenty-eight stalls survive, but there were originally more. See Kristiane Lemé-Hébuterne, 'L'église et les stalles de Saint-Martin-aux-Bois', *Bulletin de la Société des Antiquaires de Picardie*, 662 (2001), 147-76, and by the same author, *L'église de Saint-Martin-aux-Bois, stalles, peintures murales, vitraux* (Amiens: OVACAM, 2007).

wearing a headdress). Other misericords with representations of daily life
(people eating a meal, tumblers, musicians) and of proverbs (e.g. 'closing
the stable door after the horse has bolted' or 'a fool trying to shoe a
goose'), which do have a moralising intention, still rely on humour and
satire. However, the presence of this Death figure certainly is not intended
to make people laugh. Proverbs that gibe at human foolishness may have
been chosen to prompt the clergy occupying their seats in the stalls to
reflect on human foibles, but reflection can be light-hearted and some
scenes may have resulted only in a laugh without any profound impact.
Here, the mere sight of the arm-rest with the spectre of Death evokes a
more immediate and powerful reaction: the skeleton with his scythe would
have had a direct impact on the canon who sat down on his seat.

Fig. 68. Arm-rest with Death and scythe, Saint-Martin-aux-Bois (Oise, France),
very end of the fifteenth century. Photo: author.

Another misericord with an interesting reflection on death can be
found among the choir stalls of 1507-15 in Chaumont-en-Vexin (Oise),
although they are originally from the collegiate church of Saint-Gervais-
Saint-Protais in Gisors (Eure).[13] An invisible mirror seems to divide the
misericord vertically, joining or separating two distinct faces each looking
out: on the right is the face of a young lady – calm, serene, her head and

---

[13] The choir stalls were bought in 1721 by the churchwarden of Saint-Jean-Baptiste
de Clermont; the purchase included twelve low stalls and two low independent
stalls with *jouées* containing religious scenes.

hair hidden beneath a little cap and a veil – while on the left is a realistically carved skull, almost smiling (Fig. 69). The two faces are turned away from each other and it is difficult to say if the woman is aware of Death, or if Death speaks to the lady or to the beholder who is able to see both sides of this unequal couple sharing the misericord. Yet are they really partners or do we have only one Janus-like personification, representing present and future?

Fig. 69. Misericord with Death and young lady, Chaumont-en-Vexin (Oise, France), 1507-15. Photo: author.

A juxtaposition of a skull with a living being was evidently intended to provoke thought. Here, the shock is all the more powerful because of the linking of Death with a young female. Youth, femininity and Death do not seem obvious companions. Other carvings also bring together a living being and Death, but in a less provocative way, because of the character of the living person: on an arm-rest among the 113 choir stalls in the cathedral of Sainte-Marie in Auch, dating from 1520-54, it is an elderly religious who presents a skull to visitors gazing upon the stalls.[14] Here, the

---

[14] See Marie-Eve Martin-Cortes, 'Les jouées des stalles de la cathédrale Sainte-Marie d'Auch', mémoire de maîtrise (4th-year dissertation) (Université Toulouse-Le Mirail, 1995); 'Les stalles de la cathédrale Sainte-Marie d'Auch: les parcloses', mémoire de D.E.A. (5th-year dissertation) (Université de Toulouse-Le Mirail,

great age of the man is reminiscent of representations such as that of St Jerome contemplating with serenity and wisdom man's ultimate fate on earth. The old religious in Auch, in the twilight of his years, is likely to recognise in his own death his true birth into the real world – God's kingdom – instead of the end of everything, and this is the visual reminder that he holds up to the viewer like a mirror.

Fig. 70. Arm-rest showing a lady with hourglass and skull, collegiate church of Sainte-Catherine, Hoogstraten (Belgium), c.1525. Photo: author.

1997); 'L'iconographie des parcloses narratives dans les stalles de la cathédrale Sainte-Marie d'Auch', *Bulletin de la Société Archéologique, historique, littéraire et scientifique du Gers*, 375 (1999), 51-62; Jean-Pierre Suau, 'Les stalles de la cathédrale d'Auch au miroir de l'iconographie. Entre tradition et modernité (vers 1520-vers 1554)', *Bulletin de la Société ... du Gers*, 383 (2007), 7-20.

More often, however, it is a young woman or a child who convey the message to guard oneself against Death. On one of the arm-rests in the collegiate church of Sainte-Catherine, Hoogstraten (Belgium), an elegant young lady presents in one hand a skull and in the other an hourglass (Fig. 70).[15] Time runs out like sand, thereby inevitably bringing the hour of death ever closer. The hourglass aptly emblematises the finite nature of everything, including life. Yet it is not the image of the hourglass itself that might seem cruel; in fact, the hourglass illustrates only the flow of time and the reality of life running out fast. The trickling of sand may be as steady as life itself running smoothly until the end of its natural course. In contrast to the hourglass imagery, the *Danse Macabre* conveys a very different message that Death may come whenever he likes and catch whoever he wants. On the Hoogstraten arm-rest, the poignancy lies in the juxtaposition of the hourglass, the skull and the young lady – a double *vanitas* warning that Death may end not only life at whatever age, but also destroy beauty.

Another variation can be found in the church of Saint-Gervais-Saint-Protais in Paris.[16] Here a plump and dimpled putto is lying on a massive wooden coffin, his elbow resting in a seemingly casual manner on a skull (Fig. 71). The putto with a skull was a favourite Renaissance motif.[17] It also occurs on a misericord among the sixteenth-century stalls in the cathedral of St-Julien in Le Mans (Sarthe) and on a parclose from the stalls from the abbey of Saint-Victor (Paris), where a little angel displays a skull.[18] A variant of the same motif, but somewhat more complex, is found on a misericord among the choir stalls in the Grote Kerk in Dordrecht (Netherlands).[19] Here a chubby infant, loosely clad in a tunic belted at the waist, is lying on his side with his elbow resting on a skull; his left arm points to the hourglass near his feet (Fig. 72). In the background there is a

---

[15] The collegiate church of Sainte-Catherine in Hoogstraten was built in 1525; its stalls date from the same period.

[16] The church of Saint-Gervais-Saint-Protais in Paris has forty-four choir stalls, but only twenty-eight date from *c.*1540.

[17] For this motif, see also Horst W. Janson, 'The Putto with the Death's Head', *Art Bulletin*, 19 (1937), 423-49. For new insights on this motif, see Michael Overdick, cat. no. 124: Schlafender Putto mit Totenschädel, in Andrea von Hülsen-Esch and Hiltrud Westermann-Angerhausen with Stefanie Knöll (eds), *'Zum Sterben schön!' Alter, Totentanz und Sterbekunst von 1500 bis heute*, exhibition catalogue, 2 vols (Regensburg: Schnell & Steiner, 2006), vol. 2, 223-25.

[18] See n. 4 above. The stall with the skull is in the church at Les Botteraux (Eure).

[19] The sixty-seven choir stalls in Dordrecht were constructed in 1538-41. See Herman A. van Duinen, *De Koorbanken van de Grote- of Onze Lieve Vrouwekerk te Dordrecht* (Leiden: Primavera Pers, 1997).

scroll, which has been left empty; if it ever held painted text, no trace is visible today. An anonymous print attributed to the school of Dürer depicts the same subject, but with an added warning in the text: 'Hodie mihi, cras tibi' (*Today me, tomorrow thee*).[20] In the seventeenth and eighteenth centuries, the 'homo bulla' (*man is but a bubble*) motif of a child blowing bubbles was to take further advantage of the subject's potential.

Fig. 71. Misericord showing a putto leaning on a skull on top of a coffin, church of Saint-Gervais-Saint-Protais, Paris, *c.*1540. Photo: author.

Fig. 72. Misericord showing a reclining putto with hourglass and skull, Grote Kerk, Dordrecht (Netherlands), 1538-41. Photo: author.

---

[20] Van Duinen (1997), 143-44.

Death and the mirror

All these representations offer a mirror in which man must study himself; a mirror intended to help him to remember his destiny and hence change his way of life. Sometimes, in order to emphasise the message, the carver goes beyond the simple death image by giving Death a real mirror: a mere accessory perhaps, but with a meaning that is quite different from Death's other attributes of scythe, arrow and hourglass. The scythe and arrow can be used to extinguish life, while the hourglass may play a positive role by reminding man that his days are numbered and that everything must end. The mirror is more equivocal, both deceptive and revealing: it is said to be the *père des mensonges*, or father of lies; it shows man an image of this world, but this reflection is inevitably an illusion and not the reality of God's creation. It incites man to see only his own face and thus tempts him to selfishness and vanity. Yet it may also help him to look farther and deeper. We must not forget that the mirror is among the attributes of Prudence, one of the Cardinal Virtues.

We can look at one of the pendentives among the choir stalls at Amiens with the first of these allegorical meanings of the mirror in the mind.[21] The bottom of the pendentives is carved in the shape of a truncated pyramid, placed upside-down. It presents four sides that cannot be seen all at once, each showing little scenes with several personages. On one of these, a young lady, elegantly clothed in a long dress with a square-cut neck and shirring sleeves, is admiring herself in a round mirror, holding the handle in her left hand (Fig. 73a). No doubt she sees only her attractive face and her beauty, without realising that they are but ephemeral. This part of the pendentive may be intended to call to mind the sin of Pride as we find it in two works by Hieronymus Bosch, viz. *The Garden of Earthly Delights* and *The Tabletop of the Seven Deadly Sins and Four Last Things*, where the artist chose a woman looking at herself in a mirror – and a young man in the next room doing the same – to symbolise the sin of Pride.[22] On the right side of the pendentive (Fig. 73b), a young man, also

---

[21] Lemé-Hébuterne (2007), 209-10.

[22] In the right-hand panel of Hieronymus Bosch' *The Garden of Earthly Delights* (*c*.1480-90, Madrid, Prado Museum), a woman is seated before a convex mirror placed on the rear end of a devil. *The Tabletop of the Seven Deadly Sins and Four Last Things* (*c*.1500-25, Madrid, Prado Museum) by Bosch or the school of Bosch shows in the centre the eye of God and in the corners four medallions showing the Four Last Things: a deathbed scene (top left), the Last Judgement (top right), Hell with the seven deadly sins individually labelled (bottom left), and Paradise (bottom right). The centre of the eye shows Christ emerging from the tomb while the

very elegant, looks at a large skull in his right hand, pointing at it with his left hand. The shape of his lips suggests that he is conversing with the skull: he does not really hold it out to the young lady.

Fig. 73a. Pendentive showing a young lady with a mirror, Amiens Cathedral (Somme, France), 1508-19. Photo: author.

surrounding circle is divided into seven parts: *Superbia* (Pride) is represented by a woman (seen from the back) whose face is reflected in the mirror held up by a devil.

Fig. 73b. Pendentive showing a young man with a skull, Amiens Cathedral (Somme, France), 1508-19. Photo: author.

If the woman with the mirror evokes vanity or Superbia (Pride), the presence of the skull also invites us to compare this carving in Amiens with paintings in which the mirror is associated with Death. This is the case in Hans Memling's *Triptych of Earthly Vanity and Divine Salvation*, where a naked woman stands looking in a mirror that shows to her in turn her reflection, whereas on the next panel Death warns her of what awaits her.[23] It is a very rich and complex allegorical painting, but for our purpose here we shall only consider the evocation of vanity in comparison with the pendentive at Amiens Cathedral.[24] In the triptych as in the pendentive, Death does not show himself in the mirror; perhaps he is not even seen by the two young women who are bent on following their own desires and ignore him completely.

However, some carvers did not hesitate to show Death's reflection in a mirror, thereby making this attribute even more disquieting. In the choir stalls at the abbey church of Orbais, two depictions of Death can be found.[25] The first occurs on an arm-rest, similar to the ones at Vendôme or Saint-Bertrand-de-Comminges, where Death wears a veil or perhaps a shroud; unfortunately, Death's face is damaged here. More interesting in relation to the mirror imagery is the misericord at Orbais in which a skeletal Death appears as a half-length figure, covered by a veil or rather a shroud that allows us to see only his face and one hand (Fig. 74).[26] His face shows sunken eye-sockets, the jaw-bones are emphasised, and his mouth forms a large grin from ear to ear. The carver has not tried to make the skull look anatomically convincing, if we compare it to more realistically carved skulls in choir stalls elsewhere. Death holds a mirror with a handle in his right hand, just like the young woman on the

---

[23] For Hans Memling's *Triptych of Earthly Vanity and Divine Salvation*, c.1485 or later (Strasbourg, Museum des Beaux-Arts), see Dirk De Vos, *Hans Memling. The Complete Works* (London: Thames & Hudson, 1994), cat. 64, 245-47.

[24] In the central panel, a naked woman looks at herself in a mirror. In the left wing stands Death, in the guise of a still fleshy cadaver with worms in his belly, holding up a long scroll with the words 'Ecce finis hominis comparatus sum luto et assimilatus sum faville et cineri' (*Behold the end of man; clay I was and to dust and ashes I returned*). On the right wing, a devil holds another scroll with the text 'IN • INFERNO • NVLLA • EST • REDEMPTIO' (*In Hell there is no salvation*). The reverse of this wing shows a skull in a stone niche, with above it a sentence from Job: 'SCIO • ENIM • QVOD • REDEMPTOR • MEVS • VIVIT • ET • IN • NOVISSIMO • DIEDETERRA • SVRRETVRVS • SVM • ET • RVRSVM • CIRCV[M]DABOR • PELLE • MEA • ET • INCARNE • MEA • VIDEBO • DEV[M] • SALVATAREM • MEVM • IOB • XIX° • CAP°' (*For I know that my redeemer lives and that I shall rise again on the last day, when, wrapped in my skin and flesh, I will see God, my saviour, Job, 19*). The painting strongly condemns Vanity, but also Luxury.

[25] The choir stalls were commissioned between 1520 and 1525 by the first *abbé commendataire*, Cardinal Louis de Bourbon; forty-six stalls survive.

[26] For this misericord, see Sophie Oosterwijk, '*Danse Macabre* Imagery in Late-Medieval Sculpture', in Andrea von Hülsen-Esch and Hiltrud Westermann-Angerhausen with Stefanie Knöll (eds), '*Zum Sterben schön!' Alter, Totentanz und Sterbekunst von 1500 bis heute*, exhibition catalogue, 2 vols (Regensburg: Schnell & Steiner, 2006), vol. 1, 167-77, at 172 and n. 26.

pendentive at Amiens Cathedral. However, he does not offer this mirror to a human being, and so does not try to reveal himself to a mortal: he is looking at himself and, without doubt, seeing himself as we can see him, his reflection being carved in relief onto the mirror.

Fig. 74. Misericord with Death looking at himself in a mirror, Orbais (Marne, France), *c.*1520-25. Photo: author.

The motif of a reflection of Death in a mirror has often been painted, but with different meanings. In his double portrait *The Painter Hans Burgkmair and His Wife Anna* of 1529 (Vienna, Kunsthistorisches Museum), Lucas Furtenagel shows the middle-aged couple holding a mirror in which we can see their two heads reflected as two skull-like faces. The viewer can see both couple and reflection, but husband and wife are looking towards the beholder and thus not at the mirror and their ultimate destiny. In *Modesty Disarming Vanity* of 1569 (Paris, Louvre) by the Flemish Mannerist painter Jan van der Straet (or Stradanus), it is Vanity who gazes at herself in a mirror that also reflects a death's head.[27] There are many paintings that play with the reflected image of a face transformed into a skull, but paintings in which Death contemplates his

---

[27] See http://www.wga.hu/frames-e.html?/html/s/stradanu/allegory.html (accessed 16 February 2011).

own reflection in a mirror are not so numerous. However, in one version of *The Temptation of St Anthony* of *c*.1550 by the Flemish painter Jan Mandyn (1500-60), the right part shows a woman looking at herself in a convex mirror held in her right hand, in which a reflection of her emaciated face appears.[28] With her left hand, she places an hourglass on her head, while on her back hangs a quiver full of arrows. Her limbs and body are covered with slithering snakes and running vermin.

However, there are other examples of Death looking at himself in a mirror, as in the margin of a French manuscript of *c*.1300 (New York, Morgan Library, MS 796, fol. 91v).[29] In this miniature we see only the back of the mirror held by Death, and not what he himself sees there. However, a beautiful miniature at the start of the Office of the Dead in a French book of hours of *c*.1485-90 shows a skeleton kneeling on a gravestone and praying while looking at (and admiring?) himself in a mirror hanging from a branch in a tree.[30] An inscription on the tombstone reads '1484 28 SEPTEMBRIS FUIT HIC INH[U]M[ATUS]' (He was buried 28 September 1484). Two young men can be observed in the left corner of the miniature, while behind the tree we see the head of a woman wearing a black veil: is she the widow of the buried man? On the Orbais misericord, Death is looking at himself in a similar way, but for what purpose: to admire himself, as all young fashionable ladies are apt to do with a mirror? Yet when Death shows his reflected image to any human being, the intention is to remind man that he is mortal and to force him to consider his inevitable end. If Death is looking at his reflection and seeing himself in the mirror, does that mean that Death is mortal too, or is this a parody of human vanity, or even a reminder that man should be following Death's example and see his true reflection? Here the mirror seems to carry different meanings: it is both a symbol of narcissism and of wisdom.

Death is the consequence of Adam and Eve's original sin, but every Christian knows that Christ's death and resurrection cleansed that sin

---

[28] Mandyn produced several paintings of this subject, of which one is in the Frans Hals Museum, Haarlem. The version discussed here was shown in the exhibition *De Fra Angelico à Bonnard – Chefs d'œuvre de la Collection Rau* (Paris: Luxembourg Museum, 2000).

[29] See Stefanie Knöll, 'Zur Entstehung des Motivs der Tod und das Mädchen', in Andrea von Hülsen-Esch and Hiltrud Westermann-Angerhausen with Stefanie Knöll (eds), *'Zum Sterben schön!' Alter, Totentanz und Sterbekunst von 1500 bis heute*, exhibition catalogue, 2 vols (Regensburg: Schnell & Steiner, 2006), vol. 1, 65-72, and especially 68-69 and fig. 8.

[30] Hours for the use of Paris, produced in Arras or Amiens, private collection, f. 98r: see http://www.medievalbooksofhours.com/advancedtutorial/tutorial_advanced_onlinetutorial_images_dead.html#dead (accessed 3 May 2010).

away, thereby defeating earthly death and transforming it into a passage towards eternal life, like a new birth.[31] Could the Orbais misericord be meant to tell the viewer about the hope brought to mankind by the Christian faith? While the jouées of this set of stalls are carved with imagery from the Old and New Testaments (including the Tree of Jesse, apostles and saints), the other misericords do not allow us to recognise any religious message, which makes it strange that just a single misericord should carry such a profound meaning.

The Orbais misericord is even more intriguing if we consider that this mirror can be regarded as more than a mirror. Not only does it reflect the image of Death, but it also shows this image in relief, thereby evoking the fool's bauble: the kind of staff or sceptre that terminates in a fool's head at which the fool is often shown gazing.[32] By the end of the Middle Ages, fools and jesters were often depicted with such a bauble and wearing an outfit adorned with little bells that chimed with the least movement. The Amiens choir stalls are rich in arm-rests and pendentives decorated with jesters looking at their own alter ego that tops their huge baubles. The same idea can also be found in Hoogstraten, where several fools are carved on misericords and, in low-relief, on a parclose: one jester is shown confronting his bauble in the same posture as Death on the Orbais misericord (Fig. 75).

In this context, we should remember that the jester had a task that was at the same time a privilege: he had to tell the truth, not only to the king or his noble master, but also to each person he encountered. Everyone has to hear his own truth, even when that truth is sometimes hard to accept. This duality between the fool and his bauble on the one hand, and Death and the mirror on the other, could reiterate and at the same time strengthen, the traditional warning uttered by the dead in the *Danse Macabre* when facing the living: you are what I once was, and I am what you will be. Yet Death looks at himself in his mirror/bauble, mimicking the fool who sees reflected there his own folly. Likewise, Death sees reflected his own death. Death and fool thus perform a similar function towards mankind. If this is true, can we compare Death to folly, whereas wisdom sides with Life?

---

[31] In the liturgical calendar the *dies natalis* or feastday of a saint is celebrated on the day of his or her death, which is meant to illustrate that death is the birth to the true life.

[32] See Sophie Oosterwijk, "'Alas, poor Yorick': Death, the Fool, the Mirror and the *Danse Macabre*', in Stefanie Knöll (ed.), *Narren-Masken-Karneval, Meisterwerke von Dürer bis Kubin aus der Düsseldorfer Graphiksammlung "Mensch und Tod"* (Regensburg: Schnell & Steiner, 2009), 20-32.

Fig. 75. Parclose with a jester and bauble, collegiate church of Sainte-Catherine, Hoogstraten (Belgium), *c*.1525. Photo: author.

Conclusion

The imagery that we find on medieval choir stalls is a reflection of medieval society and its preoccupations. Misericords in particular have often been studied for scenes of everyday life in the Middle Ages, for the imagery on these seats in one of the most sacred parts of a church – because the most sacred part is the sanctuary where mass is celebrated – was often far from religious or even moralistic; a seeming contradiction between sacred space and profane decoration. Yet not all of these scenes on choir stalls are merely reflections of everyday preoccupations or drôleries about a topsy-turvy world: there is also a more serious side to these carvings, and more so than most people think.[33]

The carvings about Death that have been discussed here belong to the more serious side of choir-stall imagery. Yet the *Danse Macabre* is rarely to be found in the sacred spaces reserved for the clergy; instead, it tends to occur in the more public spaces, such as cemeteries, charnel houses, or the nave of a church. We could say the same about most of the carvings on stalls, however: proverbs and evocations of daily life are not often to be found in choirs, either. In fact, there is good reason for the presence of Death in choir stalls: celebrating the Office of the Dead was one of the duties of canons, especially in collegiate churches where they were expected to pray for the dead.[34] It is true that medieval choir stalls cannot compete with murals, manuscript illuminations and woodcuts in representations of the *Danse*; the *Danse Macabre* misericords in Coventry and Windsor were highly exceptional. Yet macabre imagery does occur on choir stalls in a variety of forms and motifs that sometimes reflect medieval preoccupations with death in a complex and enigmatic way.

The *Danse Macabre* served to show viewers a mirror of themselves and their contemporaries, by confronting them with their own follies typical of their age and social rank. Just as the *Danse* shows the dying looking back at their lives, the imagery on choir stalls served to remind the living not just of the follies of life but also the inevitability of death.

---

[33] As far as can be established statistically, we find in France du Nord that some 35% of imagery on stalls, *jouées*, misericords and arm-rests consists of religious motifs. Moreover, many minor scenes are no longer understood because the meaning has been lost over time, *e.g.* proverbs now unknown.

[34] In later periods *Danse Macabre* and related death imagery can in fact be found on vestments and other liturgical textiles: see Imke Lüders, *Der Tod auf Samt und Seide. Todesdarstellungen auf liturgischen Textilien des 16. bis 19. Jahrhunderts im deutschsprachigen Raum*, Kasseler Studien zur Sepulkralkultur, 14 (Kassel: Arbeitsgemeinschaft Friedhof und Denkmal e.V., 2009).

Acknowledgements

I should like to thank David L. Rosenberg for his help with turning my original draft into proper English, and to express my gratitude to Sophie Oosterwijk and Stefanie Knöll for their many suggestions.

THE ISTRIAN *DANSE MACABRE*: BERAM AND HRASTOVLJE

TOMISLAV VIGNJEVIĆ

The *Danse Macabre* has been attested in numerous places across Europe, but many medieval examples are known only through descriptions or copies, or are poorly preserved. Nevertheless, two frescoes of the *Danse* in Istria have survived in very good condition, and as such are a precious source of information on this iconographic motif within the region where Italian and Central European artistic traditions are intertwined (Pls 14-15). These *Danse Macabre* cycles are exceptional for their extraordinary compositions and iconographic peculiarities; clear signs of the ability of their authors to produce works of art in which different iconographic traditions are merged into complex and original solutions. This essay will explore this intertwinement, which gave way to a diverse and abundant artistic creativity that was evident in fifteenth-century painting in Istria.

The two Istrian *Danse* cycles are situated in Beram (in the central part of the peninsula, Fig. 76 and Pl. 14) and Hrastovlje (about 15 kilometres from Koper, in the northern part of Istria, Pl. 15).[1] Both schemes are remarkable not only for their artistic and geographic position, but also because both painters – Vincent and John of Kastav – were influenced by the iconography and style of northern European art.[2] In Istrian art and culture of the late Middle Ages, where the Italian artistic idiom and culture were heavily pervasive, this is certainly a significant occurrence because it provides a clear example of the coexistence of different cultural and artistic traditions. It is important to note that almost at the same time that

---

[1] Both schemes are briefly described and illustrated in Reinhold Hammerstein, *Tanz und Musik des Todes. Die mittelalterlichen Totentänze und ihr Nachleben* (Bern/Munich: Francke Verlag, 1980), 193-94, figs 130, 132.

[2] The two painters came from Kastav, a small town near Rijeka (Croatia), which is almost all that is known about them. They each appear to have headed large workshops as the frescoes in Beram and Hrastovlje show the hands of different painters.

these frescoes were painted, other works of art produced in Istria clearly depended on the Italian – and mostly Venetian – style.

The Venetian connection is not surprising. Whereas the eastern and central parts of Istria belonged to Carniola (which forms a central part of present-day Slovenia) and were part of the Holy Roman Empire, the west coast and some parts of the central peninsula owed allegiance to the Venetian Republic. For example, one finds clear evidence of Venetian Renaissance influences, particularly that of Jacopo Bellini, in the paintings by Clerigino da Capodistria, who was active in Koper – a city belonging to Venice. In his frescoes in the church of St Mary at Oprtalj, which are dated 1471, Clerigino created a monument to early Renaissance art with his depiction of the Annunciation with saints that was clearly based on Venetian models.[3] On the other hand, the frescoes in the church of St Mary at Beram in present-day Croatia, which are dated 1474, reveal a connection with the painting of central Europe, particularly late Gothic painting.

Fig. 76. Vincent of Kastav, *Danse Macabre* fresco on the west wall in the church of St Mary, Beram (Istria), 1474. Photo: Science and Research Centre, Koper.

---

[3] Brigitte Klesse, 'Ein unbekanntes Werk des Clerigino da Capodistria', *Pantheon*, 19 (1971), 281-91.

Beram

The church of St Mary at Škriline near Beram, in the central part of Istria near Pazin, was most probably built in the fifteenth century by the Beram brotherhood of St Mary. It was also a site of pilgrimage for many of the worshippers from this region, and served as a cemetery church for the inhabitants of nearby Beram. It has one aisle, a square presbytery, and a wooden ceiling. The frescoes, which cover all the walls of the interior, are signed by Master Vincent of Kastav and dated 1474. They were commissioned by the community of Beram and paid for by the Fraternity of the Virgin Mary of that town. On the south wall near the side entrance a text in Latin is still visible:

> In honore.domini.nostri.Y.kristi.amen.ac.glo
> riose.virginis.matris.marie.ac.domine.sanctorum.
> omium.fecit.hoc.opus.dipingere.comunitas
> Bermw.ex(pensis) fraternitatis.beate.marie.virginis.
> hoc.pinxit.magister.vincencius.d(e) kastua.et. conp
> livit.mense.novembris.die.octo.post. martini.
> anno.domini.millessimo.quadracentessimo.
> septugesimo.quarto.gr.[4]

> *(In the honour of our Lord Jesus Christ, Amen, and the glorious Virgin Mother Mary and in the name of all Saints, this work was ordered by the community of Beram to be painted at the expense of the fraternity of the Blessed Virgin Mary. This work was painted by Master Vincent of Kastav and finished in the month of November, the eighth day after [the feast of St] Martin, in the year 1474.)*

On the south wall the life of the Virgin and Christ's Infancy are painted in addition to life-size depictions of St Michael, St Florian and St John the Evangelist. The north wall depicts the Procession and the Adoration of the Magi. Underneath are five scenes from the Life of Christ and the Passion, St George slaying the Dragon, St Martin, the Church Fathers, and the Prophets. The west wall contains the *Danse Macabre* at the top, beneath which are depicted the Fall of Man on the left, and the Wheel of Fortune on the right side of the door (Fig. 76). These two scenes were severely damaged by the insertion of two windows in the eighteenth century.

The *Danse Macabre* at Beram moves from the left to the right, *i.e.* in the opposite direction of the *Danse* in Paris. The chain of alternating living

---

[4] Branko Fučić, *Vincent von Kastav* (Zagreb/Pazin: Kršćanska sadašnjost, Istarsko književno društvo 'Juraj Dobrila', 1992), 22.

and dead characters commences with a dead dancer leading the Pope and ends on the far left with a Merchant. On the far right the procession is met by Death playing the bagpipes. This is another unusual iconographic trait, since elsewhere this personification of Death as a piper is placed at the start of the procession, *viz.* seated beneath the Preacher's pulpit in Bernt Notke's slightly earlier cycle in Tallinn (Estonia)[5] and likewise in the destroyed first part of the fresco in the abbey church of St Robert at La Chaise-Dieu (Auvergne).[6] In Beram the figure of the Preacher is omitted altogether, and instead it is Death playing the bagpipes who receives the Pope. The pontiff is shown holding a money pouch in his hand, perhaps in an attempt to redeem himself – an interesting instance of anti-papal satire. The next living character behind him is the Cardinal, and then the Bishop, followed by the King wielding a sceptre topped with a fleur-de-lys, and then the Queen who holds money in her hands. The next characters are the Landlord (whose profession is indicated by a small barrel), the naked Child, the lame Beggar wearing a pilgrim's hat, the Knight in armour, and finally the Merchant who is standing beside a counter with money.

In this fresco, a singular emphasis is placed on money, an ultimately worthless commodity with which a very unusual choice of social representatives are trying to redeem themselves in vain.[7] The Beram *Danse Macabre* thus becomes a visual sermon on the uselessness of wealth in the inevitable final confrontation with Death.

The arrangement of the living dancers at Beram is remarkable. The three highest ranking representatives of the *sacerdotium* – Pope, Cardinal and Bishop – appear first, followed by the King and Queen. The model for this distinctive emphasis on the clerical estate at the beginning of the procession of the *Danse Macabre* probably came from Italy. This can still be observed in two – admittedly much later – Italian *Danse Macabre*

---

[5] Hammerstein (1980), fig. 31; also Hartmut Freytag (ed.), *Der Totentanz der Marienkirche in Lübeck und der Nikolaikirche in Reval (Tallinn)* (Cologne, Weimar, Vienna: Böhlau Verlag, 1993), and Elina Gertsman, The Dance of Death in Reval (Tallinn): the Preacher and his Audience', *Gesta*, 42:2 (2003), 143-59.

[6] Hammerstein (1980), fig. 39; also Patrick Rossi, *La danse macabre de La Chaise-Dieu Abbatiale Saint-Robert: étude iconographique d'une fresque du XVe siècle* (Le Pux-en-Velay: Éditions Jeanne-d'Arc, 2006).

[7] Such emphasis on money can also be found in some other *Danse* cycles: see Sophie Oosterwijk, 'Money, Morality, Mortality: the Migration of the *Danse Macabre* from Murals to Misericords', in Peregrine Horden (ed.), *Freedom of Movement in the Middle Ages* (2003 Harlaxton Symposium Proceedings) Harlaxton Medieval Studies, 15 (Donington: Shaun Tyas, 2007), 37-56, and also the essay by Jutta Schuchard in this volume.

cycles in the churches of San Stefano in Carisolo (dating from 1519)[8] and of San Vigilio in Pinzolo (dating from 1539), the latter painted by Simon de Baschenis.[9] In these two murals the progression of church representatives at the start of the procession also begins with the Pope and continues with the Cardinal, Bishop, Dean and Friar. This is probably because the papal curia and the clergy held a far greater significance in Italy than in the North, and the critique of this estate was therefore more topical.[10]

The mural at Beram is a synthesis of various iconographic traditions, but is closest to the examples of the so-called Basel group of *Danses Macabres*.[11] Although it has been argued that in terms of morphology it points to the later frescoes in Clusone near Bergamo, one finds very few similarities between the two beyond the most general form of procession and the direction in which it moves.[12] However, there are more differences than similarities between these Italian frescoes and that in Beram. The fervent gesticulation – which was often a visual shorthand sign of excessiveness in the medieval evaluation of gestural cultures[13] – and the presence of music-making cadavers at Beram direct us rather towards the iconographic tradition of northern examples of the *Danse*, particularly the Basel group: the Großbasel painting at the Dominican cemetery painted *c.*1440 and the Kleinbasel mural of *c.*1460 from the Klingental convent. There the entire dynamic of the procession with its wild fervency, accompanied by cadavers frolicking and playing music, likewise reminds

---

[8] Hammerstein (1980), 196 and fig. 131; Maria Giulia Aurigemma. 'Nosce te ipsum. The Representation of Death in the Countries in the Germanic Area and the Netherlands', in Alberto Tenenti (ed.), *Humana Fragilitas. The Themes of Death in Europe from the 13th Century to the 18th Century* (Clusone: Ferrari Editrice, 2002), 141-96, at 163-64.

[9] Hammerstein (1980), 197 and fig. 129; Giuseppe Ciaghi, *Nell'antica chiesa di San Vigilio a Pinzolo* (Trento: Editrice UNI Service, 2006).

[10] In contrast, the mural of *c.*1490 in the Marienkirche in Berlin shows a complete separation of clerical and lay characters on either side of the centrally placed Crucifixion.

[11] Hammerstein (1980), 77-81.

[12] Janez Höfler, 'Mittelalterliche Totentanzdarstellungen im Alpen-Adria Raum', in Markus J. Wenninger (ed.), *'du gouter tôt'. Sterben im Mittelalter – Ideal und Realität* (Klagenfurt: Wieser Verlag, 1998), 131-44, at 138.

[13] See, for example, Jean-Claude Schmitt, *La Raison des Gestes dans l'Occident médiéval* (Paris: Éditions Gallimard, 1990), 358. Gestures were supposed to be modest and obedient, so 'gesticulation' was generally frowned upon as being excessive and immoderate.

one of carnival merrymaking where the high was interchanged with the low, and the holy with the profane.[14]

Fig. 77. The Merchant and Knight in the *Danse Macabre* fresco at Beram (Istria), 1474. Photo: Science and Research Centre, Koper.

Certain similarities are particularly striking. For instance, at Beram the man who stands beside the table with money and jug (Fig. 77) is not an ordinary Merchant with wares behind him, but rather a composite figure who encompasses the Merchant, the Usurer, and the Peddler depicted in both Basel cycles. There, too, the Usurer is situated beside a counter piled with coins, while the Peddler carries an abundance of small objects offered for sale on a kind of a shelf worn over the shoulders. If we combine the motif of the Usurer sitting behind the counter and the image of the Peddler with many goods before him, we arrive at the Beram figure of the Merchant. The King in the Beram mural resembles his counterpart in Großbasel: in both images, the dead dancer accompanying the King (who has dropped his royal sceptre) plays the trumpet, and both Kings wear similar coats lined with fur at the top and open below the neck. Furthermore, the figure of the large Landlord with his small barrel of ale is

[14] Gert Kaiser, 'Totentanz und verkehrte Welt', in Franz Link (ed.), *Tanz und Tod in Literatur und Kunst* (Berlin: Verlag Duncker & Humblot, 1993), 93-118.

reminiscent of the Cook at Großbasel, who holds a jug and wooden spoon. Finally, half of the cadavers at Beram are playing instruments: trumpets, horns and lutes. This latter instrument occurs very infrequently in the *Danse Macabre*, but it is found in the hands of the dead dancer who accompanies the Duchess in the Basel group.

Fig. 78. The Knight, woodcut in the Heidelberg Blockbook, *c*.1458 (Heidelberg, Universitätsbibliothek, Cod. Pal. germ. 438). © Universitätsbibliothek Heidelberg.

The so-called Heidelberg blockbook (*c*.1458), which was probably produced in Basel, also has many similarities to the Beram painting.[15] Immediately beside the Merchant in Beram there is a Knight in armour who is similar to both the Knight (*rytter*) and the Nobleman (*edlerman*) in the Heidelberg blockbook (Figs 77-78). The Beram Knight's helmet and

---

[15] Universitätsbibliothek Heidelberg, Cod. Pal. 438: see http://diglit.ub.uni-heidelberg.de/diglit/cpg438/ and Hammerstein (1980), 189-91.

armour, which is unusually shaped particularly at the elbows and knees, were undoubtedly modelled either on the Heidelberg woodcuts, on copies of that blockbook, or a common prototype. This is not a unique instance as the *Danse Macabre* mural of *c*.1500 at Metnitz in Carinthia (Austria) is based on the same blockbook.[16] Similarly, in the Beram *Danse* one finds the ambivalent figure of a lame Beggar or Pilgrim wearing a pilgrim's hat decorated with a *vera icon*, St Peter's keys, and another pilgrim's badge, probably a small image of the Virgin. In the Heidelberg blockbook, as at Beram, the Beggar supports himself on crutches and wears a pilgrim's hat with a scallop (emblem of St James and badge of Santiago de Compostela) on his head (Figs 79-80).

Fig. 79. The Beggar in the *Danse Macabre* fresco at Beram (Istria), 1474. Photo: Science and Research Centre, Koper.

---

[16] Hammerstein (1980), 191-92 and figs 2, 97-99.

Fig. 80. The Beggar, woodcut in the Heidelberg Blockbook, *c.*1458 (Heidelberg, Universitätsbibliothek, Cod. Pal. germ. 438). © Universitätsbibliothek Heidelberg.

One particular iconographic trait of the Beram fresco, *viz.* the demonic inflection of musical accompaniment, is worth examining in detail. From the early Middle Ages the church often associated pipes and other wind instruments – particularly bagpipes – with the devil, just as drums were associated with demons, and it is bagpipes and drums that are most frequently found in the *Danse Macabre*.[17] At Beram, the crowned figure of Death plays the bagpipes while waiting for the Pope to arrive. Bagpipes were considered to be especially negative instruments since they were typically played at peasant dances, which were condemned for their supposed unruliness and lasciviousness.[18] How deeply ingrained this value-based discrimination of instruments was – in which instruments

[17] Reinhold Hammerstein, *Diabolus in Musica. Studien zur Ikonographie der Musik im Mittelalter* (Bern/Munich: Francke Verlag, 1974), and also especially the essay by Susanne Warda in this volume.
[18] Cf. Keith Moxey, *Peasants, Warriors and Wives. Popular Imagery in the Reformation* (Chicago/London: University of Chicago Press, 1989), 35-66.

used in liturgical music were imbued with entirely positive connotations, whereas others were tied to the devil's temptations and sin – is clearly demonstrated in the 1407 fresco of the Living Cross in the church of St Catherine at Lindar near Pazin. Here the Devil plays the bagpipes above a personification of Synagogue, whereas an angel plays a small organ or *portative* above the figure of Ecclesia.[19]

Fig. 81. Master with the Banderoles, *The Wheel of Fortune and the Tree of Estates*, engraving, 1464. © Vienna, Graphische Sammlung Albertina.

Finally, it is worth pointing out that the complex meaning of the *Danse Macabre* on the west wall at Beram is completely embedded in the dialogue with two adjacent frescoes. The three images form an interesting programme in which the omnipotence of Death is obviously the primary message. To the right, underneath the *Danse Macabre*, is a standing, blindfolded personification of Fortune turning her wheel on which representatives of the estates are depicted. Vincent of Kastav carefully copied the left side of a 1464 engraving by a Netherlandish printmaker known as the Master with the Banderoles, which depicts a Wheel of Fortune that juxtaposes a personification of Fortune with a Tree of Estates

---

(Fig. 81).[20] On the right side, we see a skeleton aiming his arrow at a tree full of figures who represent not the Ages (as in a Tree of Life) but the estates. Although we find no such Death as an archer at Beram, it is interesting to note that the skeleton in the engraving of the Netherlandish master had a strong influence on the dead dancers in the Beram *Danse Macabre*, particularly in the depiction of the skulls and legs.[21]

The left side of the west wall depicts Adam and Eve with the Tree of Knowledge – the crucial Fall of Man that brought sin and death into the world. It is important to note that this severely damaged fresco was also modelled after a Netherlandish woodcut, this time from the *Biblia Pauperum*.[22] The *Danse Macabre* demonstrated to the viewer the inevitability of death, whereas the Wheel of Fortune was a reminder that all worldly things are subject to the fickle will of the goddess Fortuna. With this image a fundamental Christian idea of death as a punishment for original sin was visualised. These two scenes and the image of Adam and Eve by the Tree of Knowledge located on the left highlight the delusive nature and impermanence of worldly ambition, and the omnipotence of death.

Hrastovlje

The murals by Vincent of Kastav at Beram must be counted among the most important wall paintings in Istria. In the second half of the fifteenth century the region experienced the last blossoming of the late Gothic style. More than a decade and a half later another complex mural with a similar message, albeit very differently configured, was produced by an Istrian painter, this time in Hrastovlje.

The church of the Holy Trinity, which is situated on a hill near the village of Hrastovlje, was probably built shortly before 1480, when it was

---

[20] Max Lehrs, *Geschichte und kritischer Katalog des deutschen, niederländischen und französischen Kupferstichs im XV. Jahrhundert* (Vienna: Gesellschaft für vervielfältigende Kunst, 1921), IV, no. 87, 125-29; Branko Fučić, 'Grafički listovi Majstora sa svicima u kastavskoj radionici' [Graphic sheets of the Master with the Banderoles in the Kastav Workshop], *Bulletin za likovne umjetnosti JAZU*, 10 (1962), 177-86.
[21] Fedora Paškvan, 'Prilog proučavanju Beramskih zidnih slikarija' [A contibution to the research of the wall paintings in Beram], *Bulletin za likovne umjetnosti JAZU*, 7 (1959), 53-57.
[22] Fučić (1992), 130.

consecrated by the bishop of Pičen.[23] It is now surrounded by walls that
were probably built at the beginning of the sixteenth century as protection
against frequent Turkish raids. The church includes a barrel-vaulted nave
and two aisles. Its interior is entirely decorated with wall and ceiling
paintings. Although the painter John, like Vincent, originated from Kastav,
no direct workshop affiliation between the artists at Beram and Hrastovlje
can be traced. The Hrastovlje frescoes, which had been whitewashed, were
rediscovered only in 1949, and then restored between 1950 and 1955.
They stand as an important monument to sixteenth-century fresco painting
in this region. Like the Beram frescoes, they represent a complete
narrative and decorative complex, which contains an extensive medieval
'encyclopaedic' iconographic programme.

The ceiling of the side aisles is decorated with the cycle of the calendar
year that contains the symbolic representation of the twelve months on the
ceiling above. Painted on the nave ceiling is a Genesis cycle that is again
based on engravings by the Master with the Banderoles. The north wall
features the Procession and the Adoration of the Magi while beneath this a
barely visible text contains the name of the patron, Tomic Vrhovic (about
whom nothing more is known); the date 1490; and an inscription
indicating the name of the painter, 'Johannes de Kastva pinxit'. The south
wall shows the Passion of Christ above the *Danse Macabre*.

As at Beram and the later church in Clusone near Bergamo, the
procession moves from the left (where the Child is depicted) to the right
towards an empty grave with a cross above it (see Fig. 76 and Pl. 14).
Beside it sits Death, a hoe and a shovel lying crossed before him. Heading
the procession is the first dead dancer, holding the Pope (recognisable by
his tiara) by the left hand. Unlike in the Beram mural, the King and Queen
directly follow the Pope, each with their own skeletal companion. Behind
them comes the Cardinal in a red chasuble and hat, followed by the Bishop
and the Franciscan with a book under his right arm. Next is the Doctor
who reaches into his bag in order to bribe Death with money from his
purse, while the Townsman behind him offers the skeleton a bundle
(probably containing ransom goods) with his left hand and reaches into his
bag with his right. Following them are the Knight in fashionable clothing
with a sword hanging from his belt and a shield on his back; the lame
Beggar with a crutch and rosary; and at the rear a Child stepping out of his
cradle, whom Death leads by the hand. The Child is the only figure in the
Danse to be defined by age instead of social status.

---

[23] Radovan Ivančević, 'Crkva Sv. Trojstva u Hrastovlju: romanika ili renesansa?'
[The church of the Holy Trinity in Hrastovlje: romanesque or renaissance?],
Radovi instituta za poviest umjetnosti, 12-13 (1988/89), 127-36.

In comparison with the *Danse Macabre* at Beram, the Hrastovlje cycle is almost ceremonial in its arrangement. The dead dancers do not perform any fervent movements: with their left hands five indicate the direction of the grave and what appears to be the personification of Death, toward whom the procession moves steadily, while others just raise their arms haphazardly. Four almost identical skeletons dance along; one of them is supported by crutches. No text accompanies this procession, and the Preacher, who is often found at the beginning of the *Danse Macabre*, is missing.

Fig. 82. *Danse Macabre*, Venetian woodcut, *c*.1500. © Bremen, Kunsthalle.

Several distinct iconographic traditions are synthesised in the Hrastovlje *Danse*. It shares similarities with the Beram and Clusone cycles in the direction of the procession and in the absence of a text and of the Preacher, while the figure of the lame Beggar in Hrastovlje is clearly borrowed directly from the Basel group. There are also some similarities with a Venetian woodcut produced around 1500 that was part of a cycle of several sheets of which only two are preserved. In one of these (now at the Kunsthalle in Bremen) several different social representatives are shown standing behind open graves (Fig. 82).[24] Perhaps the last (now lost) sheet

---

[24] Hellmut Rosenfeld, 'Der mittelalterliche Bilderbogen', *Zeitschrift für deutsches Altertum und deutsche Literatur*, 85 (1954/55), 67-75, at 70; Hellmut Rosenfeld,

of this cycle depicted an open grave with Death sitting on a throne, which could be based on the same lost prototype that may have been the model for the Hrastovlje *Danse*.[25] Moreover, the figure of a Knight with a sword and a shield in Hrastovlje is similar to the *cavalier* on the right in the Venetian woodcut.

Fig. 83. The Physician in the *Danse Macabre* fresco at Hrastovlje (Istria), 1490. Photo: Science and Research Centre, Koper.

Der mittelalterliche Totentanz. Enstehung – Entwicklung – Bedeutung (1954, revised edn Cologne/ Vienna: Böhlau Verlag, 1974), 358.
[25] Alberto Saviello and Uli Wunderlich, 'Ein Totentanz-Bilderbogen aus Italien', *Totentanz Aktuell*, 99 (2007), 6-8; Alberto Saviello and Uli Wunderlich, 'Noch ein Totentanz-Bilderbogen aus Italien', *Totentanz Aktuell*, 105 (2008), 4-6.

The inclusion of the Physician in the *Danse Macabre* is a standard feature of French and German *Danse* cycles, and likewise occurs in John Lydgate's Middle English poem.[26] This figure at Hrastovlje (Fig. 83) has previously been misidentified as a Merchant by Marijan Zadnikar,[27] and as a Lawyer by Reinhold Hammerstein[28] and Janez Höfler.[29] However, this figure with his long belted garment and characteristic hat is clearly a physician, for tied to his belt is his typical attribute, a small transparent glass vessel called a *matula*. Such flasks were used to examine urine and are held by the Physician in a variety of western European *Danse* cycles. Moreover, the Physician's attire is red – the traditional colour for physicians[30] – as are the robes of the Physicians depicted in the *Danse Macabre* murals at Großbasel[31] and at Metnitz.[32]

However, John of Kastav was also evidently familiar with the French model. The clothing of the King at Hrastovlje is reminiscent of the attire of his French counterparts, for instance, as can be observed in numerous prints and illuminated manuscripts based on the famous mural in Paris (Fig. 84).[33] One manuscript produced in the early sixteenth century (Paris, BnF, ms. fr. 995, fol. 3r) depicts a figure of the King that must have been modelled on that of the Parisian fresco, and it is very similar to the Hrastovlje fresco in the details of dress, *e.g.* the colours (Pl. 16).[34] Both

---

[26] Aldred Scott Warthin, *The Physician of the Dance of Death* (reprint, New York: Arno Press, 1977); Daniel Schäfer, "'Herr Doctor beschauw die Anatomay an mir ob sie Recht gemacht sey." Artz und Tod im frühen Totentanz zwischen Fiktion und Realität', *Das Mittelalter*, 10 (2005), 75-76.

[27] Marijan Zadnikar, *Hrastovlje. Romanska arhitektura in gotske freske* [Hrastovlje. Romanesque architecture and Gothic frescoes] (Ljubljana: Družina, 2002), 46.

[28] Hammerstein (1980), 194.

[29] Höfler (1998), 140.

[30] Dieter Koepplin, 'Cranachs Ehebildnis des Johannes Cuspinian von 1502. Seine christlich-humanistische Bedeutung', unpublished PhD thesis (University of Basel, 1973), 129-30.

[31] Franz Egger, *Basler Totentanz* (Basel: Buchverlag Basler Zeitung and Historisches Museum Basel, 1990), 60-61.

[32] Erwin Koller, 'Zum Metnitzer Totentanz', *Carinthia*, 170 (1980), 139-69.

[33] Hammerstein (1980), 167-70; Sophie Oosterwijk, 'Of Dead Kings, Dukes, and Constables: the Historical Context of the *Danse Macabre* in Late Medieval Paris', *Journal of the British Archaeological Association*, 161 (2008), 131-62, esp. figs 10-12. See also Fig. 16 in the essay by Frances Eustace in this volume.

[34] Uli Wunderlich, *Der Tanz in den Tod. Totentänze vom Mittelalter bis zur Gegenwart* (Freiburg i. Brsg.: Eulen Verlag, 2001), 22-24; Ann Tukey Harrison (ed.) with a chapter by Sandra L. Hindman, *The* Danse Macabre *of Women. Ms. fr. 995 of the Bibliothèque Nationale* (Kent: University of Ohio Press, 1994), 16-17.

also include a mantle lined with ermine, while the shape of the crown and the King's posture are similar in both, yet different from the image of the King in the Beram *Danse*. The Hrastovlje Doctor and the Franciscan attest to the influence of other images modelled on the Parisian *Danse*: they are especially similar to those found in the coloured graphic cycle of Antoine Vérard, produced around 1486.

Fig. 84. The King, Queen and Cardinal in the *Danse Macabre* fresco at Hrastovlje (Istria), 1490. Photo: Science and Research Centre, Koper.

Perhaps the most telling detail is the representation of the Child who, at Hrastovlje, is dragged out of his cradle by the skeleton who has taken him by the hand (Fig. 85). This motif of a cradle is typically found in French versions of the *Danse*, from its inception in the Paris mural all through the sixteenth century.[35] That the Istrian *Danse* was modelled on the French mural as recorded in print is not unusual for macabre imagery south of the Alps: there is a similar case in the church of San Silvestro in Iseo, near Brescia, where a *Danse Macabre* of *c*.1500 was copied from the Hours (use of Rome) that was printed in 1488 by Philippe Pigouchet in Paris.[36] However, a unique feature in the Hrastovlje *Danse* is that the Child is depicted in the process of stepping out of the cradle, as opposed to lying in the cradle or standing naked beside the figure of Death (Fig. 85).

---

[35] Sophie Oosterwijk. "'Muoz ich tanzen und kan nit gân?'": Death and the Infant in the Medieval *Danse Macabre'*, *Word & Image*, 22:2 (2006), 146-64.

[36] Fulvio Sina, 'L'impiego delle pubblicazioni a tema macabro d'oltralpe quale fonte di inspirazione dell' arte italiana del XV e XVI secolo: la Danza Macabra in San Silvestro ad Iseo', *Quaderni della Biblioteca*, 5 (2002), 57-66.

German depictions of the *Danse Macabre* almost always include the infant in the sequence of the estates: he is usually shown naked and standing alongside a dead dancer who is holding him by the hand, *e.g.* in the Heidelberg blockbook (Fig. 86).[37]

Fig. 85. The Child in the *Danse Macabre* fresco at Hrastovlje (Istria), 1490. Photo: Science and Research Centre, Koper.

All these evident similarities indicate that prints – most probably woodcuts – were available to the painters of the Hrastovlje mural and that they had a decisive impact on the depictions of the social representatives there. However, on the basis of visual material collected until now, it is difficult to determine precisely the models used by the Hrastovlje painters. As we have seen, the Heidelberg blockbook or some other visual source,

---

[37] See the discussion in Oosterwijk (2006), esp. 153-56.

based on the Großbasel Danse was a likely model for some of the figures in the Beram *Danse*. The *Danse Macabre* mural in Paris inspired woodcuts that decorated the margins of books of hours that were printed in Paris from the 1480s on.[38] Perhaps one of those printed hours or a copy of either the 1485 or the expanded 1486 *Danse Macabre* edition by Guy Marchant was available to John of Kastav and his workshop.

Fig. 86. The Child, woodcut in the Heidelberg Blockbook, *c.*1458 (Heidelberg, Universitätsbibliothek, Cod. Pal. germ. 438). © Universitätsbibliothek Heidelberg.

Although the stylistic and iconographic influences of the Hrastovlje *Danse* are different from those of its Istrian predecessor, its place in the iconographic programme of the church in Hrastovlje echoes that of Beram. The iconography at Hrastovlje is surprisingly complex and extensive for a subsidiary church, and the choice of this theme cannot be explained merely as repeating the example at Beram. The wall and ceiling paintings

---

[38] Hammerstein (1980), 177.

at Hrastovlje illustrate an entire Christian doctrinal belief, from the creation of the world and man (displayed in the Genesis cycle on the vault) to the coming of Christ and the cyclic course of time (represented in the cycle of the Labours of the Months). The work to be performed in each month, which is depicted in the medallions on the vaults of the side aisles, conveys the punishment that humanity has earned because of original sin as depicted in the Genesis cycle. Moreover, the outcome of original sin is Death, which is presented through the *Danse Macabre*. However, at Hrastovlje the Passion is shown on the west and south walls. It is similar to the *Danse Macabre* of *c*.1490 in Berlin, where the idea of the Last Judgement is explicitly visualised through the Crucified Christ in the centre.[39] Perhaps the patron of the iconographic programme at Hrastovlje – or his theological advisor – decided to illustrate the conclusion of human life and the Resurrection (symbolised by the cross in the grave beside Death) with the *Danse Macabre* on the south wall, rather than depicting the Last Judgement on the west wall, as was more usual in this region.

Conclusion

What accounts for the presence of the *Danse Macabre* frescoes in Istria? One might argue that their presence has something to do with the Black Death that repeatedly shook the region. While there is little information on how the countryside was affected, in the second half of the fifteenth century the Black Death was recorded in numerous cities: for example, there were outbreaks in Trieste in 1467, 1477 and 1478; in Rovinj in 1468; in Piran in 1476; and in Poreč in 1478, 1483 and 1487.[40] The connection between the plague and the *Danse Macabre* is problematic since there is no evidence of a direct influence of the epidemic outbreaks on this iconographic motif.[41] Yet these Istrian examples, especially the Hrastovlje *Danse*, may offer at least a reflection of the severe epidemics which struck

---

[39] Elina Gertsman and Almut Breitenbach. 'Tanz, Schauspiel und Gericht. Performativität im Berliner Totentanz', *L'art macabre (Jahrbuch der Europäischen Totentanz-Vereinigung)*, 5 (2004), 29-40.

[40] Bernardo Schiavuzzi, 'Le epidemie di pesta bubbonica in Istria. Notize storiche', *Atti e Memorie della Società Istriana di Archeologia e Storia Patria*, 4 (1888), 423-47; Slaven Bertoša, 'La peste in Istria nel medio evo e nell'età moderna (in contesto Europeo delle epidemie)', *Atti-Centro di ricerche storiche Rovigno*, 37 (2007), 121-57.

[41] Elina Gertsman. 'Visualizing Death. Medieval Plagues and the Macabre', in Franco Mormando, Thomas Worcester (eds), *Piety and Plague. From Byzantium to the Baroque* (Kirksville: Truman State University Press, 2007), 64-89.

the peninsula at this time. Several saints depicted on the walls of the church in Hrastovlje, for instance, were considered to be guardians against the plague or diseases in general. These include St Sebastian, St Roch and St Fabian, who are depicted in the southern apse at Hrastovlje, and St Cosmas and St Damian (patron saints of physicians), who are shown in the northern apse. The presence of these saints, combined with the *Danse Macabre*, might be construed as a response to the surrender to blind will and the inexorable reign of a Death that does not discriminate against age or estate.

These two *Danse Macabre* cycles in Istria clearly demonstrate the visual currency and the importance of print culture in the transmission of iconographic and compositional novelties produced in centres of artistic activity in the fifteenth century. It is obvious that some innovations could be transmitted through printed graphic images to different regions, where the iconographic types from the centres could be used and rearranged to form innovative new compositions and transformed according to the iconographic traditions and stylistic idioms of the recipients.

While the painter of the Beram *Danse* probably drew his inspiration from reproductions of the Basel *Danse Macabre*, in Hrastovlje John of Kastav managed to form an impressive whole by combining motifs drawn from several sources, mostly Italian and French, but also German. In this way two painters and their workshops produced two original examples of a widespread iconographic motif, which are furthermore characterised by their emphasis on the motif of people trying to bribe Death with money, be they Pope or Queen. This latter motif is an unmistakable critique of the ruling estates and a visualisation of the basic message about the equality of all before Death, regardless of power and wealth.

Acknowledgements

The author would like to thank both editors, but Dr Sophie Oosterwijk in particular, for their editorial input.

THE *DANSE MACABRE* AT BIERDZANY-BIERDZAŃSKA ŚMIERĆ (POLAND)

JUTTA SCHUCHARD

The intensive study of the *Danse Macabre* has in recent years focussed mainly on the German and French-Italian area, whereas the Eastern regions of Central Europe (Poland, Bohemia, Hungary) have attracted relatively little attention. Poland has remained largely unnoticed: only a few *Danse Macabre* schemes there have been discussed in more depth.[1] This particularly applies to the *Danse Macabre* painting in the church of St Bernard in Cracow and the reliefs in Tarłów (Central Poland), to the exclusion of other examples elsewhere.[2]

One *Danse Macabre* scene in a wooden church in Upper Silesia has so far gone completely unnoticed. It is a representation of the subject 'death –

---

[1] This is clearly shown by the few references in the literature on the *Danse, viz.* only three lines, in Hellmut Rosenfeld, *Der mittelalterliche Totentanz: Entstehung – Entwicklung – Bedeutung* (Münster/Cologne: Böhlau Verlag, 1954), 359. Hélène and Bertrand Utzinger also took no notice of the Polish examples in their *Itinéraires des Danses macabres* (Chartres: Éditions J.M. Garnier, 1996).

[2] On the *Danse Macabre* at Cracow see the exhibition catalogue *Obrazy śmierci. W sztuce polskiej XIXX-XX Wieku* (Cracow: Museum Narodowe w Krakowie, 2000). In recent years Aleksandra Koutny-Jones has worked on Polish examples in depth. See Aleksandra Koutny-Jones, 'Dancing with Death in Poland', *Print Quarterly*, 22 (2005), 14-31; Aleksandra Koutny-Jones, 'Death Personified in the Baroque Art of the Kingdom of Poland', unpublished PhD thesis (University of Cambridge, 2007). Cracow is briefly mentioned in what is still the standard *Danse Macabre* monograph in English, James M. Clark, *The Dance of Death in the Middle Ages and the Renaissance* (Glasgow: Jackson, Son & Company, 1950), 88-89. On the stucco *Danse Macabre* at Tarłów, see Jan Białostocki, 'Kunst und Vanitas', in Jan Białostocki (ed.), *Stil und Ikonographie. Studien zur Kunstwissenschaft* (Dresden: Verl. der Kunst, 1966), 187-217, at 202; Teresa Piwonska, 'Barokowa dekoracja stiukowa kaplicy Oleśnicki w Tarłówie', unpublished PhD thesis (University of Wrocław (Breslau), 1997). For a recent, detailed investigation of this *Danse*, see Aleksandra Koutny-Jones, 'A Noble Death: the Oleśnicki Funerary Chapel in Tarłów, *Journal of the Warburg and Courtauld Institute*, 72 (2009), 169-205.

old age – wealth' in the Catholic parish church of St Hedwig in Bierdzan (Bierdzany) near Opole (Oppeln) in Silesia (Fig. 87).[3]

Silesia was part of the Habsburg monarchy from 1526 to 1740. It is a rich cultural landscape with traits that are specific for this region. Characteristic for Upper Silesia until the middle of the eighteenth century was its timber construction, thanks to the extensive forests on the right bank of the Oder. Along with Little Poland, Upper Silesia has to date the largest collection of wooden churches, most of which date back to the seventeenth and eighteenth centuries.[4] These are usually built from pine logs, their exterior and interior being relatively simple in design. The walls of these churches must often have been richly decorated once, but unfortunately the buildings have been modernised, especially at the start of the twentieth century, with the mural paintings being painted over or removed. Renovation after World War II has resulted in the rediscovery and then exposure of earlier painted programmes in some churches.

While visiting various timber churches in the Opole region in August 2008, the author came upon the above-mentioned wall painting in Bierdzany, which is in a far from satisfactory state of preservation. Investigation was hampered by its condition as well as by the very dim

---

[3] In the Early Modern period the parish (Pfarrdorf) with its manor and forester's house (Försterei) belonged to the entailed estate (Majoratsherrschaft) of Turawa, which was in the possession of the barons von Blankowski (who belonged to the Bohemian nobility). In 1712 it was purchased from Martin Scholtz von Löwencron. See Konrad Blaźek (ed.), *J. Siebmacher's großes Wappenbuch*, vol. 17: Die Wappen des schlesischen Adels (repr. Neustadt a. d. Aisch: Bauer & Raspe, 1977); Konrad Blaźek (ed.), *J. Siebmacher's großes Wappenbuch*, vol. 6,8: Der abgestorbene Adel der preußischen Provinz Schlesien und der Oberlausitz, part 1 (Nuremberg: Bauer & Raspe, 1887), 12, 118, pls 9 and 71. I owe this reference to Dr Wolfhard Vahl, Hessisches Staatsarchiv Marburg. See also Oskar Brunckow (ed.), *Die Wohnplätze des Deutschen Reiches*, vol. 1,2 (Berlin: Brunckow, 1909), 74; Felix Triest (ed.), *Topographisches Handbuch von Oberschlesien*, vol. 1 (repr. Sigmaringen: Thorbecke, 1984), 108. Bierdzany was named Berdzanowitz until the end of the seventeenth century. From 1930 to c.1940 the place had the company name of Burkardsdorf, see: Herbert Dienwiebel, *Oberschlesische Schrotholzkirchen* (Wrocław: Heydebrand, 1938), 55.

[4] L. Burgemeister, *Die Holzkirchen und Holztürme der preussischen Ostprovinzen, Schlesien – Polen – Ostpreussen – Westpreussen – Brandenburg – Pommern* (Berlin: Springer, 1905); Jõsef Matuszczak, *Kóscioły drewninane nay slasku* (Wrocław: Zakład narodowy imíenía ossolińskich, 1975); Wolfgang Halfar, *Die oberschlesischen Schrotholzkirchen. Ein Beitrag zum Holzbau in Schlesien* (München: Delp, 1980); Danuta Emmerling and Alojzy Wierzgoń, *Die Oppelner Holzkirchen* (Opole: Schlesischer Verlag Adan, 2006).

lighting inside the church.[5] Unfortunately it proved impossible to carry out primary research into the history of the painting and the artist. Therefore, this paper is only an initial, sketchy investigation that may form the basis for future research.

Fig. 87. The *Danse Macabre* scene in the Catholic parish church of St Hedwig in Bierdzan (Bierdzany) near Opole (Oppeln) in Silesia (Poland). Photo: author.

---

[5] Due to poor lighting inside the church and the arrangement of the pews very close to the walls of the nave, the paintings are also extremely difficult to photograph.

Description

The log church of St Hedwig in Bierdzany is situated in the centre of the
village on a hill surrounded by a cemetery with mature trees. Its ground
plan is a Latin cross (Fig. 88). The west tower is nowadays crowned with a
lantern, but until 1930 it had an octagonal pavilion roof. Over the crossing
sits a hexagonal turret with a lantern.

The interior of the church has wooden ceilings and flat circular
galleries on three sides. The ceiling and walls are covered with paintings,
including scenes from the Old and New Testament. Underneath the
gallery, which is placed to the west of the northern entrance, there is a
representation of the Fall of Man. Adam and Eve occupy their traditional
positions, *viz.* on either side of the Tree of Knowledge with the serpent
clearly visible between them. Eve offers an apple to Adam while she
herself receives another fruit from the serpent. The Garden of Eden is
depicted as a bright scene: a meadow landscape covered in trees.

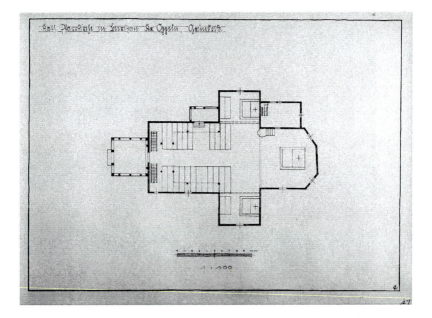

Fig. 88. Ground plan of the church of St Hedwig in Bierdzan (Poland). Sammlung
Nietsch, 1936/38. © Herder-Institut Marburg, Bildarchiv. Image No. 249576.

The juxtaposition of the Fall of Man and the *Danse Macabre* demonstrates an after-effect of traditional *Danse Macabre* schemes, such as the mid-fifteenth-century fresco in the abbey-church at La Chaise-Dieu (Auvergne) or the paintings of *c.*1440 on the wall of the Dominican cemetery at Basel. Deeply influential was also Hans Holbein the Younger's *Images of Death* woodcut series (published 1538) which inspired a huge number of later editions that were produced across Europe.

The entire northern side of the nave of the church at Bierdzany shows the viewer the Christian doctrine of Death as a consequence of original sin. The paintings may originally have been painted at the beginning of the eighteenth century, as the present church was apparently erected in 1711, as can be deduced from a foundation stone carrying that date, although there is still a debate whether the whole church was newly constructed at that time, or only the choir.[6]

On the occasion of the renovation work carried out in 1897/98, the old wall paintings were painted over, probably because they no longer appealed to contemporary taste. It was not until 1961 that the paintings were rediscovered during a renovation of the church and once again exposed. Presumably the late discovery of the paintings is the reason why the *Danse Macabre* painting at Bierdzany has so far been overlooked by researchers.[7]

---

[6] Already in 1410 and 1447 there is mention of a church consecrated to St Valentin at Bierdzany. According to the 1687/88 Visitation record of the diocese Breslau (Wrocław) the church was at that time an intact wooden construction, dedicated to St Hedwig but not consecrated, because only stone churches can receive the consecration. During periods of its history the church was in Lutheran hands and also served as a burial place.

[7] Interesting material related to the church in Bierdzany can be found in the bequest of the architect Max Nietsch (Gleiwitz/Gliwice) in the Herder-Institute in Marburg. Unfortunately, this has hitherto only been partially inventoried. Nietsch carried out an inventory of the wooden churches in Silesia during the period 1936-38. I am indebted to Dr Elke Bauer of the picture archive at the Herder-Institut e. V. for drawing my attention to this bequest and allowing me to consult it. The planned publication was not realised, but the bequest comprises a manuscript entitled 'Konstruktive Besonderheiten des oberschlesischen Holzkirchenbaues' (*Special construction features of the wooden churches in Upper Silesia*). For information on the inventory of wooden churches initiated by the 'Amt für Denkmalpflege, Berlin', see 'Deutsche Kulturdenkmäler', *Oberschlesische Volksstimme*, 3 (17 April 1938).

Iconography

The mural painting in Bierdzany displays the encounter of Death and the rich old man of the type usually referred to as the 'rich miser'. It is situated on an interior wall between the church's north door on the left and a large painted pillar on the right. In the background it shows a large rectangular opening, its blue colour perhaps reminding the viewer of Heaven and the afterlife.

The old man is sitting at a table covered with a red blanket and two bags (presumably filled with money) lying on top. He is about to write in an open book in front of him, holding a quill in his right hand. He is dressed with a cape-coat (Szlachta) of plain cloth with fur trimming, while on his head he wears a high tan cap of silky lustre. The most striking features are his moustache and the cape-coat, but these were a typical fashion among the Polish nobility in the seventeenth century (*Sarmatism*).[8] Together with the precious clothes he wears, the two bags on the table, the open coffer with papers and a bag on the floor all indicate that the figure depicts a wealthy businessman who is engaged in business activities. Perhaps the painting is not only meant to represent a certain social rank, but is also conceived as a picture of an archetypical rich man. In that case, the painting would appear to symbolise the vice of Avarice by analogy to Holbein's corresponding woodcut. The picture may thus also contain an allusion to the Ages of Man because avarice was the sin commonly associated with old age.[9]

The man looks calm and resigned in the face of Death, who appears in the traditional (post-medieval) personification as a skeleton. Death is approaching his victim from the left, yet his gaze is not directed at the old man but at the spectator. The key element that connects the two figures is a large hourglass, which Death holds out with his left hand to the old man. Positioned right in the centre of the image, the hourglass is a symbol of life that has run its course and a cautionary reminder about transience to the viewer. This emphasis on temporality is a central theme of Baroque *vanitas* images, just as the hourglass is also a standard feature in Holbein's *Images of Death* series. Striking is the central red ring of the hourglass,

---

[8] I am grateful to Dominika Piotrowska (Herder-Institut e. V., Wrocław/Marburg) for this important information.

[9] For discussion and related imagery, see Sophie Oosterwijk, 'Money, Morality, Mortality: the Migration of the Dance Macabre from Murals to Misericords', in P. Horden (ed.), *Freedom of Movement in the Middle Ages* (2003 Harlaxton Symposium Proceedings), Harlaxton Medieval Studies, 15 (Donington: Shaun Tyas, 2007), 37-56, esp. 50-55 and pls 21-23.

which corresponds to the red of the tablecloth and the cloak worn by Death. Symbolising judicial sovereignty, the colour here accentuates the role of Death as a judge. In this capacity Death appears as the main character with a sword, directed in the manner of a dart, in his left hand. The tip of the sword is aimed at the old man, especially his eyes, and at the same time at the hourglass.

It is extremely rare for a sword – ancient symbol of power and justice – to serve as an attribute of Death. Death iconography is dominated by depictions of Death as the reaper, a hunter, a grave digger or a musician. Usually, Death is associated with a sword only in representations of the apocalyptic horsemen by artists such as Albrecht Dürer and Hans Burgkmair. In the seventeenth and eighteenth centuries we find the representation of Death with a sword only in isolated cases, *e.g.* the frontispiece of Matthäus Merian the Elder's *Todten-Tanz* (1649) (Fig. 89).

Other examples are a wall painting of the early eighteenth century showing 'Death and the Maiden' at a charnel house in Unterschächen (Canton Uri, Switzerland) and a depiction of 'Death and the Nobleman' from the *Danse Macabre* panel in Emmetten (Canton Nidwalden, Switzerland).[10] The sword as an attribute of Death refers mainly to representations of the Archangel Michael at the Last Judgement and those of Justice. That a sword could be regarded both as a symbol of worldly power and as a Christian *memento mori* emblem is aptly illustrated by the sword of the Landgrave of Hessen-Kassel and King Frederick I of Sweden (1720-51) in the Hessisches Landesmuseum Kassel. It shows on one side an image of the personification of Justice with a raised sword, while the other side carries the words:

Ihr Gottlose Menschen=Kinder / Unbusfertig frevle Sünder, / Schaut aufs ende was vor Straf / treffen wird Dich Sünden=Sclav / auch Das werckZeug Glaube mir / treibe keinen Scherz mit Dir / ich Muß strafen Dass verbrechen / als wie Recht und Richter sprechen.[11]

(*You wicked creatures, unrepentant, wanton sinners, behold what punishment will befall you in the end, you slave to sin. Believe me, this weapon does not play a joke on you, for I must punish the crime and speak as both justice and judge.*)

---

[10] *Tanz der Toten – Todestanz: Der monumentale Totentanz im deutschsprachigen Raum*, ed. Zentralinstitut und Museum für Sepulkralkultur Kassel, exh.cat. Kassel 1998 (Dettelbach: Röll, 1998), 238, fig. 179; 228, fig. 160-61.
[11] Otto Rudolf Kissel, *Die Justitia: Reflexionen über ein Symbol und seine Darstellung in der bildenden Kunst* (München: Beck, 1984), 73, fig. 58.

Fig. 89. Title page of Matthäus Merian the Elder's *Todten-Tantz wie derselbe in der löblichen und weitberühmten Stadt Basel ... zu sehen ist*, *c*.1725. © Graphiksammlung 'Mensch und Tod', Heinrich-Heine-University Düsseldorf.

Death appears in the *Danse Macabre* in Bierdzany with another, more traditional attribute, *viz.* a scythe. It lies on the floor, enclosing a skull that is shown without its lower jaw, as is frequently found in eighteenth-century art. The multiple occurrence of death symbols in this representation and the implied appeal to the beholder to reflect on human transience include a *memento mori* statement that relentlessly reminds the viewer of his own finite nature. The *Danse Macabre* scene refers to the constant presence of Death in life and is a warning call for self-reflection and a pious, virtuous life. A similar admonition is to be found in the 1736

German edition of Salomon van Rusting's moralising *Het schoutoneel des doots, of Dooden Dans*, first published in Dutch in 1707:

Drum lernet doch, bey guter Zeit,
Euch zu dem Todten=Tanze schicken:
Ja, weil er so von Wichtigkeit
Muest ihr euch drauf Zeit Leben schmuecken:
Daß, wenn der Tod euch winkt und schwingt,
Ihr in den Freuden=Himmel springt'.[12]

(*Therefore, learn in good time to reconcile yourselves to the* Danse Macabre: *indeed, because it is so important you must improve your lives in time, so that when Death beckons and sways you, you will leap into joyful Heaven.*)

In the seventeenth and eighteenth centuries the skull was regarded as an important religious-moralising *memento mori* motif. The foundation of the *Toden=Kopffs=Orden* (Latin: Ordo Calvariae) by Sylvius, duke of Württemberg, in Oels (Olesnica) in 1652 is just one example of the prominence of this skull symbolism. According to the statute of the Order, members were to be constantly reminded to contemplate death and general mortality by wearing a skull ring on a black band.[13] This was to be worn on the left hand as being closest to the heart. In 1709 the Order was founded anew by the original founder's granddaughter, Princess Louise Elisabeth, widow of Philip, duke of Saxe-Merseburg. The meditation on death and dying was given even more significance by changing the emblem of the order into a white belt with a silver skull on a black-enamelled bow carrying the words 'Memento mori'.

How important the evaluation of life and death was in the early modern period is also illustrated by the instructions for meditations on death in religious texts such as Ignatius of Loyola's *Exercitia Spiritualia* of 1548. A 1687 commentary on Loyola's writings even recommended intensifying

---

[12] Closing verses of the preface to the German edition of Salomon van Rusting's *Schoutoneel*, published by Johann Georg Meintel under the title *Schau=Platz des Todes, oder Todten=Tanz in Kupffern und Versen vorgestellet: Ehemals von SAL. Van RUSTING, Med. Doct. In Nieder=Teutscher Sprache; nun aber in Hoch=Teutscher, mit nöthigen Anmerckungen* (Nuremberg, 1736).

[13] Johann Heinrich Zedler, *Grosses vollständiges Universal-Lexicon aller Wissenschafften und Künste*, vol. 44 (Leipzig/Halle: Zedler, 1745), column 689-94. On mourning rings with skulls, see Andrea Linnebach, 'Schmuck und Vanitas im Barock', in Zentralinstitut und Museum für Sepulkralkultur (eds), *Trauerschmuck vom Barock bis zum Art Déco*, exhibition catalogue Museum für Sepulkralkultur Kassel (Kassel: Arbeitsgemeinschaft Friedhof und Denkmal, 1995), 13-20.

the experience by meditating with the shutters closed because the fear of death will arise more easily in the dark. Loyola also suggested that his readers should have a skull with them.[14] Besides religious texts, many secular texts, such as works by Andreas Gryphius (1616-64) dealt with the theme of death.[15]

The painting in Bierdzany with its *Danse Macabre* scene on the theme of 'Death and Rich Man' is unusual in many respects. What makes it so remarkable? And is it really a *Danse Macabre* scene at all, or rather a painting about death in combination with a *vanitas* representation? If one allows the motif to comprise independent scenes and iconographic groups, as Johann Heinrich Zedler proposed in his *Universal-Lexicon*, then this painting may be called a *Danse Macabre* scene. Zedler defines the *Danse* ('Toden=Tantz') as 'ein Gemaehlde, welches den Tod vorstellet, und anzeigen soll, wie derselbe keines Menschen schone, sondern alle von den vornehmsten bis zum Geringsten gleichsam an seinen Tantz mit nehme' (*a painting which presents Death and is intended to show how the same [*i.e. Death*] spares no man, but instead takes everyone alike along in his dance from the most eminent to the lowest*).[16]

Unfortunately, to this day there is no universally valid definition for the *Danse Macabre*. The principle of the order and representation of all ranks of society in their encounter with Death, as well as the dialogue structure, have often been considered as the main characteristics. It is disputed whether individual scenes can also be counted among the motif, however. There are autonomous iconographic groups, *e.g.* 'Death and the Maiden' and 'Death and the Old Man', which emerged in the sixteenth century. Still, they have mostly been considered in the context of the *Danse Macabre*.

The *Danse Macabre* scene in Bierdzany is unusual particularly with regard to the location, a wooden church. To my knowledge there is only one other *Danse Macabre* painting in a wooden church, *viz.* the wall painting of a Polish nobleman and Death, which is situated in a wooden chapel of 1795 in the cemetery at Zambrów.[17] Although *Danse Macabre* iconography played an important role in surrounding countries such as the kingdoms of Bohemia and Poland in the seventeenth and eighteenth centuries, this seems to apply only partially to Silesia. It is striking that

---

[14] Białostocki (1966), 203.

[15] Friedrich Wilhelm Wentzlaff-Eggebert, *Der triumphierende und der besiegte Tod in der Wort- und Bildkunst des Barock* (Berlin/New York: de Gruyter, 1975), 70-106.

[16] Zedler (1745), vol. 44, column 711-12.

[17] Koutny-Jones (2009), 189, fig. 19.

there was only one other *Danse Macabre* image in Silesia, apart from the painting at Bierdzany, formerly at Racibórz/Ratibor in the former Dominican church of St James.[18]

The *Danse Macabre* scene in Bierdzany connects the theme of death with *vanitas* iconography and a didactic *memento mori* claim, which is characteristic for the Baroque age. The symbol of death is to be regarded as a mental image, as a religious memorial. Its core message emphasises the transience of the terrestrial world with all its material goods and calls for life in the Christian faith, in which one must not fear death; it thus stresses belief in eternal life.

Decisive for the painting at Bierdnazy is the ambivalence between Death acting with a dramatic activity and the quiet attitude of the old man who accepts his fate. He looks beyond Death towards the door, which from ancient times has been a symbol of transition between life and death.[19] However, the door is also a symbol of Christ as the gateway to eternal life and the door to Heaven, according to John 10:9: 'I am the door: by me if any man enter in, he shall be saved, and shall go in and out, and find pasture'. *Mors triumphans* (triumphant Death) is subject to Christ and to God's omnipotence so that *mors ultima* (ultimate death) becomes *ultima spes* (ultimate hope). With this prospect of hope there is a counterbalance to the accentuation of the character of punishment in the scene, which characterises the unusual presentation of Death as a judge, armed with a sword. In combination with the painting of the Fall of Man beyond the north door there is an effective depiction of the Pauline view of death as the wages of transgression.

---

[18] Hans Lutsch, *Die Kunstdenkmäler des Regierungsbezirkes Oppeln* (Wrocław: Korn, 1894), 349. Dating from the second half of the seventeenth century, the picture (0.76 x 0.94 m) was considered by Lutsch as 'bemerkenswert' (*noteworthy*) because of the Polish costume of the depicted men. It does not seem to have been preserved; at least, the *Dehio Handbook of Monuments of Art in Poland* (Dehio-Handbuch der Kunstdenkmäler in Polen), volume on Silesia (Munich/Berlin: Deutscher Kunstverlag, 2005), 789-90, does not mention the picture. The painting was also no longer there when the present author visited the church in August 2008. Still *in situ* is another personification of Death, *viz.* the figure of Death on the clock of the tower of the town hall at Olava (Ohlau) known as 'Olava death', which dates from *c*.1718.

[19] See Jan Białostocki, 'The Door of Death: Survival of a Classical Motif in Sepulchral Art', *Jahrbuch der Hamburger Kunstsammlungen*, 18 (1973), 7-32. The north door may have been the passage mainly used on the way from the church to the graveyard.

Conclusion

There are no direct models for the *Danse Macabre* scene in Bierdzany, although different influences can be recognised, including that of the motif of 'Death and the Miser' with its emphasis on the vice of Avarice. Yet the inclusion of a sword as Death's attribute is more unusual.

It is not clear for what reason this particular theme was chosen for a mural in this church. To date we know neither the patron nor the artist responsible for the painting. It is possible that the *Danse Macabre* in Bierdzany was painted to accentuate the character of the church as a burial place and a graveyard chapel.

Acknowledgements

I am very grateful to the two editors, Stefanie Knöll and Sophie Oosterwijk, for their suggestions and their support with the translation of my text. Furthermore I thank Hiltraut Schoen and Anastasia Pirogov in Marburg for their help.

THE MACABRE IN PRINT

A PHENOMENON OF PARALLEL READING IN THE OFFICE OF THE DEAD

CAROLINE ZÖHL

The starting point for the following reflections is an unusual and little-known picture cycle to the Office of the Dead that first appeared in a Parisian printed book of hours on 22 August 1509.[1] The printers and publishers of the first edition were Jean Barbier and Guillaume Le Rouge. The designs for the metalcuts came from the workshop of the Paris illuminator Jean Pichore. The eleven engravings in total form part of a sequence distinguished not only by its scale – all the hours of even the smaller offices are illustrated equally in size – but also by the specific iconographic programme of pictorial themes which have no established models in this constellation, although in the Office of the Dead they refer back individually to diverse iconographic traditions.

The most conspicuous feature of these engravings is their direct textual reference, which sets up a multi-layered system of meaning, one that can be discerned in parallel or even selectively for contemporary devotional and reading practice. Thus biblical texts from the office are included in speech banners in all the illustrations. Furthermore, in the first edition French verses not derived from the text of the book of hours have been added below each illustration. Anyone using this book for prayer was thus offered the choice between different modes of reception, which could also be taken up in parallel, each requiring a different educational background: for the prayer of the Latin office, for the understanding of the illustrations and their dimensions of meaning, and for the reading of the illustrations in connection with vernacular or Latin verses.

In the Middle Ages and early modern period the Office of the Dead was one of the most ubiquitous meditations on the thematic complex of

---

[1] For a description of this edition see Caroline Zöhl, 'Sehr bilderreicher Pergamentdruck von Jean Barbier und Guillaume Le Rouge mit 75 Metallschnitten aus der Werkstatt von Jean Pichore, in einem Einband des 17. Jahrhunderts. Unikum', in Heribert Tenschert and Ina Nettekoven (eds), *Horae B.M.V.: 158 Stundenbuchdrucke der Sammlung Bibermühle 1490-1550* (Ramsen: Antiquariat Bibermühle, 2003), 680-89, no. 85.

death, dying, repentance and expectations of a world hereafter. Not only was the prayer cycle performed on specific occasions of remembrance and Ministration to the Dead, but in the book of hours it formed part of daily devotions. It is therefore not surprising that in the course of the heightened reflection on death in new texts and illustrations of around 1400 the iconography of the illustration of the Office of the Dead acquired fresh momentum.[2]

The fifteenth century saw the development of a striking iconographic diversity in the illustrations of the Office of the Dead when compared with other texts of the book of hours, including chronological and regional emphases. Two themes dominated from the start of this development: the

---

[2] For the Office of the Dead and other texts concerning the subject of death in books of hours, see Victor Leroquais, *Les livres d'heures manuscrits de la Bibliothèque nationale*, 3 vols (Paris: Imprimerie Nationale, 1927), vol. 1, xxii-xxiii; Millard Meiss, *French Painting in the Time of Jean de Berry. The Boucicaut Master* (New York: Phaidon, 1968), figs 135-74, 230, 236, 294, 331; Millard Meiss, 'La mort et l'office des morts à l'époque du maitre de Boucicaut et des Limbourg', *Revue de l'Iart*, 1 (1968), 17-25; Friedrich Gorissen, *Das Stundenbuch der Katharina von Kleve. Analyse und Kommentar* (Berlin: Gebrüder Mann Verlag, 1973), 91-95, 118-21; F. Arné, 'Les images de la mort dans les livres d'heures (xiiie-xve siècles)', *La Maison Dieu*, 145 (1981), 127-48; Anton von Euw and Joachim M. Plotzek, *Die Handschriften der Sammlung Ludwig*, 5 vols, vol. 2, 'Brevier, Stundenbuch, Gebetbuch' (Cologne: Schnütgen-Museum der Stadt Köln, 1982), 11-47; Gabriele Bartz and Eberhard König, 'Die Illustration des Totenoffiziums in Stundenbüchern', in Hansjacob Becker *et al.* (eds), *Im Angesicht des Todes. Ein interdisziplinäres Kompendium*, Pietas Liturgica 3-4 (St. Ottilien: EOS-Verlag, 1987), 487-528 (a fundamental overview of the iconography and different levels of reality in the images concentrated on France with excursions on the iconography and development in Italy, Flanders and Holland); Roger Wieck *et al.*, *Time Sanctified. The Book of Hours in Medieval Art and Life*, exhibition catalogue, Baltimore, Walters Art Gallery (New York: George Braziller, 1988), 124-36; Danièle Alexandre-Bidon, 'La mort dans les livres d'heures', in Danièle Alexandre-Bidon *et al.* (eds), *À réveiller les morts. La mort au quotidien dans l'Occident médiéval* (Lyon: Presses universitaires, 1993), 83-94; Bodo Brinkmann, 'Zur Rolle von Stundenbüchern in der Jenseitsvorsorge', in Peter Jezler (ed.), *Himmel, Hölle, Fegefeuer. Das Jenseits im Mittelalter*, exhibition catalogue. Landesmuseum Zürich (Zürich: Verlag Neue Zürcher Zeitung, 1994), 91-100 (with documents and observations on the role of images in the use of the Office of the dead for their owners); Frank. O. Büttner, '"Ce sera moy." Realitätsgehalt und Rhetorik in Darstellungen der Toten- und Vergänglichkeitsikonographie des Stundengebetbuchs', in Bert Cardon, Jan Van der Stock, Dominique Vanwijnsberghe *et al.* (eds), *Als Ich Can. Liber Amicorum in Memory of Professor Dr. Maurits Smeyers*, 2 vols (Louvain: Peeters, 2002), vol. 2, 243-315.

Office of the Dead or the requiem mass in church (sometimes with additional stations of the Ministration to the Dead), and the dead individual as a naked corpse which, partly or even entirely liberated from the ritual context, physically embodies the expectation of death and judgement, both individually and in general.[3] Also making an appearance, usually armed, is Death incarnate in a form similar to that of the corpse, but in an advanced state of decomposition. In the following decades there was an enormous increase in pictorial themes whereby the subjects of the illustrations sprang from differing conceptions of the function of textual illustration, and were ultimately refined and combined from pictorial traditions rather than from a direct engagement with the text.

This led to the appearance of illustrations with an extremely diverse reality content: episodes from the Old and New Testaments, scenes of everyday life and rather profane representations of finitude in exampla or allegories of death, each emphasising different aspects of what was reflected in the Office of the Dead. For example, while the visualisation of the rites of death and burial confronts the prayer with its real context, themes such as the Legend of the Three Living and the Three Dead or the parable of the Rich Man and Lazarus visualise the abstract connection between death and judgement. The same goes for the Last Judgement and Purgatory. The awakening of Lazarus is one of the rare motifs in which the hope of resurrection is expressed. Representations of Job on the dung heap put a new complexion on the voice of the subsequent readings from the Book of Job, and in this respect they are reminiscent of authorial illustrations. In books of hours an amalgam of such diverse material is to be found only in the Office of the Dead.[4]

The almost unlimited diversity of pictorial themes is an inherent problem of books of hours in general, and of the Office of the Dead in particular.[5] The texts of the Office of the Dead are largely non-descriptive and offer few points of reference for illustration. An iconographic convention was enough to help locate a particular part of the text. Thus the hours of the Office of Our Lady can be identified by the stations of the Life of the Virgin, while any type of death imagery will make the Office of the Dead easily identifiable. A visual level of contemplation which is largely independent from the text is thus a general characteristic of books of hours.

---

[3] See Meiss (1968), figs 156-66.
[4] See Büttner (2002), 259.
[5] See Bartz and König (1987), 495, 500, 527.

As a direct textual reference of the images is consequently almost never taken into account in art-historical literature, art historians for the most part are interested only in the regional variants of the text which are vital to help determine where the books originated.[6] The overt textual references of the late example of an eleven-part cycle for the hours and the readings of the Office of the Dead considered here require nonetheless at least a brief consideration of the construction and content of the Office of the Dead, and its function in everyday life.

Texts in the Office of the Dead

In contrast to the official requiem mass, the Office of the Dead was used for personal devotion: initially in the monastic community and later also in a domestic context as part of lay prayerbooks.[7] Two forms of Ministration to the Dead need to be distinguished here: the vigil and the regular commemoration of the dead. Monks as well as laymen kept the vigil during the night before the requiem mass and burial of a family member, and repeated the office on the third, seventh and thirtieth days, as well as on the anniversaries. Furthermore, the Office of the Dead became a permanent feature of the liturgy at Easter and on specific feast days such as All Souls' Day. Nevertheless it was not restricted to given occasions. The adoption of the Memoria to the Dead in private books of hours ultimately shows that it did not just form part of regular monastic praying of the hours.

A concrete expectation of salvation was connected to the regular Ministration to the Dead. On the one hand relief in Purgatory was sought for the relatives, while on the other the remembrance also served to

---

[6] Transcriptions of the text of a book of hours are provided by Gorissen (1973) for New York, Pierpont Morgan Library (hereafter PML), MS M 945; Johannes Rathofer, in *Les Très Riches Heures du Duc de Berry, Kommentarband zur Faksimileausgabe des Manuskriptes Nr. 65 aus Sammlung des Musée Condé, Chantilly* (Luzern: Faksimile-Verlag, 1984); Franz Unterkircher, *Das Stundenbuch des Mittelalters*, (Graz: Akademische Druck- u. Verlagsanstalt, 1985), includes a complete German translation based on the Latin text of the Rothschild Prayerbook (Vienna, Österreichische Nationalbibliothek (hereafter ÖNB), Cod. Vind. S. N. 2844); Eberhard König and Gabriele Bartz, *Les Belles Heures du Duc de Berry. Acc. No. 54.1.1., Metropolitan Museum of Art. The Cloisters Collection New York. Transkription und Übersetzung* (Luzern: Faksimile-Verlag, 2006).

[7] On the role of the Office of the Dead in medieval life, see for example Bartz and König (1987), 495-500; Knut Ottosen, *Responsories and Versicles of the Latin Office of the Dead*, (Aarhus: University Press, 1993), 31-49; Brinkmann (1994); Wieck *et al.* (1988).

promote salvation of one's own soul and preparation for one's own death. The texts themselves give no information on expectations of the hereafter, however; Purgatory does not even appear. Instead, psalms and canticles are associated with death rather through their context.

In the main, the vigils of the Office of the Dead consist of psalmody designed to console the dead. They begin with Vespers in the evening, continue with Matins through the night, and end in the early morning with Lauds. Vespers and Lauds consist of a series of psalms, each framed by antiphons and concluding with verses, responsories and prayers that form a liturgical antiphony. To this are added canticles: the Magnificat (Luke 1:46-55) at Vespers, the Canticle of Ezechias (Isaiah 38:9-20) and the Benedictus (Luke 1:68-79) at Lauds. None of these three texts originally had anything to do with death. The Virgin's hymn of praise on the birth of Christ (Magnificat) and Zachariah's hymn on the birth of John the Baptist (Benedictus) are a permanent part of each of these hours. Only Hezekiah's song of thanksgiving on his deliverance from fatal illness refers back to the reflections in the Office of the Dead.

To understand the picture cycle designed by Jean Pichore for the letterpress print of 1509, the construction of the Matins is of paramount interest. This is celebrated in three nocturns spread over the night, but could also be celebrated – particularly by laymen – together with the Lauds at the regular morning commemoration of the dead. Each nocturn contains three psalms and three readings, of which at least eight and usually all are from the Old Testament Book of Job. The mainly fixed psalms and readings are complemented by diverse regional responsories, verses and prayers.

Alongside the invocations of David in the psalms, nine readings from Job shape the character of the nocturnal prayers. Job's ordeals and complaints against God become an allegory for the suffering of human life and, in the context of the intercession for the dead, also for Purgatory. With these thoughts Job's stricken self is transformed into the plaintive voice of the dead begging for help, which manages to be heard through the medium of prayer by others. This transformation is accomplished in the same way as the psalmists' self is transferred in older psalmody where the wake becomes a recitation *in persona defuncti*, *i.e.* on behalf of the deceased.[8] The prayer is at the same time also an intercession of the living

---

[8] See Ottosen (1993), 43-44.

for the dead, as can be seen in the change of the speaker's role, *e.g.* in the oft-repeated 'Requiem eternam dona eis' (*Grant them eternal rest*).[9]

Like the book of hours as a whole, the Office of the Dead was only to a limited extent designed to be read directly. As is evident also from the numerous abbreviations, most of the prayers and psalms – and to an extent certainly the shorter readings as well – were so familiar in their content that, with the aid of the highlighted incipits, the text was memorised rather than read word for word. A significant reason for this was that the texts in the book of hours were almost all in Latin. Lack of sources makes it difficult to estimate the extent to which the hugely enlarged readership of the fifteenth century – particularly in the last quarter-century through the development of printing – were competent enough to make accurate sense of new texts in Latin.[10] For many a book of hours must have been the only book they possessed, and this primarily demanded a form of reading in which the writing served to convey not the contents but the memory of prayer learned by heart, which was not necessarily understood literally.[11]

Only rarely were texts in the vernacular included in French books of hours, and then only outside the core body of texts. Indeed, it was most likely precisely these vernacular texts that the owners of the books knew by heart, but the addition of summaries in the vernacular of certain hours or readings points to the need for a more intimate engagement with the text than that provided in the official prayer. Often the headings with information on the use of each prayer are also in French. Furthermore, the vernacular was popularly used in the context of lavish pictorial programmes which, falling outside the customary parameters, were therefore not readily

---

[9] See the transcription of a Primer printed in Latin and English in *The Primer, or Office of the Blessed Virgin Marie, in Latin and English, 1599* (Antwerp, Arnold Conings, 1599), selected and edited by D.M. Rogers, English Recusant Literature, 1558-1640, vol. 262 (Ilkley/London: The Scolar Press, 1975); also Glenn Gunhouse, 'The Hypertext Book of Hours' at http://www.medievalist.net/hourstxt/ (accessed 10 October 2010).

[10] On the circulation of books of hours in Amiens in the early sixteenth century, see Roger Chartier, 'Culture as Appropriation: Popular Cultural Uses in Early Modern France', in Steven L. Kaplan (ed.), *Understanding Popular Culture. Europe from the Middle Ages to the Nineteenth Century* (Berlin/New York/Amsterdam: Mouton Publishers, 1984), 229-54, at 239-40.

[11] On the difference between oral and silent prayer and the role of books of hours in this development in the fifteenth and early sixteenth centuries, see Paul Saenger, 'Prier de bouche et prier de cœur. Les livres d'heures du manuscrit à l'imprimé', in Roger Chartier (ed.), *Les usages de l'imprimerie (XVe et XVIe siècle)* (Paris: Fayard, 1987), 191-227.

comprehensible and indeed also served to entertain.[12] This is also the function of the French illustrated verses in some printed editions that contain the picture cycle to be introduced here.

Pictorial programmes for the Office of the Dead

Comprehensive iconographic programmes for the Office of the Dead, such as Jean Pichore's eleven-part cycle, are rare exceptions for which no straightforward tradition can be discerned in the fifteenth century. In essence we can distinguish three types by means of the range of their illustrations. All three types originate in the development of an artistic renewal and higher productivity of pictorial invention which can be observed in Paris after 1400, and which in time spread to the Burgundian Netherlands, Holland and to the Upper Rhineland. The first and most common variant restricted itself to the border decorations of the single image page marking the opening of the Office of the dead. It was developed in Paris c.1410-15 by the Mazarine Master and the Bedford Master (who was probably Haincelin of Hagenau) in the eponymous Mazarine Hours (Paris, BMaz. ms. 468) and Bedford Hours (London, BL, Add. MS 18850), among others. Both artists appear to have aimed above all for a new, artistically ambitious page layout. This type of layout became popular in the circle of the Bedford Master and among his successors. As a rule the main miniature was thematically decisive for the pictures grouped around it, while relevant to the Office of the Dead was only the theme of death in general.

A variant of this first type, which also confined itself to the beginning of the text and only became more common in the second half of the century, were double-page illustrations with two miniatures in the manner of a diptych. Here the two pictures can extend themselves into a single scene as in the Legend of the Three Living and the Three Dead, which before 1349 was already spread across two separate miniatures in the Psalter and Hours of Jeanne de Luxembourg (New York, The Cloisters, Acc. No. 69.86, fols 321v-322). Another early example, the Hours of René d'Anjou (Paris, BnF, ms. lat. 1156A), shows completely separate subjects. In printed books as well as in manuscripts illuminated by Pichore's circle around 1500, however, we often find two episodes from the parable of

---

[12] Examples are the Bedford Hours (London, BL, Add. 18850) and the Rohan Hours (Paris, BnF, ms. lat. 9471).

Lazarus and the Rich Man (Dives),[13] or the associative connection of the poor Lazarus of the parable with the Raising of Lazarus.

Far more rarely did the text structure stimulate an expansion of illustration, as we find in the second type. That the marking of prayer times in the Office of the Dead remained the exception is certainly related to the fact that the devotions for the dead were performed as a continuous nocturnal prayer and not interrupted by other prayers, so that the marking of the hours did not have the same importance as in the Hours of the Virgin, for example.[14] Thus image programmes for the hours are also the rarest variant of this type. The Matins were only infrequently invested after Vespers with a picture of their own as well.[15] Equally rare are Offices of the Dead with three miniatures for all the hours.[16] Although early examples for the marking of two or three nocturnal hours can also be found in Paris, no established iconographic model for either variant ever evolved.

The formal variant, which was also used by Pichore's cycle, achieved a somewhat larger distribution. An illustration relating to textual content especially made sense when, in addition to the Vespers (which always had a picture), the nine readings from Job in Matins were illustrated with individual miniatures. The identification of text incipits played virtually no

---

[13] Examples from different painters in the circle of Jean Pichore are the Petau Hours in Gent (UB, ms. 234, fol. 76v) with Dives in Hell in the *bas-de-page* of the Feast of Dives with Lazarus; a book of hours in (Paris, BnF, ms. lat. 923, fols 69v-70r) – both by Pichore; and the so-called Hours of Henry IV in Paris (BnF, ms. lat. 1171, fols 55v-56r) by the Master of Petrarch's Triumphs.

[14] See Bartz and König (1987), 509.

[15] An exemption in the group of the Boucicaut Master are the St. Maur Hours (Paris, BnF, nouv. acq. ms. lat. 3107) with a funeral scene and an Office of the Dead in a private setting: see Gabriele Bartz, *Der Boucicaut-Meister. Ein unbekanntes Stundenbuch* (Ramsen: Antiquariat Bibermühle, 1999), 93. Another rare example by the Bedford Master is the Sobieski Hours (Windsor, Royal Library), where the miniature for the Office of the Dead is additionally surrounded by a cycle of small images relating to death and death rites. In the early sixteenth century, around 1508, Jean Bourdichon decorated the Grandes Heures d'Anne de Bretagne (Paris, BnF, ms. lat 9474), with the Raising of Lazarus and Job on the dunghill. A book of hours by the Master of Martainville 183 (Musée Condé, ms. 79, fols 95v and 98r) shows the same two subjects, and in the above mentioned Hours of Henry IV (Paris BnF, ms. lat. 1171) the Master of Petrarch's Triumphs chose the Feast of Dives with Dives in Hell as a diptych for Vespers and Job for Matins.

[16] This option was occasionally used only by the end of the century, *e.g.* by Maître François in the Hours of René II de Lorraine (Lissabon, Museu Calouste Gulbenkian, ms. LA 147).

part in this. It rather represents an attempt to juxtapose individual text segments with appropriate illustrations which, although not designed or able to illustrate the non-descriptive text, do certainly promote a pictorial meditation specifically related to it, one which is developed in the course of the nocturnal prayer. This was impressively demonstrated as early as *c.*1410 by a painter from the circle of the Egerton Master who used the style of the text-referential images of David in psalters to illustrate the nine readings with the appeals, pleadings and laments of Job.[17] Picture cycles of Job were more frequently to be found in the following decades, but they were restricted to a few groups of artists and regions, *e.g.* the Parisian followers of the Bedford Master around the middle of the century;[18] or Jean Colombe in Bourges from the 1470s;[19] or the circle of Jean Poyer in Tours;[20] and in manuscripts and prints around 1500, again in Paris.[21] As Job's laments largely elude visual representation, the attempt to portray his emotional state in pictures was later replaced by more accessible narrative cycles which, parallel with the text and its connection to the Old Testament account, portrayed the stages of Job's fate in an explanatory form.

In only a few, highly elaborate book projects was the parallel reading of picture and text even more complex: on the one hand where additional text segments were illustrated, and on the other – as in Pichore's graphic cycle of 1509 – where additional picture themes were introduced. An example of such an exceptional project is the Très Riches Heures (Chantilly, Musée Condé, ms. 65), which was begun for Duke Jean de Berry by the Limbourg brothers around 1410. Five full-page miniatures

---

[17] Los Angeles, Getty Museum, MS Ludwig IX, 5: see von Euw and Plotzek (1982), vol. 2, no. IX,5.

[18] *E.g.* the Master of the Munich Golden Legend (London, BL, Egerton 2019).

[19] *E.g.* in the Hours of Louis de Lavalle (Paris, BnF, ms. lat. 920) or the Hours of Guyot Le Pelet (Troyes, Mediathèque, ms. 3901), see *e.g.* Thierry Delcourt, 'Un livre d'heures à l'usage de Troyes peint par Jean Colombe. Une acquisition récente de la Médiathèque de Troyes', *Bulletin du Bibliophile*, 2 (2006), 221-44; François Avril, 'Les Heures de Guyot Le Peley. Chef d'Oeuvre de Jean Colombe', *Art de l'enluminure*, 21 (2007), 2-55.

[20] See *e.g.* Baltimore, Walters Art Museum (hereafter WAM), MS W 430, and New York, PML, MS M 12, or a Parisian follower of Poyer, see Roger S. Wieck, Sandra Hindman and Ariane Bergeron-Foote, *Picturing Piety: the Book of Hours.* (Paris: Les Enluminures, 2007), no. 2.

[21] Examples are manuscripts by Pichore (Vienna, ÖNB, cod. 1927), by the Master of Robert Gaguin (Paris, Arsenal, ms. 1191) or the Master of Petrach's Triumphs (Chantilly, Musée Condé, ms. 79). A series which appears in many printed editions by Simon Vostre was designed by the Master of the Apocalypse of the Sainte-Chapelle (also called the Master of the Très Petites Heures d'Anne de Bretagne.

combining two types of text illustration were planned: the identification of the times of prayer – effectively superfluous in the Office of the Dead (Vespers, nocturns of Matins, Lauds) – and the illustration of the psalms, hymns and canticles that runs through the whole book but is mainly set in smaller picture format as a subsidiary pictorial system. With the exception of Raymond Diocrès's requiem to the first nocturn, which the Limbourg brothers used already in connection with the Office of the Dead in the Belles Heures (New York, The Cloisters, Acc. No. 54.1.1),[22] the iconographic programme was substantially implemented only after 1485 by Jean Colombe, after which it became reflected in the work of the circle around Jean Pichore in Paris.

The introductory illustration to the Vespers shows Job on the dung heap (as in Pichore's cycle and its copy, see Fig. 99 below), added to which the *bas-de-page* shows two scenes from the rites of death. The beginning of the first nocturn of the Matins marks an incident from the Life of St Bruno, the founder of the Carthusian order, namely the requiem for Bruno's teacher, the Parisian canon Raymond Diocrès, who rises from his coffin and speaks to those present about his own damnation (as in Pichore's cycle and its copy, see Fig. 95 below). As an appeal for reversion, the *bas-de-page* also shows the Legend of the Three Living and the Three Dead in which the dead urge the living in similar terms to a timely self-reflection (Figs 90-91, Pichore's cycle and copy). In the context of the textual illustrations which follow, one could perhaps presume in the pictorial appeal for proper conduct a reference to the first antiphon of the Matins 'Dirige Domine Deus meus in conspectu tuo viam meam' (*Direct my way in thy sight, O Lord my God*), which can be seen in the space between the two pictures before the fifth psalm. In addition, the picture has border decorations of the type described above which, together with clues elsewhere, suggest the involvement of the Bedford workshop in the manuscript.[23] The third picture, as Klara Broekhuijsen has convincingly

---

[22] The legend has been illustrated in a cycle of the life of Saint Bruno accompanied by text in Jean de Berry's Belles Heures, where it appears right before the Office of the Dead. See *e.g.* Eberhard König, *Die Belles Heures des Duc de Berry* (Stuttgart: Theiss, 2004).

[23] See Patricia Stirnemann and Claudia Rabel, 'The "Très Riches Heures" and Two Artists Associated with the Bedford Workshop and Barthélemy d'Eyck', *Burlington Magazine*, 147 (2005), 534-38; Catherine Reynolds, 'The "Très Riches Heures", the Bedford Workshop and Barthélemy d'Eyck', *Burlington Magazine*, 147 (2005), 526-33.

demonstrated, shows the Legend of the Grateful Dead.[24] Both subsequent pictures are integrated in the concept of the illustration of the psalm. King David's victory over the Jebusites that illustrates psalm 29 ('Exaltabo') in the third nocturn and David's repentance illustrating psalm 50 ('Miserere') in the Lauds each show the events from which David was said to have written the psalms.

Largely earlier but no later than *c*.1430, there emerged in the Rohan Hours (Paris, BnF, ms. lat. 9471) a unique arrangement of the stations of the rite of death laid out in smaller images against inconsequentially chosen text segments, where they chronologically yet unsystematically follow the full-page main picture containing the most celebrated representation of a single dead man before his Creator.[25] Just like the main picture, the requiem for Lauds is here likewise detached from the general requiem mass, for the dead man stirring in the coffin patently resembles Raymond Diocrès, who is also to be seen in this same spot in the Très Riches Heures.

The pictorially rich variant of the second type of illustration was confined principally to the circle of Jean Colombe in Bourges, who completed the Très Riches Heures for the duke of Savoy.[26] Two further codices are distinguished by the special complexity of their pictorial programme, in which they surpass even the Très Riches Heures. The Hours of Anne de France (New York, PML, MS M 677) contains a total of twenty-four full-page miniatures to the Office of the Dead, which take up entirely different subjects and illustrate the psalms and canticles according to word illustration and other principles. To an extent these pictures are also to be found in the border decorations in the Très Riches Heures and in

---

[24] Klara Broekhuijsen, 'The Legend of the Grateful Dead: a Misinterpreted Miniature in the Très Riches Heures of Jean de Berry', in Cardon *et al.* (eds) (2002), vol. 2, 213-30. This image has long been interpreted as the Fourth Horseman of the Apocalypse.

[25] The main miniature for Vespers shows the dead man before his Judge and the column-width miniatures the dead man moving in his coffin/Raymond Diocres (Matins); a funeral procession (1st nocturne, 1st lecture); the Office of the Dead in a church (2nd nocturne); burial (2nd nocturne, 4th lecture); monks praying prior to the burial (3rd nocturne); the funeral mass and a gravedigger (3rd nocturne, 7th lecture); a deathbed (Lauds).

[26] I am grateful to Christine Seidel for helpful details concerning the below-mentioned manuscripts illuminated by Colombe and his workshop or followers from her as yet unpublished PhD thesis on Colombe and manuscript illumination in Bourges (Freie Universität Berlin, in preparation).

other books of hours by Colombe.[27] The series of illustrations of fourteen miniatures in a book of hours for Louis d'Orléans (St Petersburg, National Library of Russia, MS Lat. Q.v.I.1269) by Colombe's successors is similarly conceived parallel to the text, although less stringently. Thus it contains several double-images, which refer more to each other than directly to the text.[28]

In Paris, where Pichore's metalcuts were published in 1509, books of hours of such complexity first appeared only around 1500. Letterpress printing, which produced richly illustrated books of hours in Paris from 1485, is thought to have posed a decisive challenge to manuscript illumination. It is worth noting, however, that this pictorial richness was found above all in the border decorations and that direct borrowings from print are very rare in manuscripts. Touraine and Bourges were the sources of important stylistic and iconographic impulses for illustrators, publishers and designers of graphic series.[29] One illustrator, who had worked together in Paris with several local painters and who had been influenced by letterpress printing, seems to have been instrumental in the mediation of

---

[27] Introduced by a miniature showing a personification of Death with an arrow, the Vespers series includes David and Saul at Engedi (Ps. 119); Joseph's dream (Ps. 120); Purgatory (Ps. 129, *cf.* the Mount of Purification in the Très Riches Heures for the Office for Monday); Anne de France with her court ladies in front of a church portal (Ps. 137); a funeral procession into a church (Magnificat); a deathbed prayer (Ps. 145); Mass or a choir prayer; David taking Saul's spear (Ps. 5); David with a Lion (word illustration of Ps. 7, as in the Très Riches Heures); Dives and Lazarus (Ps. 22); Death of Dives (Ps. 24); Anointing of David (Ps. 26); the ambush from the parable of the Good Samarithan (Ps. 39); a sermon (Ps. 40); the Good Samarithan (Ps. 41), David saved from damnation (Ps. 50, *cf.* the penitent King David in the Très Riches Heures); Elijah in the fiery chariot (Ps. 64); David and Nathan(?) (Ps. 62); Elijah(?) fed by an angel (Song of Ezekiel); a prayer of a cleric (Ps. 148); the decapitation of John the Baptist (Canticle of Zechariah); Purgatory (Ps. 130, again similar to the Mount of Purification in the Très Riches Heures Heures).

[28] For Vespers: Letter of Uriah and Uriahs Death?, for Matins: King David's Grief and King David in Penance, for the reponsory 'Qui Lazarum resuscitasti': Raising of Lazarus and Lazarus an Dives, at the end of the fourth lecture: Death and Ascension of Lazarus and Dives in Hell. Additional subjects are the otherwise unknown episode of Christ with the Canaanite woman, Job on the dung heap, three scenes from the funeral rite and the Last Judgment.

[29] See *e.g.* a book of hours with miniatures by the Master of Jacques de Besançon, a follower of Jean Bourdichon and a follower of Jean Poyer with Psalter illustrations, in Wieck *et al.* (eds.) (2007), no. 2.

Colombe's ideas on layout in Bourges;[30] he is referred to as the Master of Martainville 183 after a book of hours in Rouen.[31] Under his leadership a group of highly complex books of hours was produced, which have an unconventional iconography with several picture cycles running parallel on nearly every page but, as in print, do not refer as directly to the text as Colombe does.[32] Furthermore, none of these books contain an elaborate main picture sequence for the Office of the Dead.

The third type of pictorial instances for picture sequences made use not of the beginnings of the texts in the book of hours but of the borders, which in the most lavish examples contained continuing histories on every page. The earliest manuscript of this kind was the above-mentioned Bedford Hours, which as previously in the first type was illustrated with cycles around the main miniatures.[33] Independently of the sequence of the text, it features a continuous Bible Moralisée cycle which is then elucidated through vernacular texts.[34] The Rohan Master also created a thematically related cycle in his eponymous book of hours (Paris, BnF, ms. lat. 9471).[35] It was the same artist who for the first time attempted to orientate the border cycles towards the devotional elements of the texts and thereby to assign to the text a continuing visual reading. In the Hours of Isabella Stuart (Cambridge, Fitzwilliam Museum, MS Founders 62) the three

---

[30] Isabelle Delaunay, 'Les Heures d'Écouen du Musée National de la Renaissance. Échange entre manuscrits et imprimés, autour de 1500', *Revue du Louvre*, 43 (1993), 11-24; Mara Hofmann, 'Studien zum Panissestundenbuch', unpublished MA dissertation (Freie Universität Berlin, 1998).

[31] Rouen, BM, ms. Martainville 183. The name was introduced in 1992 by Eberhard König, *Leuchtendes Mittelalter*, 4 (Ramsen: Antiquariat Bibermühle, 1992), 23; see also Caroline Zöhl, *Jean Pichore, Buchmaler, Graphikerund verleger in Paris um 1500* (Turnhout: Brepols, 2004), 46-47.

[32] London, BL, Add. MS 25696; New York, PML, MSS H 1 and M 7; Philadelphia, Free Library, MS Lewis 113; New Haven, Yale University Library, MS 411; Madrid, Biblioteca Nacional, vit. 24-3; Chantilly, Musée Condé, ms. 72; Panisse Hours, private collection (see Eberhard König *et al.*, *Leuchtendes Mittelalter*, Neue Folge, 3 (Ramsen: Antiquariat Bibermühle, 2000), no. 23.

[33] Eberhard König, *The Bedford Hours* (London: The British Library, University of Chicago Press, 2007), attributes the concept for the border cycles to the Master of the Cité des Dames. The small medaillons were executed by different artists, one of whom was the Bedford Master.

[34] For a list of the subjects, see Eberhard König, *Das Bedford-Stundenbuch, Begleitband zur Faksimile-Ausgabe* (Luzern: Faksimile-Verlag, 2006).

[35] The source for these images is the fourteenth-century so-called Anjou Bible from Naples (Paris, BnF, ms. lat. 9561): see Jean Porcher, 'Two Models for the Heures de Rohan', *Journal of the Warburg and Courtauld Institutes*, 8 (1945), 1-6.

visionary texts of Guillaume de Deguilleville's *Pèlerinages* and the Apocalypse are correspondingly set alongside the biblical texts and offices, in such a way that the *Pèlerinage de l'ame* inspires a reflection on salvation in the Office of the Dead.[36]

Comparably lavish border illustrations are again first found in the work of Jean Colombe in the 1470s. In the Hours of Louis de Laval (Paris, BnF, ms. lat. 920) an Old Testament cycle not specifically referring to the text unfolds in the Office of the Dead on the *bas-de-page*, while the outer borders correspondingly display the themes of Job, the parable of Lazarus, the ritual of death, and the hereafter.[37] Even around 1500 border cycles were still rarely found in manuscripts, but in letterpress print they became the main attraction, as is evident from the fact that publishers used them to advertise their books on the title pages. Only the above-mentioned small group of Parisian manuscripts, on which the Master of Martainville 183 worked with some other Parisian artists, can compete with print in terms of border illustration. Here it is worth noting that the leading Parisian artists who produced designs for print were not involved in this.

The Office of the Dead was most often accompanied by *Danse Macabre* imagery, in which death was visualised as a mirror image of society. As a parallel biblical pictorial meditation, narrative cycles of Job also remained popular. The text competes with psalms of repentance for *exempla* and allegories such as the parable of the Lost Son, the Vices and the Virtues, or the Fifteen Signs of the Day of Judgement.[38] To these can be added – albeit only after 1500 – *vanitas* motifs in ornamental borders, such as skulls or the allegorical figure of Lady World. Previously completely unknown in books of hours is a pictorial sequence with the title 'Accidents de l'Homme' or also 'Mors de la Pomme' which, prefaced by a

---

[36] For a brief description of the manuscript see James H. Marrow, 'Hours of Isabella Stuart', in Paul Binski and Stella Panayatova (eds), *The Cambridge Illuminations: Ten Centuries of Book Production in the Medieval West*, exh.cat. Cambridge, Fitzwilliam Museum (London/Turnhout: Harvey Miller/Brepols, 2005). For the localisation and the itinerary of the artist in different regions of France, see Eberhard König, 'Fifteenth-Century Illuminations from Angers in Cambridge: the Hours of Isabella Stuart and the Quest for a Local Style', in Stella Panayatova (ed.), *The Cambridge Illuminations: the Conference Papers* (London: Harvey Miller, 2007), 225-32.

[37] Similarly extensive programmes with only one full-page miniature can be found in books of hours in Troyes (BM, ms. 3901), in Oxford (Keble College, MS 42), and in the Heures Bureau (formerly Collection Loncle, Washington, priv. coll.): see Avril, *Heures de Guyot Le Peley,* (2007), n. 12.

[38] Both cycles were also used by the Master of Martainville 183 in the Panisse Hours: see König *et al.* (2000), no. 23.

personification of Death authorised by God, disseminates a kind of salvation history of death.[39]

Jean Pichore's cycle of 1509 and its imitations

The series of metalcuts designed by Jean Pichore in Paris by 1509 still exists in a second version, which was loosely copied from Pichore's series for the printer and publisher Thielman Kerver around 1520 by a designer greatly influenced by German graphic art after Dürer and by Holbein. Not all plates of the later series are true copies and apart from variations that also lend the pictures new semantic perspectives, it is possible to identify even some additional models. Four more versions of this cycle by different artists appeared later in the 1520s in several editions by François Regnault (the first dated 11 January 1526), Yolande Bonhomme (the first dated 2 September 1528), Germain Hardouin (11 May1532), and an undated edition from Rouen. All these are editions for the use of Sarum with variations of accompanying verses in English. Around 1532 a further version of the cycle with English verses was used for a lavishly illuminated manuscript with miniatures by the Master of François de Rohan, also for an English patron.[40] The following description is limited to the first two variants for the French market, however.

The series illustrates the Vespers and the nine readings of the Matins, the latter without thematic references to Job, nor does it form an iconographically consistent cycle. On the contrary, each nocturn seems to illustrate a thematic aspect of its own in three images, which is only clearly delimited in the first nocturn, however. The individual pictures generate not only textual references but also references to other pictures in the series, even outside these groups of three.

---

[39] See Caroline Zöhl, 'Der Triumph des Todes in szenischen Bildern vor Holbein. Le Mors de la pomme und l'Accidents de l'homme', in Andrea von Hülsen-Esch and Hiltrud Westermann-Angershausen with Stefanie Knöll (eds), *Zum Sterben schön* (Regensburg: Schnell & Steiner, 2006), vol. 1, 133-44, with a bibliographical summary on the subject; also Leonard P. Kurtz (ed.), *Le Mors de la Pomme* (New York: Publications of the Institute of French Studies Inc., 1937).

[40] For those editions, the illustrations and their accompanying English verses and for their relationship to the manuscript see Kay Sutton, 'Sources and the Sarum Hours Illuminated by the Master of François de Rohan', in Mara Hofman and Caroline Zöhl (eds), *Quand la peinture était dans les livres. Mélanges en l'honneur de François Avril* (Turnhout: Brepols, 2007), 330-43, 465.

Fig. 90. The Three Living and the Three Dead, metalcut by Jean Pichore in a book of hours (Use of Rome) published by Jean Barbier and Guillaume Le Rouge, Paris, 22 August 1509. © Ramsen, Antiquariat Bibermühle, Heribert Tenschert.

Prologue

The opening of the eleven-part series is formed by two metalcuts for Vespers which are linked to form a diptych. They have neither a concrete relation to the text that follows nor are they connected to the subsequent pictures in terms of content. The engravings depict the Legend of the Three Living and the Three Dead, which survives in several French poems of the thirteenth century, telling the story of three young noblemen whose encounter with three corpses leads to a timely repentance.[41] As can already be seen in thirteenth-century manuscripts recounting the Legend (*e.g.* Paris, BnF, ms. fr. 378), the three dead and the three living appear separately

---

[41] Two versions are linked to authors known by name, *viz.* Baudouin de Condé (active 1240-80) and Nicolas de Margival (active in the late thirteenth century). No authors are known for three other versions that survive in manuscript copies. See Stefan Glixelli (ed.), *Les cinq poèmes des trois morts et des trois vifs* (Paris: Champion, 1914), and also the essay by Christine Kralik in this volume.

in two illustrations (Figs 90-91). The theme had already been taken up in prayer books by the early fourteenth century, *e.g.* the De Lisle Psalter (Pl. 3) of *c.*1310 and the Hours of Jeanne d'Evreux of *c.*1325, but it was rare in books of hours until *c.*1500. It is only in print and in contemporary manuscripts that this theme forms part of an established pictorial thematic for the Office of the Dead, so it is not uncommon here.[42]

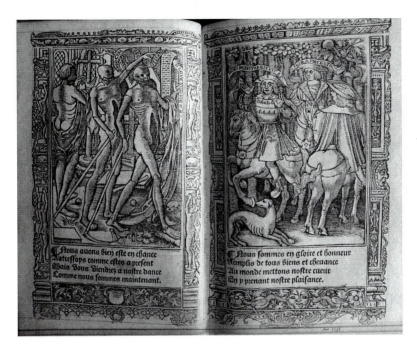

Fig. 91. The Three Living and the Three Dead. anonymous metalcut in a book of hours (Dominican Use) published by Yolande Bonhomme, Paris, 1542. © Staatsbibliothek zu Berlin.

Pichore transposes the scene to a cemetery in a town while his copyist, remaining closer to one of the textual sources – which most readers of such books were more familiar with by oral tradition, however – at least

---

[42] See again the miniatures by the Master of Martainville 183 in Chantilly, Musée Condé ms. 72. Early printed versions can be found before 1500 in books of hours by Antoine Vérard, Jean Dupré and Philippe Pigouchet: see Tenschert and Nettekoven (2003), nos 3, 7, 10.

gave the living their forest scenery back. It is interesting here that the later
designer took up the motif, but not the composition. In fact, he chose to
refer back to a different model that was equally widespread in contemporary
manuscripts.[43] Despite his stylistic training in German models, the anonymous designer thus shows himself to be rooted in the tradition of French
illustration. Both variants seem to have inverted the page order of their
models, for usually the living are shown on the left and the dead on the
right, *i.e.* following the direction of reading, whereas here this order is
reversed.

In Pichore these first two engravings are without an inscription. In
contrast his successor provides both parts with speech banners containing
the dialogue in Latin that underscore the moralising meaning of the
pictures. The dead speak in an echo of the parable of the Wise and the
Foolish Virgins in Matthew 25:13, 'VIGILATE ERGO CUM NESCITIS DIEM
NEQUE HORAM' (*Watch ye therefore, because you know not the day nor the
hour*). The living reply with the proverbial insight, 'MORS INVITABILIS EST
ET HORA INCERTA' (*Death is inevitable and the hour uncertain*), which is
not taken verbatim from any single source but often appears with
variations in late-medieval inscriptions. The Legend does not refer directly
to a text in the Office of the Dead, but rather presents a profane allegory
which also simultaneously admonishes and dramatically entertains the
observer, and generally prepares him for the requiem or memoria. As with
the later *Danse Macabre* whose message is related, the Legend was also
depicted in murals and can likewise be found as an addendum in Parisian
Danse Macabre incunabula such as Guy Marchant's expanded 1486
edition (Fig. 49).

First nocturn

To my knowledge the sequence of the first three illustrations to the first
nocturn is unique for the Office of the Dead in books of hours. The first of
the illustrations depicts the Expulsion of Adam and Eve from Paradise
after the Fall (Fig. 92). Again Pichore's composition seems to be the
wrong way round, for Adam and Eve flee to the left instead of in the
direction of reading, as a result of which the dynamic is arrested, as the
later version shows. Indeed, the picture is in any case to be read as a
representation rather than as a narrative. The Holy Trinity appears as
divine authority above the angel guarding the gates of Paradise. In
addition, Adam is given a voice through a speech banner that reads,

---

[43] See Paris, BnF, ms. lat. 1376, fol. 1v-2r.

'PARCE M[ICHI] D[O]M[I]N[E]' (*Spare me, Lord*). In terms of the pictorial logic, the quote can be understood as Adam's call to God, but in fact it is based on the following reading from Job 7:16: '[Desperavi, nequaquam ultra iam vivam:] parce mihi domine, [nihil enim sunt dies mei]' (*I have done with hope, I shall now live no longer: spare me, Lord, for my days are nothing*). The second version, in which the inscription is written out in full and in a more modern type is also not a direct copy of Pichore but refers to Dürer's *Small Passion* woodcut series.[44]

Fig. 92. Expulsion from Paradise: (left) metalcut by Jean Pichore in a book of hours (Use of Rome) published by Jean Barbier and Guillaume Le Rouge, Paris, 22 August 1509, and (right) anonymous metalcut in a book of hours (Dominican Use) published by Yolande Bonhomme, Paris, 1542. © Ramsen, Antiquariat Bibermühle, Heribert Tenschert / Staatsbibliothek zu Berlin.

---

[44] Walther L. Strauss (ed.), *The Illustrated Bartsch, 10: Albrecht Dürer* (New York: Abaris Books, 1981), no. 18.

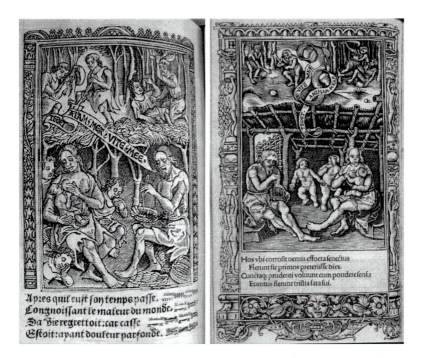

Fig. 93. Adam and Eve in the world and Cain slaying Abel: (left) metalcut by Jean Pichore in a book of hours (Use of Rome) published by Jean Barbier and Guillaume Le Rouge, Paris, 22 August 1509, and (right) anonymous metalcut in a book of hours (Use of Rome) published by Thielman Kerver, Paris, 5 December 1519. © Ramsen, Antiquariat Bibermühle, Heribert Tenschert.

In the second reading three simultaneous scenes in compartments are devoted to the wretched existence of the first people on earth (Fig. 93). Under a canopy of trees – in the later version spatially more convincingly in an open cabin – Eve can be seen with three small children and a baby, seated next to Adam who is busy weaving a basket. Above them, the crowns of trees form a floor for two later episodes from Genesis: on the left two men – perhaps Adam and Cain – are tilling the earth, while on the right we see Cain killing Abel. The later version, which seems like an inverted copy, cleverly separates the scenes above with a speech banner. The unusual motifs appear to be literally based on the third and fourth chapters of Genesis in which Adam and Eve, although still in Paradise, are fleeing from the face of God to hide among the trees. The group of children presumably illustrates Eve's curse of having to bring forth children in sorrow, while the two men hoeing allude less to specific people than to the thorny field that bears no fruit (*i.e.* part of Adam's curse). However, Adam weaving baskets is a highly unusual motif. Again his speech banner with the text 'TEDET ANIMAM MEAM VITE MEE' (*My soul is weary of my life*, Job 10:1) can be linked only to the illustration, but here it is also based on Job.

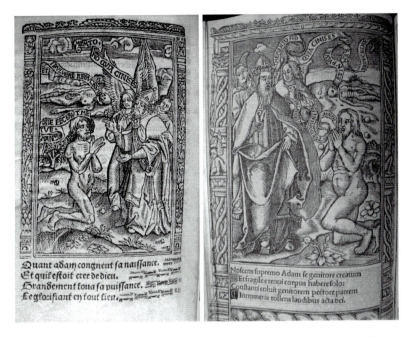

Fig. 94. Adam praying to God: (left) metalcut by Jean Pichore in a book of hours (Use of Rome) published by Jean Barbier and Guillaume Le Rouge, Paris, 22 August 1509, and (right) anonymous metalcut in a book of hours (Use of Rome) published by Thielman Kerver, Paris, 24 November 1520. © Ramsen, Antiquariat Bibermühle, Heribert Tenschert / Staatsbibliothek zu Berlin.

The third picture in this first thematic sequence shows Adam praying to God, who speaks to him in the guise of a crowned ruler attended by two angels (Fig. 94). In the background lies a human corpse who is also speaking – a rather macabre twist. This idiosyncratic iconography has no biblical or apocryphal basis, but generically illustrates Adam's penitence and, as the inscriptions makes clear, his knowledge of God's creative force and power over death. Here the text from Job 10:8-12 is split between Adam and the corpse as his unavoidable fate. Adam's prayer runs: 'MANUS

TUE [DOMINE] FECERUNT ME' (Job 10:8), and the dead Adam adds: 'ET IN
PULVERE[M] REDUCES ME' (Job 10:9). God answers this with a free
adaption of the first part of Job 10:9, 'MEMENTO HOMO QUIA CINIS ES'. In
the Office of the Dead these three quotes (with omissions) form the
contiguous beginning of the fourth reading: 'Manus tuae plasmaverunt me
et fecerunt me totum in circuitu et sic repente praecipitas me; memento
quaeso quod sicut lutum feceris me et in pulverem reduces me' (*Thy hands
have made me [and fashioned me wholly round about, and dost thou thus
cast me down headlong on a sudden?] Remember [I beseech thee that,
thou hast made me as the clay, and] thou wilt bring me into dust again*).
God's words from the Ash Wednesday liturgy or the burial rite after Gen.
3:19 are more familiar: 'Memento homo, quia pulveris es, et in pulverem
reverteris' (*[...] for dust thou art, and into dust thou shalt return*). The
transfer of Job's turn of phrase to Moses or to a generally known dictum is
on the one hand cleverly modulated to the change of speaker, while on the
other it is indeed the fitting biblical text for this image, for here Adam
(Job) is not calling to God: instead in Gen. 3:19 it is God who admonishes
Adam – and thereby the viewer – after the Fall.

   The three first images relate to the creation of Man, the origins of death
that lie in the rebellion against God, and the knowledge of God's
omnipotence over life. Starting from the Fall (which is not shown), they
depict, in the manner of a salvation history of death, how Man first
brought death into the world through sin and must painfully live as mortal
outside Paradise. Whereas illustrations of Creation and Fall are not
unknown in books of hours in particular, when they form the opening of
Old Testament cycles (as in Colombe's extensive border illustrations) or
when the Fall is typologically contrasted with the Annunciation, they are
unknown in the Office of the Dead. However, a stimulus can be found in
Pichore's own print illustrations, for as early as 1507 he had been
commissioned by the publishers Gillet and Germain Hardouin to design
the *Accidents de l'Homme* cycle for the Office of the Dead. In this work
the cycle begins with the appearance of Death incarnate in a cemetery
where God gives him the power to kill. Subsequently, starting with the
Fall that brings death into the world and then the first death through
fratricide, it presents the multiple manifestations of mortality in the world
through different types of death up to the Last Judgement. Only the killing
of Abel with a jawbone is directly comparable, although the basic idea is
very close to that of the three illustrations to the first nocturn. The theme
was first passed down in an illuminated manuscript designed at the

Burgundian court by Jean Miélot before 1470, but it was not widely disseminated.[45]

A second parallel goes back equally to Pichore himself. As early as 5 April 1504 he published a book of hours at his own initiative together with Remy de Laistre, in which he also printed the first graphic works based on his own designs. On the recto sides of this book the borders of the Office of the Dead are decorated with various illustrations in an older style that bear no relation to the text. However, placed between these illustrations is a French text which, starting with Eve grasping the apple, describes a further variant of the *Histoire du Mors de la Pomme*.

Pichore here interprets the pictures by means of speech banners which, like the readings from Job and the psalms in the text of the Office of the Dead, give a voice to the dead who are being commemorated. The pictures reduce the more complex textual content to a sequence of easily comprehensible reflections: first the invocation 'Spare me' to God in the face of Particular Judgement; then the lament over the wretchedness of life, 'My soul is weary of my life'; and finally the recognition, 'Thy hands have made me', 'Thou wilt bring me into dust again', and God's admonition to the rebellious Adam and the punishment of disobedience with death, 'Remember, man, that thou art dust'.

Second nocturn

The picture series to the second nocturn is about personal salvation but it is not as clearly delimited from the pictures of the third nocturn as it is from the cycle of the first. In the fourth reading in the second nocturnal hour, Pichore draws thematically on a pictorial motif that goes back to the Belles Heures of the duke of Berry, but without having developed into a recognisable tradition of its own over the course of a hundred years. It depicts the requiem mass for canon Raymond Diocrès (Fig. 95), which in the *Belles Heures* is found not in the Office of the Dead but in the Life of St Bruno. In the *Très Riches Heures*, which was made for the same patron, this miniature was painted by Jean Colombe although it formed part of the original concept, for the design was clearly drawn by the Limbourg brothers. Similarities of style between Pichore and Colombe lead one to

---

[45] Mailand, Biblioteca Ambrosiana, ms. S. 67 supp., fols 176r-179r, (c.1461) without images; Paris, Bibliothèque nationale, ms. fr. 17001, fols 107-114v, c.1468-70, with watercolour drawings. In print the *Accidents de l'homme* have appeared without a title in Robert Gobin, *Les loups ravissants* (Paris: Anthoine Vérard, c.1505-10). For the printed versions in books of hours, see Zöhl (2006).

speculate that the younger Parisian painter had the opportunity of studying Colombe's book art, although a direct collaboration cannot be established for certain.[46] As Colombe and his workshop did not otherwise make use of the Raymond Diocrès episode in their lavishly illustrated books of hours, the transmission of this theme in the context of the Office of the Dead remains unresolved. Furthermore, the treatment of the theme by Colombe and Pichore is not comparable.

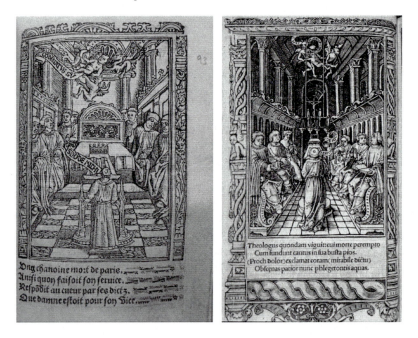

Fig. 95. The funeral mass of Raymond Diocrès: (left) metalcut by Jean Pichore in a book of hours (Use of Rome) published by Jean Barbier and Guillaume Le Rouge, Paris, 22 August 1509, and (right) anonymous metalcut in a book of hours (Use of Rome) published by Yolande Bonhomme, Paris, 5 December 1519. © Ramsen, Antiquariat Bibermühle, Heribert Tenschert

The pictorial model used by Pichore appears to have depicted an unspecified mass rather than this particular theme, for not only is the image of the rising corpse missing, but also even a coffin. Pichore's successor likewise seemed to be unaware of the original formulation of the

---

[46] In a book of hours with both styles the Parisian-style miniature is attributable rather to the Master of Meister von Martainville 183: see König (1992), no. B.

theme. The subject matter is discernible only in a soul that has been carried off by two devils in the vault of the church, in combination with the priest cry that marks the dramatic climax of the story. For according to the legend it was precisely at that moment that Diocrès arose, as the priest began the reading with the words 'RESPO[N]DE MICHI' (*[…] and do thou answer me*, Job 13:22), which can also be read in the speech banner in Pichore's engraving. The further content of the reading (Job 13:22-28), in which the cry is evidently directed at God and reflects the exclaimer's own sinfulness – 'How many are my iniquities and sins? make me know my crimes and offences' (Job 13:23) – is here remembered as a pictorial meditation and associated with the famous legend.

Fig. 96. Birth, Death and Old Age: (left) metalcut by Jean Pichore in a book of hours (Use of Rome) published by Jean Barbier and Guillaume Le Rouge, Paris, 22 August 1509, and (right) anonymous metalcut in a book of hours (Dominican Use) published by Thielman Kerver, Paris, 24 November 1520. © Ramsen, Antiquariat Bibermühle, Heribert Tenschert / Staatsbibliothek zu Berlin.

The next theme is once more not a biblical one, nor is it a legend, but rather – in this context – a highly unusual allegory. Its two bare registers consisting of a building and a landscape are reminiscent of compositions in the engraving of the first people in the world, which is also thematised here (Fig. 96). In a very low building a thin line separates two rooms, each with a bed. In the room on the left, a dying man is given the blessed candle, while on the right a mother and newborn baby lying in a bed are shown. In the register above a hunched old man walks through a landscape on two crutches. The dying, the newborn and the old man have speech banners, the reading of which quickly makes clear that here again there has been an inversion of the images, which this time actually disrupts our understanding. In fact, the speech banners should be read from left to right, then up, which then form the first line of the reading (Job 14:1-6), the baby saying 'HOMO NATUS DE MULIERE', the dying man continuing 'BREVI VIVENS TEMPORE', and the old man concluding 'REPLETUS MULTIS MISERIIS' (*Man born of a woman, living for a short time, is filled with many miseries*, Job 14:1). Here also the faulty composition is corrected by the later designer, who lets the crippled old man enter from the left into a house in which birth and death are divided between the upper and lower floors. While this change helps the reading of the picture, it does not alter the fact that the cited texts are in the wrong order. Irrespective of this, the picture presents itself as a generalisation of fate, brought on to mankind by its original ancestors shown in the first nocturn. It is reminiscent of the calendar sequence to the Ages of Man that appears in the 1509 edition, of which this is a grim overview.

The sixth reading shows a group of naked souls of both sexes in Purgatory, in which one man stands out, his voice in a speech banner addressing the Trinity who appear above him in a gloriole of angels (Fig. 97). Souls in Purgatory are rarely thematised in the Office of the Dead, but they appear occasionally in Dutch illumination, most impressively in the Hours of Catherine of Cleves (New York, PML, MS M 945) where in the Monday Matins (also dedicated to death) Hell actually appears three times, while in the Office of the Dead Purgatory appears in the context of the rite of death. In France the theme was painted by Colombe in the Très Riches Heures – again for the Monday, just as in the Hours of Catherine of Cleves. In contrast to the story of Raymond Diocrès, Purgatory also appears in other books of hours by Colombe and his workshop; indeed twice as a full page in the Hours of Anne de France, and in the borders to the Office of the Dead in other examples (Paris, BnF, ms. lat. 920, and Troyes, BM, ms. 3901). The motifs of the torments of Purgatory combined in the large miniature are here distributed across the borders in less legible single scenes. Among them there also appears a supplicant single soul not dissimilar to Pichore's formulation, although he depicts the motif with more detail in a larger size.[47] The motif is also occasionally found in Paris around 1500, *e.g.* in a stylistically characteristic book of hours designed by the Master of Jacques de Besançon and two illuminators in Tours in which a small half-size Job cycle is likewise to be found,[48] or in a very unusual iconography for Matins combining the Annunciation with Purgatory in a book of hours in New York (New York, PML, MS M 7).

Fig. 97. Souls in Purgatory: (left) metalcut by Jean Pichore in a book of hours (Use of Rome) published by Jean Barbier and Guillaume Le Rouge, Paris, 22 August 1509, and (right) anonymous metalcut in a book of hours (Dominican Use) published by Yolande Bonhomme, Paris, 1542. © Ramsen, Antiquariat Bibermühle, Heribert Tenschert / Staatsbibliothek zu Berlin.

In the sixth reading (Job 14:13-16), Job speaks explicitly for the first time about the hereafter and the hope of salvation. Of the first verse, which reads, 'Who will grant me this, that thou mayst protect me in hell, and hide me till thy wrath pass, and appoint me a time when thou wilt remember me?' (Job, 14:13), Pichore selected only the ending, which at first does not

---

[47] I am grateful to Christine Seidel for this observation.
[48] Wieck *et al.* (2007), no. 2, or New York, PML, MS M 12.

permit one to understand the context: 'CONSTITUAS MIHI TEMPUS IN QUO RECORDERIS MEI'. However, the pictorial legend had a remarkable effect on the user reading the text in commemoration of the dead, for he was not only contemplating the suffering in Purgatory and becoming aware of the dangers to himself, but he would also understand the call of the soul as being simultaneously directed towards himself, and thereby reflect upon the dead's need for intercession. For the first time the copyist here shows the composition the same way round as Pichore. Small changes reveal the ornamental graphical approach of the illustrator; they enrich the compositional balance and the readability of the speech banner, which now becomes the *titulus* of the picture and which no longer directly assigns the call to the soul.

The three illustrations of the second nocturn do not fuse into as closed a cycle as the preceding one. A very earthly lament about the misery and transience of a short life is interposed between two pictures which, even if in different ways, promote reflection on the reversion and intercession of salvation through the call of the damned and the appeal to remembrance from the hereafter.

Third nocturn

The third devotion of the Matins starts with a picture of the rite of death that had hitherto not appeared in the pictorial sequence, and generally had become rare in books of hours at that time. It depicts a death chamber, in which two clergymen are administering the last communion to a dying man (Fig. 98). The illustration forms part of a group of pictures for the Office of the Dead which add an allegorical level of reality to the rite by showing, in addition to the priests and relatives, three devils and an angel waiting to receive the dying man's soul. A window looks out onto a cemetery where we see a man with a sickle, recognisable as the Grim Reaper but in an unusual personification of Death as he is normally presented more explicitly as a cadaver. Simultaneously God the Father approaches with more angels from Heaven.

The illustration has its origins in the cycle of the *Ars Moriendi*, which presents death didactically as an alternation of stations of temptation and overcoming.[49] Two immediate comparative examples are provided by Colombe in the Hours of Anne de France, *viz.* in connection with psalm 146 where the death chamber is depicted with chaplains in the context of

---

[49] For this group see *e.g.* Wieck (1988), 124, pls 37 (Baltimore, WAM, MS W 457) and 38 (Baltimore, WAM, MS W 274).

the rite, while the struggle for souls upon the simultaneous deaths of Lazarus and the Rich Man can be seen together with psalm 40. The *Ars Moriendi* has a closer connection, however. To suit the scene the painter has also selected the exclamation of the dying from the reading, 'LIBERA ME ET PONE IUXTA TE' (*Deliver me O Lord, and set me beside thee*, Job 17:3).

Fig. 98. Deathbed – *Ars moriendi*: (left) metalcut by Jean Pichore in a book of hours (Use of Rome) published by Jean Barbier and Guillaume Le Rouge, Paris, 22 August 1509, and (right) anonymous metalcut in a book of hours (Dominican Use) published by Yolande Bonhomme, Paris, 1542. © Ramsen, Antiquariat Bibermühle, Heribert Tenschert / Staatsbibliothek zu Berlin.

The content of the reading (Job 19:20-27) must have determined the next theme, for here the text for the first time refers to Job's friends. This gives the artist the opportunity in a subsidiary place in the book to draw on a standard iconography in contemporary French books of hours – one which was also employed in examples from Bourges, Tours and Paris – in order to illustrate the new nocturns: Job's quarrel with his friends at which here, unusually, God the Father is also present. Job says to his friends,

354 Caroline Zöhl

'MISEREMINI MEI MISEREMINI MEI SALTIM VOS AMICI MEI' (*Have pity on me, have pity on me, at least you my friends*, Job 19:21). This request, like the calling of the soul in Purgatory in the sixth reading, can also be read as a challenge to the readers of the book of hours, and related to the intercession for the dead.

Fig. 99. Job on the Dung heap: (left) metalcut by Jean Pichore in a book of hours (Use of Rome) published by Jean Barbier and Guillaume Le Rouge, Paris, 22 August 1509, and (right) anonymous metalcut in a book of hours (Dominican Use) published by Yolande Bonhomme, Paris, 1542. © Ramsen, Antiquariat Bibermühle, Heribert Tenschert / Staatsbibliothek zu Berlin.

The concluding picture of the ninth nocturn (Fig. 100) is in general extremely rare, and to my knowledge unique in books of hours. It is the illustration of a concept which was widespread in proverbs and literature in the late Middle Ages, *viz.* the Three Enemies of Man: the World, the Flesh and the Devil. The picture again shows an interior entirely dominated by a bed in which a woman has just given birth to a child. A peculiar company of people are gathered about the bed: a midwife holds the baby in her arms, another woman is sitting in front of the bed, and next to her (with his back towards us) stands a gentleman in noble attire who is talking to a devil with a pig's head, towards whom the newborn is also apparently turning his face. Two of the figures, who might otherwise be seen as actual visitors to the mother and child, are identified by inscriptions as allegorical figures: the crouching woman is 'CARO' (Flesh) and the nobleman 'MUNDUS' (World). A caption for the devil was evidently not required; nevertheless the copyist surprisingly captions only this figure. Above the scene we see God the Father floating in Heaven.

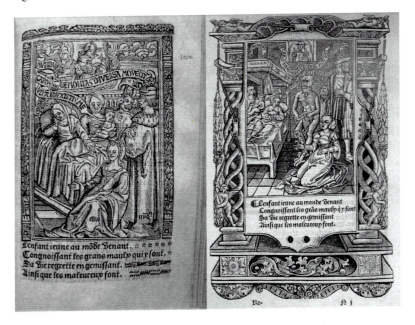

Fig. 100. The Three Enemies of Man: World, Flesh and the Devil: (left) metalcut by Jean Pichore in a book of hours (Use of Rome) published by Jean Barbier and Guillaume Le Rouge, Paris, 22 August 1509, and (right) anonymous metalcut in a book of hours (Use of Rome) published by Thielman Kerver, Paris, 10 September 1522. © Ramsen, Antiquariat Bibermühle, Heribert Tenschert.

The origins of the topos of the World, the Flesh and the Devil as a kind of diabolical trinity cannot be established with certainty.[50] Although the three powers are often separately referred to as enemies of Man in the

---

[50] Siegfried Wenzel, 'The Three Enemies of Man', *Mediaeval Studies*, 29 (1967), 47-66.

Bible, they never appear as a unified power. The three were first named
collectively in Augustine's *Sermones* (sermon 158) as powers against
which Man has to struggle, even after baptism and the forgiveness of his
sins.[51] In the eleventh century the topos was to be found in the writings of
the theologians Jean de Fécamp and Jean l'Homme de Dieu, for example,
and from the twelfth century it gained a certain currency especially
through the works of Bernard of Clairvaux and Hugh of St Victor, so that
it found its way into religious tracts and prayers. At this time the theme
also featured in the *Microcosmos* of Godfrey of St Victor in the same
metric formulation as in the speech banner in Pichore's illustration:
'MUNDUS CARO DEMONIAS [*sic*] DIVERSA MOVENT PRELIA' (*The world, the
flesh and the devil mount different attacks*). Moreover, from the thirteenth
century there is evidence of a vernacular variant with the title 'Romanz des
trois aenemis, ce est la chars, li mondes, [li] deables' (*Romance of the
three enemies, i.e. the Flesh, the World, the Devil*).[52] Finally one finds the
three powers related to the temptations of Adam through the three sins
repeated in the three temptations of Christ. Popular versions were to be
found in the *Songe de Pestilence* (1374-76/77), the second part of the
Livres de Roy Modus et de La Royne Ratio, in which the King and the
Queen make a complaint to God against the three enemies. Pichore may
have known a dramatic late-fifteenth-century treatment of the topos, which
also appeared in print under the title *Moralite nouuelle, de Mundus: Caro.
Demonia.*[53] From this it is also possible to deduce the dialogue of the
figures in the illustration.

In manuscripts, allegorical pictures of this kind are almost never to be
found. Apparently Pichore has here directly taken up a literary topos. An
equally isolated example in the Panisse Hours by the Master of Martainville
183 expresses a related idea, however.[54] Here, on the recto of an individual
sheet bound into the Office of the Dead above a French prayer, three
allegorical figures – *l'ame* (the soul), *le corps* (the body) and *le diable* (the
devil) – also encounter each other. Although here the devil again reaches

---

[51] Wenzel (1967), 49.

[52] Paul Meyer, 'Roman des trois enemies de l'homme par Simon', *Romania*, 16
(1887), 1-24.

[53] *Moralite nouuelle, de Mundus: Caro. Demonia. En laquelle Verrez les durs
assautz & tentations quilz font au Cheualier Chrestien: Et comme par co[n]seil de
son bon esprit, auec la grace de Dieu, les Vaincra, & a la fin aura le Royaume de
paradis; Et est a cinq personnages. Cest a scavoir. Le chevalier chrestien. Lesprit.
La chair.Le monde et le dyable.* (Paris(?): Pierre Sergent(?), 1540), Dresden,
Sächsische Landesbibliothek, Lit. Gall. vet. 6, misc.1.

[54] Private collection: see König *et al.* (2000), no. 23.

for the soul, an inscription defines the body not as an external temptation but as a subjection of the soul to the devil through one's own body.

Although the theme does not have biblical origins and contains no direct reference to the reading of Job, Pichore relates his pictorial version to the text by transferring the dialogue to a mother and child and by making the newborn say the first verses of the reading, 'QUARE DE VULVA EDUXISTI ME' (*Why didst thou bring me forth out of the womb?*, Job 10:18), while the speech banner for the three enemies is placed above the picture like a *titulus* instead of being assigned to any single character. The careful observer should note further textual allusion in the reference from the topos of the enemies back to the temptations of Job. In the picture God the Father reminds us that he himself gave the devil the power to tempt Job, challenging his belief by exposing him to calamities. This thought also connects the picture to the two previous ones in the third nocturn which reflect in the first reading the deathbed temptations; in the second reading Job being tempted by his friends to give up his faith in God; and finally the three temptations plaguing Man from his birth.

Editions by Barbier/Le Rouge, Kerver and Bonhomme

The edition by Jean Barbier and Guillaume Le Rouge of 22 August 1509 already features a renewed concept of illustration, compared to that of all earlier print editions and most manuscripts of the group described above. The book dispenses completely with borders and thus does not permit the second level of picture reading that was until then characteristic of books of hours. Instead, through the choice of subjects and pictorial inscriptions, the pictures take on a direct textual reference hitherto not sought in print, to which a second textual level is added by means of accompanying French verses placed outside the pictures. Around 1519 Kerver's editions were still furnished with consecutive historicised borders, especially of the *Danse Macabre* in designs by Jean Pichore, so that in addition to types of text, two pictorial levels can also be read. It was only from 1523 that Yolande Bonhomme had the picture pages set into monumental frames and, in line with the new fashion, dispensed entirely with borders on the text pages. In these editions the script décor is also printed. A painted décor, giving the print the appearance of a manuscript, is superfluous here.

As in the production of manuscripts, the creation of pictures and text in print are separate processes, although chronologically reversed. Whereas the illuminators were the last to get their hands on the loose manuscript quires, designers and block-cutters were the first to work with them, for with print the pictures must be ready before the type can be set, so that they can both be printed together in a single process.[55] Here the artist naturally knew for which text beginnings he was to create his pictures. It may well be that the publisher, who in print is the one responsible for the commission, had already determined the choice of theme. However, as far as the design of the picture themes was concerned, the main responsibility still lay with the artist.

On the other hand, for the text and layout of print editions the publisher alone was responsible. While the canonical texts could be exactly copied by means of pre-printed forms, the varying texts accompanying the pictures in the different editions were individually chosen for these book projects. Some of the later editions by Thielman Kerver, containing copies of the artwork, have the same French verses as the first edition of 1509; others replaced these with Latin inscriptions, also written in quatrains, but not rhymed.

The verses are all related exclusively to the pictures rather than to the Office of the Dead. While the speech banners with quotes from Job disrupt the picture narrative, emphasising instead their meditative function for prayer, the captions serve as explanations or even explanatory dialogue and underline the autonomy of the pictures from the text of the Office.

In the choice of language, publishers responded to the differing tastes and education of buyers, for in terms of content there were few differences with regard to the interpretation of the pictures. The French captions are catchily-rhymed mnemonics, which at times also add an unexpected dimension to the pictures. Thus the verses to the Three Living and the Three Dead in Kerver's editions provide a dialogue which can be read in parallel to the Latin speech banners, and in which the dead announce to the living the coming *Danse Macabre*: 'Nous avons bien este en chance / Autreffoys comme estes a present / Mais vous viendrez a notre dance / Comme nous sommes maintenant'. The captions to the first nocturn can indeed be read as a continuing narrative, where the pictures are also interpreted. For example, in the Expulsion from Paradise the text is about Adam's knowledge and repentence, which cannot be observed in the picture. By means of the verses the concluding allegory takes on a grim meaning of life for the child: 'Lenfant ieune au mo(n)de venant / Congnoissant les grans maulx qui y sont / Sa vie regrette en gemissant. / Ainsi que les malheureux font' (*As it comes into the world and discovers the great evils that are there, the young child groans and regrets his life just as those do who are unhappy*).

---

[55] This is a general characteristic of relief-printing techniques and also applies to the much more popular woodcut as opposed to the rare experiments with book illustration using copperplate engravings in the later sixteenth century.

No biblical or other textual sources are likewise to be found for the Latin quatrains. As they consequently could not be presumed to be known, they assume a reading knowledge of Latin and an educated taste in entertainment. In contrast to the Latin offices, the verses are not suitable for devotions.

Conclusion

The extensive cycle designed by Jean Pichore in 1509 with eleven illustrations to the Office of the Dead alone, is based on a concept of illustration stemming essentially from Bourges. Here Jean Colombe, using his knowledge of varying illustration models and pictorial programmes from the first half of the fifteenth century, had developed a number of exceptionally richly illustrated books of hours, the earliest of which had already been created around 1410. In this no single programme seems to have served as a complete model. Instead, he appears to have made free use of themes and forms of textual reference that had been handed down, so that he could develop a concept of illustration whose cyclical coherence consists primarily of a continuous connection to the intrinsically non-graphic text. In the Office of the Dead he initially chose for the iconography a sequence of three images from Genesis: the Expulsion from Paradise, Adam and Eve's fate in the world and Cain's fratricide, through to Adam's repentance. This subject, which was not normally seen in this position in books of hours, is probably primarily derived from a literary model, the *Histoire du Mors de la Pomme*, which Pichore had already used for verses and in a border cycle to the Office of the Dead.

Yet instead of extending this sequence into a complete, moralising, narrative cycle, Pichore sought completely diverse subjects for the following six illustrations, whose coherence is provided primarily by the objects of reflection highlighted by the inscriptions. Except for Job on the dung heap, all the themes are unusual. The legend of Raymond Diocrès is presumably handed down from manuscripts in the possession of the duke of Berry, probably the Très Riches Heures which was completed by Jean Colombe. The souls in Purgatory and the representation of the death chamber as scenes in the *Ars Moriendi* are also unusual subjects. Finally, the two allegorical representations of birth, senility and death, and the three enemies of Man at the mother and child's bedside are exactly as unexpected as the illustrations of Genesis. Furthermore, even in other contexts, they have no proven models in French illumination, and in the one case probably go back to cycles of the Ages of Man, and in the other to literary sources or to a widespread theological topos.

Given that the first printed edition containing this graphic series already had quatrains attached to all fifty-five illustrations, these were perhaps part of the original concept, which then could not be attributed to Pichore alone. The combination of the unusual iconography with pictorial inscriptions from the Office and edifying verses, which were available in either Latin or French, means that these books of hours can claim to be a new type of devotional book in which the traditional function of the prayer book was to be bolstered by an imaginative complexity of picture and text. At the same time, through their diverse choice of pictorial themes, their inconsequentially renewed aesthetic, and their not entirely coherent overall concept, they remained so medieval in character that from the mid-1520s they could manifestly no longer carry conviction. The last blossoming of medieval books of hours was distinguished precisely by the manifold attempts to enhance their own attractiveness – but this could not prevent their demise which was finally sealed by the Council of Trent.

Acknowledgements

I am indebted to Heribert Tenschert (Antiquariat Bibermühle, Ramsen, Switzerland) and the Staatsbibliothek zu Berlin for the permission to publish images from printed Horae in their possession. I am grateful to Clive Gordon and Sophie Oosterwijk for their help with the translation, and to Sophie Oosterwijk and Stefanie Knöll for their careful editing of this text.

LETTERS WITHOUT WORDS?
THE *DANSE MACABRE* INITIALS
BY HANS HOLBEIN AND HIS FOLLOWERS

WINFRIED SCHWAB

While working as an artist in Basel in 1523, Hans Holbein the Younger (*c.*1498-1543) designed his so-called *Alphabet of Death*, a graphical cycle of ornamental letters in which cadaver figures are shown confronting representatives of different social classes. In their treatment of the living these representatives of death give indications of how their victims have lived their lives, and thereby offer interesting insights into early-sixteenth-century society. Such ornamental initials, which are often no larger than a postage stamp, were normally used to illustrate and decorate texts. However, in Holbein's *Alphabet* the initials assume a fascinating life of their own. Irrespective of the book's content and going beyond its text, these grisly images introduce the reader to the world of the macabre and the horror of death (Fig. 101).

Shortly after its first publication Holbein's *Alphabet* was disseminated all over Europe. Copies that resemble the original woodcuts to a greater or lesser degree can be found from Spain to Romania and from England to France. Moreover, the images also exerted a significant influence on art produced in this period, which also saw the publication of several independent initials often by unknown artists who were evidently inspired by Holbein's creations. After all, Holbein's designs addressed a topic that greatly preoccupied his contemporaries: the omnipresence of death.

The theme of death was not limited to public spaces, such as medieval cemeteries with *Danse Macabre* murals (of which there were two in Basel at the time). The creation and dissemination of these macabre initials indicate that the imagery also invaded private spaces where they must have appealed to educated members of the clergy and those of higher secular rank who were literate – admittedly a small proportion of the population at the time.

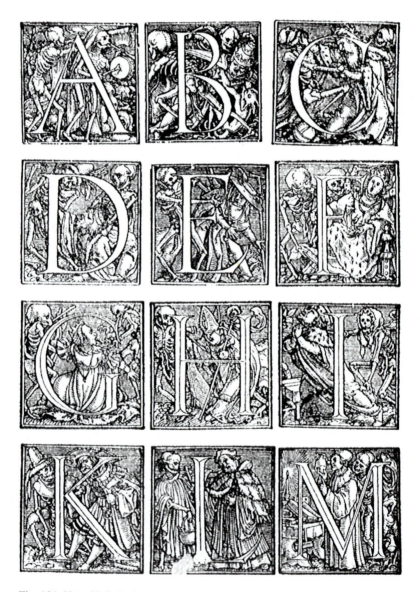

Fig. 101. Hans Holbein the Younger, *Alphabet of Death*, woodcuts, *c*.1523.

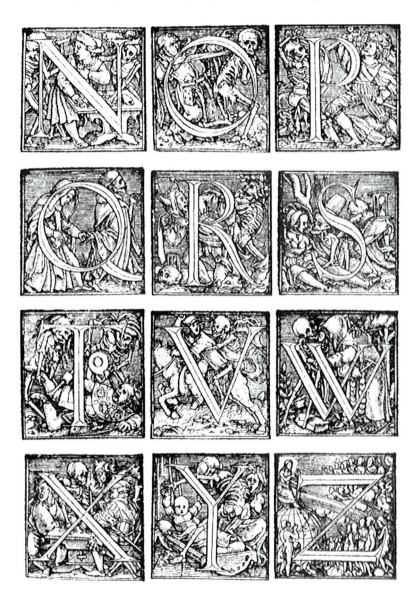

When Holbein created his *Alphabet*, probably only one or two percent of the population within today's linguistic German frontiers were able to read and write, which became just five percent by the end of the sixteenth century.[1] For those who could read, ornamental initials opened up an exciting world: when introducing words they enabled the reader to understand them correctly in the context of complex works. After all, this is what historiated initials had done in medieval manuscripts, and printed initials took over that function. However, Hans Holbein's initials are decorated with macabre motifs that emit their own moral messages, irrespective of the character of the original text that they are supposed to illuminate. Thus these initials become also interesting for people who are unable to read.

Yet this poses us with a seeming paradox, because explanatory texts play a central role in the medieval *Danse Macabre* and our understanding of the *Danse*: they might even be seen as crucial. The Germanist scholar Hartmut Freytag formulated it thus:

> Der Totentanz setzt das Miteinander von Bild und Text voraus [... und] wird bestimmt durch den Dialog des Sterbenden mit dem Tod; [...] der Totentanz versteht sich als Lehrdichtung, die das Publikum zu Buße und gottgefälligem Leben mahnt und ihm intensiv in Erinnerung ruft, dass der Tod jeden unversehens ergreifen und dem Richter zuführen kann.[2]

> *(The* Danse Macabre *requires the cooperation of image and text [... and] is determined by the dialogue between the dying and Death; [...] the* Danse Macabre *defines itself as didactic poetry that admonishes the public to repent and live devoutly and also offers a vivid reminder that Death can come unexpectedly to seize them and lead them before the ultimate judge.)*

Naturally such a bimedial interrelation between image and text is seldom found in decorated initials. After all, 'text' here means the added captions and rubrics that explain, consolidate or expand the meanings of the images. If one were to adopt Freytag's definition it would become necessary that forms of expression other than text should replace the missing didactic messages of the captions and rubrics. The imagery of the initials would then not only serve as illustrations but have the additional purpose of a dialogue that, in Freytag's words, admonishes the audience 'zu Buße und gottgefälligem Leben' (*to repent and live devoutly*) but also to offer a vivid reminder that Death may seize them when they least expect it and haul them before God.

---

[1] Marion Janzin and Joachim Güntner, *Das Buch vom Buch: 5000 Jahre Buchgeschichte* (Hannover: Schlüter, 3rd edn 2007), 160.
[2] Hartmut Freytag (ed.), *Der Totentanz der Marienkirche in Lübeck und der Nikolaikirche in Reval (Tallinn). Edition, Kommentar, Interpretation, Rezeption*, Niederdeutsche Studien, 39 (Cologne/Weimar/Vienna: Böhlau, 1993), 14-15.

However, the combination of 'image and text' does not just offer a warning about man's mortality in general. They also characterise the dying and judge their lives up to the moment of death. Holbein makes this clear through the different attributes that typify the various social representatives in the *Danse*. These may be unambiguous at first sight, but detailed study reveals much more complex layers of meaning.

This essay will debate the use of Holbein's *Danse Macabre* initials, the way they operate, and their 'afterlife'. Are they dependent on the printed texts that they illustrate, or do they emit independent messages unconnected with their context? Can they be referring to the mortality of mankind at large when they are by their very nature printed singly? Do the images represent a form of estates criticism without words, and if so, how is this expressed? For a comparison with Holbein's *Alphabet*, this essay will conclude with a brief account of the ornamental letters by the Cologne publisher Johann Quentel.

The relationship between text and image in Holbein's *Alphabet of Death*

After 1520, when the Reformation had begun to make its effects felt in his home town of Basel, Holbein became preoccupied with the theme of death in several series of graphic work.[3] Around 1523 he designed the *Alphabet of Death*, which includes twenty-four letters.[4] At around the same time he

---

[3] Hans Reinhardt, 'Holbein Hans d. J.', in Historische Kommission bei der Bayerischen Akademie der Wissenschaften (eds), *Neue Deutsche Biographie*, 9 (Berlin: Dunker, 1972), 515-20.

[4] Letters J and U are missing because at that time of letterpress printing they were replaced by I and V. Francis Douce, *The Dance of Death. Exhibited in Elegant Engravings on Wood with a Dissertation on the Several Representations of that Subject but more Particularly on those Ascribed to Macabre and Hans Holbein* (London: William Pickering, 1833), 213-20; Frank Petersmann, *Kirchen- und Sozialkritik in den Bildern des Todes von Hans Holbein d. J.* (Bielefeld: Ludwig Bechauf, 1983), 133-49; Konrad Hoffmann, 'Holbeins "Todesbilder". Laienfrömmigkeit im Todesbild der Vor- und Frühreformation', in Klaus Schneider (ed.), *Laienfrömmigkeit im späten Mittelalter. Formen, Funktionen, politisch-soziale Zusammenhänge* (Munich: Oldenbourg, 1992), 263-82; Peter Parshall, 'Hans Holbein's Pictures of Death', in Mark Roskill and John Oliver Hand (eds), *Hans Holbein: Paintings, Prints and Reception* (New Haven/London: Yale University Press, 2001), 83-95; Winfried Schwab OSB, 'Totentanz oder Lebenslust? Überlegungen zum Todesverständnis des 16. Jahrhunderts am Beispiel ausgewählter Todes- und Totentanz-Initialen der Klosterbibliotheken Admont, Einsiedeln und Ottobeuren', in *Studien und Mitteilungen zur Geschichte des*

also created the so-called *Images of Death* series, which was to remain unpublished until 1538, and he drew the design for a Swiss dagger sheath with *Danse Macabre* scenes of which several copies survive.[5] In this latter design Death is shown in different guises as he summons six social representatives divided into two groups of three each. These consist of four male and two female figures: the Emperor, the Female Ruler, the Standard-Bearer, the Aristocratic Lady, the Monk and the Child. Death himself is disguised amongst others as a military drummer wearing a peasant hat.

Holbein's interpretations of the *Danse* are usually regarded as a new Renaissance approach to the *Danse*, yet the artist was evidently influenced by earlier medieval *Danse* imagery. If we compare motifs used in his three graphic examples of the *Danse* with the imagery of the famous painted *Danse Macabre* schemes in Basel and Bern, it soon becomes clear that Holbein was familiar with them and that he derived inspiration from them for his own designs.

The Öffentliche Kunstsammlung in Basel preserves a version of the *Alphabet of Death* that specifically names Hans Lützelburger (d. 1526) as its xylographer. The text reads: 'Hanns Lützel= | burger / form= | schnider ge= | nant Franck'.[6] In addition, there are three pamphlets with explanatory biblical quotations, two in German and one in Latin.[7] These verify that the *Alphabet* was not originally nor exclusively created for use in printed books. The letter N was first used in August 1524 by the Basel publisher Johann Bebel to illustrate the introduction to a Greek edition of the New Testament, *ΤΗΣ ΚΑΙΝΗΣ ΔΙΑΘΗΚΗΣ ΑΠΑΝΤΑ*.[8] Not long after we find selected initials in use at various printing houses, but never the complete *Alphabet*. The letters were often used in combination with biblical, mythical or narrative motifs (*viz.* the *Children's Alphabet* or the *Peasants' Alphabet*).[9]

Benediktinerordens und seiner Zweige, 118 (2007), 203-68.

[5] *Hans Holbein the Younger. The Basel Years 1515-1532*, exhibition catalogue with contributions by Christian Müller, Stephan Kemperdick *et al.* (Munich/Berlin/London/New York: Prestel, 2006), 314-15 (cat. 99).

[6] *Holbein: the Basel Years* (2006), 486-87 (cat. D.25).

[7] Christian Müller (ed.), *Hans Holbein d. J. Die Druckgraphik im Kupferstichkabinett Basel* (Basel: Schwabe, 1997), 325-27 and 326 (illustr.).

[8] VD 16: B 4178. The *Verzeichnis der im deutschen Sprachbereich erschienenen Drucke des 16. Jahrhunderts* (VD 16) includes all titles in German and all printed and published works in the historical German language area during the years 1501–1600. To facilitate internet searches, the special VD 16 number will be given here: see http://www.bsb-muenchen.de/1681.0.html.

[9] Gustav Schneeli and Paul Heitz (eds), *Initialen von Hans Holbein* (Strasbourg:

The *Alphabet* opens with musical corpses in the letter A, which thus corresponds to the *dantz hus* or charnel house scenes with dancing cadavers of other *Danse Macabre* schemes;[10] the final scene is the Last Judgement in the initial Z.[11] These two initials frame twenty-two dying social representatives, comprising eighteen men and four women. They can be subdivided into three groups. In the first group, consisting of the letters B to K, church dignitaries alternate with male and female representatives of the high nobility: the Pope, Emperor, King, Cardinal, Empress, Queen, Bishop, Duke, Count. The second group, ranging from L to Q, comprises members of the clergy and the bourgeoisie, *viz.* the Priest, Physician, Rich Man, Monk, Lansquenet and Nun. The third group, R through to Y, is without any discernible order and shows especially figures on the margins of society: the Jester, Prostitute, Drunkard, Knight, Hermit, Gambler and the Child. Seven are religious characters – six men and one woman. Death himself – or his representatives – appears dressed up as an old woman, a peasant, an acolyte, and again as a monk, but always accompanying representatives from the higher social ranks.[12]

Several authors have pointed out possible similarities between the initials and the motifs they illustrate. The first of these was Eustache-Hyacinthe Langlois in 1852 who published, alongside some single initials from Hans Holbein's *Alphabet of Death*, the letter L by a Cologne publisher showing the Pope and the Emperor playing cards, and also the letter S by an unknown artist.[13] The L could stand for 'ludus' (*play*) and the S for 'sceletus'. In 1856 Anatole de Montaiglon published three editions of Holbein's *Alphabet* in Paris with commentaries in English, French and Italian. Regarding the initials M to Z he observed in the English commentary 'that each letter is the beginning of the Latin name of the character represented'.[14] Frank Petersmann in 1983 devoted a whole chapter of his PhD thesis on Holbein's *Images of Death* to the *Alphabet of*

Heitz, 1900).

[10] See the essay by Susanne Warda in this volume, esp. fig. 25.

[11] Petersmann (1983), 135-36.

[12] Winfried Schwab, '"Der anfang der sünd ist worden von eynem wyb". Zu den Todesdarstellungen Hans Holbeins', in Karen Ellwanger, Heidi Helmhold, Traute Helmers and Barbara Schrödl (eds), *Totenkleidung. Zur Konstruktion von Tod und Geschlecht in der materiellen und visuellen Kultur* (Bielefeld: transcript, 2010), 283-302.

[13] Eustache-Hyacinthe Langlois, *Essai Historique, Philosophique et Pittoresque sur les Danses des Morts*, vol. 2 (Rouen: Lebrument, 1852), 38-45.

[14] Anatole de Montaiglon, *The Celebrated Hans Holbein's Alphabet of Death* (Paris: Edwin Tross, 1856), preface.

Death. He related several initials to a combination of German and Latin terms, albeit without taking Montaiglon's ideas into consideration. As a result, in Petersmann's reading B stands for 'Bapst' (*Pope*), C stands for 'Caesar' (*Emperor*) and M stands for 'Medicus' (*Physician*).[15]

All these attempts to establish a connection between initials and visual meanings are based on the assumption that it was possible for the artist to combine these freely. However, the order of letters is naturally predetermined, just as the order of social representatives in the *Danse Macabre* is subject to strict hierarchical rules. Basically there are usually but few possible variations, *e.g.* the juxtaposition or separation of clerical and lay figures or of male and female characters. Within any one group the hierarchy had to be strictly adhered to. Moreover, the combination of Latin and German descriptors as proposed by Petersmann would hardly have been acceptable in humanist thinking. Therefore, any attempt to find a logical connection between image and letter in the *Alphabet of Death* is doomed to failure.

The relationship between the *Alphabet of Death* and the *Images of Death*

The *Alphabet of Death* presents a direct and unambiguous confrontation between Death and each of his victims: each letter is thus easy to read visually. This is in contrast to what we find in the *Images of Death* designed by Holbein not long after. In the latter series the living sometimes do not even notice Death because he is often in disguise or invisible from their point of vision, although ironically the beholder can recognise him clearly. The *Images* were first published by the brothers Melchior and Caspar Trechsel in Lyons in 1538 under the title *Les simulachres & HISTORIEES FACES DE LA MORT*.[16] It is possible that Hans Holbein received the commission for the design as early as the summer of 1524 soon after completing the *Alphabet of Death*.

---

[15] Petersmann (1983), 133-49, at 137.

[16] The title page reads: Les simulachres & HISTORIEES FACES DE LA MORT, AVTANT ELE gammet pourtraictes, que artificiellement imaginées. A LYON, Soubz l'escu de COLOIGNE. M. D. XXXVIII. See the facsimile edition Hans Holbein d. J., *Totentanz* (Wiesbaden: Fourier, 2003). The most widely available English edition is Werner L. Gundersheimer, *The Dance of Death by Hans Holbein the Younger: a Complete Facsimile of the Original 1538 edition of* Les simulachres & historiees faces de la mort (New York: Dover Publications, 1971). See also *Holbein: the Basel Years* (2006), 117-23, 471-77; Petersmann (1983).

The *Images* cycle opens with four scenes from the history of creation, *viz.* the Creation of Man, the life of our first ancestors in Paradise, the Expulsion from Paradise, and Adam and Eve's life of toil on earth. These are followed by the traditional charnel house scene that we find in other *Danse Macabre* schemes, and then the actual Images of Death. The cycle finishes with the Last Judgement and the emblem of Death.

Overall Holbein introduces thirty-four representatives, *viz.* twenty-six male and eight female figures, of whom eight men and two women represent the clergy. The cycle comprises the Pope, Emperor, King, Cardinal, Empress, Queen, Bishop, Duke, Abbot, Abbess, Nobleman, Canon, Judge, Lawyer, Councillor, Preacher, Priest, Monk, Nun, Old Woman, Physician, Astrologer, Rich Man, Merchant, Sailor, Knight, Count, Old Man, Countess, Noblewoman, Duchess, Peddler, Peasant and Child. In addition, Death himself appears disguised as a cardinal, old woman, fool, abbot, priest, acolyte, knight and peasant – sometimes more than once.[17]

Holbein's *Images of Death* contain no scenes of mourning, funerals, or figures of the bereft. Instead they focus on the moment of dying itself while at the same time characterising the social representatives. They illustrate the life-threatening hostility between people and convey social and moral criticism.

Passages from the Bible accompany the depictions of the dying in the *Images of Death* and in the three pamphlets of the *Alphabet of Death*. The choice of cited texts match each other in some parts of both cycles, but in other places Holbein varies them critically or satirically. The same texts were used for the Fool in the *Alphabet* and the Abbot in the *Images of Death*, or in the *Alphabet* for the Preacher and the Drunkard. The charnel house scene with the dancing corpses, the Emperor, Cardinal, Duke, Count, Physician, Rich Man, Nun and Drunkard are more or less related in their compositional details. The Prostitute is missing in the *Images of Death* while the Fool originally only appears as Death disguised in the encounter with the Queen.

Levels of meaning within the *Danse Macabre* initials

Holbein's initials do not appear to show any explanatory, deeper or wider sense of a 'blending of image and text' within the printed book. However, the missing message of the captions and rubrics could have been formulated indirectly, *viz.* in the depictions of the motifs themselves. As early as 1849 Adolf Ellissen discussed whether it was possible that the

---

[17] Schwab (2010), 288.

Alphabet of Death was created especially for a book with macabre content. He suspected that Holbein's initials were not intended to serve as common book decorations, but that the artist really wanted them to enhance a special text with a related context. Ellissen furthermore sought – in vain – to reconstruct this presumed text that was either lost without trace or that more probably never came to fruition for reasons unknown.[18] No such text has yet been discovered for either Holbein's own *Alphabet of Death* or for *Danse Macabre* initials by other artists.

Introductory initials might also have been matched to the text that followed in each case.[19] This would have given them a solely illustrative character. Since macabre texts made up only a comparatively small part of book production, despite their popularity, the initials would have rarely found a use. Economically speaking, it would thus not have made much sense for a publisher to acquire these initials. Approximately fifty sixteenth-century texts that include Holbein's initials were analysed for this article, but not a single one shows such any such connection.

However, the decorative initials would surely have had an associative effect on the beholder. On the one hand, they offered general reminders of well-known *Danse Macabre* schemes that the reader could have been familiar with, *e.g.* those in Paris, London and Lübeck. On the other hand, they also refer to specific macabre depictions and their special textual messages. Actually Holbein repeatedly adapted specific scenes from the graphic *Danses Macabre* schemes of the Heidelberg Blockbook of *c.*1458 and the expanded 1486 *Grande Danse Macabre* edition by Guy Marchant, as well as from the monumental *Danse Macabre* murals in Basel and Bern.

Nonetheless, such an associative confrontation with the theme, *i.e.* an examination of the specific textual contents of the monumental *Danse* schemes – was possible only for inhabitants or visitors of the two Swiss cities. To those unfamiliar with the locale the connections between these schemes and Holbein's interpretations was simply lost. An illustrated edition of the Basel *Danse* appeared only in 1621.[20] Particular similarities

[18] Adolf Ellissen (ed.), *Hans Holbein's Initial-Buchstaben mit dem Todtentanz* (Göttingen: Dieterich, 1849), 10.

[19] Christian Kiening, *Das andere Selbst. Figuren des Todes an der Schwelle zur Neuzeit* (Munich: Wilhelm Fink, 2003), 239.

[20] Johannes Jacob Merian, *Todtentantz, wie derselbe in der weitberuembten Statt Basel als ein Spiegel menschlicher Beschaffenheit gantz kuenstlich mit lebendigen Farben gemahlet, nicht ohne nützliche Verwunderung zu sehen ist* (Basel: Merian, 1621); Franz Egger, *Basler Totentanz* (Basel: Buchverlag Basler Zeitung, 1990); Zentralinstitut und Museum für Sepulkralkultur (eds), *Tanz der Toten – Todestanz.*

to the Basel cycle can be observed, for example, in the musical corpses of the letter A and the rich man of the initial N, while the stooping Death figure with the hourglass in the letter S and the physician in M are reminiscent of similar figures in the Bern *Danse*.[21] It was likewise possible for owners of the Heidelberg Blockbook or Guy Marchant's *Grande Danse Macabre* to recognise particular motifs; for example, the posture of the nuns in the Blockbook and in the letter Q are very alike,[22] and the same applies to the dress and posture of the physicians in the *Grande Danse Macabre* and the letter M of the *Alphabet of Death*.[23] Yet if we consider the often very small editions of books in this period, then we realise that the circle of recipients remains small.

Since the first two variants of a text-image relationship must be ruled out and the third has so far been found only in a few examples, we must next address the question of whether the motifs themselves assume not only an illustrative but also a dialogic purpose. In that case they would have had to use, on the one hand, non-verbal ways of reminding the public of the need for penance and a devout life, and of offering stark warnings that Death may seize anyone unexpectedly and lead them before the ultimate judge.[24] On the other hand, they would have had to characterise the dying and to describe and evaluate their former lives. Select examples will show how Holbein solved this problem.

Holbein and the characteristic attributes of social rank

Holbein uses a variety of ways to present the eighteen male and four female characters that make up his *Alphabet of Death*. On the one hand, added attributes denote their erstwhile social rank while, on the other, they often characterise the behaviour of the doomed in their lifetime. Moreover, several corpse figures appear, some of them in disguise. They often act in a surprisingly brutal manner, as if they want to punish the dying for their

---

Der monumentale Totentanz im deutschsprachigen Raum, catalogue to the exhibition in the Museum für Sepulkralkultur Kassel, (Dettelbach: J.H. Röll, 1998), 93-96.

[21] Alexander Goette, *Holbeins Totentanz und seine Vorbilder* (1897, repr. Hamburg: Severus Verlag, 2010), 183-84, 186-87, 190-91.

[22] Gert Kaiser, *Der tanzende Tod. Mittelalterliche Totentänze* (Frankfurt/Main: Insel, 1983), 318.

[23] Goette (1897), 186, 190-91; Kaiser (1983), 96; Guyot Marchant, *La grande Danse Macabre des Hommes et des Femmes* (Troyes: Jacques Oudot, 2nd edn, 1486; repr. Paris: Phénix Éditions, 2000).

[24] Freytag (1993), 14-15.

way of life already instead of leaving their fate to God's judgement. Signs of compassion or mercy are virtually absent. Typical attributes occasionally assign the dead themselves to a particular social rank.

According to Christian belief, vanity is one of the Seven Deadly Sins which lead to eternal punishment in Hell. This vice is blatantly demonstrated by the Queen whose necklace is grabbed by a corpse figure in the initial G; the letter itself frames the Queen, thereby separating her from her dead opponent. Jewellery as a symbol of luxury is also used by Holbein in his *Images of Death* where Death adorns the neck of the Countess not with a necklace, but with a chain made of bones.[25] The artist thus combines social criticism with the iconography of death, summarising cause and effect.

Avarice is another of the Seven Deadly Sins illustrated by Holbein. The two cadavers in the letter N of the Rich Man engage in activities that can only be described as theatrically criminal: while one of them diverts the victim by seizing his fur-trimmed cap, the other takes the coins from the table unnoticed.[26] For the first time Holbein chooses not to criticise a representative of a particular social rank in his *Alphabet of Death*, but a distinctly human trait. This image can be interpreted in different ways: neither can wealth protect one from death nor can possessions be defended against death. Everything must be left behind in this world. Yet another initial has possession and power as its theme. The fleeing Cardinal in the letter E is held back by a corpse holding a crutch, which is a symbol of poverty.[27] The crutch is therefore in stark contrast with the status and trappings of the Cardinal. Hans Holbein uses the crutch as a symbol once again with the Hermit in the letter W.

As one might expect, lust and excess play an important role in Holbein's work because they make the most striking images. In the initial R the Fool desperately tries to escape as he struggles in vain against the cadaver on his right.[28] The Fool wears the traditional fool's cap with bells

---

[25] Holbein, *Totentanz* (2003), 112, fig. 113.

[26] VD 16: B 4178, P 3758. Petersmann (1983), 247. Sophie Oosterwijk, 'Money, Morality, Mortality: the Migration of the *Danse Macabre* from Murals to Misericords', in Peregrine Horden (ed.), *Freedom of Movement in the Middle Ages* (2003 Harlaxton Symposium Proceedings), Harlaxton Medieval Studies, 15 (Donington: Shaun Tyas, 2007), 37-56.

[27] VD 16: B 2575, P 3758. Petersmann (1983), 183-84, 196-97.

[28] VD 16: P 3758. Francis Douce, *Illustrations of Shakspeare and of ancient manners with dissertations on the clowns and fools of Shakspeare; on the collection of popular tales entitled Gesta Romanorum; and on the English Morris Dance* (London: Longman/Hurst a. o., 1807). Stefanie Knöll, cat. no. 22, in Stefanie Knöll (ed.), *Narren – Masken – Karneval. Meisterwerke von Dürer bis Kubin aus der Düsseldorfer Graphiksammlung "Mensch und Tod"* (Regensburg:

and in his right hand he holds his bauble, the so-called *Narrenwurst*. Moreover, his genitals are clearly discernible, indicating licentiousness and immorality. On the left in the foreground lies a skull with an hourglass. Death's own head is decorated with a wreath of foliage while his legs are covered in high boots. The corresponding quotation in the pamphlets expresses very clearly the intention of the artist: 'He shall die, because he hath not received instruction, and in the multitude of his folly he shall be deceived' (Prov. 5:23). These words relate to the adulterer who gets involved with another woman.[29] In the beginning this woman is described as beautiful and alluring, but it soon becomes clear that

> Her feet go down into death, and her steps go in as far as hell. They walk not by the path of life, her steps are wandering, and unaccountable. Now therefore, my son, hear me, and depart not from the words of my mouth. Remove thy way far from her, and come not nigh the doors of her house. Give not thy honour to strangers, and thy years to the cruel. Lest strangers be filled with thy strength, and thy labours be in another man's house, And thou mourn it the last, when thou shalt have spent thy flesh and thy body, and say: Why have I hated instruction, and my heart consented not to reproof. (Prov. 5:5-12)

The initial S likewise emits a very clear moral message.[30] It shows a Prostitute sitting in front of a dry tree with her skirt pulled up, while the lower curve of the S phallically points at her abdomen. A cadaver on her left grasps her between the legs with its one hand while inserting its other hand into her cleavage. It wears a tall hat while worms or serpents wriggle out of its mouth. On the far right is another corpse figure, seemingly hunchbacked and carrying an hourglass on its back. Holbein criticises immorality and ironically reinterprets a key motif: the hourglass changes from a professional symbol – for the Prostitute time literally means money – into a sign of death.[31]

Schnell & Steiner, 2009), 126-128. Reinhold Hammerstein, *Tanz und Musik des Todes. Die mittelalterlichen Totentänze und ihr Nachleben* (Bern/Munich: Francke, 1980), 137.

[29] Compare the commandments 'Thou shalt not commit adultery' (Ex. 20:14) und 'Thou shalt not covet thy neighbour's house: neither shalt thou desire his wife, nor his servant, nor his handmaid, nor his ox, nor his ass, nor any thing that is his' (Ex. 20:17).

[30] VD 16: A 2843, P 3758. Goette (1897), 187, 190.

[31] Hoffmann (1992), 265, 267.

Excess is again starkly criticised in the letter T.[32] This time it is the Drunkard who is stumbling to the floor while holding probably a flute, perhaps as a further sign of revelry or of status. He looks in horror at a female cadaver who has taken hold of his lower right leg as if she wants to take off his shoe. A second cadaver forcefeeds him a lethal drink, thereby denouncing dissipation and licentiousness.

Naturally the fear of death affects nearly every representative of the different classes. This is especially evident with the Duke in the initial I. An old female corpse stands behind the fleeing Duke and holds him tight; her hood with its crimped edge forms an almost frivolous contrast to her flaccid breasts.[33] Almost hidden behind the Duke on the left are a coffin and bier, while a plant sprouting beside his head serves as a symbol of life. Petersmann interprets this picture as typified human behaviour when faced with mortal danger, *viz.* an anxious plea for one's own life.[34] The female corpse would thus caricature the Duke's 'effeminate' behaviour in this scene.

The Monk in the initial O also attempts to fight the ending of his life as a cadaver pulls him by his scapular towards the right edge of the woodcut. This is the only corpse in the whole *Alphabet of Death* to look straight at the reader, thereby involving him in the scene. It seems all the more questionable that it is a member of the clergy who tries to flee; after all, the religious life should have given a Monk ample opportunity to prepare himself for death. The Rule of St Benedict even counted such preparations among the instruments of religious art ('Quae sunt instrumenta bonorum operum') and he urged his followers to 'be daily aware of the unpredictable death' ('Mortem cottidie ante oculos suspectam habere').[35]

Only two characters among the living in the *Alphabet* appear reconciled to their fate in that they offer no resistance: the Nun and the Hermit. However, it is unclear whether the Nun in the initial Q understands her impending doom or whether she imagines herself to be seeing a real monk instead of Death in disguise. Death takes her by the hand and at first glance she appears to be following him humbly.[36] Yet there are details that change our initial reading of the scene. The two hold

---

[32] VD 16: P 3758. Goette (1897), 189-90; Schwab (2007), 236; Schwab (2010), 301-02.

[33] VD 16: P 3758; Goette (1897), 185; Schwab (2010), 289-90.

[34] Petersmann (1983), 144.

[35] RB 4,47, quoted from Salzburger Äbtekonferenz (eds), *Die Benediktusregel* (Beuron: Beuroner Kunstverlag, 2006), 103.

[36] VD 16: P 3758; Prov 14: 12. Hoffmann (1992), 280; Schwab (2007), 233.

hands like lovers, with her seizing his right hand with her left, which suggests a juxtaposition. The Hermit in the letter W, who is bent down with age, is led by Death out of his cell and into the open air. The cadaver almost appears to be showing tenderness as it places its arm around the Hermit's shoulder. With his crutch as the traditional symbol of poverty – used to satirical effect in the image of the Cardinal, as we have seen – the Hermit follows meekly in order to find redemption and rest.

In the initial K Death assumes a socio-critical character. With his scythe and with his leg pushed out, he topples the Count backwards.[37] The corpse wears the typical hat of a peasant, thereby alluding to contemporary debates between the nobility and the serfs at a time of peasant revolts. It is worth noting that the Peasant does not appear in his own right in Holbein's *Alphabet*, but that Death takes on this role. This is unusual because the Peasant is a stock character of the *Danse Macabre*.[38] For the early modern understanding of death it is significant that a change took place in the assessment of death in this period. Death became an event that lay within man's range of actual and even physical experience. Incidentally, one of the corpse figures in the initial D of the kneeling King wears a similar high peasant hat. Obviously there is a reference to the peasant revolts as well. Both pictures explain the abuse of power as well as the oppression of and discrimination against the lower social classes.

Devils and demons in the *Alphabet of Death*

Three of the twenty-four initials in Holbein's *Alphabet of Death* stand out by showing devils or mythical creatures. These demons can perhaps be interpreted according to St Augustine as symbols of spiritual or mental death.[39] A distinction between this and physical death has consequences for the way of dealing with the process of dying. The end of life can no longer be seen simply as a transition into another form of existence. It is rather the moment that sees a person doomed to either eternal bliss or to damnation. The Last Judgement will ultimately assess the way one has

---

[37] VD 16: B 2575. Petersmann (1983), 138-139, 253-62; Goette (1897), 185.

[38] Brigitte Schulte, *Die deutschsprachigen spätmittelalterlichen Totentänze. Unter besonderer Berücksichtigung der Inkunabel "Des dodes dantz". Lübeck 1489*, Niederdeutsche Studien, 36 (Cologne/Vienna: Böhlau, 1990), 90-91, 97. Schulte generally describes the Peasant very positively because he provides for society and he represents the typical working man. (Gen. 3:17-19).

[39] St Augustine, *City of God* (London: Penguin, 2003), 510-12. Irmgard Wilhelm-Schaffer, *Gottes Beamter und Spielmann des Teufels. Der Tod in Spätmittelalter und Früher Neuzeit* (Cologne/Weimar/Vienna: Böhlau, 1999), 42.

lived one's life and, where applicable, one's repentance at the moment of death.

A key example is the initial B. One cadaver pulls the reluctant Pope by his cape towards the left, while a second pounces on the pontiff from behind and tries to snatch his tiara – a symbol of his power. The Pope appears fat and bloated, which is indicative of a self-indulgent lifestyle and the Deadly Sin of gluttony. Lying underneath the Pope and clinging to his neck is a devil with a horned head like a goat. This initial is often regarded as denoting religious controversy. For example, Petersmann observes that Holbein's addition of a devil, which serves to characterise the Pope as the Antichrist, could only have been understood in 1523 as indicating support for the Reformation.[40] However, Holbein's religious affiliation was still unclear several years later. On 18 June 1530 all citizens of Basel who had apparently adopted a 'wait and see' policy or even a critical or negative stance towards the new doctrine, were ordered to submit themselves to a so-called Christian scrutiny (*Christliche Musterung*) by the Reformed city council of Basel. Holbein received a summons but requested more time to study the new doctrine in greater detail.[41] Incidentally the demon can also be generally understood as a tempter from whom not even the Pope is safe. Yet such anti-papal imagery was nothing new: the Pope can occasionally be found among the damned in earlier medieval art. In the *Danse Macabre* mural of *c.*1500 in Metnitz (Carinthia) he is the first to be led by Death into Hell where several devils are waiting to receive him.[42]

The second example is the initial M with the Physician, wearing the dress that pertains to his status, who is standing before an open book on a lectern.[43] In his right hand he holds a urine glass – the traditional attribute

---

[40] Petersmann (1983), 139-40; Schwab (2007), 223.

[41] Emil Dürr and Paul Roth (eds), *Aktensammlung zur Geschichte der Baselr Reformation in den Jahren 1519 bis Anfang 1534. Im Auftrage der historischen und antiquarischen Gesellschaft zu Basel*, vol. 4 (Basel: Verlag der Historischen und Antiquarischen Gesellschaft, 1941), 492; Hans Reinhardt, 'Einige Bemerkungen zum graphischen Werk Hans Holbeins des Jüngeren', *Zeitschrift für Schweizerische Archäologie und Kunstgeschichte*, 34 (1977), 229-60, at 242.

[42] *Tanz der Toten* (1998), 105-08.

[43] VD 16: B 2575, P 3758. Werner Block, *Der Arzt und der Tod in Bildern aus sechs Jahrhunderten* (Stuttgart 1966), 49-51; Daniel Schäfer, '"Her artzt thut euch selber rat." Das Erkennen des Todes in der spätmittelalterlichen Medizin', in Renate Hausner and Winfried Schwab OSB (ed.), *Den Tod tanzen? Tagungsband des Totentanzkongresses Stift Admont 2001* (Im Kontext 19) (Anif/Salzburg: Mueller-Speiser, 2002), 269-90, 273; Petersmann (1983), 140-43; Schulte (1990), 78, 97; Holbein, *Totentanz* (2003), 97; Goette (1897), 186, 190-91. For the

of the medieval physician – and he is studying it by holding it up against the light of a candle, pointing at it with his left index finger. Yet the urine sample is actually being proffered by Death looming behind him. The Physician, who is responsible for diagnosing and combatting illness, fails to recognise that he is about to become a victim himself, unaware of the cadaver peering over his shoulder. Meanwhile a mythical creature, hardly discernible on their right, is urinating into another glass. Without knowing the origin of the urine sample, he examines it and searches for signs of death – the very fate that he himself is about to experience.[44] The open book is another ironic symbol hinting at the Physician's ignorance.

The initial X is the third example in showing once again a devil in league with Death, both of them threatening a Lansquenet and a Gambler seated at a table.[45] While the latter argue about their winnings, the cadaver behind them is already reaching over to grab their money. Moreover, Death and the demon together blow out the candle standing on the players' table, which symbolises their vital force.

The Cologne publisher Johann Quentel: a comparison

Holbein used attributes, among other things, to characterise the living in the *Danse* and to illustrate their vices. These symbols partly replace the explanatory texts of the bimedial *Danse Macabre* schemes and thereby transmit the same warnings. This use of attributes is in marked contrast to the initials designed by the Cologne publisher Johann Quentel (d. 1551), which describe the conduct of the dying in scenic backgrounds full of action.[46]

From 1549, first Quentel and later on his heirs printed initials with macabre imagery, each measuring 38 x 38 mm, of which eleven have so far been identified. It is not known whether there was ever a complete alphabet. Some of these eleven known initials illustrate class representatives, while others describe behaviour. The scenes show the Merchant (A), Dice Players (E), three elegantly dressed people (two women and a man), (F), a Nobleman on a horse (G), the Pope (H), a Nobleman and Noblewoman (I), the Pope and the King playing cards (L), a robbery (M), the Knight (N), a hunting scene (O) and the Cardinal (T).

---

motif of the physician in the Danse Macabre tradition, see Aldred Scott Warthin, *The Physician of the Dance of Death* (1931, repr. New York: Arno Press, 1977).

[44] Petersmann (1983), 141.

[45] Petersmann (1983), 143-44.

[46] VD 16: B 4735, B 7361, C 5644, H 3967, K 1314, N 216, S 10254, ZV 4600. Schwab (2007), 249-60.

In Quentel's initials it is the call for responsible and moral behaviour
that comes first, while the social hierarchy loses its former importance, as
is indicated by the relinquishing of the social order. The Pope thus appears
after the merchants and the gamblers, while in the initial L the Pope and
the King are shown sharing a game of cards. Fringe groups of society are
not considered and in some cases it is impossible to identify a particular
social class. However, nature has become more important, especially the
contrast between flourishing growth and unexpected death. Animals are
introduced as carriers of meaning, whereas traditional iconographic symbols
such as the hourglass, scythe and dart occur only rarely. Moreover, Death
approaches his victims usually with a merry smile, but not malicious,
gloating or cruel as in Holbein's initials.

Nature takes up a lot of space as scenery in Quentel's initials. Eight of
the images are set in a landscape that has been rendered in great detail,
with trees and shrubs always blooming magnificently. For the first time
Quentel shows animals: horses as well as dogs. Their usually energetic
movements heighten the dynamic of each scene in contrast to the
apparently calm and composed bearing of the cadavers. Yet at the same
time the animals symbolise negative qualities of the social representatives.
Horses thus demonstrate class consciousness, arrogance and pride in
Quentel's woodcuts.

The association of horses with the sin of pride is demonstrated most
potently by the Pope riding a white horse in the initial H (Fig. 102). He
seems to be giving a blessing with his right hand, but this image of papal
status is undermined by the introduction of a cadaver who leads his steed
by the reins. Floating above the scene is a curious white cloud that may
actually indicate damage to the block. It is also likely that a demon was
omitted from the original design. Yet even without such a demon, the Pope
on his grand horse is in stark contrast to Christ who humbly entered
Jerusalem on a borrowed donkey (Mark 11:1-11; Luke 19:29-38; John
12:12-16). By association contemporary readers would also have been
reminded of the four apocalyptic horsemen in the Book of Revelation
(Rev. 6:1-8) or, if they were well versed in the bible, of the words of the
prophet Amos:

> And flight shall perish from the swift, and the valiant shall not possess his
> strength, neither shall the strong save his life. And he that holdeth the bow
> shall not stand, and the swift of foot shall not escape, neither shall the rider
> of the horse save his life. (Amos 2:14-15).

Fig. 102. Johann Quentel, The Pope
(H), woodcut, Cologne, *c.*1550.

Fig. 103. Johann Quentel, The Knight
(N), woodcut, Cologne, *c.*1550.

Quentel's initial N likewise illustrates status-conscious pride, this time
personified in the Knight riding past woodland in full armour, with opened
visor and carrying a lance (Fig. 103). On the left hand a cadaver is walking
along, shouldering a scythe, while on the right we see an old man with a
spike. Perhaps the scythe should be understood sociocritically as a peasant
symbol, alluding to the debates between the nobility and the serfs in the
way that Holbein characterises his figure of the Count.

On the other hand, dogs symbolise idleness. In Quentel's initial O a
Hunter is seen riding through the forest (Fig. 104). His armed companion
is leading two dogs on a leash, while a third dog is jumping freely about.
Walking in front of this group is a grinning cadaver. The Hunter's horse
appears to be shying and could be about to throw off its rider, who would
thus become the victim of his own passion for hunting. Holbein had earlier
used the dog as a status symbol for the Countess in his design for a *Danse
Macabre* sheath.[47]

---

[47] Schwab (2010), 300.

Fig. 104. Johann Quentel, Hunting Scene (O), woodcut, Cologne, *c.*1550.

Fig. 105. Johann Quentel, The Pope and the King Playing Cards (L), woodcut, Cologne, *c.*1550.

Fig. 106. Johann Quentel, Robbery (M), woodcut, Cologne, *c.*1550.

Two of Quentel's initials demonstrate the evil of gambling. In the initial E we see four men enjoying a game of dice together, while Death pushes the table with his left foot and uses both hands to strangle one of the men. Two of the players have pulled a weapon to attack the cadaver. In contrast to most of the other images in this cycle, Death here appears to be exceptionally brutal, as if to emphasise the reprehensible character of the game and to show how easily it can end in a lethal fight. Human passion can thus become a fatal threat to one's fellow humans. However, in the initial L Death is simply watching the card game between the Pope and the King without disrupting it; he merely watches from the sideline on the far right (Fig. 105). It is not known if this unusual motif might allude to a historic event. Like the initial L, the letter M illustrates a match between two figures, albeit here of a more violent kind (Fig. 106). In what is either a robbery or perhaps a war scene, an attacker plunges a sabre in the side of another man whose arm he has grabbed with his right hand. The victim turns his head towards his opponent as Death observes the scene without getting involved.

Fig. 107. Johann Quentel, Three Elegantly Dressed People (F), woodcut, *c.*1550.

Fig. 108. Johann Quentel, Nobleman and Noblewoman (I), woodcut, *c.*1550.

As one would expect, Quentel also denounces the sin of vanity. The initial F depicts three richly dressed figures standing in a landscape (Fig. 107). The young woman realises with dismay that the dancing cadaver with his hourglass is leading her to her death. Although she is in a merry company, at this moment she finds herself alone. A man in the background turns his back on her, as if he cannot bear to witness the scene: perhaps an early example of a repression of death? The young woman's high status cannot save her from death. This is also the fate of the Noblewoman in the initial I, who is being pierced in the side by Death's dart as she tries to defend herself with her right hand (Fig. 108). The Nobleman clasps her hand in vain. Quentel's Death reaches for the Noblewoman's necklace, which is what also happens to the Queen in Holbein's initial G.

Quentel's initials are clearly different from Holbein's in the ways in which they communicate the *Danse Macabre* message. If one takes away the Cardinal's crutch (Fig. 109), the Queen's necklace, or the peasant hat and flail in the scene of the Count's death in Holbein's *Alphabet*, the *memento mori* warning mortality remains, but all aspects of social or class criticism would be missing. If the imaginative reader were to replace the cadavers with living humans Holbein's initials would show only the social order of the Renaissance. However, if one exchanges or deletes the cadavers in Quentel's woodcuts the initials retain their scenic messages: Pope and Knight would still appear arrogant and proud, seated as they are on their high horses. The Hunter on his horse would likewise continue to indulge in idleness, while the victim of the assault in the letter M would still lose his life through a human act of violence.

Fig. 109. Johann Quentel, The Cardinal (T), woodcut, Cologne, *c*.1550.

Conclusion

Danse Macabre initials enjoyed a wide distribution across Europe during the Renaissance. Hans Holbein's *Alphabet of Death* inspired numerous artists to produce their own copies, imitations or independent designs, as did Johann Quentel in Cologne. This essay has shown that the initials transmitted their own messages independently from the texts that they decorated. Consequently no evidence was found to support any close relationship between the illustrated text and the initials.

By association, however, the initials would have reminded contemporaries of other well-known graphic or monumental *Danse Macabre* cycles. Therefore, the initials offer viewers a general warning about human mortality that transcends the fate of each depicted representative of society. Holbein's *Alphabet of Death* and the *Danse Macabre* initials by his followers formulate the same criticism of class and conduct as the bimedial *Danse Macabre*, but without words. Instead of explanatory captions or rubrics it is the symbols or scenic settings that characterise the dying persons in this way, and thus their macabre message manages to reach the illiterate, too.

Acknowledgements

I should like to dedicate this essay to my university teacher, the convent librarian of the Swiss Benedictine Abbey of Maria Einsiedeln, Dr. theol. Dipl. pal. P. Odo Lang OSB. I also owe a special debt of gratitude to Sophie Oosterwijk for translating my text into English, and to both editors for their comments and suggestions.

MIX AND MATCH:
HULDRICH FRÖLICH'S
DANSE MACABRE EDITIONS

STEFANIE KNÖLL

There are three early modern publications of *Danse Macabre* texts and images that are associated with Huldrich Frölich (?-1610), a printer and Poet Laureate born in Plauen and active in Basel from at least 1572.[1] They were published in different printing houses in Basel in the years 1581, 1588 und 1608. German *Danse Macabre* researchers refer to the 1588 and 1608 publications as the 'Bern-Basel-Holbein-mix'[2] – a term which indicates a compilation of images and texts derived from various sources. Not only is the cycle as a whole made up of scenes originating from different sources, but there is even a mixture of motifs within single scenes.

Although Frölich's editions were reproduced many times in the eighteenth century and thus have been widely distributed, historical research has largely ignored them. This may be due to the disdain in which the editions were held in the nineteenth century when they were regarded as barely true to the original. Worse still, they were held to blame for perpetuating the erroneous belief that Hans Holbein had created the *Danse Macabre* at Basel.[3]

---

[1] Rudolf Riggenbach, 'Der Buchdrucker Huldrich Frölich, "Plauensis, jetzt Burger zu Basel"', *Basler Zeitschrift für Geschichte und Altertumskunde* 58/59 (1959), 215-29; Uli Wunderlich, 'Zwischen Kontinuität und Innovation – Totentänze in illustrierten Büchern der Neuzeit', in Hartmut Freytag and Winfried Frey (eds), *'Ihr müsst alle nach meiner Pfeife tanzen'. Totentänze vom 15. bis 20. Jahrhundert aus den Beständen der Herzog August Bibliothek Wolfenbüttel und der Bibliothek Otto Schäfer in Schweinfurt* (Wiesbaden: Harrassowitz, 2000), 137-202, at 163.

[2] Wunderlich (2000), 162-66.

[3] There were two *Danse Macabre* cycles in Basel. Here I shall only be dealing with the older of the two, *viz.* the mural that was created around 1440 on the cemetery wall of the Dominican friary.

To date there is neither a detailed description and analysis of the three original editions nor of the reproductions dating from the eighteenth and nineteenth centuries. Therefore, this paper will deal with the appearance and intention of all three early modern publications. Special attention will be given to the newly invented scenes and the mixing of older motifs.

Frölich's 1581 edition

It was in 1581 that Huldrich Frölich first published his *Lobspruch an die Hochloblich unnd weitberümpte Statt Basel* (Eulogy of the highly laudable and widely famous city of Basel).[4] Embedded in a frame story, the first-person narrator informs the reader about the history and the appearance of the city of Basel by relating a dream in which a satyr prompts him to report about this town. Within this historical account the *Danse Macabre* mural in the Dominican cemetery, which dates from *c.*1440, but was restored in 1568 and 1614-16, forms a separate entity. The satyr asks for a detailed account of the mural because he has often heard the famous *Danse Macabre* verses being praised. The narrator complies and devotes the next seventeen pages to these verses. The lines of the recurring Death figure as well as the answers by the social representatives are given in the correct order, just as they were presented on the cemetery wall in Basel. In fact, Frölich's transcription is considered to be the earliest source for the *Danse Macabre* texts in Basel.[5]

Although the inclusion of Child and Turk may at first seem puzzling, it has long been argued that both were part of the mural between 1568 and 1614, *i.e.* the time when Frölich published his three editions.[6] The

---

[4] The full title reads *Lobspruch An die Hochloblich unnd Weitberümpte Statt Basel Inhaltende mancherley nam[m]haffte unnd fürneme Sachen, so darinn zu sehen: Auch die Ursachen, Warumb gemelter Statt Schlagglocken bey einer Stund andern vorlauffen; hieneben werden auch die Reumen, so am Todtentantz bey jedem Stande verzeichnet, der Ordnug nach ... eingeleibet* (Basel, 1581). For the digital version (Munich: Bayerische Staatsbibliothek, Res/Helv. 923 h), see http://dfg-viewer.de/show/?set%5Bmets%5D=http%3A%2F%2Fmdz10.bib-bvb.de%2F%7Edb%2Fmets%2Fbsb00027530_mets.xml (accessed 9 November 2010).

[5] Riggenbach (1959), 216; Franz Egger, *Basler Totentanz* (Basel: Friedrich Reinhardt, 2009 (1990)), 31.

[6] Egger only mentions the Turk and does not address the text of the Child: see Egger (2009), 31. On the basis of some anonymous gouaches (*c.*1600) and our knowledge of the so-called *Kleinbasler Totentanz*, which was created in the second part of the fifteenth century as a copy of the *Großbasler Totentanz*, Uli Wunderlich was able to show that the *Großbasler Totentanz* originally comprised the figure of

depiction of the Fall of Man, however, was probably added only during Emanuel Bock's restoration work that was carried out in the years 1614 to 1616. While all *Danse Macabre* texts in Frölich's later editions (1588 and 1608) are accompanied by illustrations, the 1581 edition includes images of only two figures, *viz.* the Pope and the Turk. Moreover, Death – a winged Reaper with an hourglass – is a re-used vignette placed next to the simple bust of the living representative. No effort is being made to create a scene in which Death meets a living person. Interestingly, the image of the Turk carries the monogram 'GS'. This already points to the collaboration between Frölich and the artist responsible for the woodcuts, who was to shape the 1588 edition decisively.

Frölich's 1588 edition

The intention and form of the 1588 edition are radically different compared to the 1581 edition. The lengthy title already testifies to this change by making it clear that this new publication is neither a general guide to the sights of Basel nor purely a true reproduction of the Basel *Danse Macabre* in word and image.[7] Instead it speaks of two murals, one at Bern and one at Basel. Frölich's stated intention is the compilation of several important *Danse Macabre* texts. In his eyes such a printed compilation is useful as he has often observed people transcribing the texts from the original. A survey of different texts also makes sense to him as it provides the reader with more and varying exempla which may be

---

the Child. The Turk was probably only included by Kluber in 1568 and replaced the earlier figure of the Mother. Frölich thus documented the state of the mural prior to the restoration by Emanuel Bock (1614-16). See Uli Wunderlich, 'Ein Bild verändert sich. Die Bedeutung der neuentdeckten Gouachen für die Rekonstruktion des Basler Totentanzes', in *Totentanz-Forschungen, 9. internationaler Totentanz-Kongress* (Kassel, 1998), 131-39.

[7] *Zwen Todentäntz Deren der eine zu Bern dem Anderen Ort Hochloblicher Eydtgnoschafft zu Sant Barfüssern: Der Ander aber zu Basel dem Neundten Ort gemelter Eydtgnoschafft auff S. Predigers Kirchhof mit Teutschen Versen, darzu auch die Lateinischen kommen, ordenlich sind verzeichnet ; Ordnung und Innhalt dieses Buchs belangende, wird nach der Lateinischen Vorrede kürtzlich erzelhet; Mit schönen und zu beyden Todentäntzen dienstlichen Figuren, allerley Ständt und Völcker gebreuchliche Kleydung abbildende, gezieret* (Basel, 1588). For the digital version (Munich: Bayerische Staatsbibliothek, 4 Im.mort. 10), see http://dfg-viewer.de/show/?set%5Bmets%5D=http%3A%2F%2Fmdz10.bib-bvb.de%2F%7Edb%2Fmets%2Fbsb00053610_mets.xml (accessed 9 November 2010).

pondered 'even more often and more seriously'.[8] His own role is that of the *Concinnator*, the creator or inventor.

Fig. 110. Death and the Senator, woodcut and text from Huldrich Frölich's 1608 edition. © Herzog August Bibliothek Wolfenbüttel (67 Poet.).

In the 1588 edition each social type is presented on two facing pages that comprise an illustration and three different texts. There are the texts of the monumental *Danse Macabre* cycles at Bern and at Basel (Fig. 110). The latter are supplemented by their Latin translations, which Frölich claims to have produced himself.[9]

---

[8] 'solches nun desto öffter un[d] ernstlicher zu betrachten': see Frölich (1588), unpaginated, p. 12 of the digitalised version.

[9] '[...] hab ich mir unter anderem, nicht allein in der Lateinischen Sprache un[d] Carminibus mich zu exercieren, den Todentantz, wie er zu Basel [...] mit Teutsche[n] Reume[n] verzeichnet, ins Lateinische, doch schlechte Vers, zu tra[n]sferieren fürgenom[m]en [...]': see Frölich (1588), unpaginated, p. 12 of the digitalised version. Massmann has already confuted this claim in 1840 by referring to the earlier publication of these Latin verses in Caspari Laudismanni *Decennalia mundanae peregrinationis* of 1584. See Hans Ferdinand Massmann, *Literatur der Todtentänze. Beytrag zum Jubeljahre der Buchdruckerkunst, aus dem 'Serapeum'*

To allow the tracking of sources for the German verses, Frölich uses a numerical system, which is explained in his German introduction as well as in a special index.[10] Roman numbers are used to indicate texts from the Basel *Danse Macabre*, whereas Arabic numbers ('teutsche Ziffern') refer to the mural at Bern. It is worth noting that the illustrations are almost always accompanied by the Bern texts,[11] while the Basel texts with their translations appear on the opposing page.[12] However, Frölich seems to have made a mistake: the Bern texts are denoted by Roman numbers instead of the announced Arabic numbers.

Roman majuscules refer to 'the added verses',[13] *i.e.* texts accompanying the few figures that are known only from Holbein's *Images of Death* and can neither be found in Basel nor in Bern. Frölich does not give a reason for the inclusion of these texts from a third source, which are likewise presented as two quatrains. Unfortunately, it is unclear where the German texts were derived from. Jobst de Necker's German edition of Holbein's *Images of Death* was published in 1544 and thus prior to the inclusion of the respective scenes. The German translations by Caspar Scheyt, which were published in several editions from 1557 on, do include the scenes. However, the texts consist of a Bible quote and three rhyming couplets instead of two quatrains.[14] The Straub edition (St Gallen, 1581) also does not qualify as a possible source for the German verses, as the figures are accompanied by much longer texts.[15] Perhaps it was the poet Huldrich Frölich himself who composed the German verses for these scenes.

---

besonders abgedruckt (Leipzig: Weigel, 1840), 30, n. 3.

[10] See Frölich (1588), unpaginated, p. 15 of the digitalised version. It is thus not comprehensible why Wunderlich (2000), 163, states that the author has failed to mention the original location of the dialogues.

[11] 'Zu dem sind vast alle Reumen des Bernischen Todtentantzes zu den Figuren gesetzt worden': see Frölich (1588), unpaginated, p. 13 of the digitalised version.

[12] There are only very few illustrations with an Arabic number (19, 37, 53, 55, 63, 65, 69, 71, 77, 83, 87). Almost all of these scenes have no text on the image page.

[13] 'Majuscul: die Carmina so zu beyden Todtäntzen kommen': see *Zwen Todtentäntz* (1588), unpaginated, p. 15 of the digitalised version.

[14] *Todtentanz durch alle Stendt der Menschen, mit d. Arzney der Seelen v. Urban Regius it. Rede Cypriani vom Sterben und Chrysostomi von der Gedult; (u. mit Reimen von Caspar Scheidt)* (s.l., 1557).

[15] *Totentanz durch alle Stendt der Menschen, darin[n]en ihr herkommen und endt, nichtigkeit un[d] sterblichkeit, als in einem spiegel zubeschawen, fürgebildet, un[d] mit schönen Figuren un[d] guten Reimen gezieret, notwendig, auch lustig allermenniglichen zu lesen, hören und wissen* (S. Gallen: Straub, 1581).

Which figures are presented in Frölich's 1588 edition, and how are the characters from the three different *Danse Macabre* cycles that are the textual basis of the publication (Basel, Bern, Holbein) combined? The work starts with the Fall of Man and the Expulsion from Paradise, two scenes which are unknown in the opening of the Basel mural but which call to mind the Bern *Danse* as well as Holbein's *Images*. Next follows the figure of the Pope. The sequence is then based on the Basel cycle and only diverges with the figures of the Nobleman, the Noblewoman and the Piper. The scenes of the Child and the Turk are still included, as they were probably part of the mural until Emanuel Bock's restoration in 1614-16.[16] The Basel *Danse* concludes with the Preacher and the Last Judgement. The first part of the 1588 edition thus adheres more or less to the sequence of the Basel cycle. However, the images are accompanied by the texts from Bern, while the Basel texts are placed on the opposite page.

The Basel figures are followed by those figures from the Bern *Danse* that are not congruent with those in Basel. Here the original sequence of the mural is often rejected. The figures presented are only allowed a single page and are as follows: Patriarch, Teutonic Knight ('Ritter mit dem schwartzen creutz'), Lawyer, Burgher and Artisan (together on one page), Astrologer, Monk, Beguine, Widow, Prostitute, Moses, Charnel house. The remark 'Ende des Bernischen Todentantzes' (end of the Bern *Danse*) is followed by five other characters derived from Holbein's *Images of Death*, *viz.* Canon, Sailor, Gambler, Drunkard, and Robber.

Overall the 1588 edition comprises sixty-one figures, although there are only forty-four independent, self-contained images. All other figures are accompanied by an image repeated from another figure, or by two separate figure-vignettes placed next to each other (cf. Fig. 110). Different woodblock carvers must have been involved with the project for the illustrations do not follow a uniform style. Some are very simple – apparently sometimes even printed from two different blocks[17] – while others show more elaborate scenes. Still only few of the images relate to the Basel *Danse Macabre*. Despite claims to the contrary, no scene is a true copy of the Bern *Danse*, but at best partly inspired by it.[18] Most of the

---

[16] Wunderlich (1998), 138-39.

[17] For example, the Cardinal: see Wunderlich (2000), 164.

[18] Eva Schuster and Mikinosuke Tanabe (eds), *Totentanz vom Spätmittelalter bis zur Gegenwart*, exhibition catalogue (Tokyo: The National Museum of Western Art, 2000), 207, see a connection to Bern in four scenes, whereas such a connection is only recognised in one scene (the Pope) in Ulrich Schulz, *Die Büchersammlung K. und U. Schulz – Die Totentänze. Eine Ausstellung der Badischen Landesbibliothek Karlsruhe* (Karlsruhe: Badische Landesbibliothek,

illustrations copy – always in mirror image[19] – scenes from Hans Holbein's *Images of Death*. Researchers have thus often pointed out that Frölich's editions played a large part in spreading the mistaken belief that Holbein created the Basel *Danse*.

More than two thirds of the illustrations carry the monogram 'GS' and they are usually set in a double frame. The carver used scenes from Holbein's famous edition but adapted them freely, *e.g.* by adding details from the Basel *Danse* or giving them a totally new twist (*e.g.* the Young Man). In the nineteenth century this unknown master was believed to be Georg Scharfenberg,[20] who was said to have copied the paintings by his friend Hans Hug Kluber 'getreu nach dem Originale' (faithfully after the original) in the year 1576: the illustration of the Expulsion from Paradise is dated 1576 alongside the carver's monogram. In the twentieth century the carver was mostly identified as Gregor Sickinger (1558-1631).[21] Stylistically different are those images by the master 'HW', which are set in a single frame and are reminiscent of a hasty sketch.[22] This carver may be credited with the following scenes, among them some relating to Basel: Cook, Pagan, Female Pagan, Abbot, the latter carrying the monogram 'HW' (Fig. 111).

2007), 150 and 212. These authors were probably influenced by the information in Massmann's survey. When Massmann (1840), 30, n. 3, writes 'Pabst, König, Cardinal, schöne Tochter mehr nach dem Berner Gemälde' (*Pope, King, Cardinal, pretty Daughter more after the Bern painting*), this seems to suggest that he saw similarities but also quite a number of differences. Egger (2009), 31-32, apparently assumed that Frölich solely employed Holbein's *Images* as a model: 'Die Illustrationen sind nicht Nachbildungen des Berner oder Basler Totentanzes, sondern Kopien des Meisters GS nach den 'Imagines mortis' (Todesbilder) von Hans Holbein d. J.' (*The illustrations are not reproductions of either the Bern or the Basle Danse, but copies by the Master GS after Holbein's* Images).

[19] This might suggest that the prints served as a direct model.

[20] *Der Todten-Tantz wie derselbe in der weitberühmten Stadt Basel ... zu sehen ist* (Basel: Mähly-Lamy, 1842), 5-6. The author refers to F. Brulliot's *Dictionnaire des monogrammes*, no. 1103. The edition which was published in 1870 by Alexander Danz in Leipzig attributes the woodcuts to the carver Sigismund Gelenius: see *Der Todten-Tantz wie derselbe in der weitberühmten Stadt Basel ... zu sehen ist. Original-Holzschnitte des 16. Jahrhunderts* (Leipzig: Danz [1870]), VIII.

[21] Riggenbach (1959), 221; Egger (2009), 31.

[22] Riggenbach (1959), 226, identifies him as Hans Wannenwetsch.

Fig. 111. Death and the Abbot, woodcut from Huldrich Frölich's 1608 edition, with the monogram of the master 'HW' below the Abbot's right elbow. © Herzog August Bibliothek Wolfenbüttel (67 Poet.).

There is also a particular group of illustrations (Pope, King, Cardinal, Daughter) that is not clearly modelled on one of the three above-mentioned *Danse Macabre* cycles. For example, the image of the Cardinal reminds the viewer of scenes from the Bern mural, but it is nothing like an exact copy. Likewise, there is no obvious model for the Daughter, which Massmann wanted to relate to Bern. The flag and the position of Death's legs might instead suggest that the scene of the King in the Basel *Danse* provided the inspiration.

The carver 'DR', who is frequently mentioned in secondary literature,[23] is not verifiable in the 1588 and 1608 editions. Apparently, he was only active in the eighteenth century for the editions published by Mechel, which will be discussed below.

There is no easy explanation for Frölich's idiosyncratic combination of the three *Danse Macabre* cycles. Although all three – Basel, Bern, Holbein – are obviously closely related, it seems improbable that Frölich set out to disclose these relations.[24] His preface rather suggests that he intended to provide the reader with a compilation of moralising texts. Still, this does not explain why the illustrations were modelled on different sources. Riggenbach assumes that Frölich bought the finished blocks from Gregor Sickinger, with whom he became acquainted in 1579 in connection with the work on Christian Wurstisen's *Basler Chronik* (1580).[25] If this were correct, Sickinger would have cut the images in 1576 – for the Expulsion from Paradise is dated – without an order from Frölich.

Nobody has ever questioned Sickinger's motivation for undertaking this task. Instead, there have been many speculations on Frölich's use of these woodcuts. Riggenbach argued that Frölich was in great distress and felt impelled to save his publication provisionally, 'although he must have been aware of the fact that the woodcuts had nothing to do with the Basel *Danse*'.[26] I have already argued that research so far has been misconceived in its understanding of Frölich's 1588 edition. The 1581 edition with its historical account of the city of Basel and transcription of the Basel *Danse Macabre* texts is one thing, but the aim of the 1588 edition was totally different from simply adorning the Basel texts with the appropriate illustrations; otherwise Frölich would not have combined the images with the Bern texts and put the Basel text and translation on the opposite page, thus combining each image with three texts. In the same way that he

---

[23] Massmann (1840), 30.

[24] 'Erklären lässt sich diese Mischung wie folgt: Huldrich Frölich muss als einer der ersten die nahen Verwandtschaftsverhältnisse zwischen den drei seinem Buch zugrundeliegenden Totentänzen erkannt haben' (*The intermixing may be explained as follows: Huldrich Frölich must have been one of the first persons who recognised the close relationship between the three* Danse Macabre *cycles on which his publication was based*): see Wunderlich (2000), 164.

[25] Riggenbach (1959), 221.

[26] '[...] obschon er sich darüber klar sein musste, daß die Holzschnitte mit dem Predigertotentanz nicht das Geringste zu tun hatten': see Riggenbach (1959), 221.

combines the images with ambiguous texts, the images themselves elude definite allocation.[27]

Uli Wunderlich advances a different opinion, however. She argues that it was simply convenient for Frölich to illustrate the Basel and Bern texts with copies after an easily available edition, *viz.* Holbein's *Images of Death*.[28] In her view only scenes that were not part of Holbein's publication were substituted by other images, *e.g.* two vignettes of a skeleton and a living person which were placed next to each other.[29] However, the images of the Pope, the King and the Cardinal testify to the fact that scenes could take a different appearance even when a model from Holbein was available.

Let us now take a closer look at some of the images: The image of the Pope (Fig. 112) poses a special problem as it is not clearly modelled on either of the three *Danse Macabre* cycles. Most scholars regard the relationship to the Bern *Danse* to be the closest,[30] which is fair enough as both show the Pope being carried on a litter, whereas Holbein's woodcut shows him enthroned. Yet the similarities to Niklaus Manuel's mural in Bern end here, for Fröhlich's Death has not approached the pontiff quite so impertinently to snatch his tiara. Instead several cadavers now carry the sedan, while there are also a number of crosses and halberds which intersect the scene in a striking way. The composition is rather reminiscent of the image of the Pope in Jost Amman's *Ständebuch* (Book of Trades) of 1568, which doubtlessly served as its model.[31] Interestingly Amman's image – which did of course not include a Death figure – was not simply reproduced but actually adapted in a fascinating way. The sedan now rests on the shoulders of clerical dignitaries. Moreover, there is a bishop, a soldier and a cardinal, who are all three clearly recognisable as masked cadavers, thereby reminding the viewer of Holbein's image of the Pope, which clearly served as the model for the figure of Death disguised as a cardinal.

---

[27] It has been stated above that Frölich introduced an elaborate numbering system but appears to have mixed up Arabic and Roman numbers. Was this simply a mistake or might we go so far as to suggest that Frölich deliberately undermined his own numbering system in order to obscure it and create ambiguity?

[28] Wunderlich (2000), 164.

[29] Wunderlich (2000), 164.

[30] Massmann (1840), 30 and 32; Paul Zinsli, *Der Berner Totentanz des Niklaus Manuel*, Berner Heimatbücher, 54/55 (Bern: Haupt, 1953), 44; Riggenbach (1959), 221.

[31] I am grateful to Martin Hagstrøm for this information. Amman himself may have been influenced by the Bern *Danse*.

Fig. 112. Death and the Pope, woodcut from Huldrich Frölich's 1608 edition.
© Herzog August Bibliothek Wolfenbüttel (67 Poet.).

Such a blending of different sources can be observed frequently in Fröhlich's 1588 edition. At first sight, the woodcut of Duke and Duchess appears to be a true copy after Holbein's scene, but Death uses his sticks not on a normal drum but on a skull. It was already in 1832 that Hans Ferdinand Massmann remarked on the absurd nature of this scene, pointing out that the posture of Holbein's Death figure in this woodcut resembles that in the scene of the Hermit in the Basel *Danse*, and noting that the drum was replaced by a skull in Fröhlich's image.[32] However, Massmann failed to observe that the curious replacement of a drum by a skull was also part of the Basel *Danse Macabre*, *viz.* in the image of the Pope.

The scene of the Blind man (Fig. 113), whom Death guides with the help of a stick, also reminds the viewer of the matching scene in Holbein's edition. At the same time, however, Fröhlich's image shows the dog from the Basel *Danse* whose leash is cut by Death. The new illustration shows the Blind man being falsely guided twice: he is cut off from his dog and – holding on to his stick – led astray by Death. The carver has thus mixed metaphors and created a visual pleonasm, *i.e.* an abundance of metaphors within one scene.

Extremely fascinating is also the invention of a new scene for the Young Man (Fig. 114). He is shown playing his lute outside a chapel-like building inside which there appear to be two female figures in front of an altar. The kneeling young woman has turned away from the altar to look in the direction of the young man making music. The lady's distraction from prayer by a lute-playing young man does of course recall Holbein's image of the Nun (Fig. 115), and indeed the figure behind her is the same cadaver snuffing the candle that Holbein included in his woodcut. The scene of the Young Man by Master 'GS' is thus a modification of Holbein's woodcut of the Nun which was achieved by shifting the perspective from the Nun to the lute player.

---

[32] '[...] Fröhlich'sche Nachschnitt (1588) [die Trommel] sinnig in einen Todtenkopf verwandelte'. Massmann in *Hans Holbeins Todtentanz in 53 getreu nach den Holzschnitten lithographierten Blättern* (Munich: Schlotthauer, 1832), 73.

Fig. 113. Death and the Blind Man, woodcut from Huldrich Frölich's 1608 edition.
© Herzog August Bibliothek Wolfenbüttel (67 Poet.).

Fig. 114. Death and the Young Man, woodcut from Huldrich Frölich's 1608 edition. © Herzog August Bibliothek Wolfenbüttel (67 Poet.).

Fig. 115. Death and the Nun, woodcut after Hans Holbein's *Images of Death* (1554, first ed. 1538). © Graphiksammlung 'Mensch und Tod', Heinrich-Heine-University Düsseldorf.

Frölich's 1608 edition[33]

In 1608 Frölich published another book of *Danse Macabre* texts through the Basel printer Sebastian Henricpetri. The title makes clear his intention to give an account of the city of Basel and its *Danse* – an aim not unlike

---

[33] *Der hochloblichen und weitberuempten Statt Basel kurtze... Beschreibung: Inn welcher nicht allein von ihrem Ursprung ..: sondern auch was fürnemlichen da zu sehen ... tractieret, sampt des Todtentantzes, Basels und Berns, Reumen, mit dartzu dienstlichen Figuren gezieret* (Basel: Henricpetri, 1608).

that of the 1581 edition.[34] The title further suggests that the Basel texts are supplemented with those from Bern. However, what happened was that the whole *Danse Macabre* section from the 1588 edition was reproduced, *i.e.* not only the figures from Bern but also those derived from Holbein's *Images*.

On the whole, the sequence of the 1588 edition was retained as well as the synopsis of different texts, the duplication of images and those cases in which no scene illustrated the text but in which two figures simply appeared next to each other.

The Mechel editions of the eighteenth century

In the course of the eighteenth century Frölich's *Danse Macabre* was distributed widely. Johann Conrad von Mechel III had already published the series in 1715, and further editions followed in 1724, 1735, 1740, 1769, 1786 und 1796.[35] The various Mechel editions hardly differ from each other.[36] The frontispiece is graced by a depiction of a young woman who is approached by Death in front of a house, while a bedridden old man inside the house is left unmolested. Changes were introduced to the sequence, however. While the 1735 edition still ended with the Expulsion and the Fall of Man in the wrong order, this error was corrected by 1786 at the latest.

It is important to take a closer look at the relationship between the editions by Frölich and Mechel. When Uli Wunderlich writes that Mechel moved the Preacher and the Last Judgement to the start and 'corrected' the order of the other scenes,[37] one might assume that the sequence in Frölich's editions had been wrong, but this was not the case. On the contrary: it was Mechel who at times introduced an arbitrary order. Not only did he omit several scenes, but he also changed their sequence: Nobleman and Noblewoman – Frölich 1608 calls them *Kriegsmann* (soldier) and *Hoffart* (haughtiness) – were brought forward, while the

---

[34] The edition contains a chronicle, the city arms, a map of Basel and a portrait of Oecolampadius.

[35] Massmann (1840), 32-33. From 1735 it was edited by Mechel's widow, and from 1769 by his sons Johann Conrad and Johann Jacob.

[36] Unfortunately I was only able to check the editions of 1735, 1786 and 1796.

[37] 'Er übernahm die Bilder nach Hans Holbein, kombinierte sie mit den Dialogversen der Basler Wandmalereien, stellte den Prediger voran, korrigierte die Reihenfolge der übrigen Szenen und wählte dafür den gleichen Titel, unter dem Matthaeus Merians Kupferstiche nach wie vor erhältlich waren.' See Wunderlich (2000), 164.

sequence of Usurer and Maiden was changed round. These changes are all the more astonishing if one considers that the Basel mural was still *in situ* during the eighteenth century. When Wunderlich claims that Mechel merely reproduced the images after Holbein and combined them with the Basel verses, this account does not do justice to the reality. As we shall see, Mechel did indeed replace and interchange some of the old illustrations and even had new illustrations cut.

The eighteenth-century editions comprise only forty-one scenes. As the Basel *Danse* consisted of forty-two scenes, one might assume that Mechel dropped only one single scene. The reality is more complicated, however. Mechel omitted seven Basel scenes that had all been part of the 1588 and 1608 editions, *viz.* the Duchess, Knight, Cripple, Herald, Executioner (*Blutvogt*), Painter, and Turk. Instead, he added six scenes (the Preacher, Last Judgement, Drunkard, Gambler, Robber, and Fall of Man), three of which were derived from Holbein.

Why did Mechel choose to omit seven scenes that were genuinely part of the Basel mural? The removal of the Turk might at first suggest an adaptation of the range of characters to the eighteenth-century state of the mural.[38] However, this theory is undermined by the fact that the Child was retained in these new editions despite its having meanwhile been removed from the actual *Danse Macabre* mural. Perhaps the figure of the Child was still too relevant for an eighteenth-century audience to be omitted. The exclusion of other scenes was probably for practical reasons. Frölich's editions had not comprised any individual scenes for the Duchess and the Painter's Wife; instead, the texts had been adorned with the duplicated images of the Duke and the Painter. For the Cripple, Herald and Executioner there had been no illustrations at all, but only two separate figures placed next to each other.

Likewise, the reasons for the inclusion of new scenes seem to be manifold: By adding the Preacher, the Last Judgement and the Fall of Man, Mechel adapts his volume to the current state of the mural. The integration of the Drunkard, Gambler and Robber makes no sense, however, as these scenes are only known from Holbein's *Images* and were never part of the Basel *Danse*. Frölich had at least separated these figures from the Basel cycle, so Mechel's inclusion of them in a publication allegedly dedicated solely to the Basel mural is more problematic. The decision must be due to the fact that Mechel did not want to repeat two identical images or include an assembly of vignettes. Consequently, he

---

[38] During Emanuel Bock's restoration (1614-16) the Turk was replaced by the Fall of Man.

either had to have new scenes cut or make use of what was available in order to reach the necessary number of 41/42 scenes. He opted for both by including the scenes from Holbein that were available and by commissioning new scenes for a former assembly of vignettes (Jew) as well as for duplicated images (Piper, Female Pagan). Interestingly, the new scenes were fashioned after the Basel mural – not after Holbein.

Fig. 116. The new illustration of Death and the Abbess, woodcut from the 1870 edition published by Danz in Leipzig. © Graphiksammlung 'Mensch und Tod', Heinrich-Heine-University Düsseldorf.

There is only one case in which an available illustration was exchanged for a new rendition without obvious reason. Whereas Frölich's editions include a reproduction of Holbein's illustration of the Abbess by the Master 'GS', Mechel exchanged it for a new illustration – presumably by the Master 'DR' – that was modelled on the Basel *Danse*. The new illustration was retained in the following editions, such as that published in 1870 by Danz in Leipzig (Fig. 116).

Further changes were due to the reorganisation of images. One example may suffice. While Frölich had illustrated the Duke with a woodcut after Holbein, Mechel combined this figure with Holbein's image of the Noblewoman that had illustrated the Duchess in Frölich's editions. In fact, Mechel used Holbein's memorable scene with the drumming Death figure who visits a young couple in order to combine Duke and Duchess in one image. Similarly, the *Danse Macabre* texts of both figures are merged: the verses of Death to the Duke are answered by the verses of the Duchess to Death.

Nineteenth-century reproductions

New editions of the 'Bern-Basel-Holbein-mix' were printed as late as the nineteenth century. Yet while Mechel's editions in the eighteenth century had not included a preface and thus quietly taken advantage of the fame of Merian's editions – the title of which they adopted – nineteenth-century editors even tried to make a virtue out of necessity. Thus, the Mähly-Lamy edition (Basel, 1842) as well as the Danz edition (Leipzig, 1870) include an elaborate preface. Mähly-Lamy opened his edition with the information that it contains 'the most accurate reproductions of the archetypes of the famous *Danse Macabre* [in Basel]'.[39] His argumentation anticipated what Danz would write in his edition thirty years later.

The title of the 1870 edition published by Danz in Leipzig largely conforms to the title of Merian's famous reproduction. At first sight the reader appears to be confronted with one of those editions. However, the subtitle *Original-Holzschnitte des 16. Jahrhunderts* (original woodcuts of the sixteenth century) should already alert the attentive reader, for Merian had created his reproductions of the Basel *Danse* only in the seventeenth century. The editor then goes on to recount that the illustrations originated

---

[39] 'Es erscheint uns nothwendig, dieser ältesten Auflage der, den Urbildern des berühmten Todtentanzes getreuesten Nachbildung einige Worte vorauszusenden.' See *Der Todten-Tantz wie derselbe in der weitberühmten Stadt Basel ... zu sehen ist* (Basel: Mähly-Lamy, 1842), 3.

in 1576, thus only eight years after the restoration of the Basel mural by
Hans Hug Kluber. Therefore, these images must be considered as 'the
oldest and most accurate [reproductions] of the famous *Danse Macabre*'.[40]
Matthäus Merian, so Danz argues, only copied the Basel mural in the
seventeenth century and thus after Emanuel Bock's restoration (1614-16).
To enhance the claim to authenticity, he points out that his volume was
printed from the old blocks and that improvements were avoided in order
not to spoil the originality;[41] only the use of new frames had been
unavoidable (cf. Fig. 116).

Mähly-Lamy and Danz pursued a clear strategy. They sold their
publications as reproductions, which were seemingly particularly authentic
and provided a nativeness which Merian's prints lacked.

Conclusion

Frölich's 1581 edition is the earliest transcription of the Basel *Danse
Macabre* dialogue. It is an accurate rendition of the sequence of the figures
and the verses.[42] Furthermore, the documentation of the state of the mural
before Emanuel Bock's restoration in 1614-16 makes Frölich's publication
an important source. The verses of the Child have been handed down even
to the editions of the nineteenth century, although figure and text had been
removed from the mural already in the early seventeenth century. Recent
research has also recognised the documentary value of some of Frölich's
illustrations which can be regarded as the earliest accurate copies after the
Basel *Danse*, *viz.* Cook, Pagan, Female Pagan, Painter, Painter's Wife.

In other respects, the editions by Frölich are too often called publications
for tourists who did not even realise what a bad reproduction they had
bought. Such a condescending attitude does not do justice to Frölich's
publications, however. It has been shown that in the 1588 edition it was
not Huldrich Frölich's prior objective to reproduce the Basel mural.
Instead, he wanted to compile different *Danse Macabre* verses and
complement them by illustrations, in order to provide the reader with
edifying exempla.

---

[40] '[...] als die ältesten und getreuesten [Reproduktionen] des berühmten
Todtentanzes gelten'. See *Der Todten-Tantz wie derselbe in der weitberühmten
Stadt Basel ...zu sehen ist. Original-Holzschnitte des 16. Jahrhunderts* (Leipzig:
Danz, [1870]), VII.

[41] *Ibid.*, IX.

[42] The idiom may have been slightly changed. Wunderlich (1998), 133, suggests
that the dialect was diffused.

The mixing of scenes from different sources, for which Fröhlich's editions have so often been criticised, must be regarded as typical of their time. The Holbein editions published in Cologne likewise introduced changes to the original, and Jobst de Necker not only altered the sequence but even added two new scenes in his German Holbein edition of 1544. The collage-like character of the so-called 'Bern-Basel-Holbein-mix' goes beyond these examples. With great attention to detail, elements from different sources have been combined to create a wholly new and idiosyncratic piece of work. Even though the artistic quality is not always convincing, the adaptation and synthesis of well-known motifs does deserve new appreciation.

Pl. 1. Burial scene with a charnel house in the background, miniature at the start of the Office of the Dead with Death on a black horse charging at a Pope and an Emperor in the lower margin, book of hours produced in Paris, *c.*1440 (London, British Library Add. MS 18751, fol. 163r). © The British Library.

Pl. 2b. Death and Bishop, sole extant stained-glass panel from a larger *Danse Macabre* window scheme, *c*.1500, in St Andrew's church Norwich. Photo: Mike Dixon.

Pl. 2a. Death and the Chess-player, wall painting by Albertus Pictor (1440-1507) in the church of Täby, Stockholm County (Sweden), 1480s. Photo: Håkan Svensson (Xauxa).

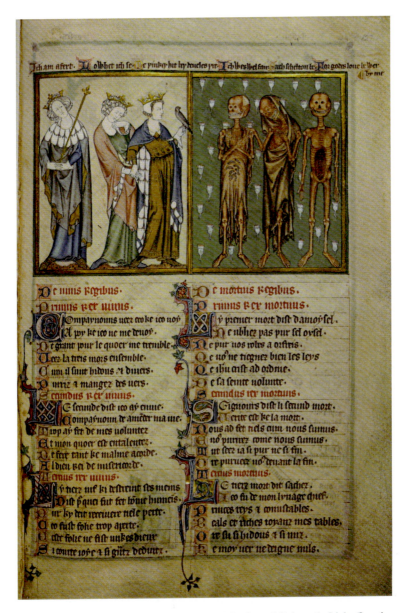

Pl. 3. The Three Living and the Three Dead, Psalter of Robert de Lisle (London, British Library, MS Arundel 83 II, fol. 127r), c.1310. © The British Library.

Pl. 4. The Three Living and the Three Dead, in a compilation manuscript probably produced for Marie de Brabant (Paris, BnF, Bibliothèque de l'Arsenal, MS 3142, fol. 311v), *c.*1285. © Bibliothèque nationale de France.

Pl. 5. *Danse Macabre* mural in the former Franciscan convent of Morella (Els Ports, Valencian Community, Spain), *c.*1470. Photo: author.

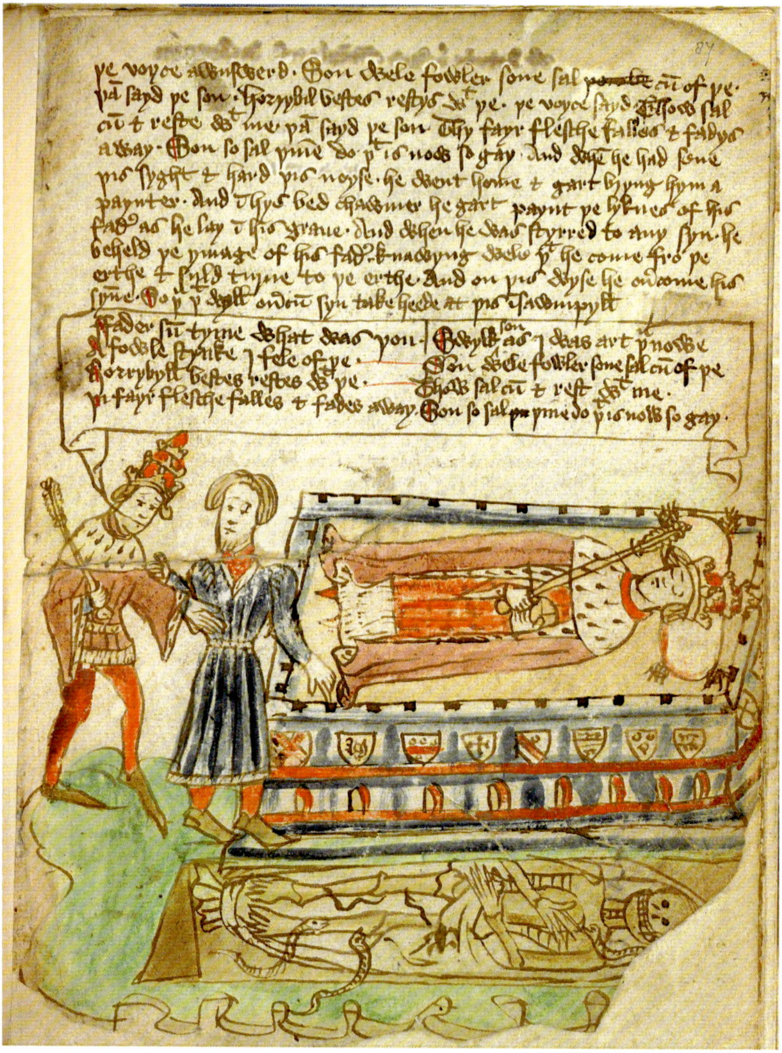

Pl. 6. The exemplum of the wicked young Emperor beholding his father's corpse, illustration in the so-called Carthusian Miscellany (London, British Library, Add. MS 37049, fol. 87r), c.1435-40. © The British Library.

Pl. 7. Hans Baldung Grien, *Death and the Maiden*, drawing, 1515. © Kupferstich-kabinett, Staatliche Museen zu Berlin, KdZ 4578.

Pl. 8. Simon Bening and workshop (Southern Netherlands), Raising of Lazarus, miniature at the start of the Office of the Dead in the book of hours of Joanna of Ghistelles (Use of Messines) (London, British Library, Egerton MS 2125, fol. 64v), early sixteenth century. © The British Library.

Pl. 9a. Encounter between death and a group of pilgrims from all walks of life, sometimes described as a 'predica della morte' (*Sermon of Death*) or 'predica dei morti' (*Sermon of the Dead*), fresco in the abbey of San Michele della Chiusa, Turin, fifteenth century. Photo: Renzo Dionigi.

Pl. 9b. Death on a cow assaulting a woman on a lion, marginal decoration in the Amiens Missal (The Hague, Royal Library, KB MS 78 D 40, fol. 91r), 1323. © The Hague, Royal Library.

Pl. 10. Death riding a bovine, miniature with the rubric of the Office of the Dead on a single sheet from a book of hours, French(?), early sixteenth century(?). © Graphiksammlung 'Mensch und Tod', Heinrich-Heine-University Düsseldorf.

Pl. 11. Death on an ox attacking a young nobleman in a cemetery, opening miniature of the Office of the Dead in the De Croÿs book of Hours (Paris, Bibliothèque de l'Assemblée nationale, ms. 11, fol. 93r), late fifteenth century. © Paris, Bibliothèque de l'Assemblée nationale.

Pl. 12. Triumph of Death, in a French translation of Petrarch's *Trionfi* by Simon Bourgouin (Paris, Bibliothèque nationale de France, ms. fr. 12423, fol. 37v), first quarter of the sixteenth century. © Bibliothèque nationale de France.

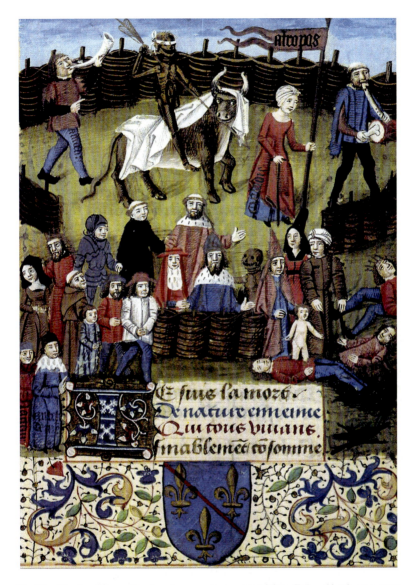

Pl. 13. Death riding a bovine, in a cortege comprising *Eaige* (Age) as a man playing tambourine, *Maladie* (Disease) holding the banner of 'Atropos', and *Accident* as a man blowing a horn, illustration of Pierre Michault's *La Danse aux Aveugles* (Paris, Bibliothèque nationale de France, ms. fr. 1989, fol. 34r), late fifteenth century. © Bibliothèque nationale de France.

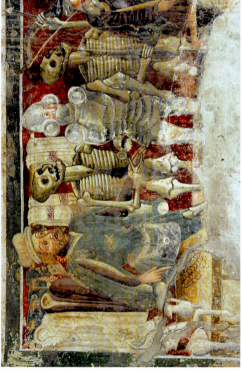

Pl. 14. Vincent of Kastav, *Danse Macabre* fresco on the west wall of the church of St Mary, Beram (Istria), 1474. Photo: Science and Research Centre, Koper.

Pl. 15. John of Kastav, *Danse Macabre* fresco in Holy Trinity church, Hrastovlje (Istria), 1490. Photo: Science and Research Centre, Koper.

Pl. 16. Death and the King, illumination in a French luxury *Danse Macabre* manuscript (Paris, Bibliothèque nationale de France, ms fr. 995, fol. 3r), early sixteenth century. © Bibliothèque nationale de France.

BIBLIOGRAPHY

Primary sources: facsimile editions

Baethcke, Hermann (ed.): *Des dodes danz. Nach den Lübecker Drucken von 1489 und 1496* (Tübingen: Laupp, 1876).

Champion, Pierre (ed.): *La Danse Macabre. Reproduction en fac-similé de l'édition de Guy Marchant Paris 1486* (Paris: Éditions des quatre Chemins, 1925).

Douce, Francis: *The Dance of Death. Exhibited in Elegant Engravings on Wood with a Dissertation on the Several Representations of that Subject but more Particularly on those Ascribed to Macabre and Hans Holbein* (London: William Pickering, 1833).

Gundersheimer, Werner L.: *The Dance of Death by Hans Holbein the Younger: a Complete Facsimile of the Original 1538 edition of Les simulachres & historiees faces de la mort* (New York: Dover Publications, 1971).

Hans Holbeins Todtentanz in 53 getreu nach den Holzschnitten lithographierten Blättern (Munich: Schlotthauer, 1832).

Harrison, Ann Tukey (ed.), with a chapter by Sandra L. Hindman: *The Danse Macabre of Women. Ms.fr. 995 of the Bibliothèque Nationale* (Kent/London: Kent State University Press, 1994).

Kaiser, Gert: *Der tanzende Tod. Mittelalterliche Totentänze* (Frankfurt am Main: Insel Verlag, 1982).

König, Eberhard, and Gabriele Bartz: *Les Belles Heures du Duc de Berry. Acc. No. 54.1.1., Metropolitan Museum of Art. The Cloisters Collection New York. Transkription und Übersetzung* (Luzern: Faksimile-Verlag, 2006).

Kurtz, Leonard P. (ed.): *Le Mors de la Pomme* (New York: Publications of the Institute of French Studies Inc., 1937).

Lemmer, Manfred (ed.): *Der Heidelberger Totentanz von 1485. 42 Holzschnitte* (Frankfurt am Main/Leipzig: Insel Verlag, 1991).

Marchant, Guyot: *La grande Danse Macabre des Hommes et des Femmes* (Troyes: Jacques Oudot, 2nd edn, 1486; repr. Paris: Phénix Éditions, 2000).

Merian, Johannes Jacob: *Todtentantz, wie derselbe in der weitberuembten Statt Basel als ein Spiegel menschlicher Beschaffenheit gantz kuenstlich mit lebendigen Farben gemahlet, nicht ohne nützliche Verwunderung zu sehen ist* (Basel: Merian, 1621).

Rusting, Salomon van: *Schoutoneel*, published in German as *Schau=Platz des Todes, oder Todten=Tanz in Kupffern und Versen vorgestellet: Ehemals von SAL. Van RUSTING, Med. Doct. In Nieder=Teutscher Sprache; nun aber in Hoch=Teutscher, mit nöthigen Anmerckungen* (Nuremberg: Johann Georg Meintel, 1736).

Sandler, Lucy Freeman: *The Psalter of Robert de Lisle in the British Library* (London and Oxford: Harvey Miller, 1983).

Tripps, Johannes: *'Den Würmer wirst Du Wildbret sein.' Der Berner Totentanz des Niklaus Manuel Deutsch in den Aquarellkopien von Albrecht Kauw (1649)*, Schriften des Bernischen Historischen Museums, 6 (Bern: Bernisches Historisches Museum, 2005).

Walther, Peter: *Der Berliner Totentanz zu St. Marien* (Berlin: Lukas-Verlag, 1997).

Primary sources: text editions

Abrams, M.H., and Stephen Greenblatt (eds): *The Norton Anthology of English Literature, Seventh Edition, Volume I* (New York: W.W. Norton & Company, 2000).

Augustine, St: *City of God* (London: Penguin, 2003).

Baude, Henri: *Dictz moraux pour faire tapisserie*, ed. *Annette Scoumane* (Geneva/Paris: Droz-Minard, 1959).

Benson, Larry D. (ed.): *The Riverside Chaucer* (Oxford: Oxford University Press, 1987).

Brown, Carleton: *Religious Lyrics of the Fourteenth Century* (Oxford: Oxford University Press, 1924).

Denzinger, Heinrich: *Enchiridion symbolorum definitionum et declarationum de rebus fidei et morum. Kompendium der Glaubensbekenntnisse und kirchlichen Lehrentscheidungen*, ed. Peter Hünermann (Freiburg/Basilea/Vienna: Herder, 2005).

Donne, John: *Poems*, ed. Herbert Grierson (London: Oxford University Press, 1933).

—. *The Sermons of John Donne*, ed. Evelyn M. Simpson and George R. Potter, 10 volumes (Berkeley: University of California Press, 1956).

Douce, Francis: *Illustrations of Shakspeare and of ancient manners with dissertations on the clowns and fools of Shakspeare; on the collection of popular tales entitled Gesta Romanorum; and on the English Morris Dance* (London: Longman/Hurst a. o., 1807).

Dronke, Peter (ed.): *Medieval Latin and the Rise of the European Love-Lyric* (2nd edn, Oxford: Clarendon, 1968).

Dürr, Emil, and Paul Roth (eds): *Aktensammlung zur Geschichte der Baselr Reformation in den Jahren 1519 bis Anfang 1534. Im Auftrage der historischen und antiquarischen Gesellschaft zu Basel*, vol. 4 (Basel: Verlag der Historischen und Antiquarischen Gesellschaft, 1941).

Dunbar, William: *The Complete Works*, ed. John Conlee (Kalamazoo, Michigan: Medieval Institute Publications, 2004).

Ellissen, Adolf (ed.): *Hans Holbein's Initial-Buchstaben mit dem Todtentanz* (Göttingen: Dieterich, 1849).

Fein, Susanna (ed.): *John the Blind Audelay: Poems and Carols* (Kalamazoo: TEAMS, 2009).

Fowler, Alastair (ed.): *The New Oxford Book of Seventeenth Century Verse* (Oxford: Oxford University Press, 1991).

Freytag, Hartmut (ed.): *Der Totentanz der Marienkirche in Lübeck und der Nikolaikirche in Reval (Tallinn). Edition, Kommentar, Interpretation, Rezeption*, Niederdeutsche Studien, 39 (Cologne/Weimar/Vienna: Böhlau Verlag, 1993).

Frölich, Huldrich: *Lobspruch An die Hochloblich unnd Weitberümpte Statt Basel Inhaltende mancherley nam[m]haffte unnd fürneme Sachen, so darinn zu sehen: Auch die Ursachen, Warumb gemelter Statt Schlagglocken bey einer Stund andern vorlauffen; hieneben werden auch die Reumen, so am Todtentantz bey jedem Stande verzeichnet, der Ordnug nach ... eingeleibet* (Basel, 1581).

—. *Zwen Todtentäntz Deren der eine zu Bern dem Anderen Ort Hochloblicher Eydtgnoschafft zu Sant Barfüssern: Der Ander aber zu Basel dem Neundten Ort gemelter Eydtgnoschafft auff S. Predigers Kirchhof mit Teutschen Versen, darzu auch die Lateinischen kommen, ordenlich sind verzeichnet ; Ordnung und Innhalt dieses Buchs belangende, wird nach der Lateinischen Vorrede kürtzlich erzehlet; Mit schönen und zu beyden Todtentäntzen dienstlichen Figuren, allerley Ständt und Völcker gebreuchliche Kleydung abbildende, gezieret* (Basel, 1588).

—. *Der hochloblichen und weitberuempten Statt Basel kurtze... Beschreibung: Inn welcher nicht allein von ihrem Ursprung ..: sondern auch was fürnemlichen da zu sehen ... tractieret, sampt des Todtentantzes, Basels und Berns, Reumen, mit dartzu dienstlichen Figuren gezieret* (Basel: Henricpetri, 1608).

Furnivall, Frederick J. (ed.): *Hoccleve's Works, I. The Minor Poems, in the Phillipps MS. 8151 (Cheltenham) and the Durham MS. III.9.*, EETS, e.s. 61 (London: Kegan Paul, Trench, Trübner, 1892, repr. 1937).

—. *Robert of Brunne's 'Handlyng Synne'*, EETS, o.s. 119, 123 (1901, 1903, repr. Montana: Kessinger Publishing, 2007).

Gobin, Robert: *Les loups ravissants* (Paris: Anthoine Vérard, *c.*1505-10).

Hanna III, Ralph (ed.): *The Awntyrs off Arthure at the Terne Wathlyn* (Manchester: Manchester University Press, 1974).

Hasenohr-Esnos, Geneviève (ed.): *Le Respit de la Mort par Jean le Fevre*, Société des anciens textes français (Paris: A. & J. Picard, 1969).

Heisterbacensis, Caesarius: *Dialogus Miraculorum*, XI, 61, ed. Joseph Strange (Cologne, Bonn, Brussels: J.M. Heberle, 1851).

Huerta, Ferran (ed.): *Teatre bíblic. Antic testament* (Barcelona: Editorial Barcino, 1976).

Jonson, Ben: *The Complete Poems*, ed. George Parfitt (Harmondsworth: Penguin Books Ltd, rev. edn 1996).

MacCracken, Henry Noble, and Merriam Sherwood (eds): *The Minor Poems of John Lydgate, II*, EETS, o.s. 192 (London: Oxford University Press, 1934).

Martin, L.C. (ed.): *Poetry and Selected Prose of Henry Vaughan* (Oxford: Oxford University Press, 1963).

Martínez de Toledo, Alfonso: *Corbacho o Reprobación del amor mundano*, Selecciones bibliográficas, 5 (Barcelona, 1949).

Marvell, Andrew: *The Complete Poems*, ed. Elizabeth Story Donno (Harmondsworth: Penguin, 1972).

Massot i Muntaner, Josep (ed.): 'Francesc d'Olesa, Representació de la Mort', *Teatre medieval i del Renaixement* (Barcelona: Edicions 62 and 'la Caixa', 1983), pp. 98-137.

Middleton, Thomas: *The Collected Works*, 2 vols, general editors Gary Taylor and John Lavagnino (Oxford: Clarendon Press, 2007).

Milton, John: *Poetical Works*, ed. Helen Darbishire (London: Oxford University Press, 1958).

Moralite nouuelle, de Mundus: Caro. Demonia. En laquelle Verrez les durs assautz & tentations quilz font au Cheualier Chrestien: Et comme par co[n]seil de son bon esprit, auec la grace de Dieu, les Vaincra, & a la fin aura le Royaume de paradis; Et est a cinq personnages. Cest a scavoir. Le chevalier chrestien. Lesprit. La chair.Le monde et le dyable. (Paris(?): Pierre Sergent(?), 1540).

Romeu i Figueras, Josep: 'La 'Representació de la Mort', obra dramática del siglo XVI, y la Danza de la Muerte', *Boletín de la Real Academia de Buenas Letras de Barcelona*, 27 (1957-58), 181-225.

—'La 'Representació de la Mort' obra dramàtica del segle XVI, i la Dansa de la Mort', *Teatre català antic*, 3 (Barcelona: Curial, 1995), pp. 17-95.

Salutati, Coluccio: *Epistolario*, II, ed. Fr. Novati (Rome: Forzani, 1891-1911).

Salzburger Äbtekonferenz (eds): *Die Benediktusregel* (Beuron: Beuroner Kunstverlag, 2006).

Scheyt, Caspar: *Todtentanz durch alle Stendt der Menschen, mit d. Arzney der Seelen v. Urban Regius it. Rede Cypriani vom Sterben und Chrysostomi von der Gedult; (u. mit Reimen von Caspar Scheidt)* (s.l., 1557).

—. *Totentanz durch alle Stendt der Menschen, darin[n]en ihr herkommen und endt, nichtigkeit un[d] sterbligkeit, als in einem spiegel zubeschawen, fürgebildet, un[d] mit schönen Figuren un[d] guten Reimen gezieret, notwendig, auch lustig allermeniglichen zu lesen, hören und wissen* (S. Gallen: Straub, 1581).

Shakespeare, William, *Complete Works*, ed. Peter Alexander (London/Glasgow: Collins, 1951).

Shirley, Janet (transl.): *A Parisian Journal 1405-1449* (Oxford: Clarendon Press, 1968).

Sidney, Sir Philip: *The Countess of Pembroke's Arcadia*, ed. Maurice Evans (2nd edn, Harmondsworth: Penguin, 1987).

Stow, John, corrected [...] by John Strype: *A Survey of the Cities of London and Westminster, and the Borough of Southwark* (London: printed for W. Innys and J. Richardson, J. and P. Knapton [and 10 others], 1754-55).

The Primer, or Office of the Blessed Virgin Marie, in Latin and English, 1599 (Antwerp, Arnold Conings, 1599), selected and edited by D.M. Rogers, English Recusant Literature, 1558-1640, vol. 262 (Ilkley/London: The Scolar Press, 1975).

Todi, Jacopone da: *Laude*, ed. Franco Mancini (Bari: Laterza, 1974).

Turville-Petre, Thorlac (ed.): *Alliterative Poetry of the Later Middle Ages* (Washington DC: Catholic University of America Press, 1989).

Warren, Florence (ed.), with introduction and notes by Beatrice White: *The Dance of Death, edited from MSS. Ellesmere 26/A.13 and B.M. Lansdowne 699, collated with the other extant MSS.*, EETS, o.s. 181 (London, 1931, repr. Woodbridge, 2000).

Whiting, E.K. (ed.): *The Poems of John Audelay*, Early English Text Society, o.s. 184 (Oxford: Oxford University Press, 1931).

Secondary sources

Alexandre-Bidon, Danièle: 'La mort dans les livres d'heures', in Danièle Alexandre-Bidon *et al.* (eds), *À réveiller les morts. La mort au quotidien dans l'Occident médiéval* (Lyon: Presses universitaires, 1993), 83-94.

—. 'Le bœuf de saint Luc', in *Aurochs, le retour: aurochs, vaches et autres bovins de la Préhistoire à nos jours*, museum catalogue (Lons-le-Saulnier: Centre jurassien du Patrimoine, 1994), 131-37.

Andersson, Christiane: *Urs Graf. Dirnen, Krieger, Narren. Ausgewählte Zeichnungen* (Basel: GS-Verlag, 1978).

Arné, F.: 'Les images de la mort dans les livres d'heures (xiiie-xve siècles)', *La Maison Dieu*, 145 (1981), 127-48.

Augé, Sylvie, Nelly Pousthomis, Michèle Pradalier-Schlumberger and Henri Pradalier: *Saint-Bertrand-de-Comminges, le chœur Renaissance – Saint-Just-de-Valcabrère, L'église romane* (Graulhet: éd. Odyssée, 2000).

Aurigemma, Maria Giulia: 'Nosce te ipsum. The Representation of Death in the Countries in the Germanic Area and the Netherlands', in Alberto Tenenti (ed.), *Humana Fragilitas. The Themes of Death in Europe from the 13th Century to the 18th Century* (Clusone: Ferrari Editrice, 2002), 141-96.

Avril, François: 'Beschreibung der Miniaturen', in François Avril *et al.* (eds), *Les Petites Heures du Duc de Berry. Kommentar zu MS lat. 18014 der Bibliothèque nationale, Paris* (Luzern: Faksimile Verlag, 1989), 225-387.

—. 'Les Heures de Guyot Le Peley. Chef d'Oeuvre de Jean Colombe', *Art de l'enluminure*, 21 (2007), 2-55.

—. (ed.), *Jean Fouquet. Peintre et enlumineur du XVe siècle* (Paris: Bibliothèque nationale de France, 2003).

Avril, François, and Nicole Reynaud: *Les manuscrits à peintures en France, 1440-1520* (Paris: Flammarion/Bibliothèque nationale de France, 1994).

Axton, Richard: *European Drama of the Early Middle Ages* (London: Hutchinson, 1974).

Bartholomew, Robert E.: 'Rethinking the Dancing Mania', *Skeptical Inquirer*, 24:4 (July/August 2000).

Bartz, Gabriele: *Der Boucicaut-Meister. Ein unbekanntes Stundenbuch* (Ramsen: Antiquariat Bibermühle, 1999).

Bartz, Gabriele, and Eberhard König: 'Die Illustration des Totenoffiziums in Stundenbüchern', in Hansjakob Becker *et al.* (eds), *Im Angesicht des*

Todes: ein interdisziplinäres Kompendium, I (St. Ottilien: EOS Verlag, 1987), 487-528.

Beaufrère, Hubert: *Lexique de la chasse au vol. Terminologie française du XVIe au XXe siècles,* Bibliotheca cynegetica, 4 (Nogent-le-Roi: Laget, 2004).

Bedaux, Jan Baptist, and Rudi Ekkart (eds): *Pride and Joy: Children's Portraits in the Netherlands, 1500-1700,* (New York/London: Harry N. Abrams, 2001).

Bellosi, Luciano: *Buffalmacco e il Trionfo della Morte* (Turin: Einaudi, 1974).

Bergdolt, Klaus: 'Der spätmittelalterliche Veitstanz', in Andrea von Hülschen-Esch and Hiltrud Westermann-Angerhausen with Stefanie Knöll (eds), *'Zum Sterben schön!' Alter, Totentanz und Sterbekunst von 1500 bis heute* (Regensburg: Schnell & Steiner, 2006), vol. 1, 85-93.

Bertoša, Slaven: 'La peste in Istria nel medio evo e nell'età moderna (in contesto Europeo delle epidemie)', *Atti-Centro di ricerche storiche Rovigno,* 37 (2007), 121-57.

Bethmont-Gallerand, Sylvie: 'De l'illustration à la leçon', *Reinardus,* 16 (2003), 47-62

Białostocki, Jan (ed.): *Stil und Ikonographie. Studien zur Kunstwissenschaft* (Dresden: Verl. der Kunst, 1966).

—. 'The Door of Death: Survival of a Classical Motif in Sepulchral Art', *Jahrbuch der Hamburger Kunstsammlungen,* 18 (1973), 7-32.

Binski, Paul: *Medieval Death: Ritual and Representation* (Ithaca, NY: Cornell University Press, 1996).

Bishop, Edmund: *Liturgica Historica: Papers on the Liturgy and Religious Life of the Western Church* (Oxford: Clarendon Press, 1918, repr. 1962).

Błażek, Konrad (ed.): *J. Siebmacher's großes Wappenbuch,* vol. 6,8: Der abgestorbene Adel der preußischen Provinz Schlesien und der Oberlausitz, part 1 (Nuremberg: Bauer & Raspe, 1887).

—. *J. Siebmacher's großes Wappenbuch,* vol. 17: Die Wappen des schlesischen Adels (repr. Neustadt a. d. Aisch: Bauer & Raspe, 1977).

Block, Elaine C.: *Corpus of Medieval Misericords: France* (Turnhout: Brepols, 2003).

Block, Elaine C., and Frédéric Billiet (eds): *Lexicon of Medieval Choir Stalls,* Profane Arts of the Middle Ages (Turnhout: Brepols, 2010).

Block, Werner: *Der Arzt und der Tod in Bildern aus sechs Jahrhunderten* (Stuttgart 1966).

Boase, T.S.R.: *Death in the Middle Ages: Mortality, Judgment and Remembrance* (New York: McGraw Hill, 1972).

Böhm, Reinhold: *Sagt Ja Sagt Nein. Der Füssener Totentanz und das Fortwirken der Totentanzidee im Ostallgäuer und Außerferner Raum: Oberstdorf, Füssen (St. Sebastian), Breitenwang, Elbigenalp, Elmen, Schattwald, Pfronten (Lithographien)* (Füssen: Historischer Verein Alt Füssen, 1990).

Böhme, Hartmut: 'Imagologie von Himmel und Hölle. Zum Verhältnis von textueller und bildlicher Konstruktion imaginärer Räume', in Barbara Naumann and Edgard Pankow (eds), *Bilder-Denken. Bildlichkeit und Argumentation* (Munich: Fink, 2004), 19-45.

Bolzoni, Lina: *Gli affreschi della Morte del Camposanto di Pisa e la predicazione domenicana, in La rete delle immagini. Predicazione in volgare dalle origini a Bernardino da Siena* (Turin: Einaudi, 2002).

—. *La Rete delle Immagini*, translated as *The web of images: vernacular preaching from its origins to St. Bernardino da Siena* (Farnham: Ashgate, 2004).

Bovey, Alixe: *The Smithfield Decretals: Tales from the Margins of a Fourteenth-Century Law Book* (Toronto: University of Toronto Press, forthcoming).

Bradley, Jill: '*You Shall Surely not Die'. The Concepts of Sin and Death as Expressed in the Manuscript Art of Northwestern Europe, c. 800-1200* (Leiden/ Boston: Brill, 2008), 2 volumes.

Brinkmann, Bodo: 'Zur Rolle von Stundenbüchern in der Jenseitsvorsorge', in Peter Jezler (ed.), *Himmel, Hölle, Fegefeuer. Das Jenseits im Mittelalter*, exhibition catalogue, Landesmuseum Zürich (Zürich: Verlag Neue Zürcher Zeitung, 1994), 91-100.

—. *Die Flämische Buchmalerei am Ende des Burgunderreichs. Der Meister des Dresdener Gebetbuchs und die Miniaturisten seiner Zeit* (Turnhout: Brepols, 1997).

—. *Hexenlust und Sündenfall. Die seltsamen Phantasien des Hans Baldung Grien / Witches' Lust and the Fall of Man. The Strange Phantasies of Hans Baldung Grien*, exhibition catalogue (Frankfurt/ Petersberg: Michael Imhof Verlag, 2007).

Broekhuijsen, Klara: 'The Legend of the Grateful Dead: a Misinterpreted Miniature in the Très Riches Heures of Jean de Berry', in Bert Cardon, Jan Van der Stock, Dominique Vanwijnsberghe *et al.* (eds), *Als Ich Can. Liber Amicorum in Memory of Professor Dr. Maurits Smeyers*, 2 vols (Louvain: Peeters, 2002), vol. 2, 213-30.

Bronfen, Elisabeth: *Nur über ihre Leiche. Tod, Weiblichkeit und Ästhetik* (Munich: Antje Kunstmann Verlag, 1994).

Brunckow, Oskar (ed.): *Die Wohnplätze des Deutschen Reiches*, vol. 1,2 (Berlin: Brunckow, 1909).

Büttner, Frank O.: '"Ce sera moy."' Realitätsgehalt und Rhetorik in Darstellungen der Toten- und Vergänglichkeitsikonographie des Stundengebetbuchs', in Bert Cardon, Jan Van der Stock, Dominique Vanwijnsberghe *et al.* (eds), *Als Ich Can. Liber Amicorum in Memory of Professor Dr. Maurits Smeyers*, 2 vols (Louvain: Peeters, 2002), vol. 2, 243-315.

Buren, Anne van: 'The Master of Mary of Burgundy and his Colleagues: the State of Research and Questions of Method', *Zeitschrift für Kunstgeschichte*, 38 (1975), 286-308.

Burgemeister, L.: *Die Holzkirchen und Holztürme der preussischen Ostprovinzen, Schlesien – Polen – Ostpreussen – Westpreussen – Brandenburg – Pommern* (Berlin: Springer, 1905).

Buttay-Jutier, Florence: *Fortuna, usages politiques d'une allégorie morale*, (Paris: Presses de l'Université Paris-Sorbonne, 2008).

Cabra, Enric: 'Reminiscències de la Representació de la Mort i d'altres peces teatrals en el cançoner de Francesc d'Albranca', *Revista de Menorca*, 2 (1990), 157-76.

Cabrol, F.: *Dictionnaire d'Archéologie Chrétienne et de Liturgie (DACL)*, vol. 5, (Paris, Letouzey et Ane, 1922-23).

Caciola, Nancy: 'Wraiths, Revenants and Ritual in Medieval Culture', *Past and Present*, 152 (1996), 3-45.

Camille, Michael: *Master of Death. The Lifeless Art of Pierre Remiet, Illuminator* (New Haven / London: Yale University Press, 1996).

Carboneres, Manuel: *Relación y explicación histórica de la solemne procession del Corpus que anualmentmente celebra la ciudad de Valencia* (Valencia: J. Doménech, 1878).

Ceretta, Luisella: *Vita del Medioevo nei dipinti della Val Susa tra X e XV secolo* (Sant'Ambrogio, Turin: Susalibri, 2004).

Chabot, André: *Érotique du Cimetière* (Paris: Henri Veyrier, 1989).

Chambers, E.K.: *The Medieval Stage* (Oxford: Clarendon Press, 1954), 2 vols.

Chancellor, Frederic: *The Ancient Sepulchral Monuments of Essex. A Record of Interesting Tombs in Essex Churches and Some Account of the Persons and Families Connected with Them* (London: C.F. Kell, 1890).

Chartier, Roger: 'Culture as Appropriation: Popular Cultural Uses in Early Modern France', in Steven L. Kaplan (ed.), *Understanding Popular Culture. Europe from the Middle Ages to the Nineteenth Century* (Berlin/New York/ Amsterdam: Mouton Publishers, 1984), 229-54.

Chihaia, Pavel: *Immortalité et décomposition dans l'art du Moyen Age* (Madrid: Fondation culturelle Roumaine, 1988).

Christadler, Maike: 'Kreativität und Genie: Legenden der Kunstgeschichte', in Anja Zimmermann (ed.), *Kunstgeschichte und Gender. Eine Einführung* (Berlin: Reimer, 2006), 253-72.

—. 'Zwischen Tod und Versuchung – Landsknechte, Reisläufer und andere Männer', *L'art macabre*, 8 (2007), 43-52.

Ciaghi, Giuseppe: *Nell'antica chiesa di San Vigilio a Pinzolo* (Trento: Editrice UNI Service, 2006).

Ciasca, Roberto: *La rappresentazione della vita e della morte nella 'laura' di Santa Margherita sul Vulture* (Todi: Accademia Tudertina, 1963).

Clark, James M.: *The Dance of Death in the Middle Ages and the Renaissance* (Glasgow: Jackson, Son & Company, 1950).

Claußnitzer, Maike: *Sub specie aeternitatis. Studien zum Verhältnis von historischer Situation und Heilsgeschichte im Redentiner Osterspiel*, Mikrokosmos, 75 (Frankfurt am Main: Peter Lang, 2007).

Claußnitzer, Maike, Hartmut Freytag and Susanne Warda: 'Das Redentiner – ein Lübecker Osterspiel. Über das Redentiner Osterspiel von 1464 und den Totentanz in der Marienkirche in Lübeck von 1463', *Zeitschrift für deutsches Altertum*, 132 (2003), 189-238.

Cohen, Kathleen: *Metamorphosis of a Death Symbol: the Transi Tomb in the Late Middle Ages and the Renaissance*, California Studies in the History of Art, 15 (Berkeley/Los Angeles/London: University of California Press, 1973).

Cooper, Tarnya: 'Memento Mori Portraiture. Painting, Protestant Culture and the Patronage of Middle Elites in England and Wales 1540-1630', unpublished PhD thesis (University of Sussex, 2001).

Corbató, Hermenegildo: 'Los misterios del Corpus de Valencia', *University of California Publications in Modern Philology*, 16:1 (1933), 1-172.

Cosacchi, Stephan: *Makabertanz. Der Totentanz in Kunst, Poesie und Brauchtum des Mittelalters* (Meisenheim am Glan: Hain, 1965).

De Vos, Dirk: *Hans Memling. The Complete Works* (London: Thames & Hudson, 1994).

Dehio Handbook of Monuments of Art in Poland (Dehio-Handbuch der Kunstdenkmäler in Polen), volume on Silesia (Munich/Berlin: Deutscher Kunstverlag, 2005).

Delaunay, Isabelle : 'Les Heures d'Écouen du Musée National de la Renaissance. Échange entre manuscrits et imprimés, autour de 1500', *Revue du Louvre*, 43 (1993), 11-24.

Delcourt, Thierry: 'Un livre d'heures à l'usage de Troyes peint par Jean Colombe. Une acquisition récente de la Médiathèque de Troyes', *Bulletin du Bibliophile*, 2 (2006), 221-44.

Desobry, Jean: 'Les Heures de Simon Vostre d'Amiens imprimées à Paris vers 1508', in *Liber Amicorum, Etudes historiques offertes à Pierre Bougard*. co-édition *Commission départementale d'histoire et d'archéologie du Pas-de-Calais*, 25, *Revue du Nord*, hors-série, collection Histoire, 3 (Arras: Université Lille 3, 1987), 123-39.

Deuchler, Florens: 'Looking at Bonne of Luxembourg's Prayerbook', *The Metropolitan Museum of Art Bulletin* (February 1971), 267-78.

Diccionari Català-Valencià-Balear, 10 vols (Palma de Mallorca: Editorial Moll, 1988).

Didi-Huberman, Georges: *La Peinture incarnée, suivi de 'le chef-d'oeuvre inconnu' par Honoré de Balzac* (Paris: Les Éditions de Minuit, 1985).

Dienwiebel, Herbert: *Oberschlesische Schrotholzkirchen* (Wrocław: Heydebrand, 1938).

Dolmetsch, Arnold: *Dances of England and France from 1450 to 1600* (London: Routledge, 1949).

Dreier, Rolf Paul, *Der Totentanz – ein Motiv der kirchlichen Kunst als Projektionsfläche für profane Botschaften (1425-1650)*, PhD thesis (Rotterdam: Erasmus University/Leiden: Brill, 2010).

Duffy, Eamon: *The Stripping of the Altars: Traditional Religion in England 1400-1580* (New Haven/London: Yale University Press, 1992).

Duinen, Herman A. van: *De Koorbanken van de Grote- of Onze Lieve Vrouwekerk te Dordrecht* (Leiden: Primavera Pers, 1997).

Ebreo of Pesaro, Guglielmo: *On the Practice or Art of Dancing / De Practica seu Arte Tripudii*, ed. and trans. Barbara Sparti (Oxford: Oxford University Press, 1993).

Eckhardt, Holger: 'Von Leichen, vom Leichaerer oder: Wie der Tanz zum Tod kam,' *Wirkendes Wort*, 44 (1994), 177-88.

Egger, Franz: *Basler Totentanz* (Basel: Buchverlag Basler Zeitung and Historisches Museum Basel, 1990).

—. *Basler Totentanz* (Basel: Friedrich Reinhardt, 2009 (1990)).

Eiblmayr, Silvia: *Die Frau als Bild. Der weibliche Körper in der Kunst* (Berlin: Reimer, 1994).

Eichberger, Dagmar: 'Close Encounters with Death. Changing Representations of Women in Renaissance Art and Literature', in Bernard J. Muir (ed.), *Reading Texts and Images. Essays on Medieval Art and Patronage in Honor of Margaret M. Manion* (Exeter: University of Exeter Press, 2002), 273-96.

Emmerling, Danuta, and Alojzy Wierzgoń: *Die Oppelner Holzkirchen* (Opole: Schlesischer Verlag Adan, 2006).

Emmerson, Richard: 'Visualizing the Vernacular: Middle English in Early Fourteenth Century Bilingual and Trilingual Manuscript Illustrations', in Kathryn A. Smith (ed.), *Tributes to Lucy Freeman Sandler: Studies in Illuminated Manuscripts* (London: Harvey Miller, 2007), 187-204.

Euw, Anton von, and Joachim M. Plotzek: *Die Handschriften der Sammlung Ludwig*, 5 vols, vol. 2, 'Brevier, Stundenbuch, Gebetbuch' (Cologne: Schnütgen-Museum der Stadt Köln, 1982).

Fehse, Wilhelm: *Der Ursprung der Totentänze. Mit einem Anhang: Der vierzeilige oberdeutsche Totentanztext. Codex Palatinus Nr. 314 B. 79a-80b* (Halle: Niemeyer, 1907).

Fein, Susanna Greer: 'Life and Death, Reader and Page: Mirrors of Mortality in English Manuscripts', *Mosaic*, 35:1 (2002), 69-94.

—. 'Good Ends in the Audelay Manuscript', *Yearbook of English Studies*, 33 (2003), 97-119.

Finoli, Anna Maria: 'La figura dell'eremita nella letteratura antici-francese', in *L'eremitismo in Occidente nei secoli XI e XII*, Pubblicazioni dell'Università Cattolica del Sacro Cuore (Milan: Vita e Pensiero, 1965).

Folkart, Balmedie: 'Structures lexicales et idéologie au quinzième siècle la *Danse aux aveugles* de Pierre Michault', *Sagi e memorie, Neolatina*, 1:2 (1977), 41-74.

France 1500: entre Moyen Age et Renaissance, exhibition catalogue (Paris: RMN, 2010).

Frey, Winfried, and Hartmut Freytag (eds): *'Ihr müßt alle nach meiner Pfeife tanzen.' Totentänze vom 15. bis 20. Jahrhundert aus den Beständen der Herzog August Bibliothek Wolfenbüttel und der Bibliothek Otto Schäfer Schweinfurt*, Ausstellungskataloge der Herzog August Bibliothek, 77 (Wolfenbüttel: Harassowitz, 2000).

Freytag, Hartmut: *Kommentar zur frühmittelhochdeutschen Summa Theologiae*, Medium Aevum, 19 (Munich: Fink, 1970).

Frigola, Jordi, and Pep Vila: 'La Bisbal tenia Dansa de la Mort', *Diari de Girona* (3 July 2005), 8-9.

Frugoni, Chiara Settis: 'Il tema dell'incontro dei tre vivi e dei tre morti nella tradizione medievale italiana', *Memorie dell'Accademia dei Lincei, Classe di Scienze Morali*, series VIII, XIII, fasc. III (1967), 145-251.

Fučić, Branko: 'Grafički listovi Majstora sa svicima u kastavskoj radionici' [Graphic sheets of the Master with the Banderoles in the

Kastav Workshop], *Bulletin za likovne umjetnosti JAZU*, 10 (1962), 177-86.

—. *Istarske freske* [Istrian frescoes] (Zagreb: Zora, 1963).

—. *Vincent von Kastav* (Zagreb/Pazin: Kršćanska sadašnjost, Istarsko književno društvo 'Juraj Dobrila', 1992).

Gay, Victor, and Henri Stein: *Dictionnaire archéologique du Moyen Age et de la Renaissance* (Paris: Picard, 1928).

Gertsman, Elina: 'The Dance of Death in Reval (Tallinn): the Preacher and his Audience', *Gesta*, 42:2 (2003), 143-59.

—. 'Visualizing Death. Medieval Plagues and the Macabre', in Franco Mormando, Thomas Worcester (eds), *Piety and Plague. From Byzantium to the Baroque* (Kirksville: Truman State University Press, 2007), 64-89.

—. *The Dance of Death in the Middle Ages. Image, Text, Performance*, Studies in the Visual Cultures of the Middle Ages (SVCMA), 3 (Turnhout: Brepols, 2010).

Gertsman, Elina, and Almut Breitenbach: 'Tanz, Schauspiel und Gericht. Performativität im Berliner Totentanz', *L'art macabre (Jahrbuch der Europäischen Totentanz-Vereinigung)*, 5 (2004), 29-40.

Gittings, Clare: 'Venetia's Death and Kenelm's Mourning', in Ann Sumner (ed.), *Death, Passion and Politics: Van Dyke's Portraits of Venetia Stanley and George Digby* (Dulwich: Dulwich Picture Gallery, 1995), 54-68.

Gliesmann, Niklas: Memento mori in der Tafelmalerei der Südniederlande zwischen 1450 und 1520, in: Andrea von Hülsen-Esch and Hiltrud Westermann-Angerhausen with Stefanie Knöll (eds), *'Zum Sterben schön!' Alter, Totentanz und Sterbekunst von 1500 bis heute* (Regensburg: Schnell & Steiner, 2006), vol. 1, 321-28.

Glixelli, Stefan: *Les cinques Poèmes des Trois Morts et des Trois Vifs* (Paris: Librairie Ancienne Honoré Champion, 1914).

Goddard, Stephen H. (ed.): *The World in Miniature. Engravings by the German Little Masters, 1500-1550*, exhibition catalogue (Lawrence/Kansas: Spencer Museum of Art, 1988).

Goette, Alexander: *Holbeins Totentanz und seine Vorbilder* (1897, repr. Hamburg: Severus Verlag, 2010).

Goldenberg, David: *The Curse of Ham. Race and Slavery in Early Judaism, Christianity and Islam* (Princeton: Princeton University Press, 2003).

Gorissen, Friedrich: *Das Stundenbuch der Katharina von Kleve. Analyse und Kommentar* (Berlin: Gebrüder Mann Verlag, 1973).

Greene, Richard Leighton: *The Early English Carols* (Oxford: Clarendon Press, 1935).

Groupe International de Recherches sur les peintures murales (eds), *Vifs nous sommes, morts nous serons. La rencontre des trois morts et des trois vifs dans la peinture murale en France* (Vendôme: Editions du Cherche-lune, 2001).

Gruzinski, Serge: *L'aigle et la Sibylle, fresques indiennes du Mexique* (Paris: Editions de l'Imprimerie nationale, 1994).

Guerry, Liliane: *Le thème du 'Triomphe de la Mort' dans la peinture italienne* (Paris: Librairie orientale et Americaine, 1950).

Guthke, Karl S.: *The Gender of Death: a Cultural History in Art and Literature* (1997, transl. Cambridge: Cambridge University Press, 1997).

Hacker, Barton C.: 'Women and Military Institutions in Early Modern Europe: a Reconnaissance', *Signs*, 6 (1981), 643-71.

Halfar, Wolfgang: *Die oberschlesischen Schrotholzkirchen. Ein Beitrag zum Holzbau in Schlesien* (München: Delp, 1980).

Halling, Thorsten, Silke Fehlemann and Jörg Vögele (eds): 'Vorzeitiger Tod: Identitäts- und Sinnstiftung in historischer Perspektive', special issue of *Historical Social Research – Historische Sozialforschung*, 34:4 (2009).

Hammerstein, Reinhold: *Diabolus in Musica: Studien zur Ikonographie der Musik im Mittelalter*, Neue Heidelberger Studien zur Musikwissenschaft, 6 (Bern: Francke, 1974).

—. *Tanz und Musik des Todes: die mittelalterlichen Totentänze und ihr Nachleben* (Bern/Munich: Francke, 1980).

Hammond, Eleanor Prescott: 'Latin Texts of the Dance of Death', *Modern Philology*, 8 (1911), 399-410.

Hans Holbein the Younger. The Basel Years 1515-1532, exhibition catalogue with contributions by Christian Müller, Stephan Kemperdick *et al.* (Munich/Berlin/London/New York: Prestel, 2006).

Harris, John, and Gordon Higgot: *Inigo Jones: Complete Architectural Drawings* (London: Royal Academy of Arts, 1990).

Hildebrand, Reinhard: 'Anatomische Darstellungen zwischen Kunst und Wissenschaft', in Andrea von Hülsen-Esch and Hiltrud Westermann-Angerhausen with Stefanie Knöll (eds), *Zum Sterben schön: Alter, Totentanz und Sterbekunst von 1500 bis heute*, 2 vols (Regensburg: Schnell & Steiner, 2006), vol. 1, 181-96.

Höfler, Janez, 'Mittelalterliche Totentanzdarstellungen im Alpen-Adria Raum', in Markus J. Wenninger (ed.), *'du gouter tôt'. Sterben im*

Mittelalter – Ideal und Realität (Klagenfurt: Wieser Verlag, 1998), 131-44.

Hoffmann-Curtius, Kathrin: *Im Blickfeld: John, der Frauenmörder von George Grosz*, exhibition catalogue (Stuttgart: Gerd Hatje Verlag, 1990).

Hoffmann, Konrad: 'Wort und Bild im Narrenschiff', in Ludger Grenzmann and Karl Stackmann (eds), *Literatur und Laienbildung im Spätmittelalter und in der Reformationszeit* (Stuttgart: Metzler, 1984), 392-422.

—. 'Holbeins "Todesbilder". Laienfrömmigkeit im Todesbild der Vor- und Frühreformation', in Klaus Schneider (ed.), *Laienfrömmigkeit im späten Mittelalter. Formen, Funktionen, politisch-soziale Zusammenhänge* (Munich: Oldenbourg, 1992), 263-82.

Hofmann, Mara: 'Studien zum Panissestundenbuch', unpublished MA dissertation (Freie Universität Berlin, 1998).

Hülsen-Esch, Andrea von, and Hiltrud Westermann-Angerhausen with Stefanie Knöll (eds), *Zum Sterben schön: Alter, Totentanz und Sterbekunst von 1500 bis heute*, 2 vols (Regensburg: Schnell & Steiner, 2006).

Hülsen, Dorothy von: 'Alfred Mahlau, Die Totentanz-Fenster der Marienkirche in Lübeck', in Hartmut Freytag (ed.), *Der Totentanz in der Marienkirche in Lübeck und der Nikolaikirche in Reval (Tallinn)*, Niederdeutsche Studien, 39 (Cologne/Weimar/Vienna: Böhlau, 1990), 385-403.

Huizinga, Johan: *The Autumn of the Middle Ages*, transl. Rodney J. Payton and Ulrich Mammitzsch (Chicago: University of Chicago Press, 1996).

—. *The Waning of the Middle Ages: a Study of the Forms of Life, Thought, and Art in France and the Netherlands in the Fourteenth and Fifteenth Centuries* (transl. 1924, repr. New York: Dover Publications, 1998).

Infantes, Víctor: *Las danzas de la muerte. Génesis y desarrollo de un género medieval (siglos XIII-XVII)* (Salamanca: Ediciones Universidad de Salamanca, 1997).

Ingrassia, Catherine: Christophe Deslignes and Xavier Terrasa, *La danse médiévale*, vol. 1 (Beauchamp: Le Local, 2009).

Ingrassia, Catherine, and Sylvie Bethmont: 'L'art de bien danser et de bien vivre', *Histoire et Images médiévales*, 29 (2010), 66-69.

Ivančević, Radovan: 'Crkva Sv. Trojstva u Hrastovlju: romanika ili renesansa?' [The church of the Holy Trinity in Hrastovlje: romanesque or renaissance?], *Radovi instituta za poviest umjetnosti*, 12-13 (1988/89), 127-36.

Jankofsky, Klaus: 'A View into the Grave: "A Disputacion Betwyx þe Body and Wormes" in British Museum MS Add. 37049', *Taius*, 1 (1974), 137-59.

Janson, Horst W.: 'The Putto with the Death's Head', *Art Bulletin*, 19 (1937), 423-49.

Janzin, Marion, and Joachim Güntner: *Das Buch vom Buch: 5000 Jahre Buchgeschichte* (Hannover: Schlüter, 3rd edn 2007).

Jones, John Winter: 'Observations on the Origin of the Division of Man's Life into Stages', *Archaeologia*, 35 (1853), 167-89.

Jungmann, Irmgard: *Tanz, Tod und Teufel. Tanzkultur in der gesellschaftlichen Auseinandersetzung im 15. und 16. Jahrhundert* (Kassel: Bärenreiter, 2002).

—. 'Warum ausgerechnet "Tanzen"? Musiksoziologische Aspekte der Totentanzikonographie', in Andrea von Hülschen-Esch and Hiltrud Westermann-Angerhausen with Stefanie Knöll (eds), *'Zum Sterben schön!' Alter, Totentanz und Sterbekunst von 1500 bis heute* (Regensburg: Schnell & Steiner, 2006), vol. 1, 119-32.

Kaiser, Gert: 'Totentanz und verkehrte Welt', in Franz Link (ed.), *Tanz und Tod in Kunst und Literatur*, Schriften zur Literaturwissenschaft, Germanistische Reihe, 10 (Berlin: Duncker & Humblot, 1993), 93-118.

—. *Der Tod und die schönen Frauen, Ein elementares Motiv der europäischen Kultur* (Frankfurt/New York: Campus, 1995).

Kettler, Wilfried: *Der Berner Totentanz des Niklaus Manuel. Philologische, epigraphische sowie historische Überlegungen zu einem Sprach- und Kunstdenkmal der frühen Neuzeit* (Bern: Peter Lang, 2009).

Kiening, Christian: 'Totentänze – Ambivalenzen des Typus', *Jahrbuch für Internationale Germanistik*, 27 (1995), 38-56.

—. *Das andere Selbst. Figuren des Todes an der Schwelle zur Neuzeit* (Munich: Wilhelm Fink Verlag, 2003).

Kinch, Ashby: 'Image, Ideology and Form: the Middle English Three Dead Kings in its Iconographic Context', *Chaucer Review*, 43:1 (2008), 48-81.

King, George A.: 'The Pre-Reformation Painted Glass in St. Andrew's Church, Norwich', *Norfolk Archaeology*, 18 (1913), 283-94.

King, Pamela M.: '"My Image to be made all naked": Cadaver Tombs and the Commemoration of Women in Fifteenth-Century England', *The Ricardian*, 13 (2003), 294-314.

Kissel, Otto Rudolf: *Die Justitia: Reflexionen über ein Symbol und seine Darstellung in der bildenden Kunst* (München: Beck, 1984).

Klesse, Brigitte: 'Ein unbekanntes Werk des Clerigino da Capodistria', *Pantheon*, 19 (1971), 281-91.

Knöll, Stefanie: 'Zur Entstehung des Motivs *Der Tod und das Mädchen*', in Andrea von Hülsen-Esch and Hiltrud Westermann-Angerhausen with Stefanie Knöll (eds), *Zum Sterben schön: Alter, Totentanz und Sterbekunst von 1500 bis heute*, 2 vols (Regensburg: Schnell & Steiner, 2006), vol. 1, 65-72.

—. '"Der Pfeifen Schall verkündet euch des Todes Fall". Zur Darstellung des musizierenden Todes in Einzelszenen', *L'art macabre (Jahrbuch der Europäischen Totentanz-Vereinigung)*, 9 (2008), 95-107.

—. 'Death and the Maiden', in Helen Fronius and Anna Linton (eds), *Women and Death: Representations of Female Victims and Perpetrators in German Culture 1500-2000*, Studies in German Literature Linguistics and Culture (Rochester, New York: Camden House, 2008), 9-27.

—. 'Maskierung und Demaskierung. Der Tod beim Maskenball', in: Stefanie Knöll (ed.), *Narren - Masken - Karneval. Meisterwerke von Dürer bis Kubin aus der Düsseldorfer Graphiksammlung 'Mensch und Tod'* (Regensburg: Schnell & Steiner, 2009), 53-61.

—. (ed.): *Narren – Masken – Karneval: Meisterwerke von Dürer bis Kubin aus der Düsseldorfer Graphiksammlung 'Mensch und Tod'* (Regensburg: Schnell & Steiner, 2009).

—. 'Schwangerschaft, Geburt und Tod', in Daniel Schäfer (ed.), *Hebammen im Rheinland 1750–1950* (Kassel: Kassel University Press, 2010), 285-300.

—. 'Die Vermarktung des Todes. Der Basler Totentanz im 19. Jahrhundert', in: Dominik Groß und Christoph Schweikhardt (eds), *Die Realität des Todes. Zum gegenwärtigen Wandel von Totenbildern und Erinnerungskulturen* (Frankfurt a.M.: Campus, 2010), 155-72.

—. (ed.): *Frauen – Sünde – Tod* (Düsseldorf: Düsseldorf University Press, 2010).

Koal, Valeska: 'Zur Praxis von Totentänzen in Mittelalter und Früher Neuzeit', in Andrea von Hülschen-Esch and Hiltrud Westermann-Angerhausen with Stefanie Knöll (eds), *'Zum Sterben schön!' Alter, Totentanz und Sterbekunst von 1500 bis heute* (Regensburg: Schnell & Steiner, 2006), vol. 1, 110-18.

König, Eberhard: *Leuchtendes Mittelalter*, 4 (Ramsen: Antiquariat Bibermühle, 1992).

—. *Die Belles Heures des Duc de Berry* (Stuttgart: Theiss, 2004).

—. *Das Bedford-Stundenbuch, Begleitband zur Faksimile-Ausgabe* (Luzern: Faksimile-Verlag, 2006).

—. *The Bedford Hours* (London: The British Library, University of Chicago Press, 2007).

—. 'Fifteenth-Century Illuminations from Angers in Cambridge: the Hours of Isabella Stuart and the Quest for a Local Style', in Stella Panayatova (ed.), *The Cambridge Illuminations: the Conference Papers* (London: Harvey Miller, 2007), 225-32.

König, Eberhard, Fedja Anzelewsky, Bodo Brinkmann, and Frauke Steenbock: *Das Berliner Stundenbuch der Maria von Burgund und Kaiser Maximilians*, exhibition catalogue (Berlin: Kupferstichkabinett, Staatliche Museen zu Berlin Preussischer Kulturbesitz, 1998).

König, Eberhard, *et al.*, *Leuchtendes Mittelalter*, Neue Folge, 3 (Ramsen: Antiquariat Bibermühle, 2000).

Könneker, Barbara: *Wesen und Wandlung der Narrenidee im Zeitalter des Humanismus. Brant – Murner – Erasmus* (Wiesbaden: Franz Steiner Verlag, 1966).

Koepplin, Dieter: 'Cranachs Ehebildnis des Johannes Cuspinian von 1502. Seine christlich-humanistische Bedeutung', unpublished PhD thesis (University of Basel, 1973).

Koller, Erwin: *Totentanz. Versuch einer Textembeschreibung*, Innsbrucker Beiträge zur Kulturwissenschaft, Germanistische Reihe, 10 (Innsbruck: Institut für Germanistik der Universität, 1980).

—. 'Zum Metnitzer Totentanz', *Carinthia*, 170 (1980), 139-69.

Koutny-Jones, Aleksandra: 'Dancing with Death in Poland', *Print Quarterly*, 22 (2005), 14-31.

—. 'Death Personified in the Baroque Art of the Kingdom of Poland', unpublished PhD thesis (University of Cambridge, 2007).

—. 'A Noble Death: the Oleśnicki Funerary Chapel in Tarłów, *Journal of the Warburg and Courtauld Institute*, 72 (2009), 169-205.

Kraus, Dorothy and Henry: *Le monde caché des miséricordes* (Paris: Les Éditions de l'amateur, 1986), 206 (translated from The *Hidden World of Misericords* (New York: Braziller, 1975).

Kully, R.M.: 'Le laboureur de Bohème et son process contre la Mort', in Claude Sutto (ed.), *Le sentiment de la Mort au Moyen Age*, Fifth Colloquium of the Institute for Medieval Studies, University of Montreal (Montreal: l'Aurore, 1979), 140-67.

Kümper, Hiram: *Tod und Sterben: lateinische und deutsche Sterbeliteratur des Spätmittelalters* (Duisburg: Wiku Verlag, 2007).

Künstle, Karl: *Die Legende der drei Lebenden und der drei Toten und der Totentanz* (Freiburg im Breisgau: Herdersche Verlagshandlung, 1908).

Laborde, Comte Alexandre de: *La Mort chevauchant un bœuf, origine de cette illustration de l'Office des Morts dans certains livres d'heures du XVe siècle* (Paris: Francisque Lefrançois, 1923).

Laforte, Conrad: *Survivances Medievales dans la Chansons Folklorique* (Quebec: Presse de Université Laval, 1981).

Langlois, Eustache-Hyacinthe: *Essai Historique, Philosophique et Pittoresque sur les Danses des Morts*, 2 vols (Rouen: Lebrument, 1852).

Larsson, Lars Olaf: *Von allen Seiten gleich schön. Studien zum Begriff der Vielansichtigkeit in der europäischen Plastik von der Renaissance bis zum Klassizismus*, Acta Universitatis Stockholmiensis, 26 (Stockholm: Almqvist & Wiksell International, 1974).

Layet, Patrick: 'La *Danse Macabre* des Femmes', in Winfried Frey and Hartmut Freytag (eds), *'Ihr müßt alle nach meiner Pfeife tanzen.' Totentänze vom 15. bis 20. Jahrhundert aus den Beständen der Herzog August Bibliothek Wolfenbüttel und der Bibliothek Otto Schäfer Schweinfurt*, Ausstellungskataloge der Herzog August Bibliothek, 77 (Wolfenbüttel: Harassowitz, 2000), 35-41.

—. 'Die bimediale Münchner Totentanzhandschrift Xyl. 39', *L'art macabre (Jahrbuch der Europäischen Totentanz-Vereinigung)*, 1 (2000), 80-96.

'Le Miroir des Miséricordes (XIIIe-XVIIe siècles)', *Les Cahiers de Conques*, 2 (February 1996).

LeGoff, Jacques: *The Birth of Purgatory*, trans. Arthur Goldhammer (Chicago: University of Chicago Press, 1984).

Lehrs, Max: *Geschichte und kritischer Katalog des deutschen, niederländischen und französischen Kupferstichs im XV. Jahrhundert* (Vienna: Gesellschaft für vervielfältigende Kunst, 1921).

Lemé-Hébuterne, Kristiane: 'L'église et les stalles de Saint-Martin-aux-Bois', *Bulletin de la Société des Antiquaires de Picardie*, 662 (2001), 147-76.

—. *Les stalles de la cathédrale Notre-Dame d'Amiens* (Paris: Picard, 2007).

—. *L'église de Saint-Martin-aux-Bois, stalles, peintures murales, vitraux* (Amiens: OVACAM, 2007).

Leroquais, Victor: *Les livres d'heures manuscrits de la Bibliothèque nationale*, 3 vols (Paris: Imprimerie Nationale, 1927).

Levy, Janey L.: 'The Erotic Engravings of Sebald and Barthel Beham: a German Interpretation of a Renaissance Subject', in Stephen H. Goddard (ed.), *The World in Miniature. Engraving by the German Little Masters, 1500-1550*, exhibition catalogue (Lawrence/Kansas: Spencer Museum of Art, 1988).

Liborio, Mariantonia: 'Il sentimento della morte nella spiritualità dei secoli XII e XIII', in *Il dolore e la morte nella spiritualità dei secoli XII e*

XIII, Todi, 7-10 October 1962 (Todi: Accademia Tudertina, 1967), 45-65.

Linnebach, Andrea: 'Schmuck und Vanitas im Barock', in Zentralinstitut und Museum für Sepulkralkultur (eds), *Trauerschmuck vom Barock bis zum Art Déco*, exhibition catalogue, Museum für Sepulkralkultur Kassel (Kassel: Arbeitsgemeinschaft Friedhof und Denkmal, 1995), 13-20.

Linton, Anna: 'Der Tod als Brautführer: Bridal Imagery in Funeral Writings.', *Daphnis*, 29:1/2 (2000), 281-306.

—. *Poetry and Parental Bereavement in Early Modern Lutheran Germany* (Oxford: Oxford University Press, 2008).

Liuzzi, Fernando: *La Lauda e I Primordi della Melodia Italiana, 1* (Rome: Libreria dello Stato, 1935).

Llabrés, Gabriel: 'Repertorio de 'Consuetas', representadas en las iglesias de Mallorca. Siglos XV y XVI)', *Revista de Archivos, Bibliotecas y Museos*, 5 (1909), 920-27.

Lüders, Imke: *Der Tod auf Samt und Seide. Todesdarstellungen auf liturgischen Textilien des 16. bis 19. Jahrhunderts im deutschsprachigen Raum*, Kasseler Studien zur Sepulkralkultur, 14 (Kassel: Arbeitsgemeinschaft Friedhof und Denkmal e. V., 2009).

Lutsch, Hans: *Die Kunstdenkmäler des Regierungsbezirkes Oppeln* (Wrocław: Korn, 1894).

Macdonald, Jeanette: 'Dance? Of Course I Can', in Helen Payne (ed.), *Dance Movement Therapy: Theory and Practice* (London: Routledge, 1992), 202-17.

Mâle, Emile: *Religious Art in France: the Late Middle Ages. A Study of Medieval Iconography and its Sources*, ed. Harry Bober, trans. M. Mathews (Princeton: Princeton University Press, 1949, repr. 1986).

Manion, Margaret: 'Art and Devotion: The Prayerbooks of Jean de Berry', in Margaret M. Manion and Bernard J. Muir (eds), *Medieval Texts and Images: Studies of Manuscripts from the Middle Ages* (Chur: Harwood Academic Publishers, 1991), 177-200.

Marrow, James H.: 'Hours of Isabella Stuart', in Paul Binski and Stella Panayatova (eds), *The Cambridge Illuminations: Ten Centuries of Book Production in the Medieval West*, exh.cat. Cambridge, Fitzwilliam Museum (London/Turnhout: Harvey Miller/Brepols, 2005).

Martin-Cortes, Marie-Eve: 'Les jouées des stalles de la cathédrale Sainte-Marie d'Auch', unpublished mémoire de maîtrise (4th-year dissertation) (Université Toulouse-Le Mirail, 1995).

—. 'Les stalles de la cathédrale Sainte-Marie d'Auch: les parcloses', unpublished mémoire de D.E.A. (5th-year dissertation) (Université de Toulouse-Le Mirail, 1997).

—. 'L'iconographie des parcloses narratives dans les stalles de la cathédrale Sainte-Marie d'Auch', *Bulletin de la Société Archéologique, historique, littéraire et scientifique du Gers*, 375 (1999), 51-62.

Martineau-Genieys, Christine: *Le thème de la mort dans la poésie française 1450-1550* (Paris: Honoré Champion, 1978).

Mas, Joan: 'Els mites autòctons en el teatre català antic', *Revista de Menorca*, 1 (1990), 45-60.

—. 'El teatre religiós del segle XVI', in Albert Rossich, Antoni Serrà and Pep Valsalobre (eds), *El teatre català dels orígens al segle XVIII*, (Kassel: Edition Reichenberger and Universitat de Girona, 2001), 17-33.

Mas i Vives, Joan: 'El gènere de la "moralitat" en el teatre català antic', *Llengua & Literatura*, 7 (1996), 91-104.

Massip, Francesc: *Història del teatre català*, 1 (Tarragona: Arola Editors, 2007).

Massip, Francesc, and Lenke Kovács: 'Ein Spiegel inmitten eines Kreises: der Totentanz von Morella (Katalonien)', *L'art macabre (Jahrbuch der Europäischen Totentanz-Vereinigung)*, 1 (2000), 114-33.

—. 'La Danse macabre dans le royaume d'Aragon: iconographie et spectacle au Moyen Âge et ses survivances traditionnelles', *Revue des Langues Romanes*, 105:2 (2001), 202-28.

—. 'Les Franciscains et le genre macabre: Les Danses de la Mort et la prédication', *European Medieval Drama*, 8 (2004), 91-105.

—. *El baile: conjuro ante la muerte. Presencia de lo macabro en la Danza y la Fiesta Popular* (Ciudad Real: Consejo Internacional de organización de festivales de folkore and Instituto Nacional de las Artes Escénicas y de la Música, 2004).

Massmann, Hans Ferdinand: *Literatur der Todtentänze. Beytrag zum Jubeljahre der Buchdruckerkunst, aus dem 'Serapeum' besonders abgedruckt* (Leipzig: Weigel, 1840).

Massot i Muntaner, Josep: 'Notes sobre el text i l'autor de la "Representació de la Mort"', in *Serta philologica F. Lázaro Carreter natalem diem sexagesimum celebranti dicata*, vol. 2 (Madrid: Cátedra, 1983), 347-53.

Matuszczak, Jōsef: *Kościoly drewninane nay slasku* (Wrocław: Zakład narodowy imíenía ossolińskich, 1975).

Maus, Heiko: 'Musikinstrumente in den Totentänzen des 15. Jahrhunderts', *L'art macabre (Jahrbuch der Europäischen Totentanz-Vereinigung)*, 1 (2000), 135-51.

Mazzatinti, G.: *Inventari dei Manoscritti delle Biblioteche d'Italia, 8: Firenze, Biblioteca nazionale centrale* (Florence, 1898).

Meiss, Millard: *French Painting in the Time of Jean de Berry. The Boucicaut Master* (New York: Phaidon, 1968).

—. 'La mort et l'office des morts a l'epoque du Maitre Boucicaut et des Limbourgs', *Revue de l'Art*, 1 (1968), 17-25.

Merlo, Enrica Zaira: 'Death and Disillusion. An Iconographic and Literary Itinerary in Christian Spain', in Alberto Tenenti (ed.), *Humana Fragilitas: The Themes of Death in Europe from the 13th to the 18th Century* (Clusone: Ferrari Editrice, 2002), 219-68.

Meyer, Paul: 'Roman des trois enemies de l'homme par Simon', *Romania*, 16 (1887), 1-24.

Meyer-Baer, Kathi: *Music of the Spheres and the Dance of Death: Studies in Musical Iconology* (1970, repr. New York: Da Capo Press, 1984).

Mezger, Werner: *Narrenidee und Fastnachtsbrauch. Studien zum Fortleben des Mittelalters in der europäischen Festkultur* (Konstanz: Universitätsverlag, 1991).

Mezger, Werner, and Irene Götz (eds): *Narren, Schellen und Marotten: elf Beiträge zur Narrenidee. Begleitband zu einer Ausstellung in der Universitätsbibliothek Freiburg im Breisgau vom 9. Februar bis zum 14. März 1984* (2nd edn, Remscheid: Kierdorf, 1984).

Michael, Michael: 'The Privilege of "Proximity": Towards a Re-definition of the Function of Armorials,' *Journal of Medieval History*, 23:1 (1997), 55-74.

Montaiglon, Anatole de: *The Celebrated Hans Holbein´s Alphabet of Death* (Paris: Edwin Tross, 1856).

Morris, Rosie: 'The "Innocent and Touching Custom" of Maidens' Garlands: A Field Report', *Folklore*, 114:3 (2003), 355-87.

Moser, Dietz-Rüdiger: *Fastnacht, Fasching, Karneval: das Fest der verkehrten Welt* (Graz: Ed. Kaleidoskop im Verl. Styria, 1986).

Moxey, Keith: *Peasants, Warriors and Wives. Popular Imagery in the Reformation* (Chicago/London: University of Chicago Press, 1989).

Müller, Christian (ed.): *Hans Holbein d. J. Die Druckgraphik im Kupferstich-kabinett Basel* (Basel: Schwabe, 1997).

—. *Urs Graf. Die Zeichnungen im Kupferstichkabinett Basel* (Basel: Schwabe Verlag, 2002).

Müller-Meiningen, Johanna: *Die Moriskentänzer und andere Arbeiten des Erasmus Gasser für das Alte Rathaus in München* (Regensburg: Schnell & Steiner, 1998).

Münkner, Jörn: 'Tote Li/ebende – li/ebende Tote. Blick unter Röcke und in Schädel', *L'art macabre (Jahrbuch der Europäischen Totentanzvereinigung)*, 8 (2007), 161-76.

Nead, Lynda: *The Female Nude: Art, Obscenity, and Sexuality* (London: Routledge, 1992).

Neill, Michael: *Issues of Death: Mortality and Identity in English Renaissance Tragedy* (Oxford: Clarendon Press, 1997).

Obrazy śmierci. W sztuce polskiej XIXX-XX Wieku, exhibition catalogue (Cracow: Museum Narodowe w Krakowie, 2000).

Olson, Claire C.: 'Chaucer and the Music of the Fourteenth Century', *Speculum*, 16 (1941), 64-91.

Oosterwijk, Sophie: 'Food for Worms – Food for Thought: The Appearance and Interpretation of the "Verminous" Cadaver in Britain and Europe', *Church Monuments*, 20 (2005), 40-80, 133-40.

—. 'Totentanzikonographie auf Chorgestühlen und Miserikordien des Mittelalters', *L'art macabre (Jahrbuch der Europäischen Totentanz-Vereinigung)*, 6 (2005), 199-214.

—. '"Muoz ich tanzen und kan nit gân?": Death and the Infant in the Medieval *Danse Macabre*', *Word & Image*, 22:2 (2006), 146-64.

—. '*Danse Macabre* Imagery in Late-Medieval Sculpture', in Andrea von Hülsen-Esch and Hiltrud Westermann-Angerhausen with Stefanie Knöll (eds), *'Zum Sterben schön!' Alter, Totentanz und Sterbekunst von 1500 bis heute*, 2 vols (Regensburg: Schnell & Steiner, 2006), vol. 1, 167-77.

—. 'Money, Morality, Mortality: the Migration of the *Danse Macabre* from Murals to Misericords', in Peregrine Horden (ed.), *Freedom of Movement in the Middle Ages* (2003 Harlaxton Symposium Proceedings) Harlaxton Medieval Studies, 15 (Donington: Shaun Tyas, 2007), 37-56.

—. '"For no man mai fro dethes stroke fle". Death and *Danse Macabre* Iconography in Memorial Art', *Church Monuments*, 23 (2008), 62-87, 166-68.

—. 'Of Dead Kings, Dukes and Constables: the Historical Context of the *Danse Macabre* in Late Medieval Paris', *Journal of the British Archaeological Association*, 161 (2008), 131-62.

—. '"Alas, poor Yorick": Death, the Fool, the Mirror and the *Danse Macabre*', in Stefanie Knöll (ed.), *Narren – Masken – Karneval: Meisterwerke von Dürer bis Kubin aus der Düsseldorfer*

Graphiksammlung 'Mensch und Tod' (Regensburg: Schnell & Steiner, 2009), 20-32.

——. 'Death, Memory and Commemoration: John Lydgate and "Macabrees Daunce" at Old St Paul's Cathedral, London', in Caroline M. Barron and Clive Burgess (eds), *Memory and Commemoration in Medieval England*, 2008 Harlaxton Symposium Proceedings (Donington: Shaun Tyas, 2010), 185-201.

Ottosen, Knut: *Responsories and Versicles of the Latin Office of the Dead*, (Aarhus: University Press, 1993).

Overdick, Michael: 'Zur Darstellung von Tod und Verdammnis in den Illustrationen zu Sebastian Brants *Narrenschiff*', in Stefanie Knöll (ed.), *Narren – Masken – Karneval. Meisterwerke von Dürer bis Kubin aus der Düsseldorfer Graphiksammlung 'Mensch und Tod'* (Regensburg: Schnell & Steiner 2009), 33-42.

——. 'Schlafender Putto mit Totenschädel', in Andrea von Hülsen-Esch and Hiltrud Westermann-Angerhausen with Stefanie Knöll (eds), *Zum Sterben schön! Alter, Totentanz und Sterbekunst von 1500 bis heute*, exhibition catalogue, 2 vols (Regensburg: Schnell & Steiner, 2006), vol. 2, 223-25.

Owst, G.R.: *Literature and Pulpit in Medieval England* (Oxford: Blackwell, 1961).

Pächt, Otto: *The Master of Mary of Burgundy* (London: Faber and Faber, 1966).

Page, Christopher, *The Owl and the Nightingale: Musical Life and Ideas in France 1100-1300* (London: Dent, 1989).

Parshall, Peter: 'Hans Holbein's Pictures of Death', in Mark Roskill and John Oliver Hand (eds), *Hans Holbein: Paintings, Prints and Reception* (New Haven/London: Yale University Press, 2001), 83-95.

Paškvan, Fedora: 'Prilog proučavanju Beramskih zidnih slikarija' [A contibution to the research of the wall paintings in Beram], *Bulletin za likovne umjetnosti JAZU*, 7 (1959), 53-57.

Perkinson, Stephen: *The Likeness of the King. A Prehistory of Portraiture in Late Medieval France* (Chicago/London: University of Chicago Press, 2009).

Petersmann, Frank: *Kirchen- und Sozialkritik in den Bildern des Todes von Hans Holbein d. J.* (Bielefeld: Ludwig Bechauf, 1983).

Pevsner, Nikolaus, and Bill Wilson: *The Buildings of England, Norfolk 1: Norwich and North-East* (Harmondsworth: Penguin Books Ltd, 1997).

Pineau-Farge, Nathalie: 'Les stalles de la cathédrale Saint-Jean-Baptiste à Saint-Jean-de-Maurienne', special issue of *Société d'Histoire et d'Archéologie de Maurienne*, 34-35 (2000-1).

Piwonska, Teresa: 'Barokowa dekoracja stiukowa kaplicy Oleśnicki w Tarłówie', unpublished PhD thesis (University of Wrocław (Breslau), 1997).

Plummer, John: *The Glazier Collection of Illuminated Manuscripts* (New York: Morgan Library, 1968).

Poli, Fernanda: *La chiesa del Castello di Bosa: gli affreschi di Nostra Signora de Los Regnos Altos* (Sassari: EDES, 1999).

Porcher, Jean: 'Two Models for the Heures de Rohan', *Journal of the Warburg and Courtauld Institutes*, 8 (1945), 1-6.

Reinhardt, Hans: 'Holbein Hans d. J.', in Historische Kommission bei der Bayerischen Akademie der Wissenschaften (eds), *Neue Deutsche Biographie*, 9 (Berlin: Dunker, 1972), 515-20.

—. 'Einige Bemerkungen zum graphischen Werk Hans Holbeins des Jüngeren', *Zeitschrift für Schweizerische Archäologie und Kunstgeschichte*, 34 (1977), 229-60.

Reynolds, Catherine: 'The "Très Riches Heures", the Bedford Workshop and Barthélemy d'Eyck', *Burlington Magazine*, 147 (2005), 526-33.

Riccioni, Stefano: 'La décoration monumentale à Rome, XIe-XIIe siècles', *Perspectives, Actualités de la recherche en Histoire de l'art* (2010-2011/2), 332-34, 359.

Rico, Francisco: 'Pedro de Veragüe y fra Anselm Turmeda', *Bulletin of Hispanic Studies*, 50 (1973), 224-36.

Riggenbach, Rudolf: 'Der Buchdrucker Huldrich Frölich, "Plauensis, jetzt Burger zu Basel"', *Basler Zeitschrift für Geschichte und Altertumskunde* 58/59 (1959), 215-29.

Robinson, David, and Dean Koontz: *Beautiful Death: Art of the Cemetery* (Harmondsworth: Penguin Books Ltd, 1996).

Roca, Jordi: *The Verges Procession and the Dance of Death*, translated into English from the original Catalan *La processó de Verges* and with commentary by Simon Furey (Melksham: F.E.P., 1997).

Röver-Kann, Anne: *Albrecht Dürer. Das Frauenbad von 1496*, exhibition catalogue (Bremen: H.M. Hauschild, 2001).

Rogg, Matthias: *Landsknechte und Reisläufer: Bilder vom Soldaten. Ein Stand in der Kunst des 16. Jahrhunderts* (Paderborn: Ferdinand Schöningh, 2002).

Romeu i Figueras, Josep: 'Francesc d'Olesa, autor dramàtic: una hipòtesi versemblant', *Randa*, 9 (Homenatge a Francesc de B. Moll, 1) (1979-80), 127-37.

Rooney, Kenneth: *Mortality and Imagination: the Life of the Dead in Medieval English Literature* (Turnhout: Brepols, 2010).

Rosenberg, Raphael: *Beschreibungen und Nachzeichnungen der Skulpturen Michelangelos. Eine Geschichte der Kunstbetrachtung* (Munich/Berlin: Deutscher Kunstverlag, 2000).

Rosenfeld, Hellmut: *Der mittelalterliche Totentanz: Entstehung – Entwicklung – Bedeutung* (1954, revised edn Cologne/Graz: Böhlau Verlag, 1968).

—. 'Der mittelalterliche Bilderbogen', *Zeitschrift für deutsches Altertum und deutsche Literatur*, 85 (1954/55), 67-75.

—. 'Vadomori', *Zeitschrift für deutsches Altertum und deutsche Literatur*, 124 (1995), 257-64.

Rossi, Patrick: *La danse macabre de La Chaise-Dieu Abbatiale Saint-Robert: étude iconographique d'une fresque du XVe siècle* (Le Pux-en-Velay: Éditions Jeanne-d'Arc, 2006).

Rossich, Albert: 'Francesc d'Olesa i la *Nova art de trobar*', in Antoni Ferrando and Albert G. Hauf (eds), *Miscel·lània Joan Fuster*, vol. 3 (Barcelona: Departament de Filologia Catalana de la Universitat de València, Associació Internacional de Llengua i Literatura Catalanes and Publicacions de l'Abadia de Montserrat, 1991), 267-95.

—. 'Dues notes sobre la Dansa de la Mort als països de llengua catalana', in Josep Lluís Sirera (ed.), *La Mort com a personatge, l'assumpció com a tema, Actes del VI Seminari de Teatre i Música medievals, Elx, 29 al 31 d'octubre de 2000* (Ajuntament d'Elx, 2002), 337-46.

Rotzler, Willy: *Die Begegnung der drei Lebenden und der drei Toten: Ein Beitrag zur Forschung über die mittelalterlichen Vergänglichkeitsdarstellungen* (Winterthur: Verlag P.G. Keller, 1961).

Ruvoldt, Maria: *The Renaissance Imagery of Inspiration, Metaphors of Sex, Sleep, and Dreams* (Cambridge: Cambridge University Press, 2004).

Rytting, Jenny Rebecca: '*A Disputacion Betwyx þe Body and Wormes*: a Translation', *Comitatus: A Journal of Medieval and Renaissance Studies*, 31:1 (2000), 217-32.

Sachs, Curt: *World History of Dance*, trans. Bessie Schonberg (1937; repr. New York: W.W. Norton and Company, Inc., 1963).

Saenger, Paul: 'Prier de bouche et prier de cœur. Les livres d'heures du manuscrit à l'imprimé', in Roger Chartier (ed.), *Les usages de l'imprimerie (XVe et XVIe siècle)* (Paris: Fayard, 1987), 191-227.

Salmen, Walter: 'Jesus Christus, der himmlische Spielmann', *Music in Art*, 22:1-2 (2008), 5-10.

Sandler, Lucy Freeman: *Gothic Manuscripts 1285-1385*, 2 vols (New York: Harvey Miller Publishers, 1986).

Saul, Nigel: 'At the Deathbed of Archdeacon Rudyng', *Monumental Brass Society Bulletin*, 108 (May 2008), 155–57.

Saunders, Alison: 'Is it a Proverb or is it an Emblem? French Manuscript Predecessors of the Emblem Book', *Bibliothèque d'humanisme et de Renaissance*, 55:1 (1993), 83-111.

Saviello, Alberto, and Uli Wunderlich: 'Ein Totentanz-Bilderbogen aus Italien', *Totentanz Aktuell*, 99 (2007), 6-8.

—. 'Noch ein Totentanz-Bilderbogen aus Italien', *Totentanz Aktuell*, 105 (2008), 4-6.

Sawday, Jonathan: *The Body Emblazoned. Dissection and the Human Body in Renaissance Culture* (London: Routledge, 1995).

Scaramella, Pierroberto: 'The Italy of Triumphs and of Contrasts', in Alberto Tenenti (ed.), *Humana Fragilitas. The Themes of Death in Europe from the 13th to the 18th Century* (2000, trans. Clusone: Ferrari, 2002), 25-98.

Schäfer, Daniel: "Herr Doctor beschauw die Anatomay an mir ob sie Recht gemacht sey." Artz und Tod im frühen Totentanz zwischen Fiktion und Realität', *Das Mittelalter*, 10 (2005), 75-76.

—. '"Her artzt thut euch selber rat." Das Erkennen des Todes in der spätmittelalterlichen Medizin', in Renate Hausner and Winfried Schwab (eds), *Den Tod tanzen? Tagungsband des Totentanzkongresses Stift Admont 2001*, Im Kontext, 19 (Anif/ Salzburg: Mueller-Speiser, 2002), 269-90.

Schiavuzzi, Bernardo: 'Le epidemie di pesta bubbonica in Istria. Notize storiche', *Atti e Memorie della Società Istriana di Archeologia e Storia Patria*, 4 (1888), 423-47.

Schleif, Corine: 'The Proper Attitude Toward Death: Windowpanes Designed for the House of Canon Sixtus Tucher', *Art Bulletin*, 69 (1987), 587-603.

Schmitt, Jean-Claude: *La Raison des Gestes dans l'Occident médiéval* (Paris: Éditions Gallimard, 1990).

—. *Ghosts in the Middle Ages: the Living and the Dead in Medieval Society*, trans. by Teresa Lavender Fagan (Chicago: Chicago University Press, 1998).

Schneeli, Gustav, and Paul Heitz (eds): *Initialen von Hans Holbein* (Strasbourg: Heitz, 1900).

Schreiber, Wilhelm Ludwig: *Handbuch der Holz- und Metallschnitte der XV. Jahrhunderts*, IV (Leipzig: Hiersemann, 1927).

Schulte, Brigitte: *Die deutschsprachigen spätmittelalterlichen Totentänze. Unter besonderer Berücksichtigung der Inkunabel "Des dodes dantz".*

Lübeck 1489, Niederdeutsche Studien, 36 (Cologne/Vienna: Böhlau, 1990).

Schulz, Ulrich: *Die Büchersammlung K. und U. Schulz – Die Totentänze. Eine Ausstellung der Badischen Landesbibliothek Karlsruhe* (Karlsruhe: Badische Landesbibliothek, 2007).

Schuster, Eva, and Mikinosuke Tanabe (eds): *Totentanz vom Spätmittelalter bis zur Gegenwart*, exhibition catalogue (Tokyo: The National Museum of Western Art, 2000).

Schwab, Winfried: 'Totentanz oder Lebenslust? Überlegungen zum Todesverständnis des 16. Jahrhunderts am Beispiel ausgewählter Todes- und Totentanz-Initialen der Klosterbibliotheken Admont, Einsiedeln und Ottobeuren', *Studien und Mitteilungen zur Geschichte des Benediktinerordens und seiner Zweige*, 118 (2007), 203-68.

—. '"Der anfang der sünd ist worden von eynem wyb". Zu den Todesdarstellungen Hans Holbeins', in Karen Ellwanger, Heidi Helmhold, Traute Helmers and Barbara Schrödl (eds), *Totenkleidung. Zur Konstruktion von Tod und Geschlecht in der materiellen und visuellen Kultur* (Bielefeld: transcript, 2010), 283-302.

—. 'Schick deine Sichel aus und ernte! Mainzer Todes- und Totentanz-Initialen im Buchdruck des 16. Jahrhunderts', *Gutenberg Jahrbuch*, 85 (2010), 163-70.

Schweinsberg, Eberhard Freiherr Schenk zu: *Die Illustrationen der Chronik von Flanderen – Handschrift Nr. 437 – der Stadtbibliothek zu Brügge und ihr Verhältnis zu Hans Memling* (Strasbourg: Verlag von J.H.Ed. Heitz, 1922).

Scribner, Bob: 'Ways of Seeing in the Age of Dürer', in Dagmar Eichberger and Charles Zika (eds), *Dürer and his Culture* (Cambridge: Cambridge University Press, 1998), 93-117.

Sherlock, Peter: *Monuments and Memory in Early Modern England* (Aldershot: Ashgate, 2008).

Shoemaker, William H.: 'The Llabrés Manuscript and Its Castilian Plays', *Hispanic Review*, 4 (1936), 239-55.

Sina, Fulvio: 'L'impiego delle pubblicazioni a tema macabro d'oltralpe quale fonte di inspirazione dell' arte italiana del XV e XVI secolo: la Danza Macabra in San Silvestro ad Iseo', *Quaderni della Biblioteca*, 5 (2002), 57-66.

Smith, Kathryn A., *Art, Identity and Devotion in Fourteenth Century England: Three Women and their Books of Hours* (Toronto: University of Toronto Press, 2003).

Solá-Solé, Joan: 'El rabí y el alfaquí en la *Dança general de la Muerte*', *Romance Philology*, 18 (1965), 272-83.

—. 'En torno a la *Dança General de la Muerte*', *Hispanic Review*, 36:4 (1968), 303-27.

Spencer, H. Leith: *English Preaching in the Late Middle Ages* (Oxford: Clarendon Press, 1993).

Spoerri, Bettina: 'Die Spiegelmetapher und das Spiegelbild in den Totentänzen von 1400 bis zur Mitte des 15. Jahrhunderts. Ein historischer Abriß', in Markus J. Wenninger (ed.), *Du guoter tôt: Sterben im Mittelalter – Ideal und Realität* (Klagenfurt: Wieser, 1998), 157-80.

Starn, Randolph: *Ambrogio Lorenzetti: the Palazzo Pubblico, Siena* (New York: George Braziller, 1994).

Stevens, John: *Words and Music in the Middle Ages* (Cambridge: Cambridge University Press, 1986).

Stirnemann, Patricia, and Claudia Rabel: 'The "Très Riches Heures" and Two Artists Associated with the Bedford Workshop and Barthélemy d'Eyck', *Burlington Magazine*, 147 (2005), 534-38.

Stolz, Michael: *Artes-liberales-Zyklen. Formationen des Wissens im Mittelalter*, Bibliotheca Germanica, 47, 2 vols (Tübingen: Francke, 2004).

Storck, Willy: 'Das "Vado mori"', *Zeitschrift für deutsche Philologie*, 42 (1910), 422-28.

—. *Die Legende von den drei Lebenden und von den drei Toten* (Tübingen: Druck von H. Laupp Jr., 1910).

Strauss, Walther L. (ed.): *The Illustrated Bartsch, 10: Albrecht Dürer* (New York: Abaris Books, 1981).

Suau, Jean-Pierre: 'Les stalles de la cathédrale d'Auch au miroir de l'iconographie. Entre tradition et modernité (vers 1520-vers 1554)', *Bulletin de la Société Archéologique, historique, littéraire et scientifique du Gers*, 383 (2007), 7-20.

Suckale, Robert: *Das mittelalterliche Bild als Zeitzeuge: Sechs Studien* (Berlin: Lukas Verlag, 2002).

Sumner, Ann (ed.): *Death, Passion and Politics: Van Dyke's Portraits of Venetia Stanley and George Digby* (Dulwich: Dulwich Picture Gallery, 1995).

Sutton, Kay: 'Sources and the Sarum Hours Illuminated by the Master of François de Rohan', in Mara Hofman and Caroline Zöhl (eds), *Quand la peinture était dans les livres. Mélanges en l'honneur de François Avril* (Turnhout: Brepols, 2007), 330-43, 465.

Targoff, R.: *John Donne: Body & Soul* (Chicago: University of Chicago Press, 2008).

Taylor, Andrew: *Textual Situations: Three Medieval Manuscripts and their Readers* (Philadelphia: University of Pennsylvania Press, 2002).

Taylor, Jane H.M. (ed.): *Dies Illa: Death in the Middle Ages*, Proceedings of the 1983 Manchester Colloquium, Vinaver Studies in French, 1 (Liverpool: Cairns, 1984).

—. 'Un Miroer Salutaire', in Jane H.M. Taylor (ed.), *Dies Illa: Death in the Middle Ages*, Proceedings of the 1983 Manchester Colloquium, Vinaver Studies in French, 1 (Liverpool: Cairns, 1984), 29-43.

—. 'Que signifiait *danse* au quinzième siècle? Danser la Danse macabré', *Fifteenth Century Studies*, 18 (1991), 259-77.

Tenenti, Alberto: *La vie et la mort à travers l'art du XVe siècle* (Paris: Serge Fleury, 1952).

—. (ed.): *Humana Fragilitas. The Themes of Death in Europe from the 13th to the 18th Century* (2000, trans. Clusone: Ferrari, 2002).

Tesnière, Marie-Hélène: *Bestiaire médiéval, enluminures* (Paris: BnF, 2005).

Thomas, James C.: *Johannes von Tepl. Der Ackermann aus Böhmen* (Bern: Peter Lang, 1990).

Tomaschek, Johann: 'Der Tod, die Welt(zeit)alter und die letzen Dinge. Bemerkungen zum "Tanz der Skelette" in Hartmann Schedels *Weltchronik* von 1493', in Renate Hausner and Winfried Schwab (eds), *Den Tod tanzen? Tagungsband des Totentanzkongresses Stift Admont 2001*, Im Kontext, 19 (Anif/Salzburg: Verlag Mueller-Speiser, 2002), 229-49.

Triest, Felix (ed.): *Topographisches Handbuch von Oberschlesien*, vol. 1 (repr. Sigmaringen: Thorbecke, 1984).

Tristram, E.W.: *English Wall Paintings of the Fourteenth Century* (London: Routledge and Kegan Paul, 1955).

Unterkircher, Franz: *Das Stundenbuch des Mittelalters*, (Graz: Akademische Druck- u. Verlagsanstalt, 1985).

Utzinger, Bernard: 'Art macabre au Mexique post-colombien', *Danses Macabres d'Europe Bulletin*, 42 (February 2011), 8.

Utzinger, Hélène and Bertrand: *Itinéraires des Danses macabres* (Chartres: Éditions J.M. Garnier, 1996).

Verougstraete, Helène, and Roger van Schoute: 'Bruegel et Pétrarque: une évocation de Laure dans le *Triomphe de la mort* de Pierre Bruegel l'ancien?', in Alessandro Rovetta and Marco Rossi, *Studi di Storia dell'arte in onore di Maria Luisa Gatti Perer* (Milan: Vita e Pensiero/Universita Cattolica del Sacro Cuore, 1999), 247-52.

Waller, John: *A Time to Dance, A Time to Die* (Cambridge: Icon Books, 2008).

Wallner, Bertha Antonia: 'Die Bilder zum achtzeiligen oberdeutschen Totentanz. Ein Beitrag zur Musikikonographie des 15. Jahrhunderts', *Zeitschrift für Musikwissenschaft*, 6 (1923), 65-74.

Ward, Susan: 'Fables for the Court: Illustrations of Marie de France's Fables in Paris, BN, MS Arsenal 3142', in Jane Taylor and Lesley Smith (eds), *Women and the Book: Assessing the Visual Evidence* (London: British Library and Toronto: University of Toronto Press, 1996), 190-203.

Warda, Susanne: *Memento mori: Text und Bild ind Totentänzen des Spätmittelalters und der Frühen Neuzeit*, Pictura et Poesis, 29 (Cologne: Böhlau, 2011).

Warthin, Aldred Scott: *The Physician of the Dance of Death* (1931, reprint, New York: Arno Press, 1977).

Wentzlaff-Eggebert, Friedrich Wilhelm: *Der triumphierende und der besiegte Tod in der Wort- und Bildkunst des Barock* (Berlin/New York: de Gruyter, 1975).

Wenzel, Horst: *Spiegelungen: zur Kultur der Visualität im Mittelalter*, Philologische Studien und Quellen, 219 (Berlin: Schmidt, 2009).

Wenzel, Siegfried: 'The Three Enemies of Man', *Mediaeval Studies*, 29 (1967), 47-66.

Wieck, Roger: 'The Office of the Dead', in Roger Wieck *et al.*, *Time Sanctified. The Book of Hours in Medieval Art and Life*, exhibition catalogue (New York: George Braziller, 1988, repr. 2001), 124-48.

—. Sandra Hindman and Ariane Bergeron-Foote, *Picturing Piety: the Book of Hours*. (Paris: Les Enluminures, 2007).

Wilhelm-Schaffer, Irmgard: *Gottes Beamter und Spielmann des Teufels. Der Tod in Spätmittelalter und Früher Neuzeit* (Cologne/Weimar/ Vienna: Böhlau, 1999).

Williams, E.C.: 'Mural Paintings of the Three Living and the Three Dead in England', *Journal of the British Archaeological Association*, 7 (1942), 31-40.

Williams, Elizabeth: '*Sir Amadace* and the Undisenchanted Bride: the Relation of the Middle English Romance to the Folktale Tradition of The Grateful Dead', in Rosalind Field (ed.), *Tradition and Transformation in Medieval Romance* (Cambridge: D.S. Brewer, 1999), 57-70.

Wilson, Blake (music), and Nello Barbieri (text) (eds), *The Florence Laudario. An Edition of Florence, Biblioteca nazionale centrale, Banco Rari, 18* (Madison: A-R Editions, 1995).

Wilson, Jean: 'I Dote on Death: the Fractured Marriage in English Renaissance Art and Literature', *Church Monuments*, 11 (1996), 42-60.

—. 'The Darlings of the Gods: Monuments to Adolescents in early Modern England', *Church Monuments*, 18 (2003), 65-89.

Winkler, Friedrich: *Die flämische Buchmalerei des XV. und XVI. Jahrhunderts. Künstler und Werke von den Brüdern van Eyck bis zu Simon Bening* (Leipzig: E.A. Seemann, 1925, repr. Amsterdam: B.M. Israël, 1978).

Winzeler, Marius (ed.): *Dresdner Totentanz: das Relief in der Dreikönigskirche Dresden* (Halle an der Saale: Verlag Janos Stekovics, 2001).

Wirth, Jean: *La jeune fille et la Mort, recherche sur les thèmes macabres dans l'art germanique de la Renaissance* (Geneva: Droz, 1979).

—. *La fanciulla e la morte. Ricerche sui temi macabri nell'arte germanica del Rinacimento* (trans., Roma: Istituto della enciclopedia italiana, 1985).

Wisman, J.A.: 'Un miroir déformant: hommes et femmes des Danses macabres de Guyot Marchant', *Journal of Medieval and Renaissance Studies*, 23 (1993), 275-99.

Woolf, Rosemary: *The English Religious Lyric in the Middle Ages* (Oxford: Clarendon Press, 1968):

Wunderlich, Uli: 'Ein Bild verändert sich. Die Bedeutung der neuentdeckten Gouachen für die Rekonstruktion des Basler Totentanzes', in *Totentanz-Forschungen, 9. internationaler Totentanz-Kongress* (Kassel, 1998), 131-39.

—. 'Zwischen Kontinuität und Innovation – Totentänze in illustrierten Büchern der Neuzeit', in Hartmut Freytag and Winfried Frey (eds), *'Ihr müsst alle nach meiner Pfeife tanzen'. Totentänze vom 15. bis 20. Jahrhundert aus den Beständen der Herzog August Bibliothek Wolfenbüttel und der Bibliothek Otto Schäfer in Schweinfurt* (Wiesbaden: Harrassowitz, 2000), 137-202.

—. *Der Tanz in den Tod. Totentänze vom Mittelalter bis zur Gegenwart* (Freiburg i. Breisgau: Eulen Verlag, 2001).

Zadnikar, Marijan: *Hrastovlje. Romanska arhitektura in gotske freske* [Hrastovlje. Romanesque architecture and Gothic frescoes] (Ljubljana: Družina, 2002).

Zahnd, Urs Martin: 'Niklaus Manuels Totentanz als Spiegel der Berner Gesellschaft um 1500', *L'art macabre (Jahrbuch der Europäischen Totentanz-Vereinigung)*, 4 (2003), 265-80.

Zedda, Corrado: 'Gli Arborea e gli affreschi della chiesa di Nostra Signora de Los Regnos Altos a Bosa', *Archivio storico e giuridico sardo di Sassari*, 3 (1996), 135-65.

Zedler, Johann Heinrich: *Grosses vollständiges Universal-Lexicon aller Wissenschafften und Künste* (Leipzig/Halle: Zedler, 1745).

Zentralinstitut und Museum für Sepulkralkultur (eds): *Tanz der Toten – Todestanz. Der monumentale Totentanz im deutschsprachigen Raum*, catalogue to the exhibition in the Museum für Sepulkralkultur Kassel (Dettelbach: J.H. Röll, 1998).

—. *Totenhochzeit mit Kranz und Krone. Zur Symbolik im Brauchtum des Ledigenbegräbnisses* (Kassel: Arbeitsgemeinschaft Friedhof und Denkmal, 2007).

Zinsli, Paul: *Der Berner Totentanz des Niklaus Manuel*, Berner Heimatbücher, 54/55 (Bern: Haupt, 1953).

Zöhl, Caroline: 'Sehr bilderreicher Pergamentdruck von Jean Barbier und Guillaume Le Rouge mit 75 Metallschnitten aus der Werkstatt von Jean Pichore, in einem Einband des 17. Jahrhunderts. Unikum', in Heribert Tenschert and Ina Nettekoven (eds), *Horae B.M.V.: 158 Stundenbuchdrucke der Sammlung Bibermühle 1490-1550* (Ramsen: Antiquariat Bibermühle, 2003), 680-89.

—. *Jean Pichore, Buchmaler, Graphikerund verleger in Paris um 1500* (Turnhout: Brepols, 2004).

—. 'Der Triumph des Todes in szenischen Bildern vor Holbein. Le Mors de la pomme und l'Accidents de l'homme', in Andrea von Hülsen-Esch and Hiltrud Westermann-Angershausen with Stefanie Knöll (eds), *Zum Sterben schön! Alter, Totentanz und Sterbekunst von 1500 bis heute*, exhibition catalogue, 2 vols (Regensburg: Schnell & Steiner, 2006), vol. 1, 133-44.

CONTRIBUTORS

SYLVIE BETHMONT-GALLERAND is a teacher of Holy Scripture and Art History in the Ecole Cathédrale de Paris at the Collège des Bernardins. Her research is focussed on proverbs and the articulations between profane motifs and their religious contexts.

MAIKE CHRISTADLER works as an art historian at the History Department of the University of Basel (Switzerland). Her current interests include graphic images of the Oberrhein region and their role in the discourse of morality on the eve of the Reformation.

FRANCES EUSTACE obtained her MA in Medieval Studies from the University of Bristol. She is a qualified dance movement psychotherapist as well as a professional musician.

HARTMUT FREYTAG is a retired professor of Early German Literature at the University of Hamburg. His publications on German and Latin literature of the Middle Ages and the early modern period include the standard publication on the Lübeck and Tallinn *Danse Macabre* cycles.

PAMELA KING is Professor of Medieval Studies at the University of Bristol. Her research interests are interdisciplinary and focus chiefly on late-medieval English culture, particularly theatre and drama.

STEFANIE KNÖLL works as an art historian and Curator of the graphic collection 'Mensch und Tod' at the Heinrich-Heine-University Düsseldorf. She has published widely on tomb monuments, representations of old age, and the *Danse Macabre*.

LENKE KOVÁCS is a lecturer at the Universitat Rovira i Virgili of Tarragona (Catalonia, Spain). Her main field of research is Catalan medieval drama, in particular Catalan Passion plays.

CHRISTINE KRALIK is completing her PhD at the University of Toronto (Canada). Her thesis examines the functions and audiences for the Three Living and the Three Dead in late-medieval manuscripts.

KRISTIANE LEMÉ-HÉBUTERNE is a French art historian whose focus is the study of French and Netherlandish choir stalls as documents of the medieval and early modern society.

SOPHIE OOSTERWIJK has published widely on the *Danse Macabre*. She was Editor of the journal *Church Monuments* (2004-11) and is currently an Hon. Research Fellow at the University of St Andrews and co-ordinator in the MeMO project at Utrecht University (Netherlands).

MARCO PICCAT is Professor and Head of the Department of Romance Philology at the University of Trieste (Italy). He edits romance texts in the French, Provençal, Catalan and Spanish vernacular.

KENNETH ROONEY is lecturer in Medieval and Renaissance literature at University College Cork (Ireland). He is author of *Mortality and Imagination: The Life of the Dead in Medieval English Literature* (Brepols 2010), and has published widely on Middle English poetry and romance.

Father WINFRIED SCHWAB OSB is subprior of the Benedictine abbey of Admont (Austria). His research focusses on graphic *Danse Macabre* cycles of the early modern period and the history of the Benedictine order.

JUTTA SCHUCHARD was curator at the Museum für Sepulkralkultur in Kassel (Germany) until 2006. Her research interests include the *Danse Macabre*, macabre prints, and many other forms of sepulchral art.

TOMISLAV VIGNJEVIĆ is Assistant Professor in Art History at the University of Primorska in Koper (Slovenia), and previously curator of medieval art at the National Gallery of Slovenia in Ljubljana (1992-2000).

SUSANNE WARDA has studied German and English language and literature. Her PhD thesis, which was published in 2011, examines the relations between text and image in German *Danses Macabres*.

JEAN WILSON taught for many years in the English Department at Boston University (USA) and now lives in the UK. She is the author of many articles on English Renaissance culture.

CAROLINE ZÖHL is lecturer in Art History at the Freie Universität in Berlin. Her research centres on medieval and Renaissance art with a focus on the transition from manuscript to print and marginal illustrations.

INDEX

Illustration references are in **Bold** type.

Albrecht II, emperor, 36
anatomy, 124-129
Anderson, Edmund, 252
Audelay, John, 17n, 197
Austria
  Metnitz, 298, 305, 376
Awyntyrs off Arthure, The, 193-206

Baldung (Grien), Hans, 106, 107,
  113, 115, **Pl. 7**
Baschenis, Simon de, 295
Beauchamp, Margaret de, 141-143
Beaujeu, Anne de, *Hours of*, 144,
  145
Beckington, Thomas, bishop of
  Wells, 31
Beham, Hans Sebald, 111, **112**, 113,
  114, 115
Belgium
  Hoogstraten, Sainte-Catherine,
  278, 279, 287, **288**
Black Death, 85, 179, 309
Bonhomme, Yolande, 339, **341**,
  343, **348**, **351**, **353**, **354**, 357
Brabant, Marie de, 136, 138, 143,
  Pl. 4
Brederode, Reynout van, 34
Brocas, Bernard, 263
Buffalmacco, Buonamico, 12, 164
Bulstrode, Lady Anne, 266
Burgundy, Mary of, *Berlin Hours
  of*, **146**, **147**, 149-153

cadaver monuments, 23, **24**, **28**, 31,
  33, 34, 35, 38
Carthusian Miscellany, 22, 32, **Pl. 6**
Charles V, emperor, 35, 215
Charles VI, king of France, 38, 39,
  42

Chaucer, Geoffrey, 3, 47, 49, 51, 54,
  202
Chichele, Henry, archbishop of
  Canterbury, 23, 31
choir stalls, 3, 269-290, **273**, **275-
  278**, **280**, **282**, **283**, **285**, **288** *see
  also* misericords
Clarence, Albert Victor, duke of,
  263
Condé, Baudouin de, 136-138
costume(s), 227-229, 246
Cotton, Sir Rowland and Lady, 253,
  254
Crashaw, Richard, 238, 239, 263
Croatia
  Beram, 17, 38, 291, **292**, 293-
  303, **296**, **298**, 308, 310,
  Pl. 14
  Lindar, St Catherine, 300

Dança general de la Muerte, 11,
  207, 210
dance and dancing, 9, 11, 17, 19,
  43-100, 103, 122, 219, 227, 228
dance-song, 50-52, 55, 57, 65
dance steps, 56, 57
Danse Macabre: characters;
  Abbess, 82, **102**, 103, 369, **402**,
  403
  Abbot, 21, 29, **76**, 86, 369, **392**
  Advocat see Lawyer
  Amorous Gentlewoman, 14
  Amoureux see Lover
  Archbishop, **62**, 70
  Aristocratic Lady *see*
    Noblewoman
  Artisan/Craftsman, **77**, 390
  Astrologer/*Maistre*, **69**, 70, 369,
  390

Bailiff, 64
Beggar/Poor Man, **64**, 82, 219-
    221, 230, 294, **298**, **299**,
    302, 303
Beguine, 390
Benedictine Monk *see* Monk
Bishop, 19, 26, **63**, 73, 209, 294,
    295, 302, 367, 369, **Pl. 2b**
Blind Man, 396, **397**
Bride, 31
Brigand *see* Robber
Burgher/Townsman, **69**, 103,
    209, 302, 390
Canon, **76**, 78, 369, 390
Cardinal, 27, **59**, 61, 65, 209,
    294, 295, 302, **306**, 367,
    369, 372, 375, 377, **383**,
    392, 394
Chevalier see Knight
Child *see* Infant
Clerk/*Clerc*, 58, **62**, 63, 65
Constable, 27
Cook, 297, 404
Cordelier see Franciscan Friar
Councillor, 369
Count, 367, 369, 375, 379, 383
Countess, 82, 369, 372
Craftsman *see* Artisan
Cripple, **94**, 401
Curé see Parson
Daughter *see* Maiden
Dean, 295
Doctor *see* Physician
Dominican Friar, 209
Drunkard, 367, 369, 374, 390,
    401
Duchess, 82, 209, 297, 369, 396,
    401, 403
Duke, 209, 367, 369, 374, 396,
    403
Emperor, 26, 27, 31, **35**, 84-86,
    172, 215, 366, 367, 369,
    Pl. 1
Empress, 101, 103, 367, 369
Evil Monk *see* Monk
Executioner, 401

Female Pagan *see* Pagan
Female Ruler, 366
Fool/Jester, 87, 93, 367, 369,
    372
Franciscan Friar/*Cordelier*, 59,
    60, 63, 209, 219, 220, 232,
    233, 295, 302, 306
Gambler, 220, 222, 227, 230-
    232, 367, 377, 390, 401
Gravedigger/Sexton, 84, 220,
    226, 227, 232
Herald, 401
Hermit, 37, **62**, 63, 67, 68, 71,
    78, **80**, 155, 161, 367, 372,
    374, 375, 396
Infant/Child/Little Girl, 31, **60**,
    70, 88, 89, **208**, 209, 294,
    302, 306, **307**, **308**, 366,
    367, 369, 386, 390, 401,
    404, **Pl. 5**
Jester *see* Fool
Judge, 369
King, 19, 21, 28, 37, 38, 58, **59**,
    60, 61, 69, 85, 209, 220,
    232, 294, 296, 302, 305,
    306, 367, 369, 375, 378,
    380, 381, 392-394, **Pl. 16**
Knight/*Chevalier*/Teutonic
    Knight, 27, **28**, 61, **62**, 68,
    294, **296**, **297**, 302, 304,
    367, 369, 377, **379**, 383,
    390, 401
Labourer/Peasant, **61**, 63, 68,
    369, 375
Lady *see* Noblewoman
Landlord, 294, 296
Lansquenet see Soldier
Lawyer/*Advocat*, 65, **68**, 87,
    369, 390
Little Girl *see* Infant
Lover/*Amoureux*, 29, 61
Maiden/Daughter, 97, **98**, 104,
    392, 401
Maistre see Astrologer
Médecin see Physician

Merchant/*Marchant*, 60, 102,
   294, **296**, 297, 369, 377
Minstrel, 17, **68**
Miser *see* Rich Man
Monk/Benedictine Monk/Evil
   Monk, 26, **64**, 78, **102**, 103,
   209, 366, 367, 369, 374, 390
Mother, 16, 36, 82
Nobleman, 209, 297, 317, 369,
   377, **382**, 383, 390, 400
Noblewoman/Aristocratic
   Lady/Lady, 82, 95, 209,
   217, 220, 222, 231, 366,
   369, 377, **382**, 383, 390,
   400, 403
Nun, 82, 209, 367, 369, 374,
   396, **399**
Old Man, 220, 225-227, 369
Old Woman, 369
Pagan/Female Pagan/Turk, 82,
   386, 387, 390, 401, 404
Painter, 36, 401, 404
Painter's Wife, 404
Parson/*Curé*, 26, 27, 60, **61**, 68,
   71
Patriarch, 63, 65, 390
Peasant *see* Labourer
Peddler 296, 369
Physician/Doctor/*Médecin*, 61,
   302, **304**, 305, 306, 367,
   369, 376, 377
Pilgrim, 298
Piper, 390
Poor Man *see* Beggar
Pope, 28, 36, **79**, 82-84, 86, 172,
   207, 209, 220, 232, 233,
   294, 299, 302, 310, 367,
   369, 376-378, **379**, **380**,
   381, 383, 387, 392, 394,
   395, 396, **Pl. 1**
Preacher, 21, 294, 303, 369,
   390, 400, 401
Priest, 102, 367, 369
Prostitute, 367, 369, 373, 390

Queen, 29, 82, **92**, 93, 101, 209,
   294, 302, **306**, 310, 367,
   369, 372, 383
Rich Man/Miser/Usurer, **64**, 87,
   220-222, 227, 229, 230,
   296, 316, 367, 369, 372, 401
Robber/Brigand/Thief, 82, 220-
   222, 227, 231, 390, 401
Sailor, 369, 390
Scholar, 209
Sergeant, 20, 27
Sexton *see* Gravedigger
Soldier/*Lansquenet*, 28n, 104,
   367, 377
Squire, 11, 27, **63**, 69
Standard-Bearer, 366
Teutonic Knight *see* Knight
Thief *see* Robber
Townsman *see* Burgher
Turk *see* Pagan
Usurer *see* Rich Man
Widow, **98**, 104, 390
Young Boy, 220, 231
Young Man, 217, 220, 222-225,
   229, 232, 233, 391, 396, **398**
Death: depicted riding on a bovine,
   173-188, **173**, **176**, **Pls. 9b-11**,
   13; as a lover, 237-266; on
   choirstall carvings, 272-290
Death and the Maiden, 82, 97, 105-
   107, **108**, 115, **116**, 231, 237,
   317, **Pl. 7**
Débat du corps et de l'âme, **22**
Denmark
   Birkerød, 38
Devanport, Lovis and Deborah, 258,
   260, **261**
Donne, John, 249, 262
drama and performance, 2, 4, 5, 11,
   19, 28, 29, 45, 65, 85, 139n,
   148, 149, 210-236, 238-247,
   356
Dunbar, William, 47, 202
Dürer, Albrecht, **35**, 36, 113, **119**,
   120-122, **171**, 317, 339, 343

Ebreo of Pesaro, Guglielmo, *De Practica sue Arte Tripudii*, 46
Elford, Anna, 262
Elizabeth I, queen of England, 237, 264
England
  Alverdiscott (Devon), 260
  Biggleswade (Bedfordshire), 23, **24**
  Bramley (Hampshire), 263
  Bristol, Lord Mayor's Chapel, 254
  Canterbury Cathedral, 23, 31
  Churchill (Somerset), **250, 251**
  Coventry (Warwickshire), St Michael, 256, 265, 271
  East Ham (Essex), 257
  Ewelme (Oxfordshire), **33**
  Eyeworth (Bedfordshire), 252
  Falstone (Northumberland), 258, **259**
  Hackney (Greater London), St John, 265
  Henfield (Sussex), 261
  Hunsdon (Hertfordshire), 27, **28**
  Lamport Hall (Northamptonshire), 40, **41**
  Langtoft (Lincolnshire), 255
  Lincoln Cathedral, 31
  London, Old St Paul's Cathedral, 37, 39, 44, 370
  Newton St Cyres (Devon), 262
  Norton-in-Hales (Shropshire), 253
  Norwich (Norfolk), St Andrew, 14, **Pl. 2b**
  Raunds (Northamptonshire), 197
  Shepton Mallet (Somerset), 254, **255**
  Stanford-on-Avon (Northamptonshire), 26
  Warwick (Warwickshire), 261
  Wells Cathedral, 31
  Wickhampton (Norfolk), 197
  Windsor (Berkshire), Albert Memorial Chapel, 263
Estonia
  Tallinn, 17, 18, 294

Felix V, antipope, 36
Ferdinand I, king of the Romans, 35
Fèvre, Jehan le, *Le Respit de la Mort*, 10
Fleming, Richard, bishop of Lincoln, 31
France
  Amiens Cathedral, 281, **282, 283**, 284, 285, 287
  Auch Cathedral, 277, 278
  Avignon, 31
  Brou (Bourg-en-Bresse), 34
  Chaumont-en-Vexin (Oise), 276, **277**
  La Chaise-Dieu (Auvergne), 294, 315
  Le Mans Cathedral, 279
  Orbais (Marne), 284, **285**, 286, 287
  Paris: Les Saints Innocents, 1, 3, 11, 17, 38, 39, 53, 66, 89, 90, 210, 293, 305, 306, 308, 370; Saint-Gervais-Saint-Protais, 279, **280**; Saint-Victor, 279
  Pocé-sur-Cisse (Indre-et-Loire), Saint-Adrien, **176**, 177, 178
  Remy (Oise), 274, **275**
  Rouen, Saint-Maclou cemetery, 26
  Saint-Bertrand-de-Comminges Cathedral, 273, 284
  Saint-Denis, 34, 35, 253
  Saint-Jean-de-Maurienne Cathedral, 274
  Saint-Martin-aux-Bois (Oise), 275, **276**
  Vendôme (Loir-et-Cher), La Trinité, **273**, 284

Francis I, king of France, 35
frescoes *see* mural paintings
Frölich, Huldrich, 82, 385-405, **388**,
   392, 395, 397, 398
gender, 12, 82, 101-129, 134n, 169,
   210n
Germany
   Berlin, Marienkirche, 84, 89,
      309
   Dresden, 35, 40, 215n
   Füssen, 36
   Lübeck, Marienkirche, **18**, 85,
      89n, 91, 370
   Nuremberg, 26n
Gerson, Jean, *De Arte Moriendi*, 70
Grange, Jean de la, cardinal, 31
Gray, James, 27, **28**
Grosz, George, **110**, 111

Halle, Adam de la, *Jeu de Robin et
   Marion*, 46
Heidelberg Blockbook, 21, 88, **297**,
   298, **299**, 307, **308**, 370, 371
Henri II, king of France, 34
Henry V, king of England, 37, 39,
   42
Hiebeler, Jakob, 36
Hoccleve, Thomas, 14; *Learn to
   Die*, 12, 13, 16
Holbein, Hans, the Younger, 5, 17,
   27, 40, 315, 316, 339, 393, 402,
   403, 405; *Alphabet of Death,*
   361-379, 383, 384, **362, 363**;
   *Les simulachres et historiées
   faces de la mort/Images of
   Death* 12, **13, 28, 35**, 368, 369,
   389-391, 394, 396, **399**, 400,
   401

Ingeborch, 14, **15**, 33
Isham, John, 40, **41**
Italy
   Atri Cathedral, 161, 162, 169
   Bosa (Sardinia), Santa Maria
      dos Regnos Altos, 164
   Carisolo, San Stefano, 295

Clusone nr Bergamo, 295, 302,
   303
Cremona, St Luca, 165
Fossanova (Latina), 160
Iseo nr Brescia, San Silvestro,
   306
Melfi, St Margarita, 160, 169
Montefiascone (Viterbo), St
   Flaviano, 163
Pinzolo, San Vigilio, 89, 295
Pisa, Camposanto, 12, 27, 161,
   164, 165, 201
Poggio Mirteto (Rieti), St Paolo,
   162, 164
Sesto al Reghena, Sta Maria in
   Sylvis, 165
Siena, Palazzo Publico, 48
Subiaco, St Benedict, 161, 162
Turin, San Michele della
   Chiusa, 165, **166**, **Pl. 9a**
Val di Susa, St Francesco, 163;
   San Giorio, 163; Madonna
   del Ponte, 163
Verona, St Fermo, 160
Vezzolano (Albugnano), Sta
   Maria, 161-163

Jonson, Ben, 240n, 260

Kastav, John of, 291, 302, 305, 308,
   310, **Pl. 15**
Kastav, Vincent of, 291, **292**, 293,
   300, 301, **Pl. 14**
Kerver, Thielman, 339, **344, 345,
   349, 355**, 357, 358
King, Henry, 252, 253
Kluber, Hans Hug, 36, 387n, 391,
   404
Knoblochtzer, Heinrich, *Der doten
   dantz*, 11, 19, 26, **75**, 76, **77**, 78,
   82, 83

Latch, John and Sarah, **250, 251**,
   252-254

Lisle, Robert de: *Book of Hours*,
    140, 141-143, 149; *Psalter*, 15,
    139, 141, 341, **Pl. 3**
Llibre Vermell de Monserrat, 45,
    49, 51
Lydgate, John, 5; *Dance of Death*,
    1, 11, 14, 21, 27, 36-39, 43, 44,
    57, 59, 60, 68, 305; *The Debate
    of the Horse, Goose and Sheep*,
    31

Manuel (Deutsch), Niklaus, 36, **76**,
    77, 97, **98**, 101, **102**, 103, 115,
    116, **117**, 118, 394
manuscripts, 15, 39, 46, 78, 133-
    154, 173-175, 213, 286, 305,
    331-341, **140**, **145-147**, **152**,
    Pls. 1, 3, 4, 6, 8, 9b-13
Marchant, Guy: *Danse Macabre*, 5,
    11, 17, **19**, 21, **22**, 26, **37**, 38,
    39, 43, 53, 55-58, **59-64**, 65, 66,
    68, **69**, 71, 87, 88, 155, **156**,
    308, 342, 370, 371; *Danse
    Macabre des Femmes* 11, 31
Marck, Philippote van der, 34
Marvell, Andrew, 256
Martínez de Toledo, Alfonso, 209
Maximilian I, emperor, **35**; *Berlin
    Hours of,* **146**, **147**, 149-151,
    153
Médicis, Catherine de, 34
Merian, Matthäus, the Elder, 36, **79**,
    80, 82, **92**, **94**, 317, **318**, 404
metalcuts, 325, 336, 339, **341**, **343-
    345**, **348**, **349**, **351**, **353-355**
Middleton, Thomas, 243
Milton, John, 248n
mirrors and mirroring, 4, 22, 29, 44,
    67-70, 90-96, 106-110, 203,
    269-271, 276, 281-287
misericords, **176**, 177, 273, 274,
    275, 276, **277**, 279, **280**, 284,
    285, 286, 287, 289 *see also*
    choirstalls
Monogrammist M, 107, **108**, 109,
    111

monuments, 243n, 247-266, **250**,
    251, **255**, **259-261** *see also*
    cadaver monuments
Munich Blockbook, 86, 97
mural paintings, 1, 11, 12, 14, 17,
    18, 19, 21, 23, 27, 38, 39, 48,
    66, 73, **76**, **79**, **80**, 83, 84, 89,
    92, 97, **98**, 101, **102**, 156, 158,
    160-165, **166**, 197, 207, **208**,
    209, 291-322, **292**, **296**, **298**,
    304, **306**, **307**, **313**, 376, 386,
    394, 401, **Pls. 2a, 5, 9a**
music and musical instruments, 9,
    16, 17, **18**, **19**, 74-81, **75-77**, 99,
    209, 295, 297, 299, 371

Netherlands
    Dordrecht, Grote Kerk, 279, **280**
    Vianen, 34
Neville, Lady Katherine, 257
Notke, Bernt, 17, **18**, 294

Office of the Dead, 135, 148, 149,
    153, 154, 174, 175, **200**, 201,
    202, 286, 289, 325-360, **Pls. 1,
    8, 11**
Olesa, Francesc d', 214-216

performance *see* drama and
    performance
Pichore, Jean, 325, 329, 331, 332,
    334, 336, 339-349, 351-357,
    359, **340**, **343-345**, **348**, **349**,
    351, **353-355**
Pictor, Albertus, 14, **Pl. 2a**
poetry, 10-13, 16, 20-22, 47, 54, 59,
    136-138, 173, 191, 192, 198,
    201, 252, 253, 262, 263
Poland
    Bierdzany, 311-322, **313**, **314**
    Zambrów, 320
portraits and portraiture, 4, 32-42,
    149, 215n, 237, 253, 254, 285
Puckering, Cecily, 261

Quentel, Johann, 365, 377, 378, **379-383**, 384

Rainsford, Meneleb, 260
Representació de la Mort, 213-227, 233
Rikelle, Jon, 37
Rudyng, John, archdeacon of Lincoln, 23, **24**, 25

Saxony, George the Bearded, duke of, 35
Schedel, Hartmann, *Nuremberg Chronicle*, 1, 9, **10**, 11, 14, 42, 101
Shakespeare, William, 5, 32, 238, 243
Sidney, Sir Philip, 249
Sigismund, emperor, 36
Sir Amadace, 193-206
Skeffington, Anne Newdigate, Lady, 256, 265
Slovenia
Hrastovlje, 17, 84, 291, 301-310, **304**, **306**, **307**, **Pl. 15**
Spain
Majorca, 207-236
Morella, 17, 207, **208**, 211, **Pl. 5**
Saragossa, Aljafería Palace, 210-212
Verges, 215n, 220n, 227, **228**
stained glass, 14, 26, 172, **Pl. 2b**
Strode, Joan, 254, **255**, 256
Suffolk, Alice de la Pole, duchess of, **33**
Sweden
Nyköping, 14, **15**, 33
Täby, 14, **Pl. 2a**
Switzerland
Basel, Dominican cemetery (Großbasel), 21, 36, 73, 78, **79**, **80**, 82, 86, 87, **92**, 93, **94**, 95, 101, 295-297, 305, 308, 310, 315, 361, 366, 370, 371, 385-391, 393, 394, 396, 399-404;

Klingental (Kleinbasel), 89, 295, 296, 361
Bern, 36, **76**, 77, 87, 89, 97, **98**, **102**, 104, 106, 366, 370, 387-390, 392-394, 400
Emmetten, 317
Luzern, Jesuit College, 36
Unterschächen, 317

Three Living and the Three Dead, 4, 15, 22, 23, 26, 29, 32, 42, 51, 70, 93, 95, 133-167, **140**, **145-147**, **152**, **156**, 170, 175, 194, 197, 213, 223, 327, 331, 334, **340**, **341**, 358, **Pls. 3, 4**
Throckmorton, Lady, 254
Tucher, Sixtus, 26n, 172
Tuke, Sir Brian, 40

U.S.A.
Little Compton (Rhode Island), 258, **260**, **261**

Vado Mori, 20, 21, 213
Vaughan, Henry, 263

Walcot, Sarah, 255
wall paintings *see* mural paintings
Warwick, Isabel Despenser, countess of, 34
Welshe, Thomas, 260
Wheel of Life/Fortune, 5, 29, **30**, 38, 128, 209, 293, **300**, 301
Williams, Henry, 26
Wolgemut, Michael, **10**, 12
woodcuts, 9, **10**, 11, 12, **13**, 14, 17, 18, **19**, 21, **22**, 26, 27, **28**, 29, **35**, **37**, 38, 42, 43, 57, 58, **59-64**, **68**, **69**, **75**, **156**, **171**, **297**, 298, **299**, **303**, 307, **308**, 315, 316, **340**, **362**, **363**, **379-383**, **388**, **392**, 394, **395**, 396, **397-399**, **402**, 403
Wyl, Jakob von, 36